THE PEOPLE'S MESSENGER

Louis Guillemette

THE PEOPLE'S MESSENGER

The Occupation Diary Guernsey 1940-45

Foreword by José Day
Introduction by Ken Tough

BLUE ORMER

MMXXII

Published by Blue Ormer Publishing.
www.blueormer.co.uk

Foreword © José Day, 2022.
Introduction and Dramatis Personae © Ken Tough, 2022.
Book Layout and Cover Design by Stephen Foote.

Front cover image: Louis Guillemette at White Rock with SS *Vega*
    (Damien Horn collection, Channel Islands Military Museum).
Frontispiece: Louis Guillemette, Greffe ID card (Island Archives).
Back cover image: Louis Guillemette aboard *Ida* with Jethou in
    background (Guillemette family collection, photographer unknown).

All illustrations, unless otherwise credited, are from the Guillemette family
    collection.

ISBN 978-1-9993415-6-5.

Printed by Short Run Press, Exeter.

Contents

FOREWORD

Louis Guillemette was appointed secretary to the newly-formed Controlling Committee when he started this diary in 1940. He had been granted permission to apply for a commission in the R.A.F. Volunteer Reserve by the Board of Administration but it was withdrawn by the Bailiff. He had been Assistant Secretary to the Bailiff, Victor Carey, previously.

Louis was thirty and married to Queenie in April 1939; both of them were born in Guernsey. His parents lived in the Bouet and had a grocery shop; by the start of the Occupation, they were both elderly and four of their six children were no longer in Guernsey. Queenie's father, George Robilliard, was a widower and lived at the Rohais here.

Louis had been involved with the evacuation; he had arranged for Queenie to be evacuated as a helper with the Vale School but at the last moment she gave her place to the mother of a young child who was going. Louis was not at all happy when she arrived at his office having had a lift in a sewage lorry. He found her a job in another office taking down names of men who were volunteering for the forces.

When they married, they moved into La Platte, Bordeaux, newly-built for them by her father. The field in which the house was built, has a fantastic view on the edge of the harbour with just the road between it and the beach. Louis hoped he would be able to go from home to work by his boat, *Ida*!

These two people were to be my doting and caring parents when I arrived at this difficult time, in August 1942. They were both very strong characters and prime examples of the saying, 'Remember the past with gratitude, live the present with enthusiasm and look to the future with confidence' [Pope John Paul II].

My brother, Nick, and I decided on the title *The People's Messenger* as the title for our father's diary as it describes his responsibilites to the Controlling Committee for dealings with the German Civil Administration. He received orders most days for the Guernsey community to follow the next day. The Bailiff relied on him for his friendship and for information. Louis was always able to talk with everyone in a level-headed and friendly way with a smile.

Louis died on his boat in Sark when he was just 67 and Queenie lived until her 99th year in Guernsey. Their son Nick was born in 1947.

Louis was appointed Assistant States Supervisor in October 1944 and then became States Supervisor in 1948 until 1975.

José Day (née Guillemette)
Guernsey, February 2022.

INTRODUCTION

Louis Guillemette ('Louis') was a senior civil servant who was at the heart of the daily negotiations between the civilian government of Guernsey and the German authorities throughout the Occupation from 1940 to 1945. He kept a personal diary which he made available to post-War historians, beginning with Alan and Mary Wood in 1955. That diary is a key primary source on the government of the Island during the Occupation and is here published in full for the first time, together with the supporting official documents which Louis carefully filed with each diary entry.

The Diarist

Louis was born in Guernsey in 1910, the second of six children of Auguste and Edith Guillemette. His family was of recent French origin; the founding matriarch of the Guernsey Guillemettes, Marianne Hamelin was born at Carrefour (otherwise Carfo) near Plémy in Brittany in 1839. She ran away from home at the age of 15 after an altercation with the parish priest. She settled in Jersey, where she married one Louis Auguste Désiré Guillemette and had two children, Auguste, born in 1864, and Marianne, born in 1868. Marianne moved to Guernsey as a widow and by 1891 was in business as a grocer at the Vrangue, St Peter Port. Auguste married a Guernsey girl, Edith Sauvarin, and by 1911 was a grower and running the family general store in the Bouet, adjacent to the gasworks. The house names Plémy and Carfo survive in the Bouet to this day. In 1939 Louis married Evelyn ('Queenie') Robilliard; their new home, 'La Platte', beside the fishing harbour at Bordeaux, was built by his father-in-law, George ('Skipper') Robilliard. Bordeaux was then an industrial landscape, dominated by the steel towers of the cable-way serving the great quarry at Les Pétils and by a patchwork of tomato vineries. The uneasy proximity of glasshouses and blasting for granite was a fact of life in the Vale and St Sampson's; Louis's daughter José, born in 1942, recalls La Platte being shaken by quarry detonations in her youth.

After attending Amherst School, the Boys' Intermediate School and Elizabeth College, Louis had joined the civil service in 1928. In 1934 he became assistant secretary to the Bailiff and he was still in that role in the months leading up to the Occupation in June 1940. He plainly made his mark although his diary gives no detail of his personal contribution at that time. However from other accounts – which explicitly drew on his memory – we know that he was in telephone discussions with the Home Office on 18 June, as the British Cabinet were debating whether to demilitarise the Islands, and that on 21 June, now acting as secretary to the president of the new Controlling Committee ('the C.C.'), Louis telephoned the British authorities to request that ships be sent to evacuate Alderney. The evacuation of Guernsey, especially of Island schools, was initiated by the Bailiff's Office, and Louis later recalled that he had no more than three hours' sleep each night from 18 to 22 June (Durand (2018) pp.7 & 25, and Packe & Dreyfus (1971) p.21). His emerging status as a key public servant was reflected in the withdrawal of the permission previously granted to leave the Island and join the R.A.F.; quick decisions were having to be made to ensure that vital personnel stayed at their posts – for example eight medical doctors were specifically asked by the C.C. to remain in the Island.

Writing the diary

On New Year's Eve, 1940 Louis typed a summary of the events of that year. However the diary proper begins abruptly on 27 April 1942, with daily entries up to the end of June; later they are made every week or ten days. Frequent entries were made again during the invasion in June 1944 when it seemed as if the shooting war was about to engulf the Islands. On 25 May 1942 he regrets not having started the diary at the beginning of the Occupation; he looks forward to post war reunions with family and friends and 'to read once again the outline of what will then seem quite an interesting chapter in our lives'. We know that at the time Louis showed his diary to trusted people; on 24 April 1945 he records that 'somebody said the other day that this diary is not so interesting as it used to be.' Nevertheless in view of the candid comments he made, and the official documents he included in the diary, he kept it under wraps at home. Moreover he was careful not to disclose any new detail in his diary which might incriminate individuals; for example on 19 August 1943 he describes 'from information which is common property' the latest escape by fishermen from nearby St Sampson's Harbour. Of course many other Islanders also kept diaries, including a junior colleague, Ken Lewis – who typed many of the documents attached to Louis's diary. In addition two independent researchers, Ralph Durand and Violet Cortvriend, were given access to 'live' official records during the Occupation, and each subsequently published an account of that period. (Durand (1946) and Cortvriend (1947)).

All civilian radios having been requisitioned permanently in June 1942, Louis was circumspect in his diary references to war news, saying only that it came 'through roundabout channels'. Many people, including Louis, listened illicitly to B.B.C. broadcasts and undercover newsletters were also circulated. Louis's sister Madeleine, who worked in the Bailiff's Office, was a courier for the *Guernsey Active Secret Press* and he would have known of her activities. The Germans were also well aware that civilians listened to the B.B.C. (Diary 2 August 1943 and 13 December 1944).

The diary was typewritten at home in the evenings, except during March 1945 when Louis found it impossible to work by candlelight and typed it at the office on Thursday afternoons. A typical entry would consist of his personal narrative of recent exchanges with the German authorities, accompanied by official correspondence or memoranda – much of which was drafted by Louis himself – followed by a summary of the war news, an account of his latest outing in his boat and finally domestic dramas, often involving his wife Queenie and baby daughter José. The enclosures normally detail grim encounters with the occupier over food reductions etc, but some lighter items are included (see Appendix Items 11, 18 and 19). Louis rarely re-read his diary entries, he did not revise it after the war and he made it available to researchers in its original form.

Executive government

These were extraordinary times which demanded swift improvisation at the top of Island government. On 19 June 1940 the British government withdrew its armed forces from the Channel Islands, having wisely decided that the Islands could not be defended against enemy-occupied France. The Germans hesitated for ten days before landing on the Island and during that interval Guernsey cleared the decks for what was to come. First, 19,000 people, out of the population of 43,000, chose to be evacuated to England in ships provided by the British government. Second, the administration was transformed almost overnight. Instead of government by several committees of States members, each reporting to the States as the legislative assembly, the States delegated all their administrative powers to an emergency cabinet, called 'the Controlling Committee' ('the C.C.'). The powers of the C.C. were in fact much wider than those of the States, because by Order of the Royal Court, under the Emergency Powers (Guernsey Defence) Order, 1939 – an Order of the King in Council – it could take almost unlimited control over any goods or undertakings whenever deemed by the C.C. 'necessary for maintaining supplies and services essential to the life of the community' (Tough (1978)).

On 21 June the States appointed Ambrose Sherwill, H.M. Procureur (H.M. Attorney-General) as President of the C.C., and he chose a team of seven, all but two of whom were sitting members of the States, each with relevant expertise, and each with executive powers over his specific portfolio – finance and economics, essential commodities, health services etc. Louis was appointed secretary to the president of the C.C. and, at just thirty years of age, became one of the most influential civil servants in the new emergency régime. In its valedictory message to the Islanders the British government had directed that the Bailiff and the Crown Officers should remain at their posts, as clear an indication as could be expected in the turmoil of late June 1940 that the welfare of the Islanders required that government should carry on.

Coming to terms with Occupation

In addition to grappling with a collapsing economy – which soon demanded overnight nationalisation of the dominant tomato industry – the C.C. found time, in the week before the Germans arrived, to speculate on what the future might hold. Perhaps the Islands would be treated, as they had been between 1483 and 1689, as quasi-neutral territory? Perhaps they would be allowed to receive monthly supply ships from the United Kingdom? There could be no doubt that, even with a reduced population, Guernsey could not feed itself. Any hope that the war would pass them by was soon dispelled by the air raid on St Peter Port Harbour on 28 June and the German military occupation two days later. Far from being a neutral bystander, Guernsey became one large fortress; by mid 1943 there were 13,000 German troops, 1,600 German builders and technicians and 5,100 foreign labourers. For the 24,000 Islanders who remained, the Island effectively became a 24 square mile internment camp; farmers and growers lost much of their productive land and glasshouses, and many dwellings were commandeered by the military.

In theory, the C.C. had been handed all the levers of government; in practice they were subject to German dictation and supervision as the occupiers exercised to the full, and on occasion over-stepped, their powers under international law. Overnight the Presidents of the C.C., first Sherwill and from December 1940 his successor Jurat John Leale, began what was to be five years of negotiation with the occupier; generally the best they could hope for was damage limitation – as with the arbitrary deportations in 1942 and 1943 – but sometimes, by invoking the Hague Convention and exploiting divisions between the military command and the Feldkommandantur (military government/civil affairs unit) they were able to obtain concessions.

In the privacy of his diary Louis focussed on the negotiations between occupier and occupied from a privileged position as adviser to the President of the C.C.; he was ever present, notebook in hand, at critical meetings between Island leaders and Germans at all levels from junior military government officers to the commanding general – a combination of fly on the wall and recording angel. In his report to the States in May 1945 Leale made the interesting point that Louis's note-taking of all important meetings with the Germans was made easier by the reliance on interpreters at all official meetings. The diary proper is supplemented throughout by minutes and letters, often drafted by Louis himself. There is a marked contrast between the style of the civilian correspondence and the typically terse and abrupt German responses. General von Schmettow concluded one exchange with the Bailiff with a request that if agreement cannot be reached with the Platzkommandantur the Bailiff should '...apply to Lt-Col von Helldorff, in order to avoid long-drawn correspondence.' That reply would no doubt have been drafted by von Helldorff for signature by the General (see Appendix Item 83).

The rules of engagement

All human engagement requires a set of rules broadly agreed by the parties if it is not to descend into chaos and brute force. The German and Island authorities alike invoked the 'Regulations on the Laws and Customs of War on Land' annexed to the Hague Convention of 1907 ('the Hague Rules'). These devote only eleven short sections to military occupation, are expressly not a complete code on the duties and obligations of occupier and occupied, and have to be read together with the customs and usages of war in general 'as they result from the usages established among civilised peoples, from the laws of humanity and the dictates of the public conscience recognised between civilised nations' – to quote the optimistic preamble to the Convention. There is no definitive text of those customs and usages; typically each belligerent nation will set them out in the form of a commentary, often incorporated in a manual of military law. The Guernsey authorities relied on the 1929 edition of the British Manual of Military Law ('the British Manual'); they soon discovered that the German equivalent differed, and in August 1943 Louis borrowed a copy of the that German manual and had it translated to assist in countering the German interpretation of the Hague Rules (Leale (1945)).

Article 52 of the Hague Rules stipulated, *inter alia*, that any requisitions and services demanded from the civilian population by an army of occupation 'shall be in proportion to the resources of the country'. The Guernsey authorities frequently objected to requisitions of civilian food stocks, especially butter and potatoes, on the grounds that they were out of proportion to the Island's severely limited resources. These objections were usually overruled, leaving Louis to fume in his diary that in such disputes the German view prevailed, for there was no neutral umpire to whom the Islanders could appeal. Sometimes the dispute was between national governments. In February 1945 Guernsey civilians were to endure three weeks without any bread. Louis was in no doubt that this was caused by a difference of opinion between the British and German governments over the interpretation of Article 52.

Under international law a population under enemy occupation must remain peaceful and afford the occupier 'such measure of obedience as is necessary for the security of his forces, the maintenance of order and the administration of the country'. On the other hand the occupying army, having temporarily supplanted the national government, is under a duty 'to restore and ensure, as far as possible, public order and safety'. The occupier may not destroy or seize enemy property, whether private or public, 'unless it is imperatively demanded by the necessities of war'. That is of course a key qualification – time and again Louis complains at the German reliance on 'Military Necessity'. The rights of the occupier include control of all means of transport and communication. The invader may also impose press censorship, restrict movement of civilians and require them to carry identity cards. The Occupation of Guernsey was to see all those controls imposed by the German authorities.

Civilians are under a duty to go about their usual trades and professions peacefully and can be required to serve the occupying forces in their civilian roles. They cannot be required to work on fortifications 'but may be offered payment to undertake such work voluntarily'. Government officials 'will at times best fulfill their moral duty towards their own people if they remain in office in the presence of the invader. For if they withdraw there will be disorder and confusion; while if they remain at their posts order and safety are better secured'. The occupier is entitled to remove or appoint officials and even judicial officers may be removed 'if they refuse obedience to the occupant'. The dismissal from office of Sherwill in 1940 was an example of that power being exercised.

The examples in the preceding two paragraphs are taken from Chapter XIV: 'The Laws and Usages of War on Land' of the British Manual and may reasonably be taken as an authoritative statement of the British view of the respective rights and duties of an army of occupation and of an occupied population.

Dealing with the occupier

Until the final year of the Occupation all civilian dealings with the Germans had to be directed via their specialised military government/civil affairs unit, known as Feldkommandantur 515 ('F.K.'). This was based in Jersey, with a branch or Nebenstelle in Guernsey, housed in Grange Lodge, a substantial neo-Tudor villa and peacetime hotel on the outskirts of St Peter Port. The F.K. had its own line of command up to the German military government headquarters in Paris. It was staffed by lawyers, career civil servants and specialists in economics, agriculture etc., provided administrative and logistic support for the military, and supervised the civilian authorities (Cruickshank (1975) chapter 6 and Bell (2002) chapter 8). F.K. officers wore quasi-military uniforms but would not have undergone full military training. In German army slang they were known as 'narrow-gauge officers'. The F.K. was often seen as a nuisance, obstructing the military by their insistence on due process;

for example the F.K. had to be notified in advance before civilian houses were demolished, so that the States Billetting Officer would have time to rehouse the unfortunate occupants. To Louis and his colleagues the officers of the F.K. were all too often the bearers of bad news, portraying themselves as constrained by orders from above which they could not ignore, however much they expressed sympathy with the civilian population.

The new C.C., rapidly expanding its staff as it took over supervision of most aspects of daily life, was initially housed in the vast Tudor-Gothic Revival building of Elizabeth College, the school having been evacuated to England days before. Louis was given a remote room high in the north-western turret. In 1941 the German Fortress Engineers took over the building and the C.C. moved down the hill to Hirzel House and the adjoining Maison Allaire where it stayed until Liberation in 1945. This was a stone's throw from the Bailiff's Chambers in the Royal Court House, where Louis had been assistant secretary before his move to the C.C. From March 1944, as a cross-Channel invasion became more likely, the military took greater control of civil affairs and meetings were held at the army quartermaster's HQ at Summerland, a neo-Tudor villa in Mount Durand. From July 1941 the Commanding General of all German forces in the Islands resided at La Corbinerie, a Regency villa set in wooded parkland, conveniently near the military hospital in Guernsey, a short drive from St Peter Port. Conferences with the Red Cross delegates during the visits by the relief ship S.S. *Vega* took place at Rozel, a Georgian villa in Mount Durand.

Louis, or a colleague such as Ken Lewis, was in daily contact with the F.K. at Grange Lodge, a few minutes' walk from the C.C.'s offices. He records relaxed discussions with interpreters and other English-speaking officers on, for example, the progress of the war. They would accuse him, apparently in jest, of being 'the States' spy' and of eavesdropping on conversations at Grange Lodge; after two and a half years Louis had in fact picked up very little German but his F.K. interlocutors 'think my ignorance is entirely feigned' (Diary 5 February and 19 July 1943). He discusses in the diary the difficulty of the C.C. in dealing with the occupiers who, until the final weeks before Liberation, held all the cards. Faced with orders to reduce meagre rations still further, the C.C. considered resignation more than once. Each time they concluded that would not be in the best interests of Islanders; as Louis put it '...wisdom returns to take the place of more theatrical sentiments.' (Diary 30 April 1943). They opted for compromise rather than posturing; having protested in vain against the mass deportation order of September 1942 they decided to assist in the process to minimise the suffering of the deportees. One of the longest diary entries describes the practical support given to the families awaiting departure – and the help given by F.K. 515 officers (Diary 26 September 1942).

'We know what the public does not and that is that the Feldkommandantur are the only friends we possess...'. Louis made this entry on 28 January 1943, in the midst of the crisis over the second, even more arbitrary wave of deportations. A swathe of key Island figures had received notice to attend for medical examination, including the Bailiff, Sherwill, Leale, Raymond Falla and five doctors. Louis and Leale were impressed by the support offered by F.K. 515; Knackfuss came over from Jersey and together with von Aufsess made direct representations to General Müller, the commanding general in Guernsey who had signed the orders. Several names were removed from the list, although Sherwill and his family remained. In the event his wife and children were exempted, after unofficial intervention by von Aufsess (see Wood (1955) p.148). If Louis knew of that intervention he would certainly not have mentioned it in his diary. However his initial belief in the good faith of F.K. 515 waned during the disputes over requisitioning of civilian food stocks, such that by 8 March 1945 he records that he and Leale were impressed by Reich, the new naval quartermaster appointed by Hüffmeier; although a Nazi, Reich 'is obviously intelligent, he does not shout and he is direct'. To which Louis adds the caveat: 'We have, of course, been favourably impressed by Germans before'.

Unusually, there exists a private German assessment of Louis himself. In December 1944 von Aufsess accompanied Bailiff Coutanche to Guernsey for the first visit of the Red Cross relief ship S.S. *Vega*. In his diary for 28 December von Aufsess describes Louis as 'rather pushing, but very able and intelligent'. Later, on 1 May 1945, he is 'bright and industrious, assuming a great deal of responsibility in a comparatively junior post'. (von Aufsess (1985) and (2020)).

Co-operation with Jersey and France

The people of Guernsey and Jersey faced similar challenges from 1940 to 1945 under enemy occupation. The Germans controlled all communication between the Islands and played one Island off against the other. Post between the Islands depended on a ship being available and could be censored; during the crisis over cuts in food rations in April 1943, the Bailiffs of Guernsey and Jersey were, exceptionally, permitted to confer by telephone – but only by attending at the F.K. offices in each Island. From Guernsey's point of view Jersey had the advantage of more farmland in relation to population; for example Jersey was self-sufficient in wheat and produced a surplus of potatoes. By contrast the Guernsey landscape was dominated by tomato glasshouses; conversion of these from a luxury salad crop to general food production was hampered by shortages of fertiliser and fuel for irrigation. Guernsey was both more densely populated and more heavily fortified than Jersey. In July 1942 the Germans permitted a C.C. delegation to visit Jersey for discussions with their Jersey counterparts on the Superior Council to seek agreement on food supplies, imports from France and preparation for a possible Allied siege of the Islands – which of course came to pass two years later. On 16 July 1942, Louis describes that week in Jersey, with a graphic account of occupied St Helier, its streets deserted in mid-Summer; he met the mother of Peter Hassall, a 15 year old escapee deported to Germany, and also one of the Jersey hostages recently released by the Germans. Appendix Item 8 is the official report of that visit.

The best example of effective co-operation between Guernsey and Jersey was the organisation set up in the nearby French port of Granville to purchase food, seeds, fuel and other necessities for the Islanders – by legal means where possible and, where not, on the Black Market. Louis devotes some of the most vivid writing in his diary to accounts of the free-booting Granville operation. On 17 October 1942, when the current diary had been under way for some six months, he reminisces about trips to Granville in August 1940 and June 1941. The Germans and their auxiliaries were spending large quantities of francs and Occupation marks in the Islands; in accordance with Gresham's Law, workers and shopkeepers would hasten to deposit those doubtful currencies in Island banks where they would be credited to their accounts in sterling. This system relied upon a guarantee by the States of both Islands that they would buy surplus foreign currency from Island banks at the official rate; this guarantee was itself financed by ever-increasing overdrafts from Island banks. In turn the States used that German and French currency to finance the Granville purchases. This was all on a strictly cash basis so suitcases of banknotes had to be taken by sea to France. Louis relates colourful anecdotes of the Granville office; by June 1941 they had obtained a safe to keep some millions of francs 'with a piece of cardboard to separate the Jersey money from that belonging to Guernsey'. The safe was borrowed from Sherwill's office back in Guernsey and was a considerable advance on the hotel wardrobe originally pressed into service (Diary 17 October 1942).

The currency régime imposed on the Islands by the Germans was of course unsustainable. It was open to speculation by anyone able to bring French and German currency into the Islands and was only partially mitigated by the ability of the States to spend that unwelcome currency in Granville on food and fuel. The diary tracks the twists and turns of German financial policy towards the Islands. When the Germans eventually stopped the export of currency to France, Louis commented in his diary on 8 March 1944 that 'Alice in Wonderland is pure logic to our present financial mess.' The German view was that the Island's parlous financial state should not be seen in isolation but in the context of the war debt of the British state and empire as a whole on the conclusion of hostilities. In a sense that is what happened, for in the post-war settlement the UK government made a grant to Guernsey of £3.3m to help the Island meet its indebtedness of £6m, the price of survival during the Occupation; these were huge sums, as in a normal year the entire revenue of Guernsey was only £700,000 (Sanders (2005) pp.53-55). The balance of the Island's debt to the banks was paid off by 1960.

Coping with isolation

Indefinite isolation from family and friends overseas is a recurring theme of the diary. The Island community was fractured by the departure of men into the armed forces, including both Louis's brothers, then the mass evacuation of June 1940 and finally the deportations of 1942/43. One half serious/half frivolous response was to resort to spiritualism for news of absent relatives and friends; on 28 October 1942 Louis records a séance over tea hosted by Dr Symons and attended by the Sherwills. From early 1941 it had become possible to exchange messages to and from the UK via the International Committee of the Red Cross. These had to be strictly personal in content, were limited to 25 words and transit time was measured in months. Ironically, correspondence to and from Guernsey with prisoners of war held by the Germans was much less restricted; long letters, photographs and even parcels could be exchanged with prisoners of war in Germany. The same postal opportunities existed between Germany and the UK, subject of course to censorship and delays. The 887 civilians deported from the Island in 1942/43 were treated the same. By May 1943 Channel Island internees at Biberach were so well supplied that they began sending bulk shipments of cigarettes, chocolate, tea and even food parcels to people in Jersey whose need was greater than theirs (Bailiff of Jersey's Biberach file). For a time at least, Island PoWs and internees alike were able to act as unofficial forwarding agents between the UK and the Islands and vice versa (Harris (1979) and Mayr (2017)). By 19 July 1943 Louis had received photographs of all his nephews and nieces in England. The Allied invasion of France in June 1944 interrupted all these exchanges; months of silence followed until February 1945 when a new batch of messages was delivered by the Red Cross relief ship S.S. *Vega*. By then almost a year had passed since the last messages from the UK had been written. For example, it was not until 12 February 1945 the Guillemettes were to learn of the death in action on 8 August 1944, south of Caen, of Louis's younger brother Vic, a tank commander.

Boating was Louis's favourite relief from the anxieties of Occupation. The diary records at least 24 trips to Herm, usually in his 18-foot fishing boat *Ida*. Combining business with pleasure, Louis would ferry F.K. officers such as Dr. Brosch and Inspektor Oser, on tours of inspection; the Germans had insisted, against local advice, on sheep being farmed in Herm; they were dismayed to find that the animals did not thrive. German officers also treated Herm as a hunting preserve, just as Lieutenant-Governors of Guernsey had done over the centuries (Le Page (1995)). To Louis and his boating companions, such as Dick Johns and Raymond Falla, trips to Herm were an opportunity to enjoy the hospitality of the caretakers, Mr and Mrs Le Page, and for shoregathering, especially of ormers which were available in numbers which later generations could only dream of. There was always plenty of firewood to be collected from the pines planted by earlier Tenants. Some of the best writing in the diary describes fishing trips (under sail when possible, because fuel was in short supply). On just two occasions, in February 1943, Louis records taking his wife Queenie to Herm. The Island had always been a Crown property, with access strictly limited by successive Tenants; these wartime visits, when Herm was run by the States of Guernsey, may have inspired the States to buy the Island in 1949 and to create, in effect, a national park for Guernsey.

The afterlife of the Diary

Unfortunately the diary ceases on 2 May 1945, one week before the Liberation. Louis would then have been extremely busy, not least in assisting Leale in the drafting of his 20,000 word report delivered at the States' meeting on 23 May. From internal evidence it is very likely that Louis relied on his diary and the attached documents in working on that report. It was then put aside as he embarked on his post-war career as States Supervisor and Treasurer of the States – in the modern jargon 'Chief Executive' – until his retirement in 1975. Although in the diary he envisaged referring to it in his circle of family and friends in future years, he never seems to have done so. The earliest known comment on the diary by an outsider is by Desmond Hawkins, features producer for the B.B.C. On 15 October 1946 he wrote to Louis: '... it is quite obvious [the diaries] would interest many people. Why don't you make them the basis of a book? You obviously have unusual detachment towards the whole history of those years, with at the same time the closest grasp of what was happening'.

That diary now appears in full and must speak for itself.

Ken Tough
Guernsey, February 2022

ABBREVIATIONS

A.E.F.	Allied Expeditionary Force
C.C.	States of Guernsey Controlling Committee
CIOR	Channel Islands Occupation Review
C.T.S.	Civil Transport Service
F.K.	Feldkommandantur (Military Government Unit) replaced by P.K. in May 1944)
G.U.B.	Greenhouse Utilization Board
H.M.	His/Her Majesty
H.U.V.	Heeresunterkunftverwaltung (Army Quartermaster's Dept)
I.A.S.	Island Archives Service
I.C.R.C.	International Committee of the Red Cross. Based in Geneva, the I.C.R.C. organised the transport, via Lisbon, of the supplies donated by the British Red Cross.
K.Ass.	Kriegsassessor (Military Government Officer)
K.V.I.	Kriegsverwaltungsinspektor (Military Government Officer – junior to K.V.R. and M.V.R.)
K.V.R.	Kriegsverwaltungsrat (Military Government Officer)
M.V.R.	Militärverwaltungsrat (Military Government Officer)
N.C.O.	Non-Commissioned Officer
N.N.E.	North North-East
O.K.V.R.	Oberkriegsverwaltungsrat (Senior Military Government Officer)
O.T.	Organization Todt
P.K.	Propagandakompanie (Army News Reporters and Photographers)
P.K. I	Platzkommandantur I (Front-line military government unit, under tighter military control, which replaced F.K. 515 in May 1944.)
PoW	Prisoner of War
R.A.F.	Royal Air Force
R.C.A.F.	Royal Canadian Air Force
R.M./R.K.M.	Reichsmark/Reichskreditkassenmark (terms used interchangeably) – German unit of currency as issued for use in occupied territories.
S.K.H.	Soldatenkaufhaus (Retail shop for the troops – cf. the British N.A.A.F.I.)
T.B.	Tuberculosis
U.S.A.A.F.	United States Army Air Force

DRAMATIS PERSONAE

(These notes supplement the information given in the Diary, giving the full names, year of birth etc., where known, of people mentioned. See the Introduction for more background information. The surnames, occupations, ranks etc. are those current during 1940-1945; people born after the Occupation are not included).

The Diarist

Guillemette, Louis Auguste b. Guernsey 1910. (Hereafter referred to as 'Louis').

The Guillemette family

(In order of birth; all were born in Guernsey except where stated otherwise.)

Guillemette, Auguste Désiré b. Jersey 1864. Father of Louis.

Guillemette, Edith Mary (née Sauvarin) b. 1872. Mother of Louis.

Sauvarin, Fannie Isabel ('Auntie Fan') b. Jersey 1878. Aunt of Louis. Ran Les Gravées Post Office and General Stores.

Robilliard, George Shave ('Skipper') b. 1880. Building contractor of Sarel Villa, Rohais & Le Foulon. Queenie's father; built La Platte.

Winterflood, Marguerite (née Guillemette) b. 1909. Sister of Louis. Married Hubert Winterflood (b. Guernsey 1908) in 1937. They evacuated to England in 1940.

Sims, Madeleine Edith (née Guillemette) ('Mads') b. 1911. Sister of Louis. Proof-reader for *The Star* newspaper in 1940. Later a proof-reader in the Bailiff's Office. Kept a diary. Married Irwin Edward Sims (b. 1909), printer with The Guernsey Star & Gazette Ltd., in 1939.

Williams, Adèle May (née Sauvarin) b. 1913. First cousin of Louis. Married Herbert Frederick Williams (b. 1897) in 1943.

Collins, Marie (née Guillemette) ('Babe') b. 1916. Sister of Louis. Married Leonard Walter Graham Collins ('Len') (b. England 1913) in 1939. Evacuated to England in 1940. Len stayed, was shipwrecked off Jersey in May 1942 and deported to Germany in September of that year. He escorted returning internees to Guernsey in November 1943 before himself returning to his camp at Laufen. See the family group photograph taken on that brief visit.

Guillemette, Evelyn Marjorie Tillett (née Robilliard) ('Queenie') b. 1914. Married Louis in 1939 and set up home at La Platte, Bordeaux.

Guillemette, Victor George ('Vic') 1915-1944. Louis' youngest brother. A civil servant in Guernsey before volunteering to join the army. Married Phyllis (née Browne) in 1940. They had two daughters, Bernadette and Margaret. Vic was killed in action in Normandy, serving with the 8th Battalion, The East Lancashire Regiment. Commemorated on the Bayeux Memorial to the Missing. 'Captain Kiki' was a family nickname, probably from his role in *The Mikado*.

Guillemette, John Désiré ('Des') b. 1913. Journalist pre- and post-war. Joined the Australian army and fought in New Guinea. Married Marjorie (née Loaring) and they had a daughter, Michelle, in 1941.

Guillemette, José b. 1942. Daughter of Louis, in 2019 she initiated the publication of this Diary.

Bailiff and Controlling Committee

Carey, Victor Gosselin b. Guernsey 1871. Bailiff since 1935; sworn Lieutenant-Governor 'as far as civil duties only appertain' on 20 June 1940, after the swift departure of Maj-Gen F.R. Minshull-Ford the previous day. Resided at Le Vallon, St Martin's. As President of the States and of the Royal Court, which then had legislative and administrative as well as judicial functions, the Bailiff was head of Island government. He was not a member of the new C.C. set up in June 1940 but, accompanied by its president, he represented the Island at the highest-level meetings with the German authorities.

Sherwill, Ambrose James b. Guernsey 1890. HM Procureur (HM Attorney-General). President of the C.C. from June to December 1940. Suspended in October then removed from public office by order of the German authorities. Briefly permitted to resume a public role in 1942. Lived with his wife and two sons at Havelet House, St Peter Port until he was deported to Germany in February 1943. See Sherwill (2006).

Leale, Jurat Rev John b. Guernsey 1892. Economics Officer then succeeded Sherwill as President of the C.C.; Methodist minister and Cambridge graduate in Economics.

Lainé, Jurat Sir Abraham (James) b. Guernsey 1876. Vice-President of the C.C. and President of the Essential Commodities Committee. Retired – Indian Civil Service.

Symons, Dr Angelo Nelson b. Nelson, New Zealand 1875. Health Services Officer.

Drake, Jurat Aylmer Mackworth b. England 1872 d. 1941. Horticulture Officer until his death.

Dorey, Percy b. Guernsey 1881. Succeeded Jurat Drake as Horticulture Officer. President of Glasshouse Utilisation Board. Leading tomato grower; Managing Director of the Fruit Export Co. Ltd.

Falla, Raymond Ogier b. Guernsey 1901. Leading bulb grower, at The Meadows, St Andrew's. Agriculture Officer. Led purchasing expeditions in France. Family friend of the Guillemettes. Robust sense of humour.

Sayer, (Michael) Wynne b. England 1885. Agriculture Officer, deputising for Falla. Mission to Jersey 1941 and supervised work in Alderney in 1942. Retired – Indian Agricultural Service. Deported to Germany in September 1942.

Johns, Richard Henry b. Guernsey 1878. Labour Officer. Owner of Johns Butchers, South Side, St Sampson's. People's Deputy for St Sampson's and the Vale.

Raffles, Stamford b. England 1885 d. 1942. Information Officer until his death. Retired – Malayan Government Service. People's Deputy for St Peter Port.

Ridgway, George John Proctor b. Guernsey 1881 d. 1942. Advocate of the Royal Court 1911; HM Comptroller 1935. Legal advisor to the C.C. until his death.

Martel, John Edmund Leopold b. Guernsey 1893. Advocate of the Royal Court 1919; succeeded Ridgway as Acting Attorney-General and legal advisor to the C.C.

Marquand, Henry Edward b. Guernsey 1886. States Supervisor and Treasurer of the States. Head of the Civil Service.

Other Civilians

Ash, Fanny b. England 1890. Lived with her farmer husband, Henry Hubert Ash, at Ashleigh, Grand Bouet, St Peter Port. Family friend.

Audoire, (John) Nigel b. Guernsey 1910. Lived with his wife Maisie Emmeline (née Brache) at Bordeaux Lodge and later at Windfield, New Road. A radio and electrical engineer, he built a radio transmitter/receiver, hidden in his home, capable of contacting London in case of dire emergency. It is believed that he did this with the knowledge of members of the C.C. Friend and neighbour of Louis; sailed his own fishing vessel *Frypan*.

Barnett, Roland James b. England 1910. Posted to France as a supplies clerk for the Granville purchasing operation.

Béghin, Louis Charles b. Jersey 1889. Shoe retailer; became part of the Granville purchasing team.

Bell, Very Rev Thomas b. Guernsey 1820 d. Guernsey 1917. Rector of the Vale 1859-1914 and Dean of Guernsey 1892-1917.

Bertrand, Ludovic Edmund Peter b. Guernsey 1897. Carpenter and grower, living at Gas Lane, the Longstore, St Peter Port. Editor of the *Guernsey Active Secret Press*, an underground newsletter. See Bertrand (1945).

Bichard, Henry Robin ('Harry') b. 1890 Guernsey. Grower, of Les Hautgards, Vale. Chairman of the Potato Board under the C.C. Friend of Louis.

Bird, Mary b. Guernsey 1920. Daughter of Wilfrid and Elise Bird. Mary Bichard (née Bird) died in January 2022 at the age of 101. She was the last survivor of the friends and relatives of the British commandos, Hubert Nicolle and James Symes, taken to Paris for interrogation in 1940. See Bell (1998).

Bird, Walter b. Guernsey 1858 d. 1942. Merchant and corn agent.

Bird, Walter Arthur b. Guernsey 1916. Bulb grower, employed by his father Wilfrid.

Bird, Wilfrid John b. Guernsey 1887. States official then self-employed grower. Le Profond Val, St Peter's then Apsley, Brock Road, St Peter Port.

Bisson, Henry Charles b. Guernsey 1910. Fisherman, of Le Mouillage, Bordeaux. Neighbour of Louis. See Sauvary (1990).

Blaikie Webster, John Philip b. Wales 1884. In 1940 described as retired; later grower and chairman of *The Star* newspaper.

Bougourd, Alfred John ('Alf') b. Guernsey 1889. Managing director of Bougourd Bros Ltd, motor dealer. Escaped to England in the *Kate*, 14 August 1943. See Kreckeler (1978) and Bell (2002).

Bougourd, Stephen b. Guernsey 1891. Coal merchant in 1940, later grower and fisherman, of Grande Rue, Bordeaux. Neighbour of Louis.

Broughton, Henry George ('Harry') b. England 1900. Chartered Accountant with Messrs Black, Geoghegan and Till. States Auditor and financial adviser. Friend of Louis.

Brousson, Lt-Col Frederick b. England 1876. Government Secretary. Deported to Germany 1943 and repatriated to England via Sweden March 1945. See Harris (1990) pp.176-181.

Buckingham, Graham Walter b. Guernsey 1920. Mechanic. Escaped from German custody July 1944 and recaptured 6 months later. See Bell (2002) pp. 294-5.

Cambridge, William Russell b. Scotland 1902. Doctor with his surgery at The Bridge, St Sampson's. Friend of Louis..

Carey, (Victor) Michael (Graham de Vic) b. Guernsey 1900. Son of Bailiff Carey; Advocate of the Royal Court 1927. War service as a major in the Somerset Light Infantry; officer in Anglo-American military government in north Africa, France and the Low Countries.

Carrington, Adolphus Edward Alfred b. England 1876. Managing Director of Leale Ltd.

Chambers, Sir Theodore, KBE b.1871. Vice-chairman of National Savings Committee. Chairman of Welwyn Garden City Ltd 1920-50.

Cheesbrough, Herbert b. England 1906. Grocer's assistant. Deported to Germany 1942. See Bell (2002) pp.96-8, 226 and 403.

Chilcott, Ralph Edgar b. Guernsey 1902. Manager of the States Dairy.

Collings, Bernard Stanley b. Guernsey 1895. Doctor, with his surgery at Paradis, the Grange.

Corbet, John Edwin b. Guernsey 1882. Fisherman, living at Les Grippios, Vale. He is probably the Jack Corbet referred to by Louis on 13 December 1942. See also Sauvary (1990) p.40, who refers to a Jack (otherwise 'Ginger') Corbet.

Corbet, Wilfrid John b. Guernsey 1894. Grower at Balmoral, Vale. Assistant to Labour Officer. People's Deputy for St Sampson's and the Vale.

Corbet, William Henry ('Bill') b. Guernsey 1912. Fisherman and lorry driver; lived at Les Croutes then at 2, Tertre Lane, both in the Vale. Escaped to England on the *Kate* on 14 August 1943. See Kreckeler (1978) p.14 and Bell (2002) pp.256-7.

Corfield, Leonard James b. 1893 England. Manager of Barclays Bank, Fountain Street.

Cortvriend, Violet Victoria Edwina (née Gerry) b. England 1893. Wife of Gustave; given real time access to Louis's office and files to write an account of the Occupation. See Cortvriend (1947) and Sauvary (1990).

Coutanche, Alexander b. Jersey 1892. Bailiff of Jersey since 1935; presided over the Superior Council, the equivalent of the Guernsey C.C. Regarded by the Germans as a formidable negotiator. See von Aufsess (1985) and (2020).

Cranch, Donald George b. England 1904. Bank clerk. Deported to Germany 1942. With Len Collins and Willliam Reid, he escorted three fellow deportees being repatriated to Guernsey in August 1943, before returning to Laufen. See Harrris (1980) p.168.

Cross, Charles Henry b. England 1873. Proprietor of the North Cinema and People's Deputy for St Sampson's and the Vale. Deported to Germany in 1942 but later repatriated to Guernsey.

De Coudenhove, Henry Edward, Baron b. France 1871. Grower at La Falaise, St Martin's. Consular agent for France and Belgium and representative of the City of Paris at Hauteville House.

De Garis, Ernest b. Guernsey 1878. Farmer and grower at Myrtle Place, Castel. Elected Jurat of the Royal Court in 1928.

De Garis, Francis Henry b. Guernsey 1892. Deputy Inspector, Potato Board.

De Garis, John Alfred b. Guernsey 1903. Farmer; Organiser for the Farm Produce Board.

De Putron, Harry Lloyd b. Guernsey 1880. Owned Caledonia Nursery, St Peter Port.

De Putron, Pierre b. England 1886. Elected Jurat of the Royal Court in 1940. Custodian of Business and Industry, responsible for abandoned premises and stock. Later Food Controller, Essential Commodities Committee.

Dickson, Francis Martin ('Frank') b. Guernsey 1901. Farmer and caretaker of Herm on behalf of the Farm Produce Board from June 1940. Germans ordered his return to Guernsey in November 1942. See Le Page (1995).

Doig, Alexander Irvine b. Scotland 1879. Plasterer. Deported to Germany 1942 but repatriated in August 1943 to his old house at 12 Cliff Street. See Harris (1990) p.168.

Domaille, Daniel John ('Dan') b. Guernsey 1883. Fisherman. Rescued Quinain brothers on 9 June 1943.

Dorey, Albert Victor ('Vic') b. Guernsey 1896. Grower, employed by Fruit Export Co. Ltd. Friend of Louis.

Dorey, Edward Arthur ('Ted') b. Guernsey 1896. Farmer at Oatlands, St Sampson's and grower at Belgrave Vinery. Boating companion of Louis.

Dorey, Frank Leale b. Guernsey 1890. Grower for P.F. Dorey & Sons Ltd., Fontaine Vineries. See Sauvary (1990).

Dorey, John Nicholas b. Guernsey 1884. Farmer at King's Mills; Head Agricultural Organiser under the C.C.

Dubras, Charles Edmond b. France 1869. Coiffeur and parfumier at 22 High Street.

Duquemin, Hansel Alfred John b. Guernsey 1909. Driver for Organisation Todt, the German fortress builders in Guernsey. Made one unsuccessful attempt to escape by boat from Guernsey; in 1943 sent by the Germans to fish from Alderney. Escaped to England with Henry Ingrouille 8 April 1944.

Enticott, William Stanley ('Bill') b. Guernsey 1909. Fisherman (a Greffe ID form required him to state his place of employment, to which he replied 'On the Sea'.) Lived at South Side, St Sampson's and Beau Séjour, Vale Road. Escaped with Fred Noyon 3 November 1944. See Kreckeler (1978) and Bell (2002) p.307.

Finey, Rev John Harold b. England 1896. Rector of the Forest.

Foote, George William b. Guernsey 1853. Veterinary surgeon at Rohais de Bas. Refused to allow building on his land at what became known as Foote's Lane.

Fox, William Burton b. Eire 1897. Physician, surgeon & obstetrician. Surgery at St Damian's, St Sampson's & also resident at the Emergency Hospital, Castel.

Frampton, Wilfrid b. Guernsey 1885-1944. States Accountant. His wife, Ella, kept a diary frequently quoted by Bell (2002).

Frossard, Rev Edward Louis b. France 1887. Rector of St Sampson's.

Garbett, Most Rev Cyril Forster b. England 1875. Bishop of Winchester 1932-42 and Archbishop of York 1942-55. Sherwill recounts a dramatic trip to Sark with Dr Garbett, Dean Giffard and the Lieutenant-Governor in 1934 on the Rev Peter Mignot's boat. See Sherwill (2006), pp.29-32.

Gardner, Charles William b. Guernsey 1899. Accountant & company secretary at *The Star* newspaper. Pianist; Occupation entertainer with his brothers Cyril ('Cyd') and Roy.

Garland, Garnet Garfield b. England 1893. Manager. Deported to Germany in 1942; elected Camp Captain at Biberach. See Harris (1990) and Bailiff of Jersey's Biberach file.

Genet, Auguste Pierre Achille b. France 1868. Master baker at Four Cabot, St Andrew's.

Gibson, Richard Edward b. England 1891. Surgeon, practising at Paradis, The Grange and at the Emergency Hospital. See Gibson (1945).

Giffard, Very Rev Agnew Walter Giles b. Guernsey 1869. From 1932 Dean of Guernsey and Rector of St Peter Port.

Godwin, Ivon David b. England 1908. Shop assistant. Deported to Germany in 1942 with his wife Joyce (née Collins) and twin sons Ralph and Neville. See Harris (1980) p.198.

Golding, Raymond Wallace Henry b. Guernsey 1912. Clerk at the Labour Office, Hirzel House.

Green, William ('Billy') b. Guernsey 1909. Cycle dealer. Keen motorcyclist and swimmer. See Bell (1992) p.168 on swimming in quarry near Bordeaux.

Greville, Patrick Ernest Michael ('Pat') b. Guernsey 1902. Licensee of Pat's Bar, Fountain Street.

Grignard, François. Based in Caen. Supplied cycle and vehicle tyres and charcoal power units to Guernsey and Jersey 1942-43.

Grut, Allan Norman b. Guernsey 1912. Photographer and photographic dealer.

Guillemet, Maurice b. Guernsey 1897. Vimiera, Rohais, St Peter Port. Grower/farmer. Became part of the purchasing team at Granville.

Hart, Jack b. England 1901. Manufacturing and dispensing chemist at New Road, St Sampson's. See Sauvary (1990).

Harwood, Ronald ('Ron') b. Guernsey 1908. Civil service colleague and Best Man at Louis's wedding in 1939. Flew to England in June 1940, with instructions to assist Guernsey evacuees. After the War became managing director of Leale Ltd – the position which Louis had been offered, initially accepted and ultimately declined. See Diary 22 and 28 October 1943.

Hathaway, Sybil (formerly Beaumont, née Collings) b. Guernsey 1884. Dame of Sark from 1927. See Stoney (1978).

Heggs, George b. England 1898. Engineer and Manager, States Water Board. See his report in Lainé & Loveridge (1946), pp.95-102.

Henry, Ernest John b. Guernsey 1885. Coal merchant & ship broker, of Uganda, Vale. Deported to Germany in February 1943 and repatriated to Guernsey the following August.

Henry, Ernest Thomas b. Guernsey 1880. Farmer at The Hermitage, L'Ancresse. His son, Thomas Stephen, b. Guernsey 1913, a grower at Eastbourne, Vale, was a friend and neighbour of Louis.

Hickey, Canon Thomas Grant b. Guernsey 1877. Catholic Priest in Charge, Rector of St Joseph's Church and Rural Catholic Dean.

Hill-Cottingham, Frederick Thomas b. England 1878. Retired civil engineer; People's Deputy for St Peter Port. Vice-President of the Committee for the Control of Essential Commodities. See Bell (2002).

Hills, Major Francis Barritt b. England 1880. General Manager, States Electricity Board.

Hodder, Charles Henry b. Guernsey 1912. Friend and neighbour of Louis from their childhood in St John's. Formerly joint owner with Louis of *Ida*. Career civil servant; chartered secretary. Unlike Louis, he was permitted to leave and join the army in June 1940. See Bell (2002) p. 27.

Hollard, Pierre Paul b. France 1890. Official translator for the C.C. In 1940 lived at Sunnycroft, The Grange and from 1942 at St Mihiel, Belmont Road.

Hubert, Francis John ('Frank') b. Guernsey 1922. Lived at father's house, Sefton, Doyle Road. Worked in the family seed and vegetable growing business. See Hubert (2001).

Hubert, Nicholas b. Guernsey 1864. Farmer & grower at Grande Rue, Bordeaux. Friend & neighbour of Louis.

Hubert, Nicholas John ('Nick') b. Guernsey 1893. Grower and later fisherman at Grande Rue, Bordeaux. Owned quarry at Rue Godfrey.

Hubert, Jean Thomas Daniel ('Jack') b. Guernsey 1905. Clerk; later a grower. Escaped on the *Kate* on 14 August 1943. See Corbet, William Henry above.

Hubert, Wilfrid George b. Guernsey 1892. Lived at Sefton, Doyle Road. Seed trade expert and seed merchant. By 1942 Imports Officer under the C.C.

Ingrouille, Alora Hilda (née Le Noury) b. Guernsey 1893. Mother of John. Lived with her husband John Alfred at La Miellette then La Moye from 1941.

Ingrouille, Henry Trevail ('Harry') b. Guernsey 1902. Fisherman (entered 'Fishing Summer, Land Work Winter' on his Greffe ID form).

Ingrouille, John Henry 1920-45. Lived with his parents. Falsely accused of organising resistance, imprisoned in Germany and died in June 1945 before he could be repatriated. See Sanders et al (2014) pp.217-8.

Jehan, Bertie b. Guernsey 1904 d. 1944. A greenhouse hand and farm worker, he lived at La Favourite, Les Crabbes, St Peter's. Shot on 23 August 1944 while guarding his potato patch by night. See Bell (1992) pp.292-293.

Johns, Richard ('Dick') b. Guernsey 1910. Butcher at South Side, St Sampson's, employed by his father Richard Henry Johns (See C.C. above). Friend of Louis.

Kilshaw, Rev William b. England 1888. Vicar of St John's. People's Deputy for St Peter Port.

Lambert, Pierre Louis Victor b. France 1894. Electrical engineer. Acting French consul. Recruited the Le Page brothers – see below – to escape with information for the Allies in January 1945. It is believed that members of the C.C. were aware of, and approved, the plan. See Kreckeler (1978) pp.15-16 and Bell (2002) pp.337-8.

Langlois, Major Edwin Mauger b. Guernsey 1898. Electrical contractor; Constable of St Martin's. States Billetting Officer, responsible for rehousing civilians ousted by the German forces, often at short notice.

Langmead, Arthur John b. Guernsey 1898. Police Inspector. Deported to Germany 1943.

Lean, David b. England 1876. Retired – Royal Canadian Mounted Police. Deported to Germany 1942; repatriated to Guernsey from Laufen in August 1943. See Harris (1980) p.168.

Le Maître, Lewis b. Guernsey 1896. Master baker of Belle Vue, Bordeaux. Neighbour of Louis.

Le Maître, Vernon McCrindell b. Guernsey 1906. Civil servant and billetting officer. Neighbour of Louis.

Le Page, Ernest b. Guernsey 1884. Farmer and caretaker of Herm with his wife Marguerite, in place of his brother-in-law Frank Dickson, from 1942 onwards. See Le Page (1995) and Marshall (1958).

Le Page, James Ewald b. Guernsey 1908. H.M. Deputy Greffier, responsible for the Register of Identifications.

Le Page, John William b. Guernsey 1913. Fisherman, of 2, Gas Lane, St Peter Port – see Lambert above.

Le Page, Thomas John b. Guernsey 1908. Fisherman, of 1, Gas Lane – see Lambert above.

Le Poidevin, Clifford b. Guernsey 1907. Greenhouse worker of Les Grippios, Bordeaux. His wife, Leah Annie (née Le Tissier) b. Guernsey 1903, ran the grocery shop attached to Bordeaux Bakery. Neighbours of Louis.

Le Tissier, James Edwin ('Jim') b. Guernsey 1883-1944. Grower, of Bordeaux. Neighbour of Louis.

Lewis, Kenneth George Hilary ('Ken') b. Guernsey 1922. Junior colleague of Louis and assiduous diarist.

Loveridge, John Henry ('Jack') b. Guernsey 1912. Secretary, States Committee for the Control of Essential Commodities. See Lainé & Loveridge (1946). Colleague of Louis. After 1945 pursued career in the public legal service: Bailiff of Guernsey 1973-82.

McCulloch, Henry b. Scotland 1890. Master tailor. Deported to Germany 1942 and returned to Guernsey August 1943.

MacDonald, George. Caretaker, with his wife, of Jethou. Originally from Alderney, they had moved to Herm and Jethou c.1921 to work for the novelist Compton Mackenzie.

Machon, Roy Noverraz b. Guernsey 1920. Cinema projectionist. Deported to Germany for making 'V-sign' lapel badges; later imprisoned for further term for holding 'a political meeting' – namely the farewell party mentioned by Louis. See Sanders et al (2014).

Malbon, George b. England 1886. Greenhouse hand. Killed by anti-aircraft shell on D-Day, 1944.

Mallett, Frank b. Guernsey 1889. Master coach builder; ran St Sampson's Coach and Motor Works.

Mallett, Ronald Archer b. Guernsey 1912. H.M. Deputy Greffier; seconded to become Secretary, States Potato Board.

Margot, Francis Swiss hairdresser. Lodged at Woodlawn, Doyle Road. Neighbour and friend of Frank Hubert. See Hubert (2001).

Mentha, James b. Switzerland 1876. Manager of the Royal Hotel.

Nicolle, Emile W. b. Guernsey 1892. Secretary to States Committees. Father of Hubert Nicolle. See Bell (1998).

Nicolle, Frank Hubert b. Guernsey 1900. Harbourmaster. Uncle of Hubert Nicolle; Germans ordered his dismissal, together with his brother Emile.

Nicolle, Hubert Frank b. Guernsey 1919. See Bell (1998) for Nicolle's two missions to Guernsey in 1940. An unintended consequence was the dismissal from office, by the Germans, of Ambrose Sherwill, first president of the C.C.

Noel, Stanley Arthur b. 1899 Guernsey. Motor engineer and garage proprietor. Manager of Military Transport Service 1941. Detained in relation to the escape of the *Kate* and deported to Germany in September 1943.

Norman, John Francis ('Jack') b. Guernsey 1912. Haulage and agricultural contractor.

Noyon, Frederick William ('Fred') b. Guernsey 1878. Retired sea captain then fisherman, of West View and later Vale Avenue, Vale. Escaped November 1944. See Enticott above.

Ogier, Thomas James ('Tom') b. Guernsey 1901. Grower, of 1, Myrtle Lodge, Hougue Jehannet, Vale. Grower manager for the G.U.B. and seed expert.

Oliver, William Douglas b. 1888 England. Chief Officer, Fire Brigade. Discharged by German order August 1943 and reinstated December 1944.

Ozanne, Thomas ('Tom') b. Guernsey 1870. Shop assistant at Bordeaux Stores. People's Deputy for St Sampson's and the Vale. Founder of Bordeaux Wesleyan Mission. Neighbour of Louis.

Peek, Gervase Foottit b. Guernsey 1855 d. 1943. Prominent builder and founder of the *Guernsey Evening Press*.

Penstone-Franklin, John Trevor b. England 1882. States Harbourmaster.

Pommier, Clement Leopold Jean b. Guernsey 1900. Employed in family charcuterie at 28 Fountain Street.

Prins, Hendrik Warmold b. Netherlands 1896. Grower, of The Bungalow, St Martin's. Employed by G.U.B.

Quinain, Henry James ('Harry') b. Alderney 1917 and **Quinain, John Alfred** ('Jack') b. Alderney 1914. Fishermen brothers, of Surprise House, St George's Esplanade and later 4 Candie Road. Came to Guernsey with their father Jean-Louis Bienaimé Quinain (another 'Jack', b. Alderney 1881), when Alderney was evacuated in June 1940. See Bell (1995) p.245 for details of the destruction by sea-mine of the Quinains' boat *Sunrise*.

Randall, Group-Captain Charles Russell Jekyl R.A.F. (ret'd) b. Guernsey 1879. Brother of the following.

Randall, Lt-Col Robert William b. Guernsey 1878. Managing Director, R.W. Randall Ltd (Vauxlaurens Brewery). Deported to Germany 1943.

Reid, William Percival b. England 1905. States Vermin Destroyer. Deported to Germany 1942; with Donald Cranch, escorted repatriates to Guernsey August 1943.

Riderer, Auguste Hedwig b. Germany 1883. 'Language stenographer; translator for German and local authorities'. Working from home.

Robin, Ambrose Collas b. Guernsey 1886. Administrator, States Insurance Authority.

Rose, Alistair Westland b. England 1903. Physician, of Paradis, later Kilravock, Doyle Road, the 18 New Street. Friend of Louis. See Rose (2001), (2002) and (2008), and Cortvriend (1947).

Roussel, Alfred John b. Guernsey 1879. H.M. Greffier; member of the United Club, whose premises overlooked St Peter Port harbour.

Rowe, William James ('Bill') b. South Africa 1916. Grower. Deported to Germany 1942.

Rumball, William Norman b. Jersey 1906. Bank clerk. Ran the accounting operation at Granville on behalf of both Jersey and Guernsey.

Santangelo, Domenico b. Italy 1882. Violinist & music teacher. In 1911 wrote score for Guernsey's unofficial anthem 'Sarnia Chérie'. See Marr (1984).

Sarre, Alfred Cyril ('Alf') b. Guernsey 1899. Accountant; produce merchant & fuel importer. Representative of the States of Guernsey in Jersey. See Bell (2002) pp.111, 305.

Sebire, Archibald Reginald b. Alderney 1916. Fisherman. Killed on the Quinains' boat.

Short, Ronald Terry ('Ron') b. England 1910. Civil servant. Secretary, States Dairy.

Skinner, Daniel b. England 1881. Labourer. Deported to Germany 1942; repatriated to Guernsey from Laufen August 1943.

Smith, Frederick John b. Scotland 1878. Dental surgeon at Rosewood, The Grange. Apparently a 'character', he posed for his ID photograph wearing a full beard and smoking a pipe.

Stockwell, Alick Stronach b. England 1873. Retired – Royal Army Pay Corps. Set up the Identity Card system in 1940-41. Deported to Germany 1942. See Tough (1995).

Stroobant, Frank Edward b. England 1907. Businessman & proprietor of the Home from Home Restaurant, St Peter Port. Deported to Germany 1942. See Stroobant (1967). Friend of Louis.

Sutcliffe, Richard Brook b. England 1904. Medical practitioner and general surgeon at Westbourne, The Grange & 18 New Street. Friend of Louis.

Tidd, Hugh b. England 1911. Grower at Les Naftiaux & Le Varclin Farm. Married Nancy Ida (née Guilbert) b. Guernsey 1922. Friends of Louis.

Timmer, Gerrit Jan b. The Netherlands 1903. Market gardener, of Timmer Ltd., The Suntrap, Forest.

Toms, Charles Henry b. Guernsey 1887. Photographer and later Linotype mechanic, for the Guernsey Press Co. Ltd.

Travers, Henri b. Guernsey 1914 & **Travers, James Le Patourel** b. Guernsey 1906. Hotelkeepers at The Prince of Wales, Smith Street.

Van Katwyk, Johannes William b. 1893 The Netherlands. Fisherman & metal dealer of Le Maresquet, Vale.

Vaudin, George Martin b. Guernsey 1887. Grower and merchant, of Vaudin & Keates, The Bordage. Led the States of Guernsey purchasing mission in Granville.

Warry, George Samuel b. Guernsey 1916. Baker at Warry's Bakery. Married Zelia May ('Zu') (formerly Arnold, née Carpentier) b. Guernsey 1914. Friends of Louis.

Wheadon, Edward Thomas b. Guernsey 1875. Fruit grower. People's Deputy for St. Peter Port. President of the States Insurance Authority.

Williams, Maj-Gen Weir de Lancey b. Guernsey 1871. Retired from the army 1923. In May & June 1940 briefly led a force of Local Defence Volunteers in Guernsey intended to deal with enemy airborne troops. See Durand (2018) p.5.

Wilson, Walter Melvin b. England 1891. States Maintenance Engineer.

German Personnel

(Military or naval ranks are given in English, except when there is no clear English equivalent, when the German term is given. The documents are inconsistent in the spelling of 'Schneberger' and 'von Helldorff' and the preceding forms are here used throughout.)

von Aufsess, Hans Max, Freiherr (Baron) b. Germany 1906. Studied law and forestry; Bavarian landowner. Led the civil affairs branch of F.K. 515 in Jersey 1943-45. Transferred to Guernsey in April 1945. Intellectual and fluent in French and English. See von Aufsess (1985) & (2020).

Brosch, Dr Richard. Lawyer; second in command of F.K. 515 civil affairs branch at Grange Lodge from 1940; led the Guernsey branch from October 1941 to March 1943. Acquired fluent command of English. Sherwill found him 'invariably courteous' and 'a kind, likeable person'. See Sherwill (2006) p.144. Others, including Louis, were frustrated by his food production schemes and demands for statistics.

Casper, Dr Wilhelm. b. Germany 1902. Lawyer and regional administrator in civilian life. O.K.V.R and chief administrator of F.K. 515 civil affairs branch, based in Jersey, from September 1941 to autumn 1943, when he was succeeded by his subordinate von Aufsess.

Göttmann, Sonderführer Kurt. German press officer and censor from January 1941. For his chequered career, including shipwreck and later imprisonment for corruption, see Falla (2018).

Hauschild, M.V.R. In March 1945 made the hazardous flight from Germany to the Islands. His role – to advise on agriculture. His grandiose scheme to reorganise milk production in Jersey 'was doomed to failure' – see von Aufsess (1985) p.159.

von Helldorff, Colonel Hans, Graf (Count). Quarter-master and chief of staff to General von Schmettow. Replaced when von Schmettow was removed on 28 February 1945, and ultimately banished to Herm.

Hüffmeier, Vice-Admiral Friedrich b. Germany 1898. Career naval officer. Commanded battleship *Scharnhorst* from March 1942 to October 1943. A committed Nazi, he then had a desk job overseeing 'National Socialist Leadership' appointments in the navy. Naval commander of the Channel Islands from July, 1944. Replaced von Schmettow as commander in chief on 1 March 1945 and appointed naval officers to key positions.

Knackfuss, Colonel Friedrich b. 1887. Feldkommandant (overall head of F.K. 515 and based in Jersey) from February 1941 to January 1944. Stoutly defended the prerogatives of military government in disputes with army units in the Islands. See Cruickshank (1975) chapter 6.

Krafft, Herr Friedrich. A professional interpreter who spent five years in Guernsey working for F.K. 515 at Grange Lodge. During that time he was in almost daily contact with Louis. Sherwill described him as 'always kind, patient and courteous'. See Sherwill (2006) p.144. In 1946/7 Krafft interpreted at war crimes trials in Nuremberg.

Kratzer, Major Dr Jacob. Head of the F.K. 515 civil affairs branch in Guernsey from March 1943 to May 1944 when he was transferred to Saint-Lô. Required an interpreter. Sense of humour. In civilian life had been a civil servant in Munich.

Krefft, Sonderführer Alfred. A junior liaison officer at Grange Lodge, fluent in English. Not to be confused with Friedrich Krafft.

Melzer, M.V.R. A senior officer at Grange Lodge from March 1943 to May 1944. Required an interpreter.

Müller, Maj-Gen Erich. Commander of 319 Infantry Division and German commander in chief in the Channel Islands May 1941 to September 1943. Based in Guernsey.

Obermeyer, Captain. German harbourmaster; got on well with the Guernsey harbourmaster, Captain Penstone-Franklin.

Oser, Inspektor. Agriculture specialist at Grange Lodge, reporting to Brosch. Some command of English. Often critical of Guernsey farming standards. Left September 1943.

von Oettingen(-Wallerstein), Rittmeister Eugen, Fürst (Prince) b. Prague 1885. Headed the military branch of F.K. 515 in Guernsey from March 1941 to April 1942. Louis found him diplomatic and co-operative.

Reffler, K.V.R. Dr Wilhelm. Headed F.K. 515 civil affairs branch in Guernsey from its inception in August 1940 until his departure in October 1941. Agriculture specialist. Ella Frampton described Reffler in her diary as 'a good friend of this Island.'

Reich, Korvettenkapitän. Replaced von Helldorff as chief of staff 1 March 1945. In civilian life a banker from Cologne. 'More at home with figures than with people'. See von Aufsess (1985) p.146 et seq.

von Schmettow, Lt-Gen Rudolf, Graf (Count) b. Germany 1891. Professional soldier. Transferred from Jersey to Guernsey on 1 September 1943 to become German commander in chief in the Channel Islands. 'Outstandingly able, conscientious and humane' – von Aufsess (1985) p.147. Dismissed 1 March 1945.

Schneberger, M.V.R. Replaced Kratzer as head of the Guernsey civil affairs branch of F.K. 515 in May 1944. 'Dictatorial' and failed to 'promote team spirit'; in April 1945 posted to Jersey to fill vacancy left by von Aufsess. See von Aufsess (1985) pp. 95, 172.

Zachau, Inspektor Hermann. Officer at Guernsey civil affairs branch of F.K. 515 from 1941-45. His duties included supervision of the civilian police.

Red Cross Personnel

Callias, André. Swiss Assistant Delegate at Lisbon of the I.C.R.C. Travelled on the relief ship S.S. *Vega* to the Islands from December 1944 onwards.

Iselin, Colonel Frédéric. Aged 65. Swiss Delegate at Lisbon of the I.C.R.C. Led the I.C.R.C. delegation in December 1944 on the S.S. *Vega*; impressed Louis by his ability to 'get his own way' with the Germans. von Aufsess found him 'formidably well-read and well-informed ... irreproachably correct'. Between 1932 and 1935 Iselin had served on League of Nations missions to resolve boundary disputes between Burma/China and Syria/ Iraq.

Family group in the back garden at Plémy, Bouet.
(back row: Louis, Marguerite, Madeleine; front row: Marie (Babe), Désiré, Victor)

Guillemette Stores, Bouet – with Auguste and sister, Marianne.

Guillemette family photo in the garden at Plémy, c. 1930.
(standing: Victor, Marie (Babe), Madeleine, Désiré, Marguerite, Louis;
seated in front: Auguste and Edith)

Louis, Marjorie and Désiré outside Plémy, Bouet.

*Wedding of Louis Guillemette and Evelyn 'Queenie' Robilliard, 27 April 1939
(front row (left to right): Edith (Louis's mother), Gwen Robilliard, Henri Travers,
Betty Robilliard, Louis, Queenie, flowergirl Ann Down, Marie (Babe), Ron &
Meta Harwood; back row: Victor, Auguste, George Robilliard (Queenie's father))*

*Wedding of Victor Guillemette and Phyllis Browne, 29 Feb 1940
(left to right: Edith, Louis, Victor, Phyllis, Irwin and Madeleine Sims and Auguste).*

Louis Guillemette

Queenie and José, 1942

Guillemette Family photo, 1942 (back row (left to right): Len Collins,
Madeleine & Irwin Sims, Louis; front row: Auguste, Edith, José and Queenie)
Len Collins had returned from Laufen to Guernsey accompanying a
sick deportee. This photo was taken during his stay and copies were
sent from Laufen to evacuated members of the family in England.

Santangelo's Choir and Orchestra present 'The Two Painters' ('Old Japan' poem by
Alfred Noyes, music by Coleridge Taylor), Central Hall, March 1942.
(Zelia 'Zu' Warry, soloist, behind and to the left of Santangelo,
Irwin Sims is the furthest to the right; Madeleine Sims is the first woman
in the same row as Irwin, Louis is on back row second from left).

Louis aboard "Ida"

Louis at the piano

Bordeaux Harbour showing Vale Mill (right)
and La Platte far left (Photo: Priaulx Library)

Raymond Falla and Louis in Granville (Photo: José Day)

Hirzel House and Maison Allaire (Photo: Steve Foote)

Summerland, Mount Durand (Photo: Graham Jackson)

Grange Lodge, Grange (Photo: Graham Jackson)

La Corbinerie (Photo: Priaulx Library)

*German officer, Louis, Admiral Hüffmeier and Bailiff Victor Carey
beside the SS Vega (Photo: Damien Horn collection,
Channel Islands Military Museum)*

*Admiral Hüffmeier, Alexander Coutanche (Bailiff of Jersey),
Victor Carey (Bailiff of Guernsey) and Colonel Iselin at Rozel, Mount Durand
(Photo: Priaulx Library)*

States of Guernsey in session, 8 May 1945
(photo: Occupation Archive)

Victor Carey, Louis, R.H. Johns and Bill Arnold,
Liberation Day 9 May 1945 (photo: Sir de Vic Carey)

Royal Court Steps, Liberation Day 9 May 1945
(Louis far right) (photo: Sir de Vic Carey)

Some Controlling Committee members and officers
back row: John Loveridge, Wilfrid Bird, Louis, two unidentified
front row: Percy Dorey, Pierre de Putron, R.H. Johns, Dr Angelo Symons

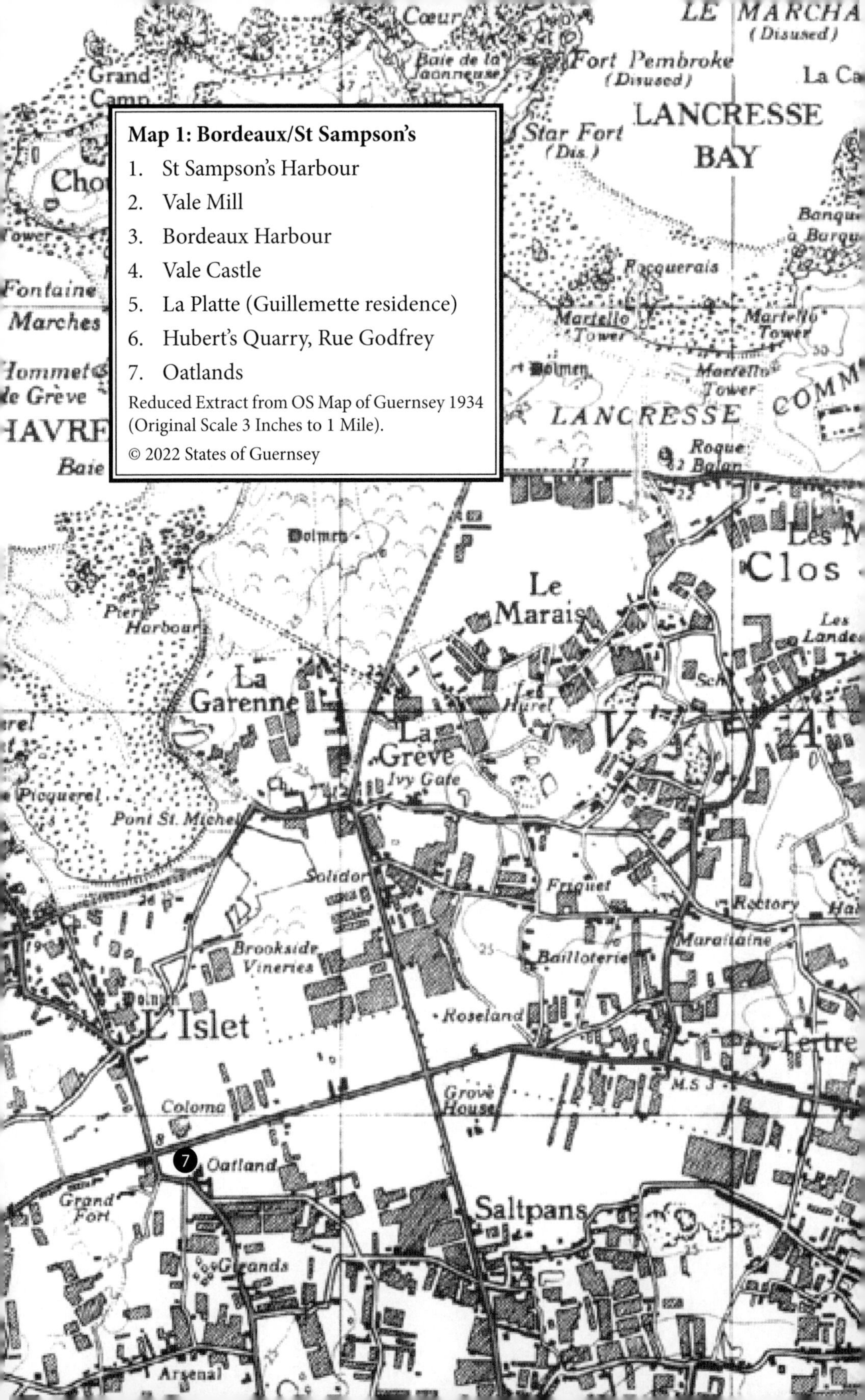

Map 1: Bordeaux/St Sampson's

1. St Sampson's Harbour
2. Vale Mill
3. Bordeaux Harbour
4. Vale Castle
5. La Platte (Guillemette residence)
6. Hubert's Quarry, Rue Godfrey
7. Oatlands

Reduced Extract from OS Map of Guernsey 1934 (Original Scale 3 Inches to 1 Mile).

© 2022 States of Guernsey

Demie de Fontenelle

Le Roulier

Vieille du Nord

Banque au Mouton

FORT DOYLE
(Disused)

Fontenelle Bay

Fontaine es Boeufs

Hougue Patris

39

Grand Hougue

57

La Lande

La Fontenelle

Omptolle

Mares à Fils

Homptole

Pierre

Moulière

Mou

Paradis

69

La Rochelle

Croix Besnard

Petit Omptolle
(Homptole)

Ch.

25

The

Vadle

La Blanche
Carrière

Miellette
Bay

60

Drhus
Dolmen

Port de Noirmont

Hommel
Paradis

Corbet
Beac

La
Marquise

②

⑥

24

Cocagne

Pétils
Bay

Bretoridu

Bordeaux

⑤

③

La
Vieille

Fortelrie

BORDEAUX
HARBOUR

Hommet

Les Jumelles

Hommet
Benest

Béquets

Sous les
Hougues

Rocques
Barrées

Le Poincon

La Banque
Imbert

Le Gros Rocher

Maresquet

Vale Castle

④

18

La Pl
Light

①

HARBOUR

Smy.

Pier

Black Rock

Ch.

St. SAMPSON

Map 2: Little Russel

1. Rocque au Nord
2. Les Brayes
3. Platte Fougère
4. Tautenay
5. Grande Amfroque
6. Godin
7. Houmet Paradis
8. La Vielle Rocque
9. Bordeaux Harbour
10. St Sampson's Harbour
11. La Platte beacon
12. Roustel beacon
13. Les Rocqueries
14. Corbette
15. Brehon Tower
16. Vivyan
17. Passe Percée
18. Rosaire
19. Les Ferrières

Reduced Extracts from contemporary Admiralty Chart of Guernsey and Herm (Crown Copyright).

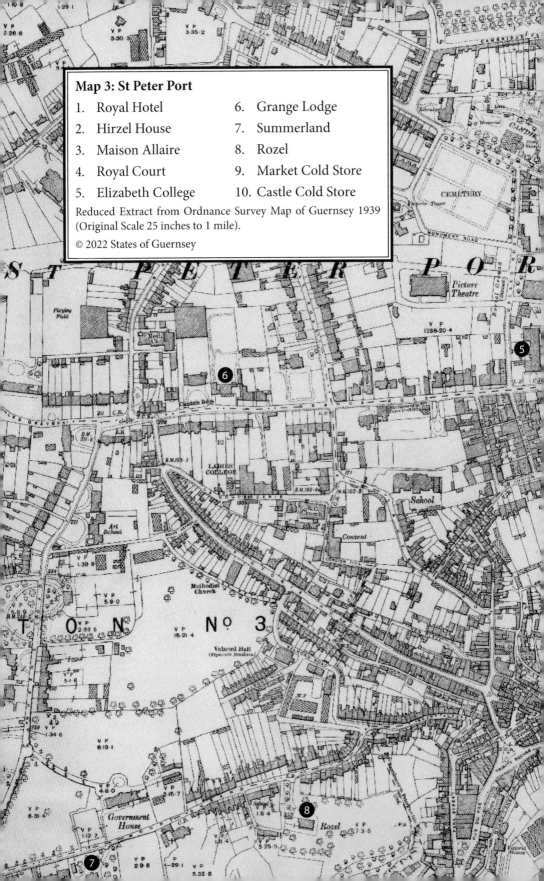

Map 3: St Peter Port

1. Royal Hotel
2. Hirzel House
3. Maison Allaire
4. Royal Court
5. Elizabeth College
6. Grange Lodge
7. Summerland
8. Rozel
9. Market Cold Store
10. Castle Cold Store

Reduced Extract from Ordnance Survey Map of Guernsey 1939 (Original Scale 25 inches to 1 mile).

© 2022 States of Guernsey

ACKNOWLEDGEMENTS

Special thanks to the staff of the Priaulx Library and the Island Archives, as well as to Mary Sims (Madeleine Guillemette's daughter) and Nick Guillemette.

I would also like to thank my children, Sarah, Oliver and Estelle and their families for their encouragement.

The following people have given assistance with information about their deceased relatives: Mary Bichard (née Bird) and her daughter, Jeanne Gathercole, Sir de Vic Carey, Nicholas Drake, John & Alison Foley, Geoff Norman, Mike Tidd, Eileen Davis, Rosemary Henry, Isobel Mauger, Margaret Smith (née Corfield), Michelle Nash, Peter Warry, Mavis Duquemin, Joan Roussel, Mrs Todd and her daughter Sue Payne, Dawn Madell, Jeanne Langford, Bernadette Williams, Gary Blanchford and Elizabeth O'Brien (née Harwood).

I would also like to thank Sir de Vic Carey, the Priaulx Library, Island Archives, Simon Hamon and Damien Horn for their permission to reproduce photos from their collections; States of Guernsey Mapping Team and Digimap Ltd for their assistance in sourcing and supplying the historic maps; John Nettles and Sir de Vic Carey for kindly reading the diary and providing generous quotes for the back cover; my daughter, Sarah, for proof-reading the book before publication; Richard Heaume of the German Occupation Museum and the Committee of the Guernsey Literary Festival for their support of the book launch.

Many other people have helped me when I was delving into tracing those mentioned in this diary. Thank you very much for your interest.

My sincere thanks to Ken Tough; without his diligent attention to detail and perseverance this diary may never have been published and printed. It is the complete text as it was written by my father, Louis Guillemette. I am also grateful to Ken's wife, Lee, for her patience and consideration.

Steve Foote has been so encouraging with the publishing and printing that I owe him a special thank you too for his hard task.

José Day
February 2022

THE DIARY 1940-45

1940

I've never before made a New Year's resolution with any hope of carrying it out, so in deciding to keep a diary during the coming year I have no illusions about the possibility of its petering out during the next two or three weeks. The fact remains, however, that having spent the last half hour or so in thinking over the events of the past twelve months, I feel convinced that although they seem ordinary enough in these extraordinary times, after a few months of Peace they will appear like the plot of some extremely extravagant melodrama. And if past happenings give some idea of the upheaval which has occurred in the life of our little community, the immediate future promises further daily happenings which, at the time seeming of little importance, may often grow and have repercussions which may change the life of hundreds of us. It is really to trace the history of such incidents that I am beginning to write.

Nineteen forty started in Guernsey with most people beginning to feel very bored with the war, with some hundreds of the younger men already in England in the fighting forces and with those of us who were still at work here leading more or less normal lives, except for a large dose of extra work. We were still, at that time, struggling with the legal complications of Compulsory Military Service and talking too much and doing too little about the planning of Island agriculture. And we even thought the war might fizzle out! My brother was at home on leave and I remember being despondent because I considered my work here so important that my duty was obviously to stay on here for the time being. We were, in fact, still playing at War.

At the end of January I went to London to attend a conference at Great Scotland Yard and was very impressed with the submarine net and barrage balloons at Southampton. That conference was a leisurely affair and when we came away we felt little nearer to the promulgation of our law to make it compulsory for us to fight for our country. And we were quite right.

It was then I met Sir Theodore Chambers and talked over the possibility of introducing the National Savings Movement into the Channel Islands. By the beginning of April the campaign had started in earnest and at the end of May we had caught up, proportionally, with England. To us it was obvious that Guernsey was just as patriotic as any other part of the Empire. What did we know of patriotism then?

I had great fun working out a most complicated scheme for the blacking out of the lighthouses in the Bailiwick, but it was never tried out. Anyway, I flew to Alderney once, went to the Casquets with some charming Alderney pilots in their ancient motor boat, and paid Alderney an emergency visit in an R.A.F. speedboat.

By the beginning of June some of us began to see that the Channel Islands were not the harbour of refuge that we had imagined them to be and our fears crystallized that night we heard our first German bomber flying up the Russel and became a conviction when two bombs, dropped out at sea, shook our secure houses.

Before we could gather our wits the Germans were over the Seine and into Normandy and the Home Office said our tentative suggestions for the evacuation of the children from the Islands were not so ridiculous as we had been told. Within a day or so orders came to get the children <u>ready at a day's notice</u>. I am just beginning to understand what that meant to families which were separated for the first time. Panic reigned and it was soon apparent that everybody must be given an opportunity of leaving the Island. That week was a nightmare of inadequately organized work and almost uncontrollable mass hysteria. It ended at last and tomato exports began again. For a few days life was almost normal and a few people even came back to the Island but one day an aeroplane with black crosses plainly visible on it flew low over the Town and harbour. Many people thought it was Polish but some saw its sinister significance and were not surprised to hear the first burst of machine-gun fire next evening and then the first German bomb. The harbour was crowded with growers' vans and people saying goodbye to their friends at the Southampton boat and we were lucky to lose no more than fifty people. The war had arrived, though, and we knew that at last we had to face facts. We crouched in the basement at Elizabeth College and I, for one, was terrified. When we dared to come out into the open we saw great columns of smoke rising from the harbour and a St. John Ambulance with bullet holes all over the body abandoned outside St. James' Church.

Two days later the Germans arrived, a few first in two or three military aeroplanes and next day in hundreds in troop carriers which roared to and from the Airport. I was lucky enough to meet the Germans at a conference at the Royal Hotel a few hours after they landed and ever since hardly a day has passed without a similar meeting. But the Island was cut off and communications with England were silent.

The Island soon settled down to the Occupation and counted itself fortunate in having Mr Sherwill, as Liaison Officer and President of the newly constituted Controlling Committee of the States. For his part, he took a pride in the very correct relations which started immediately between the Island and the Germans and never spared himself in maintaining them.

German orders began to pour in – orders for the administration of the Island, for the safety of the occupying forces, orders for housing and food for them at the expense of the Island.

It began to be obvious too that if something was not done soon, food would run short. At first this did not seem very serious to the Germans, as they were certain that the war would be finished by the end of August, but as delays in their campaign began to occur, arrangements were made for a local representative to be sent to France. Raymond Falla and I volunteered to go but I was not allowed to leave my work so Wilfred Hubert went. The success of his efforts is apparent from the fact that we still have sufficient food, six months later.

I had a comic trip to Granville with 105,000 R.M. in an old suitcase and spent a few days in Jersey en route, where I gathered the impression that control of the life of the community there was not nearly as successful as it is here.

Real tragedy made an appearance with the landing of two Guernsey army officers.[1] For eight weeks they were hidden by their nerve-racked relatives and friends. The news of their plight reached Mr Sherwill and he tried heroically to save them from the fate which he realized would be theirs if they were discovered – because they had landed without uniform! In his efforts to save their lives, he involved himself to such an extent that when they eventually gave themselves up he was incriminated together with fifteen other people who had helped them.

They were all taken off to Paris for trial – a further pitiful splitting up of families – and as a punishment to the Island an order issued for the confiscation of all wireless sets on the Island. Five days was allowed for the collection of all the sets and nearly thirteen thousand were collected and registered with copious details in this time.

Christmas Eve saw the publication of a notice giving back the wireless sets to the civilian population and making known the fact that all concerned with the harbouring of the officers had been pardoned, with the exception of Mr Sherwill who was to relinquish his position of President of the Controlling Committee, and the two Nicolles who were no longer to be employed by the States.[2] The officers were to be treated as prisoners-of-war.

On this the last day of the year I have had the privilege of welcoming home these friends and of realizing how like a large family our community is, with its little quarrels and the genuine affection which we all feel for one another. I took home three members of a family to the sole member who

---

1   Lieutenants Hubert Nicolle and James Symes were landed at Petit Port on 3 September 1940 – however their return rendezvous failed and they were forced to surrender on 21 October. See Bell (1998).

2   These were Hubert Nicolle's father, Emile, and his uncle, Frank.

had remained here, the mother, and I had to come away quickly to avoid making a fool of myself.

We have learned many lessons through this Occupation and the severance of communication with England and our friends. The good and evil in characters have been brought to light to an incredible extent, class distinction has almost disappeared, the difficulties of planning the life of even a small place like this have been brought home to us very forcibly, but we still hope very vigorously for peace and better times.

1942

The Prince called me in to his office this morning to tell me that he would be leaving the island permanently in the course of the next few days.[1] I said that I had already heard a rumour to this effect and that the local government would be sorry to lose his help. He has really fought well on our behalf when the military have been insistent on taking more than they should under the provisions of the Hague Rules and in countless other cases where local food supplies and buildings, etc were at stake. He is a very capable diplomat and has kept the peace when it would have been very easy for relations to break down completely to the detriment of the civilian population. He realizes too, what so few Germans seem to understand, that efficiency is no more than a means and is never an end, and that virtue, coupled with a lively sense of humour, makes him so like our own people that I have often enjoyed my interviews with him.

Today he confessed to me that it was sometimes with sadness, and he implied it was sometimes with anger too, that he was forced to insist on the carrying out of German orders vis-à-vis the local population. He thought they were often quite unnecessary. We agree on this point, but the excuse, "military necessity" which the Devil introduced into the Hague Rules gives the Germans the last word in many battles which we think we would otherwise win hands down.

This is the third anniversary of our wedding and this evening Zelia and George came to supper and are staying here for the night. We had a delicious little meal with a bottle of Château Neuf du Pape and then did our best to get mellow on liqueurs.

TUESDAY, 28TH APRIL

Had a talk with Percy Dorey this morning on the future of the glasshouse industry after the war. He hopes for drastic measures to cut out waste of time, labour and transport and visualizes a co-operative organization to undertake the collection, transport – or rather shipment – and perhaps marketing of Guernsey tomatoes. This would mean the payment of an average price to growers and cut out the choice of markets as far as the grower is concerned.

---

1   The Prince referred to is Rittmeister von Oettingen.

I discussed with Jack Norman and later with Captain Franklin the collection and transport of timber from Herm. Submitted to Grange Lodge an application for the wide use of water from the domestic mains in greenhouses. Dr Brosch said we must submit such matters to the F.K. again and again and must not wait for suggestions from them. I pointed out that as far back as January we had told them how vital was the question of water supply as far as the glasshouse industry was concerned.

Controlling Committee this afternoon. The main subject of discussion was the revision of wages and salaries and it was decided to appoint a Committee to make a full investigation into the matter. Mr Leale then asked me to introduce the question of the transmission of official mail to and from Jersey and it was decided that all mail for Jersey should come through our office. The discussion then turned on the general question of relations between the two Islands and it was perfectly clear to me – as it was before – that the idea of an eye for an eye is deeply engrained in some of our people. There are probably more people in Jersey with this idea, but the fact that two wrongs do not make a right is one which is of greatest importance to me. It was suggested that Jersey uses the F.K. to get goods and privileges from us, but I pointed out that the Jersey people are quite convinced that this is our policy. In some cases they maintain they have been told by members of the F.K. that we have suggested measures which are injurious to Jersey and which they were about to put into operation. In my opinion much of the bitterness between the Islands is due to misunderstandings.

We have decided to plough the rest of the field at Bordeaux and this evening I asked Lewis Le Maître whether he would care to graze the land before we plough. We now have about ten perch in cultivation and have started levelling for a lower terrace, leaving trenches for the foundations of a retaining wall for the upper terrace.

The war news is very confusing, but I find that quite a number of Guernsey people to whom I have spoken today have a presentiment that there is unrest in at least one European country. Certainly I do not find the people with whom I come into contact any happier than they were a week ago.

WEDNESDAY, 29TH APRIL

Went with Mr Leale to the Bailiff this morning for formal leave-taking of Prince. Stayed with the Bailiff for an hour after the others had gone and we talked about Guernsey. I told him about the misunderstandings which are always occurring between Guernsey and Jersey and the steps the Controlling Committee were taking to stop them. He asked that if matters became serious I should let him know and this I promised to do.

Perhaps I am making a mountain out of a molehill, but I think the President should take immediate steps to put matters right with Jersey by letting the Bailiff of Jersey know, either by a visit to that island or by letter, that a strong line is to be taken here in future regarding anything resembling unfair dealings with Jersey and that we expect him to do the same in that Island.

Went to Oatlands this afternoon with Harry Bichard to see how Ted Dorey was progressing with the boat. He has added a false keel, put in strengthening floors, risen one plank and given her a very attractive sheer. He has also fitted new knees and has got rid of a bad twist. He says that the planking is quite sound. When he has finished the boat should be better than new. He is doing all this free on the understanding that he is allowed to use her this summer. Of course, I shall be a member of the crew.

We are told on good authority that, although the food situation is bad here, it is worse in Germany in many ways. It is proposed that the potato ration this year should be 5 lbs per person, per week, and Inspector Oser says that we shall have to supply potatoes to the forces.

THURSDAY, 30TH APRIL

It looks as if the Germans mean to do their utmost to enforce the potato rationing scheme. Oser told Bichard that he wanted every patch of potatoes checked for area. This will, of course, be the most difficult commodity that we have had to ration so far, since, with the exception of one person, everybody I have asked during the last week has planted a fairly substantial patch of potatoes for their own use. There is no doubt that last year's terribly bad crop and the resulting shortage during this winter have made us realize that each member of the community must help himself. Many people, especially those living in St. Peter Port, have been without potatoes since last Christmas or before. A contributory factor was the seizure by the Germans of 600 tons of potatoes last autumn and many people think the same thing will happen to any potatoes held by the States this year.

I went along to the Douzaine Room this afternoon to vote for Jack Domaille in the ballot for the election of a Vale Constable and when I crossed the crest of the hill and lost the full force of the easterly wind, I suddenly realized that spring had arrived with all its distinctive sights and smells and sounds. It was a very pleasant realization.

When I arrived home again, I took my spade and pick and attacked afresh the beginnings of the lower terrace which I am making behind the house. I dig out the trench to a depth of about eighteen inches, uncovering pebbles and sand which were obviously part of the beach at some time; then I fill it in again with quarry rubbish until the surface is just above the level of the grass. Next I skim the turf off the next trench and start the process all over again. It is a very slow job, but, strangely enough, I enjoy it more than anything else I have done in the garden up till now. At six o'clock I stopped to hear the news and heard that the R.A.F. had bombed shipping off the coast of north Brittany. What a combination! Laying out a garden with the threat of instant annihilation hanging constantly over us. Hope does certainly spring eternal.

FRIDAY, 1ST MAY

Today's great event at Bordeaux was the arrival of the Pram. It was delivered by George and left on the terrace for the evening. It made me feel very strongly the imminence of fatherhood. It was bought from the States' Custodians[2] for the lump sum of £4–1–3, including tax, and apart from a slight rattle is in good running order.

For the past day or two a rumour has been gathering speed and by this morning it went as follows:–

The German doctor in Sark has been battered to death in his bed by a Sarkee.[3] The weapon used was a hammer and it served him right for he had made himself hated both by the garrison and the civil population. He had even, whilst under the influence of drink, ordered a visiting barber off his premises and when the man tried to explain why he was there had fired a revolver over his head and chased him through the garden into the road. If the culprit was not found within twenty four hours, Sark would be entirely cleared of civilians.

Wynne Sayer received a letter from Mrs Hathaway during the morning in which she mentioned that a German doctor had committed suicide.

SATURDAY, 2ND MAY

We have decided to have the field ploughed and so this evening we started preparations. The first difficulty to be overcome is the question of drainage. At present all the road water from the north side of the valley comes in through the front of my neighbour's property and discharges from a pipe into the field. Added to this, all the greenhouses on the north side of the field unload their water into it. We are therefore going to make a new trench round the north and west boundaries to join up with the present douit and

---

2   Custodians were appointed by the States to take charge of properties and goods abandoned during the evacuation in June, 1940.

3   On 29 April 1942, the German medical officer in Sark, Dr August Göbel was found dead. A German medical orderly was convicted of his murder and executed. See Le Tissier (2006).

thence to the sea. We hope all water will flow through the trench and thereby keep the field reasonably drained.

SUNDAY, 3RD MAY

Started the day with a visit to the Bouet to wish mother a happy birthday. As a present I took her a bunch of flowers from Queenie, our barley flour ration for the week and about a dozen of last year's potatoes! And she was delighted.

We did good work in the field, making the new trench, and then spent an hour stripped to the waist amongst the willows. The wind whistled through the tops of the willows but near the ground there was not a breath of wind. It was fine.

Tonight Queenie told me that she was looking out of the window yesterday when she saw a French workman – of which there are hundreds in our district – pick up a little girl, give her two hearty kisses and put her down again. I had not realized before just how homesick some of those poor devils must be. We are two of the lucky ones in Guernsey because we have not yet been turned out of our house and so we know very little about homesickness. What we do know about though, is our longing for freedom and above all for reunion with all our friends (including relations) who are out of the Island. I can imagine that, on a perfect spring day like this one, they must dream the rosiest of dreams of Guernsey.

MONDAY, 4TH MAY

Sure enough a Red Cross message arrived today from Babe to Mother, saying how homesick everyone is for Plémy and all that it stands for!

I started getting the boat engine ready today and I almost forgot the war for a few hours. What a rich pleasure is to be extracted from pottering about with boats, especially at the beginning of a season when, added to the pleasure of working with the hands is the fact that good work done now will mean less trouble when the real business begins.

TUESDAY, 5TH MAY

After much manoeuvring, I have today taken possession of a motor cycle which is a distinct improvement on the one I was riding before. At least, I hope it is.

This afternoon I went with Inspector Brandt of the German Customs to see whether something could be arranged so that it would be possible to fish from Perelle. He promised that he would do all he could and it looks as though we shall be successful.

The evening I spent with my northern neighbours digging a new douit round the north boundary of the field. They are a friendly lot and worked well and quickly. I think they regard me as being mentally deficient but they are very kind.

WEDNESDAY, 6TH MAY

Visited the Albert dock today to talk to the Perelle fishermen. They are quite ready to go back with their boats. I saw workers in a new industry while I was there. Two men were in a dinghy, one sculling and the other knocking limpets off the harbour wall into a basket with a small hammer. Limpets fetched such high prices this winter that it paid fishermen to spend whole days on the rocks off Herm collecting them for the market.

I reported at Grange Lodge that Dr Symons had been told by two N.C.O.s from the Vauquiédor Hospital that in future no drugs were to be ordered from the German firm of Krause but that they should be procured from Langlois of Rennes. I asked whether the Feldkommandantur knew anything of such instructions being issued. They knew of a general instruction to that effect and said that the trouble was that the supply of such goods in Germany was in a more serious condition than it is here.

This afternoon Jack Norman came down with his tractor to plough the field. It is a compact and very powerful little machine and made a very satisfactory job considering that the land has not been ploughed in living memory.

I came down to see him start and then went straight off with Mr Johns and Queenie to see what must surely be one of the most beautiful gardens in Guernsey. It is at the Village de Putron and belongs to Dr and Mrs Symons. It extends over the edge of the cliff and practically down to the sea. At the top is the house and a lawn surrounded by trees and flowering shrubs and the slopes of the cliffs are covered with trees, shrubs, bluebells and primroses. The wild sweet smell of spring mingles with the heavier scent of the cultivated shrubs and the whole is rounded off by the background of the sea and the islands. It was a perfect afternoon and I am left with a memory of blue and green and gold, all in delicate shades, and of a host and hostess who fitted into the picture. The war, the secret police and the noise of aero engines and anti-aircraft fire faded completely from my memory like a bad dream.

THURSDAY, 7TH MAY

This morning we were back in harness, meeting Dr Pelz and Inspector Oser on the question of control of fish sales. They wanted to introduce a completely new system, on the lines of one which has just been put into operation in Jersey but I received the impression that they knew little, if anything, about the Guernsey system at the beginning of the meeting. However, an hour's talk, mostly in very bad French (on my part), appeared to show them that our system is fundamentally sound and we parted on the understanding that we should consider a tightening-up of our regulations, which, I must admit, seem to have become rather slack during the past winter with an almost total lack of fish of any kind.[4]

It seems strange that even nature seems to work against us in times of stress. Last year's potato crop was one of the worst in living memory and the fishing during the winter when the food shortage in Guernsey amounted almost to famine, was the last straw.

This afternoon Nigel and I went to work early forking our potatoes. It was so hot that we stripped to the waist and were perfectly happy. Clearing up the mess caused by the plough seems absolutely hopeless but I suppose that with perseverance we shall get it straight eventually. Anyway, we planted a few rows of beans – 'Masterpiece' they are called by their proud originator.

FRIDAY, 8TH MAY

Tonight I sowed an ounce of cabbage seed, Coeur de Boeuf, if you please! I carefully prepared a bed roughly eighteen inches by ten feet and had just finished my sowing when Tom Ogier, expert in chief, strolled up to inspect my work. His astonishment knew no bounds when he heard of the quantity I had sown. Apparently they should have been spread over a perch of land. I saw the joke.

It was reported at the Controlling Committee this afternoon that a 3½d packet of soap powder had been sold for 25/–.

SATURDAY, 9TH MAY

Frank Mallett was tried yesterday by a German Court for assaulting a German soldier who apparently was working in his workshop and did not agree with him over the use of some tool or other. Mr Sherwill defended him but he was found guilty and sentenced to one year's imprisonment. Today, Mr Sherwill submitted a plea for clemency and the sentence was varied to three months with a fine of 5,000 marks – over £500.

The B.B.C. reminded us tonight that today is the eve of the anniversary of the invasion of the Low Countries by the Germans in 1940. To me this means the anniversary of the realization of what war means and of the

---

4   See Item 2: Meeting with FK: Fishing, 7 May 1942, p.286

surprising heights and depths of human achievement. I think of the violent overthrow of our settled, pleasant and sometimes smug way of living in our Island, of the great acceleration in administration and of the way in which the reins of government have changed hands.

I hope that, if ever peace comes again and I can overcome my repulsion sufficiently to read these notes, I shall be reminded that there comes a point – and the earlier the better – when discussion of difficulties is fruitless and action is the sure and surprising way to overcome those difficulties.

Ernest Henry and I were discussing this evening the amount of pleasure we get from working on the land and we decided that the reason was that we had to do this work to provide essential food. He is certain that as soon as peace is declared he will give up keeping cattle and for my part I fear the consequences of having my boat moored once again outside the front door. How obvious it is that some discipline in life is essential not only to our health but to our happiness, and how we hate this discipline! What a pity.

We had news from Len Collins today. He crossed to Jersey early this week and was wrecked off Jersey. I am attaching the story of the journey to this page.[5]

SUNDAY, 10TH MAY

The rain arrived today and I had to stop indoors, so I went through some papers in a suitcase which Queenie will soon be needing. I found a letter from Charles, written the week after the evacuation and just after he had arrived in England. Nearly two years ago! I thought of the day I received that letter in my new office in the north west turret at Elizabeth College and of the very scanty time I had in which to read it. And I remembered a half-crazy soldier – a Guernseyman – who came to see me that morning to ask whether I could find his wife and family. He had escaped from St. Malo by fishing boat and said that he had seen a private from the Black Watch crucified with bayonets by the Germans just outside that port. I never knew whether the story was true because his nerve was completely shattered. When he arrived here he found that his wife and children had gone to England and I managed to get him a passage on a boat which was going there. I gave him the Home Office address at Whitehall and eventually packed him off. The sun shone in a deep blue sky.

---

5   See Item 1: A Brief History of our Trip to Jersey, 6 May 1942, p.284. A more detailed account of this adventure has been written by Frank Hubert. He confirms that the trio were himself, Len Collins and Charlie Gardner. Collins and Gardner were travelling on business for their employer, *The Star* newspaper. Hubert went for a 'jolly'. See Hubert (2001).

I went over again the rest of that week up to the Friday evening when I was with Mr Sherwill in his office talking to the Home Office about the possibility of invasion by the Germans. The air raid – our first – started during that conversation and I heard for the first time the clearcut sound of machine-gun fire from aircraft and then the explosion of the first bomb. That raid was like a long-drawn-out motor car accident on a summer's day, with fire and black smoke and destruction. I was never so terrified in all my life as we gathered in the basement and waited for the building to tumble about us. Although it sounded as though the town was being bombed and the bombs screamed low over our heads, it was the harbour that suffered and we escaped.

How I should like to see Charles again and how we all long for the end of our imprisonment and reunion with our friends in exile. It seems incredible that this nightmare will some day come to an end and our first wish is that we may all be spared to meet again.

Mr Churchill made a memorable speech this evening and gave us all new hope. He has been Prime Minister two years today.

MONDAY, 11TH MAY

Much discussion of the Prime Minister's speech at Grange Lodge. I maintained it was our turn this month to stick our tails up. Our bombing offensive is getting stronger every day – or rather night – and the Russians are admitted by the Germans to be infinitely stronger than they ever imagined, America is now working at full pressure, the food situation in Europe is getting worse, and I have been told by a high officer that at present it is worse in Germany than it is here, and practically every German to whom I have talked during the past few weeks is confident that there will soon be an English invasion of the Continent. Herr Hitler's last speech, with hints at the possibility of another winter campaign in Russia, has had a depressing effect on the occupying forces here.

In all our discussions on the war, it is pleasing to see that both the German officers and I respect each other for our staunch adherence to our respective countries. They are all – at the Feldkommandantur at any rate – men who can think for themselves and our discussions never descend to the level of arguments.

TUESDAY, 12TH MAY

Several Red Cross messages arrived today. One from Babe told us that Michael had fully recovered from bronchial pneumonia. What a lot of worry the lack of news saves us. We had no idea he had ever had such an illness. But how our hearts went out to Babe who was left to go through such an ordeal without Leonard at her side. Another message said that Captain Kiki was working hard. I feel very proud and a little scared of this surprising small brother of mine.

Two subjects which came up for discussion by the Controlling Committee today give some indication of conditions in the Island at present. Firstly, there was draft legislation to control barter shops which at present have free rein. It is suspected that much stolen property finds its way to these shops and rationed foodstuffs are offered in exchange for luxuries like cigarettes. Cases were cited, too, of such necessities as children's footwear being offered for goods which fathers of large families could not produce. Many of the foreign labourers who are here in their thousands manage to find the goods asked for and the result is that our own people have to watch articles which they badly need being obtained and exported through the shortsightedness, or worse, of Guernsey men and women.

The second subject was a draft letter from Mr Leale to the Bailiff of Jersey suggesting a joint application from the two Islands for a relief ship from England. This is necessitated by the alarming rise in the death rate and the sickness rate since the beginning of the year. Added to this both men and employers complain that work is slowed up by lack of energy due to malnutrition. I wonder how this suggestion will end?

This morning an N.C.O. came to see the President of the Glasshouse Utilization Board while I was with him. He was sent by the officer in charge of an anti-aircraft battery to ask for the discontinuance of an action which was being brought against a soldier of the unit for the theft of potatoes from a greenhouse worked by the G.U.B. This greenhouse had been broken into several times recently and potatoes had been taken. As on so many occasions during the past winter no trace of the thieves had been found, but when the greenhouse was being dug last week an identification disc was found just under the surface of the ground.

This was, of course, very clear evidence and it was to plead for the owner of the disc that the N.C.O. had been sent. He pointed out that the theft was a small one but that if the action was pursued the punishment would be very severe and might have a lasting effect on the life of the man concerned. Mr Dorey asked for my views and I explained that thefts had reached very large proportions in the Island. When we caught our own people we punished severely and as such thefts brought us always nearer starvation, it seemed that the policy should be the same in the case of the Germans who did not have to depend, as we do, on local products for the greater part of their diet. The N.C.O. said that the battery had been very lenient in not taking over all the greenhouses which were very near to their station. We let that pass for the time being and Mr Dorey said we had no wish to be vindictive and would

16

discuss the matter with the appropriate authorities. The N.C.O. added that if Mr Dorey agreed to cancel the action the matter could be arranged with the Field Police. This we naturally refused to do and I mentioned the matter to Dr Brosch when I saw him later in the morning. He said that so few thieves were caught that it was essential to make examples of any of which the guilt could be proved. I mentioned about the leniency of the battery in the matter of taking over the greenhouses and told him that if they became any less lenient I should report the matter to him immediately. He agreed.

WEDNESDAY, 13TH MAY

Mum and Dad came down to Bordeaux this afternoon. They travelled by horse-bus (a covered van) and walked back to the Bouet. Such a feat would have been considered far beyond them before the war, but the fact remains that some months ago Mum walked to Bordeaux and <u>back</u> by herself.

THURSDAY, 14TH MAY

We heard over the wireless that the East Lancs had sent men to Madagascar and we are wondering whether Vic is amongst them. It looks too as if the spring offensive has started on the Eastern Front and reports so far show that the Germans are advancing in the Crimea with the Russians doing the same around Kharkov. Will the Russians advance southwards and cut off the advancing Germans on the Black Sea coast?

This afternoon we banked the potatoes and weeded the peas. Then we planted the rest of the Masterpiece beans and went to Oatlands to see how the boat was progressing.

FRIDAY, 15TH MAY

I spent an hour with Inspector Oser this morning and he told me stories of the toughening process for younger men in pre-war Germany. It must have been kill or cure.

I had to have some teeth attended to today and went to Smith this morning. He filled a front tooth and gave me the comforting news that one other must come out and that there is one more to be filled. When we had finished the business part of the visit we started on local politics. He is a very bitter critic of the ways of the Controlling Committee and of the Bailiff. He instanced an advertisement issued in the papers about a year ago when the Bailiff offered a reward of £25 (or it may have been £20) for information regarding the V signs which had begun to appear in various parts of the island. He said that he realized that the Bailiff had probably done this under pressure but he thought that, as a British subject, he should have refused. I have no excuse to offer to this suggestion. I said that very often it would be most spectacular and very easy for the Controlling Committee to refuse to obey German orders which were contrary to the interests of the population but that such a refusal was not always the wisest course. As an example I told him the story behind a recent requisition by the Germans of 150 bicycles. It started with a verbal instruction to me by the Prince to produce these bicycles. I flatly refused to have anything to do with such a measure and obtained confirmation of my action from the Controlling Committee. The Prince said he would have to report my reply to Jersey and, sure enough, we eventually received written orders to obtain the bicycles. Mr Leale and I went to see the Prince about it and again refused to obey the order. We were then told if we did not cooperate the German police would take the first 150 bicycles they met in the roads and that it would therefore lessen the hardship on the population if we took the bicycles from people who needed them least. We thereupon agreed to select the bicycles, feeling that it was our duty, especially as bicycling is practically the only means of transport and footwear is wearing out fast, to protect the more hardpressed of the population. We also obtained agreement on the valuation of the bicycles by local as well as German valuers.

Smith thought that our action was unjustified and though I agree that such a decision must be a matter of opinion, I feel that we are in office to lighten the burden as much as we can for our people and that we therefore did the right thing.

This afternoon Dr Brosch asked me to go and see him. When I arrived he was in a furious temper and I gathered that he had telephoned to the States' Office this morning and asked for the figures of French imports during 1941. He said that it appeared to him to be not more than half an hour's work and that although he spoke English badly he thought he could not possibly have been misunderstood. The figures were urgently needed for a conference which was to be held in Paris, presumably in connection with the victualling of the Channel Islands. The only reply he had so far received was a letter from Sir Abraham, which arrived at 3 o'clock, asking him for more precise details of the figures required. Such action was a provocation (against Germany, understood) and I was to see that he had the figures within two hours. I made no promises except that I would make enquiries, but I felt that if a conference was to be held it might mean more food for the civilian population and so I made the necessary enquiries and collected the figures, somewhat approximate, I'm afraid, with the help of some of the Essential Commodities, Farm Produce Board and States' Office staff. Tonight all is quiet once more and again it appears to me that I have done my duty to the population by obeying a German order. I wonder if they would think so? The Feldkommandantur do try to help us on the food question and it seems ridiculous to hamper their efforts.

I think that statistics of this sort should be readily available and I shall take the matter up with Mr Leale tomorrow.

SATURDAY, 16TH MAY

I spent practically the whole morning with Mr Leale discussing with Sir Abraham, Mr Broughton, the Supervisor and Mr Frampton the question of the recording of transactions connected with importations from France. It was agreed by all present that the present system, or lack of system, is most unsatisfactory and that an adequate one must be installed. We decided to get from Granville a detailed statement of how the office is run and what records are kept and then to make such alterations as are necessary before reorganizing the systems used by Essential Commodities and the States' Office.

I spoke to both Broughton and Mr Leale today of my wish to spend a couple of years in England immediately after the war possibly as a liaison with the Home Office. I could then finish my degree and make such studies as might be useful here in administration. At present, nobody in our little Civil Service knows anything more than the running of the States' Office, Guernsey and it needs no great imaginative brain to see how inadequate must be our methods as a result of this deficiency. They both thought my plan a good one.

We received from Grange Lodge instructions that fishing would not in future be allowed in three of the best fishing grounds because of continuous danger from small-arms practice. This appears to me to be 'Military Necessity' carried to extremes and I am hoping that the Controlling Committee will record the strongest of protests.

SUNDAY, 17TH MAY

I spent the morning planting beans in the wilderness. I stopped every quarter of an hour or so to stretch and dream of the garden which should some day take the place of the horrible mess left by the plough. As I bent to work again – and by the way, what a fiendishly uncomfortable position the standard spade requires of the gardener – my mind automatically switched back to that latest order about fishing grounds. I thought of all the occasions on which the comfort, the food supply and the health of our people have been sacrificed to the god of 'Military Necessity', until I marvelled at their patience and at the efforts of the Controlling Committee to keep the peace. I kept rigidly before me my faith in the wisdom of the administration in refraining from kicking against the pricks, but I found myself wondering, not for the first time, whether the explanations given us and accepted in such good faith were always as irreproachable as they appeared. Of course we have protested on countless occasions to the Feldkommandantur and have sometimes enlisted their help successfully, but when we have lost a fight we have known that they have appreciated our difficulties and reasons but have been overruled by the military. We have felt that they are the spokesmen for the Military and we have been advised many times that it would be useless to take the matter further. But would it be useless, I thought, and would it be possible that our acceptance of rulings encouraged the Military to use 'Military Necessity' as a cloak to achieve ends which could not be legitimately grouped under that heading? Was it time to make a firm stand and let wisdom – or caution, if you will – take second place for a time.

This evening I wrote down all the occasions I could think of when 'Military Necessity' worked directly against our people and when protests to the Feldkommandantur were unsuccessful. They made a formidable array and I shaped them into a letter to the General pointing out the hardship to the population which would result from the new fishing order and ending with a request to him to remember that as far as we are concerned the necessity to keep our population in a reasonable state of health and the Island intact ranks as least as important as 'Military Necessity', and asking him to consider our point of view in the same way that we have always considered his.

MONDAY, 18TH MAY

This morning I took my draft letter to Mr Leale and explained my reasons for writing it. He agreed that such a letter should be sent, but did not like my wording. I admitted I had written it in a hurry and he set about redrafting it, using the points I had made. This afternoon he showed me the final draft and it seemed to me that although the English was better it had lost some of its force in the process. However, I may be prejudiced in my own favour.

One thing which worries me more than any letter is that Mr Leale admits to feeling the strain of his work. He, like many other members of the Controlling Committee is getting tired and I cannot see any way in which he can get a real rest. He cannot leave the Island except to go to Sark and a holiday there does not attract him. The rough and tumble of a trip to Jersey and France would not brace him as it does me and so he must keep on without rest until either the end of the war comes or he becomes so tired that he gives up trying to help our most ungrateful people.

I called on the Ingrouilles this afternoon to break the news to them that our application for the release of their son who was sentenced to five years imprisonment – by a German Court – has been unsuccessful. He is their only child and the pride of their hearts but it did me good to see the bravery with which they accepted my news. They are not rich or clever but they are natural and proud and they are *grateful* to me for my tiny efforts! There were no tears but an optimistic hope that the end of the war will set John free long before his term is up. I have little doubt that they are right.

TUESDAY, 19TH MAY

I had rather a stormy morning at Grange Lodge. Inspector Oser asked me to go with him to Dr Brosch to discuss cold storage in Guernsey. The Germans are importing security stocks of perishable foods for themselves and therefore want more cold rooms. Oser had inspected the two cold stores with Sayer and the Supervisor and apparently had not succeeded in finding a way to get more of the space which we still retain and need. Dr Brosch asked me for my views and I said that it appeared that 'Military Necessity' again was about to operate. The cold stores, I said, belonged to us and we needed them – or such of them as we still had – to store perishable food for our population. If the Germans needed more cold stores it was obvious to me that they should build them. I did not know, I said, how many troops and civilians they had imported but certainly the number of our own people was much larger, yet already they had taken from us much more than half our cold storage and were now asking for yet further space. I think they saw the point of this argument, although they were tactfully silent on the subject. They put forward certain suggestions for the joint use of some of the cold chambers but I insisted on discussing the matter with the experts. They said they would advise the Military to build further cold stores but the trouble was that the food was either arriving or about to arrive and some arrangement must be made for the time being. I admitted that I saw their difficulties and I knew the Feldkommandantur would do what they could for us but I did not see why our people should have to be sacrificed because of errors of omission on the part of the Military. It was decided that I should put their suggestions before our experts and let them know the results.

We went on to discuss other minor matters and Inspector Oser, as he often does, began to make sarcastic remarks about the Controlling Committee. I asked him to remember that the Committee was composed almost solely of unpaid members who had given up the last two years to most strenuous work for the Island. They had no opportunity, like the Feldkommandantur, to take three or four holidays every year, but were obliged to remain at work the whole time except for a couple of weeks each year when they were still available for advice. Moreover, they were all oldish men and I objected most strongly to his remarks. I asked whether he thought the organization of the

Feldkommandantur was beyond reproach and instanced one case in which a complicated organization had been set up, with the help of one of their officers, for the preparation of timber to meet the demand for coffins. The last stage in the system was the granting by the Standortkommandantur of permits to cut the trees required and I knew when the permits had been granted by that office. Yet it was not until about a week later that the Feldkommandantur delivered the permits to us, the reason for the delay being that they had nobody available to type the covering letter to us. I also asked whether it was a case of good organization when important Orders of the Controlling Committee were sometimes in the Feldkommandantur's hands a month before they were granted their approval.

Then I went off to lunch.

John Loveridge came back from France yesterday evening. Two things he said impressed me. Firstly, he saw the Renault works and they are absolutely flat; secondly, he formed the opinion that the food situation in Guernsey is worse than France and worse than Jersey.

WEDNESDAY, 20TH MAY

I had no sooner arrived at the office this morning than I was told that Inspector Oser expected an answer from me regarding the cold store not later than 9.50 a.m. I had had no opportunity of seeing Sayer about the matter but I managed to catch him on the way to the office and we went straight to Grange Lodge. Oser told us that he had had a stormy meeting with the Intendant – chief of the revictualling department here – and for his pains in stating our difficulties fairly, he had been accused of being one hundred per cent for the British. He thought that further discussion was useless and asked for a decision from us as to whether or not we would give up more cold storage space. We talked it over, Sayer and I, and gave the answer that as the Controlling Committee was responsible for the food supply of the civilian population, it was quite impossible for us to give up more space. Oser went off to report to Dr Brosch and I busied myself with other matters. Later in the morning I heard that Dr Brosch and Oser had met Sayer, the Supervisor and one of the Revictualling officers at the cold stores for further discussion of the matter. Feldkommandantur could quite easily have given our answer to the Intendant and let us take the consequences which would probably have been the wastage of much of our food supply. Instead they went further into a matter which obviously has increased their unpopularity with their own people.

At the end of the morning Doctor Brosch called me into his room and said he was sorry he had to order the clearance of one of the rooms at the Castle Cold Store. I refused to take a verbal order and he thereupon dictated

22

a letter containing the order and handed it to me before I left the building.

We had a further discussion at Hirzel House after lunch and Sayer, Mr Johns and myself went to inspect both cold stores. We obtained the measurements of all the rooms and I worked out the cubic capacity of the space occupied by both the Germans and ourselves. They have much more than we have. It was obvious to us that as they were bound to find storage for perishable commodities which had actually arrived here, we should, at least as a temporary measure, suggest any compromise which would save our own stocks. I suddenly thought of the corridor between the cold rooms at the Castle store and the rest of the story is told in the letter which Mr Leale sent to the Feldkommandantur.[6]

THURSDAY, 21ST MAY

One of our fishermen was hit by a rifle bullet off L'Ancresse Bay yesterday and I went to St. Sampson's at 7.15 this morning to see Langlois who runs the German Customs Patrol boat and asked him to make certain that fishermen did not go west of Fort Doyle without due warning of the danger involved. We received a letter from the F.K. shewing three danger areas last week[7] and I made arrangements with the Customs chief for his harbour guards to shew a map marking the danger areas to every fisherman on leaving the harbour. I know that the guards received instructions because I asked them to shew me the map which had been given to them. Captain Franklin and I decided that to make doubly certain that the fishermen know the areas, we should put a notice in the newspapers. This we did today and I was told by Dr Brosch that I should have received Feldkommandantur approval before doing so.

This morning I handed to Mr Leale a draft letter to F.K. on the subject of cold storage, making a strong protest against the action taken. We discussed the possibility of his resignation and once more his wisdom brought out plainly my own weakness in that direction. He said that he had thought the whole matter over during the night and he had made up his mind that if he did resign it must be on the grounds that he had been unsuccessful in his efforts to uphold the rights of the civilian population and not as a protest against German orders. If he resigned for the latter cause it would be impossible for any other islander to take on the Presidency without being branded as a traitor and he thought it was quite likely that somebody else might be more successful than he had been. He is quite right of course, in his reasoning.

---

6 See Item 4: Leale to F.K.: Cold Storage, 23 May 1942, p.290.
7 See Item 3: Leale to Mueller: Fishing, 19 May 1942, p.288.

I had to call at Grange Lodge late this afternoon and Dr Brosch spoke to me once more about Mr Leale. He asked whether I thought he wished to resign because he was tired or because of the cold store decision. He did not think the latter sufficient cause for resignation. I said it was the last of many unsuccessful fights and that Mr Leale felt that he had failed in his duty to the civilian population by having such a long list of failures during his term of office. Dr Brosch said he would have to report the matter to Jersey and was not sure what he should tell them. He asked what Mr Leale's reactions would be to the return to duty of Mr Sherwill. Colonel Knackfuss had been interested in the granting of such a permission. I said that I thought that Mr Leale would welcome Mr Sherwill's return and that it would relieve him of much work. Mr Sherwill could become Procureur again and Mr Leale would remain President of the Controlling Committee. I said I would speak to Mr Leale on the matter and tell Dr Brosch his views. I also said that, in my opinion, nearly every member of the Controlling Committee was getting tired and that if our difficulties became worse during the coming months several of them would find it necessary to give up their work.

The boat is practically finished and it is a delightful relaxation to me to be able to go to Oatlands and potter about. We hope to get her to St. Sampson's on Sunday.

FRIDAY, 22ND MAY

The Bailiff called me in this morning to talk about two major matters which he thought should have been dealt with by him or at any rate with his full knowledge. They are the payment by Jersey of part of the costs of Occupation of Alderney and the request for a food ship. In the former case the matter was decided by Grange Lodge and we had no chance of discussing it. Mr Leale, however, did write to Grange Lodge saying that, in disputing Guernsey's responsibility for Alderney, he did not intend to force Jersey into payments in connection with that Island. In the latter case Mr Leale wrote to the Bailiff of Jersey asking what his reactions to such a request would be. The Bailiff, on seeing the minutes of the Controlling Committee, immediately wrote to the Bailiff of Jersey on the subject. It is obvious to me that there should be closer liaison between the Controlling Committee and the Bailiff, although Mr Leale does report to the Bailiff once a week at least. The Bailiff wants me to visit him more often, but, as I explained, my mornings are so full that I can seldom find time to go over to the Court and he is not there in the afternoons. I must try to go more often, though.

I spoke to Mr Leale about the return of Mr Sherwill and he told me to tell Dr Brosch that he would be delighted to work either under or over Mr Sherwill. This I did this morning.

24

This afternoon I delivered our formal protest regarding cold storage. Dr Brosch read it and said that he could not accept the third paragraph from the end, which is as follows:–

"In your last paragraph you say that foodstuffs must not be allowed to spoil. We shall do our utmost to avoid this, but unless we have adequate facilities we obviously may fail."

He said he would write to the Controlling Committee insisting that the responsibility still remained with them and if any food was spoiled he would regard it as sabotage. If there was any question of lack of space we must report the fact to him in good time to save waste of food. I said the paragraph was the result of his hint to us that more cold storage might still be taken from us. We had already accepted the present arrangement. He answered that no further space would be taken and repeated the phrase about sabotage. I replied that in my view the sabotage would be on their part if they took more storage space and I asked him to include in his warning letter to us the statement he had just made about not taking more space. He said he could not make such a promise.

I asked what would happen if there was a breakdown in the freezing plant at either of the cold stores. The plant at the Castle Emplacement is new but that at the Market is very old. He said that the view taken by the Germans would depend on the facts of the case and I undertook to let him have a full report on the condition of the plant at each store. He is going to the General tomorrow with the week's two important letters. I wonder what the outcome will be?

I discovered this evening that the petrol tank belonging to the boat is in a shockingly dirty state. It looks as if someone has emptied paint into it and it will have to be taken to pieces for cleaning.

SATURDAY, 23RD MAY

Ted launched the boat this morning.

I saw the Supervisor this morning and asked him for a report on the machinery at the cold stores. I explained the reason for the request. It appears that the Maintenance Engineer had already received instructions from the Supervisor on the matter and that several matters of urgency should be put right. We met Mr Leale, Sir Abraham, Sayer, Johns and Loveridge and decided to report verbally to Grange Lodge this morning. This we did and I am including a memorandum of the meeting.[8]

8   See Item 5: Meeting with F.K.: Cold Storage, 23 May 1942, p.292.

A railway clerk named Barnett is going to Granville to organize the shipment of goods for the Islands and he is to receive £270 a year plus board and lodging. Both Loveridge and I feel that we should receive pay nearer this figure than we do at present and I have spoken to Mr Leale and Sayer about it.

SUNDAY, 24TH MAY

More trouble about the Cold Stores and Markets. As arranged at Grange Lodge, a soldier went to the Castle Cold Store yesterday to let Wilson into Room No. 1. This morning he asked for admission to the room again and had to wait for an hour and a quarter before the soldier arrived. When he did arrive it was found that they could not get at the machinery because meat was piled against it and the soldier refused to move the meat. Obviously it is impossible for Wilson to work under such conditions. Then the question of handing over the keys of the Markets came to a head with an order from the Military saying that they were to be handed over this evening. Sayer telephoned to me and I advised him to get in touch with Dr Brosch. This he did with some difficulty and was told not to hand over the keys but to report with me to Grange Lodge at 9 a.m. tomorrow. This evening he tells me that he went to the Markets at the time appointed for the handing over and refused to give the keys to the N.C.O. who appeared. He says that the N.C.O. went away muttering "tomorrow". I wonder what will happen. At least this life is not dull and Sayer goes up still further in my estimation for his tenacity. It is remarkable to find a man with so few ties in the island – he only came to live here a few months before the Occupation – fighting our battles so valiantly.

Mr Krafft called to see us this afternoon. He is probably the most conscientious German I have met and has been very helpful to us in our difficulties. He believes in his country as much as we do in ours and we respect him for it, especially as he sees only the good on his side.

George Warry has operated on the petrol tank. He took one end out and cleaned out the inside thoroughly. This morning he rewired the ignition and we made the engine more in keeping with the perfections of Ted's work. We are hoping for a trial sail tomorrow.

MONDAY, 25TH MAY

Sayer and I went to Grange Lodge this morning as arranged and after discussion with Dr Brosch and Oser we went down to the chief of the Revictualling Department to discuss cold stores and markets. They agreed to all our suggestions.

Oser said he had had no sleep last night and there is a strong rumour that the Germans expect something big to happen today. Coupled to this an enormous force of German bombers passed over here last night and the English wireless says that they raided points on the South Coast. The German wireless says that they raided the bases of light naval craft on the south coast. We wonder if something really is happening at last.

I inspected Oser's vegetable garden at Grange Lodge this morning and it certainly is a pattern. He thinks that, in general, people do not know how to get the best out of the land in Guernsey and although I do not agree with him I must admit we do not always seem ready to profit by ideas which we have not thought of ourselves.

This evening I discovered one letter from Vic, written just after a first-rate choral concert in London and two from Des sent to us in the autumn of 1939. I had almost forgotten what appreciative and sensitive minds my two brothers have and I feel grateful once again that they ever took the trouble to entrust us with their innermost thoughts. I would not part with those three letters or with the one that I received just before the Occupation from Charles for any money. I dream of a day in the boat with those three and the talk we will have and the lack of talk. So when they come back after the end of this nightmare, and if they ever take the trouble to read these silly little notes, perhaps they will forgive my clay feet for a short time and realize I am very proud of them and all their doings. Des especially has developed his talents since he left home and I wonder whether he will have the good fortune to get the appreciation he deserved from many people who have the culture – his own word – necessary to read his work. He says that one must have humility to have culture and Christ said the same thing two thousand years ago about the qualifications for entrance into the Kingdom of Heaven. Tonight I feel that I possess at least this one virtue, for as I look out of the window and see the potatoes which are the pride of my heart at present, I do feel humble for having forgotten much of the beauty which used to be my staple diet. I must claim, though, that I see a very beautiful old stone hedge behind the potatoes and that their greenness and sturdy health mean more to me than their potential food value.

The war and the lack of plentiful supplies of food have made a great, if perhaps temporary, change in our sense of values and I discover that I get real pleasure in purely utilitarian gardening. It is very satisfying to grow food which alone stands between us and real hunger and perhaps starvation. In our case especially, it has been a real struggle to trench in grassland, plough up a marsh and drain it and fight most obnoxious weeds. My health, and especially my liver, has improved out of all knowledge and I hope I will have the guts to discipline myself to continue the good work when peace comes.

Writing this diary is not difficult now that I have made a proper start and I wish that I had had the foresight to start with the beginning of the Occupation. Sometimes I manage to realize that the war is not eternal and then I know that for me, at any rate, there will be some interest in normal times to read once again the outline of what will then seem quite an exciting chapter in our lives. It is my constant hope that those of us who are left here and our friends – including relations – who are away will live to meet and talk and enjoy ourselves together again.

TUESDAY, 26TH MAY

Today at Grange Lodge Inspector Zachau told me that it had been suggested that part of the Soldiers' Cemetery at Fort George should be made into a burial ground for Germans only. In the proposed section there are some graves of English soldiers and he asked whether we would rather remove the bodies or just the headstones. I said my opinion was that the Controlling Committee would not be prepared to do anything at all in the matter and would probably look upon the scheme as an insult to our dead. It was obvious that he had not wanted to mention the matter at all and he said it was not intended as an insult. I said I would mention the matter to the Committee. Messrs Leale, Johns and Dr Symons confirmed my opinion.[9]

WEDNESDAY, 27TH MAY

This morning I mentioned the matter of the cemetery to the Bailiff and he agreed with me. I therefore told Mr Krafft that we were not prepared to give permission for the removal of either bodies or headstones.

One thing I forgot to mention was that recently at Grange Lodge Dr Brosch and Oser informed me that we did not have any experts in the Island. I retorted that we were thankful there were so many at Grange Lodge!

It looks as if we may be able to open Perelle Bay for fishing after all. Dr Brosch has asked for a list of the boats and fishermen who would fish from this point and I gave in the list this morning.

It has rained so much during the last week that the bottom of the field is under water. I still think, however, that it can be drained if we bank up the sides of the douit and let the land slope towards the centre of the field. I propose to dig out a trench about five feet wide right down the centre and about eighteen inches deep and to fill it in with clinkers and a coating of gravel. This ought to provide the necessary drainage, but if it is not sufficient it will not be difficult to make some cross paths on the same lines.

---

9   See Item 6: Meeting with F.K.: Fort George Cemetery, 26 May 1942, p.295.

THURSDAY, 28TH MAY

This morning we received a reply from the General to Mr Leale's letter. I am enclosing a copy of it.[10] Tuesday afternoon Loveridge and I spoke to Mr Leale about our pay. We think that as we are doing special work we can justly ask for adequate pay, especially as Barnett is to be paid a fairly high wage for his new work in Granville.

Until today it has been too rough and too rainy to try the boat. However, we went aboard this afternoon and succeeded easily in getting the engine going. Then we hoisted the sails! We ghosted down the harbour on a very light breeze and near the entrance a fairly heavy puff caught us. That was the crucial moment. Would she go about? Ever since we first bought the boat eight years ago I have dreamed of owning a boat that would go about without having to put an oar over the stern. The helm went down and the bowsprit swung steadily without that sickening slowing down which has always disgusted me. The jib flapped, the mainsail flapped, the jib filled on the other tack and she was round. "It's a miracle!" I said and for me this was not an overstatement. I tasted bliss this afternoon, to the great amusement of Ted and Nigel, and I almost forgot the war until we made a tack so near the entrance to the harbour that the German guard thought we were going out and ran out of his hut with his rifle, determined to put an end to any attempt to sail for England.

FRIDAY, 29TH MAY

Drafted a letter asking for a rise in pay and handed it to the President. No great excitement.

SATURDAY, 30TH MAY

I forgot to mention that yesterday I applied for permission to become master of my own boat when it is not being used by Ted. I received a permit from the German Harbourmaster entitling me to take charge on each Sunday this June. The actual dates are given on the permit! Today Sayer and I were asked to go to Grange Lodge at two o'clock and we discussed Pigs, Poultry and Potatoes at great length. Then we went down to Mr Foote's fields at the bottom of the Rohais to inspect the French cattle which we have imported as security stock in case communication with France is cut off for any time. How the Guernsey experts would have held up their hands in horror in peacetime. A Colorado Beetle was discovered at St. Sampson's today.

---

10 See Item 7: Müller to Leale: Fishing, 26 May 1942, p.296

SUNDAY, 31ST MAY

This morning Dick Johns and I went to St. Sampson's and boarded *Ida* for a sail. The wind was due west and therefore blowing straight down the harbour. We cast off the moorings east of the clocktower and tacked up through the narrows to the Bridge. She showed no signs of misstaying and is remarkably stiff. There is still a leak in the stern when the motor is running.

On the 1 o'clock B.B.C. news we heard that more than one thousand R.A.F. bombers raided the Cologne area last night. The effect is beyond my imagination.

Tonight the B.B.C. said that 3,000 tons of bombs were dropped on Cologne and district.

Three thousand tons of stones would have done very considerable damage.

MONDAY, 1ST JUNE

The Feldkommandantur are very anxious that we should produce yet more food here. On Saturday they suggested that an effort should be made to increase the pig population. Their idea is that every farm of 50 vergées or over of cultivated land (as opposed to waste land) should be required to keep one breeding sow and that a boar should be kept in the centre of the most important farming area. We said that unless it is made profitable for farmers to keep pigs they will not do so. We explained that roots fetch such high prices as human food that the farmer, at present, finds it more profitable to sell them direct to the consumer than to pass them through a pig. Sayer claimed that it would be necessary to let the price of pork find its own level if farmers were to be encouraged to keep pigs. Dr Brosch said that then the poor man, who now has nothing, would be unable to buy pork. In Germany the scheme was working well already. We pointed out that the question of the relative food values to the population of roots fed to pigs and roots eaten by humans had already been considered by the Controlling Committee and that their opinion had been that, under present circumstances, the latter was the better proposition. However, we promised to reconsider the matter carefully.

In the same way with poultry, the F.K. put forward a scheme for the keeping of poultry on farms. The eggs of one fowl would be kept for each member of the farmer's household, on a basis of 80 eggs per bird, per year, and the remainder would have to be delivered to a central depot for distribution to the rest of the population at reasonable prices. Here again we said that without the incentive of profit we thought that farmers would not keep fowls, especially with the present shortage of poultry food. Apparently, once again, the scheme is working smoothly in Germany and we said we would examine it carefully.

With regard to potatoes, they are very keen on a strict rationing scheme on a basis of 5 lbs per person per week irrespective of whether individuals grow potatoes for their own consumption or not. To do this, a near estimate of the area of potatoes planted by each householder should be taken by States' inspectors and the estimated crop deducted from the total ration allowable to each individual. This will be the most difficult rationing scheme we have yet had to put into operation and frankly it looks hopeless. The fairness of the scheme, of course, is obvious to me, except that some people have grown no potatoes through laziness.

We discussed these problems with the President this afternoon and it was decided that Falla and Sayer should draw up a report on them.

Nigel and I spent a very pleasant evening trying to sail the boat in St. Sampson's harbour with an almost complete absence of wind. It has been an almost perfect day, spoilt of course by the war and the thought of mad destruction. Truly these years are bearable only by thinking constantly of the heavenly peace to come.

Mr Dorey submitted a letter to the President a day or two ago pointing out that thieving in G.U.B. properties is on such a large scale that the total crop will be affected, especially as immature potatoes are being dug. It was suggested that this letter should be forwarded to Grange Lodge so that they would be aware of the facts and would be prepared for shortages as compared with our estimated totals. I said I thought we should put forward some concrete proposals for stopping the thieving and after discussing the matter with Inspector Langmead, Mr Leale and Mr Dorey we are going to have a meeting with the Constables of the parishes on Wednesday afternoon.

TUESDAY, 2ND JUNE

Dr Brosch told me this morning that there were further bad things coming to the civilian population. He would tell me no more except that it was not punishment.

This afternoon I went to Herm with Mr de Putron to inspect the timber-felling. We left St. Sampson's at 2.30 in the patrol boat which is in as bad a condition as any boat I have ever been aboard. The engine has to be coaxed the whole time, the stem is rotten and as anchor cable they have 10 fathom of chain and a short length of rotten rope. I am speaking to Captain Franklin about it tomorrow.

It was a lovely afternoon, though, and I soon forgot my indignation when we landed. We went up to the copse where the trees are being felled and the smell of pines was everywhere. De Putron and Norman began to mark the trees which have still to be felled and I strolled over to Dickson's vegetable garden where I found him working. I lay full-length on the grass in my shirt sleeves and we chatted amateur philosophy. Artillery and anti-aircraft practice was going on the whole time in Guernsey but it did no more than accentuate the peaceful silence of the place. Then we strolled through the huge neglected upper gardens and down the hill to Dickson's cottage where we met Mrs Dickson, looking very spruce and I had a glass of buttermilk and a cigarette. This led me automatically to the piano and I performed my tricks with two or three Bach preludes that I begin to know.

We arrived safely back in Guernsey at eight o'clock and Mr Johns, who met us, told me that the subject of my salary was brought up at Controlling Committee this afternoon. No decision has been reached so far.

WEDNESDAY, 3RD JUNE

I have left the writing of this day until Friday and I am afraid I can remember nothing about it.

THURSDAY, 4TH JUNE

Apart from work which was not especially interesting, I spent the morning watching the weather and wondering whether it would be suitable for boating this afternoon. It was, and we left St. Sampson's at 2.30. There was a perfect breeze from the north and we made for Brehon on the last of the flood. The boat settled into her stride as we left the harbour and it was a very satisfactory stride. In no time at all we were south of Brehon and then we furled the jib and put out the whiting lines. There was no difficulty at all in handling her at whiting speed, but we caught only one. An hour later we set the jib again, got out our sandwiches and made for Vivian which we reached long before we had finished tea. Talk about a kid with a new toy! I forgot the war completely and tasted perfect bliss. We caught four more whiting while handling the pots on the Banques and then beat back to St. Sampson's against wind and tide, taking the inside passage. Both Ted and I were most impressed with the boat's performance.

FRIDAY, 5TH JUNE

I played for a funeral at St. Stephen's this afternoon so I spent half an hour at the organ early in the morning. The smell and general atmosphere of the church still holds me and I itched to hear the organ the moment I walked in. Needless to say the results of my efforts soon brought me back to earth.

We had a conference at the Crown Hotel this morning to discuss fishing on the west coast and it was decided that Portelet Bay, Pleinmont should be opened. We are to see the fishermen concerned and to give them each a map of the danger zones in their area. This concession is the result of months of fighting on my part and I do hope it will be a success.

SATURDAY, 6TH JUNE

I recently received hints from the Feldkommandantur that we were to receive orders which we would not like and sure enough they were handed to me today in the form of a letter and order from the Feldkommandant requisitioning all radio receivers in the Bailiwick. I asked the reason and was told there was no reason and that the order had been received from Berlin. I gathered the impression that the F.K. were extremely sorry to have to issue the order.

I took the correspondence down to Maison Allaire and obtained a quick verbal translation for the information of Mr Leale and myself. My first reaction was that we should refuse to have anything to do with the collection, but Mr Leale reminded me that if we did not the sets would probably be irreparably damaged. Dr Brosch had already told me that they were to be kept in the care of the F.K. and not taken away from the Island.

We called an emergency meeting of the Controlling Committee at the Bailiff's Chambers and it was decided that the Bailiff, Mr Leale, Mr Martel and myself should go to Grange Lodge at 12.15. We saw Dr Brosch and the Bailiff put our case very strongly, pointing out that we had, as a population, done our best to abide by German orders and that he was certain that this order, taking from us, as it did, the last link with our friends and fellow countrymen, would cause great suffering and discontent in the Island. Dr Brosch said he realized this and that, if we wished, we could put our case to Colonel Knackfuss. We therefore arranged to meet him tomorrow morning. Dr Brosch also said that they would help all they could with regard to transport. The members of the Controlling Committee that had been consulted all agreed that we should do the collection.

This afternoon Mr Leale and Mr Martel drafted the necessary Controlling Committee Order and wrote to Mrs Hathaway in Sark and I collected together all the officials who would be engaged in the collection and went through with them the details of the scheme. We came to the conclusion that we must ask for 1,500 gallons of military petrol as we have none at all to spare and that as very little labour is available we must ask for an adequate extension of the time limit of one week which we had been given to complete the collection.

This evening, I received a phone call from Dr Brosch. He said that he had spoken to the Colonel who said that an interview with him would be useless. I said that we had several points to raise and that I thought we should see him tomorrow even if we could not see the Colonel. I told him of our transport difficulties and he replied that we did not need transport since people could be required to deliver the sets to a centre in their parish. I reminded him of his promise to us on the matter and protested that the collection was not a matter which was pleasant to us and that he must help us. I also pointed out that we could not possibly do the work in one week. He said that we must do it as soon as we could if we could not abide by the time limit. I also said that an alteration would be needed to the German notice. He said he was sorry but that he could not help us.

I telephoned to Mr Leale and we are to meet at 10 a.m. tomorrow at Maison Allaire to discuss the alteration of our plans.

I wonder if this is a foretaste of what we must expect as our country gets stronger in this war. However, we have not lost our dignity and I for one do not intend to let the Germans see what a blow this will mean to our population. Once before they took our sets, but that time it was as a punishment and then nobody cringed and we all managed to smile. I hope we all behave the same way this time, especially as the first reaction of everybody to whom I have had to break the news has been that the Germans must be getting weaker if they are afraid of what we may hear from the B.B.C. Nevertheless, the feel of the mailed fist can be a little disturbing when our own fists are so woefully naked.

The Bailiff is not signing the Order which we are issuing because, as Bailiff, he does not possess the power to issue Orders.

SUNDAY, 7TH JUNE

I arrived at the office at 10 o'clock and met Mr Leale, Mr Martel and Vernon Le Maître. We worked out details of the revised scheme for the collection of the wireless sets and Vernon went off to find centres. I saw Goettmann about the translation of the F.K. order.

This afternoon Dick Johns and I went out in the boat. There was a very strong breeze from the north and we reefed right down before leaving St. Sampson's. We reached Brehon in no time and tried for whiting in the eddy north of the tower, with no success. The tide was full and with the wind against it there was a very lumpy sea running. In gybing the gaff cracked and we had to take down the mainsail to strengthen it with whipping. In taking in the sail we made the first tear in it – not a very bad one. We had to sail very close to the wind on the way back, but we arrived without further mishap.

Mr and Mrs Sherwill called to see us early this evening and he told me that when he saw Colonel Knackfuss some weeks ago he was told that the Colonel regarded me as "the best of the bunch". I am not sure that I welcome this compliment but in any case whatever work I have done since the Occupation has been entirely in the interests of the population and my conscience is quite clear. I think the F.K. must realise this. The Colonel thinks very highly of the Bailiff of Jersey and if he thinks that my very small efforts are made with the same aims as those very much greater ones of Mr Coutanche, I need not worry about what my countrymen think of me.

Vernon came in this evening to report on his day's work. He must have worked very hard and the results are most satisfactory.

MONDAY, 8TH JUNE

Having spent the last two days trying to organise the wireless set collection, I was told at Grange Lodge this morning that organisation would be necessary and they proceeded to criticise my plans. I told them flatly that as far as I was concerned it was impossible to change the scheme at all. They said no more.

This afternoon we met the wireless experts at the Supervisor's office and allotted collection depots. We decided that all necessary details of sets should be noted and that valuations should be done afterwards by a small committee of the experts. We also met the Constables of the parishes and made arrangements for labour and writing at the depots.

TUESDAY, 9TH JUNE

I met Dr Brosch at Grange Lodge. He was very busy and so was I but he agreed to come with me to see Victoria Road Chapel to decide whether it would be suitable as a centre for the storage of sets. We went in his car and agreed to use the chapel. When we came out he sat in the car and said, "Where shall we go now? I have never been to Victor Hugo's House, let us go there now!" In the middle of one of the busiest mornings I have had for months! We went and found the place locked, so we went for a ride round St. Martin's and back to Grange Lodge. On the way he said he thought he would give up work and become a chauffeur. I said I thought it was a very good idea, because the Guernsey people were not grateful for our efforts and had a very poor opinion of both the Controlling Committee and the Feldkommandantur. He coolly told me that they had a very poor opinion of the Controlling Committee, believing it to be the worst institution ever invented but that they realized the sterling worth of the F.K.

Oser and I were talking about the war while I waited to see Dr Brosch. He was in the front line of the Western Front in the winter of 1939 and he told me that the Germans and the French talked to each other regularly across no man's land. At Christmas the Germans had a concert which was being broadcast. A Frenchman called through a megaphone and asked the band to play "*Parlez moi d'amour*".

They played it and told their wireless audience that they did it by special request of a French soldier. Oser is sure that the war is only wanted by the Jews. The answers to this statement were so obvious that I did not bother to give them.

I asked for the military petrol which Dr Brosch had said he would procure for the collection of the wireless sets into the two Town centres. Not only was I refused but was told that the States would have to pay for the transport.

I said that if the F.K. would give us a promise that the sets would be kept for return to their owners we would be willing to supply the transport. Dr Brosch said he would like to be able to give such a promise but did not have the authority to back it if the military decided that they wanted the sets. I protested strongly but he pointed out that transport was only provided to help the population. As far as the Germans were concerned it was the duty of owners to deliver sets to the two centres in the Town. I retorted that we would, in due course, send in an account to the F.K. for the full cost of the collection and he accused me of trying to terrorize him. This evening I went to some of the depots and discovered that the sets were not coming in as fast as they ought because many people think they need not deliver them till the 17th. I have already asked permission of Grange Lodge to issue a notice drawing attention to the fact that the Controlling Committee notice must be obeyed strictly, but they refused. They also refused the publication of three alterations in the schedule of depots so that some of the addresses published are wrong. They say that our draftsmen should have foreseen these alterations when the original notice was issued. And we had 48 hours to organize the whole affair!

WEDNESDAY, 10TH JUNE

We have been allowed to ask for an editorial in the newspaper impressing on people the necessity for adhering strictly to the Controlling Committee notice.

This morning all fishermen were summoned to the Hafenkommandantur because it seems that it is suspected that somebody has left the island by boat. I must try to get the full details tomorrow.

THURSDAY, 11TH JUNE

Some days ago Mr Leale told me that Sayer was going to Jersey to discuss several matters, including potatoes and food ships and had asked that I should go with him. Mr Leale told him that there were private reasons why I should not go at present. I agreed that I should not go unless it was absolutely necessary. Today, however, Sayer tackled me on the subject and asked whether I would change my mind. He said that he wanted me especially as the subjects to be discussed were very delicate ones. I said I would speak to Queenie since I was not prepared to go if she did not wish me to do so. I discussed the matter with her this evening and she has no objections whatever, although the baby is expected in six weeks time.

I took our radio set to the depot this evening on a trailer towed behind Jim Le Tissier's bicycle. That set was a wedding present from my brothers and sisters and it hurt a lot to give it up. However, the pain was less severe when I suddenly struck the idea of trying to sell it at a really high figure to some of our Visitors and I asked the radio dealer at the depot if he could get £25 for it. If we get this amount we shall be doing quite well because it only cost £17 and is three years old.

FRIDAY, 12TH JUNE

I saw a Jersey newspaper today containing the notice concerning the collection of wireless sets in that Island. All sets have to be given in by tomorrow. I managed to get an extension to next Wednesday for Guernsey. They only have 12 depots as against 23 here and they have no scheme for spreading the collection over the time allotted as we have here. I was not surprised, therefore, to hear this afternoon that no sets have been delivered up to today and I do not envy anybody connected with the collection tomorrow evening. They will never cope with the rush.

I also heard that the order for the collection had been cancelled in Jersey and I went post-haste to Grange Lodge to find out if there was any truth in the rumour. According to Dr Brosch there is none. I told him that I intended trying to sell the set and he said that he did not blame me. He would not be at all surprised to receive an order from the Division as soon as the sets are collected for the delivery of 100 sets to the military. That is no more than I expected and it does not improve my opinion of the Occupying Forces. I told him how I felt about giving up the set and he said that he understood. He said that he thought the discipline of the troops was very good and he also agreed that the behaviour of our people was excellent, considering the vexations they had to bear, especially with regard to the evacuation of their homes and orders like this one on the collection of radios. We went on to speak of the administration and he said he thought the administration in Jersey was superior to that in this Island. I explained that their civil service was almost intact whereas here we had not only lost many of our younger men but had also been deprived of the services of both Crown Officers. Then we came on the question of food production and he said we did not take the initiative and we put obstacles in the way when the F.K. made suggestions. I said he must agree that some of the F.K. proposals were impracticable and he asked for an example. I gave his recent suggestion for the keeping of pigs and pointed out that a breeding sow ate as much as a cow and that we could not stretch the food and land available. He thinks we should concentrate on intensifying all cultivation.

Oser came in and we began to speak about potato rationing. Only a few days ago both Dr Casper and Dr Brosch assured Mr Leale that they did not intend taking potatoes from the civilian population as they did last year. They submitted to me their calculations whereby we are expected to ration our people strictly to 5 lbs of potatoes per person per week throughout the year, taking into consideration home production. After making provision for seed and wastage, they calculate that we shall be able to hand over to the troops 1,320 tons of our potatoes. This calculation and arrangement was made without consulting us at the beginning of March and until today I, at any rate, had heard nothing of it.

I expressed myself somewhat forcibly on this point and was told that the Germans bring us much of our food from outside and we must therefore be prepared to give something in return. I said that it was obvious to me that the Germans gave us nothing at all and that the French were the ones who made the sacrifice and that with a bad grace. We would be quite willing to export what we could to them. Dr Brosch said that they did not want what we could provide and I had to correct him there. A few weeks ago we had a visit from a French official who told us that if we could supply France with some tomatoes they would be much more willing to help us. How I long sometimes to be given a chance to fight a battle before an independent umpire and how much I learn every day about the methods of the Occupiers!

SATURDAY, 13TH JUNE

I told Mr Leale this morning about the scheme for taking potatoes from the civilian population and he took the news really badly. He has always believed, as I have, that Dr Brosch is honest and, unless there is some explanation which we have not heard, it now looks as if he told the President an untruth the other day on this subject.

We received a Red Cross message from Beata yesterday and one from Babe today. Apparently they write to one another and Beata and her husband – she has married Bunny – are living in Wales. Bunny has been in a sanatorium and from this we gather that he has had some accident in the submarine in which he was serving. Babe says her little boy is a real comic.

SUNDAY, 14TH JUNE

A light N.N.E. breeze this morning, so Dick Johns and I left St. Sampson's intending to go to the Brayes where mackerel have been caught recently. The wind proved too light and instead we made for Roustel where we caught two whiting. Then we went on to the Rockeries for lunch and to the eastwards of Herm. It was really fine to be at sea under sail and we managed to catch nine whiting altogether. We beat back to St. Sampson's in the late afternoon and arrived home a little before eight o'clock.

MONDAY, 15TH JUNE

Since we shall have to ration potatoes very strictly to ensure there are enough for everybody this winter we decided on Saturday to check the areas under potato cultivation including small garden patches. This check will start either today or tomorrow.

I am getting really worried about Mr Leale. He told me this morning that he sometimes feels as though he will not be able to finish the Occupation as President. Up to a short time ago he thought he could go on indefinitely but now he feels that he will one day just stop. I told him I thought he should consult a doctor but he says he has no symptoms except that he thinks he is becoming more forgetful and his legs go to sleep more easily. When I hear people criticising him and think of his scrupulous honesty which stops him from obtaining much of the food consumed by his critics I wonder if Guernsey people will ever realize what he has done for them and whether they will show him the gratitude he deserves.

This afternoon I visited some of the wireless collection depots and at one of them entered into a discussion with a man whose name I do not know on the subject of the government of the Island. He seemed to me to be typical of the average more intelligent Guernseyman and he knew nothing of the struggles of the Controlling Committee on behalf of the population. He knew all about the Committee's failures and then some. (I can think of no more apt phrase).

I called at Grange Lodge to see Dr Brosch and found Raymond Falla and Oser with him. They were having a heated argument on agriculture and the policy to be adopted and Dr Brosch was once again advocating intensification. He is annoyed because his pig-breeding scheme has been turned down and blames Sayer who, he says, turns down every suggestion made by Grange Lodge – with a smile. We explained that the breeding of pigs had been the subject of many discussions by the Controlling Committee and that that body had long ago decided that it was better for the population to consume the products of the soil direct instead of through the medium of the pig. He seemed rather shaken when we told him that all our doctors were of the same opinion as the Committee on this subject. He told Raymond, however, that as agricultural officer it was not enough for him to put notices in the newspapers. He must become a leader and teacher and convince our people that they must strain every nerve to grow food for their own sustenance. Of course he is right there, but, as Raymond pointed out, we have lost 12½% of our agricultural land to the Germans and our farmers have much to discourage them in these days. He said that only today he had received a message from one of his men that several German horses were grazing on some of his fields. Dr Brosch said he knew all about these difficulties and had even been told by Germans that it did not matter about the food of the local population as long as their horses could find food. The General, however, went so far as to insist that the gorse should be uprooted and crops grown in its place. He, Dr Brosch, said that Dr Symons wrote every week about the lack of calories and sent in statistics of sickness and deaths. He wanted to see no more of these reports as long as there was uncultivated land in the Island. I am, of course, very much a layman in agricultural matters but I wonder whether there is not some truth on both sides. It is very easy for Grange Lodge to criticise, but it is much more difficult to keep enthusiasm for food production at concert pitch with the setbacks the producers are encountering the whole time from the Germans. Further, the lack of food has for some time been telling on heavy workers and it is now impossible to get a full day's work from most of the people in the agricultural industry.

Raymond said that if the Feldkommandantur had lost confidence in him, they could find somebody else and he would go back to his farm. Dr Brosch said he must please himself on this matter but that while he was agricultural officer he must do his utmost to produce food.

Everyone said much more but I cannot remember it all and anyway it has all been said *ad nauseam* before.

I finished spraying my potatoes tonight and blew away the cobwebs of bureaucratic argument in the process. How lucky are those of our people who do not have to take kicks from two sides at once.

TUESDAY, 16TH JUNE

This morning I asked Dr Brosch why he had told Mr Leale that the troops would not be taking potatoes from us this year. He said that he did not remember doing so and added that if Dr Casper had supplied this information it must have been while he was alone with Mr Leale. I reminded him that he must have known it was intended that potatoes would be requisitioned since the correspondence shewn me by Oser was dated March last. I also said it was impossible to work without frankness on both sides.

The Controlling Committee met this afternoon and decided to give me a rise of £67 a year, starting from last January. Added to this I have sold our radio for £25 and since it looks as if the Germans are going to have it in any case, I feel very pleased to receive payment instead of giving it to them. We can now have the house painted.

To complete the day I went to a play this evening, *A Quiet Wedding*.[11] To my untutored intellect the acting was perfect and the substance of the play excellent and it was a real stimulus to me to live with the actors and enjoy their brilliant talk – or perhaps chatter is a better word – and duly lap up the character-studies so neatly set before me.

WEDNESDAY, 17TH JUNE

Fishing was the main topic at Grange Lodge this morning and after thinking that they had found a really inefficient industry, Dr Brosch and Oser had to admit that they could find little fault with it. I wonder sometimes whether Oser is trying to improve our food supplies or just to make trouble. He certainly thinks he can teach everybody in Guernsey something about their respective métiers.

This afternoon I went to most of the radio collection depots in the north of the Island and called at the Vale Church on the way to run over the music for the wedding at which I am playing tomorrow. It was a breezy afternoon and the mixture of salt tang, blue sky and ancient stonework and trees and strong sunshine was exhilarating. I walked into the vestry and found the organ key in the second drawer down in the very solid and handsome chest-of-drawers. And I noticed the picture of Dean Bell, Rector of the Vale from 1857 to 1914. Then I started up the box of tricks and listened wonderingly to the hideous noise which came from it. Really, I don't understand how I have the cheek to offer to play at serious functions. When I could stand the noise no longer I shut up the box and walked out into the sunshine again. I went to the next depot through the lanes and had to pull up to watch a very lively tree with every leaf quivering in the breeze. It really was good to be alive this afternoon.

The delivery of wireless sets by our people is now finished and I am

11 *A Quiet Wedding* was a 1938 comedy by Esther McCracken. It was performed by the Regal Players at the Lyric Theatre, New Street. According to Madeleine it was 'very good'.

surprised to see the bold front they shew even in this time when their last link with our country is being taken from them.

THURSDAY, 18TH JUNE

The main event today was the wedding of Leah our next door neighbour.[12] It took place at the Vale Church and I played the organ. The Church was nearly full and the transport was composed of four carriages, one van and one Guernsey carriage. By dint of much arrangement an adequate tea was provided for the guests afterwards and everybody turned out in their best clothes – an unusual and awe-inspiring array. I weeded the beans during the lulls in the merriment.

We hear that Mr Churchill is in America and it looks as though the much-talked-of Second Front is to start soon. Is it a move of desperation or are we really ready for it?

FRIDAY, 19TH JUNE

I arrived in Town at 8.20 this morning to get through my work as early as possible. We then made for St. Sampson's Harbour to go to Herm in *Ida*. The party consisted of Sayer, Jurat de Garis, Ted Dorey and myself and we were subjected to a minute examination before being allowed to get aboard. I made the fatal mistake of taking my attaché case to carry my food and, of course, the guard insisted on seeing what it contained. I laid out for his scrutiny sundry old papers which were hanging about in the case and he seemed especially interested in one containing recipes for various wartime dishes. He did not understand any English. We had dense fog all the way across but made a perfect landfall to the secret delight of Ted and myself. Needless to say we preserved a true professional casualness in front of the other two. I went to see the timber which has been cut and the others inspected the animals and I had my first bathe of the year from the harbour slipway. We were exactly half an hour on the trip in each direction.

SATURDAY, 20TH JUNE

Dr Brosch thinks that the Controlling Committee are taking advantage of him because he does not use the Iron Hand. He told me with some heat today that if things went on like this he would use other methods with us. He is under the impression that Guernsey people are lazy and that there is a definite movement afoot to cause trouble in official circles. We should not

---

12 Leah Le Tissier married Clifford Le Poidevin.

use machinery, and certainly not petrol, for mowing hay, every greenhouse should be cultivated, boats should sail whenever there is wind and we should appoint a man to decide each day whether or not it is suitable weather for boats to go out. He recently ordered us to produce five ladies' bicycles for the nurses from the Soldatenheim and Mr Leale wrote and said we were attending to the matter but that neither he nor the Bailiff possessed the power to requisition for such a purpose. This morning he said that he did not care where we obtained the cycles and that he was fully aware of the fact that power was not given to the Bailiff or Mr Leale. He did the ordering and it was the job of the Controlling Committee to produce the cycles. He does not seem to understand that unless he gives, in his order, the names of the owners from whom the machines are to be taken, he is asking us to do more than we can. He asked whether we expected him to go out into the road and take the bicycles he wanted. Actually, we have asked a cycle dealer to build the machines and they are being delivered today. He asked whether I thought he liked having to order that the potato ration should not exceed five pounds a week. The ration had been fixed and there was no room for further discussion. This was too much and I asked him what he thought the Controlling Committee's functions were. If they were to have no say in such matters they might as well resign. All he needed was a civil service to carry out his orders. The discussion came to a full stop then, but it is difficult to work with this total lack of confidence. It seems to me sometimes that the Germans are unable to see far into any subject. We get the same sort of criticism from totally uninformed Islanders and many of the suggestions which they put forward are obviously the result of this lack of appreciation of the details of working in the trade or industry under consideration. In other cases, I do admit, they throw light on matters which need improvement and they act as the States used to in more democratic times. I fancy that this lack of confidence is the result of Oser's presence and I wish they could be required to put into operation some of the schemes they put forward and that they could attend Controlling Committee meetings and more informal meetings with the President when everybody concerned ends up with a headache trying to find the best way to serve the interests of the population. As for the suggestion that the Controlling Committee or any of its members try to sabotage the food supply, etc. that of course is ridiculous and makes our work many times harder than it would be otherwise.

SUNDAY, 21ST JUNE

Spent the day sailing in company with *Frypan*. We beat up to the Brayes in the morning and tried for mackerel without success then met at the Platte Fougère after lunch. We raced from the lighthouse to Rousse with a fine north-easterly breeze and we beat *Frypan* by about 200 yards. Nigel is now determined to get bigger sails and so I suppose we have won our one and only race.

MONDAY, 22ND JUNE

More arguments with Grange Lodge and more criticism from Oser. I have given the substance of all the arguments before and it is not worth while repeating them. Dr Brosch is obviously not pleased with us because for the last two days he has shewn no inclination to shake hands!

TUESDAY, 23RD JUNE

Group Captain Randall was thrown out of his house some time ago and was refused permission to cultivate his garden. We asked F.K. to obtain permission for him to do so and they did not grant it. He, therefore, wrote to Mr Leale setting out the position of Island food supplies and health as he sees it and asking once more to be allowed access to the garden. We transmitted his letter with a covering note to F.K. and the reply has taken the form of a summons to Randall to appear at Grange Lodge at 9 a.m. tomorrow to make good in writing certain statements he made in his letter regarding the incidence of deaths and sickness due to malnutrition, etc. Dr Symons has given him a note signed by himself and all the practising doctors stating that Randall's statements are substantially true. I foresee more and very fierce arguments tomorrow.

This morning before work and this evening I have been trying to learn to use a scythe on our tiny hay crop. As usual I have had plenty of advice from many nationalities.

WEDNESDAY, 24TH JUNE

I received a telephone message at half past eight this morning ordering Sayer and myself to be at Grange Lodge by nine o'clock. I arrived at five minutes to nine and met Oser on the landing. He asked why Sayer was not there yet and I pointed out that there were still five minutes to go. He said that he had ordered us to be there by nine at the latest. I thought this was a very poor start and matters did not improve as the interview proceeded. From the way we are being treated recently nobody would guess that we are doing our best.

The main subject was Herm. Apparently Oser and Dr Brosch went there yesterday to inspect the animals and the first thing they discovered was that Pritchard, our new shepherd, had left for Guernsey last Saturday and had not returned. Oser said he would make an example of the man and that as Sayer was responsible for him they would both be put in prison. "En prison!" he shouted two or three times at the top of his voice. Of course Pritchard should not have left Herm for more than a day but Sayer was not aware that he had left at all and I only heard casually late last night when I met Henry Bisson. According to Oser the sheep were in a bad state and both they and the cattle were neglected. We submitted to an hour's criticism and threats and were then handed over to Dr Brosch who went over much the same ground and gave us new instructions regarding the treatment of the animals. One instruction, namely that all the ram lambs were to be castrated, was directly opposite to Oser two or three days ago. Much of the criticism was obviously just because agriculture is far from perfect in the Island, but as Sayer pointed out it is very nearly impossible to train our farmers who have concerned themselves in the past with the production of pedigree cattle, to become perfect arable farmers. Perhaps propaganda would help but from what I know of the opinion of themselves held by our farmers, I am very doubtful.

In any case, the result of our interview was that Sayer and I were a mass of frayed tempers. We both felt that either the efforts of the Controlling Committee during the past two years were of no use at all or that Grange Lodge had not even begun to understand our difficulties. We also felt that Oser regards everything we do with such suspicion that it will soon be impossible to work with him at all. He has even hinted that the members of the Controlling Committee take advantage of their official positions to get extra food.

To add to our difficulties, our own people and especially some of the greengrocers, serve Germans with larger amounts of vegetables than they will give to Guernsey people.

THURSDAY, 25TH JUNE

Dr Brosch is in Alderney today and I did not see Oser this morning. I feel like a schoolboy on holiday. Mr J.N. Dorey was at Bordeaux this afternoon and he told me that while he was out with Oser the other day they came across a man using a scythe. He was working neither fast nor well and Oser asked him where his sharpening stone was.

"Over there on my coat," said the man.

"We carry them in our pockets in Germany," said Oser and sent the man to fetch it.

He took it and very expertly sharpened the scythe. Then he began mowing and Dorey said he used it extremely well. This little episode does not count for much, perhaps, but to me it shews that Oser is not merely a theorist and

I have been wondering afresh since, exactly how backward our people are in farming and how much truth there is in the criticism we receive.

This afternoon I sowed some sugar beet seed in the front garden and enjoyed a race between *Ida* and the *Frypan* in a stiff breeze while I worked.

Some time ago Jersey agreed that they could supply us with some potatoes if we needed them later this year. Soon afterwards Grange Lodge showed me their figures of the quantity of potatoes to be delivered to the Occupying Forces by the two Islands and I suggested that we should tell the Bailiff of Jersey what that Island would have to supply and ask whether he still thought that Jersey could let us have any. We received a letter from him today saying that they had not been informed of the German requirements but that he thought a visit from us to approach the F.K. in Jersey with him would still be a wise plan. I am supposed to go over with Sayer and Dr Symons if the visit materializes. Mr Leale is going to see Dr Brosch on the matter tomorrow.

FRIDAY, 26TH JUNE

Dr Brosch did not come back from Alderney today so Mr Leale could not see him.

Group Captain Randall went to Grange Lodge on Wednesday and was told by Dr Brosch that he must produce his own evidence proving the statements he made in his letter.

I felt so weary today that I took the afternoon off and went out in *Ida* with Ted and Frank. We went to the Brayes and caught eight mackerel. Everyone else caught four or five times as many as we did.

Mr Leale is going to see his doctor tonight. He tells me that when he is tired and relaxes one side of his head sometimes becomes quite numb. He has a practically permanent feeling of tiredness.

SATURDAY, 27TH JUNE

Mr Leale and I went to see Dr Brosch this morning. The first subject discussed was the very severe criticism which we have been receiving from Grange Lodge recently. Mr Leale said we were all doing our best and Dr Brosch must remember that all the members of the Controlling Committee were getting tired. The Committee made mistakes, as we were all aware, but its successes were of no mean order. The production of foodstuffs was much higher than before the Occupation. He put his points in a masterly way and the whole interview was carried off without any loss of patience or temper. Dr Brosch said there were many things they could not understand, especially regarding an apparent slackness in agriculture and horticulture.

We explained that maximum production cost money and reminded him that Grange Lodge had insisted on cutting down budget deficits.

Another thing which annoys the Feldkommandantur is the constant stream of correspondence on the incidence of sickness which, it is claimed, is due to lack of food. Dr Brosch thinks that in the Islands we are in a better position than anywhere else in Europe. He said that last winter in Germany people queued for hours to buy one or two roots. Mr Leale pointed out that the same thing happened in Guernsey in the first months of this year. Group Captain Randall's letter has apparently caused much annoyance too, and they are certain it was inspired by somebody else. I am wondering whether we have heard the last of this matter. Mr Leale asked if it would be of any use applying for permission for Mr Sherwill to return to power and Dr Brosch said he would recommend such an application to Jersey.

We next spoke about the supply of potatoes to us from Jersey and of our proposed visit to that Island to make a joint application with the Bailiff of Jersey for permission to buy potatoes. To my great surprise Dr Brosch raised no objection to our visit and we shall probably be crossing towards the end of next week. Oser told Harry Bichard today, by the way, that they would probably be taking 700 tons of potatoes from us this year – less than half the figure he quoted to me recently. He also seems to have said that the figure is not settled.

They are firmly convinced that our farmers and farm workers do not work as hard as they should and Dr Brosch even went so far as to say that if Mr Leale went out with him this afternoon he would see for himself that no one was working in the fields.

During the course of the conversation we reminded Dr Brosch of the great discouragement to our farmers which the loss of agricultural crops and land meant. He said that they were our enemies and he could not understand why such requisitions did not make our people all the more determined to cultivate intensively to keep starvation at bay, when it was caused by the action of the enemy.

I came away feeling that the Feldkommandantur would never fully appreciate our point of view and our difficulties, and although we could never forgive the Occupying Forces for many of their actions, we had come nearer to making them see what we have to contend with than we have for many months. It is sad to think that the public will probably never appreciate all that Mr Leale is doing for them every day.

SUNDAY, 28TH JUNE

Exactly one hundred and four weeks ago today the first Germans landed at the Airport and the Occupation had begun. That we have become used to the present state of affairs is obvious from the fact that I can scarcely call to mind the heaven in which we used to live.

However, I spent no time today soliloquising as I was much too busy catching mackerel. *Frypan* and *Ida* went over to the Humps this morning on a fine westerly breeze and arrived back with considerable difficulty at half past seven this evening, the wind having freshened throughout the day. We had great difficulty in weathering Tautenay against the strong easterly tide and when we did get into the Russel we had to take a tack right down to St. Peter Port, just managing to pass to windward of Rousse and Brehon. We tacked right up St. Sampson's Harbour to Dredge's shop where we weighed in. We caught 73 fish, kept twenty and sold the rest for 30/–. Altogether a very successful day.

MONDAY, 29TH JUNE

Last night we were reminded that the war is still on by the almost constant roar of aeroplane engines. Some shewed lights and so must have been German and some apparently did not because the guns went into action a few times. This afternoon a British plane came over and wrote a V in the sky. It was promptly fired at without visible effect.

We received notification today that all cameras and photographic materials are to be collected as a result of a recent attempt by three Jersey boys to escape to England. Apparently they took with them photographs of military objectives.

A notice appeared in the Jersey papers stating that ten hostages had been taken in connection with tampering with telephone wires and the issue of leaflets and that if the culprits did not give themselves up these ten would be sent to a concentration camp. I am proud to say that the culprits were men enough to confess.

We had a preliminary conversation today on the subject of potatoes from Jersey. We are expecting to cross to the other Island at the end of this week.

TUESDAY, 30TH JUNE

The Germans are taking radios from those collected recently. Nothing else of importance today.

WEDNESDAY, 1ST JULY

This morning I handed in to Grange Lodge an application from the Bailiff for the reinstatement of Mr Sherwill as Procureur. I had a long talk with Dr Brosch on the subject and he thinks that if Mr Sherwill comes back he cannot become a mere member of the Controlling Committee after having been President before. I pointed out that the trouble at present is that Mr Leale has too much to do and that having a really experienced legal adviser would be a great help to him. I also said that, in practice, the Procureur acted as general adviser to the Controlling Committee and that Mr Sherwill's brain would boost the work of all members. Dr Brosch said several times that as Procureur Mr Sherwill would have no responsibility for the administration of the Island. I pointed out that we did not want him to have responsibility but would welcome his brain. Dr Brosch immediately took up the point and and said that if we did not want to make Mr Sherwill responsible, they did, rather than give the responsibility to a man who wrote to them saying that he did not consider himself responsible for the agriculture of the Island. (Mr Leale wrote recently to the F.K. in answer to a letter from them holding him responsible for some detail of agricultural policy, and said that he could not accept responsibility for this detail, pointing out that he was not an agricultural expert: the language difference apparently led Grange Lodge to misinterpret Mr Leale's meaning.) Coupled with Colonel Knackfuss' statement to Mr Sherwill at a recent meeting that the F.K. thought the Controlling Committee hardly strong enough, Dr Brosch's remark leads me to think that they want to get rid of Mr Leale. The trouble is, of course, that Mr Leale does his work quietly and with a complete absence of window-dressing and the F.K., therefore, do not appreciate what he is doing.

We talked over again the agricultural policy and the difficulties encountered and I said that, in comparing us with Jersey they must remember that the changes necessary in that Island are nothing compared with those which we have had to initiate.

I told Mr Leale of my conversation with Dr Brosch, not omitting the hint (involuntary) that a new President of the Controlling Committee would not be unwelcome to the Feldkommandantur.

THURSDAY, 2ND JULY

Mr Leale told me this morning that he had been thinking about the course he should take if Mr Sherwill was allowed to come back into office. He thought that he should send his resignation to the Bailiff so that the States could decide between himself and Mr Sherwill as President. Mr Sherwill came while we were discussing the point with Mr Johns and we all decided that Mr Leale's decision was the right one. Mr Sherwill added that, in his opinion, Mr Leale should continue as President and said that he would make that plain to the States. Mr Johns thought that Mr Leale should continue as President after taking a rest. I am to make the position clear to Grange Lodge tomorrow.

We told Mr Sherwill of our present difficulties especially with Grange Lodge and warned him that our relations with F.K. had deteriorated since the influx of troops and O.T. workers and the beginning of fortifications.

This afternoon I went fishing and we caught no more than two mackerel.

The war news is very bad at present and there seems to be great dissension in the British Government.

Our baby should arrive within the next three weeks and I am not very happy about leaving Queenie to go to Jersey. However, I must go and Dr Sutcliffe has promised to do everything he can to look after her. I suppose I should be very little use here in any case.

FRIDAY, 3RD JULY

Monsieur Grignard of Caen is here. He is the agent for the charcoal-burning apparatus which we are fitting to the lorries in order to dispense with petrol and he buys machinery, cycle accessories, etc. for the Island as well. He tells us that the French authorities are asking that we send scrap metal in return for the new metal used in the agricultural machinery etc. which we import. He came with me to Grange Lodge this morning to discuss the matter and Dr Brosch agreed to help provided that M. Grignard would give assurance in writing that we would receive new machinery in proportion to the scrap we export.

This afternoon I went to Grange Lodge again with Mr Dorey to discuss questions concerned with Glasshouse Board produce. We started our conversation at 2.30 and finished at 5.45. Dr Brosch says his primary interest is that the G.U.B. should be run without any deficit. Once again we explained the difficulties but even the necessity of recognizing the effects of supply and demand on markets for very perishable commodities is of such secondary importance to him that he suggests making one price for the whole crop and thinks that this will work. We were asked to estimate how many tomatoes would be available for export to France, for the troops, and what price we should ask for them. Mr Dorey suggested 10d per kilo for first quality tomatoes from 15th to 31st July and Dr Brosch told Oser to ask for 1/–! They also suggest that we, in Guernsey, should not eat our first tomatoes but send them to Jersey to be sold at a price to be fixed by us beforehand. We are very keen on selling some tomatoes to France if only as a gesture of gratitude for all we are getting from the French but apparently we must ask France for the same price as the Germans in France are willing to pay.

We brought in our little crop of hay tonight and put it in the rabbit house for the winter.

The war news sounds very bad these days, with the Germans only a few miles from Alexandria, but the troops here say very little about it. In Russia they are having small successes, but I am wondering whether they are so quiet because of the losses they are suffering in making the headway which they have made. The end does seem a long way off yet, and everybody, German and English and French, to whom I speak, is very tired of the war and all it means.

SATURDAY, 4TH JULY TO THURSDAY, 16TH JULY

My excuse for not keeping a daily record during the past twelve days is that I have been to Jersey and have only just settled down again.

Last Sunday week we took Grignard fishing with us, having, with some difficulty, obtained permission to do so from the German Naval authorities. Two points which stand out in my memory are that we were nearly all seasick and that he is certain that the French government will never allow the Germans to make use of their fleet against the Allies.

On Monday the 6th Dr Symons, Mr Sayer and I left here for Jersey on the *Paul et Jeannine*, a small steamer of uncertain age and very definite limitations of speed. It is strange to go on to the Jetty to board a boat feeling that there is always a possibility of being bombed in the process. Our poor old harbour where we used to think ourselves mighty tough in the old days when we had battled against the wind and the rain from the Weighbridge to the Duty on Goods Office! The queer thing is, that once under way, there is no longer any feeling of danger and we thoroughly enjoyed the crossing which took three hours and a half. We arrived at a quarter past eight and went to the hotel through deserted streets. Of course we have become used to the air of forlornness in our Islands, but I often wonder what our friends would think if they suddenly came back in the height of summer and found not even the ghost of the holiday spirit which we have since childhood associated with summer. And what, I wonder, would they think of our reception at the hotel? The proprietor and his wife greeted us with consternation and regretted (with their tongues in their cheeks, we thought) that they could not put us up. After a little domestic wrangle they changed their minds and decided they could give us beds but no food. They explained that they had no spare butter and said that they were sure we would realize that nothing could be done without that essential commodity. We had to agree, of course, and they cheered us by saying how fortunate it was that we had not come on a Saturday night, because then the Rationing Office would not be open until Monday and we would therefore have to go without food for more than a day instead of doing without only one meal. We wondered. Luckily I had brought some sandwiches and we ate those and washed them down with what were claimed to be double brandies at 4/2 a time. Our official work is all contained in my report to the Controlling Committee.[13]

During our visit we mixed with all types of people and gained some impression of Jersey life under present conditions. We went to a very good little play. These entertainments are a feature of the lighter side of our lives during the Occupation. They are put on in both islands by amateurs and they are so well patronized that it is very difficult to buy tickets. However, we succeeded and enjoyed ourselves thoroughly. Then, luxury of luxuries, we borrowed a car and went out into the country to see the crops. How very wholesome it looked to see field after field of wheat and oats, a symbol of our very real effort to ward off starvation and of the forcible return to stark realities. We asked several quite ordinary people about their food supplies and were told that rations were very short but that they thanked God for the Black Market. Perhaps it is because I am an official in Guernsey, but it appears to me that the Black Market is much more flourishing in Jersey than in Guernsey. And the prices asked, and paid, in this trade! Five pounds a pound for tea, one pound a pound for strawberries, four and six for blackcurrants and various intermediary prices for other soft fruits. Three pounds fifteen for a bottle of whisky, two shillings and a penny as a minimum for all drinks, a terrific figure, I think up to five shillings per egg, twelve and six and over for a pound of veal.

We heard the story of the attempted escape of the three boys in a boat from the mother of one of them. It appears that they bought the boat from an Italian and that it had not floated for eighteen months until they launched it on the night of their attempted escape. The eldest boy was eighteen and I think the other two were fifteen. They gave the harbour guard something to drink which dulled his wits and rumour has it that he even helped them to launch the boat, without realizing what they were going to do, and he has since been shot for his part in the affair. However, they were three or four miles out at sea before they discovered that the boat was making so much water that they could not cope with it. They began to throw things overboard and these included suitcases containing photographs of military objectives. These suitcases were washed ashore and were damning evidence against them. Finally the boat sank and one boy, who could not swim and was already almost out of his mind with fear had to be abandoned by the other two after they had made frantic efforts to save him. Then the other two swam ashore and were found next day in a deserted bungalow, naked and huddled together for warmth, with their soaked clothes in a heap on the floor. The boy whose mother I spoke to thinks her son has been taken off to Germany but she has received no news at all of him. And he is fifteen years old!

---

13 See Item 8: Report to C.C.: Visit to Jersey, 11 July 1942, p.297.

Then we spoke to one of the ten hostages who were taken by the Germans because of the leaflets which were distributed advising people not to give up their radios during the recent collection. They were not treated harshly and were so well fed at the expense of the States of Jersey that they were sorry to come out of prison. The man who issued the leaflets, named Gallichan, was forced by his brother-in-law to give himself up and received five years imprisonment with one year's sentence to his brother who distributed them.

Our conversations with the Jersey authorities were finished at last and we went to see Colonel Knackfuss, the Feldkommandant, to lay before him our requirements and our difficulties. He seemed very pleased to see us and the meeting went off most jocularly and in English and rather bad French. He called Dr Symons the Uncle Doctor and laughed when I said that we were not at all satisfied with our catches of fish in Guernsey, although he had just complimented us on them. He said, teasingly, that we were never satisfied.

During our last evening we went to a birthday party and drank cognac and champagne and then we came back to the hotel and had a sing-song with old Gervase Peek who, at eighty six or so, had crossed to Jersey for treatment for cancer and at 11.30 p.m. could still sing a very loud solo.

I thought often of Queenie at home and hoped desperately that she was still well and that there would be no bombing raids while I was away. What a time to bring a child into the world and how I hope the iron of war will not enter into its soul.

Saturday morning came at last and we were to leave for Guernsey at 7.30. We were on the pier at that hour and actually left at 8.45. It was blowing hard from the west and while we were waiting and listening to the singing of the rigging and the telephone wires we had time to compare the size of the ubiquitous *Paul et Jeannine* with the probable size of the seas outside the Island. As we left St. Aubin's Bay with the tide under us and the wind dead ahead we met the first patch of steep short seas and a batch of Germans went down before them stricken with seasickness and destined to remain shorn of all dignity for the next three hours. Then a Guernsey girl who was with us went to the side and I went to stop her disappearing overboard. We had not left our seats two minutes when a twelve foot stove pipe, nearly red hot, came down with a crash on the place where she had been sitting. Up and down we went, practically in the same hole, for nearly an hour until we rounded the Corbière and shaped our course for Guernsey and then we began a corkscrew motion which did not cease until after we had passed St. Martin's Point. How I longed to be comfortably sick and how determined I was not to give way to my longing in front of the King's enemies. My patriotism won the day.

At a quarter to one we tied up in St. Peter Port and when all our luggage and documents had been thoroughly examined by the German Customs we were free to go back to our normal wartime existence. So up I climbed to Hirzel House, reported our safe return to Mr Leale and pointed my motor cycle for La Platte. I did not know how much I loved Queenie until I saw her face light up in welcome and could put all my groundless fears behind me. The doctor had examined her the day before, however, and told her that she must be prepared to go to hospital any day so I did not come back any too soon.

Sunday morning I spent at sea in *Ida* and went to the Humps where we caught ten mackerel. We came back in time for lunch and I spent the rest of the day at home, and very happy I was to be there.

Monday I spent in preparing and dictating the report of our visit to Jersey and since then I have been making myself acquainted with the happenings during our absence.

Yesterday we dug the first of our early potatoes and discovered an average crop. It was thrilling though, to collect the results of our gardening efforts and to know they are vitally necessary.

FRIDAY, 17TH JULY TO TUESDAY, 21ST JULY

This has been a time of waiting for the baby to arrive and we are still waiting. Sunday we went to the Ferrières in the morning in a strong north-west breeze and anchored off the south coast of Herm for lunch. I had a bathe over the side and *Frypan* tied up behind us. We had a long beat back to St. Sampson's and did not have one bite throughout the day.

On Monday I saw Dr Brosch for the first time since my visit to Jersey. We did our routine business in an atmosphere which was somewhat strained and then I told him of my conversation with Colonel Knackfuss regarding Mr Sherwill's return to office. He said there would be no need for further conversations on the subject since the Colonel had already given his approval. I asked in what capacity Mr Sherwill would return and he replied that for the present he would return as Attorney-General.

On Monday afternoon I received a telephone message to the effect that two German police were searching Colonel Randall's house for food. After some difficulty I managed to get hold of Dr Brosch and asked him whether there was not some mistake as I thought he probably wanted the police to search Group Captain Randall's house. He said he would see about it and, sure enough, they searched the Group Captain's house later. They also searched Dr Symon's house for the same purpose. On Tuesday morning we received a letter from Colonel Knackfuss stating that they would not prosecute Captain Randall although the statements made in his recent letter were false.

Tuesday morning I telephoned to Mr Sherwill and later went to see him regarding his return to duty. He received the news, as he said, without enthusiasm. He is quite determined that his return shall not result in the displacement of Mr Leale and there are several members of the Controlling Committee – in fact I think all of them – who want no change of President. We talked over present conditions and difficulties and then I took the official letter to the Bailiff.

I spent an hour or so with Dr Brosch in the afternoon. We were very friendly this time and talked of things other than the details which cause the friction. He thinks it is time that a new policy, very definite and designed to serve as more than a temporary measure, is put into operation in Guernsey. At last we were clear of misunderstandings caused by the language difficulties and I saw what he was thinking. I said it was very difficult for our President to work out new policies and to look years ahead when he was constantly harrassed by matters of detail and he agreed that he found the same thing in his work at Grange Lodge. He thinks that the President should have somebody to do all the detail work for him. He said that he had attended a lecture given in Guernsey by a very famous German. Apparently it was on the decadence of the British Empire and it fitted in with the Doctor's observation in Guernsey. In India we have done nothing for the people – in Guernsey our agricultural officers have made no step to bring production into line with present day requirements. I think what makes him so frantic sometimes is that he thinks we are so far gone that we cannot see the slough of indolence in which we wallow. I pointed out that often it was the detail, like the loss of an eighth of our agricultural land which caused a slackening of enthusiasm on the part of both the farmer and the official and he agreed this did make for less effort. What the Feldkommandantur do not realize is that it is the hindrances which we discover at every turn which stop the forward progress for which they look. Dr Brosch thinks the President should be a man who would go out into the country and see for himself what is happening, who would talk to our people and hear their difficulties, who would, in short, formulate his policy from first hand information. How noble a conception – if you can have a noble conception of Policy for an Island of 20 square miles – and how impossible to carry it out when the President has to interest himself in the collection of wireless sets, cameras and bicycles! However, my conversation gave me a new idea of Dr Brosch's capacities although I could not help remembering all the time that the day before he had ordered the searching of the house of a man who, since the beginning of the Occupation, has worked at full pressure, through health and ill-health, to protect the food-supply and the health of our people.

WEDNESDAY, 22ND JULY TO SATURDAY, 25TH JULY

Mr Sherwill is back at work and seems to be full of vigour. Everybody with whom I have spoken during these past few days is heartily glad to see him back, not least among them being Mr Leale who feels that now he really can relax and enjoy his few weeks of rest.

Even more important to me is the fact that we are still waiting for the arrival of our baby. Queenie is extremely well and we are hoping that all will go well. Crowds of people ask every day how she is and to all I reply, "Still complete."

On Thursday it was too rough to go out in the boat and Nigel and I spent the afternoon and evening in the garden planting cabbage and weeding beans – and I was extremely contented! Friday evening we sowed a perch of swede seed.

Pat Greville and several other people have been arrested but I have not yet heard definitely what the charge against them is.

I was speaking on Saturday morning to Percy Dorey and Prins about the difficulties of administering the Glasshouse Utilization Board and Prins gave it as his opinion that one of the reasons for lack of control on the part of their officials is that they are all temporary employees. It is therefore natural for them, in their dealings with growers, to remember that after the war they will probably have to work with the growers again in their ordinary capacities – many of them having businesses which are dependent for their success on the goodwill of the growers. Added to this many of them have personal friends among the growers and in any case their pay as G.U.B. officials is so small that they do not really care whether they are sacked or not. I fancy this the main reason for whatever slackness still remains in the administration of Mr Dorey's department.

We have asked for an official receipt from the Feldkommandantur for the radio sets delivered to them recently and they have ordered their officers here to count the sets. This, of course, is a terrific task and they have asked us for three men to help with the work. I am seeing Dr Brosch on the matter at the first opportunity.

The war news seems as bad as it can be from our point of view, except that we are holding out well in Egypt. On the other hand the Germans here do not seem as happy about the news as one would expect. Perhaps the reason for this is even if the summer campaign in Russia is successful the cost in men and material will be enormous and will not bring the end of the war in sight. War weariness on both sides seems very apparent to me.

SUNDAY, 26TH JULY TO SUNDAY, 2ND AUGUST (11.30 AM)

Our long wait for the baby is nearly over now. I woke at four o'clock this morning and Queenie told me quite casually that she had begun to have pains at half past one. She is a permanent example of courage to me. Not only did she not complain about the pain, but she would not let me telephone to the doctor until six o'clock. He sent the ambulance down just before seven and Queenie gave all the attendants (three of them) cups of tea. Then she climbed in and disappeared from my view. I am still waiting like every husband since the first in the world, and wondering just how much she has to bear before she can relax and forget her pain.

This week at the office has been a comparatively quiet one. I have not been to Grange Lodge as often as usual, but yesterday I went to see Dr Brosch with Mr Leale and the Supervisor. The main subject was a new scheme which threatens to come into operation whereby we will not be allowed to pay for our purchases in France with the Reichsmarks which accumulate in our banks. Instead our buyers will have to send accounts to a central bank (Barclays) in Jersey and the French merchants will be paid by them. Apparently a debt will pile up in France which the Islands will be expected to pay at the end of the war. Both the Feldkommandantur and ourselves are very much against the scheme since not only will we have to meet this debt, but we will be inundated with money which will probably be useless after the war. Dr Brosch also talked about intensifying production in the Island so that we shall not only have enough to eat but will have a considerable surplus for export.

Last Sunday Dick and I went to the Brayes and caught 55 mackerel. The mackerel fishing this year is very successful. Catches of five or even six hundred are quite common and Ernest Henry tells me he does not remember mackerel being so plentiful so early in the season. We are to have a meatless week, this week, since we feel that the meat thus saved will be needed much more next winter. Fishing has started at last at Portelet – the result of six month's insistence on my part and on the part of other officials who are interested – and here the catches have justified our efforts.

War news dribbles through rather slowly these days, but it appears to me that the attitude of the Germans we meet belies the claims made on the propaganda pages of our newspapers. We hear too that the R.A.F. made a fairly heavy raid on St. Malo on Friday afternoon. There must be a fair amount of activity at that port since all heavy traffic for the Islands comes through there. We shall probably hear more anon about the damage done.

In the garden we have planted lettuce and celery and have begun weeding the carrots.

SUNDAY, 2ND AUGUST TO MONDAY, 10TH AUGUST

The hospital telephoned at lunchtime to ask whether I would like to see Queenie during the afternoon (Sunday) since there was no likelihood of the baby being born for some hours. This was a bitter blow since I had expected to get news by then that all was over. All Sunday I waited and every phone call – and there were many – made my heart leap. When I rang the hospital early on Monday morning the baby was not born yet and it was not until 11.30 that Dr Sutcliffe rang up to congratulate me and tell me we had a daughter and that both Queenie and the baby were quite well. Then the fun began! Phone calls to all our friends took nearly an hour, two or three stiff drinks put a rosier complexion than ever on life and I received permission to see Queenie as soon as I wished. I forgot all about eating and made for the hospital as fast as my motorcycle would go.

I walked up the hospital steps feeling very thankful that Queenie's ordeal was safely over but otherwise little impressed by recent events. Then I opened the door of the ward and saw my wife. Somehow she was a new person, triumphant and yet so defenceless I could have wept and there was a glamour about her that I had never seen before, even on our wedding day. I don't think we said anything very suited to the occasion but we knew that whatever happened we belonged to each other. Then I was taken to see my daughter and if ever she comes across these silly notes and takes the trouble to read them, I hope she has a strong enough sense of humour to appreciate the fact that, although I suppose I felt proud of her, I was most struck by her total lack of beauty. From the time I left the hospital until now, and I suppose for many months to come, I have been asked by ladies of all ages to describe the child and to all of them I have answered: "She weighs seven and three quarter pounds, is about fifteen inches long, as far as I can judge and looks exactly like Billy Prout. (Note by the diarist: Billy Prout was a most disreputable old itinerant fishseller with a permanent scowl). The looks of profound dismay and disgust on the faces of such ladies repays me adequately for their other question, "Don't you feel proud to be a father?" thereby relegating me immediately to the company of bowler-hatted, blue-serge-suited, lemon-gloved and patent-leather-shoed Sunday morning trundlers of perambulators.

Definitely my first feelings were of thankfulness that Queenie is safely out of danger but I am beginning, after a week during which I have seen José several times, to have a regard for her which, something tells me, will rapidly develop into overpowering love.

During the week I have been on holiday and have spent very little time either sleeping or in solitary contemplation. I started off on Monday evening at a dance organized by the Huberts, complete with my own bottle of cognac.

I arrived late and as I walked in I was greeted with handshakes from scores of friends and drinks with and from dozens. Sutcliffe told me that Queenie had been really wonderful and had not complained once through a really long period of intense pain. Then I *was* proud and I have continued to be more and more so as nurses and sisters and matrons have also borne witness to her courage. What a start for a child, to have a brave mother! By the end of the dance, having emptied the cognac bottle with a chosen few and consumed many miscellaneous and wonderful beverages, I was gloriously tight. An hour later, alone in the dark in the garden at Sefton, a most violent physical reaction set in, but repentant I was not and not even the passage of my brother-in-law Leonard, with bicycle, over my recumbent form could shake my new-found and, I fear, temporary dignity.

Since then I have been to one more dance which was a sorry anti-climax, two supper parties which were quietly enjoyable, and a very short weekend party at Albecq which confirmed friendships already very close. I have also spent several mornings fishing, getting up at dawn and seeing the sunrise from the boat. Once, at the Brayes, the Germans began artillery practice and their first shell landed so close to us that we used a pint or two of our precious petrol in travelling half a mile in what must be record time for *Ida*.

I went to the hospital to see Queenie every evening until the other maternity patients discovered the fact and objected so strongly that, by mutual consent, it was decided by the Matron, Sister, Queenie and myself that I must adhere strictly to official visiting times. Last Saturday and today, therefore, I have not seen my wife and I marvel to think that married men manage to live here through the whole Occupation without their spouses.

As far as I can ascertain the war news is no better than it was a week ago, with the Germans continuing to advance in southern Russia and reports of violent unrest in India. Rumour has it, too, that the recent British raid on St. Malo did very little damage to any military objective.

I have neglected the garden shamefully and it has rewarded me by growing weeds twice as fast as ever before.

Today I went back to work and discovered that quiet reigns throughout local official circles.

TUESDAY, 11TH AUGUST TO TUESDAY, 25TH AUGUST

Queenie is still in hospital because her recovery has not been as rapid as is usual and the fact that my diary has not been written up for a fortnight shews that I have had very little spare time. Actually I have been to one or two dances and a party and have spent a few evenings at home with Bill Rowe who now plays the violin extremely well.

José is beginning to look more human now and I never miss an opportunity of looking into the nursery. I used to think that all babies looked alike but they don't! Our baby, I begin to see has imitated the features of both of us to some extent, but apart from actual likenesses her expression of solemnity and supercilious aloofness is unique in the nursery and too comic for words. Neither Queenie nor I have yet descended to baby-talk and I am hoping most sincerely we never shall. How I hope that our daughter who, of course, is the first and most important baby that ever was born, is endowed firstly with a rich and delicate sense of humour and secondly with intelligence above the average. If it is possible for her to be affectionate and friendly as well that will be just too perfect.

The most striking news during the last weeks is the recent raid on Dieppe and district by troops from England. The English radio said from the beginning of the raid that it was not an invasion and our withdrawal is said to have gone according to plan. The Germans, of course, say it was an invasion and that it failed completely. The fact remains, however, that a landing was effected and that the main body of our forces returned safely. The effect on the population here was astounding. Everybody was exhilarated and I found myself wishing I was flying a fighter plane, not because I want to kill Germans, but just to be in the fun. The Germans are still advancing in southern Russia but the effect of this remarkable move forward is having no visible effect on the troops here who seem to me to be getting more and more war-weary.

I have been fishing only once during the past fortnight and we caught nothing at all.

Dr Casper, who has taken the place of Dr Brosch temporarily, has written us to the effect that our measures to keep prices down are not strong enough to give the poorer people a fair chance. Dr Brosch wants us to raise vegetable prices to such a point that the G.U.B. can produce them without loss.

Meanwhile we are finding it impossible to get rid of the vegetables and tomatoes which are available except at a most uneconomic price. The two main causes are the falling off in local demand because nearly everybody is producing vegetables for themselves and the very poor sea transport which makes it almost impossible to export sufficiently quickly to save our products before they become overripe or rotten.

WEDNESDAY, 26TH AUGUST TO SATURDAY, 29TH AUGUST

Queenie is at home again. She returned from the hospital in a Gazogène ambulance which began life as an ordinary petrol-driven furniture van. It is now a perfect ambulance and apart from the gas-making apparatus, which was imported, the whole conversion was carried out in the Island. Maisie and

I worked hard for two days to make good the depredations of three weeks of holiday from housework and our care and zeal could not have been greater if a General's inspection had been in the offing. We scored full marks.

José was carried in by a fat old woman in St. John Ambulance nursing kit and when she had deposited our supercilious daughter on the the the settee she said, "Well, my dear, here's your bundle and a very nice bundle it is. I hope you have a good night." Her first words irritated me, calling anything so dignified a Bundle! The bit about having a good night sounded ominous but my fears were unfounded and we all slept most of the night.

It was strangely moving having Queenie back and the presence of a daughter as well made me realize – with a start is scarcely too strong an expression – that I am Happily Married. I felt my responsibilities to such an extent that I did several hours weeding and picked food for the accursed rabbits almost with enthusiasm.

I am on holiday this week and we went fishing on Friday. We caught fifteen mackerel with great difficulty.

War news includes the fact that the Russians are counter-attacking very strongly in the Moscow sector and seem to be driving the Germans back. It is also said that the B.B.C. announced that early on Friday morning the R.A.F. attacked a convoy south of Guernsey in bright moonlight, setting two ships on fire. Wilder and perhaps to some people, more attractive, rumours include one claiming that the boats were full of troops and that one ship reached Jersey burning fiercely.

SUNDAY, 30TH AUGUST

We had a quiet night with the crump of bombs and the boom of guns in the far distance to lull us to sleep. This morning I was up early and having produced breakfast and fed the rabbits I went off to St. Sampson's where I met Dick. What a ridiculously intense pleasure there is in hoisting the mainsail in our little tub and casting off the moorings and gathering speed to run silently down the harbour! Coming up neatly to the steps at the entrance is as satisfying to me as a good meal and the procedure of reporting to the German guard on leaving and returning gives a feeling of importance to the whole expedition.

This morning we had a fair tide and the wind behind us right up to the Platte Fougère and there was a feeling of peace and contentment abroad which it was difficult to reconcile with the daily loss of thousands of young lives throughout the world. We in these Islands are spectators – unwilling perhaps – of this great madness which has overtaken our modern world and except at times like this morning we live only for the time when it will be all over. I think sometimes that we have learnt already the lesson which it teaches so clearly, that we had grown selfish and soft and had drifted far from the reality of working directly for the food we eat and the satisfaction which goes with such labour. We can look objectively, too, at our former way of living and see that frills like motor cars and and new clothes must never regain the exaggerated importance which we used to attach to them. We now know the value of good food and many of us are determined that when once again we can buy as much as we want we are going to treat it with the respect it deserves and not make ourselves permanently unfit by eating like pigs. But most glaring of all are the faults in the administration of our little community and we look forward to the opportunity of using the power given to our government to improve the material and perhaps also the cultural welfare of our people.

José cried for about an hour this evening and we amateur parents felt a bit helpless and wondered whether she had enough food. Doubtless we shall learn by experience but meanwhile this kind of worry is something new to us and we do not enjoy it. We often think of Babe having her baby and bringing it up in England without Len beside her and then we hate the war more than usual.

MONDAY, 31ST AUGUST

It is said that today, for the first time since the outbreak of war, the news on all fronts is favourable to us. The Russians are taking the initiative over most of the front and even in the south seem to be checking the German advance. The bombing of Germany is continued by the English and Americans on the west and by the Russians in the east. The Americans have consolidated their positions in six of the Solomon Islands. I wonder whether this week will see the beginning of an invasion of France. The early part of the nights will be moonless and the summer is ending, and the Russian drive coming directly after Mr Churchill's visit looks to me as if it may be the beginning of an all-round offensive.

Meanwhile José holds the stage at Bordeaux. She slept fairly well last night but Queenie did not.

TUESDAY, 1ST SEPTEMBER TO THURSDAY, 10TH SEPTEMBER

We now go to bed immediately after José's 10 o'clock feed and the result is that there is no quiet period in which to write up my diary. That's one excuse for not noting down each day's events. The other is that the novelty has worn off and I have to exert myself to continue writing.

To take the news in its order of importance: José now is fed every three hours during daytime instead of every four because she never seemed satisfied and usually spent the last hour between feeds yelling at the top of her voice. Last Thursday she was christened at St. Sampson's Church by Mr Frossard. It was an impressive little service and it made us all feel the responsibility of bringing up our baby. Zelia, Maisie and Dick were the godparents. The Rector gave us all furiously to think when he prayed for all those who, but for the war, would have been with us in Church and I, for one, nearly wept. We had a little celebration at home afterwards. Those present were Skipper and Mum and Dad, Zu and George, Maisie and Nigel, the Rector and Mrs Frossard, Dr Sutcliffe, Mrs Marquand, Mads and Irwin, Auntie Fan, Dick, Len and Gwen Falla. Having laid a good foundation of carefully stored champagne and the older people having gone home at 6 o'clock, the rest of us felt that it would be wrong to waste our happy state, so we unearthed some food and cooked supper. To our disgust curfew came too soon at 10 o'clock, but we all enjoyed ourselves. Mum, Dad and Fan hired what, as children, we used to call a Country Carriage and they looked too cute for words arriving and leaving. On the way here they took the wrong turning and ended up in either a quarry or a stone yard.

The late potatoes which we have dug so far have been about half either diseased or spoilt by wireworms and we have lost quite a quantity through theft. The thieves are probably foreign labourers who are always so hungry that robberies are an everyday occurrence throughout the Island. There are some thousands of these people in the Island. The spring tides at the beginning of the month coincided with heavy rain and the result is that the bottom of the field flooded.[14] All the carrots which were planted there have gone rotten in the ground.

Dr Brosch is back from leave. He is still trying to make Percy Dorey suggest vegetable prices for next year at a level which will ensure a balanced budget for the G.U.B. He suggests a standard price, to be maintained throughout the season, for each sort of product and says that the Germans will take any surplus which we cannot sell at that price. At the prices necessary to balance the G.U.B. budget the amount which the local people will be able to afford to buy will be a small fraction of what is produced and we feel rather doubtful whether Germans will be able to distribute the rest, especially as most of it will have to be exported with the very poor shipping available.

Apparently Cologne is very badly damaged but the cathedral is untouched except for very minor scars.

The Germans now speak of their plans for their winter campaign in Russia and I think it is safe to say that although they have advanced in some sectors, the resistance of the Russians is stronger than they ever expected.

---

14 The flooding in the field was the result of seawater from the beach across the road, flowing through the outfall and into the back at high tides. It still does.

On our local paper yesterday there was a German account of the recent raid on Dieppe. One thing which stood out for me was that the reporter, after interviewing British wounded and prisoners, was amazed to find that our men seemed to treat the war as a kind of sport. I felt proud of that and it gave me back in full the British spirit – and I longed to be with our men.

We went fishing last Sunday, leaving St. Sampson's at 8.30 and getting back at 4.45. We went first to Tautenay, then back to Rousse and the Rocqueries and on to the Ferrières and up past Brehon on the flood in the afternoon. We caught one mackerel, five whiting and an abundance of fresh air and contentment.

The bombing of Germany must be very heavy because hardly a day passes without somebody mentioning that a German of their acquaintance has had news of the loss of his home – and sometimes of his family as well. If the men concerned have been fair in their dealings with us we find ourselves feeling sad to think that the war has brought grief into their lives.

FRIDAY, 11TH SEPTEMBER TO TUESDAY, 15TH SEPTEMBER

On Sunday we went fishing complete with a conger trot which we had been given by Henry Bisson. We made first for the Brayes to catch mackerel for baiting the trot. The wind was blowing strongly from the north east and it was high tide. The result was very short seas in the overfalls which we had to cross north of Corbette and we broached-to just as an extra big one came up on our beam. The top of it came aboard and the boat heeled so much that the water poured in over the lee gunwale. We were soaked and remained wet throughout the day. When we had caught enough mackerel we went over to the Rocqueries and lost a few rubber baits trying to pull whiting. Then the time came to bait and set the trot and we dropped anchor between the Creux to get ready. We paid out around a cluster of rocks east of Creux without much difficulty and spent a couple of hours round the Ferrières waiting to pull up the trot again. After much delay and some complicated manoeuvres we managed to get one float aboard and began to pull. The first two hooks came in with baits intact – and then there was nothing more except a tail end with a clean break.

The tide was still so strong that the float at the other end of the trot was under water, so we went off to Brehon and caught half a dozen mackerel, and lost a line. When we returned, to our great excitement, the float was showing and we approached it very gingerly. We pulled it aboard and the engine stopped! Before we could get it started again we had drifted down with the tide and had to throw the float overboard so that the weight of the boat would not break the cable. Three times we tried and three times the engine failed us. Then at last we succeeded in pulling the weight aboard –

plus about a fathom of trot. The rest remained securely in position at the bottom of the sea and we held the broken end in our hands and laughed like fools. Thus ended our first attempt at trotting and we had a glorious sail back to St. Sampson's getting in at half past seven.

Today (Tuesday) Mr Krafft of the Feldkommandantur telephoned to me at half past eight in the morning to say that he had a very important and urgent letter from the Colonel for the Bailiff.[15] I asked if it was good or bad and he said, "Bad," so I said I would pick it up on my way to the office. For days now I have been feeling that we would soon be getting news that some of our people would be transferred to the continent after the bombing in Germany and, sure enough, the letter gave notice that all English people who were not residents of the Bailiwick and all men of 'the English people' between the ages of 15 and 70 *with their families* were to be transferred to Germany. I accepted the letter for transmission to the Bailiff and asked Dr Brosch for a definition of 'English'. He did not know whether it meant people born in the British Isles, excluding the Channel Isles, of course, or all persons of British nationality, with the same exception. We were ordered to prepare lists of such persons and Dr Brosch said we should make two lists, one including all the former category and the second the rest to make up the latter. I was perfectly formal and thought it best not to discuss the matter further until we had a translation of the letter made and discussed it with Mr Leale, Mr Sherwill and the Bailiff.

It was decided it was in the interest of our people to accept the letter and to ask for an interview with Dr Brosch this afternoon. Meanwhile, a notice appeared in the newspaper over Colonel Knackfuss's signature setting out the order contained in the letter.

This afternoon the four of us went to Grange Lodge and discussed the matter with Dr Brosch. He was obviously very upset about the order and pointed out that it came from a very high German authority. The Bailiff expressed our concern (that is a very mild word) and asked whether anything could be done to alter the order. Dr Brosch held out no hope at all even though he realized that many of those who would be taken away had lived in the Bailiwick for the major part of their lives. We asked whether the maximum age could be reduced and he said there was no hope at all of this. The Feldkommandantur have no idea at all of the reason for the order.

It is very probable that, in the changed atmosphere after the war, it will be thought that a most unheroic attitude was taken by the administration of the Island in consenting to take any part in the preparations for the evacuation of part of our community but we know that the Feldkommandantur have not the staff to deal with the matter in the way which will make for the

---

15 See Item 9: F.K. to Bailiff: Deportations, 15 Sep 1942, p.302.

alleviation of suffering and that by keeping in close contact with them we will not let any opportunity pass to save our people.

We said we assumed that the destination of the evacuees would be an internment camp in Germany, but Dr Brosch did not answer. Mr Sherwill asked again, and again no reply was forthcoming. I ask myself whether the Germans will fall so low as to use our people as hostages, or billet them in towns which are likely to be bombed and I cannot believe they would treat innocent people in this way.

Dr Brosch said the first batch would be leaving Jersey tomorrow, about four hundred strong, he thought, and that we must be prepared for the first batch to leave Guernsey by Sunday next at the latest. Mr Sherwill pointed out that, under international law, it was necessary to allow people time to set their affairs in order and to prepare themselves. It appears that individual notices will be served on people by the Feldkommandantur and that about a day's notice will be given them. Mr Sherwill pointed out that this was not nearly sufficient notice and was, in fact, extremely harsh on people who, after all, were not criminals. Dr Brosch said that all people affected by the order should start making arrangements immediately.

So much for the official aspect, in which the striving to save a couple of thousand people from terrible suffering amounts to a bout of argumentative jugglery. At the end of the day, though, and when talking unofficially to Mr Leale and Mr Sherwill it begins to dawn on me how friends will suffer and I think of the terror to women and children and old people of the sea crossing, the endless train journey and the arrival in an enemy country. Queenie saw three women at St. Sampson's this afternoon crying openly and I am told that people were sitting in Candie Gardens weeping bitterly and alone. It is one thing to leave your home and friends to fight for your country or to seek refuge in a country peopled by your own race, but it is quite another to be torn against your will from everything you hold dear and to be submitted to the indignity of being herded together by the enemy and taken to a quite unknown destination and to unknown terrors. One line from the Old Testament repeats itself over and over again in my mind – "By the waters of Babylon we sat down and wept" – wept tears of utter helplessness and homesickness. And the mother of one family consisting of father, mother and twin boys of four who are likely to be taken was sitting happily in our lounge yesterday afternoon, taking tea with Queenie.[16]

I think also, though, of the Frossards where Queenie went this afternoon. They had just heard the news and Mrs Frossard kept everybody laughing all the afternoon with her ideas for overcoming probable difficulties. Dr Fox

---

16 The family taking tea at La Platte were Mr and Mrs Ivon Godwin and their sons Ralph and Neville.

came in too and they proceeded to amuse themselves by thinking of all the very worst things which might happen to them. Mr Frossard is determined to be brave and I am certain that they will both prove towers of strength to the whole tragic party. I believe our people will take even this bitterest of all blows without showing their fear or sadness to the enemy and already the spirit of comradeship which has gradually disappeared since the Occupation over two years ago is shewing itself again. It seems that it is in dire trouble that the best in human nature comes out on top.

WEDNESDAY, 16TH SEPTEMBER TO SATURDAY, 26TH SEPTEMBER

Until today I have been too busy to discover what my impressions of the past ten days have been, but this evening I managed to get home by six o'clock and the wind has died down and the seas are breaking within thirty yards of where I sit – and there is a feeling of peace once more. I know the spell will be broken directly I leave home tomorrow morning, if not before, but I must use it to set down as best as I can some immature notes on what has been a particularly painful week, even in these tragic days of war.

Real work started last Wednesday, the 16th, when a form appeared in the local newspapers to be filled in by all those affected by the order. We put a staff in the Police Court, in charge of Raymond Golding, to receive the forms and prepare them for the extraction of the lists required by Grange Lodge. We had promised them for Saturday morning but we knew that the sooner we delivered them the longer notice the unfortunate evacuees would receive and with a little organization and much hard work we managed to get them to Grange Lodge by six o'clock – six hours after the closing time for declarations.

We were asked for lists of key men employed by the public services and administration and we gave them in without delay. We were told by the F.K. too that people who were medically unfit would not have to leave the Island provided that the German doctors were satisfied that they were unfit to travel. Our doctors saw all sorts of difficulties about giving medical certificates ad lib. and we therefore arranged for some of them to meet the chief of the German medical staff to discuss the standard of unfitness which would exempt people from evacuation. Roughly, the German doctors' decision was that exemption would be granted to persons with 65% disability or over; to women more than seven months pregnant and to families one member of which was a baby of not more than six weeks old. In practice, if any member of a family has come within the above category, the whole family has been exempted. Our doctors formed a medical board and interviewed all persons applying for medical certificates. This work took a whole day and some 280 people were examined. A list of those who, in the opinion of the board, should be examined by the German doctors was submitted to Grange Lodge and on Friday the St. John Ambulance Brigade began its work of transporting people to the Vauquiédor Hospital for German examination. The Brigade did magnificent work and Dr Symons and one other Guernsey doctor were present throughout the examinations. In some cases we thought the German decisions harsh but there were many scenes of family rejoicing when sick members were told they might stay in their own homes.

Each family or person to be evacuated received an individual order from the Feldkommandantur and the first batch was delivered on Friday afternoon and evening by a member of Feldgendarmerie accompanied by one of our Island policemen. From that evening until now Grange Lodge has been filled with people asking for exemptions and we have fought tooth and nail for sick people and for people whose absence would upset the life of our little community. Often we have failed, sometimes we have succeeded and time after time we have been astounded to hear of exemptions granted to people who in our opinion are useless or worse. We have had reason to be grateful to every officer at Grange Lodge at some time during this week and to be exasperated with most of them too, but there is one man who, though a loyal German – perhaps the most loyal I know – has proved himself a true friend to every man and woman who have been to him in their trouble. That man is Herr Krafft, a serious and sometimes gloomy humanitarian who is the father of a small boy in Nuremburg and an idealist who lives up to his ideals always. He has listened to stories of illness and trouble all day long and worked with his officers far into the night to get individual orders out as early as possible. And in the middle of all this headaching rush he has received news that his home has been damaged by British bombs AND HE HAS CONTINUED TO BE KIND AND POLITE TO HIS ENEMIES. I can only say to those of my fellow countrymen who maintain that the only good German is a dead one that Herr Krafft is the exception which proves their rule.

Of course there has been no time off for anybody and we worked right through Thursday and Sunday. The first transports were due to leave last Monday and transport was arranged to bring people in from one centre in each parish to the Gaumont Cinema, which I chose as the most comfortable depot in which the evacuees could await embarkation. My original idea was that they could wait there until the boats were almost ready to leave but the Feldkommandantur did not agree and used it merely as a centre for the writing up of lists of passengers.

I found that I had no time to organize details of transport with all the general work which it fell to me to do, and Vernon Le Maître was given the duty of dealing with this section. This he did admirably and obtained the use of Monro's store[17] for the temporary storage of luggage while people were passed through the Gaumont. When they came back to Monro's they were passed on to Essential Commodities Committee staff, under Jack Loveridge of course, who issued each individual with a tomato basket containing a two pound loaf, a quarter pound of butter, some cheese and other eatables, including chocolate and a tobacco ration for the men. They then crossed to the White Rock with their luggage and were examined by German customs officials and afterwards were carried by bus to the Jetty where they sat and waited in the dining room which has been boarded off in the open shed. We had been given the use of two field kitchens, with attendants, and magnificent soup was prepared with the help of the Pommiers and Frank Stroobant. Stroobant also produced ham sandwiches and hardboiled eggs and coffee and it was quite embarrassing to hear the organization praised. Those of us who have to organize big jobs at high speed are more used to abuse than praise.

By eight o'clock on Monday evening all evacuees ordered to leave the Island that day were safely aboard their boats and by eight thirty I was having my supper at home.

At nine thirty the telephone rang and Dr Brosch informed that it was too rough for the ships to put out that night. We were to have breakfast ready for everybody for half past six next morning!

I had no night pass and we had no food at all prepared.

I telephoned Vernon Le Maître to come down and contacted Stroobant. George Warry was with us and guaranteed to supply the bread. At ten minutes to ten we left La Platte on our motorcycles with George on the pillion of mine and made for the private quarters of the Standortkommandant in Doyle Road. We arrived without being stopped and asked for night permits. He asked how many we wanted and we said one for each of us plus about a dozen for helpers. He demanded the names and identity cards of these helpers and as I had not even thought whom we could ask to help I had to work quickly. I telephoned Sefton and found that the Huberts were throwing a party. There were six of them and they all came along. On the way they met Margot and he fell in too. Drs Rose and Sutcliffe agreed to help but they already had night passes and – very useful – motor cars. We decided on the spot to do our work at the Prince of Wales Hotel[18] and rang Jimmy Travers to ask if we could. He agreed and he and Henri and their wives offered to help too.

Next we went to the Standortkommandantur with a junior officer to get the passes and from there on to our rendez-vous. Raymond Falla and Dr

17 Monro's store was near the Royal Hotel.
18 Prince of Wales Hotel is at the top of Smith Street.

Rose went on to the Dairy for milk and butter, George Warry went on the back of Vernon's motorcycle to the bakery to get a van-load of bread and Frank Hubert went with Dr Sutcliffe to find a bread-cutting machine.

We decided to make sandwiches with tinned beans, bread and butter and then had to wait for the ingredients to arrive. Margot suggested that we might find it easier to work at the Royal Hotel and as the Travers did not mind us changing, I telephoned Mr Mentha – at 11.30 p.m. – and obtained his permission. So, off we went to the Royal, with Henri and his wife in the back of the van since they did not have night passes. The butter and milk arrived soon afterwards and we started work. We had two bread cutting machines and slices of bread were produced at high speed and at great danger to the limbs of the manipulators. We opened a whole case of tinned beans and mashed them into a paste in whatever receptacles we could find. Most of the men worked stripped to the waist and apart from a few minor interruptions, like the immersion of Stroobant in the sink by the doctors, we worked non-stop to 4.15. The hotel provided us with half a dozen bottles of red wine to slake our thirst, but those working nearest had most of that.

Nearly everyone went into the lounge for a couple of hours sleep when we had finished work, but Raymond, Rose and I talked until half past five and then made ourselves a cup of tea.

At six o'clock we went down to the harbour to see whether the field kitchens were there. I have walked the quays of our harbour at all hours of day and night but never have I seen such a scene of desolation. The Germans are laying railway tracks everywhere and the harbour's spick and span appearance which was our pride in peacetime has disappeared completely. Add to that a howling southwesterly gale, with pelting and nearly horizontal rain, inky darkness, the occasional loom of a tin hat and rifle and you may, if you have a vivid imagination, get some idea of the scene which confronted us. To get at our feelings you must add a sleepless night, the aftermath of sandwiches made with fresh bread and cold beans and the smoke and spark laden atmosphere under the open shed where the Germans were stoking the field kitchens and their horses were pawing the concrete. The tide was high and ships of all shapes and sizes were heaving about all round the Jetty. We stayed only long enough to make sure that the evacuees were still asleep on their ships and that water for tea and coffee would be ready for seven o'clock.

With daylight St. John Ambulance workers came down and breakfast was served. Then we went on to the office to get on with a very hard day's work.

At one o'clock it was decided that the weather was too bad for the ships to put out for at least twenty four hours and all the evacuees were taken back to their homes. On Wednesday at 3.30 p.m. they all assembled at their parish centres only to be told it was still too rough. On Thursday the same thing happened and it was not until Friday that they were brought back to the harbour, via the Gaumont and the Customs shed, and given a meal before boarding their transports once more.

They eventually sailed at one o'clock on Saturday morning and arrived in the Bay of St. Malo at 7 a.m.

This is a very rough outline of the trials which beset the first batch of evacuees, but the second batch which were due to leave on Wednesday, are still here and are due to leave tomorrow (Sunday) if the ships return from St. Malo in time.

SUNDAY, 27TH SEPTEMBER

The boats arrived back from St. Malo during the night and the embarkation of the second batch of evacuees has been carried out quite successfully. Tonight they are all aboard, full of hard-boiled eggs and soup and sandwiches and coffee and fruit – and such courage as I have never seen in my short existence. I had no idea that people I had known all my life could be uprooted from their homes and surroundings and herded together for an unknown destination in an enemy country – which is being bombed night after night – and still appear as if they were looking forward to a rather special holiday. The Germans make no comment but this evacuation has not lessened their respect for our nation.

Wynne Sayer came back from Alderney yesterday. He has been there for the past month gathering the harvest. Alderney is not a very healthy spot just now and none of us make the trip for fun. I myself have not visited the Island since the Germans came here two years ago. When the party was ready to go, the men asked whether they could travel on the *White Heather* since they thought they would be safer than on a German boat. Sayer made the necessary arrangements but the harvesting machinery was too bulky and had to be shipped on a German ship. Sayer thought that the machinery might go on to Cherbourg or be damaged if someone did not travel with it and so, in spite of the danger, he went with the machinery. While in Alderney he and the men saw a German motor ship sunk by a flight of British planes. He never asks his men to do what he will not do himself and he worked with them throughout the harvesting.

The Feldkommandantur sent a telegram for him to return last Saturday week and as he had not returned last Friday they were getting very restless. I discovered they had decided in his absence that he must go with the evacuees and the Bailiff and the Attorney-General wrote one letter and Mr Leale another, asking for his exemption. These I delivered to Colonel Knackfuss himself on Friday.[19] The Colonel said he could not give me an immediate

19   See Item 10: Leale to F.K.: Deportations protest, 23 Sep 1942, p.303.

answer so when Sayer put in an appearance on Saturday morning I reported to Dr Brosch by 'phone and asked when he would like to see Mr Sayer. He said he would let me know later and within half an hour a policeman delivered an evacuation order to Sayer without any interview being granted.

The Bailiff, Mr Leale, Mr Sherwill and Dr Symons went immediately to Grange Lodge and interviewed Colonel Knackfuss but without success, and it was with very heavy hearts that the whole staff – with the Controlling Committee – gathered at Hirzel House to say goodbye to a brave and clever man and a rare gentleman.

This evening at the White Rock, Mr Sherwill made a presentation to Frank Stroobant who, though leaving the Island tonight, has elected to cater for the evacuees throughout the week and up to the very last moment. He was given a silver beer mug with the inscription, "From the Bailiff and people of Guernsey to Mr Frank Stroobant in appreciation of his services during the evacuation, September, 1942".

When we met Dr Brosch at the Gaumont this morning he told us he was convinced that that the evacuees would be in England within a fortnight. He said he knew that the proposed arrangement for the exchange of internees between Germany and England had been agreed and he thought that probably our people would go first to Frankfurt and then through Switzerland, Spain and Portugal to England. To us it seems too good to be true.

Nearly a fortnight ago a fishing boat failed to return to St. Sampson's Harbour. It was last seen near Rocque au Nord and as it was a very small boat (about fifteen feet overall) and the seas were such that larger boats put back, it was generally assumed that the occupants had been drowned.[20] Today it is reported that the B.B.C. has announced that someone near Weymouth has come into possession (by roundabout means) of a tattered newspaper giving details of the escapades of the eighteen Guernsey policemen who were sentenced to terms of imprisonment for robbing German stores. Is there any connection between these two little items of news?

MONDAY, 28TH SEPTEMBER

We heard today that yesterday's evacuees arrived in St. Malo at 6.15 this morning. Dr Brosch told me that he was on the White Rock at midnight and that the boats had not left then. Our people were singing and nobody seemed to be asleep. It was a perfect moonlight night and for anybody with a love of either adventure or beauty the crossing must have been a memorable one.

20 On 15 September 1942, four people escaped in GU.266 *Whynot*, a 16-foot fishing boat. See Kreckeler (1978).

Today the weather has deteriorated steadily and tonight the wind is once more howling around the house with a driving rain which makes our cosy home more dear to us even than usual. It needs little imagination to picture the feelings of our friends who have been torn away from their homes and do not know where they are being taken. For my part I think of the happy times I have had with many of those who have gone and of the evenings we had planned to spend together this winter, and I am filled with something very akin to remorse for not appreciating more fully their friendship while they were with us.

There is abroad a very definite feeling of loss and we have talked of the miserable duty of filling the gaps left in the administration by the evacuation of several who we counted as friends as well as colleagues.

Looking back over the past three years, it is easy to see signs of the disintegration of our little community. When the war started Guernsey was certainly a prosperous Island and, on the whole, a happy one. Most of the more vigorous young people left during the first six months and with the evacuation in June 1940 came the first really painful split. Then we settled down for a year and learned how to heal that wound as best we could. Next, came the big influx of military and O.T. and the compulsory evacuation of many homes, often at a few hours' notice. Many people – and especially the older ones – suffered terribly when they found themselves wrenched from the surroundings in which they had passed the major part of their lives and even now the knowledge that any one of us may be the next to be called upon to take our portable luggage and surrender our home lends an uncertainty to our existence which makes our other burdens no easier to bear.

The huge defence works which are springing up in many parts of the Island and the laying of railways to the harbour and quarries and the great shiploads of building materials make us wonder what the Island will be like if the war lasts much longer and those of us who love Guernsey (and most Guernsey people do) have moments of sadness when we realize that the Island will never be quite its old beautiful self for us or for those who are away and must be dreaming of their home. And now this latest evacuation has torn another limb from the mutilated body of our community and if we allow ourselves to think at all we cannot but wonder whether it was worth stopping here after all. But the Germans see only the mask of our smiles.

José is eight weeks old today and weighs nine pounds five ounces. She has milk rash and already yells with temper when she is put back into her cot after feeding, but to her fond parents she is the only baby in the world. And I thought myself the hardest and most rational of persons!

Last night some friends who dabble in amateur spiritualism and sometimes have a friendly chat with a group of spirits, asked where the first set of evacuees were. They were told they were at Dijon and that is on the way to Switzerland! Are they really going to England?

TUESDAY, 29TH SEPTEMBER AND WEDNESDAY, 30TH SEPTEMBER

I've just read the last entry in this diary – a thing I can seldom coax myself to do – and I wonder whether my liver was badly out of order when I wrote it or if our position here is as grim as I then thought.

Really, we do have lots of fun. There are dances nearly every evening for those who can stand the pace, theatrical companies are more dense per head of population than anywhere else in the world, all night parties are almost a weekly occurrence in the lives of wartime bachelors and spinsters, swimming is more popular even than in peace time and for the women the abundance of scandal occasioned by temporary alliances makes a teatime dish more succulent than any they ever dreamed of in more balmy days.

Our amateur spiritualistic friends have now conjured up a spirit whose sense of humour has more than made up for the loss of the radio and Tommy Handley. The other evening they asked whether there would be any more evacuations and the reply was that the young men would be taken within two months. Each asked whether they would have to go and when they had received their replies – mostly in the affirmative – someone asked whether I would be included in the party.

"No," said the spirit.

"Why not?" they asked.

"Because he is a twister," replied the planchette board.

Now that we cannot listen to the B.B.C. the war news comes to us through roundabout channels and so improves during the journey that we are in a state of continuous optimism. Stories of manipulators in the Black Market, arguments with the Germans on the cause and outcome of the war, fantastic rumours and criticism of all governments provide a constant source of amusement.

Of my own work I can say truthfully that it is never boring and for both Queenie and myself little José is so amazing and her wants are so exacting that we scarcely have time to realize how happy we are.

I think that for nearly everybody the fact that the more we work in natural surroundings to produce food the better we feed has cured us of mental as well as of physical constipation and if only the tragedies which go with war could be removed – with the war as well, of course – I think that our present way of life would soon toughen us into people of the same stamp as our Channel Island ancestors.

On Tuesday Mr Sherwill and I went to Grange Lodge and spent two hours discussing with Inspector Zachau the new Price Regulation Order which will some day soon be put into operation. The whole savours of shutting the stable door after the horse has bolted but perhaps it may have some effect on profiteering. We shall see.

The R.M./£ rate of exchange has been altered from R.M. 9.60 to £1 to R.M. 9.36 to £1. The new rate is stated to be the one now in operation on the Berlin Bourse.

THURSDAY, 1ST OCTOBER

Yesterday morning Dr Brosch said he wanted me to go to Herm with him for a whole day, preferably today. I said I had to do my work at the office first and suggested meeting him there this afternoon with my own boat. Eventually as a compromise we agreed to go at 11 o'clock in my boat. Raymond Falla was also to come with us.

I woke early this morning before the sun was up and rushed to the window like a kid on the day of the Sunday School treat to see what the weather was like. It looked as if it would probably rain all day, with the wind from the south and heavy black clouds right across the sky. Before giving up hope completely I went downstairs and discovered that the glass had risen considerably during the night, but I went to the office quite resigned to another day of too little fresh air and too much smoking (this week being tobacco ration week). By ten o'clock the sun had broken through and the wind had died down and I had prevailed upon Dr Brosch to chance it. By half past ten I had collected Raymond, obtained permits for Raymond, Dick and myself to land in Herm, called at La Platte for sandwiches and was on my way to St. Sampson's. Dick was already aboard *Ida*, the sun was by now shining in a cloudless sky and we motored down the harbour to wait for Dr Brosch. We poured a gallon of our precious pre-Occupation petrol into the tank and went ashore to telephone Grange Lodge to make sure that he was coming. Mr Krafft said that he had left and by half past eleven we were all aboard with the engine running noisily but well.

When we came to the harbour entrance we discovered that the boom was in position and we had to call to the guard to lower it so that we could get out. What a difference a German officer's uniform makes! In two minutes we were free and pointing for Herm.

There was scarcely any wind and we had to use the engine all the way across. It was high tide and we ran right into the harbour and tied up. Raymond jumped ashore, stripped and jumped into the water. I had no bathing costume, but the water was so clear and generally inviting that I undressed and dived off the side of the boat with no costume at all. I hoped Mrs Dickson was not looking but would not have been very concerned if she had been.

Dr Brosch went off with his gun and we sat on the pier and ate sandwiches. Then Raymond went off to inspect the sheep – we have about a hundred on the island – with the shepherd and Dick and I went up to see the Dicksons. Frank Dickson produced a fat hen pheasant for Queenie and me and a rabbit each for Dick and Raymond and we stored these carefully aboard. Then we set off with Frank for a walk round the gardens and then down to Rosaire to pick blackberries.

All these details may seem rather childish but to anybody who knows Herm and loves it like we do they will conjure up the heavenly peacefulness which I have never experienced elsewhere. For me, heaven is Herm harbour at high water on a perfect autumn day, like today, with the rich golden sunlight turning the sea into a marvellous transparent green.

There was an abundance of blackberries and by two o'clock we had picked several pounds. Then we went back to the harbour to get the boat away before she grounded and taking Raymond and Frank Dickson aboard, we set sail and drifted towards the Rockeries. We caught no fish and came back to Rosaire. We went ashore and met Dr Brosch who wanted to go to Jethou, so waiting only for Frank to collect some milk and apples for the caretakers, we crossed the Percée and ran alongside the rocks on the north side of the Island. Everybody landed except me and I sculled the boat few yards from the shore and stood looking down into water so clear that I had the impression I was standing on a floating platform some twenty feet from the ground. I took off my clothes and lay in the bottom of the boat for an hour while the other paid their respects to the Macdonalds. I closed my eyes and listened to the lazy little waves breaking on the rocks and the cries of the seabirds – and the dull thud of gunfire in the far distance.

We put Frank and Dr Brosch ashore again in Herm and tried to catch whiting on the east side of the island, without success. We ourselves went ashore at six o'clock and sat in the Dickson's cosy dining room, with its log fire and brick hearth, and drank coffee and talked of nothing in particular while waiting for Dr Brosch to return from his second hunting expedition. Eventually he came in with a couple of rabbits and we left soon after seven.

We crossed the Russel uneventfully until we were well west of the Platte and then the carburettor developed a choked jet which led to the last quarter of a mile being covered in fifty yard spurts with much swinging of the starting handle by Dick.

By the time we had landed the others – the boom having to be let down again to allow us to get in – there was enough water for us to reach our moorings and the securing of the boat for the night seemed a neat way of ending a truly memorable day.

I have had a well-cooked supper with my wife to talk to while I ate it, I have said good-night to my daughter who I swear is already trying to talk to us, and I am going to bed now to dream of peace and of spending a day in the boat with my two brothers, one of the most pleasant of all my dreams.

FRIDAY, 2ND OCTOBER TO SUNDAY, 4TH OCTOBER

Dick went aboard the boat today (Friday) to see what was wrong with the engine and discovered that the carburettor was half full of water. He cleaned it out, replaced it and gave the engine a trial run. The boat went once round the harbour and then the engine stopped. The tank was empty! We had no spare petrol and with the strong ebb and the wind practically dead ahead we would never have reached St. Sampson's before dark yesterday if we had fished for another quarter of an hour earlier in the day.

It appears that in Jersey the authorities have refused to help with any further evacuations. Here we have made no such declaration as the official attitude is that the primary motive governing the actions of the Controlling Committee must be the easing of the lot of the population and it may well be that conditions will be such that the work done by us may help people who may be required to leave the Island. We know that our efforts were not in vain last time.

Apart from a letter from Mr Sayer, written in St. Malo when he arrived at 7 a.m. last Monday morning we have received no news of our evacuees.

We are again going into the question of cultivating Herm and I am supposed to be taking Inspector Oser, Mr De Garis and Mr J.N. Dorey over tomorrow. Dick and I went aboard the boat today (Sunday) to make sure that everything is in order and we discovered that she had quite eight inches of water in her. It was coming through the stern tube and a slight adjustment of the stuffing box soon put matters right.

There has been a general tightening up of fishing regulations and as a result only twenty boats from St. Peter Port, ten from St. Sampson's and seven from Portelet are to be allowed out in future. Fishermen whose families are in England have their licences taken away from them.

We recently received from France the regulations regarding the rationing of toilet paper and as it is the most perfect example of bureaucracy gone mad that I have ever seen I am including a translation of it in this diary.[21]

I weighed José this morning. Her weight is now 9 lbs 7½ ozs. This afternoon we finished sowing mustard which we hope to trench as green manure later.

It appears that Stalingrad is still holding out and the Germans no longer appear to have the least hope of finishing the Russian war this season. It is

---

21 See Item 11: Memo: Toilet paper rationing [nd], p.304. Given the timing that this order is due to take effect, 1 May 1942, it seems likely that this was an April Fool's joke.

rumoured that cannibalism is not unknown amongst both the German and Russian prisoners in Russia but I have no confirmation whatsoever of this.

MONDAY, 5TH OCTOBER TO FRIDAY, 9TH OCTOBER

The most exciting happening during the last few days has been the raid on Sark. I first heard about it on Monday morning but only as a very garbled rumour, but when I went to Grange Lodge later I asked what it was all about and gathered from lack of answers to my perhaps indiscreet questions that a British boat landed some men early Sunday morning and killed two Germans, apparently without loss to themselves. I also gathered that Sark – of all places! – is regarded as a hotbed of espionage.[22]

As the week has advanced further information has dribbled through, first in rumour form from Sark, then apparently over the English radio and lastly in the local newspapers.

As far as I can gather, the landing took place at four o'clock on Sunday morning, probably at Dixcart Bay and ten English officers and men took part. They went to a house where four Germans were sleeping and routed them out of bed. They hurried them down to the sea in their night clothes with their hands fastened somehow. Three of the Germans managed to get away from their captors but two were killed in the attempt. The fourth man was taken off to England with some document signed by Colonel Knackfuss (probably a newspaper) ordering the evacuation of British born subjects. The prisoner is supposed to have stated that some nine hundred people had gone from Guernsey and that the Jersey figures were not available and that they were being taken to Germany for forced labour. Nobody in Guernsey believes this last statement.

Since then the Germans have put the English Dieppe prisoners in chains as a reprisal for the fastening of the hands of the men captured in Sark and apparently the English are retaliating by tying up German prisoners in their hands. It is also said that questions have been asked in the Commons concerning the names of the people evacuated and that Switzerland is to be asked to procure such names.

For the first three days of the week it was extremely foggy and guards were out day and night around the coasts.

Altogether we have the feeling that the war is much nearer than it has been for some time.

On Thursday evening there was an extremely noisy anti-aircraft practice and we were very pleased to see that José took no notice at all. She is quite

---

22 On the night of 3-4 October 1942, the British launched Operation Basalt, a commando raid on Sark with the aim of reconnaissance and taking prisoners.

used to the noise of blasting in the quarry, of course, and this is probably the reason for her indifference.

Last Monday Queenie and I went to a dance for the first time in twelve months. It was a great adventure and we started off with a race to Town with a German dispatch-rider. It was a very happy little dance and it was good to see Queenie welcomed back to normal pleasures. We came back gingerly with scarcely any lights in the inky blackness.

On Tuesday evening I paid my first visit to Jack Hart's séance with the planchette. We had a friendly and most comic chat with three spirits, two of which possessed a most highly developed sense of humour. We asked many leading questions. On the subject of Sark we were told that the purpose of the raid had been to find out whether there were any guns in that Island pointing towards the French coast which might interfere with landing operations on the Cherbourg peninsula. Our spirit said that he thought the name of the skipper of the boat was Carter and that Michael Carey was there as guide. We asked what Winston Churchill was doing and the answer was that he was talking to Mr Eden about Sark and saying that there would be no need to bother about the Islands since there were no guns in Sark. Des has apparently been in Inverness for the past eight weeks and Vic may be in Uganda.

We have checked through the potatoes and find that the crop amounted to nearly ten hundredweight of sound ones.

The weather has been so bad that I have not yet been to Herm with Inspector Oser.

SATURDAY, AND SUNDAY, 10TH AND 11TH OCTOBER

On Friday afternoon Dr Brosch and two other officers from the Feldkommandantur came down to the Greffe to inspect the filing system in connection with the Identity Card registration forms.[23] They seemed very surprised at the efficiency of the system and went on to the Labour Office to see the index cards kept for all persons over fourteen for the purpose of recording the regular and sparetime work of every individual. The recent evacuation and their first practical insight into our statistical routine has obviously made them realize that the local administration is not as inadequate as they fondly imagined.

They want to be in possession of the statistical information necessary to avoid the difficulties they experienced during the evacuation. The statistics we possess do not give all the data they want and they asked me whether we could get it for them if we took the necessary powers by an amendment to

---

23 See Tough (1992).

the Registration and Identification of Persons Order. I gave no direct answer, firstly because I did not know whether we could do it by such an amendment and secondly because I thought that the Controlling Committee might not be willing to help in such work.

Saturday morning Mr Leale, Mr Sherwill and I spent an hour or so discussing the matter and we decided that since it would be quite hopeless to obtain a cancellation of any order for evacuation, it was in the interests of the population to see that arrangements went through as easily as possible. Furthermore, the information we would gather through a new return would be of great use to us in other ways. We therefore went into the details of the form to be issued, having ascertained that an amendment to the existing Order would give us the necessary power.

Saturday afternoon Mr Sherwill and I went to Grange Lodge and discussed the necessary arrangements. We discovered that the Feldkommandantur had no knowledge of a further evacuation at present.

We also discussed at length the new Price Regulation Ordinance which is at present in draft. It provides for the setting up of a Price Regulation Committee which will have the duty of examining all prices. We tried to explain that it was unnecessary to make the new Committee overlook the price regulation work at present undertaken by the Essential Commodities Committee and the Glasshouse Board but without success. They want a member of each of these Committees to be members of the new Committee although, as we pointed out, this would involve wasting the time of men who already have more work than they can do. They think that the criticism which will be offered by the new Committee will be very helpful to both the Glasshouse Board and the Essential Commodities Committee, even though the members will have no detailed knowledge of the work of either the Board or the E.C.C. Further, we said we lacked men of the calibre necessary to make useful members of the new Committee. We talked from two o'clock to a quarter to six or thereabouts.

Today (Sunday) has been delightfully quiet and I have been in the garden nearly the whole day. The weeds are seeding and I have collected hundredweights of them. After an hour's work I was really tired but by the late afternoon I was beginning to get into my stride and was sorry to finish.

A man passed on a cycle and asked me casually if I wanted to buy some ormers. I was not long in dropping my tools and getting him indoors and we bought nineteen dozen ormers at three shillings a dozen.[24] They were not all for us, of course, but we took six dozen and intend using them as the foundation for our supper for the crews of *Ida* and *Frypan*.

---

24 See Item 97: Ormers and Ormering, p.487.

José submitted to her weekly weighing today and turned the scale, as they say, at 9 lbs 15 oz, a gain of 7½ ozs this week. She is beginning to take real notice of things near her and especially of lights and bright colours and of Ma and Pa. Her grin warms our hearts and to us her little throaty noises are obviously extremely intelligent efforts at speech.

Jack Carré of Sark has been brought over under armed escort and everybody thinks it must be in connection with the Sark Raid. I wonder!

MONDAY, 12TH OCTOBER TO THURSDAY, 15TH OCTOBER

The Sark raid has brought serious repercussions here. During the past week some scores of families have been forced to leave their homes in order that German units may be collected into more compact groups. It is heartrending to see people with vans and handcarts moving their furniture and valuables, sometimes a whole street moving at once. Our Billeting Office has been worked to death and it is a constant marvel to me to see them working unflaggingly after two years.

On Tuesday I received a telephone call from Inspector Oser saying that he wanted to go to Herm at ten o'clock. This was at twenty minutes to nine and I was just on the point of leaving for the office. I managed to get in touch with Jurat de Garis and Mr J.N. Dorey who were to accompany us and then with Ted Dorey who was to come as the second member of the crew. Then I went off to get the boat ready.

We left St. Sampson's just before eleven o'clock with Inspector Oser rather sulky because we had had to wait for the two members of the Farm Produce Board. I reminded him that he had given them no time to rearrange their work for the day, but this seemed to make very little impression. However, we arrived in Herm without any mishap although I felt a bit nervous with six people aboard (Oser brought a friend of his) and the full power of a twenty eight foot tide under us.

Ted and I walked to the top of the Island and returned to the boat for lunch. Then we spent an hour fishing under sail – with no success – and returned to pick blackberries and gather fir cones.

We left at 6.55 with over a hundredweight of cones, a basket of mushrooms, one of apples, four or five pounds of blackberries and a rabbit apiece. I expect this will not sound very marvellous when peace and prosperity comes again, but at present it represents a cargo worth its weight in gold and many times its weight in Reichsmarks.

The end of season supper was waiting for us at La Platte, so we opened our old engine right up and did the journey in 33 minutes.[25]

---

25 See Item 12: End of Season Supper Menu, 13 Oct 1942, p.306.

The supper was a great success and all but Frank Dorey stayed for a chat with our spirit friends afterwards. Maisie, Nigel and Jack crossed to Bordeaux Lodge at midnight and it was looked upon by all of us as a very daring adventure! My stories of the wisdom of the spirit world have so fired Dr Symons that he insisted on seeing the board. Mr Johns and I therefore took him to see Jack Hart on Wednesday afternoon and he took all the measurements of the moving parts. The board proper, however, was still at Bordeaux Lodge but he came to us to tea and we were able to put the apparatus together and try it. Although we were all newcomers – Dr Symons, Mr Johns, Nan Guilbert, Queenie and myself – it began to work after twenty-five minutes but nothing of very great interest came through.

Later in the evening, however, Queenie and Nan and I tried on our own and it started working within five minutes. We spoke with two spirits, each of them very interesting. We hear that Charles is second clerk in London in connection with the Guernsey evacuees, Ron being in charge; that Charles would come back with the first batch of returning Islanders, that he has two more children and that he is not in the forces.

We asked about Beata and were told that her baby – a girl – was born on October 2nd and that she had named it Queenie Anne and that both her mother and Anne were killed in an air raid on September 29th. The possibility of this last news being true brought back such memories of these sweet friends of ours that for the rest of the evening we felt more keenly our isolation than we had for many a long day.

Vic apparently is in Uganda and Des in Ireland. Once again we heard that our latest evacuees are at Tolz.

At a meeting of the Controlling Committee on Tuesday afternoon it was decided to return all glasshouses worked by the G.U.B. to their owners, when such owners are still in the Island. The main reason for making this decision is the extreme difficulty of controlling so unwieldy an organization with the present lack of transport for overseers, lack of suitable men to act as overseers, inertia of employees working for a States Department and consequent financial loss.

Mr Leale and Mr Dorey went to see Dr Brosch on Wednesday afternoon to explain the position to him but they did not receive sanction to take any immediate steps since Dr Brosch wants to see what arrangements will be made for the export of produce before he arrives at any decision.

This afternoon (Thursday) while I was at Hart's shop a Belgian came in and asked for a special kind of purgative. He explained that he wanted these little pills so that he could put one in his eye to produce inflammation. He hoped by doing so to be sent back to France and then his tale came out. He comes from Brussels and has a wife there. It is impossible to send her money from here because the Occupation mark is no longer legal tender in Belgium. She is going to have a baby next month and he shewed me a letter from her imploring him to come back because she can no longer work and having no money sometimes goes a whole day with nothing to eat. He cannot get permission to return and told me that so many Frenchmen have refused to come back to Guernsey when they go on leave that the Germans refuse to let their workmen go on leave unless the same number come back to work. He is seriously considering cutting the end of his finger off, hoping that as he will not then be able to work for some time they will send him back. He told us that one of his friends, to feign tuberculosis sucked an eighth of a cigarette into his lungs. He died from the effects. He told us too of several other desperate ruses adopted by workmen in order to get back to their homes, mostly without success. How they hate the Germans and the War generally.

Apparently Stalingrad is still holding out and there are rumours that the Russians have gained considerable successes in this sector. The Americans also appear to have fought a very successful naval battle near the Solomon Islands.

José continues to enjoy a very considerable popularity and she finds no difficulty in procuring nursemaids. This week she had had three different ones for her afternoon outings.

FRIDAY, 16TH OCTOBER AND SATURDAY, 17TH OCTOBER

The popularity of amateur spiritualism grows apace. George has made a board and we tried it out on Friday evening. Within five minutes we were obtaining results and we spoke with a Greek woman who told us that the pilot on the Sark raid was one de Carteret and that Michael Carey was in charge of charts, being sent by the Admiralty. We were also honoured by a visit from Old Nick himself, but his language was so frightful that he soon wore out his welcome. We noticed that he used many of the expletives of those sitting round the table, doubtless in order to make us feel at home.

George Vaudin and Rumball arrived from Granville late on Thursday evening on the barge which brings our fuel oil. They told us that it was only by special permission that they were allowed to come straight from Granville instead of having to travel through St. Malo. Prices seem to be rising the whole time in France and the Black Market goes from strength to strength.

Talking to our Granville people always brings back for me memories of my two or three visits to that town since the Occupation. I have not been to France since June 1941 but how that fortnight stands out in my memory.

We left here in the *Normand*, a steamer of some 2,000 tons built during the last war and showing many signs of the rough handling she has received during the past few years. Her bows were crumpled and kept watertight with masses of concrete, her ironwork was practically devoid of paint and you could easily pick out the brass by its gorgeous green tint. She was run by a Jersey crew and was supposed to be solely for the provisioning of the civilian population so she flew the Jersey flag and had another one painted on the roof of her deckhouse. Her skipper was Ted Larbalastier, a young Jersey pilot with plenty of dash and an intimate knowledge of Black Market procedure. Having let go fore and aft, it was obvious that the next step was to put her engines vigorously ahead and it hardly seemed worthwhile stopping them again when it became clear that the fore end of her poop deck was going to join forces with one of the fenders on the Jetty. Sure enough the connection was purely temporary and a few extra twists in ironwork on quay and ship will never, I am sure, be brought home to that gallant crew.

We made ourselves at home on the bridge and in the saloon and soon learned to appreciate the Will Hay atmosphere so that when a laughing Jersey boy came running up the ladder and addressing the skipper said, "Afternoon, Ted, there's some tea going now." and the skipper replied, "OK, Bill, just aim for that rock until I come back." We thought ourselves the honoured guests of the captain of some crack liner and marvelled at his wondrous navigation.

We were invited to take tea in the galley and having picked our way thither over the recumbent forms of sundry teutons we soon learned that once having put one's shoulder to the grimy walls, the part of one's clothes in contact with same was the only section that was likely to get dirty. After the first sip or two, we likewise learned the peculiar technique of half eating, half drinking necessary to convey the tea from cup to the gullet. A most filling and satisfying brew. None of us needed a second cup.

I climbed down the thirty feet or so of iron ladders into the engine room without once slipping off the beautifully greased rungs and watched with all due awe the astounding antics of those massive engines. It needed little imagination to transport oneself back to the South Kensington Science Museum. The engine room staff were mainly proud of the fact that they had removed an inch of grease from the floor WITHOUT SOAP.

We were thankful that we had to visit some of the officials in Jersey before going on to France but the day came when we found ourselves ready to proceed with the *Normand* the only means of transport. Once more we went aboard, but this time about five hundred troops came with us and there was scarcely room to stand on deck. Until we were at sea we thought once or twice of the very successful sweeps which the R.A.F. had been making over the French coast, but once the ship was in motion, as always it became our little world and quite a secure one at that.

Halfway across to Granville I beheld with some amusement what seemed to me to be some sort of war dance being performed on the fore hatch and thought how clever it was of the dancers to have smoke issuing from the centre of their ring. Skipper Ted asked me casually to tell the Chief Engineer to turn on the water in the forehold and explained that a FIRE had broken out there! I yelled down the engine room grating but my news had a most disappointing reception and I believe it was only because the Chief and I liked each other that he agreed to do what I asked – in his own time, of course. By the time I arrived back breathless on deck the fire was out.

Granville, charming as ever, came into view eventually and we slid easily into the inner harbour. I was stared at by the German harbourmaster who, three months before, had thrown me out of his office for smoking and lounging in his presence and he ordered the Customs to search my luggage.

How we enjoyed that visit, with marvellous meals at Helary's in the company of perfect hosts. I remember vividly our trip to Saint-Lô to meet an ogre called Genelot, the Intendant who has the power to fill or keep empty the bellies of we Islanders. That was a successful interview and we celebrated at the Hotel de la Gare in company with a husky American-German who thought Sayer a typical English gentleman and was pitifully happy to renew the acquaintance of Englishmen. We were equally happy to have him with us. We sat down to lunch at a few minutes past one and rose to go home at half past six. It was hot and the cars were like ovens. I found it impossible to keep my eyes open but my head span at such a speed when I closed them that I knew not what to do. Eventually I stopped the car and a few minutes in private in a lonely part of the road brought instant and very welcome relief.

I remember too, a dinner we gave to our Granville friends one Sunday evening at a big restaurant at Juluville. Our only conveyance from Granville was the States of Guernsey lorry with lettering on its sides and back which left no cause for ambiguity as to its owners. We broke all rules in using it on a Sunday, for pleasure, and without the regular driver, and in being out of Granville without a German permit.

The restaurant courtyard was full of German cars and buses when we arrived, but we gaily parked our lorry in the centre of the group and sauntered in for an apéritif. Eventually we were summoned for our meal and entered the main dining room. Here we found we had been given the big centre dining table which had been specially decorated with flowers and creepers and the best china and cutlery. In one corner of the room was a high German officer – we felt certain he was at least a General – with his staff, in another some very grim-looking individuals who, without doubt, belonged the most secret of secret police. The remainder of the surrounding tables were filled with Germans of all types eating their somewhat frugal meal. Eight or nine Englishmen, with their French friends, taking the place of honour at what was obviously a favourite German resort, in enemy territory and without permits! Until the effects of the meal and the wine began to show themselves we either spoke in French or remained silent – except for Sayer who spoke to me in a loud voice in Hindustani. What a meal and what speeches when the Germans had gone and what a rollicking ride home in the moonlight with violent community singing in French!

Yes, we have had some fun during these two years in spite of all our troubles, and magnificent work has been done in Granville in spite of that awful little office at the Villa Hirondelle which was our first headquarters, with five people trying to work in one room, interviewing traders, answering German questions, making out cargo lists, paying bills, filing and writing letters and endeavouring to keep some millions of francs within the confines of our mutual safe with a piece of cardboard to separate the Jersey money from that belonging to Guernsey.

That safe was a great improvement on our first coffers which consisted of the bottom of the wardrobe in Raymond's bedroom at the hotel. When I arrived with a suitcase containing about fifty thousand pounds worth of francs in August 1940 we simply turned it upside down on top of the money already there and went downstairs to get a drink. We did not lock the wardrobe because it had no lock.

Today (Saturday) Rumball, Raymond and I went to visit a friend of ours in the Town with the skipper of a German ship who has been very helpful to us over cargoes coming to the Island. In the room behind the shop we met four members of the military section of the Gestapo who had business to do with the owner and were now enjoying a drink. There was nothing very satanic about them, in fact one was a missionary in China before the war, but it was strange to me to be talking to them almost as to friends with the constant thought at the back of my mind, "Perhaps, one day I shall see the other side of them".

I discovered that the skipper of the ship knew Hans Forster very well. Forster was here in 1934 at the beginning of a voyage across the Atlantic in a 22 foot boat with his wife and he came for a ride one Sunday afternoon with Queenie and me. We liked them very much and often wondered what had become of them.

This afternoon Rumball and I saw Mr Leale about a loan of German currency to Jersey. Strangely enough we always have much more currency than we need for purchases in France and Jersey is always short. We have about 57,000,000 francs in Granville at present. The only explanation we can give is that we have much more vegetables and fruit to sell to the Germans and foreign workmen than Jersey has and we estimate that our local sales of grapes alone must bring in nearly a million marks this year.

SUNDAY, 18TH OCTOBER TO WEDNESDAY, 28TH OCTOBER

My only excuse for not writing up my diary during the last ten days is that I have had a charming book to read and many even more charming friends to entertain.

The most important orders issued to us by the Feldkommandantur have concerned the collection on their behalf of a hundred bicycles, the stoppage of fishing from November 1st until further notice and the third is not really an order but simply a notification that billeting charges 75% of which are at present paid by the Germans, must be met entirely by the States from 1st November.

The bicycle order brought up once more the old question of the local government's lack of power to requsition for the Germans. It brought forward, too, the first reaction to all such orders, namely to tell them to do their own dirty work and the less spectacular but much stronger reaction in the form of a reminder from the conscience that the Controlling Committee's *raison d'être* is the protection of the interests of the population and if we make no effort to produce the bicycles with the minimum of hardship the Germans will take the first hundred they meet on the roads. The value of a bicycle to almost any type of person but more especially to manual workers is infinitely more than it was in peacetime. Not only does it enable a man to reach his work throughout the Island but it saves his almost irreplaceable shoe-leather, it allows him to come home for his midday meal and thus save extravagant use of the bread ration and it gives him an opportunity of searching out those little extras which a visit to the country sometimes produces. With trailer he carries firewood, seaweed and his lighter furniture when he is turned out of his home. The loss of his bicycle may be more serious to a man than the loss of his home.

We decided that in this case the fairest way of carrying out the order was to call in all bicycles left behind by evacuees and we asked Grange Lodge to issue an order to this effect. First, Dr Brosch refused and said that we should adopt the same procedure as was used for the collection of motor cars for purchase by the German authorities. I therefore looked up the files to see how this collection was done – two years ago already – and discovered that the order was given and signed by the Feldkommandantur! Naturally I showed him the order with some glee and he telephoned Jersey about it. The Colonel said that no notice of any kind whatsoever was to be published in the newspapers on the subject. I asked Dr Brosch the reason for this refusal to what seemed to us a most obvious request but he gave me none. And we knew that we still had to produce those bicycles, that many of them were practically untraceable except through a direct order to their present owners whose names we did not know and that if we ordered people to produce them and they refused, we had no power to enforce our order. Eventually we obtained permission to send a letter to the custodian of the property of each evacuee stating that German authorities had requisitioned a number of bicycles and that all bicycles belonging to evacuees had to be given up. Our only remedy if people refused to give up the bicycles was to report them to Grange Lodge and this, of course, we could never do. The result of this bluff was that we received a number of cycles, enough, we hope, to satisfy the German demand and once again we ate humble pie until we felt extremely bilious.

The order for the stoppage of fishing was issued because of the extreme petrol shortage. We are allowed to buy – at a fantastic price – 10,000 litres of petrol per month to meet the requirements of agriculture and fishing and now that catches are getting smaller the Feldkommandantur think that petrol at present used for fishing would produce more food if saved for agriculture. We have asked for the continuance of fishing for at least another two months, on a limited scale, since longnose are still plentiful and shellfish are being caught in promising quantities. We are saving and processing the livers of ray, conger and dogfish and the oil produced is of great medicinal value. The loss of this supply would be very serious. However, up to now the fishing order remains in force and we are hoping that if the German patrol boats, which use our petrol in comparatively large quantities, can be prevailed upon to supply their own, we may yet succeed in some measure.

The Feldkommandantur notification that it has been decided not to pay anything towards the costs of billeting is something of a shock and we have wondered why this decision has been made. Does it mean that Germany has lost interest in the finances of the Islands and if so are we to conclude that she no longer means to hold them IF she wins the war? From the purely financial aspect it is questionable whether the loss of this apparent source of income is really serious. We have well over fifty million francs in Granville now to meet the cost of our purchases in France and the amounts received in German money by our banks every month are colossal. It seems certain that the Occupation mark will be valueless after the war and it is questionable whether it is better to have received more of them than we can spend instead of having a debt against Germany to tender when the Occupation is over. I suppose it must finish one day.

Last Thursday Queenie and I went to tea with Dr and Mrs Symons. The Sherwills were there too and we worked the Doctor's new planchette board. It had not worked before and when we left it stopped again.

On Saturday we went to the Sherwills for lunch and Queenie made her first appearance in Town complete with José who, being an expert window-dresser, smiles benignly on all and sundry. I'm afraid we are completely the proud young parents.

A friend of ours who some months ago received a Red Cross message telling him his wife had died in England, sent letters to her parents through a prisoner-of-war and he has received from them letters in their own handwriting. He showed us these letters and we gazed and marvelled. They seemed like messages from heaven.

We have not yet received any news of our people who were taken off to Germany in September but the Feldkommandantur are trying to get some information as to their whereabouts.

The war news is getting a little more exciting and the Germans are worried about North Africa where we have begun a large-scale offensive. They seem afraid of an Italian crack-up and its effect upon the German people. We are raiding North Italy heavily from England.

Stalingrad is still holding out and we hear rumours that the Germans have asked for a four day armistice to bury their dead and collect the wounded. Apparently the Russians would accept if Germany would broadcast her request over the radio but up to now she has been unwilling to do so.

THURSDAY, 29TH OCTOBER TO TUESDAY, 3RD NOVEMBER

On Sunday we pulled up our parsnip crop which was very poor and some of the sugar beet which seems quite satisfactory.

During the last week or so José has not been quite her happy self and to discover how much feed she is getting we have weighed her before and after meals. She never seems to get more than four ounces and as the book of rules says that at her age she should receive six ounces she has been introduced to bottle feeding. She is taking more notice of her surroundings every day and to our great delight seems to have a passion for trees. We now have three small pines in the south east corner of our garden as well as seventeen others ready to be transplanted. Dr Symons is giving us some sycamores and five of the poplars are flourishing. We hope that José will realize that our efforts in this direction are as much for her enjoyment as for our own.

WEDNESDAY, 4TH NOVEMBER TO SATURDAY, 7TH NOVEMBER

Ever since the defence works were started with foreign labour a year ago we have been bothered by thieving which has now taken on quite important dimensions. Not only are a considerable portion of our crops lost in this way but everybody is inclined to harvest before produce is ripe, especially in the case of vegetables. The result is that the yield is considerably smaller than it should be. Many people too are definitely discouraged from working as hard as they should.

The Feldkommandantur in an effort to stop thieving are rounding up all foreigners who are not working during working hours. Usually these men live in labour camps but some stay away from the camp, do not turn up at their work and live on the country. We are hoping that the punishment of these men will lessen thieving.

Nothing of great importance has happened here in official circles during the past few days and I have found myself slack enough to spend several hours chatting loose philosophy with sundry officers at Grange Lodge.

How everybody on both sides longs for the end of the war! And how well propaganda news protects us from the full brunt of war news! This week it seems that the Allied Offensive in North Africa is really successful and that the enemy is in full retreat. According to the Germans with whom I come in contact the fighting is so confused that the Germans have retired to their second line in order to clear the air! The impression I get from them is that this step was taken by them as much to help us as to give them a better chance!

We are still owed something like £24,000 for tomatoes exported and we have asked to be paid in seed potatoes instead of German currency. We received a few tons of Polish potatoes last year and planted them. The crops have been very successful.

We hear that an Irishman has been sent back to Jersey from Germany. He was one of the evacuees and says that our people are in a camp in southwest Germany and receive the same food as the Germans. We are hoping for more news shortly.

José has now settled down to her new diet of half bottle and half natural feeding and is much more contented. She now amuses herself – and us – by making noises when she is left alone which may be attempts at speech, as we like to think, or merely the result of wind in the tummy. Whatever the cause we stand and worship.

SUNDAY, 8TH NOVEMBER TO TUESDAY, 10TH NOVEMBER

Sunday was a lovely day and by ten o'clock Nigel and I were hard at work collecting seaweed. We heard a drone in the sky and thought it was was one of the infrequent German planes which pass over the Island until suddenly there was the sound of cannon-fire. Soon afterwards we saw a small plane across the south of the Island, WITHOUT ANY ANTI-AIRCRAFT FIRE, and we knew there had been an airfight and that if anyone had been hurt it was the British plane. That afternoon we heard that a British plane had been shot down on the south coast and that the pilot had baled out and had landed safely.

Apparently the Americans have landed in French North Africa, in several places, and have overcome opposition from the French fleet. An armistice has been signed in Algiers and there seems little doubt that the operation has been entirely successful. We feel exhilarated and already for some optimists the war is as good as finished. Directly we have taken the North African coast, they say, we will take Italy and march through France. This will cause the Germans to withdraw troops from the west coast of Europe, we will make successful landings at several points, Russia will start a full-scale offensive and Germany will be beaten. If only this could come about! Apparently we are raiding northern Italy very heavily already.

A French engineer has arrived here recently to discuss the purchase of new machinery for the Dairy and he came to see us at home with Ron Short on Monday evening. He was in Dakar as recently as 1st October and thinks that the French in Africa will welcome the Americans. On his way back to Spain by air a Spitfire accompanied the plane in which he was travelling across the Mediterranean but did not attack them. He said he did not feel too comfortable. He thinks that nine out every ten persons in France are pro-British and are longing for a British invasion of the Continent.

At last we have received news of our evacuees. About fifty cards arrived from them through the Field Post and we hear from Jersey that they are in Biberach in Württemburg. They seem to be comfortable and we hear of dancing and swimming. Apparently they are in some kind of officers' camp.

Tonight Raymond Falla telephoned to say that the Germans are making a military zone round the west and north-east coasts of the Island and it looks as though the result will be the evacuation of many more families from their homes.

José gained eight ounces last week and a very high percentage in intelligence. The sight of herself in the mirror is a constant source of amusement.

WEDNESDAY, 11TH NOVEMBER TO SATURDAY, 14TH NOVEMBER

Apparently the North African campaign is a great success because the Germans make very little mention of it in their propaganda. We hear rumours of Tobruk having fallen to us once more and of American troops entering Tunisia in the west. In Russia there is still no sign of a German victory although all the Germans to whom I speak assure me that this is inevitable.

A photograph of Michael[26] has arrived and he has been duly and genuinely admired by all of us. Mother is already planning a children's party and I am wondering whether the various cousins will take to each other

---

26 Michael was sister Babe's son. The photo came through Field Post probably via Laufen, the men-only camp to which brother-in-law Len Collins was deported.

better than we did with ours or whether they will find the fond plans of the older generation a most horrible bore.

The original plan for the new military zone involved the evacuation of some 130 families but the Feldkommandantur has been busy and has prevailed upon the military so to alter the plan that about 70 houses have been saved. In addition all properties within the area may be cultivated. We have cause to be grateful to the F.K. for their efforts on behalf of the civilian population. Inspector Oser thinks that the F.K. may soon be withdrawn from the Islands. We hope he is wrong.

A letter arrived from George Vaudin today (Saturday) saying that Rumball and the manager of Barclays Bank, Jersey had been summoned to Paris regarding the project which was mooted last summer for the creation of a debt in France in place of payment in German money for our purchases in France. The whole subject is lacking in clarity but doubtless we will hear more than we wish about it in due course.

This week I have started transplanting my little pines to form a copse at the bottom of the field. Even with the future as uncertain as it seems at present we still automatically plan years ahead.

SUNDAY, 15TH NOVEMBER TO MONDAY, 16TH NOVEMBER

Sure enough we have received a further letter from George Vaudin enclosing a protocol drawn up by the Germans and French regarding payments for imports and exports between France and the Islands and a report from Rumball on meetings held in Paris on the subject a week or so ago. When I was in Jersey last July, Jurat Dorey, President of the Jersey Finance Committee promised to let us know of any developments in the matter and although Benest, Manager of Barclays Bank, Jersey, left for France a fortnight ago we have heard nothing from Jersey yet.

The scheme, as far as we can see, involves the payment of all purchases in France through the Bureau des Changes in Paris. All invoices would have to be passed by them and we would pay Barclays in Jersey by sterling cheque. The result would be that we could never unload the money we receive for goods sold to foreigners in the Islands – a huge sum.

I told Dr Brosch of the protocol today (Monday) and he was shocked. He thinks it will ruin the Islands. I said that obviously we would protest, after due consideration, but that the matter was so involved that we needed time to study it properly. Rumball's explanation of the protocol is excellent.

The Feldkommandantur have been ordered to leave their dwelling houses and asked us today to try to find them alternative accommodation. Oser and I went to see some houses in Doyle Road and when he discovered a baby in one of them he refused to discuss that house further. We both hated the job and came to no conclusion and for my part it was only the fact that the Feldkommandantur had saved 70 families from evacuation in the new military zone that led me to take even the minute part I did take in the visits.

Vraic, in the absence of other fertilizers, is of the utmost importance to us this year and we have been badly hampered in its collection by the blocking up of nearly all the slipways on the beaches. However, where there's a will there's a way and most people have found ways and means of getting the seaweed over the sea walls. To supply farmers in the middle of the Island we have made arrangements for a contractor to have petrol and lorries for the collection of sea weed at L'Erée and today he telephoned to say that the only slipway on that bay is partially blocked by loose stones. He asked if O.T. men could clear those stones away so that his lorries could enter the beach. Oser telephoned for me and was told that very soon that slipway was to be blocked by a wall. Such difficulties face us at every turn and have to do best we can to solve them. Sometimes we succeed.

José gained 7 ounces last week.

Everybody including Germans agrees that the North African campaign is of major importance but the Feldkommandantur officers think that the Germans will march through Spain this week and probably attack Gibraltar. Meanwhile we hear of the evacuation of troops through Benghazi.

TUESDAY, 17TH NOVEMBER TO THURSDAY, 19TH NOVEMBER

We visited L'Erée on Wednesday and discovered that the slipway will not be blocked permanently for about five weeks. Norman is therefore going ahead as fast as he can in the time allotted to him.

I hear from the Feldkommandantur that a British plane made a forced landing in Jersey on Wednesday afternoon and that it was filled with newspapers printed in England. The pilot was saved. They tell me also that British naval vessels were off Alderney on Wednesday night and that the artillery opened up on them although the results could not be seen.

I went into the engine house of the blondin at the quarry near our house this week and watched fascinated as the driver, whom I have known for some months, threw off his disguise of commonplace respectability and performed fantastic wonders of jugglery. He had just finished hoisting two tons of stone from the bottom of the largest hole I have ever seen when we arrived and he then proceeded with little fuss on his part but a mighty whirring and rattling from the huge engine to deposit a scaleboard on to a truck slightly smaller than itself some two hundred feel below us and so far horizontally that I honestly would have needed field glasses to see the detail of the operation. I came away astounded at my ignorance of the interesting things which go on all around me.

The Feldkommandantur think that they may have decided on two houses in which the five officers involved will live. That is the nearest approach I can give to their domestic condition at present. I have spent several hours this week visiting houses with them, but their choice made difficult by their reluctance to turn out civilians, the insistence of one on a house the appearance of which will uphold the dignity of the F.K., the demand of another for a good garden and above all by their outraged feelings at the fact that though they are the oldest German inhabitants, they are being ordered to move by and for comparative newcomers. My foremost feeling for them is pity – the same sort of pity that I would extend to any other Guernsey family which had been forced to leave their home.

Needless to say the main topic of discussion in the President's room at Maison Allaire this week is the protocol regarding the new finance arrangements with France. What official dignity remains to the Controlling Committee is outraged by the fact that this agreement has been signed by the French and German governments without discussion with the people whose whole financial future is involved. I told Dr Brosch this today and he saw the argument but suggested that perhaps the German answer would be that the Channel Islands are now part of Germany and that we were not in the same position as the French who had signed an armistice with Germany. I gave the obvious answer that as the nation of which we form part is still at war with Germany we must be regarded as occupied territory within the meaning of the Hague Convention.

It was suggested this morning that a strong delegation be sent to Jersey to discuss the matter with the States of that Island and up to now it looks as if Messrs. Sherwill, Marquand and Broughton – and perhaps myself – may form the party.

As regards imports, the States of course act only as agents and are paid by the public for such commodities. It is therefore simple for them to pass this money on to Barclays Bank, Jersey, thus discharging once and for all our debt to France. The trouble arises, however, because Barclays apparently will not accept payment except in sterling and marks will accumulate here at a fantastic rate. Up till now the States have bought all the marks the banks have received in order to pay for imports but if they stop doing so there is little doubt that the banks will be quite unwilling to accept marks for crediting to cusomers' sterling accounts. The result is almost bound to be inflation with everybody doing their best to have no marks in their possession and therefore offering ever higher prices for any holdable commodity.

The alternative is for the States to continue to guarantee German currency and this will cost the Island, at the present rate of increase of marks, at least £750,000 per annum.

It seems ludicrous that the government of this little Island should be expected to bear such a burden and no doubt we shall reach some agreement with whoever we meet on the matter.

FRIDAY, 20TH NOVEMBER TO TUESDAY, 24TH NOVEMBER

Last Sunday night a Lancaster four-engined British bomber made a forced landing in Sark, apparently on its way back from a raid on Stuttgart. I understand all its seven occupants were saved and that it landed because of a shortage of petrol. That same night a motor yacht which is being used by the German navy met either a patrol vessel or a convoy off this Island and gave either the wrong signal or none at all. The result was that it was fired on and landed several dead when it arrived here. Many of our people professed to receive this news with glee – that is rather fashionable – but it seems to me that anyone with any sporting instincts at all must, at the bottom of their hearts, be appalled at such a tragedy befalling even their enemies.

José only put on three ounces last week and we are not sure whether this is due to too much water in the milk or an overdose of opening medicine. She now chuckles delightfully and a chance smile of hers bestowed on my wine-merchant has resulted in a more than usually generous ration from him this week.

The war news is good. Apparently the Russians are advancing both on the north and south of Leningrad – it is said, up to fifty miles in a westerly direction – either the whole or nearly all French Africa has come over to us and there are rumours of a most uneasy feeling in Italy.

We have not yet received any news from Jersey about the new financial arrangement with France but Mr Leale has written to the Feldkommandantur on the matter setting out our main objections to it. On Monday morning I asked Dr Brosch to arrange for a telephone conversation between Mr Leale and the Bailiff of Jersey to discuss the possibility and urgency of an inter-island conference on the matter and he telephoned Jersey to make enquiries. He spoke to Dr Casper and told me afterwards that F.K. Jersey did not want any delegation to go down for the present and apparently would not even allow the telephone conversation. I explained once more that we did not want to discuss the matter with F.K. Jersey, but with the States of Jersey but did not receive permission.

WEDNESDAY, 25TH NOVEMBER AND THURSDAY, 26TH NOVEMBER

It appears that only three R.A.F. men were in the bomber which landed in Sark, the other four having baled out either over Germany or France.

Discussions on the protocol and its effects and of the implied stoppage of payment for French imports in Reichsmarks have taken up most of our time this week. On Wednesday morning Mr Leale, Mr Sherwill, Mr Broughton and I spent a couple of hours discussing the matter with Dr Brosch. We went over the main points as we see them and he asked that they be set out in a letter to him. He sees quite clearly the disastrous effects on the Island's finances and is quite as appalled as we are about them.

Apparently in the occupied countries – the Channel Islands being the exception – the costs of the Occupation, including the pay of the occupying forces are paid in the currency of the country. The money required seems to be obtained as a contribution from the government of the country and we suggested that perhaps it might be possible for the occupying forces in these Islands to be paid in francs. If the French 'contribution' is at present spent in full and if part of it could in future be used for the payment of the forces occupying these Islands and therefore not spent by the Germans in France we think it would make no difference to France since the same amount of goods would be taken from the French as before, only a small part of them would go to us instead of to the Germans. Dr Brosch is not very hopeful of this arrangement being agreed to by the Germans in Paris and read to us parts of a letter from Berlin on the stoppage of the payment by the Germans of 75% of the Occupation costs here. In this letter it was pointed out that the cost of the war per head of population in England was much higher than it was in the Islands and this was given as one of the main reasons for the stoppage of the payment. Although there are several answers to this argument, no opportunity has been given to the governments of these Islands to put them forward.

Another danger which we are facing at present is that of becoming a dumping ground for R.M. and francs as confidence in those currencies diminishes. Already a French firm which runs a sort of bazaar for the benefit of the Germans here has stopped sending its takings to France for the purchase of stocks. It has an account with a local bank and formerly it transferred funds by means of a cheque to the States which caused the release of a like sum in Granville. It has now instructed its bankers not to forward any more funds to France. The result will be that all its takings will be left in its account in Guernsey IN STERLING. Presumably it will be financed for purchases in France by someone who prefers a sterling balance to either francs or R.M. We fear that vast quantities of francs and R.M. will be smuggled into the Island on visiting vessels and will be paid into local banking accounts either direct or through some unpatriotic islander.

The only apparent way of averting this danger is by converting bank balances in R.M. The awful effects of such a measure if put into effect in its simple form are obvious; complete loss of confidence in the mark and inflation. Up to date we are sorting out the details of how and why such inflation will come and toying with methods of avoiding it. If it seems possible to succeed in avoiding inflation it may be that an attempt will be made to switch bank accounts to R.M. – an experiment against all the known rules of economics.

Meanwhile I am implored by Grange Lodge to find a lavatory basin for Dr Brosch's bedroom in his new house – and I have found him one.

FRIDAY, 27TH NOVEMBER AND SATURDAY, 28TH NOVEMBER

By far the most exciting news during the past two days is the scuttling of the French fleet at Toulon. To many of us here it seems terribly sad that the end of these proud ships should come in such a way, but it has showed us that France still has plenty of spirit left and that at any rate she does not intend her arms to be used against the Allies. I should imagine that this action has had a most heartening effect throughout France and has lifted men's hearts from the misery they have suffered through the indignity of having to bow to German orders.

I asked Dr Brosch yesterday (Friday) to try once again to get permission for some of us to go to Jersey to discuss the protocol with the States of that Island and this morning he told me that Dr Casper – who is in charge of the F.K. in the absence of the Colonel – is in Paris. We presume he is taking the matter up on our behalf. I pointed out that before writing a final letter on the subject we feel it imperative to talk the matter over with Jersey, since, if both Islands do not decide on the same measures in the event of a stoppage of R.M. purchases in France there is a very real danger of complications. He sees this point but seems unable to grant the necessary permission.

Today we have talked again around and about the subject at Hirzel House and have to some extent picked our way through the maze of complications arising from the stoppage – or otherwise – of the present policy of the States of purchasing all surplus Reichsmarks in the banks.

I have been reading Negley Farson[27] lately and find that he brings home to me very vividly the fact that a junior civil servant in Guernsey knows very little of the world he lives in and should take infinite pains not to become too smug at an early age. Too many possessions and too little discipline do not give depth of character, of thought or of experience and it is almost with impatience that I wait to see the effects of a spartan existence on brother Des.

We were talking this afternoon of the dullness of peacetime existence to the bulk of young Englishmen and I suggested that it is bad for the young of a country to feel that that their native land has all that it needs. I even went

---

27 Negley Farson (1890-1960) was an American journalist and keen fisherman.

so far to suggest that it is bad for anybody to have a surplus of eatables and when I made that statement I had in mind the pleasure I get nowadays from producing food in the garden and from the sea. If therer were no longer any vital necessity to work in this way I am sure I would soon lose interest. It seems to me that there should be some positive and adventurous aim, apart from the killing of their contemporaries, to occupy the energies of our young men and women if we are to stop wars in the future. We must not let boredom reign again. The astounding results of a nation working for one end is shewn in the history of Germany during the past decade. If only that aim had not been war!

SUNDAY, 29TH NOVEMBER TO THURSDAY, 3RD DECEMBER

We received two Red Cross messages this week – one from Babe and one from Ron Harwood – and one of them took nearly four months to get here! Of course such delays do not seem strange to us and if a message takes less than two months on its journey we are much more impressed. I should imagine that two centuries ago letters came to Guernsey much more quickly and regularly and in many other ways we have gone back several centuries without noticing very much hardship now that we have become accustomed to the fact. Practically all articles of food which come from the tropics, for instance, have all but disappeared, but many of us are putting on weight. Tea is so scarce that I bought some for a friend a few days ago for £5 10s a pound – and that was dirt cheap. The current price is more like £12 to £14. We still have a pound or two but we have become so accustomed to coffee substitute that we do not drink tea more than once a week. I believe that many people would be quite happy to live as they do at present indefinitely if they could have peace and their liberty and could get away from the Island as often as they liked.

Raymond Falla, Dr Brosch and I went to Herm in *Ida* on Tuesday. Dr Brosch brought his gun and a bagful of cartridges but half way across he discovered that only five of the cartridges fitted the gun. There was a strong westerly breeze and we tied up snugly in the harbour. I spent a happy couple of hours climbing pine trees for cones and came back with two hundredweight. After lunch Dr Brosch wanted to shoot at some wild duck and geese on the west coast, so we went out in the boat to chase them. One of the precious cartridges went into a group of about a hundred birds and he winged an oyster-catcher. Raymond chased the poor thing halfway across Rat Island and we just scraped back into deep water in time to save grounding on the falling tide. The other four rounds sprayed the waters around us and the heavens to no effect and I put the others ashore for tea. I myself went fishing and in moving a bag I heard a squeak and the bird flew ! On the way home Dr Brosch said it had not been a very successful day apart from the bird which he meant to keep at Grange Lodge as a pet. I was afraid of an outburst when I told him it too had gone. We reached St. Sampson's at 5 o'clock soaked to the skin after a crossing in the teeth of the wind.

The protocol is still the subject of much discussion and an elaborated letter has now been drafted by Mr Leale for submission to Grange Lodge.[28] We have not yet received permission to visit Jersey but we hear from the Bailiff that the matter has been discussed by the States and the F.K. in that Island. The S.K.H. – the French firm who run the German bazaar here – have withdrawn all their marks from their local banking account and apparently are sending them to Granville.

When we weighed José on Sunday we found that she had put on ten ounces during the week. She now shows her displeasure most emphatically when she is put to bed and her yells would not disgrace a steam whistle.

The war news is still very heartening although I suspect we lost a great many ships in the North African landing. No German now thinks the war will be a short one and many are even more pessimistic.

FRIDAY, 4TH DECEMBER TO TUESDAY, 8TH DECEMBER

José has had her ten o'clock feed and Queenie has taken her crowing to bed. Skipper and I are having a nightcap and final smoke before the fire before turning in. Everything is silent and very peaceful and when I locked up just now I saw that the night was quite black and that rain was falling gently. I sit down at the piano and play something which fits the atmosphere. Suddenly there is a sound like the moving of furniture upstairs and we wonder what Queenie is doing. I stop playing and there are booms and ear-splitting cracks everywhere. The anti-aircraft guns have opened up. I look out of the back window and hear the drone of aero engines and see the low cloud lit up by the searchlights. There are gun-flashes everywhere and shells burst almost vertically overhead. I go upstairs to see if Queenie and José are all right and we look out of our bedroom window. The searchlights on Brehon Tower are zigzagging enthusiastically over the clouds. Quite pretty. The plane passes on and a few minutes later another takes its place. More noise and a shell whistles overhead on its way out to sea. There are flashes from Alderney and Jersey as well as from the west of this Island and we gather from that that a large number of planes are passing over the Islands. We turn out the lights downstairs and go to bed. The noise continues until we are almost asleep. José goes to sleep as soon as her light is put out, just as usual.[29]

28 See Item 13: Leale to F.K.: Currency Transfer Protocol, 4 Dec 1942, p.307.
29 Search lights from the Vale Mill on the hill behind the house which was fortified. Shooting practice involved shooting between La Platte and the hedge between the two fields next door. Sometimes it meant moving out of the house with José in her pram.

That was Sunday night and we hear on Monday that one plane was shot down in Alderney and wonder why the R.A.F. pass over these Islands when they could save themselves from the risk of destruction by making a detour of three or four miles.

On Monday afternoon, according to German reports, twenty Spitfires carrying bombs appeared off the southwest of Jersey and sank one large vessel and damaged others in the convoy. Travelling is no longer a pleasant adventure and we would hate to be killed by our own people.

Last week Sayer's aunt received a letter from him, from Laufen in Bavaria. Apparently our people are fairly comfortable although their extra luggage has not yet been shipped. It is said that the delay is caused by lack of transport in France but F.K. say they hope to send it on during the next few days. Sayer asks in his letter that I make some arrangement for the transfer of money for the use of the poorer of the evacuees. We took this matter up some time ago with F.K. but have not yet received any reply from them. Sayer asks his aunt to send him some Occupation Marks in her letter to him and says that these can be used in the camp. Dr Brosch thinks it would be useless for us to send large quantities of money direct like that since it would probably be returned or even confiscated. We are therefore going to ask George Vaudin to try to transfer money through a French bank, to the camp, in Sayer's name, the amount being 100,000 francs. There is apparently some clearing system between French and German banks and we hope this scheme may work. We are also asking him, if this fails, to call at the Red Cross headquarters in Paris and ask them to help us. Apparently Red Cross parcels arrive from England because Sayer says that they smoke Players and English tobacco. I am writing to Sayer to tell him what we are doing as regards money.

Our list of guests at La Platte during the past week is as follows:-

Sunday: Zu and George to supper, Skipper to supper and sleep.
Monday: Zu, George, Dick and Henry Bisson for the evening.
Tuesday: Dick and Mary Bird to supper and sleep.
Wednesday: Zu and George for the evening and sleep.
Thursday: Nobody.
Friday: Zu, George and Dick for the evening.
Saturday: Nancy Guilbert and Hugh Tidd to supper and sleep.

This is not such an exceptional week and having our friends with us makes life quite bearable and sometimes very enjoyable.

Most of the greenhouse properties in the Island are now run by their owners once more, the Glasshouse Utilization Board retaining only those belonging to evacuees and people who can prove that they are not in a position to work them. We have now received a letter from the private growers' organization asking whether the States will guarantee a minimum price for tomatoes next year. This seems a just request since growers are forced to grow a certain proportion of tomatoes under the Island cropping plan. It is hoped to export about 6,000 tons of tomatoes next year and since under the protocol exports will be credited to us by the Bureau des Changes it is important that the export should be a success. I asked Dr Brosch what he thought about the States giving such a guarantee but he gave no definite answer. He says there is to be a conference in January and that the French firm, Chatam, are almost certain to buy the tomatoes delivered to Guernsey quay. We wonder whether anyone will be foolish enough to take the risk of delays in transport and losses in transit for a crop worth £240,000.

We have received from the F.K. a letter and map showing a new military zone around the coasts of the Island. The creation of this zone will mean the evacuation of fifty one families and only those who have experienced the loss of their homes in this way can realize what it means. In this case the people will be allowed to take their furniture with them, but this is not always the case when the houses are to be occupied by troops. Naturally we have an organization which undertakes such work under the direction of Major Langlois and they are kept busy. They do wonders in finding accommodation for evacuated families but their work is becoming increasingly difficult as empty houses become fewer. The spirit of evacuees is marvellous and I am constantly surprised at their calmness. It seems to me that I would be embittered for life if I had to leave my home. Major Langlois and his staff are public benefactors and must have earned the gratitude of hundreds of people during the past two and a half years.

José put on four ounces last week and we are waiting breathless for the appearance of her first tooth.

We have just finished our first batch of syrup made from sugar beet. The process is as follows:– Cut the beet into slices and cover with water in a saucepan. Boil for as many hours as your patience will allow and strain, either through muslin or a fine sieve. Boil the pulp again for three quarters of an hour and strain again. Boil all the liquid collected for three quarters of an hour. The result should be a thick syrup. Ours tastes like sweet ground. Sugar beet is in such demand that it fetches 2½d per pound.

We harvested our sugar beet and swedes last Sunday. Neither of these crops was large, apparently because we planted too late.

Today (Tuesday) Jack Corbet and a crew of three started the collection of seaweed by boat. They cut it at the Rocqueries[30] and used an old lifeboat for the purpose of transport. Their cargo weighed five tons, six hundredweight.

---

30 The Rocqueries are a reef, uncovered at a spring low tide forming a lagoon between the rocks on the west coast of Herm.

WEDNESDAY, 9TH DECEMBER TO SUNDAY, 13TH DECEMBER

There is no interesting local war news and apparently nothing spectacular has happened anywhere else.

We hear stories from time to time of the terrible plight of the Russians who are working in Alderney. One man saw a number of them unloading cement at the harbour and said that some of them had nothing on their feet. They were all caked with cement from head to foot, with their eyes showing through the cement dust and on the ladders they were using to get aboard the ship care had to be taken not to put your hands on the blood from their feet on the rungs. Another story is that one of these men was knocked from a twenty foot wall and broke his legs. He was left where he fell all day.

In Guernsey too, one of the foreign labourers was seen by hundreds of Guernsey people lying in the plantation at the Half Way. He was there all one day and I do not know whether he died or not. A local doctor who saw him said he was dying and it was quite certain that he was covered with lice.

On Wednesday I attended a meeting consisting mainly of bank managers to discuss the possibility of foreigners dumping foreign currencies in local banks. I am attaching a minute of the meeting.[31] These currency problems fascinate me, but we all feel the need of a real expert here.

I spoke to Dr Brosch again about the export of tomatoes and he feels certain that Chatam will be willing to buy our crop delivered on Guernsey quay. He thinks the transport risks will be taken either by the German government or by some insurance company.

On Wednesday night there was a very high tide and a southerly blow. The result was that at La Rocque, St. Peter's, about twenty feet of sea wall collapsed on the beach and a small part of the road went with it. O.T. have been taking thousands of tons of shingle and sand from this beach and undoubtedly this the cause of the collapse. I went out with the States Engineer and Inspector Zachau of the F.K. to see the damage and all three of us thoroughly enjoyed ourselves saying, 'I told you so,' to the O.T. They promised to repair the wall but if they do not do the work properly it is quite likely that with the high tides in February and March some hundreds of vergées of low-lying ground will be flooded with sea water.

Most mornings this week we have spent half an hour before work collecting seaweed for the garden. It gives one a fine appetite for breakfast. What a lot I didn't know before the war about Guernsey agricultural methods – and how little I know now.

---

31 See Item 14: Meeting with Bank Managers: Foreign Currency, 9 Dec 1942, p.310

José now weighs exactly thirteen pounds and takes a definite interest in her surroundings. When she cries in temper she looks like a proper hard little Breton woman. When she smiles she is charming.

MONDAY, 14TH DECEMBER AND TUESDAY, 15TH DECEMBER

Altogether we collected about 25 cwt. of vraic on Sunday. With the lack of other manure it is worth a shilling a cwt. this year. We have spent half an hour before breakfast for the past two mornings collecting a load and an appetite.

During the summer Mr Sherwill received a letter from Berlin stating that the sentence of five years imprisonment passed on John Ingrouille two years ago had been revoked. Two or three months passed and nothing further was heard of him so Mr Sherwill wrote to Berlin asking what had happened to him. We have had no reply but three weeks ago two women who were witnesses at his trial were taken off to Berlin, it being rumoured that they were wanted as witnesses again in connection with Ingrouille. Tonight Ingrouille's mother and father came to see me and say that Ingrouille has been sentenced again to five years imprisonment. We do not know all the facts, of course, but there is certainly something strange about the whole matter. Meanwhile the parents are almost shaken out of the brave calm with which they have faced the last two years. Mrs Ingrouille says she no longer believes in either God or hell but she does believe her son to be innocent and wants justice. We have never been allowed to see the full evidence in the case. John is the only son and the apple of his mother's eye.

We have made the final arrangements today for the shipment of the evacuees' baggage to Germany and hope it will leave tomorrow.

At Grange Lodge this morning Inspector Oser was speaking with Falla, Norman and myself. I asked some question and Oser said I knew the answer already. In fact, he said, I was the States' spy at the Feldkommandantur and knew everything. When we laughed he said that he had been told this, not by Germans, but by English people. Often lately, they have told me at Grange Lodge that I understand German perfectly and only pretend not to understand when they speak in that language. As a matter of fact I am ashamed of my small knowledge of the language after two years and a half of daily talks with the F.K., but when I know what the conversation is about and know the facts I can sometimes pick up enough words here and there in the conversation to understand the gist of it. The fact remains, however, that their erroneous belief in my histrionic powers may be dangerous one day.

Auction sales are now the only officially recognized medium of sale in which there is no limit to prices. Recently an Ordinance relating to price regulation was approved by the German authorities and is now in process of consideration by the Court. Today the Controlling Committee decided to bring auction sales under the provisions of the Ordinance and the result will probably be the stoppage of all such sales. Actually bidders at auction sales today are mainly dealers and they give fabulous prices for articles for resale to foreigners. This practice has the effect of increasing our takings of R.M. in the Island and since we already have enough for our requirements, our policy must be to stop it.

WEDNESDAY, 16TH DECEMBER AND THURSDAY, 17TH DECEMBER

We hear that, owing to the fact that there is very little left to buy in Germany, there is a definite trade in the exchange of the internal German currency and the Occupation Mark; it is said that 100 internal marks exchange for 60 Occupation Marks. Apparently the Occupation marks are then given to soldiers returning to the occupied territories after leave for the purpose of buying goods for sale in Germany. Even with the huge prices paid on the black market in the occupied countries there is still a very big margin of profit to be made in Germany. If this is so – and it is only hearsay as far as I am concerned – it would account in some measure for the enormous quantities of marks carried by some soldiers and foreign workmen and for the high prices paid in Guernsey for all kinds of goods which, before the war, would with difficulty have been sold at all. Does it also show a wholesale flight from the mark and, if so, what is the inference as far as German public opinion goes?

George and Zu were married today (Thursday) at St. Sampson's Church. There was a choir composed of eight of the little choir recently started by Reginald Le Prevost of which Zu and I are members. I played the organ. Afterwards we went on to their new home and about twenty of us drank their health. I did the toast of the bride and bridegroom and made a completely fatuous speech. Mads, Irwin, Skipper, Queenie and I stayed on to lunch and helped entertain further guests during the afternoon. I firmly believe they are going to be very happy together.

We received Red Cross messages from Marguerite, Marie and Beata today, all saying how thrilled they are to hear we are going to have a baby! Beata says she is expecting her baby on September 19th. Talk about stale news! Mother had a message from Des. That seemed almost a miracle.

FRIDAY, 18TH DECEMBER

Dr Brosch told me today that the Colonel is coming over very soon. He thinks there is something in the wind and when I asked if he thought it might be something unpleasant for us, he did not say no. We hope it is not some fiendish Christmas present for us.

About a month ago we asked for a five days extension of curfew over the the holidays. We heard today that, owing to altered conditions, there would be no extension whatever.

Raymond Falla has been asked to go to Sark tomorrow, to buy a landau. It is said it is for the General. Nix benzine? Apparently food for the troops is not too plentiful because I was asked today whther it would be possible for one of our boats to do a day's fishing for the F.K. before Christmas. Apparently the petrol would be supplied from civilian stocks.

Prices at auction sales continue to soar. At a sale held by Fuzzey's this week, one tin of pilchards went for 25/–, a pound tin of custard powder, £4-11-0, a sixpenny tin of boot polish, 12/–, three pounds of candles, 30/–, small tins of cream, 17/6 each, a quarter pound of tea, £2-7-6, tins of fruit in the neighbourhood of £2.

FRIDAY, 18TH DECEMBER TO TUESDAY, 29TH DECEMBER

These last eleven days opened with a visit from Colonel Knackfuss. He asked to see the Bailiff, Mr Leale and Mr Sherwill and invited me as well. When we arrived at Grange Lodge, wondering what new nightmare was in store for us we found that the object of our visit was to be wished a happy Christmas! Then the Colonel asked whether we had anything to discuss and of course the currency question came up immediately. I am including a minute of the discussion.[32] We discussed several other relatively minor matters and left soon after one o'clock after what we looked upon as a short meeting lasting only just over an hour.

During the afternoon I slipped down to the Royal Hotel on my own to see whether I could get the Colonel to grant us even one night's extension of curfew. We originally asked for five nights extension over the holidays and were refused them all – owing to altered conditions. The Colonel told me that, although he was in favour of granting the extension, General Müller was not willing to allow civilians on the streets after nine o'clock and he is responsible for the defence of the Island. However, the Colonel promised to take the matter up again for us.

They asked at Grange Lodge what we thought of conditions generally in the Islands and Mr Leale said certainly the food supply was better than last winter. He reminded the Colonel, however, that the worst months, February, March and April, were still to come. The Colonel said that his unofficial opinion was that the sinking by the R.A.F. of ships between the Islands and the French mainland was bound to have an effect on our food supply.

---

32 See Item 15: Meeting with F.K.: Currency Problems, 21 Dec 1942, p.313.

The news has come through that Darlan has been shot. I wonder whether we shall ever hear his story in full and whether he is really the biggest rogue in history? It is probably too early to judge, especially without full knowledge.

Last Wednesday Nigel and I went to Herm in *Ida* with Dr Brosch and Taborsky. We went right around to the Shell Beach and altogether it was a very pleasant day. I thought how delightful it would be to make such a trip with my friends as in the days before the war.

We went to the pictures on Saturday to see a second-rate American film – a great treat these days – and there was a German news film. When Stalingrad was mentioned there was a very distinct titter right through the house.

José is flourishing. For the past two weeks she has gained twelve ounces per week. She now does her exercises each evening to accompaniment of the Andante from Haydn's Surprise Symphony.

George Vaudin is back from Granville for Christmas and says that last Sunday week there was some machine gunning by the R.A.F. at the station. About four French people and four Germans were killed. The French people take such affairs as a matter of course and 99% of them are pro-British, especially since the beginning of the North African campaign. Another acquaintance of mine who has just returned from France tells me that he sold a sovereign there for 4,500 francs – about £22-10-0. Apparently British pound notes are selling for 600 francs.

Tonight (29th) Queenie and I went to the annual reunion of the Cherchemidians – those people who were taken off to prison in 1940 in connection with the arrival in the Island of Nicolle and Symes. We met at Mr Sherwill's house and had a very merry evening. Being with them all again recalled vividly for me the nightmare days of that terrible affair. We came back in the inky darkness on my motor cycle against a terrifically cold and strong north wind.

Our third Christmas under German Occupation has come and gone. We all believe it will be the last – and the Germans think that is impossible. They think the war will last at least two more years and perhaps even longer, and they are already very war-weary. They asked me at the Feldkommandantur the other day whether I thought that conditions in England were bad too and whether the English people were tired of war. I said that I had no information except that all the photographs I had seen of friends in England – and we get hundreds through prisoners-of-war – showed them fatter than they were when they left Guernsey. I also mentioned that I heard that insurance rates on the North Atlantic route had fallen recently.

On Christmas Eve we had a little supper party here. Madeleine and Irwin, Zu and George, Maisie and Nigel and Dick Johns came and we laughed from 8 p.m. till 3 a.m. I found myself in a corner once or twice, thinking of Christmas 1939 when all my family except Des were here, and I longed with all my heart to see them again. Queenie said afterwards that she would give anything to look in on them all even for half an hour – and we flatter ourselves that they have a similar longing.

Madeleine gave the Bailiff a two ounce tin of Player's Navy Cut tobacco as a Christmas present and he was completely overcome.

The Bailiff received a letter from Frank Stroobant who is the head of one of the internment camps in Germany, asking for regular food parcels. Other people here have received letters expressing the wish that the evacuees could send us some of the food they are having. It is difficult to know what conditions are really like for those of our people who were taken to Germany last September but we all feel that they are probably suffering severe hardships. Meanwhile we have consulted the Feldkommandantur about sending them both money and food and are informed that an F.K. officer was sent to look after the luggage which was sent off recently and is to contact our people and bring back a report on conditions generally and the possibility of sending money and goods to them.

1943

Having been refused any extension of curfew over the holidays most people have made the best of a bad job and organized all-night parties. Any change of address has to be notified to the Greffe and many people have complied with this formality. Some have not. We went to one of these parties on New Year's Eve at Sefton the home of Wilfred Hubert. This was quite an adventure for us and meant a fair amount of preparation and organization. First we had to arrange for someone to look after José during the dance which preceded the party. The Birds very kindly consented to do this and we deposited her there at 5 o'clock. Then we placed our transport – obtained after much wangling – under lock and key and moved off to Sunnycroft in the Grange. The dance room was full of our friends and we were presented with vouchers entitling us to five drinks apiece. These were not very strong, of course, but they were adequate with the intoxicating happiness which enveloped the party. There was a very good little cabaret, with four men converted into a dance chorus. Two of the performers were erstwhile dignified doctors. At half past eight we all went home like good children and Queenie and I fetched José along to her new quarters. She had been a little difficult earlier in the evening but she was sporting enough to behave properly for the rest of the night. How we all enjoyed ourselves. We ate and drank almost as though there was no shortage of food, we toasted our King and country at midnight from a table covered with the Union Jack, we played childish games and forsook our better halves and went to bed at five o'clock.

On Saturday night we had a party at home. Twenty of our friends turned up. We made it as near non-stop as we could, starting with Beetle[1] and going on to ukelele and vocal duets from Drs Sutcliffe and Rose. We had supper with as much wine as we could drink and a real Christmas pudding and while nearly everybody helped with the washing up a few of us rigged up the surprise of the evening – a talkie cinema. George Formby himself entertained us for an hour and a half and then our favourite Will Hay came on. The show, with extras, lasted from midnight to three o'clock and everybody was fresh and ready for anything at the end of it. So we played charades, with more gusto than skill. At half past five we turned over to Sardines, after a few

---

1   Beetle is a party game with dice in which the players draw a schematic beetle.

choruses and cup of coffee and eventually turned in soon after six o'clock.[2] All the girls slept upstairs in various beds and on mattresses on the floor and the men made themselves comfortable on the floor and armchairs in the lounge. Everybody had a scratch breakfast at ten o'clock or thereabouts and those who did not have to leave at once set to with a will to clear up the mess. By the time they left at 11.30 the house was like a new pin in my eyes and quite presentable in Queenie's.

The two doctors flirted with José and, to her great delight fed her and attended to her more personal requirements. She seems to have little if any native modesty.

About three o'clock in the morning most of the anti-aircraft guns went into action but apart from, "Whoopee, there's the R.A.F.!" nobody took any notice at all.

On Friday night there was a heavy explosion which turned out to be a mine washed up on the beach at Portinfer by a very strong west wind. We turned over and went to sleep again.

Even now after all our talk, we are not certain whether we will continue to be allowed to make all our purchases in France with the German money which accumulates here. The Feldkommandantur say they are trying to obtain this concession. One thing we do know is that the protocol is not operating yet.

Now we are into the New Year and are awaiting almost with certainty the early end of the war and thinking of the problems which will confront us when the Germans leave the Island.

TUESDAY, 5TH JANUARY TO TUESDAY, 12TH JANUARY 1943

A thirteen hundred ton steamer bound from the Islands to St. Malo was wrecked this week somewhere south of Jersey.[3] Apparently the accident happened at night and was due to faulty navigation. It is said that over one hundred and eighty people lost their lives and some of those rescued had been in the water as long as thirteen hours. Goettmann, the propaganda journalist from Guernsey, was in the water for three hours. Such a disastrous wreck has not occurred in these waters for several decades.

François Grignard, of Caen, who supplies the gazogènes and charcoal for our lorries and makes other purchases for us in France, is in the Island again. He says, like all other Frenchmen, that 90% of his compatriots are pro-British now and believe that a landing will be made on the Continent this

2   Sardines is a variation of the game of hide and seek.
3   The SS *Schokland*, a Dutch freighter pressed into German service, was wrecked off Noirmoint Point, Jersey, at midnight on 4/5 January, 1943. Some 250 German troops were on board. See Falla (2018) pp.48-9.

spring. Apparently the R.A.F. are very busy, because he says at Caen they see '*des quantités*' of British aircraft. They have had as many as 43 air-raid alerts in 48 hours. As regards the destruction of the French fleet at Toulon he feels that by this means France has shewn that she still retains her national self-respect. He still believes in Pétain and says that Laval is a true Frenchman and that even if he does not like the English he likes the Germans less. After speaking to him I feel more than ever the futility of making sweeping statements about the French and that they are not as decadent as is usually imagined. A good Frenchman loves his country as much as a patriot of any other nationality.

I was interested to note that he has foreseen the advantage of keeping some funds in a banking account in Guernsey for use after the war.

It has been blowing hard for some days and on Monday night a small floating dock which is kept in the Old Harbour broke adrift and destroyed fifteen of our fishing boats by sinking them and then grounding on them.

We are toying with the idea of keeping a large stock of French francs in the Island if the protocol comes into effect, so that Barclays will be able to pay the French Government in their own currency after the war without having to buy francs on the money market. If this is possible we will avoid the difficulty of having to incur a sterling debt with Barclays to be met after the war.

WEDNESDAY, 13TH JANUARY TO SUNDAY, 17TH JANUARY

Last night, (Saturday) we went to a play, *While Parents Sleep*, put on by the Old Amherstian Players at the Lyric.[4] It was excellent. For a year now the Lyric has been open to the public for all kinds of stage shows by local artistes and they have been very successful and a great factor in lightening the monotony of the Occupation.

After the play we went to an all-night party given by the two doctors at New Street.[5] For Queenie and me these parties are landmarks in our existence and we set out to enjoy them to the full. We arrived home at half past eleven this morning and spent the afternoon sleeping. Of course we took José with us to the party and she behaved very well, but she has become a little more difficult recently, due, so we are told, to the imminence of teething.

Just before Christmas we were asked by Grange Lodge for lists of all persons punished in Guernsey for criminal offences during the past ten years. We gave them in and heard no more on the subject until Saturday when I met Charles Gardner, just back from Jersey. He told me that all

---

4   The Lyric Theatre was in New Street.

5   Dr Sutcliffe's surgery was also in New Street.

persons punished for crimes in Jersey since, I think, 1927 had received individual notices to present themselves at the Feldkommandantur for an interview, presumably in connection with some further evacuation nightmare. Ex-British officers had received similar notices. During the last few days there have been numbers of British planes over at night and the anti-aircraft guns have been in action. The noise, added to José's peevishness have meant broken rest, especially for Queenie. The baby does not wake me, the guns do.

MONDAY, 18TH JANUARY TO THURSDAY, 21ST JANUARY

The question of exporting tomatoes during 1943 is one which has worried the Controlling Committee considerably. It is most likely that the fruit will feed Germans and not the French and this is an obvious reason for lack of enthusiasm on the part of any patriot. On the other hand if the protocol comes into force the value of the crop will be offset against our imports from France and will reduce our debt to that extent. Added to this there is always a possibility that we may be able to sell in France. The scheme is that an important fruit wholesaler named Chatam, who is an Alsatian, will buy the tomatoes on the Guernsey quay and will shoulder all risks from that point. We have been sceptical concerning his willingness to take such a risk and the ability of the Germans to supply the necessary transport. Oser has recently seen Chatam and he told me today (Thursday) that insurance and the provision of shipping permitted to travel without convoy protection are the two difficulties which have yet to be overcome. He believes that they will find a way out.

News from our internees in Germany is coming in much better now. Mother had a letter from Leonard which took only ten days to come and he says that he has received one from Babe in her own handwriting. That seems almost miraculous to us after more than two and a half years. Dr Brosch tells me that arrangements are being made to enable us to send money to Germany but as yet he does not know the details. There is tragedy as well as comedy in some of the letters received here. One well-bred woman is suffering with her back because of sleeping on straw; a man we know writes to say that if he was a Red Indian his name would be either Running Water or Rushing Wind.

There have been two cases which apparently have been identified as typhus amongst the O.T. foreign labourers here during the past week or so. Last Thursday Dr Symons, Dr Revell and I met one of the German doctors to discuss measures to be taken to prevent the spread of the disease. He assured us that all possible precautions had already been taken and that, if necessary, Dr Symons would be consulted. Meanwhile we have heard nothing of further cases and the Health Department have prepared themselves for any such emergency.

This week we have received from the F.K. a letter which amounts to an order to teach German to all children over twelve in our schools. This is directly opposed to the English interpretation of the Hague Rules and we shall probably protest. The letter begins, however, by saying that the measure is already in operation in Jersey and once more we find ourselves without the possibility of consulting the Bailiff of that Island before making a decision. It is true that we can write Jersey on the matter but we should probably have to wait a fortnight at least before before getting a reply and that is too long when a pistol is held at one's head. The Secretary and President of the Education Council have already had preliminary talks at the F.K. and have been told that the measure is recommended by the Germans but that if it is not accepted we shall have to take the consequences when the matter is reported to headquarters in Paris. So the game goes on with the local administration as an ever more badly bruised buffer between our population and the Germans.

Apparently the Russians are meeting with spectacular success in their push forward and in North Africa we are doing extremely well. Inevitably we are thinking again of the end of the war and the most gloomy pessimists are forecasting the end of the war this year. Certainly the Germans are not happy and there is little talk from them of offensives. They seem tired and they all think the war cannot end (in their favour of course) in less than two years.

To me Peace and all it means seems no more than an extravagant and heavenly dream and the relaxation it would allow our keyed-up nerves would be almost dangerous. I suppose the war must end sometime but I can scarcely remember what life was like before September 1939 and the full realization that an end will come is as far from my comprehension as infinity.

FRIDAY, 22ND JANUARY TO SATURDAY, 23RD JANUARY

Next Wednesday there is to be a very large scale artillery practice with Lihou Island, Herm, Jethou, the north end of Sark and Houmet Paradis as the targets for most of the guns on this island, except the very heavy ones. It is bad enough having the shells whizzing overhead en route for Herm but when the guns from the west of the Island aim at Houmet Paradis a shell falling three hundred yards short on a distance of about eight miles will land in a large block of greenhouses. If they are short by seven hundred yards they will go clean through our roof! The Bailiff has written General Müller asking whether some other target, not so close to valuable glasshouses and other property could be chosen.

Today (Friday) Jim Le Page, Allan Grut, Mr Edmonds and I went with Krefft to Victoria Road Chapel to examine the locks on the doors and the catches on the windows. Apparently someone has broken in recently and some valuable cameras are missing. The F.K. asked me again recently to take over the keys of this building but I refused on the grounds that the F.K. requisitioned the radios and cameras and, under the Hague Rules, were responsible for their replacement intact or the payment of indemnity to the owners whether they win the war or not.

Queenie and I received a letter from Leonard today and one arrived at the office for me from Major Stockwell. It gives so much detail of camp life that I am including it in these notes.[6] We have also received from the F.K. details concerning transfers of money to internees and the sending of letters and parcels. We are going to set up an organization of sorts to work in conjunction with the Post Office to do the necessary work.

I met a distinguished Belgian today (Saturday) who, in peacetime was the Secretary of the International Committee for combating the Colorado Beetle. He is in the Island in connection, apparently, with measures against typhus and he thinks conditions here are very bad and that the risk of infection is a real one.

SUNDAY, 24TH JANUARY TO WEDNESDAY, 27TH JANUARY

The war news is getting better and better, with the Russians advancing in many sectors and North Africa going well. The German communiqués are despondent and so are those Germans with whom I come into contact.

On Sunday Dick and I went to Herm, collected about two hundredweight of fir cones and sailed back to St. Sampson's in 37 minutes.

The arrangements for the sending of parcels, letters and money to internees are completed as far as we are concerned and I have prepared everything to go into the paper tomorrow. The Post Office, as usual, is offering free help in collecting letters and parcels.

Today at Grange Lodge Zachau asked me to make arrangements at the Regal Cinema for medical inspections of certain of our population. I asked whether we could furnish civilian doctors to be present with the German doctors who are carrying out the examination and was told this would not be necessary. I said I could not be responsible for making the arrangements and insisted on an officer from Grange Lodge taking charge. I asked a few leading questions about evacuations but received no direct answer. It looks, however, as though some of the persons on the list of people punished for criminal offences are to be evacuated, together with some men who have

---

6   See Item 16: Letter from Major Stockwell: Conditions in Biberach [nd], p.316.

served as officers in the British Army. I pointed out that we would be wanting to make arrangements for their comfort, etc., and would like to know the exact number concerned, but here again I drew a blank. Doubtless we shall learn more during the next few days. Meanwhile, our long-suffering population is to be subjected to more worry and sorrow.

We are sending in a protest against the order regarding the compulsory teaching of German in our schools.

Queenie and I went to a performance of *The Ghost Train* and thoroughly enjoyed it, especially the magnificent Heath Robinson effects by Jack Hart.

THURSDAY, 28TH JANUARY

This morning when I reached the office I went over to the Bailiff and obtained his signature to a letter and notice for the papers concerning communications with our internees, then I went on to *The Star* office and handed them in with a short verbal explanation.

When I arrived back at Maison Allaire Madeleine was waiting outside for me. She held a letter and said that the Bailiff had received it and wanted to know what it meant. I took it from her and read that, by order of General Müller, Officer Commanding the Channel Islands, the Bailiff was required to present himself at the Regal Cinema with the members of his family, at 5.30 p.m. on Saturday next for a medical examination. At the bottom was a footnote to the effect that arrangements would be made to prevent the Bailiff having to wait his turn for examination. I was so dumbfounded that I laughed and ran in to Mr Leale with the letter.

In his dark and cheerless little room with the sham oak panelling and a surfeit of draughts were Mr Leale, Mr Sherwill, Dr Gibson and Raymond Golding. I handed the letter to Mr Leale and he read it out incredulously. There was no doubt in the minds of any of us as to the reason for the examination and we wondered whether we were dreaming. I telephoned the Bailiff and told him that I would go immediately to Grange Lodge and ask for an explanation. This I did, and having first seen Inspector Zachau regarding the arrangements for the Regal Cinema I went on to Baron von Aufsess and asked why the Bailiff had received the letter.

He assured me that the letter did not mean that the Bailiff would be evacuated but that the General had ordered that all persons considered as possible evacuees were to be examined. He added that, in his opinion, the Bailiff would not leave the Island. I asked whether the Bailiff of Jersey had also been examined and he replied that in Jersey the orders were issued by another General who worked in a different way. I thanked him for the explanation and calling for Zachau left the building and went on to the Regal. I had not been in this cinema for quite a considerable time and I

114

was astounded at its delapidated condition. Holes are not infrequent in the luxurious carpets in the gangways, the velvet armrests on the seats show signs of heavy wear and, in many cases, have even lost their padding. It is difficult to imagine how such a dingy atmosphere can have taken the place of the spruce comfort in this new building. All English signs have disappeared from the walls and great patches of damp are showing through in the lobby. The whole place reminded me of an ancient and untended railway waiting room. We arranged for the rooms we needed and I went off back to the office where I reported the information I had received and went over to the Bailiff to set his mind at rest.

While I was in the office, talking to Colonel Brousson, the Colonel's clerk came in with the mail and sure enough, he too had one of the fatal envelopes. He opened it and accepted the news like a true soldier with a laugh.

Back in Mr Leale's room I discovered that reports of summonses had been coming in all the morning. Five doctors had received them, including Dr Symons. So had Colonel Randall and an old soldier of over eighty. Soon we heard that one had arrived at Mr Sherwill's home and then Mrs Leale telephoned to say that one had arrived for him. News continued to pour in, Vic and Ted Dorey, Mr Frossard and later Raymond Falla and Major Langlois reported receiving letters.

This afternoon Mr Leale, Mr Sherwill, Dr Symons and I went to Grange Lodge and had quite a friendly chat with Baron von Aufsess on the subject. It may sound strange to say that the conversation was friendly when it must affect adversely so many of our people but we know what the public does not and that is that the Feldkommandantur are the only friends we possess and the talk was mainly an assurance from the Baron that he would do his utmost on our behalf. And I know that he will.

So today has passed, bringing worry and grief to many innocent people and sympathy for them from those of us who are exempt – so far. Perhaps one day it will seem strange to read about all this. To me, at present, it seems almost part of the daily routine and to most of those who have to submit to the examination it is, to judge from the way they have accepted the news, rather in the nature of an adventure.

FRIDAY, 29TH JANUARY TO SUNDAY, 31ST JANUARY

All the letters summoning people for medical examination have now been sent out and the actual medical examinations are finished too. I was at the Regal on Friday afternoon to see that there was nothing to complain about in the arrangements and one of the first arrivals was an old soldier who has spent quite a long time in the mental home as a patient. The fact of having to submit himself for examination by German doctors brought on a bout and his roars and struggles in the empty theatre, with three or four people, including a German soldier, holding him, lent a weird and hellish atmosphere to the whole proceedings.

The examination was most cursory; in fact, only those who said they had something wrong with them were examined at all.

Inspector Oser is looking after the interests of agriculturalists who are affected and Taborski is writing on behalf of Major Barritt Hills, Heggs and Bertram Bartlett. In addition we drew up a list yesterday (Saturday) of members of the administration, doctors, dentists and clergy, whom the Controlling Committee look upon as important to the running of the Island and I gave it to the Baron this morning with a covering letter signed by Mr Johns. Mr Johns signed it because Mr Leale's name appeared on the list.

Now we have to await developments obediently, like good little children.

The war news seems very good. Goering made a speech yesterday in which he said that up to now the German people had had great victories but that they were receiving set-backs and must be prepared to die for their country. Such a message to a country which is already war-weary can surely have no very heartening effect. The F.K. these days seem more friendly and understanding than I have ever known them before.

On Saturday evening we went to a dance at Sunnycroft and a few of our friends came back for an impromptu party. We went to bed at four o'clock. We have plenty of fun of our own making.

José today weighs 15 lbs 12 oz. No teeth yet, but a few bumps in her gums which we believe will sprout soon.

MONDAY, 1ST FEBRUARY TO WEDNESDAY, 3RD FEBRUARY

Monday and Tuesday I spent talking at Hirzel House, generally expressing horror at the upset in our administration and trying to find ways and means of repairing the breaches which looked like appearing and mooning around Grange Lodge asking for whatever information they had to give. The Baron told me on Tuesday that Vaudin and Barnett would be interned but that they would be allowed to remain in Granville for a month to teach our new agents their work. He asked that we should immediately set about finding men to replace Vaudin and Barnett. I reported the news to Mr Leale and we called George Vaudin in to break it to him. He took it like nearly everybody else – with a smile and a shrug of the shoulders. Raymond Falla and I went to Grange Lodge early in the afternoon to ask whether anything could be done to obtain their release and suggested that we should write on the matter. Back we came to Mr Leale and together we drafted a letter explaining how difficult it would be to replace both of them and especially George who has been in France for more than two years, speaks French well, understands the French character and is known to all the French and German officials who are concerned with feeding the Islands and has an extensive business experience. When I handed the letter to the Baron he said that he had already made the same points to the General in a report but would send on Mr Leale's letter.

The Baron promised to give me full details of the internees today and this morning I was at Grange Lodge by half past eleven. He did not have the list with him but he told me that the Bailiff and Mr Leale, Dr Symons, Major Barritt Hills and Heggs would remain here. Mr Sherwill, however, is to go and while I was with him he telephoned to him to let him know. It was obvious to me that the Baron did not like the job but he behaved like any gentleman would and did not shirk an obvious duty, saying how much he regretted having to make known this decision.

I then went on to Inspector Zachau and asked whether the people who had had a medical examination were to be told if they were to be interned. He said that directly they had obtained a boat and knew when it would be available they would send notices giving the internees details of their departure. I pointed out that everyone concerned was on tenterhooks and it would be a kindly act to put their minds at rest. He agreed but said that he did not see how this could be done since they could not use the newspapers and had too much work to do to send out preliminary letters. I asked whether we could help and he agreed that I should copy out a list of those who had been examined medically. This I did and was then given the names of those on the list who would be exempted.

By ten minutes to one I was back at the office and reading out in Mr Leale's room the names of many of our friends who would be disappearing soon. We were back again in one of our periodical crises, with our little world crumbling before our eyes. What a painful operation it is!

Then Mr Leale telephoned the Bailiff to make an appointment to see him this afternoon. At half past two we met at the Bailiff's Chambers and I read the list once more. We discussed the possibility of doing something to save Mr Sherwill and the clergy and decided that the Bailiff and I should make an appointment to see the General. I therefore telephoned the Baron and he said that he doubted whether the General would see the Bailiff and asked whether the Bailiff would go and see him on the subject. All three of us went and I introduced the Bailiff who had not met the Baron before. He said he would try to make an appointment for the Bailiff but did not think the General would change his mind. After a short and very friendly talk, the Baron being genuinely sympathetic, we left, after the Bailiff and Mr Leale had thanked him for his efforts on behalf of our population. Mr Leale suggested that we should go and thank Inspector Oser too, but he was not in the building and we went on to Inspector Zachau who said that he did not deserve any thanks since he did only what he was told to do by the head of the Feldkommandantur.

Back at the office we sent off letters from the Bailiff to all those who would have to go, expressing regret at having to impart the news and advising them to make all their preparations forthwith. I telephoned, too, to many people I know so that they would have as much warning as possible and once more I was proud to belong to a nation whose people could take such disastrous news so gallantly.

Tonight I have had to answer the telephone quite a number of times and I have wished each time that I could give some reassuring news instead of confirming fears.

Even now we know that the war has not shewn us more than the hem of its hideous garment and we think with profound pity of women and children in both friendly and enemy cities who run screaming for shelter at the very sound of aero-engines. Surely, this horrible and somehow inevitable war will not last much longer.

THURSDAY, 4TH FEBRUARY AND FRIDAY, 5TH FEBRUARY

Thursday opened for me with a telephone call from Inspector Oser at 9 o'clock to tell me that no arrangements had been made for the Bailiff's interview with the General since they had received word that Colonel Knackfuss was coming over. The Baron was of the opinion that the results might be more in our favour if the Colonel was left to take up our case. I agreed and breathed a sigh of relief at the news that the man whose duty it is to safeguard the interests of the civilian population would be on the spot to help us, or, at any rate, to state our case and to see that the grave consequences to the community which would result from the internment of key men is fully realized before any final decision is made. The Colonel arrived, I believe, at 5 p.m. today (Friday) and there have therefore been no further developments in the situation as yet.

Today Inspector Zachau told me that he had received a message from the Hafenkommandantur to the effect that they might be ready to take the evacuees next Sunday. He told them that he could not possibly be ready by that day and I thanked him for saying so.

Several times lately I have been told by members of the F.K. that they are surprised that my name did not appear on the list of persons to be evacuated. They say, laughingly, that I am the States' spy, that I express my views too strongly and one of them even suggested, unless I misunderstood him, that I was given to listening to conversations from outside rooms at Grange Lodge. It was on the tip of my tongue to protest angrily at this last remark, but I saw it was said banteringly so I said nothing. I did wonder, though, whether they really believe I would lower myself to adopt such methods to hear conversations which cannot be any business of mine. Anyway, even after more than two and a half years I understand practically no German at all although they think my ignorance is entirely feigned. It may very well be that I shall one day be caught up in the net despite the fact that in all my dealings with the Germans I endeavour always to to act correctly and with an entirely open mind.

This afternoon I went to see the Sherwills at their home and the full significance of internment was brought home to me when I saw household valuables being packed and Mrs Sherwill working at full pressure to prepare herself and her family for departure. War is certainly cruel to innocent people and doubly so when they are being taken away by their enemies to an enemy country. No longer do I imagine that the sufferings of humanity – at any rate their mental sufferings – have become less with the growth of Christianity. I know, of course, that they will be treated as well as possible in the internment camp and that similar conditions must prevail with the internees of all nations. My complaint is not against Germany but against war in general. Last night, and often recently, the night has been made hideous with the noise of aero-engines and anti-aircraft guns and I have lain in bed hoping that no plane would be hit and thinking of the human beings whose nerves would soon be torn to shreds by the scream of falling bombs and the hum of aircraft hovering overhead looking for their targets and I have thought that the urge to bring children into this world owes nothing to reason.

SATURDAY, 6TH FEBRUARY TO MONDAY, 8TH FEBRUARY

On Saturday morning at Grange Lodge I was told that the notices to individual evacuees were ready for delivery and that they wished me to arrange for our police to do this work. I was pleased to do so since it gave us an opportunity to make a list of those to whom notices were being sent and to include in the envelopes a note from the Supervisor regarding arrangements for custody of property etc., one from Mr Johns about arrangements for transport from homes to boat and one drawn up by me to explain the meaning of 'dependent children' since this was not clear in the German notice.

Today (Monday) a subsidiary set of notices has been issued to people whose cases were not decided on Saturday and we have been notified of five people who have been exempted. In addition, Mrs Sherwill and the two boys are allowed to stay here.

Yesterday the Bailiff, Mr Leale and I went to Grange Lodge and saw Colonel Knackfuss and Baron von Aufsess. They had just spent two hours with the General trying to get exemptions for some of the proposed internees whose presence in the Island is vitally important to the satisfactory working of Island life. They had met with no success and said that Mr Sherwill would have to go. The Bailiff expressed his consternation at this decision and said he could not administer justice in the Island without Mr Sherwill, in view of the fact that we have only two other lawyers here and neither of them experienced in the duties of a Crown Officer. Eventually the Colonel asked whether the Bailiff had written on the subject and as he had not it was suggested that a letter be sent in today. This the Bailiff did and I delivered it to the Colonel this morning. He said it was quite satisfactory and this afternoon he and the Baron went once more to the General to fight our battles. I have not yet heard the result.

This morning the Baron said the population was like a chicken, the Feldkommandantur wanting it to carry on laying eggs and the General wanting to eat the bird.

The people of St. Sampson's have signed a petition asking that Mr Frossard be allowed to remain in the Island and I delivered it to the Colonel with the letter about Mr Sherwill. The petition was addressed to the General.

Today we hear that one or two people here have received letters from our September internees hinting that there is a possibility of repatriation and this news will undoubtedly cheer those who have to go this time.

TUESDAY, 9TH FEBRUARY AND WEDNESDAY, 10TH FEBRUARY

It has been decided that Mr Sherwill must go to Germany. I think that the Feldkommandantur officers are almost as upset as we are but there is nothing more to be done. Mr and Mrs Frossard are to stay, together with several other people whose cases have been taken before the General by the F.K.

The evacuation has been put off three times so far because of the weather and is arranged at present for Friday. Meanwhile, today we have received the ominous order to see that luggage belonging to men is packed separately from that belonging to women and children. Apparently families are to be split up and all men under 64 years of age are to be put in a separate camp. What this means can only be imagined by putting oneself in the place of those who are leaving the Island and when I think how I would feel if I was going into a strange country and leaving Queenie and José to fend for themselves miles and miles away, my heart sinks. The Bailiff and Mr Leale are to see the Colonel tomorrow to ask whether any other arrangements can be made or, at any rate, to discover the reason for this measure. We think there may just possibly be a chance that the old men and the women and children are to be sent to England – but that chance seems pitifully remote. Mr Bartlett and his family were exempted at the last moment last September and were actually taken ashore when on the boat. If they had gone together then they would not have been parted. Now it looks as if he will be separated from his wife and child when they get to Germany. Meanwhile I can well imagine the feelings of all those who are waiting to go.

We hear rumours of the spread of some disease among the foreign O.T. workers and the F.K. have issued an order that no foreign worker or uniformed member of the O.T. are to visit places of entertainment or public bars in the Island. Besides being a measure against the spread of infection, this will help the financial position, since quite a large amount of German money is spent here in this way.

We have found two heroes to take the places of Vaudin and Barnett in Granville – Louis Béghin and Maurice Guillemet and they will be crossing to France either at the end of this week or some time next week.

Today I delivered to the F.K. a petition signed by about 500 inhabitants of the Vale asking for the retention of Mr James, the Rector of the Parish. The Baron accepted it but pointed out that Mr Frossard had been allowed to stay here not because of his ministry but because of his public work. He thought that the petition for Mr James would prove absolutely useless.

THURSDAY, 11TH FEBRUARY AND FRIDAY, 12TH FEBRUARY

Yesterday morning the Bailiff, Mr Leale and I went to Grange Lodge to see Colonel Knackfuss. We told him we understood that the families to be evacuated were to be split up, the women and children going to one camp and the men to another: the only men to remain with the women being those over 64. We said that this would cause great suffering and asked whether something could be done to alter this decision. He said that he realized how disagreeable this was and that he could imagine if he were in the position of the head of a family. He explained, however, that the order came from the authorities who would be taking over the evacuees when they reached the mainland and that the difficulty was that there was no room in the camp where the women were going for the men as well. Apparently this camp is something rather special, with facilities for the education of the children. The men will probably go on to Laufen. He regretted he could do nothing in the matter. We also spoke about Mr James, the Rector of the Vale and the Colonel promised to try once more to get him exempted. Unfortunately this attempt came to nothing.

There is apparently another outbreak of typhus here and the Colonel assured us that he was taking all possible measures to stop it from spreading. He said he was especially strict because his father died of this disease in the last war.

And now, today, we have seen about a hundred and fifty more of our friends go off and, as before, we have found it difficult to part. I saw one toddler going off to the medical examination with its mother and another being carried, crying bitterly, by a friend. I suppose that to communities which have had to submit to bombing the sight of a child crying with fear means very little, but to me it seemed the essence of the cruelty of war. I saw another woman going off with three children and no man to help her and I felt sick at heart.

Thirty five people were brought across from Sark but seven were exempted at the last moment because of ill-health. They are to return to Sark tomorrow, feeling, I am sure, that they have been snatched from a nightmare.

Once more I feel proud of my compatriots who show such courage and cheerfulness in the face of calamity and once more I feel grateful to the German Feldkommandantur which has done everything possible to help us. The war and patriotic hatred are forgotten when trouble is abroad and the sailors and German doctors join with us in trying to make the lot of the evacuees as easy as possible.

Mr Sherwill received from the F.K. a letter stating that he is head of the Guernsey contingent and asking anyone to whom he shows it to give all possible assistance. An F.K. officer is also travelling the whole way with the party to supervise transport and so, when the boat finally drew away from the quay into the strong wind and drizzle we felt all that could be done had been performed.

There was some delay in getting the evacuees to the boat, due in some measure to the fact that the buses which picked them up at their homes were late in arriving in Town. This in turn was caused by the fact that many people were not ready when their bus arrived, although they had all been warned to be prepared by 1.30 in order to arrive at the Gaumont by 3 o'clock.

SATURDAY, 13TH FEBRUARY TO MONDAY, 15TH FEBRUARY

We hear that our people arrived safely in St. Malo early on Saturday morning.

On Sunday Queenie, Dick, two F.K. officers and I went to Herm in *Ida*. There was a really strong westerly wind and we sailed across in less than half an hour. We collected pine cones and spent half an hour with the Le Pages. At five o'clock we motored back and were thoroughly soaked with spray and drizzle.

We have received news that the protocol is now in operation and also that we can send money to internees through Barclays, Jersey.

TUESDAY, 16TH FEBRUARY TO SUNDAY, 21ST FEBRUARY

News from St. Malo is that the evacuees were there during a visit from the R.A.F. but that only three bombs were dropped and that nobody from our party was hurt. I can well imagine the effect on people already frightened by the sea-journey and now told they are to be separated from their spouses. Many of them are old people who have left in Guernsey property which is the material manifestation of their life's work and the business-like sound of aero-engines and bombs must have seemed to them like the end of their world.

When the banks here sent in their January reports to the German department which overlooks their work, they reported the dangers involved in the present monetary conditions in the Island, and especially in regard to the piling up of R.K. notes. Barclays has now been asked by Herr Caesar of that department for a full report on the matter. They have also asked for details of the balances of persons who evacuated to England in 1940, among others.

MONDAY, 22ND FEBRUARY

Today I hear that Dr Reffler is in Tunisia, that Dr Brosch is leaving the F.K. and that the Prince is back in civilian life. I also received a letter from Alf Sarre in which he says that only 45 people left Jersey in the recent evacuation and that there was only one ex-officer amongst them. He was in charge of the internment camp in Jersey before the Occupation. He also says he has heard officially that some of the September evacuees – old people and children – have already been repatriated to England and have arrived there.

Six men came back from the Laufen camp today and I hear that they are looking anything but well.

Apparently the Russians are still advancing at an enormous rate and in North Africa where the Americans recently were pushed back, they have stopped losing ground. It is difficult, however, without radios to get a clear picture of what is happening, since we have to read between the lines of the German communiqués which naturally put the best complexion on events from their point of view.

TUESDAY, 23RD FEBRUARY TO FRIDAY, 26TH FEBRUARY

On Thursday there was a further small evacuation, the unfortunates comprising 25 people from Sark and 13 from here who received temporary exemptions recently. Among the Sark people was one family of nine children and mother – the father is dead – and I have not been able to discover the reason for their inclusion in the party. There was another family of seven children and mother and father and from Guernsey one ex-policeman left with his charming little family of four children and his wife. He only arrived back in the Island two weeks ago after nearly a year in prison.[7]

I think this was the most tragic evacuation we have had so far, because nearly all those leaving were poor people and so helpless. Some of the Sark children had never left that Island before and one small boy told me how thrilled he was with his ride in a bus to the Ladies' College where they were fitted out with clothes. I sent him off in transports of joy at the thought of a ride in a train!

Now that the protocol is in operation, the local Paymasters can no longer get German money from our banks by making available funds in Granville for us and since we shall now be cutting down our French purchases to a minimum there will be less in the shops for the occupying forces to buy. This is said to have annoyed the Division somewhat, and we hope they will for their own sakes, try to stop its operation. Meanwhile we are writing F.K. asking them to arrange that the millions of francs which we hold in Granville, something like seventy million, shall be accepted by the Bureau des Changes as payment for purchases in the near future, on the grounds that they were placed in Granville before we received notification that the protocol was in operation.

To add to our difficulties we have received notification of higher wage-rates to be paid to civilians, both foreign and local, in the employ of the Germans. As commodities purchase-able are ever fewer, this new money is bound to lead to some measure of inflation and it will also mean more R.K. notes finding their way to the banks to be piled up as an ultimate States debt.

There are now several cases of typhus amongst foreign workers here, twelve so far as I am told and in addition there are more than twenty under observation. Some weeks ago we received permission to refuse admission to public houses and all entertainments to foreign workers and men in the uniform of the O.T. and now dancing has been stopped. No public announcement of this latter measure is to be published in the local newspapers. It is a grim sight to see guards stationed outside the quarters where typus is either suspected or has been found and we wonder what the end of this outbreak will be.

---

7 Former Police Constable Alfred Le Gallez, his wife Nora and four children were deported on 25 February 1943.

SATURDAY, 27TH FEBRUARY TO TUESDAY, 2ND MARCH

We have now heard from Rumball in Granville that he has been informed that the Bureau des Changes will take all the francs we have in Granville and will give us a sterling credit at Barclays Jersey, in exchange. This is a magnificent concession and will probably save the Island something like half a million pounds. It is probably the result of Rumball's diplomacy. It now becomes unnecessary to send our letter to the F.K.

On Monday Queenie, Dick, Dr Brosch and I went to Herm and saw the sheep. It is lambing time and already there are about fifteen lambs. When we went to see the sheep in the paddock we discovered that two lambs had just been born. Both the babies and their mother were yelling at the top of their voices and galloping about. The birth could not have taken place more than three hours before. It is really thrilling to walk about a piece of unspoiled parkland right away from all signs of war and when to this pleasure is added the little voyage in one's own boat, the result is a day which leaves us all with something good to ruminate upon. We borrowed three saws and cut up about four hundredweight of pine and eucalyptus logs from dead trees and these we brought back with great satisfaction. Dr Brosch is leaving the Island soon and will be working in France. I think he loves Herm almost as much as we do and he did not want to come back to Guernsey. He looked back at Herm for the first mile of our return journey and I think he was wondering whether he would ever be able to visit it again. Somehow he seemed a tragic figure and when I thought of all his efforts to help the population of our Island I felt really sorry for him and hoped that he would come back again one day when we have the means of entertaining him and showing our appreciation.

Last year we brought over from Herm some fallen pine trees and a few that we cut down from the copse towards the southern end of the island and I am suggesting that we plant young trees now to take their place.

José now weighs 16 lbs 11 oz. Her smile warms the heart of all who see it. She is not extremely forward and does no tricks but she is healthy, good-tempered and not lacking in intelligence.

A man called Brunt has been practising abortion here and one of his "patients" has died. She was little more than seventeen years old and apparently was expecting a German baby. He has been charged in the Police Court with murder. I hear he has performed some remarkable cures here and that many people feel desperately sorry for him.

WEDNESDAY, 3RD MARCH TO TUESDAY, 9TH MARCH

Saturday, Sunday and Monday were ormering tides[8] and I obtained permission to use the boat on Sunday and Monday. Sunday, Raymond Falla, Dick and I went to Herm and took two F.K. officers with us. Dick and I spent the rest of the morning, as usual, gathering firewood and then we walked out to the Plat Houmet to hunt the elusive crustacean. We all had large baskets and Dick had a sack as well and we set to, somewhat casually at first, turning over small rocks and hoping that underneath would be found ormers in quantities. Raymond found the first one and several more before Dick was successful. Then Dick's score began to mount up and my feet and legs to get wet. In my limited experience of the sport I have found that about one in a hundred of the rocks I overturn has on its underside an ormer about an inch and a half in length and I began to get frantic as the others picked merrily at their stones while I slithered and bumped on the long seaweed like a beginner at skating. I found one eventually and felt my cup of happiness overflowing. Then I found another and that was all for the next twenty minutes or so of agony. My underpants were now thoroughly saturated and I began to feel more professional and as the others decided that their two or three dozen made it hardly worthwhile stopping where we were, we walked a mile or so roughly in a southwesterly direction until we came to the sea again. Here Raymond quietly left us and we plunged once more into the icy and slippery depths. Miracle of miracles, I found another! I was so excited that I laid my hook on the surface of the sea in order to get to grips with the monster. I slipped him a fast one and whipped him off his perch before he realized the enemy with which he had to contend. Then I reached out for the hook and discovered that, being iron, it had not floated. This was my lucky moment for in rearranging the seabed in search of the hook I found no less than twenty more ormers. Dick had collected sixty one in the same time and we suddenly discovered that we were almost frozen stiff. Herm was faintly visible in the middle distance and we set off for food and a change of clothing. We loaded a cart with our four hundredweight or so of wood and having unloaded it halfway and lifted it, truck and all, over a stile we eventually arrived at Rosaire where we loaded it on to the boat. By the time the operation was completed there was almost enough water to take the boat back to the harbour and this I did. It was now blowing really hard from the north and I hurried the others aboard the boat and started off for St. Sampson's, hoping to get there before the flood began to make against the wind. We actually were within half a mile of our destination before we met the flood, with short and steep seas which lifted our starboard

---

8   For an explanation of ormering, see Item 97: Ormers and Ormering, p.487.

quarter and drove her onwards in a smother of foam with her lee shoulder almost buried and the gunwale on that side awash. After quarter of an hour of violent corkscrew motion we got in at six fifteen.

On Monday Dick and I repeated the performance in a flat calm. This time I had ten and Dick thirty ormers.

We had another letter from Rumball this week in which he says that he has been to the Bureau des Changes again and that there is a possibility that we may, in addition to getting our present stocks of francs accepted, be able to continue to send over our surplus German money.

We have received notification from the F.K. that it becomes necessary in view of present conditions to conscript labour and that we must be ready for this. For some time past I have been told at Grange Lodge that people here are not working hard enough and when we have said that we have no unemployed we have been told that there are many people, especially in shops, who have not sufficient to do. It seems that lists of such people will have to be given to the F.K. so that if the military insist on the requisition of labour, under Article 52 of the Hague Rules, they will be able to choose names from the lists and so disorganize the life of the community to the smallest possible extent.

Dr Brosch has left F.K. 515 and sailed from Guernsey on Monday evening. It is said that he wept at the harbour and when I think of his very real affection for the Island – and its people – and of all his efforts to help us, and of the fact that he has been taken from his colleagues and is going to Caen, I am not surprised.

An F.K. order appeared in the newspapers during the week ordering the collection of all electric fires. We are looking after them when they are collected and they are to be stored at Leale Ltd in the Bordage. Mass collections and evacuations are now mere matters of routine and we take them in our stride.

WEDNESDAY, 10TH MARCH TO FRIDAY, 12TH MARCH

The military have given orders for fifty more radio sets to be taken from the central store for the use of the troops. This means two or three experts and a clerk in attendance to find sets in working order and record them. Up to now the States have had to pay such labour costs but I asked at F.K. today that the military pay in future and also on this occasion. I said we were tired of paying such charges when we had already lost our sets and they saw that point. I am to be informed soon regarding their decision.

We have two new officers in Dr Brosch's place. Major Kratzer who has been the Feldkommandant's Adjutant since they came to the Islands and is therefore not a stranger to us and Herr Hertig who has been in Jersey for six months. They both appear easy to work with and I think will fight well for us. I suppose that after the war even I will find it strange that I now look upon the F.K. – all Germans and therefore our enemies – as friends. On my daily visits to Grange Lodge there is little formality, considerable laughter and, especially during the last six months, a feeling of mutual understanding which I shall never be able to explain to my critics among evacuated friends, but if this ever brands me as a lukewarm patriot I can only refer my accusers to any member of the F.K. who will not be able to deny that I have always worked to the limits of my capacity for our population and have never by word or deed shown myself to be other than a staunch Britisher. Nevertheless, during the past few days I have felt really sorry for Herr Krafft whose family is in Nuremburg which has had two or three tremendously heavy air-raids recently.

I hear that during a recent daylight raid on Rennes about three thousand French people were killed when a bomb dropped on an open-air market. Surely such warfare is too terrible ever to be repeated in the history of mankind.

Meanwhile everybody here, English and German alike, is waiting for the second front to start and for our part we long for it as the beginning of the end of the war.

Rcently at least two sets of German officers have been making enquiries regarding the capacity and equipment of the hospitals which are still in our hands. I asked at Grange Lodge what this signified and was told that they think it possible that some sort of emergency measures are contemplated. I said that if there is any question of their being taken from us we shall certainly invoke the Hague Convention. The commentary on the Convention in the English Manual of Military Law says quite definitely that hospitals must not be taken over. Already our new Mental Home and the Victoria Hospital are in German hands.

Today we received two letters from Leonard enclosing three snapshots which he has received from England. In each of them his son is the central figure and is being held by Babe, Marg and Norman Simon respectively. It is almost like seeing Babe and Marg in the flesh again and it revives once more family affections which we hardly realized existed when we could see them every day. Little Michael looks a bonny boy and the incredible fact that we shall probably meet them again one day is the star to which we hitch our wagon.

SATURDAY, 13TH MARCH TO THURSDAY, 18TH MARCH

Mr Krafft has received news that his family is safe and all those of us who know him are glad.

128

I am informed by the F.K. that they will pay labour charges in connection with the examination and recording of radios and that they have been successful in saving our hospitals for us.

Three British airmen were sighted off the Hanois in a rubber boat and were rescued by German boats from here last Tuesday. They had apparently been at sea all night.

Rumball writes that he has handed over to the Bureau des Changes all cash surplus to our immediate requirements in Granville – from memory, the amount is 65,000,000 francs and that we are to receive a sterling credit at Barclays for it. He also asks that we continue sending him R.K. notes.

FRIDAY, 19TH MARCH TO SUNDAY, 21ST MARCH

We had four rabbits ready to eat until Friday night when they were all stolen. There are very few rabbits left in this neighbourhood now.[9]

Mrs Sherwill has received two letters from Mr Sherwill giving news of Laufen. Apparently there is sufficient to eat and life is not too uninteresting. Being in constant touch with friends in England must be very thrilling and I could almost wish that, if I had no responsibilities here, I had been shipped off.

José becomes ever more interesting. Four teeth are now visible to the naked eye and her smile and giggle are worth conjuring up. She sighs with joy when the piano strikes up and Zu's singing carries her straight to heaven. She delights in her mother's version of nursery rhymes and generally makes life worthwhile to several of us.

MONDAY, 22ND MARCH TO FRIDAY, 26TH MARCH

Yesterday and today there has been artillery practice with the sea a quarter of a mile east of the Town Harbour entrance as the target and guns from all over the Island firing. For safety's sake the General ordered the evacuation of the whole Town as far up as Lukis House in the Grange and from St. John's Church to the Val des Terres. This area included the Town Hospital and Asylum, the Platon and Victoria Homes and the Prison and accommodation had to be found for the patients of the hospitals. The prisoners with the exception of Dr Brunt were given their freedom since there was nowhere to put them and as far as I know they all came back when the danger was over. For the bedridden patients of the Town Hospital we were allowed to use the Victoria Hospital which, incidentally, is not in a bad condition. The Brock

---

9   The rabbits were kept in hutches under the kitchen window at the back of La Platte, so could not have been closer to the house.

Road and St. Stephen's schoolrooms were made available for other patients. All went well as far as we know.

Continental summer time begins next Sunday and a few days ago Mr Leale asked me to find out from Grange Lodge whether the curfew can be extended at the same time. I pointed out, on Mr Leale's suggestion, that many people cultivate gardens away from their homes and that as it would soon be daylight at nine o'clock production would begin to be delayed by the curfew. Dr Kratzer informed me today that the military did not intend to extend the curfew for the time being but he promised that the matter would be discussed further as the days lengthen. We had a friendly and rather comic argument on the matter but it was obvious that the decision had already been made and that we would have to wait a week or two before bringing it up again.

The conscription of labour has begun and over a hundred men have been called up. Most of them have come from Town shops and as far as I can gather they are given easy jobs to do. There was a story in circulation some weeks ago about eight men – Guernseymen – in German employ who were seen in a certain building in the Town by a passer-by. It was ten o'clock in the morning when he passed and he heard a piano playing and saw men leaning out of the windows.

"You don't seem to be working very hard," he said.

"No," was the reply, "we've been here since half past seven, eight of us, and our job is to sweep out this room but we've only one broom. And we get £3 a week, £3-5-0 this week, with overtime." At present it looks as though the labour which is being conscripted is not really needed but we are wondering whether the men will be given harder work to do later.

This week we have had four Red Cross messages, one from Marg and one from Beata which are replies to messages from us announcing José's birth, one from Babe and one from Des. Des says that his life is an excellent preparation for many yarns and beers. One interesting point about Beata's message is that it contains news of her baby. According to the planchette the baby was a girl called Queenie Anne. It now turns out that it is a boy called Bill!

We went to a 21st birthday party on Tuesday. It was a real Occupation party and ended at 5.30 a.m. when everybody tried to get two or three hours sleep before starting work.

There was a charming domestic scene here this afternoon with Queenie feeding the baby, myself sawing logs and a German N.C.O. painting the view from our lounge window in oils. He came the other day to ask permission to do a picture and we felt that granting such permission could do no harm to the British war effort.

SATURDAY, 27TH MARCH TO SUNDAY, 28TH MARCH

On Saturday morning while I was at Grange Lodge Major Kratzer told me that he intended ordering the Labour Office to supply conscripted men instead of issuing individual notices through the F.K. He asked what my reaction to such an idea would be and I said that my personal opinion would be that the Controlling Committee would object most strongly to undertaking such duties. I continued that the Controlling Committee had cooperated so far to the extent of supplying lists of men whose withdrawal from civilian work would disorganize such work to the least possible extent, but they regarded their duties as consisting of looking after the interests of the civilian population and would probably view more direct action in such a matter as unpatriotic. Further, it would be impossible to explain to each person called up, and to the general public, the reasons underlying apparent aid to the enemies of our country and this would make the civilian population think that the Controlling Committee was not doing its duty. I suggested that Major Kratzer must see our point of view and he answered that he certainly did. He pointed out, however, that the Labour Officer had the power to issue orders to civilians to present themselves for duty under German control, that the F.K. was not a Labour Office and that the notices sent out by the Labour Office could begin with the words "By Order of the F.K." No further discussion took place and when I returned to the office I reported to Mr Leale. He reminded me that we had received a letter from Colonel Knackfuss stating quite clearly that the F.K. would send out the notices and this point I shall bring up at Grange Lodge tomorrow.

Mrs Cortvriend has now obtained permission to use our files and minute books and she is to work in my office in the afternoons.

A British plane came over at dusk last night and apparently took photographs, since several flashes were seen in the sky at the time.

MONDAY, 29TH MARCH TO FRIDAY, 2ND APRIL

This week it was discovered that our stock of insulin had almost run out, supplies not being sufficient for more than three or four days.

Since the beginning of the Occupation we have received insulin from a German firm, Krause of Hamburg, a very small quantity from the Red Cross and some from France. Up to last May we depended mainly on Krause but then we received a communication from the F.K. saying that they had received instructions that no more of the drug was to be obtained from German firms. Despite this fact several more consignments have been received from this firm. Meanwhile, orders were sent through to our Granville buyers to procure insulin in France and two parcels were obtained from French chemists at reasonable prices. The rest has been obtained on the French black market at terrific prices. The F.K. have lately adopted a new method whereby the firm Langlois of Rennes have been appointed official suppliers of drugs for the Island and one order has been placed with them, with F.K. backing, for insulin. No insulin has come into the Island from any source this year and this is the cause of the shortage. It appears to me, however, that drastic steps to procure supplies should have been taken weeks ago and such action is our affair.

Luckily the F.K. staff doctor was in Guernsey this week – he is stationed in Jersey – and he is asking Jersey to help us out temporarily. The Bailiff has also written to the International Red Cross asking for 100,000 units (our consumption is 5,000 units a week) to form an emergency stock to meet delays in delivery of our allocation: and a telegram has also been sent to Vaudin asking him to expedite delivery of the order on Langlois. F.K. are also writing Langlois asking them to deliver immediately. I don't think anything else can be done for the time being, but if French supplies do not materialize during the next two or three weeks we shall have to take up the matter again and even more strongly.

At about half past one on Thursday afternoon Queenie was looking out of the front window when suddenly a British plane appeared flying up the Russel at a tremendous speed and so low that it disappeared behind the rocks outside Bordeaux. Apparently there were actually two planes and two more appeared today, flying south this time. Jack Corbet and Henry Bisson were fishing south east of the Town Harbour at the time and they lay down in the bottom of the boat and heard bullets from guns ashore whizzing over them. Most unpleasant for them.

Dick and I spent the first few evenings this week drawing a new plan of two terraces to be made behind the house and yesterday afternoon we started work. I wonder whether we or the work will win? There must be at least a hundred tons of soil and rubbish to move.

SATURDAY, 3RD APRIL TO WEDNESDAY, 7TH APRIL

Saturday was a magnificent day and we were full of the thought of our trip to Herm next day. At midday we went down to Bordeaux to dig cat-bait and then went back to Town. I went on to St. James' Church which was crowded for the funeral of Gervase Peek. It was delightfully quiet with the organ playing softly and everybody sitting day-dreaming and possibly thinking about their contacts with the old man who claimed their respect, and perhaps their love, despite all his little failings. He received a send-off into the next world which must have pleased him very much.

Sunday was just as perfect as the day before and we left for St. Sampson's – Dick, Raymond, Herr Krefft and I – at ten o'clock. We landed before 10.45 and began preparing wood to bring back. By 11.30 we were aboard the boat again and went off to the Rocqueries to fish for whiting. I sculled about, stripped to the waist and we caught nothing at all. We listened to some bombing in France, to the drone of aero-engines in the Great Russel and to air raid sirens in Guernsey and I wondered if we would see something of the excitement. However, nothing happened and we went back to Herm for lunch. Then we strolled up to the pinewoods again, past masses of primroses and violets and bluebells and smoked a very satisfactory pipe before finishing our work. Altogether we collected about seven hundredweight of pine and took it down to the harbour where we met Raymond who, during an hour's stroll on the beach had collected three dozen ormers, thirty crabs, three lobsters and a conger. We walked over the island to Belvoir where we bathed and then loaded the boat and came back to Guernsey full of sun and contentment.

This week the main subject of discussion at Grange Lodge has been the intensification of work by the civilian population. On Tuesday morning I spent an hour with Major Kratzer and Inspector Taborski, explaining our difficulties and today Colonel Knackfuss has arrived and the Bailiff, Mr Leale, Mr Martel, Mr Johns and I went to Grange Lodge where we went over the same ground again and heard from Mr Johns a detailed account of what he has done so far to meet the demands of agriculture, horticulture and the Germans. The Colonel said he was delighted with everything that had been done etc. and altogether was most diplomatic. A minute of the meeting will probably be an interesting record.[10]

This morning nineteen Frenchmen and their boat were brought into St. Peter Port Harbour. They were obviously trying to escape to England and I think everybody – the Germans as well as ourselves – were sorry that so gallant an attempt had failed. Two years ago sixteen Frenchmen on a similar attempt were brought in here and the leader was shot in Jersey. We hope that the same fate will not overtake any of this party.

THURSDAY, 8TH APRIL TO MONDAY, 19TH APRIL

I suppose I should make some excuse for letting twelve days pass without writing up my diary. My only reason is a spell of magnificent weather which has kept me out of doors until dark and left me too lazy to do any writing when eventually I have settled down indoors. I have been to Herm four times – twice with Dr Casper from the Jersey Feldkommandantur who is

---

10 See Item 17: Meeting with F.K.: Intensification of Work, 7 Apr 1943, p.317.

the German with the most understandable outlook that I have met so far. He is a civil servant in charge of an area in East Prussia with a population of 60,000 and he understands the difficulties of administration.

He was like a boy at play on our trips and knows something about boating and other good pleasures. I found it difficult at times to remember to treat him like an enemy and he has gone back to Jersey promising to hurry on a few matters which are outstanding but very urgent as far as we are concerned.

We are having considerable trouble with the sheep in Herm, which are dying off wholesale. The lambs too, are not thriving. There seem to be various causes for our lack of success. One is that there is not enough food for them in Herm in the winter. Last autumn they were in very good condition and we asked permission to kill off the thirty or so young rams. We were not allowed to do so and certainly they ate food this winter which should have gone to the ewes which have lambed recently. Another reason is that some of the ewes are bad mothers and were almost certainly shipped to us by the French authorities on this account. It is thought too that there is some form of disease among the sheep and many old Guernseymen have told us that in years gone by every attempt to rear sheep in Herm has been a dismal failure. Whatever the reasons the cost to the States has been prohibitive and as we were never keen on the idea of keeping sheep there at all, we feel rather sore.

Arrangements for the export of tomatoes have been proceeding during the past fortnight. M. Chatam, an Alsatian fruit merchant who is to market the tomatoes has been to the Island and has met Mr Dorey. He is to buy the fruit loaded on the ships in Guernsey but will not take responsibility for it until it is landed in Granville. We have therefore had to arrange for a 5% charge to be made on the produce, the proceeds to form an insurance fund to be held by the States. Meanwhile the twine we need for tying the plants in the greenhouses has not yet arrived and if it is not here soon the crop will spoil. It is being made specially for us and is of paper. Nobody knows whether it will withstand greenhouse conditions throughout a whole season.

British planes have passed over or near the Island nearly every night and we are almost getting used to the hideous sound of anti-aircraft guns in the small hours. The air-raid sirens seem to be sounded now every time a plane comes near the Island during day or night and their wail adds to the weird din.

It appears that the fighting in Tunisia is nearing an end and everybody is wondering what will happen next.

Something that surprises me very much is the fact that with all the bombing of Germany the Germans with whom I come into contact show very little bitterness, even though some of them have lost their homes and all know that their families are in danger. I have a feeling that most people now look on the war as something permanent and outside human control and that it is this almost subconscious outlook which kills bitterness.

José continues fascinating but has contracted the deplorable habit of grinding her four teeth together and producing a sound altogether out of proportion to her small size. Most people walk away in horror when she starts.

TUESDAY, 20TH APRIL TO WEDNESDAY, 28TH APRIL

A week of anniversaries and birthdays. Mine on the 21st, Vic's the 23rd, Queenie's the 25th, Brook Sutcliffe's the 26th, Raymond Falla's the 27th. Raymond's little boy's was on the 25th and the Sutcliffe twins' a little earlier in the month. Our wedding anniversary was on the 27th. We decided that such a crop of events called for a celebration and Queenie, Raymond, Brook and I therefore threw a party here last Saturday night. There were twenty two of us altogether without counting José who, nevertheless, made the most of whatever audiences she could collect at the beginning and end of the session. We hosts spent days collecting raw materials and managed to find adequate supplies of eats and drinks, even including half a dozen bottles of champagne which we mixed into cocktails with a very black bottle of cognac, a few lumps of sugar and a little bitters. We poured this fiery mixture into our guests when they arrived and then sat down to supper at half past eight. By the time Dr Rose had proposed the health of the hosts and Brook had replied and Rose had rounded off the subject and the patter and banter had subsided, it was half past ten and all hands set about the washing-up. This is always one of the most popular items on the programme and gives scope for a certain amount of slap-stick which is excellent fun but somewhat hard on the crockery.

Of course we had to play Beetle next and by the end of it were all worked up to a frenzy of excitement. Then came the *pièce de résistance* – two minutes entertainment per head by everybody at the party. On being invited everybody had been warned of what was expected of them and weird and wonderful were the turns produced. I am trying to collect copies of some of the items and shall pin them to this page. They seemed brilliant to us even if they appear sketchy in cold blood.[11]

The rest of the night was spent playing a few minor games and an attempt at sleeping from five o'clock onwards, all the girls sleeping in beds upstairs and the men in one long row on the floor of the lounge.

---

11 See Item 18: Birthday Entertainment 1: Doctors Sutcliffe & Rose, p.320 and Item 19: Birthday Entertainment 2: Controlling Committee au Cabinet, p.322.

If the war has done nothing else, it has taught us how to play with gusto and I sometimes wonder how long it will take us to return to our more insipid and sophisticated forms of pleasure.

There has been more activity than usual round these waters lately. Last week a British plane laid some mines near the north of the Island and minesweepers have found and blown up three of them. We hear there are several boats in St. Malo which show signs of fighting and yesterday afternoon a convoy, presumably coming from Granville to Guernsey, was attacked by aircraft off Jersey. It seems that two of them were sunk and a third damaged and as we are expecting Vaudin and Rumball on a visit, we were all very worried this morning. However, Grange Lodge very kindly telephoned Jersey for us and discovered that both of them are safe and well in Jersey. Until they arrive we will not know whether they were on one of these boats or not. There is also a possibility that the tomato twine which we need for our crop was in one of the wrecked ships and if this is so about half the plants in our greenhouses will be useless since it is most improbable that fresh supplies of twine will be available in time. The twine was ordered in France and had to be made specially for us.

A few days ago I met a Scotch girl who left here in the January evacuation and has just been sent back from the internment camp at Compiègne, near Paris. She says that food and quarters were not too good and that Red Cross parcels were extremely welcome. In the camp were the women and children and men of over 64. She thinks they have all been sent on to Germany where the women and children will be in a camp with their husbands and fathers. They have seen no air raids at the camp and apparently the discipline is very strict.

There is very little to report on Island life in general except that during an artillery practice recently a shell which exploded prematurely did considerable damage to a bungalow at Rocquaine.

At Grange Lodge all is peaceful.

THURSDAY, 29TH APRIL AND FRIDAY, 30TH APRIL

At Grange Lodge all is peaceful!!! What a temptation to Providence and how Providence has jumped at it! This morning before I left home I received a telephone message from Grange Lodge asking me to arrange for the Bailiff and Sir Abraham Lainé and myself to meet Major Kratzer at 11.45. We guessed at once that the meeting would have something to do with food supplies and we were not mistaken. The memorandum of the meeting gives full details.[12] We came away from Grange Lodge at 12.30 fuming, and I

---

12 See Item 20: Meeting with F.K.: Reduction of Food Rations, 30 Apr 1943, p.325.

made arrangements for the Controlling Committee to meet the Bailiff this afternoon at three o'clock. Then I took the letter to Mr Leale and heard a quick verbal translation before dictating my notes.

At three o'clock we met in the Bailiff's room and had a very frank discussion of the order.[13] Some members of the Committee thought it time to give up trying to help our population, or perhaps it would be better to say that they thought the interests of the population would best be served by resigning. However, they arrived at no decision but decided to meet again when a letter to the Germans had been drafted by Mr Leale. It was also suggested that an effort be made to obtain permission for the Bailiff to talk to the Bailiff of Jersey over the telephone and I went to the Feldkommandantur to see what I could do. I was ushered into Major Kratzer's room and he said he had no objection but would have to ask the Colonel's permission. He tried to get in touch with him immediately and while we were waiting for the call from Jersey he asked whether we had discovered any difficulties in putting the order in operation and whether these difficulties would form the subject of the conversation between the two Bailiffs. I said we had found many difficulties and that the Bailiffs would probably discuss them.

He also asked whether we intended calling for the aid of the Protecting Power. This was suggested at the meeting this afternoon but I was not authorized to say so and I therefore hedged by saying that we did not know who our Protecting Power was. He smiled and said surely the Bailiff must know but I explained that we were occupied very early in the war and as that we were the first part of the British Empire to be occupied by the German forces the question of a Protecting Power had never arisen before. He seemed so incredulous and amused at our ignorance that I asked which country was the Protecting Power for Germany. He coughed a bit and said he thought Switzerland was. I grinned and he said that he didn't have to know such things as he was not the member of the Government.

A bread ration of under three pounds a week for the greater part of our population and there I was talking to a German – and laughing with him too – who I knew to be hating the very thought of the task he was called upon to do. And as a background to this grim Alice-in-Wonderlandish conversation I looked out of a first floor window into an expanse of sunlit greenery with the wind playing magically in it. And in one corner of that cheerful-looking room the radio was reproducing a perfectly delightful 'cello concerto. Eventually they got through to Jersey and discovered that the Colonel was not available but tonight I hear that the conversation has been arranged for 12.45 tomorrow.

---

13 See Item 21: Meeting Bailiff & C.C.: Reduction of Food Rations, 30 Apr 1943, p.328.

The local doctors have had a meeting today to discuss the effects on the population of the reduction in rations.

Mr Leale read me the first draft of his letter when I returned to the office and I thought it was masterly.

Yesterday afternoon I met Major Kratzer at Rousse, Grand Havre where the military are pulling down three cottages which are apparently in the firing line for some of the guns. When we arrived the work of demolition was in full swing, with the occasional sound of breaking glass and the thud of iron mallets smashing through the interior walls of a cottage which some poor Islander had scraped together enough money to build. The wallpaper still clung pitifully to the broken walls and the roof was a mass of broken slates forming a carpet round the remains of the house. I'm not an expert at analysing emotions but I felt an overpowering anger that this should be going on in our little Island and in a place which, as children, we looked upon as our especial province.

I asked Major Kratzer whether it was really necessary to break every slate – costing 1/6 each nowadays – when we have few if any supplies of new ones in the Island and offered to send men down to take off the roof of the remaining cottage. This we are going to do and we may also collect any materials except wood!

Usually in cases where houses are demolished – and there have been a considerable number – we are informed beforehand and in some cases we have been able to salvage part of the fabric, but in this case I can find no trace of any information being received by us.

There is a general feeling abroad these days that a crisis in the war is very near at hand and we wonder, quite objectively so far, how much of it we shall see here. That Germany is still very strong there can be no doubt, but I cannot help feeling that as a nation, they are more war weary than we are and I find myself wondering whether any attack now on the continent, especially if not initially successful, will not give them renewed strength instead of causing a breakdown.

SATURDAY, 1ST MAY AND SUNDAY, 2ND MAY

Most of yesterday morning (Saturday) was spent in discussion of the rationing order and the principles involved.[14] All members of the Committee agree that the line to be taken must be a strong one but the question of resignations has faded out again, as it always does when wisdom returns to take the place of more theatrical sentiments. If the whole Committee resigned it simply means that the Bailiff would have to ask the States to elect another President

---

14 See Item 22: Meeting Bailiff & C.C.: Reduction of Food Rations, 1 May 1943, p.330.

and it is most unlikely that the new President and Committee would be nearly as good as the one already in power. As for the Bailiff he has orders from the British Government to look after the interests of the population through the Occupation, so there is no question of his resigning. Also, since the members of the Committee are chosen by the President, who alone is elected by the States, the resignation of any member would merely be an embarrassment to the President under most circumstances.

Dr Symons submitted a draft of his report on the probable effects of the reduction in rations on the health of the population and this will accompany the Bailiff's letter to the Germans.

One point on which there is some difference of opinion among the members of the Committee is clause 5 of the German letter, the continuance of full rations to local civilians and their families, working for the Germans directly. Some members think that such unfair treatment will cause trouble among the population and that in any case everyone should be treated alike. The opinion of the majority, however, is that almost certainly a protest would mean a reduction of everybody to the reduced rations and this would do nobody any good.

At 12.45 I went with the Bailiff and Mr Leale to Grange Lodge. We were received very politely and in a very short time Herr Krafft was in touch by telephone with Feldkommandantur Jersey where the Bailiff of Jersey was waiting. Our Bailiff's first question was,

"Have you put the rationing order into operation yet?"

The answer was,

"No, and we do not intend to do so."

The Bailiff then went on to explain that their view was that, since the order was confined in its operation to British subjects and excluded Irish and French it appeared to be a reprisal and since the sinking of the shipping involved is a legitimate act of war the order was contrary to International Law. If it was not a reprisal it is not justified in Jersey on economic grounds, since they can produce enough wheat and butter to continue the present bread and fat rations indefinitely. A letter to this effect is to be handed to the Feldkommandant in Jersey together with copies of the correspondence for transmission to the Swiss Ambassador in Berlin, Switzerland being the Protecting Power for our nation.

Mr Leale read a draft of the Bailiff's proposed letter to the F.K. and the Bailiff of Jersey agreed with nearly all of it except that we had quoted Article 50 of the Hague Convention which states that no collective penalty, pecuniary or otherwise, may be inflicted on occupied territory on account of the acts of individuals for which it cannot be regarded as collectively responsible. He thought that this Article was intended to apply to acts of sabotage, etc, and not to the acts of either of the belligerents. With this view we agreed. The Bailiff of Jersey said further that Jersey did not need to ask for help from the Red Cross but agreed that we must.

There was a further meeting of the Bailiff and Controlling Committee in the Bailiff's room during the afternoon, when the Bailiff and Mr Leale reported on the telephone conversation. One matter which the meeting discussed, almost to the exclusion of all others, was what appears to be a weakness in the Bailiff of Jersey's argument, namely that his claim that reprisals for legitimate acts of war are forbidden depends on the commentary in the British Manual of Military Law on the Hague Convention and, as far as we can gather, on no actual law which has international application. (See page 343 of Manual of Military Law.) Further, we wonder whether, if we claim that the sinking of ships containing food for the civilian population is a legitimate act of war, the Germans will use the argument at some time in such a way that it will be an embarrassment to us. The meeting broke up without the draft letter being approved and Mr Leale went off to find some form of words which would avoid the difficulty. It was decided, however, that we must back Jersey's arguments in our letter.

I gather from conversations at Grange Lodge that they look upon the order as being of some political importance and that it will not continue indefinitely.

We regard the fat ration as excluding any reduction in the butter ration, especially as we do not import butter.

One point which I find very interesting is the difference between the attitude adopted at our Friday meeting at the the F.K. when there was a quibble over the words 'reprisal' and 'retorsion' and the tone of the notice in Friday's newspaper when the cut in rations was made out to be necessary because of the loss of foodstuffs in transit.

Since my visit to F.K. on Wednesday we have understood that Vaudin and Rumball were both in Jersey but when Mr Leale asked the Bailiff of Jersey how they were he said that as far as he knew they were not in that Island but that Louis Béghin was. We were very mystified until we heard that some luggage had arrived in the Island on an oil barge which arrived here on Friday evening with diesel oil for the Electricity Department. She was lying at St. Sampson's and on Saturday afternoon I called on the skipper in his cabin. I introduced myself and explained our anxiety regarding our people from Granville and then asked whether he had any news of them. He told me they had travelled on his vessel from Granville on Tuesday and were involved in the R.A.F. attack, his ship suffering slight damage. However, his three passengers were Vaudin, Barnett and Béghin: Rumball, apparently, staying in Granville. After the attack they put into Jersey and he received so little notice before leaving Jersey again on Friday afternoon that he could not get into touch with them. They therefore remained in Jersey. During

140

his journey to Guernsey the convoy was attacked again but he suffered no damage. Some of the convoy, however, put back to Jersey again. As far as I could gather all his crew want to leave the ship as soon as he gets back to Granville and I must say I do not blame them. The skipper, however, like so many seamen is a fatalist and says he is not afraid. He does not think these waters will be very pleasant this summer. He was mainly concerned over a pair of shoes which he left here last voyage for repairs and which had not yet been returned to him by the O.T. officer who had taken charge of them.

If the order does come into force – and it is possible that we will have no option but to enforce it whatever the Germans say, if sinkings continue – it is proposed that we ask the Red Cross for a supply of flour to make up for the reduction in the total used in the production of the reduced bread ration, and for some type of meat.

Today I received a telephone message from Grange Lodge informing me that two ships had arrived and they contained 22 tons of tomato twine.

MONDAY, 3RD MAY TO WEDNESDAY, 5TH MAY

On Monday morning when we met at the office it was discovered that during the week end Mr Leale had redrafted the letter to the F.K., that Mr Martel had drafted a new one and that Sir Abraham had drafted a section on the question of reprisals. The Bailiff had drafted one to the Swiss Minister in Berlin and Mr Leale had also drafted one to him and one to the Red Cross. We went over to the Bailiff's office, Mr Leale, Mr Martel, Sir Abraham and myself, and the result of two hours work was a rehash of the letter to the F.K. incorporating sections from each draft and some new ideas as well. Before all this work was finished I was called to Grange Lodge on routine business and while there I heard a whisper to the effect that there were to be some amendments to the German order.

However, work went on and the afternoon saw typists and translators hard at it preparing the three letters, to the F.K., to the Swiss Minister in Berlin (Protecting Power), and to the International Red Cross; and Dr Symons' report to the Bailiff.

Early on Tuesday morning I was informed by telephone that the F.K. had received definite news of amendments to the order and that these amendments would take the form of a letter which we would receive during the day. Meanwhile we were to stop the work of preparation. I also learned that the amendments were in our favour. Later in the morning the letter was handed to me and translated in my presence so that I might put questions which I thought might arise.[15] In effect the amendments were that the only

15 See Item 23: F.K. to Bailiff: Food Ration Order, 3 May 1943, p.332.

real cuts would be in the bread ration and that these cuts would affect the whole community regardless of occupation or nationality, with the exception of persons under 21 who would receive full rations. As we had based our main argument on reprisals on the fact that there was some differentiation in the treatment of different sections of the community the letters already prepared were no longer suitable and every one of them had to be redrafted. This was done on Tuesday afternoon and the whole correspondence was completed and handed in to Grange Lodge late this afternoon. The Bailiff, Mr Leale, Mr Martel and I are to meet Major Kratzer tomorrow morning to talk over the whole matter before the letters leave the Island.

On Tuesday afternoon I called on Major Kratzer and said we trusted he did not regard us as discourteous in not discussing the matter with him before, but reminded him that at our Friday meeting he had said that matters of principle were the subject of orders from Paris and therefore could not be discussed at the F.K. He said that he had not regarded our silence as discourteous and I explained that the new order had led us to think that the Bailiff of Jersey had had discussions with the Colonel in Jersey. He answered that the amendments came from Paris and not from Jersey. One F.K. officer had expressed to me his admiration for the Bailiff of Jersey on Tuesday morning.

Our translators were: German: Messrs. Hollard and Dobrez; French: The Reverend E. L. Frossard. Their work has been excellent.

This evening Mr Leale telephoned and asked me to think over the advisability of telling the Swiss people that two of our foremost administrators – Messrs Sherwill and Sayer – are interned at Laufen and suggesting that, if it is impossible to come here, the matter should be discussed at Laufen. We are to ask Major Kratzer's advice on this matter tomorrow.

Meanwhile, and as usual, the most conflicting rumours are current in the Island and one section of the community seems to be satisfied that at last the Controlling Committee is is fighting the Germans and that if they had done so before the population would not have suffered as it has. Another section say that at last the Controlling Committee is fighting, having been brought to their senses by the fact that their own bellies are involved this time.

THURSDAY, 6TH MAY AND FRIDAY, 7TH MAY

Thursday morning found the Bailiff, Mr Leale, Mr Martel and me at Grange Lodge where we met Major Kratzer and Hertig. The minute of the meeting is very full and I need not repeat here the substance of the discussion.[16] What I could not put into the minute, however, is the effect on us of the

---

16 See Item 24: Meeting with F.K.: Reduction of Food Rations, 6 May 1943, p.333.

various phases of the discussion. I was told that the Major had had a very long discussion over the telephone with Jersey earlier in the morning but I attached no importance to it. We went into Grange Lodge thankful that the letters were safely delivered and looking forward to the relaxation of dotting the 'i's and crossing the 't's in the form of ramming home subsidiary arguments. Instead we were allowed to talk for a little and the F.K. trump card was gradually introduced into the conversation and finally thrust under our noses. Jersey did not intend to appeal at all and had signed the order for the reduction of the bread ration. Furthermore, the Bailiff had issued a notice saying that he had received an assurance from the F.K. that the cut was in no way a punishment to the population. They followed up this bit of information by asking whether we wished to proceed with our appeal and stating that the Colonel ordered us to put the cut into operation by next Monday. We were completely taken aback. We had couched all our correspondence with a view to making an appeal in company with Jersey and had taken pains to make certain we did not clash with the Jersey arguments. We asked for a day to think out our course of action and we also asked that arrangements be made for our Bailiff to speak to the Bailiff of Jersey by telephone, hoping thereby to find out why Jersey had suddenly taken up an attitude which was totally inexplicable to us, especially as they are self-supporting in wheat and could therefore claim that the cut in rations was not necessary on economic grounds. We were told soon after the end of the meeting that the Colonel would not allow the conversation to take place and this made us more uneasy and suspicious than ever. Up to now we have heard nothing from Jersey but I am wondering whether, since the second German order does not alter the total flour saved but is simply a redistribution of the cut throughout the population, and since Hertig says the Bailiff of Jersey is a marvellous man, the second order is really the result of his negotiations. As far as Jersey in concerned, once the cut is evenly distributed over the population, and in view of the fact that the flour is on the Island, it should be possible to issue the extra flour in some form other than bread. I can well understand that if this is so the Bailiff would be quite willing to give up the idea of appealing to the Protecting Power.

But what about Guernsey? Whatever we do, we have not much more than one half Jersey's area of land per capita and much of that is either under glass or in the hands of the troops or the O.T. so it is quite impossible for us to produce our requirements in wheat. In fact we only have about twelve weeks' supply of flour in the Island and we cannot distribute extra flour without the fact becoming evident to anyone who may scrutinise our statistics of stocks. We must therefore either make the strongest possible appeal or accept rations which we know to be altogether inadequate for the maintenance of the health of our population.

Of course we have chosen the former alternative. There was a meeting of the Bailiff and the Controlling Committee on Thursday afternoon when this was decided and when the order reducing the rations was drafted. This order states quite clearly that the reduction is the result of F.K. orders and care was taken to let the public know that it is to be regarded as a temporary measure. The Bailiff is signing no notice at all.

I took the order up for F.K. approval late in the afternoon and Major Kratzer came out into Krafft's office and taking it from Krafft's hands passed it to me with a bow, saying, "*C'est une action célèbre.*" I must have looked a bit glum, because he added, "*Vous n'êtes pas content?*" I said I was not and that we regarded the cut as something calamitous. He stopped smiling and said he was sorry and hoped that the cut would be purely a temporary measure. Tonight he has spared no pains in making arrangements for a German boat to go to Sark post-haste to bring back a Sarkee who has to undergo an urgent operation for appendicitis.

Today we have concentrated on the redrafting of all the letters of appeal to meet the new situation, omitting altogether the legal aspect, concerning which we were never very happy about. What a tiresome business it has been, pulling letters about for the third time and wondering whether they would ever reach their destination.[17]

Mr Leale has written to the Bailiff offering to go to Geneva to put our case before the Red Cross and the suggestion that we send a delegation has been incorporated in the latest draft.

It is intended that, while the order is in operation, all possible will be done to boost other rations from whatever sources we can find.

SATURDAY, 8TH MAY AND SUNDAY, 9TH MAY

Saturday morning the Bailiff signed all three letters once more and I took them to the F.K. where I saw Major Kratzer. I told him that the main difference in the redrafted letters was that all mention of reprisals had been omitted. He sat back in his chair, his eyes twinkling and said, through the interpreter, "I will now tell you the legal definition of reprisal, a reprisal is an unfair punishment for an unlawful act." Then he continued, "You maintain that the sinking of our ships by the R.A.F. is a lawful act and therefore you cannot use the reprisal argument." This apparently was an argument he was keeping up his sleeve and, quite understandably, he did not want to let his ingenuity go unnoticed even though he did not have to use it. I roared with laughter and said that

---

17 See Item 25: Bailiff to F.K.: Reduction of Food Rations, 7 May 1943, p.337; Item 26: Health Services Officer report, 7 May 1943, p.339; Item 27: Bailiff to Swiss Minister: Reduction of Food Rations [nd], p.341; Item 28: Bailiff to Red Cross, Reduction of Food Rations, 7 May 1943, p.343.

the only answer I could give was that to understand such an argument one would have to stand on one's head. I feel certain that everybody at F.K. hates having to take a hand in cutting down rations, but I think the Major is rather proud of carrying out his orders without more trouble from us. He was very insistent that the order should be in Sark on Saturday so that it could come into operation there on Monday and to me it is obvious that he wants to be able to report to Jersey that the matter is rounded off completely. I told him that we were asking that permission be sought to send a delegation from here to Geneva and he thought it was most unlikely that such permission would be granted. I also asked whether he thought the appeals would be forwarded to the proper quarters and he said that, although he could not give any guarantee, he thought they would reach their destinations.

Now we have done all we can for the time being and have to wait for results. Meanwhile a gale is raging and it is quite certain that the letters will be delayed through lack of communications with the Continent. What further delays they will encounter nobody knows.

We hear that a German troop ship was sunk between Jersey and St. Malo on Thursday night and we are wondering whether this is the British reply to the measures taken at our expense to stop attacks on shipping between France and the Islands. Everybody seems quite ready to suffer the reduced rations if the British Government thinks it necessary to sink ships.

The Tunisian campaign seems to be nearly over and everybody is asking, "What next?"

The high winds of the last few days are doing considerable damage to crops here and my potatoes are so burnt that it seems impossible that they will ever recover. Anything which may affect our food supply causes us considerable worry now and we all hope for rain and calm weather soon.

MONDAY, 10TH MAY TO THURSDAY, 13TH MAY

The North African campaign is over.

In Guernsey the first days of the week were uneventful, except that the German vet has examined all our horses, apparently with a view to knowing where suitable horses may be found in emergencies, for military purposes.

Today, however, Vaudin, Béghin and Barnett arrived and we talked for more than an hour this morning. Meeting them and hearing their stories makes one realize that we are a very small Island and not really the centre of the universe. It is easy to forget that we have men taking their lives in their hands getting food for us in France but the story of their voyage from Granville to Jersey brought it home to me as never before.[18]

---

18 On 27 April 1942, a convoy from Granville was attacked by R.A.F. fighter-bombers

They spent the first part of the journey on the oil tanker sitting against three barrels of petrol in the stern and as they did not know whether they would be calling at Jersey or not they decided to wait until they were sure before having their meal. It became obvious that they were coming straight on and George went into the cabin to open a bottle of wine. The popping of the cork was the beginning of many more pops and realising they were being attacked he dropped flat on the floor. Béghin did the same and Barnett, thinking he did not have time to reach the cabin, stretched out on the deck. The planes, of which he saw five or six, zoomed over the boat at mast-height firing as they went and although he buried his face in his hands he suddenly saw a white flash and something dropped alongside him with a thud. He looked up and saw it was a spent cannon-shell. That was enough for him and he dived head first down the three steps into the cabin where he landed on his hands and face.

The attack only lasted a very few minutes and when it was over and they were breathing a little more easily the captain came to them and told them to put on their lifebelts as they were sinking. Luckily this was a false alarm and they circled round a steamer which had been hit in the engine room by bombs and was powerless to move. They saw a lot of wreckage floating and discovered that a motorship had gone down. Eventually they reached St. Helier and had to remain there fifteen days before they could get a boat for Guernsey. During the gale last weekend they did try to get to St. Malo because there seemed to be more chance of getting here through that port but the boat they were on went no further than the roads outside St. Helier where they were anchored all night in a howling gale with one anchor chain between them and a lee shore of dangerous rocks. Then they returned to Jersey to contine their wait.

They still have to face the journey back to Granville, except Béghin who stays here. Vaudin and Barnett had been ordered to an internment camp at the beginning of the year and were allowed to go back to Granville only to teach Béghin and Guillemet the work there. This order has now been cancelled and they are allowed to continue to represent the Island in Granville.

We have two lorries in Granville and they have Island registration numbers. Béghin tells a good story of an incident during a journey undertaken by one of them. A French gendarme, puzzled by the number plate, stopped the lorry and asked our French driver what the number meant. He replied, *"Je peux seulement vous dire Monsieur, que c'est un camion américain, appartenant aux anglais, conduit par moi, un français, sous l'autorité allemand."*

---

near Jersey. One vessel, the motor schooner *Helma*, was sunk and the SS *Maas* badly damaged. The team from Granville were on another vessel in this convoy.

"*Passez!*" was the gendarme's only reply.[19]

Transport is difficult now that our gazogène lorry goes to Paris every week to bring back textiles. We have forty tons to transport and the lorry can only carry five tons each time.

Mother and father received a letter from Leonard today, enclosing a photograph of Babe and Michael and another of Marjorie and Michelle. How I long to see those charming children in the flesh. Apparently Des has gone back to Australia again. A trip across the world must be a mere matter of routine to him now. I wonder whether we shall both speak the same language when he returns.

FRIDAY, 14TH MAY TO TUESDAY, 18TH MAY

On Friday evening we were dancing at Sunnycroft in the Grange when suddenly there was a burst of anti-aircraft fire which developed into a terrific volley. Through it came the sound of aircraft and rushing to the window we saw the silver shapes of British fighters twisting and turning over the Russel. Everybody went mad with excitement and for the rest of the dance wore permanent smiles. So did we until, walking down the Grange, German ambulances began to roar past us on their way to and from the harbour. Sitting next to the driver of one ambulance on its way to hospital was a young sailor with a wounded shoulder and a look of stunned amazement which we could not forget. We went home soberly after that remembering that in this war it is mainly people even more innocent than that boy who are suffering most. If ever this war ends and I am still alive I shall look upon it as the highest honour I can attain to work in any way, however small, for the evolution of some means other than war for the settlement of differences between nations. And surely this time there will be a strong enough majority of statesmen – and not mere idealists – to ensure that the seeds of another upheaval will never take root. Such observations probably sound trite and stale but they are none the less sincere for that and I am certain that not one person in a million throughout the world still has any pleasure in this war. We all know war settles no international problem satisfactorily.

Saturday night at midnight a British plane flew up the Russel and we were awakened by a terrific anti-aircraft barrage. How it escaped being hit I do not know.

Last night we were kept awake by the noise of hundreds of aircraft and of anti-aircraft fire. How I hate it all!

---

19 "All I can tell you, sir, is that it's an American lorry, belonging to the English, driven by me, a Frenchman, under German authority."

We are still concerned here at the shortage of insulin. We have been informed by F.K. that no more drugs are to be bought in Germany and since, in practice, insulin can only be bought on the black market in France – in small lots and at exorbitant prices – I have pointed out to F.K. that our only means of obtaining supplies is through the Red Cross. The Bailiff wrote Geneva on the matter some weeks ago and F.K. are telephoning their doctors in Paris and the Red Cross in that city too in order to hurry on supplies.

There is a good story current about a Guernseyman who was told by two O.T. officials of his acquaintance that the war in Africa was over.

"Oh, really?" said he, "I have no wireless now, so I know nothing about it. Who won?"

WEDNESDAY, 19TH MAY TO FRIDAY, 21ST MAY

We have received further news from Rumball regarding the working of the protocol and I am pinning the letters to this page.[20] Whether we shall ever receive our sterling credit from Barclays after the war depends, I suppose, on whether the French authorities supply the necessary funds. Meanwhile we continue to unload all surplus marks and so the question of introducing mark accounts in the local banks is shelved for the time being.

The mornings have been delightful today and yesterday and we have been out of bed and in the water before breakfast. Even in wartime Bordeaux looks as lovely as ever in the mornings with the tide right up.

The Germans are worried about the dumping of refuse on the coast! This morning Inspector Zachau asked me to bring to the notice of the public any legislation we have on the subject. I said we would do so but reminded him that the worst offenders were not our own population. I am to give him a list of recognized dumps and he will inform the German authorities of their whereabouts.

The question of tomato production came up before the Controlling Committee this afternoon and letters from the President and Mr Dorey are going to Grange Lodge as soon as possible.

SATURDAY, 22ND MAY TO TUESDAY, 25TH MAY

The most spectacular event has been a raid by the R.A.F. on a convoy in the Little Russel on Sunday morning. We were still in bed at half past eight and had heard the drone of planes for some little time before it became louder and, looking out of the window, we saw a score or so of planes flying past the Platte Rock a few feet above the water. The anti-aircraft all along the coast

---

20 See Item 29: Rumball to Leale: Currency Transfer, 7 May 1943, p.345.

opened but they went on steadily, some of them firing at Brehon as they went. Some people on the sea side of the road shouted that a ship had been hit but long before we were dressed she had sunk.[21] As far as I can gather two other small ships and an anti-aircraft ship were damaged and none of our people saw any planes shot down. On Monday morning at Grange Lodge I was told that about six o'clock on Sunday morning four British fighters flew up the Russel and that one of them had come down in the water with engine trouble. The pilot was saved by German boats. We presume they gave notice of the convoy which they must have seen on its way here. One ship – the only one with any supplies for the civilian population aboard – had just entered the harbour when the attack took place and so, once again, we lost nothing. I asked this morning at Grange Lodge whether they had any news of the result of our petition to the Red Cross and the Protecting Power and Major Kratzer answered that he had heard nothing. He added that he had hoped that the cut in our rations would have been restored by now but after the attack on Sunday he would be pleased to hear that no further cut was to take place. I pointed out than none of our supplies had suffered and he replied that it was not a question of our supplies but of shipping in general. If they lost all their ships they could not import anything at all for us. He added that boats flying the French and even the Jersey flag had been attacked and I said I was surprised to hear that there were still boats flying the Jersey flag. We have heard of none since the *Normand* and the *Spinel* two years ago. I think he is mistaken. I also added that I thought that ships flying the French flag actually carried war materials and he said that the same ships carried supplies for us on other occasions.

We hear that Stroobant has been taken to Smolensk in connection with the 40,000 Poles who have been discovered dead in that district. Why he went and what his mission was we do not know as yet.

The question of the removal of certain graves at the Soldiers' Cemetery at Fort George has been raised again by the F.K. Apparently they wish to remove three or four graves from the section in which the Germans bury their dead to another part of the cemetery. They point out that this section is becoming full and that they wish the removal to be done so that they can keep all their graves together. They said they could do the removal themselves but that they would rather we did it. I pointed out to them that the cemetery is a British Government one and that it is doubtful whether anybody here has the power to permit the removal of bodies. They suggested that the Bailiff in his capacity of Lieutenant Governor possesses the power. I have spoken to the Bailiff and to Mr Leale on the subject and we all feel that it would probably be a good

---

21 M.V. *Oost Vlanderen*, laden with cement and guns, was sunk by the R.A.F. off St. Peter Port Harbour on 23 May 1943. Relics are displayed at the German Occupation Museum.

thing for all the German graves to be kept separate from the British. Before giving a final decision on the matter the Bailiff is going to speak to the Dean and will probably visit the cemetery with Major Kratzer. I am convinced there is no thought of insult in this German suggestion and it does seem petty to refuse to grant a concession – unless there is some good reason against it – towards men, even if they are enemies, who have died for their country.

I asked today whether the F.K. had considered the letters from Mr Leale and Mr Dorey on glasshouse production and whether they were ready for discussions on the subject.[22] Major Kratzer said that the letters would have to be submitted to Jersey for decision and Inspector Oser told me he was writing a long explanatory letter to F.K. Jersey. He added that he now knew all about our glasshouse production and was satisfied that good growers could make it pay. He saw no objection to the planting of beans and potatoes in July and August but was dead against any form of subsidy on such crops. He also disagreed with the suggestion that the G.U.B. should be enlarged again. Our experts contend that these crops cannot be made self-supporting and that a subsidy, besides encouraging growers to plant them will also give full control over the produce. At present one of the chief difficulties which we have to meet is the fact that a very large proportion of the produce grown in greenhouses never finds its way to the civilian buyer but is sold, by our own people, to foreigners of all types at prices much higher than the controlled prices. Private growers who sell in this way are, naturally, making a profit – but at the expense of our own population which is suffering from a shortage of vegetables. The obvious remedy of raising the controlled prices is one which will cause untold dislocation to our already unbalanced Island economy. The too-great purchasing power of our imported population is an evil against which we fight a constantly losing battle. We foresee chaos in the industry if Mr Dorey's suggestions are not put into operation. I hope we are wrong.

WEDNESDAY, 26TH MAY TO FRIDAY, 28TH MAY

We received a frantic message from Jack Loveridge that the German officer in charge of food stores intended taking over the main Essential Commodities food store – Young's at Glategny Esplanade – and that he was providing transport for the removal of the contents to St. George's Hall which the Germans were vacating. Mr Leale, Jack and I went to Grange Lodge to ask for their help in saving the store and when we had put our case we discovered that the F.K. had already given their consent. The memorandum of the meeting gives the main details of the discussion.[23]

---

22 See Item 30: Leale to F.K.: G.U.B. Concerns, 22 May 1943, p.347.
23 See Item 31: Meeting with F.K.: Requisition of Food Store, 26 May 1943, p.351.

On Wednesday afternoon I went with Major Kratzer and Inspector Zachau to look over St George's Hall and Young's and then we went on to the Paymaster. The Major went in to interview him alone and when he came out he said that if we could find alternative accommodation for German flour we need not vacate Young's. I pointed out that the reason given at the morning meeting for the changeover was that it would save guards and the Major replied that this was one reason but that the Paymaster also wanted to have a store farther from the sea and the harbour. I went back to the office to report and with the help of the Billeting Department we drew up a list of four buildings whicch we thought might be suitable. This morning I took Inspector Zachau and the Paymaster to see Elizabeth College gymnasium which turned out to be already in use, Morley Chapel which they turned down as being too small and La Villiaze Chapel which they would not accept for the same reason. I went back to the office with Jack where we discovered that the Quartermasters had been busy on the fourth suggestion – J.F.G. Williams on the Esplanade – and had discovered that the Germans were not using it. They thought it suitable for flour. We went back to Grange Lodge and Inspector Zachau came with us – in a steel helmet on the back of my motor cycle – to see Bragg's store at Rougeval which we offered in addition to Williams's. They said they wanted 1,000 square metres of floor space altogether and these two stores only measured 600 square metres. We therefore took him on to a garage in St. John Street belonging to W.A. Martin. At present it is used as a garage for five or six German cars and, as the unit concerned is quartered at Hotel Normandie, we suggested that the cars might be garaged at the Royal Court garage. We are still awaiting a verdict and meanwhile Mr Leale's letter of protest has not been sent. Major Kratzer himself is in Alderney.

SATURDAY, 29TH MAY TO MONDAY, 31ST MAY

Apparently we have lost the fight over the food stores. On Saturday morning Inspector Zachau informed me that the Paymaster concerned insisted on the whole 1,000 square metres of floor space being in the one building and that therefore none of our suggestions so far were acceptable. I replied that obviously there was no store of those dimensions available and the Inspector said he would submit the whole matter to Jersey by telephone for the Colonel's decision. I added that it appeared to me that the Paymaster had decided long ago to have Young's store at any price and although the F.K. do not admit this I have an idea that I am right. On Saturday afternoon I handed in the protest from the President of the Controlling Committee, copy of which I am including here.[24] This morning the Major who is back from Alderney informed me that the Colonel had decided in favour of the Paymaster and that we should therefore have to leave Young's. We are to do nothing until we have the requisition in writing from Jersey. I thanked him formally for the news and hoped that my face did not betray my feelings which were – I suppose murderous is too strong a word. Essential Commodities say the only place they can move into is St. George's Hall and that they will have to arrange for two men to sleep there each night. This will not do away with the vermin pest or with the danger of fire. F.K. seem to think that we shall be able find alternative accommodation and it is in vain that I explain that the stores I showed them, while suitable for flour are quite unsuited to less bulky and more valuable goods such as are at present stored at Young's and which are so much more easy to pilfer.

On Saturday morning about a hundred and fifty American bombers passed over the Island flying south and it is said that they attacked Rennes and some of the submarine bases on the Atlantic coast. Yesterday again some of our fishermen reported scores of British planes at the head of the Russel and it looks as though aerial activity generally is speeding up. Is the climax of the war coming at last?

We receive news from England very frequently through the Red Cross and our internees in Germany and they all seem to be very worried concerning conditions here. If they get no worse we shall count ourselves lucky.

We have pulled the boat up for painting. She has been in the water a whole year and there is not much paint left on her.

We have had three meatless weeks following due, not to attacks on shipping, but to the fact that the French will not supply us, maintaining that we should be producing enough for our own needs. This contention is ridiculous, of course, but although we have explained the position to them, supplies do not arrive. Luckily for the population, however, the fishing season is beginning well and there have already been some big catches of mackerel. Spider crabs are abundant and there are considerable supplies of ray and whiting. Fishing at Portelet has started again and we have several consignments from Sark.

Every month we hear of people being caught with wireless sets – and they are generally betrayed by anonymous letters written by Guernsey people. Both the German authorities and ourselves are disgusted.

We have to supply patrol boats to control our fishing boats at sea and this year they have been painted with the yellow nose which indicates they are German naval craft. The Guernsey crew, two men, have protested, especially in view of the increased air activity in these waters and on Saturday I took

24 See Item 32: Leale to F.K.: Requisition of Food Store, 26 May 1943, p.353.

up the matter with the F.K. while Captain Franklin saw Captain Obermeyer. The result is that this morning the yellow nose is being painted over.

TUESDAY, 1ST JUNE TO THURSDAY, 3RD JUNE

On Tuesday morning the Bailiff, the Dean,[25] Major Kratzer, Inspector Zachau and I went to the Soldiers' Cemetery to see what the German request in connection with the transfer of graves involves. I have written a memorandum of the whole matter for record purposes.[26]

Two or three days ago the United Club was raided by the Germans and field glasses and steward were taken away. Now we hear that Mr Roussel, H.M. Greffier and a member of the Club, has also been put in prison. More anon.

On Wednesday morning I saw Major Kratzer and reminded him that nearly a month had passed since the letters to the Red Cross and the Protecting Power were handed in. I said that our people were finding the reduced bread rations very inadequate and asked whether any useful purpose would be served by submitting duplicates of all the correspondence involved in case the originals had been lost. He said this was not necessary and that he had forwarded the documents to Jersey by the first available boat; he promised to speak to the Colonel as soon as possible to see if he could find out what had happened.

It is rumoured that a statement was made some days ago over the English radio to the effect that the Channel Islands are blockaded and that we had sufficient food for two months: whether this is true or not, we have no means of finding out.

FRIDAY, 4TH JUNE TO MONDAY, 7TH JUNE

The United Club affair has been settled and nobody has been detained. Apparently the fact that members use field glasses at the windows overlooking the harbour has raised suspicions.

On Saturday morning Mr Krafft telephoned to say that he had messages to convey to me from Major Kratzer. The Major was at his elbow and had evidently been telephoning to Jersey.

The first message was that, in reply to my enquiry about our letters to the Protecting Power and the Red Cross, they could not tell me that the letters were being sent on. I asked what exactly that statement meant. Had they already been sent or not? There was more talk in German and then Mr

---

25 The Dean was the Very Rev Agnew Giffard.
26 See Item 34: Memo: Soldiers' Cemetery, Fort George, 6 Jul 1943, p.355.

Krafft said that they had been held up in Jersey as the F.K. thought at first that the ration cut was a very temporary measure. As, however, the rations were still in force the Colonel was sending on the documents on the next boat with a covering letter from the F.K.

The second message was that 52 head of cattle were on their way from Granville for us.

The third was that the Major had seen Le Riche's store where we store the cheese and thought we might use it instead of Young's. The answer to that which I conveyed to him this morning is that we shall use it for some commodities but that it is not big enough for the whole of our stocks.

The fourth message was that, after such a long conversation, the Major wished me a happy weekend. I returned the compliment.

Today a letter arrived for the Bailiff in reply to the letter sent to the F.K. on the evacuation of Young's Store. It orders us to get out as soon as possible and disallows our protest that the requisition is against the Hague Convention. We have no appeal from this decision.[27]

TUESDAY, 8TH JUNE TO FRIDAY, 11TH JUNE

At about half past two on Tuesday morning everybody in this part of the Island was awakened by heavy artillery fire – as far as we were concerned we could hear the shells screaming over the house – and we heard later in the day that a British ship of some kind had been operating off the north coast. Apparently it was not hit.

On Wednesday afternoon some Alderney fishermen named Quinain who are fishing from St. Peter Port lost two members of the crew of their boat when it was blown up by a mine near Grand Amfroque. Apparently the mine was entangled with some French fishing net which they were trying to salvage and as they pulled on the cable they could feel something grating. A big black object appeared below them and then the explosion occurred. It seems miraculous that any of them survived. We wonder whether the mine was laid by the ship which was fired on on Monday night. Up to now the land mines which the Germans have put down around the coast have killed several Germans and this is the first accident which has occurred due to British mines.[28]

On Monday afternoon all the local bank managers were summoned to Grange Lodge for a meeting with a German from Paris. He, apparently, comes from the German Foreign Currencies Control Board and has

---

27 See Item 33: Knackfuss to Bailiff: Requisition of Food Store, 1 Jun 1943, p.354.
28 The Quinain brothers were fishing in GU.120 *Sunrise*, a 30 foot motor boat. They were rescued by Dan Domaille, who was fishing nearby. The crew members who died were Archibald Sebire and Herbert Dunn. See Bell (1995) p.245.

demanded details of the contents of all strong boxes in the banks. No Controlling Committee member was asked to be present at the meeting and on Wednesday I asked Major Kratzer whether he could throw any further light on the subject. He apologized first for not asking someone from Hirzel House to attend the Monday meeting but explained it had been called at very short notice. As far as he knew, he said, the idea was to get information concerning securities, gold bullion and uncut diamonds in the Island. I asked whether there was any question of removing such valuables from the Island and he said he had not heard of any such intention. I reminded him that under the Hague Rules only valuables belonging to the State could be taken and he said that the control was conducted under a law which was made for the whole of Germany as well as the occupied territories. He added that if the German Government wished they could make it a law that everybody must wear top hats. I asked whether he meant that his Government could make laws which would supersede the Hague Rules and he said they could, provided that such laws applied to Germany as well as to the occupied territories. I said I did not agree with him and in any case I had never found anything in the Hague Rules about top hats. We parted chuckling.

SATURDAY, 12TH JUNE TO THURSDAY, 24TH JUNE

I have had a week's leave and Dick and I have fitted out the boat, started the retaining wall for the terrace and practically finished the haymaking in the field. I thoroughly enjoyed my holiday.

F.K. say the Bailiff's letters to the Protecting Power and the Red Cross are now well on the way with a strengthening letter from their staff doctor stating that it is impossible for the health of the Islands to be maintained indefinitely on the present bread ration. Mrs Sherwill has received a letter from Mr Sherwill saying that he has received one from the Archbishop of York, formerly the Bishop of Winchester and therefore well known here, and that he has replied stressing our need for Red Cross aid and asking him to use his personal influence to get it for us.[29] Mr Sherwill has also written to the Headquarters of the Red Cross (presumably Geneva) on behalf of the Islands.

K.Ass. Hertig who has been at the F.K. since Dr Brosch left and whom I have come to like for his liberal outlook and comfortable philosophy is leaving for the army and being replaced by a new officer who looks very fierce. I rather suspect, however, that his bark will prove much worse than his bite.

I hear through roundabout sources that I have made a personal enemy of the German Press Censor and I cannot imagine the cause. However, there is nothing I can do about it.

---

29 Dr Cyril Garbett (1875-1955).

A fund has been opened by the two newspapers to help the dependents of the two fishermen who lost their lives the other day and to fit out the two survivors with a boat and gear. It has reached the amazing figure of more than £1,200.

From the beginning of the Occupation the Controlling Committee has advanced money to persons entitled to pensions from the British Government and to others who normally receive their income from English sources. It has been the practice not to advance the full amount of British Government pensions, firstly because at the beginning of the Occupation every effort was made to keep down purchasing power in view of the decrease in purchaseable goods and secondly, to make some reserve in each case for delays in notification of decrease in pension. For some time past the *The Star* has been running a fund, called "Help the Children Fund", which is designed to help poor persons who cannot afford to pay for food and clothing for their children. The managing director of *The Star* wrote a week or two ago to the Bailiff criticising the policy of the Labour Officer who controls advances to pensioners, on the ground that he was too niggardly in his advances to women who are entitled to dependents' allowances. The letter was not couched in the most diplomatic of terms but the Bailiff acknowledged its receipt and said he would answer in full as soon as he had received all the relevant information. Without waiting for his full reply, *The Star* printed their criticisms and when they did receive the Bailiff's letter the managing director replied in terms which can only be described as insolent. It appears to me that this paper sets out, not to be constructive, but to cause unrest by publishing criticisms without taking the trouble to get official answers. Time after time I have myself offered to obtain for them official reasons for policies which may seem contrary to the public interest but they never take advantage of the opportunity and the result is they use their power over public opinion to worry unnecessarily people who are already perplexed.

FRIDAY, 25TH JUNE TO THURSDAY, 1ST JULY

The export of tomatoes has begun and I believe that some of them will find their way to Germany. Whether it will be possible to maintain the necessary shipping service remains to be seen.

These days we often hear the sound of low-flying fighters on their sweeps over the Channel and last Saturday evening, just before dark, eight or nine flew up the Little Russel. They were met by a really intense barrage of light anti-aircraft fire all up the coast. One or two passed inside Platte rock and the flak was bursting right amongst them. How they managed to escape being hit I do not know and the Germans claim they shot down two.

Three years ago today the Occupation of these Islands began. Reason insists on the probability that three years hence it will be over but the impression which most of us have is that the Germans have been here for generations and that Guernsey without them is a heavenly daydream which sensible workaday folk should not waste their time in conjuring up. But we do talk and think often of the god-like existence which was ours before the deluge and we leave our German acquaintances open-mouthed at the thought of the contentment and amenities which used to be our heritage before they came. As the months and years pass these visions become ever brighter and more extravagant and our friends in England more god-like. May we never be disillusioned.

One thing is certain, Guernsey and Guernseymen for better or for worse have been subjected to forces and conditions which will leave their mark for centuries. We have learned to know privations, insecurities and dangers never imagined in our insular little lives. We have met subjects of a great continental power at very close quarters, we have seen poverty and misery undreamed-of amongst the foreign labourers who are here in their thousands. We have been driven right back to nature in our struggle to find enough to keep us alive. We have had proof once and for all that necessity is the mother of invention. We know the grief of forced partings, the longing for reunion with loved ones, the tragedy of losing our homes. And we know that life is very sweet.

FRIDAY, 2ND JULY TO SUNDAY, 4TH JULY

On Friday Colonel Knackfuss arrived from Jersey and asked to see the Bailiff and Mr Leale on Saturday morning. I went with them and the meeting was little more than an excuse for polite conversation. Of course, both the Bailiff and Mr Leale dwelt on the question of the return to normal bread rations and the reply was that as soon as local supplies of vegetables, etc., became scarcer a strong plea would be put up by the F.K. In vain did Mr Leale point out that tuberculosis – usually taken as indication of the general health of the population – is increasing in the Island. They replied that T.B. patients could have extra bread! Mr Leale asked, too, how it came about that they had to reduce bread rations because of lack of shipping space, when they could find boats for the export of five thousand tons of tomatoes. They replied that much more was shipped to the Islands than was shipped from them. They talked about supplying us with a thousand tons of seed potatoes from France for next year's planting! We shall certainly need seed next year, whatever happens. There was no sign of racial or any other kind of hatred throughout the session.

There has been plenty of mackerel this season and yesterday morning on the way to the office I decided it was about time I caught a few. At eleven o'clock I walked into the office of the German Harbourmaster and asked if I could have a permit to use my boat for one day. I had, of course to give the names and addresses, place of birth, date of birth and identity card numbers of Dick and Nigel who are my crew and I received the permit the same afternoon. Full of excitement I came home and collected Dick and Nigel to help get the fishing lines ready but luckily a fisherman friend of ours came in during the evening and did the job for us.

This morning at a quarter to seven we were up and admiring a perfect morning – with hardly a breath of wind. We made for St. Sampson's hugging a can and a half of precious petrol and a few tomatoes. As usual, most of the boats were already on the fishing grounds before we had found a dinghy and cast off from the moorings. Then we upended the first can and a mixture like muddy coffee flowed into the petrol tank. We reported to the guard who said we had too many petrol cans aboard and made for the harbour mouth where the motor stopped. Having drained carburettor and sump and knocked the skin off one thumb against the floor-boards when the beastly thing started, contrary to all expectations, we managed to struggle up to the Brayes where we were treated to the spectacle of dozens of boats with crews dripping sweat over their exertions in pulling in the fish. Then the motor stopped again just as Nigel hooked a mackerel which promptly escaped. We hoisted the sails and the wind dropped. We took off the petrol tank and drained it. We lost some of the screws which hold it in position. We spread grease and oil all over the freshly painted floor-boards. We got in each other's way. We felt slightly sea-sick, all of us, and ate some tomatoes. The wind sprang up and we decided to try fishing under sail and the wind took us half a mile from the place where fish were being caught. We cadged a mackerel from another boat and with all due ceremony cut magnificent baits from it. Then we caught a fish on the only line with an old piece of rag as bait. We poured the contents of the other can into the clean tank and the engine started so we joined the other boats whose crews were sitting about earning a well-earned rest and trailing their lines idly now that the tide had turned and there were no more fish to catch. When we thought we had burned enough petrol we followed the other boats back to the harbour and had an interesting discussion on the way about the catches we had had in the past and the reason for our lack of success today. We each had our own theories on this latter subject and it was noticeable that each theory involved only two people – and they did not include the speaker. We were glad to be back on *terra firma* and went home proudly with four mackerel which we had caught and one which we had cadged.

We asked one other boat how many they had caught and when they said they did not have more than a hundred we gave up asking.

[There are no entries for the 5-6 July 1943.]

The Feldkommandantur have asked for two sets of figures. Firstly the number of men of British nationality born in 1922 and secondly the number of men – plus dependents – working in occupations vital to the life of the Island. I saw Inspector Zachau on these two matters and he said that while he knew that some movement was afoot in France for the removal of the 1922 age group, he did not know whether this measure would be applied here but thought the Colonel was asking for the figure so that he would be informed on the subject. With regard to the second set of figures, he said that I could definitely banish from my mind any thought that they were to be concerned with contemplated evacuations. He was not at liberty to tell me why they were wanted. We have had to ask our staff to work overtime to get out the figures. Inspector Zachau ruled that dependents should include all children living with parents coming within the categories involved and being born after the end of 1924.

A few weeks ago, Mr Leale, in asking Colonel Knackfuss for reversion to full bread rations, mentioned that tuberculosis was increasing in the Island, saying that in medical circles this was always taken to indicate a falling-off in the general health of the community. Since then the F.K. have paid visits to the States' Dairy and ordered the installation of wash basins and have also ordered the examination of the staff by German doctors for infectious diseases and tuberculosis. They also suggested that, as they had taken over two thirds of the King Edward VII Sanatorium – by the way, this leaves us with insufficient room for our tuberculosis cases and some have to live at home – we should use the White House in Herm as a sanatorium. We decided to go into the matter and yesterday afternoon Dr Symons, Dr Sutcliffe, Dick, Inspector Zachau and his clerk and I went over in *Ida*. It looks as though it will be possible to clean up the house sufficiently for the mild cases and the suspects to be sent there for rest although the setting up of a hospital with a full nursing staff and organization – with medical attention on the premises – presents insuperable difficulties under present conditions. Inspector Zachau is to ask for the General's permission and if this is forthcoming we will go ahead with our enquiries. While we were there yesterday four German vessels came in with a considerable number of troops and their equipment. They are to remain on the Island and so, as far as we are concerned, the last spot where we could go to forget the war has been lost. We enjoyed our afternoon and went to the Ferrières to see if we could find a mackerel. We did not have one bite and the motor broke down. Anyway we had a memorable sail from St. Sampson's to Herm with a fresh south westerly breeze and a bright sun which put just the right sparkle on the water.

German officials from Paris have been going through the private strong boxes at the banks and have broken open the boxes belonging to people who have left the Island. They have taken nothing away but have put certain valuables in the custody of the bank managers.

We have landed in Sicily and have not been driven out again. In Russia apparently the fighting is intense in the central sector of the front and here too the success of the Germans is not very clear.

Mr Krefft lives in Cologne and since the recent R.A.F. raids on that city he has been waiting to hear whether his family and home are safe. He has now heard that his family was not in the city during the raids but that his home is destroyed. I must admit I have felt sorry for him while he has waited for several days in suspense for news and that seeing Germans I know suffer in this way gives me no satisfaction at all.

FRIDAY, 16TH JULY TO MONDAY, 19TH JULY

Apparently we are more than holding our own on Sicily and the Russians are attacking on the eastern front.

Mr Hertig has left Guernsey and is going back to the army.

This afternoon I had quite a long talk with Inspector Oser. He started off by saying that all the spies in Guernsey would soon be rounded up as they had made a fatal mistake. He grinned as he said it and I realized that, of course, he was having a rub at me. Some time ago he told me that Guernsey people had told him that I was a spy and although I know he is joking it is not altogether a comfortable feeling even having one's leg pulled on such a question by a German. I told him that espionage was not my job, luckily, and indeed I can imagine no work which would be more distasteful to me. I think that the work of a government agent must be the most nerve-racking of all wartime occupations. He also said that Captain Obermeyer had said that I was a little fox. There was little flattery in the conversation. Apparently it was contemplated, earlier in the Occupation, to appoint Mr Blaikie Webster as President of the Controlling Committee in the place of Mr Leale.

José is nearly a year old now and is a really happy little soul. She sits up on her own, is a really dirty eater and wriggles with delight at the first note I strike on the piano. She loves to hit the keys with all her might and we take this as the first signs of a budding musicianship! We have now received from England photographs of all the nephews and nieces.

Frank Stroobant who has acted as Camp Senior at Laufen since the arrival there of our contingent, has had to give up the position for reasons of health and Mr Sherwill has taken his place. Stroobant has made a name for himself for popularity and leadership.

TUESDAY, 20TH JULY TO MONDAY, 26TH JULY

The most important news this week is that Mussolini has resigned. Whether this is the best news of the war so far remains to be seen but we read in it the beginning of the end as far as the Axis is concerned. I have spoken to only two or three Germans today but I detected no sign of despondency in them although they had heard the news. I wonder sometimes whether their dearest wish is that the end should come as soon as possible. In Russia the Germans are meeting with no success and the submarines are doing nothing at all. Meanwhile the bombing of Germany goes on by day and night.

The question of Children's Allowances came before Controlling Committee last week. Everybody felt that some help to the poorer parents is badly needed, but they all realize that, once started, it will be impossible to discontinue these allowances – without much unrest. The financial position of the Islands after the war is such an unknown factor that the only reason to be taken into account in giving allowances at present is the alleviation of want. The rate which the Controlling Committee will advise the States to grant is four shillings per child, although some of the Committee's advisers, and especially Mr E.T. Wheadon, asked for a rate of six shillings.

Garland, from the married camp at Biberach, has written to the Bailiff asking for the shipment of two or three tons of tomatoes to them. I have taken the matter up with the F.K. but they say that although they are making enquiries they think difficulties of transport – or rather, a shortage of transport – will make this impossible.

TUESDAY, 27TH JULY TO MONDAY, 2ND AUGUST

F.K. inform us that it is impossible to get permission to send tomatoes to the camps in Germany.

On Friday Inspector Oser told me that the bread ration was to be restored as from the first of August. This news has delighted the population who were feeling the effects of the reduced ration. The reason given for the restoration is that marine traffic between the Islands and the continent has not been interfered with recently.

I managed to get a permit to use the boat over the August holidays and on Sunday my father-in-law, Dick and I went to the Brayes. We were up at six o'clock and went up the Russel before a strong south east breeze. All the time we were out the wind made and we thoroughly enjoyed a soaking on the way back. Actually there were scarcely any fish about and we caught four – and were not the most unsuccessful. It is quite three weeks now since the first schools of mackerel disappeared from these waters and the period of waiting for them to come back has been specially hard for us with every other week a meatless one. How health is maintained throughout the Island is a source of constant wonderment to everybody. When Colonel Knackfuss was here a few weeks ago Mr Leale impressed upon him the seriousness of the ration-cut and pointed out that tuberculosis was increasing. Apparently the Colonel was impressed because when he was inspecting a school next day – he takes an enthusiastic interest in the children – he asked one little boy what he had had for breakfast. To the horror of the teacher the boy replied, "An egg!" The Colonel was delighted and asked every child in the class the same question. As might be expected he never heard the first answer repeated.

When I walked into Grange Lodge the other day one of the staff said, "Good morning, Mr Guillemette. I have been so busy yesterday and today that I have had no time to listen to the news. What is it please?" "Hang on a minute," I replied, "I may seem friendly but I'm not as friendly as all that. I come here to get the news from you, not give it to you." "Ah, yes," he said, "I usually hear any news that's going but you get it a little before me."

The war news seems to be a little less spectacular this week. Apparently the bombing of Italy has ceased for the time being – perhaps to give the Italians time to make up their minds to stop fighting. In Sicily the advance has slowed up and in Russia the fighting does not seem to point to any spectacular success for either side although I rather suspect the Russians are getting the best of the fight.

TUESDAY, 3RD AUGUST TO THURSDAY, 5TH AUGUST

There are persistent rumours in the Island that both Orel and Catania have fallen. This news, coupled with tales of horror brought back by Germans living in the bombed areas of Germany make one feel we are on the eve of terrific events.

José was one year old on Wednesday. She had a birthday party composed of worshipping grown-ups and basked in their attentions. She giggled and talked incessantly and generally showed off and was very sweet. At one o'clock next morning she was yelling so hard that Queenie brought her into our bed. She lay back comfortably between us in the inky darkness and prodded me vigorously to find out what I was.

"Goodnight," I said, and we both swear she answered, "It's Dad," in a voice which could not disguise her disappointment at discovering I was nothing more exciting.

Mr Krefft is back from Cologne. He tells me that the main roof of the cathedral has collapsed but that the spires are still standing. He has lost his home. He told me too, about a school friend of his who, when our bombers visited his town, hurried his wife and two children into their car to escape, when a phosphor bomb fell on them. Later Krefft's brother saw a newspaper laid out on the side of the road with a little pile of debris on it and card saying, 'Family So and So. To be collected for the cemetery.' That was the end of that family.

Our chief fireman, Mr Olliver, has been discharged by the Germans because a Guernseywoman reported him for swearing about the Germans during a quarrel which he had with her. The Fire Brigade at present is half German and half Guernsey in personnel.

Recently we received from a German department some invoices for goods bought in France for the use of the occupying forces here. Mr Leale wrote to the F.K. expressing surprise at receiving such accounts and asking them to put the matter right. Instead we received the reply that it was quite in order for the States to be ordered to pay such accounts, since the articles mentioned came under the heading of billeting articles and were not available here. The letter ended with the whimsical remark that the finances of the States were still sufficiently strong to meet such claims. That we should be expected to meet such charges without any opportunity of checking the accounts or of placing orders, apart altogether from the fact that the Hague Rules say quite plainly that requisitions are only to be levied in proportion to the resources of the country, is a matter which cannot be allowed to continue without the strongest possible representations being made, and Mr Leale is continuing the correspondence.

FRIDAY, 6TH AUGUST TO SUNDAY, 8TH AUGUST

Mr Sherwill recently wrote to his wife saying that he had spent two hours, the day before, with members of the International Red Cross and that he had made a special report on Island conditions. Copious notes were taken and he was promised they would be sent immediately to Geneva. He believes that they will help us and says that he now has excellent opportunities periodically for direct contact. He stressed the fact that the Island Authorities should keep him posted regarding food and medical requirements. Mr Leale has obtained from the departments concerned full lists of goods required here and has sent them on to Mr Sherwill, explaining that the lists were made out in order of priority and asking him to use his own discretion in placing them before the Red Cross. I have reported to F.K. what has happened and we are giving them a copy of the letter and enclosures from Mr Leale. Major Kratzer told me that the F.K. have no objection to what we are doing provided it is done through the proper channels.

About eighteen months ago Mr Leale submitted to the F.K. a scheme for children's allowances. This was turned down by Dr Brosch who thought that if any extra income was given to wage earners it ought to come from the employer and not from the States. At about the same time the Jersey States put up a somewhat similar scheme and did not obtain German approval. On the 14th of July we received a letter from the F.K., enclosing the Jersey scheme and saying that it had been approved by them and asking for a similar scheme to be put into operation in Guernsey. It is to be discussed by the States tomorrow and yesterday *The Star* contained an article criticising the scheme submitted to the States and also the way it is being introduced. The uninformed and spiteful criticism of the local administration which is published in this paper can only be looked upon as the effort of a man – Mr Blaikie-Webster – who is quite without experience in administration and if the paper had a more serious following his efforts at causing strife at such a difficult time could be construed only as a danger to the peace to the Island.

Today I was called to Grange Lodge and asked how the States proposed to finance the Children's Allowance scheme. I pointed out that it would be taken from General Revenue and that the cost would be taken into consideration in fixing the rates of taxation at the next budget meeting. Major Kratzer asked whether some new source of revenue could be created to meet the cost of the scheme and I pointed that it was not customary for the States to introduce separate taxes for the financing of each new expenditure. The present system of taxation was designed to obtain funds from the sources best able to contribute and we saw no reason to alter that policy in this case. The suggestion that adult rations should be raised in price in order to reduce the price of children's rations would mean that all adults, whether rich or poor, would have to pay more. If the poorer members of the community were asked to pay less than the more wealthy then complications of administration would arise and in any case the result would be the same as a small rise in Income Tax. I think the Major saw the point, but he asked that the question of raising special taxation be carefully thought over.

The Major also spoke to me about Mr Leale's letter in connection with the costs of billeting services and said that although the F.K. letter on the subject had been written in his absence from the Island he was in full agreement with it. I said that we thought it was unjust to ask the Island to pay for imports for the occupying forces since the cost of Occupation was already more than in proportion to the resources of the Island and that we might be called upon to pay for all such imports. The Major said that in any case it was the duty of the F.K. and H.U.V. to restrict expenditure under this heading. He lent me a copy of the German commentary on the Hague rules and we are going to have it translated.

While I was at Grange Lodge two of the people who were sent to Laufen came in. They were McCulloch and Cheesbrough. Apparently the latter acts as liaison officer at the camp and he came over to see McCulloch safely home. He offered me an English cigarette and when I hesitated about taking it assured that there were plenty at the camp and that he smoked between four hundred and five hundred a week!

MONDAY, 9TH AUGUST AND TUESDAY, 10TH OF AUGUST

The States on Monday adopted with one small amendment the measure on Children's Allowances. Mr Leale's introduction and answers to various critics of the scheme were masterly and as the scheme was put forward by the Controlling Committee it appeared to me that the unanimous vote in favour was not far short of a vote of confidence in the Committee.

It was Mr Leale's silver wedding on Monday and after office hours the Committee and staff met to present him with a huge basket of fruit – no more durable present being procurable. Dr Symons made a very witty little speech and took the opportunity of showing the President the affection and respect in which he is held by Committee and staff alike. When it is remembered that it is now more than three years since the whole team started working together, it is a great tribute to Mr Leale that he not only has no serious critics in the building but is appreciated more and more as time goes on. What a pity the public does not know him better and what a pity that there are so many people with minds so small that they cannot grasp what his work means to their well-being!

Today the Bailiff, Mr Leale and I went to Grange Lodge to talk over the States decision on Children's Allowances. Major Kratzer is still keen on the introduction of some special tax to meet the cost of the scheme although Mr Leale repeated the explanation which I gave on Sunday morning for taking the necessary funds from General Revenue. The other points the Major made were that the payment of allowance should not stop at the fourth child and the allowances are not generous enough. Regarding the former, Mr Leale said that the main reason for stopping at the fourth child is to discourage larger families amongst poor people. He thinks it is better to encourage more families of four children rather than larger families in fewer cases. The Major was most insistent that in Germany there was no limit to the number of children for which allowance can be claimed and that we should adopt the same principle here. I asked whether the German government really wanted to encourage the production of a greater number of British children. The Major laughed and said he was concerned with the large families already in being in the Islands. Mr Leale said that of course Public Assistance was available for large families in case of need and agreed that this question of the encouragement or other wise of large families was one on which it is possible to argue for ever.

Sark is asking for Mr Finey, the Rector of the Forest, to go over for their Harvest Festival and to administer Holy Communion on Sunday 22nd.[30] The Dean therefore asked me to obtain permission from Grange Lodge for Mr Finey to stay in Sark over the week-end, and eleven o'clock last Wednesday morning found me shaking hands with the beaming Major Kratzer. When we had completed our ceremonial – I'm sure we amateurs are much better at it than any professional diplomat – I started, in terrific French, to lay my weighty case before him. I explained that there was to be a Harvest Festival and special Communion and when I came to the bit about wanting a permit for a priest to go over to do the work he scratched his head and said that he had already issued a permit for a priest to go to Sark. I said I knew nothing about that and asked the name of the priest. He called for a clerk to fetch the file and produced the name of Tardiff. I explained that Mr Tardiff was a Methodist minister. "*Mais il peut faire ces devoirs,*" said he. "*Mais non, Monsieur*" I replied. "*Pourquoi pas, c'est le même Dieu?*" "*Ah non, Monsieur*". "*Pas le même Dieu! Eh, bien combien des Dieux y-a-t'il?*" he asked. "*Je ne sais pas, mais ici je crois environ vingt.*" He nearly fell out of his chair with mirth and then continued, "*Eh bien, vous voulez un permit pour un veritable prêtre,*" he said. "*Oui, un prêtre du vrai Dieu,*" I replied.[31] The permit was granted.

Mr Krafft is back from leave. He told me all about his meeting with his little boy, who is nearly four years old and who had only seen his father for a few weeks so far during his short life. Mr Krafft beamed as he spoke of the little boy's joy at seeing his father and how well they got on together. Since leaving, his home town has been heavily bombed and now, instead of enjoying memories of a happy holiday, Krafft is anxiously waiting to hear whether his family is still alive. When a kindly and simple hearted man like Krafft is seen in such agony of mind, the full horror of war comes home very forcibly to one, even if he is the enemy.

Apparently the evacuation of Axis forces from Sicily has begun and on the eastern front the Russians still seem to be pressing forward.

It is claimed that José has begun to move under her own power but careful checking of positions on the floor minute by minute is necessary to

---

30 The Vicar of Sark, the Reverend Richard Phillips, had been deported to Germany in February 1943.

31 Translation: "But he can take those services." "No sir" I replied. "Why not, it's the same God?" "I'm afraid not." "Not the same God! How many gods are there?" he asked. "I don't know but I think about twenty here". He nearly fell out of his chair with mirth and then continued. "So, you want a permit for an authentic priest" he said. "Yes a priest of the true God" I replied. The permit was granted.

prove the accuracy of this statement, since movement is not visible to the naked eye.

I have now been able to talk again with Cheesbrough and to smoke several more of his English cigarettes. Apparently the September evacuees had a very bad time of it during their first six weeks in Germany when they were shockingly housed and fed in a camp in the Ruhr. They saw bombing raids almost every night. At Laufen they are now much more comfortable and some of the men work on farms with the consent of the British government. Apparently the camp at Compiègne where the women of the January evacuation were kept for several months was heavily bombed four days after they left it for Germany.

SATURDAY, 14TH AUGUST TO THURSDAY, 19TH AUGUST

The outstanding item of news this week is the escape from the Island of a boat load of Guernsey people. Dick and I meant to spend Sunday morning at sea and we arrived at St. Sampson's at nine o'clock. There were quite a few fishermen lounging on the Bridge and they called to us that we would not be allowed out. We stopped and they were simply bubbling over with the news that Jack Hubert, Alf Bougourd and Bill Corbet had left in the *Kate*. So we came back home.[32]

From information which is common property, I gather that Alf Bougourd went aboard while she was still high and dry on Saturday afternoon and that when the patrol boat came in to moor at about four o'clock he was sitting in the stern waiting for her to float. He called out to Langlois, the skipper of the patrol boat, and asked whether he had been given the rest of the day off. When Langlois said that he had, he said he was glad to hear it. He advised another fisherman to follow his own example and get rid of water in his petrol by passing it through chamois leather. When the boat floated Jack Hubert and Corbet joined him and they reported to the guard and left the harbour. Apparently, once clear of the guard, they ran alongside the rocks near either the Vale Castle or Houmet Paradis and picked up Corbet's wife and mother-in-law and a man named Le Page and his wife. It is also said that they had hidden petrol in crab-pots but whether this is true I do not know. However, they were last seen near Rocque au Nord at about half past five but as the fishermen go as far as this for mackerel no one thought anything amiss. The weather was thick with quite a strong breeze and they must soon have been out of sight of land. Since then nothing has been heard of them but they have been the main topic ever since.

---

32 See Kreckeler (1978) for the details of this escape. The boat, GU.28 *Kate*, can be seen in the German Occupation Museum in Guernsey.

Van Katwyk, a fisherman, reported that they were not back at half past ten and apparently a plane and one or more boats were sent out to search for them soon afterwards. By then it was brilliant moonlight but I do not think they were found.[33]

On Monday, everybody was on tenterhooks, wondering what punishment would be meted out to the Island and I went to Grange Lodge wondering what sort of reception I would receive. I walked into Inspector Zachau's room and he looked at his clerk and then at me and we all grinned but nothing was said. However, when I had done the work I had to do with him, we could keep off the subject no longer and he said he did not think what the escaped men had done was very clever. I said that I thought all responsible people in the Island agreed with him, since the only good which could come of the escapade was the benefit to those who had actually escaped. I said that if there had been any Island reason for their escape, such as ill-treatment of the population, I might change my opinion.

Corbet's father and mother were put in prison on Sunday morning with Alf Bougourd's housekeeper and are still there and we have received a letter from the F.K. saying that the property of those who escaped is to be regarded as enemy property under German law.

On Wednesday morning Mr Leale, Mr Martel and I went to see Major Kratzer. We were well-received, as usual, and the memorandum of the meeting gives a resumé of what took place.[34]

Opinion is very strongly divided on the question of whether or not it was right for these people to escape but I think many more than half the population are against them. Those in favour say that every man has a right to decide a question like this for himself and that they can no more be called selfish than can anybody who has a store-cupboard and does not help his neighbours who are short of food. They think it is the duty of those left in the Island to take the punishment without cringing.

Those against the escapade say that it is selfish to bring punishment on the Island when the only reason for escaping is comfort and personal glory. They add that to go when the war seems more likely to end soon than it has ever done before is not only selfish but silly. They quote the threat made by the Germans that punishment for escape may be the evacuation of some of the male population and they point out that the actual result has been the imprisonment of the father and mother of one of the escapees. Personally, I am sure that I could never bring myself to subject my parents to an experience which must be nothing short of terrifying to old people, even if they are only kept in custody for questioning.

---

33 Van Katwyk, of course, reported their absence in case they had come to grief and a search needed to be mounted, not because he wanted them to be caught.

34 See Item 35: Meeting with F.K.: Escape, 18 Aug 1943, p.357.

Meanwhile the general opinion is that the punishment is a fair one and not too severe, although the young people of the Island will feel it as a very real one.[35]

Fighting in Sicily has ended and we are wondering where and when the next blow will fall.

FRIDAY, 20TH AUGUST TO THURSDAY, 26TH AUGUST

On Tuesday evening we heard the sound of aero engines and then all the anti-aircraft guns on the east coast, on Brehon Tower and in Herm opened up. We rushed upstairs and sure enough there were four aeroplanes flying about the Russel. One dived and we thought it would crash in the sea but we watched it flatten out and fly off towards Jersey. Then we looked towards Herm and saw, over the low land at the northern end of the island an ominous black cloud beginning to appear. At the same time we heard a shout and realized with horror that it came from the Germans and was a cry of victory. I had never before heard human beings cheering over the death of one of their kind and I felt physically sick. It now appears that the plane which was shot down as well as the other three, were German and not British!

Mr E.J. Henry arrived in the Island on Monday morning but I have not yet heard details of his ordeal.

On Wednesday morning I was called up by the police at 7 o'clock because some men had arrived back from Laufen and Mr Sherwill had told them to get in touch with me on arrival. I went into Town at once and found that the men were Messrs Lean, Skinner and Doig who are remaining here and Reid and Cranch who came across with them and are returning to the camp. Mr Sherwill sent a note by them to Mr Leale saying that he had been given to understand that he was only to discuss camp matters with the Red Cross and that he was afraid he could, therefore, do no more for the Island through that channel.

Fishing has been stopped completely since the recent escape and it is now necessary to obtain a permit even to go aboard the boat to pump out. Billy Green and Dr Rose went to the bathing pool the other day, assuming that it was not a beach and therefore they could bathe there. A German officer of most ferocious mien caught them and they had to appear – or rather Billy had – at Grange Lodge. Apparently he is not to be punished but they made it quite clear that the pool is out of bounds.

I have been on holiday this week and we have lifted our potatoes. From

---

35 The Germans stopped all fishing for five weeks and restricted access to the beaches. See Bell (1995), pp.251-2.

just under five perch the crop was five hundredweight of edible potatoes. No disease, thank goodness.

FRIDAY, 27TH AUGUST TO WEDNESDAY, 1ST SEPTEMBER

The end of the war seems so much nearer these days that Mr Leale and I have amused ourselves by going over a list of matters which will have to be discussed with the Home Office as soon as contact is made with England. They include food supplies, financial aid, supplies of British currency, control of travel to and from the mainland, the repatriation of foreign labourers, supplies of furniture and building materials for the restoration of buildings damaged during the Occupation, British soldiers needed to guard German supply dumps and to render harmless the mines which have been laid throughout the Island and any booby-traps which may have been set, presentation for approval of all legislation which has been passed since the beginning of the Occupation and, most important, the immediate return of Mr Sherwill.

We talked too of the winding up of the Controlling Committee. Mr Leale thinks that its work will finish soon after the end of the Occupation and that in any case, as it is purely an emergency committee, the President should tender the resignation of the Committee to the States at the earliest possible opportunity. We both think, however, that for a long time to come the old States system of administration by committees will be much too cumbersome a method of dealing with the bigger and more pressing matters which will be cropping up and Mr Leale suggests some form of Cabinet. The ideal seems to be the Head of the Cabinet appointed by the States and the members appointed by him. Whether the States would ever allow so much power to pass from their hands is questionable. The Cabinet would be a small one and would consist of members who would each be the head of a department – perhaps such departments would be confined to finance, labour, horticulture, agriculture and industry. If once the old committee system starts again for all matters it may never be possible to break away from it. Less pressing matters might continue to be administered by Committees apart from the Cabinet.

It is obvious that reconstruction and the return to normal conditions of trade and Island life in general must be hampered to the least possible extent by red tape. What a relief it will be to throw state control overboard!

We hear rumours that a new section of the army is being formed in England for the administration of occupied territories. This will be somewhat similar to the German Feldkommandantur system, which works very well. Feldkommandanturs are set up behind the front lines in occupied territories as a sort of connecting link between the fighting forces and the civilian population. As far as I can gather the F.K. takes its orders from its Headquarters – in the case of the Channel Islands the headquarters being in Paris. The officers consist to a large extent of men with some legal qualifications, coupled often with some years of experience as civil servants. Some of them are men of learning and vision, some are more parochial than most Guernseymen. The head of an F.K. is, I think, always an army officer and there may be other army men as well on the staff. In F.K. 515 there are two agricultural officers, one in Jersey and one in Guernsey, and a medical officer besides a Paymaster and an officer who is head of the F.K. court which tries civilians for offences against F.K. orders. Apparently if the fighting forces make orders which are against the rights or interests of the population of the occupied territory and the F.K. does not get satisfaction when they protest against such measures, they may appeal to their headquarters which in turn take the matter up with the headquarters of the branch of the fighting forces concerned.

Some weeks ago the Bailiff appealed to the Colonel for the return of civilian radios. He has now received a reply to the effect that the conditions which made it necessary to requisition the radios have not altered and that they cannot, therefore, be given back.

Since the departure of Alf Bougourd and Co., fishing has been prohibited. Some days ago, however, the fishermen were asked to fill in a form giving very full details of their families – including their whereabouts – and their private means. A list of those fishermen who may continue to fish has now been published and the younger single fishermen as well as others with members of their families in England have been left out. They came to see us this morning and at Mr Leale's suggestion they are signing a petition asking for a reconsideration of their case. Only men who were *bona fide* fishermen before the war will be asked to sign the petition. Luckily Colonel Knackfuss is here and we are to speak to him on the matter tomorrow.

One of our food ships went on the rocks off Jersey in bad weather early this week. I believe it contained wheat and cognac – two of the staffs of life.

THURSDAY, 2ND SEPTEMBER

Inspector Oser, who has been in charge of horticulture and agriculture at the F.K. for the past two years, came down to wish us goodbye yesterday. He said that he hoped to come back to Guernsey for a holiday after the war.

The Bailiff, Mr Leale, Mr Ambrose Robin and I went to Grange Lodge this morning at the request of Colonel Knackfuss who has been here for two days. Our scheme for children's allowances had been altered by the F.K. in such a way that the anomalies which we had wished to avoid had been introduced. After half an hour's explanation he grasped our point and we are allowed to introduce our original scheme except that an allowance is to be made for every child whereas in the original scheme payment was made only up to and including the fourth child. In my opinion this amendment is a great improvement.

We spoke to the Colonel about fishing and he promised to help us but he has gone back to Jersey tonight. However, the petition will be completed tomorrow and we will hand it over to the Germans.

FRIDAY, 3RD SEPTEMBER TO THURSDAY, 9TH SEPTEMBER

This week has given us the best news we have had since the war began. It started off on Friday with the landing of British forces in the extreme south of Italy and yesterday it was announced that Italy had signed an armistice with us. We wondered why the advance in Italy had been so slow during the week, especially as the Germans said that opposition was very weak. It now transpires that the armistice was signed on the day that the landing took place.

Even the most loyal Germans look upon the collapse of Italy as changing completely Germany's position. Some of them have been reputed to have been seen playing leap-frog and it is said that one group of Austrians sang their old national anthem. They all feel that they cannot allow the Russians to overrun their country. Stories of the effects of the bombing in Germany are horrible and now that we shall have bases so near their southern and eastern boundaries I fail to see how the morale of the German people can ever stand up to the expectation of what the winter holds on store for them. They feel that they will all have a turn. Personally, coming into contact with them as much as I do, I find myself hoping that they will ask for peace at once and so save many very ordinary and very human men from the horror of hearing that their families have perished. My forecast is that the war will finish in Europe before Christmas.

José now chatters incessantly in a complicated and quite incomprehensible language of her own, crawls at speed, hampered only by a superfluous leg and plays the piano equally well with hands and feet. It has not really sunk in yet that we may see her cousins within the next few months.

FRIDAY, 10TH SEPTEMBER TO WEDNESDAY, 15TH SEPTEMBER

At about three o'clock on Saturday morning we were awakened by the sound of gunfire and looking out of the window we saw tracer shells whizzing over the water between Sark and Jersey. We also heard then, and for half an hour afterwards, the sound of high-powered engines. An hour afterwards we heard gunfire again but were too lazy to look out of the window again.

It appears that some ships which left here earlier during the night were attacked by British E-boats off Jersey. None of them were sunk. At Grange Lodge they told me that a parcel of two and half million francs which we were sending to France was on one of these boats and it would have been just too funny if it had been lost by the action of our own side. I agreed that it would have given Lord Haw Haw something to laugh about for the rest of the war.

This week there have been exceptionally high tides and on Tuesday evening the wind was blowing hard from the south west. This has the effect of making the tide higher than it would otherwise be and Dick and I therefore went to l'Erée to see what the effect of wind and tide would be on a piece of sea wall which had collapsed some time before because of the taking of sand from the beach by the Germans and which had been repaired temporarily by them. If it had collapsed some hundreds of vergées of low land would have been flooded. However, all was secure.

We came back via Vazon and found that for at least a quarter of a mile the spray was sweeping continuously across the road. We decided to ride through it and for the first hundred yards we dodged each wave. Then we caught one, fair and square. It was almost solid water and we could not see for some seconds. A hundred yards further again and the engine suddenly cut out until we were travelling at not more than eight miles an hour. Then it cut in again and saved us from walking the last two hundred yards.

It looks as if we are having a stiff fight in Italy, especially near Salerno where we are having difficulty in holding even our bridgehead on the coast. In Russia the Soviet troops appear to be continuing their advance.

Today there was a States meeting at which the main item was the Projet de Loi on Children's Allowances. This was passed and I took it to Grange Lodge this afternoon for approval. They are sending it on to Jersey and hope to get approval by Saturday so that the Projet can be presented to the Court on Saturday. If everything goes well we should have the scheme in operation by the week after next. Mr Corbet asked a set of questions about the advance by the States of British Government pensions and allowances. These questions were raised because of repeated criticism in *The Star* of the policy of the Controlling Committee on the matter and in my opinion they gave complete answers to this criticism.

THURSDAY, 16TH SEPTEMBER TO MONDAY, 20TH SEPTEMBER

The Law on Children's Allowances has received German approval and was adopted by the Royal Court last Saturday. In the *The Star* of Thursday some astounding statements were made in an article headed 'Unrepentant'. Many people think that this paper should be suppressed on account of its policy which is so obviously against the government but Mr Leale's opinion is that no notice should be taken and that its policy will do the paper much more harm than good.

Since the ban on sea-bathing many people have begun bathing in quarries and for the last two Sundays we have had a plunge in Nick Hubert's quarry near Bordeaux.[36] Somebody has put up a pulley on a wire rope with one end about twenty feet above the surface of the water and the other three feet up on the other side of the quarry. This provides quite a thrilling aerial flight. There is a springboard for diving, too, and with a depth of about a hundred feet of clean water there is quite an attractive bathing pool. At least twenty people were bathing on Sunday with some forty spectators.

Last week we received a letter from Grange Lodge giving a list of motor cycles which were to be taken off the road. They included all cycles used by doctors and on Saturday morning I went to see Major Kratzer with four of the doctors. We were told that it was not permissible for any individual to be allowed the use of two vehicles, the doctors holding permits for their cars as well as for the motor cycles. We explained that the idea of using two vehicles was to save petrol, since motor cycles were used whenever possible. The fact that the doctors were granted, concurrently with the withdrawal of motor cycle permits, half a gallon of petrol each extra showed that the saving of petrol was not the reason for the order and Major Kratzer said the reason was probably the shortage of vehicles which might make it necessary to hand the surplus vehicles over to the German forces. In the face of this argument there was nothing more to do, but as the saving will not amount to more than three or four motor cycles in very indifferent condition, we could not see much force in the German argument.

Fishing on a restricted scale has started again and there were some quite good catches of longnose and shell-fish over the weekend. Some of the most valuable weeks of the season have, however, been lost and with the great shortage of meat this is serious to our population.

George Vaudin, who is here on leave from Granville, says that in France there is plenty of black market meat, but obviously with difficulties of transport little or none reaches the Islands. Although, in theory, the food situation is supposed to be at least as good as it is in France, the smallness of the black market owing to transport difficulties, makes the total food available much smaller than it is there.

It looks as though we are consolidating our position in southern Italy and we hear that in Jugoslavia the patriots are in possession of quite a long

---

36 Nick Hubert's quarry in Rue Godfrey is still full of water. He lived in La Turquie, north of Bordeaux harbour. See Map 1.

strip of coastline. In Russia the advance seems to be continuing and reports of sinkings in the Atlantic are now few and far between.

TUESDAY, 21ST SEPTEMBER TO SUNDAY, 26TH SEPTEMBER

Smolensk has fallen, the Russians are said to have crossed the lower Dnieper in several places, we are advancing in Italy, bombing of Germany has started again after a week or two of quiet and we are all wondering whether the war will last over Christmas. On the other hand the German submarine campaign has reopened with a surprise attack on a North Atlantic convoy after many weeks in which they had done nothing at all. Although they are our enemies, I must admit to some admiration for the crews of these submarines especially now we have such deadly methods of fighting them.

What is of vital importance to us here is that we should be ready to take full control in the Island when the war ends or when the Germans leave, whichever takes place first. It is almost impossible to foretell what problems we shall have to face, but efforts are being made to have the best possible control ready to put into operation.

Another matter which we are thinking and talking about is the system of administration which will operate after the war. Mr Leale thinks he should tender his resignation and therefore that of the members of the Controlling Committee at the earliest possible moment but it seems obvious that the old committee system cannot possibly cope with the work which will have to be done. There are many of us who think that this system should never come back in full and the Bailiff is asking a few members of the States to form an informal committee to discuss and examine the question of setting up some form of Cabinet as a permanent measure to take charge of the most important administrative work.

For my part I am trying to ensure that the records of the administrative work which has been done during the Occupation shall be up to date and I have also pressed for an enquiry into the finances of the Civil Transport Service. We have already set up a basis of valuation for all requisitioned vehicles and boats and the Controlling Committee has elected a sub-committee, of which I am a member, to go into C.T.S. affairs.

MONDAY, 27TH SEPTEMBER TO WEDNESDAY, 29TH SEPTEMBER

Adèle Sauvarin was married on Tuesday afternoon. I had a suspicion I had not made a very successful job of the music and when I met Santangelo at the reception my suspicion was confirmed. "Ah, hallo, my boy," he said, pumping my hand up and down, "how are you? Now that's an organ you're not used to."

F.K. have sent forms through the post to young men born in 1922 to 1925 inclusive. They have to give information as to whether they are married or single, giving details of their families, if married, their usual work and whether they are working for Germans or civilians at present. They have to return the forms personally to Grange Lodge where they are asked a few questions.

I called on Major Kratzer this morning and asked him, on behalf of the Bailiff and Mr Leale, what the reason was for the collection of this information. He said that they had received orders to do this work but did not know the exact use to which it was to be put. I asked whether he could give me an assurance that it did not involve an evacuation and he asked whether I wanted him to give a personal promise to that effect. Of course he could not give me one and I asked for his opinion. He said that he felt fairly certain that there would not be an evacuation but thought that the same measure had been put into operation in France to set to work young men who were not fully employed. I said that I understood that in France the men called up in this way had been sent to other parts of the country or to Germany and he said that he did not think that this would happen here.

Stanley Noel and Stephen Bougourd, both of whom were detained in connection with the escape of Jack Hubert and Co., and a man named Machon who made V signs in his spare time from coins, are to be sent to Laufen at the beginning of next month. Bougourd came with me to Grange Lodge to ask whether there was any possibility of his being allowed to remain here because of his mother, aged 82, who is dying slowly of cancer. We explained that the shock of hearing that he was leaving the Island had caused a relapse and that it was feared that his absence would cause her death. We asked that at any rate he should be allowed to remain here until she had become accustomed to the idea. It transpired during the interview that Bougourd's sister lives with their mother. He even offered to stay in prison here rather than leave the Island. Major Kratzer said he was very sorry he could not grant the request but that he had been ordered to send Bougourd away and had no power to rescind the decision. He said that the order must be looked upon as the result of the war and he wished Bougourd good luck. One more failure!

THURSDAY, 30TH SEPTEMBER TO SATURDAY, 2ND OCTOBER

By far the most important event during the past three days is the carting off of Queenie to hospital. She has been ailing for some weeks and Dr Sutcliffe decided on Friday that she should go into hospital for observation and a possible operation. He called at the office to tell me this on Friday afternoon and naturally I came straight home. Going to hospital was the joke of the afternoon – on the surface. This afternoon Dr Sutcliffe came to fetch Queenie in his car and they went off with Queenie just as gallant as I expected. José and I waved goodbye from the window and when I had conquered a most embarrassing desire to weep we set to with a will to make one another laugh. We succeeded for an hour and half until Uncle Dick and Auntie Maisie came in and gave me a breather. I'm very much more than fortunate in my choice of a wife and daughter. This evening I have been to the hospital where I found Queenie safely in bed in a small ward with two suffering women and a small crowd of extremely cheerful nurses. She had, before turning in, made a tour of inspection of the hospital, greeting kindly matrons, masters and smaller fry of her acquaintance and such patients as she happened to know. She arrived back in her ward the richer by four figs which she had purloined from a weaker woman. She is to be examined and perhaps operated upon on Monday morning.

Mrs Sherwill has received a most amazing letter from Mr Sherwill. He says that they will be home again by next March or April at the latest, that they know much more than we do, that the exact date is not yet determined, that he has full liberty within ten miles of the camp and that Mrs Sherwill is to send him a Union Jack and to ask no questions. I advised Mrs Sherwill not to send the flag because even if there is no objection to its arrival at the camp I feel certain that its inclusion in a parcel from here would be frowned upon – if not worse – by any censor at this end. I shall probably be cursed for a busy-body but I cannot think that Mr Sherwill wants to place his wife in any danger. Other messages hinting at good news have arrived from Laufen and we all wonder what it can be. It has been suggested that if the Russian advance continues much further the Germans may wish the British to enter German territory before the communists and may abandon the western front. There are no signs of such a move in this neighbourhood. There can be little doubt, though, that we are on the eve of great events.

In Italy Naples seems to have fallen and we are advancing up the east coast even faster. In Russia there is no sign of a slowing up of the advance. There does not seem to have been so much bombing over Germany recently.

Apparently the Machon man gave a farewell dance at Stroobant's restaurant on Thursday evening and because his guests sang 'We'll hang out the washing on the Siegfried Line' with such gusto that it was heard outside, there was a German police raid and identity cards were taken from all who had them. Those who had left them at home were put in prison for the night. Apparently after individual questioning, the identity cards were handed back to their owners.

SUNDAY, 3RD OCTOBER AND MONDAY, 4TH OCTOBER

Saturday night Dick slept in the back bedroom and I in the front. All went well until about four o'clock when José set up a yell which brought us both into her room at the double. We did the necessary and went back to bed for quarter of an hour or so, until the next howl. Until six o'clock we rushed backwards and forwards, both of us, at every yell, and when we were not on the move we lay awake listening. At seven o'clock I took her into my bed. At eight she had her bottle, at nine we brought her downstairs and at eleven when Maisie came into relieve us we were both stretched out, one on the settee and one on the floor of the lounge, down and out.

Last night we decided it would be better for one person to be on duty and I took first turn. We had a magnificently quiet night with no disturbance until six o'clock when José took her bottle like a lamb and having submitted docilely to the other rites went happily back to sleep until it was time for us to get up.

This morning at a quarter past eight Queenie was operated upon. By 9.20 Sutcliffe had telephoned to tell me that everything was in order and ten minutes later I was in his consulting room hearing the details. The operation was quite successful and I felt very appreciative of the kindness shewn to both of us by our friend the doctor. I don't know whether it is the same with everybody else but when Queenie is suffering I know exactly what my feelings for her really are.

TUESDAY, 5TH OCTOBER TO SATURDAY, 9TH OCTOBER

Queenie is recovering fast. Tonight when I went out to see her she was in high spirits and full of hospital news. José has behaved perfectly all the week and I have learned more about the running of the house than I ever knew before.

On Wednesday afternoon the Bailiff, Mr Leale and I paid a formal visit to the new General at La Corbinerie – a return visit for the one paid by the General a few weeks ago at the Vallon. The Bailiff went in his car and Mr Leale and I met him there in one of the gazogène taxis. The house is very imposing, a Georgian mansion in quite spacious grounds and we were met by a manservant in a white coat and an officer interpreter. We were ushered into a charming room where the General was waiting. There was a fine fire and three little tables set out for afternoon tea for three people – obviously the General, the Bailiff and the interpreter. Mr Leale and I were not expected but were welcomed very politely, nevertheless. We did not feel embarrassed.

The General is tall and extremely well-groomed and we bowed and shook hands in keeping with the dignity of the occasion. I hoped that Victor's (my brother's) Montague Burton suit would stand the strain! Then we sat down and made polite conversation as one always does at tea parties. To anyone looking on the afternoon might have appeared rather a silly waste of time. In reality the result was that if, on some future occasion, we need to interview the General on any work connected with the welfare of the Island, we will not be complete strangers. We were still at the very polite stage when we were ushered out again. The Bailiff sat in his car and was driven off. We jumped into our taxi and sat there for about four minutes while a fan like an air raid siren shrieked in its efforts to generate enough gas to allow us to move off. By the time we were ready, the General, the interpreter and even the manservant had disappeared into the house.

Sarre is over here from Jersey. He thinks food is more plentiful there than it is in Guernsey, mainly because of the much greater amount of land per head of population.

SUNDAY, 10TH OCTOBER TO THURSDAY, 14TH OCTOBER

Queenie is still in hospital and Maisie is still day-nurse with Dick and I doing alternate night shifts. José is behaving really well, beaming on friend and foe alike. I hope that she develops some powers of discrimination as she grows up!

We managed to buy a load of firewood from an O.T. firm which is leaving the Island. We had three and a quarter tons for just over £2. The usual price of firewood at present is £1-2-6 per hundredweight. While the lorry was being loaded a rather good looking German boy sat on a pile of wood playing idly with one of the heavy iron staples they use for fastening logs together. He brought it down smartly on his left leg and it embedded itself in the leg. He laughed and left it there for a few seconds. We were all aghast and when he told us with a pitiful smile that his leg was of wood and he had lost his real one in Russia the horror of the war somehow struck us afresh. He looked too young to have to shoulder the burden of such a handicap for the rest of his life.

Guillemet is home on leave from Granville. He has been in three air-raids in Paris recently. He was running into Paris one morning with the lorry when a French policeman stopped them and said there was an alert and that Guillemet and the driver must leave the lorry and go to an air-raid shelter. The policeman turned to stop a cyclist and while his back was turned Guillemet told his driver to drive on. The policeman was too late to stop them and they went on to the factory which was their destination. They found the staff in the road looking up at some British fighters which were circling overhead. They began to dive almost vertically – all at the same point – and to climb again. This went on for twenty minutes and the spectators explained they were indicating the target to be bombed. Sure enough they heard eventually a roar which increased in volume and the bombers came into sight and plastered the target. One big bomber was hit and began to lose height and disappeared from view behind the surrounding buildings. On the way back Guillemet passed through the street in which he had encountered the policeman and there, within a hundred feet of the place where he had been ordered to remain, was a fire engine and firemen putting out the fire and clearing up the debris caused by one of the bombs.

At the Granville cinema a speech by Laval was put through the sound apparatus during a performance. Somebody coughed and the irritation of the throat spread so rapidly through the audience that not a word of the speech could be heard. The cinema was closed for a fortnight.

Apparently the Russian advance continues and in Italy there is really hard fighting.

FRIDAY, 15TH OCTOBER TO FRIDAY, 22ND OCTOBER

The cameras confiscated by the F.K. in June 1942 are in such a bad state owing to damp and pilferage that they have written to the Bailiff asking that he take them over. He wrote back saying that as the occupying forces were obliged under article 53 of the Hague Convention, to restore them at the end of the Occupation and to pay indemnity, he did not see his way to take responsibility for them at this stage. Major Kratzer asked to see the Bailiff and the memorandum of the meeting indicates the result of the meeting.[37] Meanwhile the cameras are being transferred to a store placed at the disposal of the F.K. by us.

Another subject discussed at Grange Lodge was the issue of a new 2½d stamp and here again the whole matter is set out in the minute of the meeting.[38] It does seem a pity that Blaikie Webster is such a troublemaker. I feel sure there is some good in him somewhere. Perhaps he will learn some day that he is not the only man in Guernsey with the interest of the public at heart and that others with more experience of administration than he will ever have are doing their utmost.

During the week Mr Leale offered me a job to start after the war. It is that of assistant managing director of Leale Ltd., the idea being that the present managing director, Mr Carrington, should remain in office for a few years until I have learned the business and should then retire, leaving me to manage the whole business if I prove capable. It is probably the biggest of the purely local businesses and the pay will be more than I can ever hope for

---

37 See Item 36: Meeting with F.K.: Storage of Photo Apparatus, 22 Oct 1943, p.359.
38 See Item 37: Meeting with F.K.: New Postage Stamps, 22 Oct 1943, p.361.

in the States. To say the very least I was surprised to receive this offer and regard it as the finest compliment ever paid to me. I shall miss public work. Shall I enjoy business as much?

Queenie is still in hospital. She was critically ill over the weekend, but thank goodness she is definitely on the mend now. It will be marvellous to have her at home again.

José now stands easily by herself and we enjoy our little jokes together. Dick and I are still night nurses. The first Sunday we were alone, we scrubbed and polished everything. Last Sunday we dusted and wiped things over with a wet rag!

SATURDAY, 23RD OCTOBER TO THURSDAY, OCTOBER 28TH

We have been so busy entertaining our friends during the past week that there has been little time for writing up diaries. In fact this is the first evening Dick and I have had alone since last Saturday. However, Queenie is getting better and José is behaving excellently, so we feel we can relax.

We received orders from the F.K. recently to reduce rations of butter, milk and sugar. Instead of carrying out the orders, letters from Messrs. Leale, R.O. Falla, Sir Abraham Lainé and Dr Symons were sent in showing why we should not do so and today we went to Grange Lodge to emphasize the points already made. We hope we have been successful but the matter has to be referred to Jersey.[39]

At a meeting of the States last Wednesday, an excise duty on locally grown tobacco was approved. It was introduced without previous notification to the States and was carried without opposition.

Apparently the Russians are still going ahead fast and everybody is wondering whether the Germans will ever be able to check their advance. If this proves impossible it may be that the war will end sooner than we think.

I have accepted Mr Leale's offer of a post in Leale Ltd., but not without some regret at giving up a career which means more to me than I ever realized before. In fact, if there were someone from whom I could get an assurance that my services in a senior position in the States would be welcome even at a considerably later date I would not hesitate to remain on at my present salary. However, as things are there is nobody from whom I can get such an assurance and I cannot afford the luxury of turning down a very well-paid post on the chance of getting the one I want in the Civil Service. Whether the carrying of a big responsibility in business will be as attractive to me as some power in directing the administration of this Island remains to be seen. At present, at the risk of seeming pompous, I admit that my conscience

---

39 See Item 38: Meeting with F.K.: Reduction in Food Rations, 26 Oct 1943, p.363.

is not quite clear about throwing over my public work for business which must consist mainly in looking after my own financial interests.

FRIDAY, 29TH OCTOBER TO MONDAY, 8TH NOVEMBER

Queenie came back from hospital last Wednesday and seems well on the way to recovery. We have taken on a girl to do the housework. José can almost walk, can say several words, eats like a horse, shows much more restraint and discipline in going to stool, loves her mother vigorously and recognized her the moment she came in from hospital.

Apparently Jack Hubert and Co. have arrived in England, because news has come through the internment camps that they had a very cold reception. Jack is supposed to have said that he would like to be back here. A week ago Mr Leale, Major Barrit Hills and I went to Grange Lodge at Major Kratzer's request. We were told that the new electric station was almost finished and that it was proposed that the States should take it over and run it, charging in the ordinary way for all current sold. They asked whether we agreed to the scheme and Mr Leale said that he could give no opinion until Major Hills had examined the plant and gone into costs of production. It turned out that it is very improbable that we shall get any more diesel oil and that as the new station is run entirely with coal as fuel there is no alternative. The station consists of three sets of suction gas apparatus, each of 300 kilowatts output and one steam turbine of 1,000 kilowatts. The whole is already connected to our cables and when in full operation will take the full present day load. At the pre-war cost of diesel oil and indeed at a very considerable increase in price the new station would not be a very economic proposition so there is no apparent permanent advantage to be gained from the capital invested in it. As a coal supply is already in the Island, however, it will be useful until the end of the war. It is interesting to note that the suction gas plant used formerly in Guernsey was scrapped twenty years ago. Steam turbines are not commercially successful under a minimum load of 5,000 kilowatts. There has been no mention of the States paying anything towards the costs of erection of the plant.

The war continues as much in our favour as ever. Kiev has fallen, we are advancing in Italy, the submarine seems to have lost the whole of its advantage and there is talk of bringing into use an eight ton bomb filled with a new super-powerful explosive.

The Controlling Committee want me to go to Jersey to discuss several matters and to have a general talk on post-war problems. One of the principal stumbling blocks is going to be the changeover from German to local and English currency.

TUESDAY, 9TH NOVEMBER TO WEDNESDAY, 17TH NOVEMBER

Last Wednesday morning the telephone bell rang at seven o'clock. Len Collins wished me good morning and said that he had arrived from Laufen during the night. They were eight days on the journey, nearly five of them in St. Malo waiting for a boat. This is not unusual nowadays with shipping dislocated by bombing, mines and weather. Len says they have no special knowledge at the camp to make them more optimistic than they are here and so the thrilling mystery of those last letters has disappeared. The camp seems to be in a safe spot but they missed a heavy raid in Munich by a couple of hours. The Red Cross and other parcels they receive from England and America simply amaze us. Butter, real tea, bacon, cocoa, cigarettes, good soap. He brought photographs and letters from Marguerite and Babe in England – in their own handwriting. Thoughts of pre-Occupation friends and relatives are almost impersonal sometimes and Island life before 1940 is a matter of history. Three and a half years of separation has proved a strain for nearly all separated couples and for some the strain has been too great. The percentage of births in the Island which are illegitimate has risen from 4% in 1939 to 19.1% so far this year. Many of these babies have German fathers. The fact that principles of morality are not fundamental is brought home to us day by day.

Two or three weeks ago the British cruiser *Charybdis* was sunk in a night engagement in the Channel between Ushant and the Channel Islands. Last Friday bodies – nearly all engine room ratings – began to be washed up on the west coast and altogether eighteen have been brought ashore and one in Sark.

When I reported the matter at Grange Lodge on Friday morning they were immediately interested in making arrangements for a funeral with military honours. This is customary, apparently, amongst all countries at war. At first we thought that the men should be buried at Fort George but the Soldiers' Cemetery has so few unoccupied graves that as the number of bodies grew we decided to bury them at the Foulon where each man could have a separate grave. A special section of the extension was therefore set aside for the purpose and today the funeral took place. Everything went well and seemed quite simple. I have seldom taken charge of a job with more detailed work to attend to.

For some reason I was not in the least impressed by the ceremony.[40]

Grignard has gone back to France after waiting about two weeks for a boat.

---

40 The Germans accorded the dead full naval honours and a very large number of Islanders attended the ceremony. 721 wreaths were laid. The event continues to be commemorated to the present day.

This morning some British fighters flew up the Russel while I was dressing. We watched spell-bound as they banked and dived and one deliberately turned back and flew in a circle, as though inviting the anti-aircraft gunners to try again. As he came north again in front of the St. Sampson's guns he climbed and did a complete roll. Then he went on to England, chased by flak and we went on with our work.

THURSDAY, 18TH NOVEMBER TO TUESDAY, 23RD NOVEMBER

We took Queenie back to hospital today for more treatment and a particularly grey pall has settled over the house. It's blowing hard, too, and Len is leaving for Germany again tonight.

High spirits are far away.

The only fun this week has been a minor fight with the F.K. over some radio accumulators they want us to find for them. They wrote saying that they wanted 130 accumulators[41] and that the States were entrusted with supplying them. They added that this should not be difficult since all those originally used for radios were still in the Island and were not all in use. Our first reaction on reading the letter was that to order us to find accumulators when they had already taken the radios was the last straw. However, we said that, in our opinion, the only way to get them, if there were any available at all, was to advertise for them in the newspapers. Actually we did not think we would get any offered, firstly because all accumulators on the Island have far outlived their efficient life, especially if they have not been used since the radios were confiscated in June 1942, and secondly because those which are still usable are in great demand for bicycle lamps and for lighting in country houses without gas or electricity. They agreed to the advertisement but telephoned later to say that they could not allow any mention to made of the fact that they were needed by the German authorities. Mr Leale and all the members of the Controlling Committee with whom he discussed the point were against any measure which might deceive the population and I therefore went to Grange Lodge to explain the position.

I was ushered into Major Kratzer's room and having discussed some other small matters I said I had a delicate question to place before him. Accumulators. He ordered Mr Krafft to fetch Mr Melzer and when he arrived we started. I explained that Mr Leale was unwilling to help in finding the accumulators unless he could make it clear in his notice that they were needed by the Germans. They both shook their heads and said we must put in the notice without mentioning the Germans. I said Mr Leale felt very

---

41 These were large, heavy, rechargeable wet batteries which were used to power a radio when there was no electricity in the house. They could be taken down to the local garage to be recharged.

strongly on the matter and was unwilling to deceive our people. They asked how the deceit would arise and I explained that accumulators were in such demand that it would be a definite sacrifice on the part of anyone giving up an accumulator. It might be that some people would be willing to make the sacrifice if they knew the accumulators were for the Germans, others would help if the civilian population were to benefit. Mr Leale thought that everyone should know, before they made the sacrifice, who they were making it for. I went on to explain that although there must be thousands of accumulators in the Island, a very small number would still be in working order and I added that unless a really good price was offered I did not think any would be forthcoming at all.

Major Kratzer said that if we could not procure the accumulators on a voluntary basis the F.K. would have to order us to find them. I said that perhaps this would be the best way, but they would then have to issue a requisition order. They said this was unnecessary and as at the beginning of the meeting they had said that they could not shoot with accumulators and as their letter to us did not say that the accumulators were needed for military purposes but for 'special purposes' I gathered they did not fancy issuing a requisition order. However, they said they would write to us again on the subject and I said we would do nothing until we had received their letter. We are now awaiting their letter and I telephoned to remind them that as the Bailiff alone has the power to requisition they should address the letter to him. This makes the whole matter horribly official from their point of view.

The fact remains that with the very limited numbers of accumulators available now, we cannot spare any without some sacrifice on the part of those who are required to give them up. Major Kratzer said they would requisition under the same article of the Hague rules that they used for radios, since accumulators could be regarded as part of a radio. I asked whether an accumulator used for a cycle lamp could be regarded as part of a radio and he said that originally they had been bought for this purpose. He asked whether I knew that the article referred to radios and I answered that I knew that the Hague rules were drawn up before radios were used commercially. Of course F.K. are willing to pay fair prices for the accumulators.

We parted after an hour and a quarter of argument which I am sure we both enjoyed to the full. The Major dearly loves an argument and we both have sufficient sense of humour to prevent too grim a note creeping in during our meetings.

Meanwhile the war continues with the Russians still advancing and the Germans saying we are launching a big new offensive in Italy. Berlin is now getting a big share of the night bombing and the Americans are attacking in huge daylight raids. Our wave of super-optimism in the Island has died down again and the end of the war seems quite a long way off.

WEDNESDAY, 24TH NOVEMBER TO SATURDAY, 27TH NOVEMBER

Major Kratzer informed on Wednesday that they were dropping the accumulator question and we have received a letter to the same effect. They say they are managing to get the accumulators without our help.

On Wednesday morning Mr Krafft telephoned me to say that it had become necessary to take down the De Saumarez monument at Delancey Park for military reasons. The Major wished me to find out whether the States would undertake the demolition or if the military should blow it up. I said that such a measure would be badly received by the population since Admiral de Saumarez was one of the greatest Guernseymen in history. Mr Leale and I went to see the Bailiff on the matter and it was decided that I should see the Major and ask for an interview between the Bailiff and the General.

I realized that I knew scarcely anything about Admiral de Saumarez' life and accordingly I spent half an hour before going to Grange Lodge in reading up his life in Duncan.[42] By the time I had finished I was convinced that the destruction of the monument would be a major Island calamity although I must admit that for the past six months I have thought of the fact that quarrying in the vicinity was stopped many years ago because of the danger of the monument falling and have waited with expectant interest to see whether the tunnelling which has been going on underneath the monument would have any exciting effect.

When I asked the Major to arrange the interview he told me that the General was out of the Island. He telephoned the Staff office, however, to find out whether the demolition could be postponed until the General came back and was told that the General had already given his consent after months of argument and that it was certain that nothing could be done to rescind the decision. I launched into an oration on the virtues of the late Lord Admiral and ended by saying that his memory was even more revered in Sweden than it was in England and that I did not know whether international complications might not arise from interference with the monument.

By the way it is quite impossible for the States to undertake the removal of the monument as we have not the necessary apparatus.

The Bailiff received a letter from the F.K. on the 24th on the matter and wrote a protest next day. This correspondence, together with the F.K. reply, speaks for itself.[43]

We have removed the bronze panels from the base of the monument and doubtless it will fall during the next few days.[44]

---

42 See Duncan (1841).
43 See Item 39: Kratzer to Bailiff: De Saumarez Monument, 24 Nov 1943, p.364.
44 The recovered panels are now displayed at Castle Cornet.

SUNDAY, 28TH NOVEMBER TO TUESDAY, 7TH DECEMBER

The De Saumarez Monument was blown up today. Stones fell as far away as the Vale Road and the bottom of Mont Morin. At Mr Leale's house, Ormond, in the Grandes Maisons Road, two windows were blown out.

I was not as clever as I thought over radio accumulators. We have received orders to produce 100 by the 15th of this month. I am hoping to collect them without having to requisition any actually in use and I have asked the trade to help me.

Two more bodies from the *Charybdis* were washed up – one here and one in Sark – just over a week ago. The one found at the Chouet was buried at the Foulon with full naval honours, last Saturday. It was horribly wet and stormy. The Sark one will probably be buried in that Island.

We have had many robberies in various parts of the Island lately and up to now the thieves have not been caught. Their methods suggest that they are experts.

Mr Toms has been appointed by the F.K. to keep the requisitioned cameras in order. They are going to pay him for his work.

Queenie is back from hospital and is to have treatment at home for three weeks. We hope she will then be cured.

José says several words now and can walk if someone holds one of her hands. We have made no effort to teach her to walk. She is almost out of babyhood now and we find her very lovable.

Zelia gave birth to a veritable Warry last Sunday evening.[45]

WEDNESDAY, 8TH DECEMBER TO THURSDAY, 16TH DECEMBER

The trade have produced 139 accumulators.

The body which was washed up in Sark was brought here for burial and the funeral was last Saturday. There was no German guard of honour since the body could not be identified. We presume that he was a navy man since he wore the standard naval lifebelt.

There is quite a shortage of milk at present and for the first time during the Occupation it has been found necessary to cut the normal daily ration to less than half a pint. Added to this the Germans want us to cut down the butter ration to the French ration so that we can maintain a three month security stock of something over thirty tons. We have pointed out to them that our security stock is actually in the cattle and that even if shipping between the Islands and France were to stop completely we could still supply the population with butter. We usually build up a stock in the summer to

---

45 See Diary entry 27 January 1944 for christening of John Warry.

carry us over the lean winter months. They say that if there were a siege, they would take some of our cattle for meat and this would mean that the butter production would fall. They have also asked for a list of all civilian food stores. They have not told us why they want this information.

Inspector Zachau told me yesterday that when I go to England after the war I shall be put in prison. I asked him why and he said that Guernsey people had told him that I gave up everything to the Germans. I replied that after working with the F.K. for three and a half years I was thankful to say that I had never done anything detrimental to our population. He said he was well aware of that and had often told people so. So, I find myself in the comic position of being defended by the Germans for my work in favour of Guernsey critics.

Occupation Reichsmarks are being withdrawn from circulation in France. I have spoken with Grange Lodge on the matter and they have now sent down the German order for registration with a footnote to the effect that it does not apply in the Channel Islands. There seems to be some talk of making French francs legal tender here and such a step would probably rid us of one of the greatest of post-war dangers, namely the possibility of dumping German money into our banks where a sterling credit would be granted at the expense of the States. Of course this would only be a short-term danger as we would take immediate steps to counteract it.

FRIDAY, 17TH DECEMBER TO THURSDAY, 23RD DECEMBER

There is much talk of an influenza epidemic in England and America and it is said that it has also spread to Germany. There can be little doubt that if it comes to these Islands it will be disastrous with the population in its present state of health and with food and fuel short. The threat of a cut in the butter ration in these circumstances is causing much worry and I suggested at Grange Lodge that the matter should be dropped for the time being. They said we must prepare for siege conditions. I replied that in my opinion the danger of epidemics was far greater than that of a siege. The Major said that I could not have a very high opinion of my country-men and I said that as the obvious reply might land me in prison I thought it better to say nothing at all.

We are hurrying on the amendments to the Children's Allowance scheme so that more families may become eligible and the Bailiff is calling a special meeting of the States instead of waiting, as arranged, for the Budget meeting.

The withdrawal of German money from France has caused dislocation in the local black market for goods imported from France. The bargees will only accept French money and this is very scarce in Guernsey as it is not legal tender here.

Saturday will be our fourth Christmas under German Occupation and coming in the midst of a period of reaction from the superoptimism of last autumn it looks like being a gloomy one for many people. To most Germans and to many of us too, the war seems endless and the happy days of peace nothing more than history. How millions of people in Germany can stand up to the terrific bombing raids and perhaps to epidemics as well, with grief for the loss of their friends and relatives in Russia added, I cannot imagine.

These waves of extravagant optimism and pessimism are a feature of the Occupation and apparently at the internment camps the loss of a sense of proportion is even more pronounced. We often wonder what our reactions will be when we hear the war has ended. Although the strain on the nervous system is not apparent from day to day, it must be terrific and some sign of this will surely become evident.

Meanwhile, quite a large proportion of the population set themselves out to provide entertainment and some of it is very good indeed. We went to see 'Charley's Aunt' Saturday evening and the acting was excellent even if the play was rather a disappointment. We went to hear the Little Choir at the Regal Cinema on Monday and thoroughly enjoyed their carols and on Sunday evening Dick and I walked to St. James' Church to a carol service in aid of the St. John Ambulance. I have never seen the church so crowded. There was hardly room to stand. We enjoyed the walk even more than the service.

José is growing rapidly. She cannot walk by herself yet, but she says a few words and has a charming sense of humour. Her greatest passion is for hammering at the piano – she plays as well with her feet as with her hands.

From the day that Queenie left the hospital she has recovered and is putting on weight and looking really well. The difference in the running of the house is indescribable.

FRIDAY, 24TH DECEMBER TO WEDNESDAY, 29TH DECEMBER

The spirit of Christmas is irrepressible. The girls decorated the telephone room at Hirzel House – this is really a common room for Committee members and staff alike – and I managed to find enough drinks for everybody to have one or two on Friday afternoon. Queenie came and set out immediately to kiss all the men in the room, more than thirty of them. One boy standing next to me chuckled delightedly and was obviously so taken with her that he asked me who she was. He had the grace to blush furiously when I told him. When the last bottle had been drained we left and after calling at George Warry we arrived home in time to put José to bed and eat a hurried supper. Then we changed into evening clothes, climbed back on to the motor cycle and made for town. We went first to the Travers to deposit extra clothes and walked up to Sunnycroft to a dance given by the

Wellingtons. It was a magnificent evening with more than enough to drink, even without the flask which nearly everybody carried. We arranged with the Cambridges to wake up George and Zu and make them give us a drink on the way home and having sung our way across Belgrève Bay, we were glad to find that the motorcycle pulled up obediently outside their house. We called, first softly and eventually much louder until George put his head out of the window and said quietly but very grimly that if we woke up the baby he would wring our bloody necks. We whistled unconcernedly and decided to continue our journey, which we did at a moderate speed and an entirely original song on our lips. We found ourselves at home eventually without mishap, thanks entirely to the fact that the motorcycle had done the journey so many times before.

We decided against a Christmas dinner next day and even on Boxing Day we did not really do justice to the joint.[46]

The banks have received written instructions from the F.K. to the effect that all British notes held by them are to be sent through Grange Lodge to Paris and that when they arrive there they will be paid for in marks. The manager of the Westminster Bank asked that the States should guarantee them against loss of the money in transit to Paris and the matter came before the Controlling Committee this afternoon. The Committee thought there was no reason for a States guarantee but asked me to offer my services in explaining the banks' position to the F.K. This I did and the manager of the Westminster Bank asked me to take the matter up for them. Major Kratzer said that the letter had been written in that form because the F.K. were not bankers and had not the funds available to pay for the sterling on delivery at Grange Lodge. They offered to give a receipt for the money which would mean that the risk of transit to France would be borne by them. I asked what the Germans were going to do with the money but F.K. did not know. The banks are satisfied to receive proper receipts.

While I was at Grange Lodge the Major reminded me that we had sometimes criticised the strict control exercised regarding permits for travel to and from Sark and asked whether I knew about an attempted British landing on that Island. I said that I knew of the landing in September 1942 but of no other, whereupon he informed me that there had been one last Tuesday morning at one o'clock.[47] I said that I had heard nothing whatever

---

46 José recalls that Queenie, on reading this diary in 2005, added that their 'Christmas joint was a rabbit we had reared!'

47 This was Operation Hardtack 7. It took place on the night of 25/26 December and consisted of five men led by Lt. McGonigal. They tried and failed that night to climb the Derrible cliff, landed again two nights later and reached the Hog's Back where they walked into a minefield which alerted the Germans to their presence and killed two members of their party, both from the Free French force.

of it and was surprised that the news had not yet reached Guernsey. He said that he too was surprised and thought that I must have heard about it. He added that this time none of their men had been killed but that at least two of ours had walked into a mine field and been blown up. I asked whether they could be buried here with the naval people but they said that no decision had been reached on the matter. Inspector Zachau told me afterwards that two Guernsey people had told him about the landing this morning and I am surprised that the news had not spread throughout the Island by this afternoon. Anyway we had heard nothing about it at Hirzel House when I left there this afternoon.

The order to cut down the fat ration to 310 grammes per month arrived yesterday and at a meeting of the Controlling Committee held during the afternoon it was decided to submit an alternative proposal to F.K., namely that the ration, now 6 ounces a week, be cut to 4 ounces.[48] The Committee felt that they could not countenance a cut below the latter figure and I was instructed to collaborate with Mr Martel in drafting a suitable letter to the F.K. The Committee met again to consider the draft and my version was toned down a little, the refusal to carry out the order being cut as undiplomatic at present.[49]

THURSDAY, 30TH DECEMBER

I was extremely disappointed yesterday to find that the Committee did not mean to refuse to carry out the fat reduction order immediately and when Dr Symons came into my room this morning I gave him my reasons for thinking that the Committee's decision was a wrong one. Being convinced that we can issue a four ounce fat ration during siege, even if a quarter of our cattle are slaughtered to feed the troops and our own people, it is obvious that a cut to three ounces cannot be in the interests of the population but for the benefit of others. That being so the Controlling Committee cannot conscientiously carry out such an order and I believe that the Germans will respect them more for saying so immediately rather than asking for a change in the order without making their next step clear. Dr Symons saw my point and called in Mr Martel. He agreed and called Mr Johns who also agreed. Then Sir Abraham arrived and we all went down to his room and changed the letter back practically to its original form.[50] I took it to Grange Lodge late this morning and told Mr Krafft that the Major ought to see it as soon as possible.

---

48 See Item 40: C.C. Meeting: Reduction of Fat Ration, 28 Dec 1943, p.366.
49 See Item 41: C.C. Meeting: Reduction of Fat Ration, 29 Dec 1943, p.369 and Item 42: Lainé to F.K.: Reduction of Fat Ration, 29 Dec 1943, p.370.
50 See Item 43: C.C. Meeting: Reduction of Fat Ration, 30 Dec 1943, p.372.

This afternoon I spent stirring a copper full of minced sugar-beet in the depths of a very dark barn, smelling strongly of rabbits and cats.[51] I was called very soon after six o'clock by Grange Lodge who said that they had a very important letter which should be dealt with tonight.

So back to town I went on my motorcycle.

At Grange Lodge I saw Major Kratzer who handed me the letter in question, which, as I expected, contained instructions to carry out their previous order on the reduction of the fat ration. He also made the six following points:–

1. The order is an order and not a wish of the F.K. (This because the Controlling Committee's letter mentioned that our alternative proposal went a considerable way towards meeting their wishes).
2. Urgent military reasons are the cause of its being issued.
3. Had the Controlling Committee effected economies in the previous consumption of fat the order would not have been necessary.
4. If there is any difficulty in weighing 310 grammes the ration may be increased but not beyond 3 oz per week.
5. The order would work in favour of the civilian population in case of siege.
6. The sooner the order is put into effect the sooner we shall attain the 36 tons reserve and be able to revert to our present ration.

He said that the amended order must be in tomorrow's newspaper. I said that the Controlling Committee regarded the whole matter as being one of vital importance and they must be given time to discuss the latest development. I said I could not make any promise about tomorrow's newspaper but would waste no time in laying the F.K.'s views before the Controlling Committee.

I called to see Mr Martel at his home and we arranged to ask the Committee to meet the Bailiff tomorrow morning at ten o'clock. I telephoned all the members and sat down to supper. Before I had finished Dr Symons telephoned to say that he wanted the Committee at the same time to meet in Mr Leale's bedroom (Mr Leale has been ill since last Friday), so I sat down and telephoned everybody once more.

---

51 Sugar beet was minced and boiled until it was palatable for sweetening. A labour intensive task.

1944

At the meeting this morning it was decided to issue the order reducing the ration to three ounces. Two reasons for this decision were:–

Firstly, the only practical continuation of the refusal would be the resignation of the Committee and rightly or wrongly the members feel that this would not be in the interests of the community. Even if the Bailiff could find a successor to Mr Leale (who, alone, is appointed by the States) willing to sign the rationing order, the new President would be regarded as unpatriotic in acquiescing. This means that the new President would almost certainly be an F.K. nominee.

Secondly, there is a danger that if the Committee refused to reduce the ration the Germans might take over the Dairy and perhaps even the Essential Commodities Department. Disadvantages are obvious.

So, once more the spectacular and much more satisfying method has had to be abandoned and the wise counsel of Mr Leale has been followed.[1]

I took the new order to Grange Lodge for approval. The first paragraph had been altered to make it quite clear that it was issued on F.K. instructions. Major Kratzer telephoned Jersey to get the Colonel's approval and he told me that the Colonel was very relieved that the ration was to be reduced here as he is extremely worried over the matter. I said that the F.K. might be pleased but that the Controlling Committee certainly were not and could not agree that it was in the interests of the population, especially with the present shortage of food. The Major claimed that if the population knew all the facts – as we do not – they would be quite happy. He was taking steps immediately to obtain potatoes for us. I said they would have to be quick as there would be no potato ration after next week.

Two facts which we cannot overlook are that even if some cattle are killed we can still continue a four ounce ration and the reserve which they insist upon, 36 tons, is over four months ration at 3 ounces. All reserves are based on a three months siege. I have not yet been convinced that they do not want us to create a reserve which they could draw upon in case of siege. As I said before leaving Grange Lodge, time will tell.

So the year ends with another failure on the part of the Controlling Committee in a fight in the interests of the population and it is not

---

1   See Item 44: C.C. Meeting: Reduction of Fat Ration, 31 Dec 1943, p.373.

surprising if the public, without full knowledge of the situation, think that the Committee could do more for them.

We went to a dance at the Ladies' College on Friday evening.[2] There was no bar and so practically every man took a flask of some horrible concoction. The result was that the motor cycle developed a decided wobble on the way home.

Friday and Saturday were especially fine days and Allied planes passed over and off the Island almost incessantly during daylight. Two American planes came down near the Island and several members of the crews were taken prisoner. One plane crashed near Rocque au Nord in full view of many of our people and some of the crew landed on the rock and were taken off by German boats. Today the Police Inspector telephoned to say that two bodies had been washed ashore and on enquiry at the F.K. I learn that they will be buried by the German air force.

MONDAY, 3RD JANUARY TO WEDNESDAY, 5TH JANUARY

The funeral of the two airmen took place at the Fort George cemetery this morning. Six Island representatives were invited to attend and the Bailiff, J.E.L. Martel, General Williams, Dr Symons, Reverend E.L. Frossard and the Police Inspector went. As the bodies were those of members of a bomber plane, no wreaths were allowed, either from us or from the Germans, and there was no firing of salutes. Whether it is more or less gallant to carry our orders and give your life in a bomber or on a cruiser is a question which I do not feel competent to answer.

Today the States passed amendments to the Children's Allowances scheme whereby more families become eligible and the allowances granted are generally higher than before. It was intended formerly to bring the matter forward on Budget Day but it has been hurried on so that families may get the benefit as soon as possible during the winter. The F.K. insisted on an amendment of their own whereby every family eligible for any allowance at all gets the full four shillings allowed for each child. Thus a man earning 68/– weekly, with four children, now gets 16/– allowance. A man earning 68/6 gets nothing at all since 68/– is the maximum wage entitling a man with four children to an allowance. Under our scheme a man with four children would be granted an allowance which, with his wages, would make his income up to 68/–.

After the meeting the Bailiff invited the members of the States into the Jurats' Room to wish them a Happy New Year and while they were there he asked me to read to them a letter which he had received from Jurat Leale

---

2   The Ladies' College was then in the Grange. It moved to Les Gravées in 1965.

explaining the Controlling Committee's action in regard to the cut in the fat ration and asking for a vote of confidence from the States.[3] The vote was given unanimously – and I should think so too! Mr Leale himself read a letter which he is sending to the F.K. on the matter.[4]

Bombing over the Continent is almost incessant and we are wondering whether at last there is to be an attack from the west. Everybody is convinced that 1944 will be the last of these strange years of hatred and misery and grief and for my part I wonder whether we, in these Islands, will be lucky enough to come through to peace or will be the ignominious mice in the fight between our friends and our foes. There can be little doubt in the mind of anybody who troubles to think at all that if these Islands are attacked the civilian population will suffer more than either combatant since we have no shelter of any kind. It is not a pleasant thought that we may be called upon, not to defend ourselves and our families, but to run like rats out of the way of the fighting. I pray very often that we may be spared such an indignity.

Meanwhile, we forget such threats as often as we can and dance and drink (when we can find something to drink) and read and work and listen to as much music as we can – and dream of happy times with our friends whom we have not seen for more than three and a half years.

THURSDAY, 6TH JANUARY TO FRIDAY, 14TH JANUARY

José now walks – up to ten paces. Unfortunately she cannot walk without giggling and after ten steps she is so helpless she sits down suddenly.

On Saturday Mr Hill-Cottingham was tried by the Royal Court for attempting to get rationed goods illegally. A lorry which was searched by the police at the Essential Commodities flour store at Vauvert School was found to have loaded upon it some flour which the driver said he had been ordered by Mr Hill-Cottingham to deliver to the latter's house. It turned out that the flour, with which was mixed sundry pieces of string, etc. had been swept up from the floor and although a sample of this, when sifted, was declared by two bakers to be good flour and fit for human consumption, the fact remains that it might have been contaminated with T.B. or other germs left there by spitting workmen. However, the Court found him guilty and fined him £200 and costs. Public opinion seems to be divided on the Court's verdict; some people thinking it an unfair one and others that he should have been punished much more severely. Grange Lodge seem to hold the latter opinion.

---

3   See Item 45: Leale to Bailiff: Reduction of Fat Ration, 4 Jan 1944, p.375.
4   See Item 46: Leale to F.K.: Reduction of Fat Ration, 4 Jan 1944, p.376 and Item 47: Kratzer to Leale: Reduction of Fat Ration, 6 Jan 1944, p.377.

Two German soldiers have arrived here to make arrangements for the transfer of all requisitioned radios, with the exception of those lent to the forces, to France. We valued each set when it was taken into store, or soon after, and they appear to be willing to pay for them at our valuation. The result will be at least £60,000 worth of marks which will eventually find their way to the banks and will have to be bought by the States.

With the exception of Mr Leale and Mr Martel I have not discovered one member of the States who understood the details of the amended Children's Allowances scheme which they passed last Wednesday. The reason appears to be that the explanation in the Billet d'Etat was not full enough. I should think that this is a unique case in the history of the States. Actually, many members studied the question carefully and there was quite a long debate before the measure was adopted but they all started with a false impression of the subject and this misled them.

Dick and I went to a delightful two piano concert, yesterday afternoon. The pianists were Miss Lilian Walker Clarke and Mrs Bond and their performances gave us a real thrill. It did my pride no good and I have not looked at the piano since.

Mr Frampton of the States' Office is very ill and it is questionable whether he will ever work again.

SATURDAY, 15TH JANUARY TO MONDAY, 17TH JANUARY

At Grange Lodge this morning Major Kratzer asked whether Mr Hill-Cottingham had already given up his public duties (we had two letters from the F.K. on Saturday, one asking this question and the other asking for a record of the trial). I said he had given up such duties. The Major said that if he had been tried by a German court he would have received several years of imprisonment on his own confession without taking into consideration the indictment. I explained Mr Hill-Cottingham's defence, both as he had put it and what he had omitted to place before the court but the Major said that did not alter his views. I asked whether the Germans were thinking of pursuing the matter further and he said that would be decided in Jersey. He added that as the goods were imported ones the F.K. were interested.

I asked about the payment for radios. I wanted to know whether the Germans were going to pay for them now or were going to give us an acknowledgement of their debt and pay after the war. The Major said that upon requisition the radios had come under the control of the F.K. and the decision was, therefore, theirs.

I explained that I was concerned whether our valuations would be accepted, because, if they were not, the whole matter must be settled before the sets left the Island. It would be hopeless trying to right the matter if there

196

was any tangle after they had been shipped. He said that he understood that our valuations would be accepted but that we might write and ask for a formal acknowledgement. The matter would then be submitted to the appropriate German authority outside the Island.

There is some question of mining the road opposite our house and if this happens they will have to transfer the railway to run through our front garden. I asked at Grange Lodge that if the matter comes before them, they ask that it be kept as far from the house as possible. The vibration cannot but harm the building.

I think I mentioned that all the British notes in the banks here have been taken by the Germans and that all the banks have protested although they have had to give them up. I heard a few days ago from Sarre that in Jersey the States refused to hand over their notes which amount to £86,000 as against £16,000 here and that the matter had not yet been settled. This morning I asked the Major, who has been in Jersey recently, what had been the outcome of the protest. He said that he did not know but that our notes were in Jersey. I said that, of course, if Jersey were not required to give theirs up, we took it for granted that ours would be handed back to us. He laughed and said that this case showed how much better we (I took him to mean the F.K. and the Controlling Committee) were in Guernsey than in Jersey. I answered that it showed us nothing of the sort, but simply that we would have to be much more careful in future.

TUESDAY, 18TH JANUARY AND WEDNESDAY, 19TH JANUARY

The Germans have ordered that a civilian dentist be appointed to attend to the teeth of foreign civilians employed by O.T. Dr Symons, Mr Bowen and I went to see Inspector Zachau yesterday afternoon and explained that the few dentists we have left in the Island are already working very hard and that in any case if one of them is forced to attend to foreigners whose cleanliness is questionable he will undoubtedly lose his other patients. Eventually we compromised by arranging that a surgery and apparatus be provided by the O.T. authorities and that each dentist take his turn.

Major Kratzer informed that Jersey has handed over the British notes in possession of the banks.

F.K. informed us that as from January 1st it will no longer be possible for us to sell our marks to the paymaster in return for francs in France. We have stopped S.K.H. from transferring their marks to France through us as they have done in the past and this afternoon the F.K. asked me why we had stopped such transfers. I said that as we could not export any marks we could not export those belonging to S.K.H. I also said we had a limited surplus of funds in the Barclays Bank account and that when these had been used we would have to borrow from France to pay for our purchases in that country. We did not intend to use such funds to pay S.K.H. bills. The Major saw the point and agreed with our decision.

As from tomorrow both the local newspapers are to be reduced considerably in size and they have notified the public that they are raising the price of the paper from twopence to twopence halfpenny. Mr Martel telephoned *The Star* on the subject this morning and was told that they had received the approval of the German censor. Working on German orders we instituted a Prices Determination Committee some time ago and all rises in price have to be submitted to them. This afternoon I asked Grange Lodge whether they knew anything about the censor's approval and they telephoned him in my presence. He answered that he had not given approval but had told Mr Webster that he had no objection (or that he was not interested, I am not sure which). F.K. said they were surprised that the price of the paper should be raised with a decrease in size and I said that it might be because of a fall in revenue from advertisements. The Prices Determination Committee wanted to examine the case before granting any rise in price. (I happen to know the Guernsey Press Co. are making considerable profits). The Major agreed that it was entirely our affair.

I saw Mr Martel who telephoned Mr Webster. The latter said that he would not change his mind and that the price would be raised. Mr Martel warned him that he was inviting prosecution and he said that he invited it and he was very tired of the whole administration and especially of the Controlling Committee. This evening I telephoned the Managing Director of the Press Co. and he told me that his firm had not been in favour of the rise but had been talked into it by Webster. He is coming to see me tomorrow morning.

THURSDAY, 20TH JANUARY TO MONDAY, 24TH JANUARY

The managing director of the Press Co. told me that his paper would not be raised in price and *The Star* also appeared on Thursday at twopence.

Last Wednesday the Bailiff wrote to F.K. informing them that he had received Mr Hill-Cottingham's resignation as Deputy and in accordance with local law he would submit it to the States at their next meeting. He received a letter back from them asking him to order Mr Hill-Cottingham to divest himself of all his public duties. I saw Major Kratzer on the matter and asked whether, in view of the fact that the Bailiff was following the constitutional method by placing the resignation before the States, they wished him to take any further steps. The Major said that the matter was merely a formality but that as the F.K. were interested officially in the control of imports they wished to order Mr Hill-Cottingham's resignation themselves. I asked whether that meant that the constitutional method was to be superseded and he replied that the F.K. had that power always and if it had not been exercised here it had been in other occupied territories. The matter is still under discussion by the Bailiff and the Controlling Committee.

Mr Frampton, the States Accountant, died this morning.

We have made another landing in Italy, about thirty miles south of Rome.

TUESDAY, 25TH JANUARY TO WEDNESDAY, 2ND FEBRUARY

On Monday I went with Mr Leale to Grange Lodge to discuss the reduction of the fat ration, etc. A memo of this meeting should be pinned to this page.[5] From what I can gather from unofficial conversations the Major is in a minority in advocating such a large reserve of butter. He is the perfect stone-waller and we would give much for the arbitration of the Protecting Power at these meetings. We would certainly not lose as often as we do.

The F.K. have ordered eight motorcycles, four cars and three lorries to be taken off the road and to be handed over to the military. My motorcycle is one of the unfortunates. The remarks shouted at me as I ride my pedal cycle to Town are varied and sometimes original. In addition, 105 cars, 28 motorcycles, 20 vans and 15 lorries have to be produced for purchase by the Germans and it looks as though Vic's car, which I have tried to hold for him, will have to go this time.

Harry Broughton came down to supper on Monday and brought with him the Grieg and Rachmaninoff (no. 2) piano concertos. We still have them and have played them each evening on Dick's gramophone. Not only have I forgotten the war for two or three hours at a time, but I have retasted the bliss which I had not known since I first discovered big music.

José now walks so well she accompanies her mother to get the milk and the bread. Her babyhood is over.

Last Thursday, John, George and Zu's son, was christened. I am godfather and we spent the evening together and ate and drank well.

THURSDAY, 3RD FEBRUARY TO MONDAY, 7TH FEBRUARY

The Bailiff has received a letter from the F.K. stating that the British notes handed in recently by the Savings Bank are not to be taken over by the Germans but will be retained in Paris for the time being. Yesterday at Grange Lodge we asked whether they were to be returned, since it seemed unfair that the Savings Bank should receive neither payment nor notes. The Major explained that they were to be kept in Paris although they still belonged to

---

5   See Item 48: Meeting with F.K.: Reduction of Fat Ration, 31 Jan 1944, p.378.

the bank, thereby avoiding the risk of transport. Mr Leale asked whether the Major looked upon this measure as advantageous to the bank and the Major said that of course it was. We can only gather from this that British money is more valuable than marks, even in German eyes. When the Major gave this answer, Mr Leale looked at me and put out his tongue in astonishment and the Major caught him in the act. He said he did not understand why Mr Leale looked so surprised.

The radios which are to be taken to France are still here for lack of suitable shipping space.

We have asked several times recently whether the Bailiff's letters of May 1943 to the Red Cross and the Protecting Power ever reached their destination. Yesterday the Major told us that Jersey had not been able to find out and Mr Leale thereupon pointed out how unsatisfactory this was from our point of view. The Major promised to take up the matter again on our behalf.

The body of a British airman, a sergeant, was washed up on the north coast last Saturday. Apparently he had on him British, Belgian, Dutch and Spanish money.

Little John Warry is very ill with congestion of the lungs.

TUESDAY, 8TH FEBRUARY TO FRIDAY, 11TH FEBRUARY

On Tuesday the Bailiff received a letter from the F.K. stating that, in future, the surplus marks which the States have always bought from the banks here are to be made available to the occupying forces.[6] Until the beginning of the year we had always done this, the German paymaster using the marks to pay the troops and handing us francs in Granville in return. In this we did not have to make any physical transfer of money to Granville and thus saved the risk of transport. Now, however, we are no longer permitted to transfer funds in this way and the result is that the Paymaster, in taking our marks, has nothing to give us in return. The letter means that he will continue to take them. We had budgetted for a large sum in marks in hand by the end of 1944, but now we shall have none and our deficit will rise by nearly a million pounds. In fact, of course, this step makes no difference to our financial position, since if we held the marks which we buy from the banks they would be useless to us whilst the amount we hand over under the new arrangement will be put to Occupation Account.

Mr Leale and I talked over the matter at Grange Lodge today and from hints dropped it looks as though the German policy may be that it does not matter frightfully if they tax us beyond the possibility of recovery since the

---

6   See Item 49: Melzer to Bailiff: Occupation Costs, 8 Feb 1944, p.380.

British Government is bound to help us out after the war! WE EXPLAINED THAT we are financially independent of England but they seemed a bit incredulous. However, they suggested that Mr Leale put his arguments in writing when they would be sent on to the higher authority which issued this last order.[7]

Yesterday Hugh Tidd married Nancy Guilbert at the Castel Church. The church was nearly full of people and I played the organ. We went to Mrs Massy-Dawson for the reception and ate and drank up to pre-war standards.

Dr Symons has asked the German staff doctor for permission to issue extra rations of fat to hospital patients and staffs and I think he will be successful. We are so short of nurses, especially properly trained ones, that this concession should make the work much easier.

We are expecting a visit from a lady of the French Red Cross within the next day or so. We do not know whether this is in response to our much-repeated appeal for help.

SATURDAY, 12TH FEBRUARY TO WEDNESDAY, 16TH FEBRUARY

Madame Danel of the French Red Cross arrived in the Island early on Monday morning to visit French North African prisoners of war who are working here. I met her first with Mr Martel at five o'clock on Monday afternoon and I have spent most of the past two days in her company. We were very disappointed to find that she had not come here on our behalf but she is in constant touch with the Paris representative of the International Red Cross and she is going to put our difficulties before him. Incidentally we wrote to him last August but he never mentioned our letter to Madame Danel and we wonder whether the letter ever arrived in Paris.

During her visit I took her to Baron de Coudenhove and the Pommiers on Monday afternoon, Raymond Falla, the Bailiff, Mr Leale, our Red Cross department, Genet the French baker, Dr Symons (to tea), the Dubras and the Frossards on Tuesday and then on to supper here, where she met Sutcliffe and Lambert; and today to Canon Hickey and the Sisters of the Sacred Heart, to the States Meeting and to Blanchelande this morning. This afternoon while I was busy at the Gasworks on an enquiry Heggs and I are making, she had to leave suddenly by boat and I have not been able to finish the work we were doing together.

Everybody who met Madame Danel found her charming and Queenie and I are hoping to see her and the rest of her family both here and in France after the war. She says the French people are still full of spirit and she thinks we in the Islands are like snails who have disappeared into our shells until

7   See Item 50: Meeting with F.K.: Occupation Costs, 11 Feb 1944, p.381.

the war finishes, that some of the allied bombing is causing havoc in France – especially American bombing – and that the centre of the French Red Cross in Paris was completely destroyed recently by bombs, that the war should finish this year, that there is sufficient to eat in the country and that town populations are helped by their country friends in France and that generally control is not as tight in France as it is here. She took with her a list of medical supplies which we need urgently to complete the three months security stock which we need to hold in case of siege. I hope that she realizes, after talks she had with us, that we are in a bad way as far food is concerned.

THURSDAY, 17TH FEBRUARY TO MONDAY, 21ST FEBRUARY

On Saturday evening I received a telephone call from the Supervisor who told me that Barclays Bank had been informed by the manager of the German brothel (a Frenchman) that F.K. had given instructions that about 40,000 marks were to be transferred to various addresses in France. Apparently this money represents the earnings of the girls and is being transferred on their behalf. The procedure would be for this money to go through the clearing in Paris, but as far as the actual cash is concerned, the marks would remain in the local bank and would have to be bought by the States in the same way that all other surplus marks are bought. Thus the transfer would cost the States the full amount transferred and we get nothing from the brothel! I took the matter up at Grange Lodge this morning and was informed by Inspector Zachau that he had already put our case to Jersey and St. Malo on several occasions, using exactly those arguments put forward by me but had been told that there was no other way in which the money could be transferred. I said that we had told Barclays to do nothing for the time being and that we were expecting something in writing from Grange Lodge. I added that when we received their letter we would send in our protest and would wait for their reply before giving Barclays further orders. The Inspector said we could protest but he advised us not to hold up the transfer. Later in the morning I saw M.V.R. Melzer and asked whether we might get the money, paid in to Barclays by the brothel (and by the Soldatenkaufhaus which is a French firm selling small articles to the Germans) for transfer to France, changed by the Paymaster into francs in Granville so that we could obtain from France goods in return. He promised to find out for us.

We have also received today a copy of a letter sent by our accountant in Granville, Hall, to an official at the Bureau des Changes in Paris. In it Hall states that he has been informed by Baron von Aufsess of the F.K. that in future we shall no longer be allowed to transfer credits to France for purchases there. This I take to mean that our credits at Barclays here, amounting to three quarters of a million sterling, will be useless for the remainder of the Occupation and that from now onwards we will have to borrow from the French Government for all purchases we make. If this is so it means the end of all hopes of unloading on France the surplus marks we have collected in the past through our purchases of marks from the banks. France's objections to giving us goods for such money is, of course, quite understandable and I am surprised that it has not been stopped long ago. What appears so objectionable to me, however, is that the whole matter has been negotiated by the F.K. without any discussion with us at all. After all we have to foot the bill.

When Mr Leale discussed the reduction of the fat ration with Major Kratzer some weeks ago he said that in the event of very cold weather setting in he would ask for a temporary increase. With the great shortage of food this winter – the potato ration stopped weeks ago and meat is very scarce – the reduced fat ration is very serious and today I submitted to Grange Lodge a draft order giving a temporary increase of 2 ounces per head per week. I was promised a reply tomorrow.

They told me at Grange Lodge today that some ships were attacked outside Granville last week. Apparently they were empty and none were sunk although some damage was done. I hope that Madame Danel was not aboard any of them.

Several people have been put in prison recently for having radio sets in their possession. It is said that the Germans receive many anonymous letters giving information on the matter and it is also rumoured that civilians give verbal information as well. I do not know whether this is true or not.

TUESDAY, 22ND FEBRUARY TO WEDNESDAY, 23RD FEBRUARY

We have been granted permission to issue an extra two ounces of fat per head this week.

The attack on the ships at Granville took place last Tuesday week so that Madame Danel could not have been aboard.

The Bailiff has received a letter from the F.K. ordering the issue of a 2½d postage stamp. This has been opposed by us for some time and the reason given, the saving of paper, is not a very convincing one.

THURDAY, 24TH FEBRUARY TO WEDNESDAY, 1ST MARCH

We have received orders from the F.K. that the S.K.H. and the brothels are to be allowed transfer facilities through Barclays and the French clearing.

José now climbs the stairs by herself and trots everywhere.

There was an attack by E boats on a German convoy off Jersey last Saturday night. Mr Krafft who was going on leave was on one of the ships in the convoy.

Queenie went ormering last week and came back with nineteen ormers and a broken fingernail.[8] We bartered the packet of cigarettes which I am due to receive next Tuesday for another dozen ormers and we are having mighty meals.

I ride a bicycle now that I have lost my motorcycle and so far nobody has passed me on the road on a similar mount. The result is that I always arrive at the office delightfully warm.

THURSDAY, 2ND MARCH TO WEDNESDAY, 8TH MARCH

Arising out of our interview of the 11th of February at Grange Lodge, the Bailiff wrote to the F.K. protesting against this taking over of R.K. We have now received a reply in which they state that the debt incurred is to be looked upon as an Empire debt and not an Island one. At last we have received from them written confirmation of their financial policy towards the Islands and we regard the letter as of extreme importance in post-war negotiations. Copies of the correspondence are attached hereto.[9]

Heggs and I have just finished an investigation, on behalf of the Prices Determination Committee into a claim put forward by the Gas Company for a rise in the price of gas. The work has been fascinating and, with my somewhat scanty knowledge of practical accountancy, has taxed my ingenuity to the full.

The Controlling Committee decided last Friday to grant to all civil servants the first £200 of salary in full. Up to the present everything over £150 was subject to a 50% cut and the Controlling Committee decision therefore means a rise of £25 per annum. In view of the fact that doctors' and hospital fees have just cost me nearly £50 the rise has come at the right time.

A German fighter crashed at the Castel a day or so ago.

The war drags on with continuous advances by the Russians, terrific air attacks on Germany both by day and night and no sign at all of any dramatic change in German morale. In Italy we seem to be having difficulty in doing more than hold our own.

Dr Kratzer, M.V.R. Melzer and Mr Krefft came to Hirzel House a few days ago to inform us that the F.K. as such is to be disbanded and that civil administration is to be taken over by the military.

Apparently the Major and Colonel are leaving the Islands but some of the other officers will be staying on. What the effect of this move will be on the treament of the civilian population remains to be seen but it appears to me that in effect there will no longer be any appeal from a military decision.

---

8   See Item 97: Ormers and Ormering, p.487.
9   See Item 51: Bailiff to F.K.: Occupation Costs, 18 Feb 1944, p.383.

Up to the present the F.K. could appeal to their Paris Headquarters if they thought any military decision was against our interests.

Motor cars, vans, lorries and motorcycles have been taken off the roads lately for purchase by the military. They will probably be paid for in R.K. which will find their way to the banks to be purchased by us and taken back once more by the Germans. Alice in Wonderland is pure logic to our present financial mess.

THURSDAY, 9TH MARCH TO WEDNESDAY, 15TH MARCH

Father's birthday was last Friday. He was eighty. We had a tea-party at the Bouet and those present were:- father, mother, Mads and Irwin, Dick, Zu, Mrs Henry Ash, Fan, Mr Kilshaw (who came late), Skipper, Queenie and myself. It was almost like old times and Dad told his unique stories about his horses. (I forgot to mention José among the guests). We thought about the rest of the crowd and longed to have them with us and assured each other that next year would be altogether different. Dad declares that we shall have a party of at least seventy – just like a Guillemette wedding reception.

This week we have been allowed to issue an extra two ounces of fat again and a pound and a half of macaroni. The shortage of food is serious, many families being without potatoes and roots being very scarce. Timmer, who buys vegetables for the Germans, is taking much of the food that is badly needed by the civilian population and growers are selling to him because he can offer high prices.

Dr Symons was successful some time ago in getting extra fat for the patients and nursing staffs of the hospitals.

It seems to be generally agreed, both by the Germans and ourselves, that an invasion of Europe will be begun soon. I wonder? The Russians are still moving forward and not much of Russia is still left in German hands. What the effect of their advance on the Balkans will be we should soon know if the advance continues at its present rate. American daylight raids on Germany are in full swing. It appears as though they are trying to cripple the German fighter force before the invasion begins.

Little John Warry has recovered completely. For a time the doctors feared for his life.

THURSDAY, 16TH MARCH TO WEDNESDAY, 22ND MARCH

We have planted sixteen boxes of potatoes during the past week of which eleven were Polish seed. The weather has been very dry for some weeks and the ground is in good condition. We hope for a downpour of rain now that the planting is finished.

Mr Krafft is back from leave and he told me of his adventure on the way to St. Malo. When their convoy was off Jersey during a very dark night, a sailor came running downstairs shouting that there were British E boats about. They rushed on deck but could see nothing. One of the patrol vessels apparently could see the E boats which were stationary and fired tracer shells at them. The British boats opened up with their machine guns and killed and wounded several men. The boat Mr Krafft was on was not hit but one of the gunners told him he had seen two torpedoes pass close under their stern. They put into Jersey for the night.

Mr Leale and I went to interview Colonel Count von Helldorff at Summerland on Monday morning, (see memorandum attached).[10] He asked Mr Leale to discuss the Fire Brigade question and when I told F.K. of the interview they were annoyed we had not told them we were going. They are very keen on keeping control of civilian affairs, and rightly so, in my opinion, but we were glad of an opportunity of talking with the staff officer who apparently is responsible for the work of the F.K. He seemed very interested in the production of foodstuffs in the Island and said that he had talked the matter over with F.K.

Today I am told that Major Kratzer is returning to Guernsey.

The Russians seem to be pressing forward on all fronts and it looks as though they are going to open a full scale offensive against Finland. They offered Finland peace terms recently but these apparently were refused. It is said that there has been some trouble in Hungary and that the Germans have taken control there. The bombing of Germany and of factories in France continues day and night.

THURSDAY, 23RD MARCH TO MONDAY, 3RD APRIL

Major Kratzer is back here in charge of the F.K. He told me this morning that it is not quite decided whether he will stay but that the F.K. remains in being. The Islands have been declared fortresses and this apparently means that in the cause of defence the military can claim more of their own way than formerly.

Last Saturday week being a very good tide for ormers I obtained permission to use the boat. Dick, Nigel, Harry Bichard, Raymond Falla and I were all allowed to go! The control at St. Sampson's Harbour is very strict, all the boats having to report on the south side and wait for the patrol boat before leaving the harbour. By half past eleven about ten boats were ready, most of them edging up to the harbour mouth or puffing impatiently about. A guard was laboriously checking names. The boats were filled with a most

---

10 See Item 52: Meeting with F.K.: Firemen's contracts, 20 Mar 1944, p.385.

piratical-looking assortment, nearly all of whom had taken advantage of the occasion to shirk shaving. The sun shone brilliantly and the water was just the right shade of green. At last, after a few false alarms we were allowed out and every throttle was opened wide. The guard boat was nowhere near first in the race and what is more as soon as we were outside the breakwater we could go where we liked. I did not see the guard boat again that day. We revelled in the luxury of being afloat once more and crossed to Herm, chatting happily and filling ourselves with memories of the way the east coast and the islands looked on such a perfect day. We thought only a little of all the automatic anti-aircraft guns which line the coast and would open a death-dealing fire at the first sign of a British plane in the Russel. No such plane appeared.

We landed Raymond in Herm and slid quietly across to Jethou where we anchored off the east coast, ate our lunch and went ashore. I am not good at ormering, mainly because I always think there is a better spot just round the corner. I turned tons of heavy rocks in my ramble and eventually as the tide turned came back towards the boat. Dick had not moved more than a hundred yards and had fifty ormers. I had five. I decided that I might as well try to find a few more and by the time it was too late I had found a good place. My total catch was fifteen. A boy collected ten dozen from the creek where we moored the boat. A party of twenty German sailors came methodically across the beach, turning every stone and collecting buckets full of ormers.

We went back to Herm and picked up Raymond who brought his catch down to the steps in a wheelbarrow. Besides three dozen ormers he had two congers as long as he is tall and five lobsters.

We came back to Guernsey without incident and crawled home, luxuriously tired, to talk of our day and the pleasures of our simple Island life.

Queenie did not come with us but went down to the low water mark in front of our house and came back with thirty ormers. Skipper had a dozen ormers given to him.

On Monday night just as the new moon was going down, there was a roar of many planes and guided by searchlights and controlled by flares sent up from the airport scores of German planes went echoing across the deathly still night to attack south west England. They came back, flying very low, an hour or so later. A sinister night.

We have received a letter from Hall, in Granville, saying that in Paris they know nothing of the arrangement whereby the French government is to allow us unlimited credit for the purchase of goods in France.

We have planted another four boxes of potatoes and have started erecting fencing to limit the wanderings of José.

TUESDAY, 4TH APRIL TO THURSDAY, 13TH APRIL

Queenie telephoned me at the office this morning to say that José had pulled the hot iron off the table and had burnt her hand badly on it. I felt sick. When I arrived home she was in bed asleep but soon after she woke up and was brought downstairs just as happy as usual. Luckily Queenie does not lose her head in emergencies and had bound up the burns properly. This afternoon Dr Sutcliffe came down and put on a dressing. José submitted like a hero.

The new 2½d postage stamp was on sale for the first time yesterday, Wednesday 12th. By F.K. orders and in view of the fact that the object of issuing this stamp is to save paper, sales were restricted to ten at a time. Everyone went in more than once and I should imagine that most of the 120,000 printed so far have already been sold.

This evening just after we had finished supper we heard a roar and rushing to the front window we were in time to see eight British planes fly down the Russel. None appeared to be hit by the hundreds of shells aimed at them. It was queer to think that by the time we had finished washing up they might be back in England and that their crews might be drinking good beer.

We have finished our trellis fence and some temporary gates so that José will now have to give up her bad habit of sitting in the middle of the road. As always in the spring the urge to work is with us and we hope to finish off the levelling of a lower terrace which we began last summer. The Germans, meanwhile, are knocking down walls right and left near the bay.

A Red Cross message from England says that Marguerite, Hubert and Jack have visited Malcolm. We can only imagine that Jack must be Jack Hubert. I wonder what tales he tells of our doings here.

Last December the Germans insisted that two men, Harry Ingrouille and Duquemin should go to Alderney with their boat to fish for the garrison. On Monday morning Major Kratzer said that I might be interested to hear they had gone fishing from Alderney on Saturday and had not been seen since. He added that when their boat was landed in Alderney in December it had been badly damaged and that the repairs done to it had been of a temporary nature. It was feared that they might have been drowned. I said that, for the men's sakes, I hoped they were drinking whisky in England.[11] The Major hoped, for the safety of the fortress that they were not.

No payment has been made yet for the British notes taken from the banks some months ago and it appears now that the German authorities in France are of opinion that there are still large numbers of notes in the Island. Mr Leale was asked on Wednesday to estimate how many notes

---

11 For the details of this escape see Kreckeler (1978) and Bell (2000).

208

were in circulation before the Occupation and how many had been taken by evacuees to England. If there are any English notes left here it will take a better organization than we could ever hope to put into operation to find them. Even with the mark guaranteed by the States as it is at present, British notes command about double their value for purchases on the French black market. George Vaudin says that every bargee on the run from Granville to the Islands is a millionaire and that their women folk all walk about Granville in fur coats!

On Good Friday I played the organ at St. John's for Steiner's Crucifixion and enjoyed myself thoroughly. The day before I played at the Vale for the funeral of our neighbour, Jimmie Le Tissier, who was the finest neighbour anybody could wish to have. When I arrived at the church a girl we know was getting married and I played the Wedding March for them.

The Russians continue their advance. Odessa has fallen, the Germans in the Crimea are being attacked ferociously, the advance into Rumania and Czechoslovakia continues. Our bombing of Germany and Austria as well as of occupied territories never ceases during suitable weather. In Italy nothing spectacular happens. The U boat has lost its news interest. We all wonder how and when the war will end.

FRIDAY, 14TH APRIL TO TUESDAY, 18TH APRIL

Over eighty thousand stamps were sold on the first day of issue.

On Saturday morning during a conversation with Major Kratzer through Mr Krafft as interpreter, he reminded me that F.K. had ordered that dogs were not to be admitted to the Markets. I said that I remembered the order. Mr Krafft continued with a deprecatory smirk, that while in the meat market the day before a dog had appeared and done his BUSINESS right in front of him.

"Good Heavens!" I exclaimed, "he could not have realized that you were Major Kratzer." "No," he replied, "and if I had been able to speak English I would have given him a good dressing down!"

An enormous pair of silver candlesticks appeared in a shop window in the town recently with an explanation of their quality in German. Obviously it was hoped to find a German buyer. After a chat with Mr Leale I called on the proprietor and explained that if they were bought by a German and paid for in marks, those marks would find their way to a bank, be bought by the States and be reclaimed by the German paymaster to pay the troops. In other words, the candlesticks would be a gift from the States of Guernsey. The price asked was three thousand marks. The proprietor had not realized the position and said that they were being sold on commission. I suggested that the owner be told that the Controlling Committee were surprised at the fact that an attempt was being made to sell such valuables and that she be given an explanation of the loss to the States if the deal went through.

The candlesticks were taken out of the window and the owner was spoken to by the proprietor of the shop. She said she was only doing what hundreds of other people had been doing throughout the Occupation and that she would sell them through another dealer. The proprietor of the shop pointed out to me that through my talk with her she had lost commission and the States would be no better off. I told her that until the beginning of this year we had been able to get rid of most of our surplus marks for goods purchased in France but that the position had become much more serious since we received nothing at all for marks taken by the Germans.

I spoke to members of the Chamber of Commerce on the subject and an effort is to be made to bring before traders the effect of continuing to sell valuables to Germans. It is not fair to accuse sellers of a lack of patriotism until we are sure that they are aware of the effect of sales of this kind.

Recently we received from France a consignment of seed potatoes. The Germans claimed about forty-three tons as the share due to military units which cultivate land. Whether this is fair or not I do not know but they told us that, of course, they would pay us in full for what they have taken. Actually we have paid for the consignment in France in francs and I therefore asked that we should be paid in the same currency. I pointed out that as we now owed the French Government for the potatoes it was useless giving us marks since we could not transmit them to France. F.K. promised that they would be paid for in francs.

WEDNESDAY, 19TH APRIL TO THURSDAY, 27TH APRIL

Five years ago today we were married. We do not know yet what married life under settled conditions is like.

During the past few days scarcely an hour of daylight has passed without our hearing the R.A.F. either overhead or a few miles off the coast. At night terrific explosions have shaken the house. The weather has been gorgeous and this morning as I cycled to the office I thought what a perfect day this would be to end the war. Instead, everybody is on tiptoe waiting for the invasion to start. There is a lull in the fighting in Russia, in Italy no great effort seems to be made to press forward, in Yugoslavia the patriots are keeping the country in an uproar and the tension is becoming ever more intense. Bombing all over Europe is crippling transport. For our part we hope that whatever operations have to take place will start soon and finish quickly and we shall be alive and whole to see the end.

We went to Sutcliffe for drinks yesterday afternoon and had champagne and WHISKY! I had almost forgotten the taste.

FRIDAY, 28TH APRIL TO MONDAY, 8TH MAY

On Friday Major Kratzer told me that he wanted me to go with him to see some of the communal kitchens and we went round in the F.K. car that afternoon. We visited the St. Peter Port one first. It is run by the staff of Le Noury's and is in the firm's bakehouse in Berthelot Street. Everything was spotless and the Major would not believe I had not warned them of his coming. The same happened at Cobo and at the Vale. These kitchens serve a very useful purpose in supplying meals especially for men who are living alone. Of course there are hundreds in this position with their wives and families in England.

The Major has taken it into his head to see how we are running the Island and without any warning or any invitation to anyone to escort him, he went to see the hospitals the other day. He said he was surprised that such a rich Island should be so poor in hospitals and I explained that a new General Hospital was due to come before the States when the war started. I added that he should remember that the Germans had taken over our two best hospitals, the Vauquiédor and the Victoria. Some time ago when typhus broke out amongst the foreign workers here, we made a special effort to get back some of the King Edward Sanatorium, then in the hands of the military. F.K. took up the matter on our behalf and after a long struggle we regained possession of the building in question. When the F.K. officers visited the Sanatorium they discovered that not only were we not using the block in question, but it had not even been put into a proper state of repair. They pointed this out to me later and I had to swallow this reproof with an uneasy feeling that they were probably right. I have suggested to Mr Leale that he make it a practice to visit States' institutions weekly.

Last night was as bright as day and from 2 a.m. onwards until after four o'clock the sound of planes and light naval artillery made the night hideous. This morning we are told that there was a naval engagement off the south of the Island and that a ship in a convoy on the way here was sunk. She carried a cargo consisting of manure and a sewage cart! I understand that out of a crew of 21 only 15 were saved.

The lull in the land fighting continues everywhere. What it means, nobody knows. Meanwhile bombing continues from Rumania to France.

TUESDAY, 9TH MAY TO FRIDAY, 12TH MAY

We have been informed this week that the motor cars which were taken recently and the British notes taken from the banks are being paid for in marks. Mr Leale has protested about the cars. It is perfectly obvious that the Germans have not the slightest interest in maintaining the solvency of the Island.

Today at Grange Lodge Major Kratzer wished me goodbye once more. He is being transferred to a Feldkommandantur in France. Apparently Raymond Falla suggested to him that he might like to restore the butter ration before he left and this evening he told me that if we prepared an order to this effect he would sign it, provided we attained the reserve of 36 tons before putting the order into operation. The order will be ready for his signature tomorrow.

Contrary to expectations the Russians have not started an offensive against the Finns but Sevastopol has fallen and fighting in the Crimea has virtually finished. There is no sign yet of any invasion in the west but we know from experience that the bombing of northern France is playing havoc with the railways.

SATURDAY, 13TH MAY TO TUESDAY, 23RD MAY

No invasion yet. The Germans here long for it and some sort of decision in the war. For our part the Occupation has gone on so long now that it is with difficulty that we can imagine any other existence. We work in our gardens to produce enough food to live on, we ride to and from town on cycles to see an amateur show or to hear a concert, we drink liqueurs costing £1:5:0 and cognac at over £2 a bottle and on special occasions we drink a little of our remaining tea which we could sell for £24 a pound. We pass the word round about the latest girl who has 'gone Jerry' or who is going to have an illegitimate child, we read heavy political works and organize parties to listen to good music on records. We seldom go to the cinema. We dance sometimes, either at L'Ancresse Lodge Hotel or at Sunnycroft in the Grange and we have even been known on such occasions to treat ourselves to a bath at a friend's house where there is plenty of hot water. We, of course, can never bath at home since our gas ration will not run to hot water in such quantities.

Just recently we have had quite a little excitement. They were fortifying the bay in front of our house and we now have so much barbed wire about that we cannot get out of the front gate. Gaps have been made in the side walls of three front gardens to the north of us and that is how we reach the road.

Very often now British planes fly down the Russel during the day and E Boats hum about the sea at night. We have two or three times looked out of the window in the middle of the night to see tracer shells flying in two continuous arcs between two sets of light naval craft. Next morning we hear the result of the attack on a convoy coming to the Island and the Germans will tell us we cannot expect supplies from France when the British are sinking the ships. The obvious answer to that is that we can do without the supplies if it helps to finish the war.

The fuel situation here is very serious now. We learn that we cannot expect any more coal or diesel oil and that we must make arrangements for communal cooking and perhaps feeding too. We all hope that the war will be finished before we have to come to this but nevertheless we have to take the matter in hand. At the beginning of the war such a measure would have been an exciting novelty. Now the thought of it bores us to tears.

In Italy a new drive has started and from the German communiqué it looks like being successful for us.

The Feldkommandantur is no more.

In its place there is a Platzkommandantur which consists of most of the officers from the F.K. The difference is apparently only one of size and seniority of staff, the reductions in staff made recently resulting in the office falling below the strength required in an F.K. Meanwhile we have a new senior officer at Grange Lodge, M.V.R. Schneberger.

WEDNESDAY, 24TH MAY TO TUESDAY, 30TH MAY

Two or three British planes flew very low down the Russel a few mornings ago and in their excitement a gun crew behind our house peppered the upper storeys of some of the houses near here.[12] They did not hit our house but the danger of their doing so cannot be overlooked. There is a blank wall between José's room and the gun so she cannot be hit while in bed, but of a bullet came in the back bedroom window it would certainly hit anyone in bed in that room and might pierce the dividing wall and put an end to us in the front room. The risk does not worry us much.

Last Saturday afternoon we had an air raid. At least sixteen planes, said by the Germans to be American Thunderbolts, attacked Fort George and there were some German casualties.13 No civilians were hurt but several houses near the Fort were hit by cannon shells. The noise of anti-aircraft fire was tremendous. It seemed horrid to witness death and destruction on such a fine day.

José has fallen in love with the telephone. Queenie found her the other day talking to the telephone operator who said that she had for some minutes been trying to make out what was being said at our end of the line. She loves to play in the sink and thoroughly enjoyed receiving the whole of the soapy water from the washing in her lap a couple of Saturdays ago. Queenie, of course, had no idea she was sitting under the downpipe.

We had our first bathe in the quarry yesterday afternoon. The water was really warm.

We are still waiting anxiously for rain.

---

12 The gun crew behind La Platte refers to the Vale Mill on the top of the hill.
13 These were in fact rocket- and bomb-carrying Typhoons of the R.A.F.

There have been air attacks on Fort George on Friday, Saturday and today. Apparently they are after the direction-finding apparatus and we think it must be part of a network which extends over northern France and which gives valuable information to the Germans as to the whereabouts of our planes. Up to now there have been no civilian casualties and, considering the number of bombs dropped, very little damage to property outside the Fort. One house in the Strand which was hit in the German air attack in 1940 was hit again this morning. At least one plane crashed into the sea outside the harbour this morning and took some of the thrill out of the attack, as far as we are concerned. We have no doubt that we must be prepared for a much more exciting life this summer than we have had so far during the Occupation.

Last Friday morning two fighters fired at Brehon Tower as they passed down the Russel. One of them was hit and after climbing steeply the pilot took to his parachute. The other plane circled round the parachute and then made off. Soon other planes appeared and flew over the spot and our north coast for the rest of the morning. Fred Noyon and his two nephews went out in their boat at one o'clock to put down their trots and while they were out they decided to investigate. The planes passed over them and they waved to the airmen who waved back and pointed in the direction of Sark. Eventually they found the airman in his rubber dinghy which had been dropped to him by a bomber with his own smaller boat tied alongside. When they had him safely aboard their boat the planes sank the other craft by gunfire. He was an American named Wagner and twenty-eight years old and he dearly wished to have another shot at the Germans who had brought him down. He gave the Noyons some chocolate and some of his iron rations and asked if we had good beer in the Island. He thought it terrible that we did not and when he heard that bread was so strictly rationed he could not understand how the population kept alive. As they passed Brehon on the way to St. Sampson's the flak soldiers waved to him. "Look at the b......s," he said, "I'd like another shot at them." But he returned their greeting and was handed over to the Germans at the harbour entrance.

In one of the most badly damaged houses on the Fort Road a canary still sang lustily when its owner returned although its cage was battered beyond recognition and the room was a shambles.

José finds it quite exciting to watch air attacks now. I hope she never tastes their bitterness.

It is rumoured today that we have occupied Rome. Certainly, from the German news we are making good progress in Italy.

There is a temporary officer at the F.K. who is a graduate of Edinburgh University, has taught in Scottish schools for some years as well as lectured at his university, knows Eric Linklater and Compton Mackenzie personally and has the best command of English that I have experienced in talking to any German.

Mr Staad has been invited to examine the question of communal feeding and cooking and this morning we had a preliminary meeting at Grange Lodge on the matter.

We are painting red crosses on the roofs of the Sanatorium, the Emergency Hospital, the Town Asylum and Blanchelande.

TUESDAY, 6TH JUNE

From the time we went to bed last night until half way through this morning there was a constant roar of aeroplanes. We saw very few because the sky was overcast. There was a firework display in the sky over Alderney and Cherbourg at midnight and the sound of guns at sea. José came into our bed and stayed there all night, to her great delight.

This morning at daylight I looked out of the front window and saw our guards patrolling, armed to the teeth. When the time came for the lifting of curfew the guards remained on duty and they did not take away the barrier across the road. We knew then that there was a general alarm and guessed that all those planes, more than we had ever heard in a single night, were part of the beginning of some sort of invasion. It was very soon afterwards that we heard that our troops had landed in northern France and everybody I met on the way to the office greeted me with a broad smile. Little more authentic news has filtered through during the day but rumours are without number. I have been told that the British have landed at Dunkirk, Calais, Boulogne, Dieppe, Le Havre, Caen, Cherbourg, Granville and Saint Brieuc; that all the higher staff officers have left the Island, that we are to have a twenty four hour curfew.[14] Certainly all shipping had disappeared from the harbour this morning and the telephones have been out of operation all day.

We all regard this as the last lap of the war and wonder how long it will take and what will happen to us before it finishes. Nobody dreams that we shall be other than successful and frankly I should not like to be a member of the other side.

A man was killed near here this morning by an anti-aircraft shell which fell short.[15] What a sad end on the eve of such great happenings!

14 This was partly true, General von Schmettow had in fact been summoned to a meeting with other senior German commanders at Rennes on 5 June, and had to return suddenly when the invasion occurred.

15 George Malbon, of 5, Rue Flère, Vale, was killed by a falling anti-aircraft shell at his home at 7:30am. He was Guernsey's only civilian casualty on D-Day.

At Grange Lodge this morning, where everything was normal on the surface, I met an officer who has been asked to write an article on life in the Channel Islands for the newspaper which is issued in prisoner of war camps. The paper is called *The Camp* and according to him it contains articles mainly from the pens of the prisoners. He asked to be introduced to the Bailiff and Mr Leale and we told him all our troubles. I asked him to send us a copy of the article and I shall be interested to see what he makes of the information we gave him. He certainly cannot paint a very rosy picture. The article is to be written at the request of some of the prisoners – I suspect that they must Channel Islanders.

Dr and Mrs Symons are in Sark. I am sure he is making valiant efforts to get back but I suspect he will find it very difficult.

Of course all fishing has been stopped for the time being and we are told that there will probably be no ships coming to the Island during the next fortnight at least.

WEDNESDAY, 7TH JUNE

There was a constant roar of engines for at least three and a half hours last night. It is said that airborne troops landed during the night on the Cherbourg peninsula.

This morning I had just arrived at the office when there was a sound of falling bombs and a terrific flak barrage. Planes had attacked ships which had arrived here during the night. They sank none but there were German casualties. One of our boys, on the Sark boat, is suffering from shrapnel wounds but I do not think they were serious.

The Germans I have met today are all pleased that the invasion has started and that a decision must be reached fairly soon.

The German radio announced yesterday that parachute troops had been landed in Jersey and Guernsey. This, according to the Germans here, is to be corrected.

It is quite an adventure to go to town these days, taking note of possible cover all along the coast road. Life is no longer boring in Guernsey.

I understand there have been no air raids in Jersey.

We sowed some sugar beet seed more than two weeks ago. One patch has come up, the other shows no sign of life whatsoever. Perhaps this is not as serious as it seemed a week ago.

Curfew is now at nine in the evening instead of eleven but nobody minds at all. We are all waiting for the end.

The planes passed as usual last night taking troops to the front. Apparently things are going well but we are meeting with stiff opposition. It looks as though Cherbourg is the objective of the attack and if this is so we should see something of the attack, at any rate at night. There are two opinions here. One is that the Allies will land here soon, the other is that the Islands will be ignored for the time being. I incline to the latter view because it appears necessary to put shore batteries completely out of action before making a landing from the sea and if the same weight of bombs would be necessary here as in France, thousands of tons would have to be dropped. To a layman it seems improbable that Guernsey is strategically important enough to call for such action.

We all feel that the Occupation as we know it is over. Four years of stagnation have passed and a new phase has begun which must end with our relief. What will happen to us during this period we cannot imagine but we are on our toes, looking for changes in the behaviour of the Germans. As yet we find no bitterness in our contacts with them but we imagine that those of us whose work brings us into contact with them will have to be ready for some very grim meetings.

This afternoon the Bailiff, Mr Leale, Mr de Putron, Raymond Falla, Stead, Loveridge and I went to Grange Lodge where we met M.V.R. Schneberger, Spann, Taborsky and Krefft and an officer who, I think, is the chief of the victualling authority and a staff officer. We discussed our difficulties in regard to rationing and the safety of our food stores. Flour and wheat in the Island should last about four months, meat is so short we shall have to depend on local supplies after next week, butter is plentiful although the only suitable cold store is on the Castle Emplacement and has already had bombs within a couple of hundred yards of it. Sugar will last several months but fuel is so short that we know that gas will have to be cut off before our stocks of food give out. We are working hard on schemes for both communal cooking and feeding and the Germans promised us 160 tons of coal. They are also taking less coke than they have done in the past. We shall see what happens.

Certainly today there was a noticeable absence of interference with the plans we have already made and they asked if we were thinking of cutting down any of the present rations. We said that the rations were already so small that we thought it inadvisable to make any reductions. They agreed.

Meanwhile they have ordered a census of cattle to be taken on the 15th of this month (R.O.F. had already arranged for this to be done) and none are to be slaughtered without German permission.

All entertainments have been stopped and churches are not having any special services which would tend to attract crowds.

I wonder all day long what Vic is doing and whether he is in France. I hope more than I ever thought I should that he comes through safely. I wonder too what is happening to François Grignard and his crippled wife in Caen.

FRIDAY, 9TH JUNE AND SATURDAY, 10TH JUNE

We hear from the Germans that Granville was bombed a day or so ago but I believe that it was no more than we have had here. We hope our people there are safe and that they will come through the next few weeks without harm. It should certainly be exciting for them.

Planes pass here each night for France and this evening we saw several large ones towing gliders. We thought of the boys in those gliders, keyed up with the knowledge that within a few minutes they will be in France and face to face with the enemy. And we thought of the Germans tense too with the knowledge that in a few minutes another batch of Tommies will be at them. All human beings with a fine zest for living and a readiness to die for their country. And all certain that their cause is the right one. I think that the role of looker-on in this struggle gives one altogether too much time to think.

We seem to be doing very well in France. We hold a large strip of coast and have taken Bayeux. Fighting around Caen is very fierce and the Americans are fighting in the peninsula itself.

SUNDAY, 11TH JUNE TO SATURDAY, 17TH JUNE

We are still pouring troops and supplies into Normandy and have extended the beach head until now it includes part of the east side of the Cherbourg peninsula. We have advanced as far as Montebourg and westwards almost to La Haye du Puits. Apparently the biggest battles have not yet started but it is estimated that the Germans have about 300,000 men against us. The Germans are using a new weapon against England. Apparently it is some kind of flying machine which is pilotless and controlled by radio from some other plane. It is full of high explosives and crashes with its load. Whether it is a serious menace or not remains to be seen. The Germans I have spoken to seem quite excited about it.

The chief local news is that a damaged submarine which put in here during the week was spotted by our planes and was the cause of five raids and two reconnaissance flights over the harbour within eighteen hours. Thank God there were no civilian casualties! The fate of the submarine is unknown to me.

Mr Leale and I were on our way to the office when one of the raids occurred (if I had not walked with him from the Half Way I should have

218

been rounding the Salerie Corner when the planes came) and we watched it from a house near the Red Lion. The din of the hundreds of anti-aircraft guns, the roar of engines and the swoop of the great black planes shooting rockets ahead of them made a picture which no one but the Devil could have painted. Old ladies, small boys and girls, Germans and general traffic continued on their way to town directly the planes had passed. Dense clouds of smoke arose from the damaged shipping in the harbour. We are fast becoming war-minded.[16]

Now that the fighting is coming so close to the west of the Cherbourg peninsula an hour seldom passes without the sound of aeroplanes and all this afternoon and evening the rumble of artillery or bombs has been unceasing. Last night we watched bombs exploding on the French coast and about four o'clock we saw three huge fires.

There is a rumour that Jersey is being evacuated of German troops but I think it untrue. We have heard nothing from Granville for several days and it is thought that our buyers may be in St. Malo. We hope they are safe.

Meanwhile we continue to build our wall, to plant sugar beet and to weed the potatoes.

SUNDAY, 18TH JUNE AND MONDAY, 19TH JUNE

It is said that the Americans have completely crossed the Cherbourg peninsula and have arrived at Carteret, just behind Sark. The almost continuous noise of gunfire leaves us in little doubt that they are somewhere near.

Some of the coastal guns on Les Vardes fired a few rounds yesterday evening. Apparently two British warships were seen by many people about five or six miles out and when the firing started they put up a smokescreen and made off. They are the first British ships seen here for four years.

About half past eight this morning some planes flew over and we watched them circle the town and heard the flak going up. When I arrived at nine o'clock the streets of town were carpeted with plate glass. Hardly a shop window had escaped in the Pollet, Smith Street and High Street and as far distant as the Grange Club and St. Peter Port Garage had suffered. All this was caused by one bomb which dropped either near the entrance to or just inside the Old Harbour. It must have been a big one. Some of the shops and offices with windows on both the quay and High Street looked as though a tornado had been through them. Raymond Falla said that in the Alliance Club one portrait had been speared by a broom and many more of

---

16 On the morning of 15 June, R.A.F. Typhoons, escorted by Spitfires, targeted a German U-boat sheltering in St Peter Port Harbour. This was the first of a number of raids on U-boats using the harbour. None of the submarines were damaged.

distinguished former presidents showed whiskers most untidily awry. The Electricity shop front was blown through Lipton in the High Street.[17]

During the night a plane, presumed to be German, jettisoned some mines. They made a most frightening din as they swept down at the ends of their parachutes. The first landed in the road near the Longstore, one came down in a back yard in Bosq Lane, another in Kinnell's Yard and I think a fourth in the Plaiderie. Luckily none of them exploded. The only casualty, thank God, was the grave-digger at St. Sampson's cemetery who had some shrapnel in the chest and is now in the Emergency Hospital.

I obtained permission for the doctors to wear their white steel helmets during emergencies.

Apparently all recent rumours of large-scale bombing in Jersey and the evacuation of that Island by the Germans are untrue. A German returning here says that nothing untoward has occurred there.

There is no news yet of Vaudin and Co.

TUESDAY, 20TH JUNE TO THURSDAY, 22ND JUNE

We had our first night raid on Tuesday night. The planes dropped flares and then bombed the harbour. No civilian casualties. Today we have heard the heaviest explosions yet. They seem to come from Cherbourg and it is said that the Americans are within two or three miles of that town. Planes are passing the north of the Island all day long and most of the night.

FRIDAY, 23RD JUNE TO SUNDAY, 25TH JUNE

I am told that the orders issued to the Germans here are that they are to fight to the last man. We are trying to get used to the idea of fighting on the Island and I think very few people have any wish to be protected at the expense of the efficient prosecution of the war. Luckily only those who have seen warfare before can imagine what fighting in this confined space would mean and the rest of us tell each other that we are ready for whatever may come. Perhaps the most serious point from our side is that we have no adequate shelters and must therefore bear the full brunt of any attack while the Germans are underground waiting to fight when the preliminaries are over. This would surely mean thousands of civilian casualties and we have no medical service big enough to cope with such numbers. Added to this is the fact that our telephones have been taken from us, except in a

---

17 There were two raids on St Peter Port Harbour on 19 June. Overnight 12 parachute anti-submarine mines were dropped by R.C.A.F. At about 8am a U.S.A.A.F. aircraft dropped a 1,000 lb bomb on the Old Harbour creating spectacular blast damage in the Town centre.

very limited number of cases, so that the delay in summoning doctors and ambulances would be terribly serious. We would not even be allowed on the roads to go for help. We hope it will never happen.

The Germans have requisitioned a ton and a half of butter per week until further notice. They promise to substitue pork fat if the need should arise. The Bailiff is protesting. Copies of the correspondence herewith.[18] Meanwhile we are moving about half our butter stock to the Market cold store where it may be a little safer than on the Castle Emplacement.

The attack on Cherbourg has begun and we are wondering how long it will hold out. Some ships have arrived here, either from Alderney or Cherbourg and Allied planes hover round the harbour, presumably keeping an eye on them. At night we hear the sound of propellors and ships' engines and the thud of naval gunfire. We see flares in the east and tracer shells and turn over and go to sleep again.

Four years ago we were listening to explosions in Cherbourg and waiting for the Germans to come. Once again we are hearing explosions from the same quarter and waiting for – what?

It is a strange thought that, if we are lucky, we may be seeing our friends (including relatives) within a few weeks and we wonder what they are thinking about it all. Doubtless they are worried about us and we wish we could let them know that we are still very much alive.

José sleeps between Queenie and myself nearly every night now. She hates the sound of planes at night and we think it better to spoil her a little rather than let her spend hours of terror in her own room.

All day today the weather has become steadily more overcast and this evening there is a definite promise of rain. It is rather late now for the crops to get the full benefit and we are thankful that it is so unlikely that we shall have to depend on our own food supplies this winter.

MONDAY, 26TH JUNE

Some hundreds of civilians and political prisoners have arrived here from Alderney. All the Guernsey and Jersey contingents have come as well as Frenchmen and women and only a few pre-Occupation Alderney people are remaining with the garrison. It appears almost certain to us that Alderney will be taken. Some came in open boats towed by larger vessels and I am told that one small motor ship had a cargo of four hundred people battened down in the hold without room even to sit down. It is also said that one ship with 180 people aboard was sunk on passage.[19]

18 See Item 53: P.K. to C.C.: Delivery of Butter, 22 Jun 1944, p.386.
19 The political prisoners from Alderney were subsequently shipped overnight to Jersey and from there to St Malo. On 4 July, one vessel, SS *Minotaure*, was torpedoed off St

Apparently the German news has announced the fall of Cherbourg but we have heard nothing official. At any rate we no longer hear explosions from that direction.

It has rained steadily all day and we have enjoyed it.

TUESDAY, 27TH JUNE AND WEDNESDAY, 28TH JUNE

Four years ago we had our first air attack – a German one. We shall never forget it.

I spoke to a Guernseyman who came down from Alderney in the motor ship I mentioned the other day. He said that they were packed into the hold until there was no room to move. There were still some people on the gangway who could not find room below. They were pushed on top of the others and the gangway was taken away. The mass found its level eventually. He said they knew nothing of the journey as the hatches were on but the worst feature was the heat. It was like being in a Turkish bath. There were women as well as men in the hold. Luckily it was not rough.

M.V.R. Schneberger and Mr Krafft called at the Bailiff's Office this morning to give him a verbal explanation in connection with the requisition of butter. The Bailiff was not in and they are calling again on Friday. Mr Leale, Mr Johns and I were at Grange Lodge this afternoon and Mr Schneberger explained that the butter was being requisitioned because a consignment of ten tons had been sunk on the way here and the troops had no other reserve. He said that at first he had been against the requisition but he saw it could not be helped. Mr Leale said we had been forced to create the butter reserve very much against our will and had understood that the sacrifice had been made so that the butter would be available for the civilian population later. As regards the promise of pork fat if needed, he asked what these words meant. Did they mean that as soon as we found it was impossible to continue the present butter ration from production we would be given fat to make up the ration? They have not been told at Grange Lodge what the words mean.

They have requisitioned fifteen more bicycles today and that is why we went to Grange Lodge. Mr Johns explained the great difficulty the civilian population had in keeping their bicycles in commission because of the shortage of parts and tyres. Schneberger said that he had told the military that there would be great difficulty in finding bicycles but these were needed for ambulance men who would be needing them badly. He asked if we could supply even six bicycles and we said we would see what we could do. If we refuse altogether they will probably take away fifty instead of six!

Malo with heavy casualties (Bryans (n.d.), pp.54-55).

Mr Leale asked on behalf of the doctors, if the civilian population could be informed if any ultimatum is received from the Allies. We should certainly want to take whatever precautions we could before fighting began here. They promised that we should be so informed and Schneberger said that Grange Lodge was there to look after the interests of our population. We asked whether there was any truth in the rumour that an ultimatum had been delivered in Alderney with regard to the evacuation of civilians. This was denied categorically.

THURSDAY, 29TH JUNE AND FRIDAY, 30TH JUNE

It is said that the Russians are advancing faster than ever before. In Normandy bitter fighting is going on round Caen. The German flying bomb is still being sent over England and we should soon be using Cherbourg as a port.

I saw the Bailiff for a few minutes before Schneberger and Krafft arrived and stayed on with him for the interview. They gave the Bailiff the same reasons which were put forward on Wednesday at Grange Lodge for the requisition and the Bailiff gave the same answers – which are the only rational ones – as Mr Leale. He asked whether the Germans intended taking other foodstuffs from us and said they must know how little we have. They answered that there was no talk of any other requisitions.

The general opinion here now, both German and civilian, seems to be that there will be no attack on the Islands. It is thought probable that military decisions on the continent will occur before it becomes necessary to drive the Germans from the Islands.

We have been talking about the first contacts with the allied forces landing here. How will they come? By plane or by sea or by flying boat? I think by flying boat since we do not know whether booby traps have been set at the airport and the danger of mines at sea may preclude arrival by ship. (I surmise of course that the Germans will have evacuated the Island and that the war is not over).

There was a comic bit of propaganda news in the Jersey paper on the 20th of this month. It said that recent attacks on Guernsey had been confined to light bombing raids and that the anti-aircraft here had shot down twelve planes and damaged (I think) six more. We know of one certainly brought down and a possible. The article did not appear in our papers.

SATURDAY, 1ST JULY TO THURSDAY, 13TH JULY

Two boats came in from Jersey last Sunday week and until today no others had arrived. A convoy came in this afternoon in broad daylight.

The accumulation of German money in the banks during June is the biggest on record (I think £98,000 worth). We presume the news is leading people to hold less cash than usual.

The tomato crop is now bearing in maximum quantities and as there are no boats huge amounts are going to waste. The G.U.B. had 150 tons surplus last week and even after offering them free to whoever wished to collect them from the Fruit Export stores, many tons had to be dumped over the sea wall. Thirty miles away are thousands of troops who are fighting for us and who would certainly be delighted to have them.

On the 3rd of the month a notice appeared in the local paper to the effect that farmers who had not cut their hay crop by the 5th would lose it as the troops would cut it themselves and use it for their own animals. Since then each German unit has collected hay and many farmers have lost invaluable feeding stuffs through no fault of their own. In some cases grass left for grazing has been cut, in others meadows unfit for cutting have been reaped. In many cases with the shortage of petrol and horses, farmers have been unable to get anybody to cut their hay in time and have lost it. At the last minute the Germans lent eighteen horses and drivers but of course they were too late to be of any real help. This is a clear case of what happens when the military are left to carry out orders, no account being taken of individual hardship and on Tuesday the Bailiff came to Grange Lodge with Jurat de Garis, R.O. Falla and myself to complain. We explained the injustices which had occurred and said that, even if the hay could not be given back, it must be obvious that such action could only result in a straining of relations between occupiers and occupied, and we hoped that it would not occur again. The Bailiff suggested that it might be best for him to write to the General, setting out our grievance but Schneberger undertook to do it personally for us. He agreed that the matter should never have been dealt with as it was and I think that the interview did what it was intended to do – make them understand that we do not intend to take such action lying down.

Many people are building air raid shelters and hideouts to be used if street fighting occurs. I still doubt very much whether any fighting will take place here.

Fishing has begun again but the first mackerel have passed on to the spawning grounds and the next lot are not here yet. So we have not much fish. There has been no meat ration for several weeks.

The curfew has now been put on to 10 p.m. and the telephones are in full use.

Alderney has not been attacked.

Flying bombs are still being sent over England almost incessantly.

In Normandy we are still fighting around Caen but I think we are breaking up the German armour reserves there instead of trying to push on yet. On this side of the peninsula the fighting is around La Haye du Puits. In Russia the northern front is very successful and the Russians are within a few score miles of East Prussia. In Italy we are not far from Leghorn.

There is a rumour abroad that an agreement has been signed between England and Germany for an exchange of internees. We hope that our people may be sent back to England that Mr Sherwill will be amongst those repatriated. He could do much work which would ease things for us when contact is made.

I am hoping for the end of the war before the position becomes too serious here.

FRIDAY, 14TH JULY TO FRIDAY, 21ST JULY

The most spectacular news this week is that an attempt has been made on Hitler's life. Very few details are available but it seems that the attempt was made at his headquarters and by a general. Several staff officers were present and I think at least one was killed by the bomb which landed about six feet from its target. What a scene for historians and movie producers, coming as it does after more than a year of retreats and in the middle of wholesale losses on three fronts. What is behind it and what will be its effect on the war? It seems to me that unless the general concerned is mad, there must be some plot and organization, big and strong enough to fight the SS and secret police and if this is so there may very well be civil war in Germany. What is the dispute about? The lack of air support on all fronts and the sacrifice of aircraft production for pilotless bombs which are nothing more than a form of terror-warfare, or the fact that the Russian front has obviously been weakened to find reserves for the western battle? Or is it something deeper about which we cannot even guess?

It looks as though we are becoming more successful in our advances in France and there is little doubt that the French are causing havoc behind the lines. In Russia, of course,the advance is colossal and in Italy we are pressing on.

If people pay anything at all for tomatoes they give up to a penny a pound. The crop is excellent!

The submarine has gone and tonight there are only a couple of barges left in the harbour – one loaded with tomatoes for Jersey. At least a dozen ships must have left here last night and they must have had a very dirty crossing to France.

This week there have been fine catches of mackerel and longnose and fishing is in full swing again.

Some time ago we asked permission to issue emergency rations of some controlled foodstuffs so that people would have something to eat if confined to their houses during an attack on the Island. We were refused. When our last batch of Jersey papers arrived we saw that the States of Jersey had issued free rations of nearly all foods and I naturally applied again for this Island. After a long argument, during which I flatter myself that I countered every reason put up by the Germans against such an issue we were refused again but received a verbal assurance that if the present quiet period ends they will take the matter up again. I said that neither the Bailiff nor Mr Leale felt that they could shoulder the responsibility should an emergency occur suddenly and find the population without food.

As a special treat we have a meat ration this week.

The Bailiff followed up his interview about the cutting of hay with a letter of protest which I am enclosing, with the reply from the Germans.[20]

This week an advertisement appeared in the newspaper asking for somebody to adopt a baby TO BE BORN NEXT OCTOBER.

SATURDAY, 22ND JULY TO SATURDAY, 29TH JULY

On Monday evening we were working in the garden when we heard planes and spotted them diving towards the harbour. There was a terrific flak barrage and a minute or so later they came into view again flying over the sea close in to St. Sampson's. They twisted and turned quite leisurely in front of our bay and José, who woke up danced about with excitement on her window sill. They hit an escort vessel just outside the harbour mouth with four bombs and by the time smoke and débris had cleared only a tiny part of the hull was still above the surface. This disappeared almost immediately. It is said that the next ship in the convoy, still in the harbour mouth, had about forty tons of ammunition for Alderney aboard. They just missed this one!

Some days ago a friend asked what had happened to the Bailiff's recent letter to the Red Cross regarding the continuance of messages. She also asked whether we contemplated making any move to get supplies of food from the Red Cross if we were cut off completely for any considerable period. I had already asked at Grange Lodge for news concerning the Bailiff's letter and had told them that we would probably send them a reminder about it as we regarded it as extremely important. They assured me that it had been passed on to Jersey and from there to France. I now drafted a letter to Grange Lodge, for the Bailiff's signature, asking to be informed of any delay in delivery of the Bailiff's letter and adding that as we considered the time opportune for taking steps to secure Red Cross supplies of food we should be glad of an interview with the Platzkommandant and the General. When I showed this draft to Mr Leale he told me that he had meant to take up the

---

20 See Item 54: Bailiff to P.K.: Taking of Hay, 15 Jul 1944, p.387.

matter at the beginning of August but agreed that I should approach the Bailiff at once. This I did and the letter was duly delivered.[21] The result was a meeting between the Bailiff, Mr Leale and the General and members of his staff at La Corbinerie yesterday afternoon.

The General agreed at once to help us in getting a letter delivered to the International Red Cross and suggested (or perhaps the suggestion came from Mr Leale) that a similar one should be sent to the Swiss Minister in Berlin, as representative of our Protecting Power. Both Mr Leale and the Bailiff telephoned to me at home after their meeting asking me to make the necessary drafts and they have been agreed today.[22]

At Grange Lodge on Wednesday I was told that George Vaudin is in hospital in Granville with sciatica and that nobody appears to know the whereabouts of Guillemet and Barnett. The branch office of the P.K. has been transferred from Granville to St. Malo and Taborsky and Pelz are going over to set up the necessary organization for our revictualling through Brittany instead of La Manche. Nobody has much hope of this organization ever being put into operation.

Meanwhile we hear that the Americans are well south of Coutances. In the Caen sector the Germans are apparently very strong and we are not moving ahead fast. We are, however, holding down reserves while the Americans go ahead and I should imagine that if Rommel weakens Caen to stop their advance we shall make a drive there. In Russia the advance is as sensational as ever and there is only a little over a hundred miles between the Russians and Germany in one sector. In Italy we are still advancing steadily.

There are no further sensational developments in the plot to kill Hitler.

SUNDAY, 30TH JULY TO THURSDAY, 3RD AUGUST

On Monday morning I went to Summerland to deliver the Bailiff's letters to Colonel von Helldorff and to discuss with him any alterations he might suggest. Last time Mr Leale and I went to that office we were left waiting in a stifling outer office for at least half an hour and I had no wish to repeat that ordeal. For a long time past I have been intending to have some cards printed and I gave the order last week. They arrived on Monday morning in time so I determined to try them out forthwith.

I walked into the clerks' office at Summerland and announced that I wanted to see the Colonel. Before they had time to raise objections or to ask my business I produced a card and told them to take it to the Colonel. It worked splendidly. An officer came out to usher me into the august

---

21 See Item 55: Bailiff to P.K.: Letter to Red Cross, 26 Jul 1944, p.389.
22 See Item 56: Bailiff to Red Cross, 29 Jul 1944, p.390

presence, instead of being left to wait as one generally is in an office where one is not known.

There were only two very minor suggestions regarding alterations to the draft and the letter was finally delivered to the General on Tuesday morning. Whether it ever arrives at its destination remains to be seen.

Last Friday a young man named Buckingham was being escorted to the boat for the Continent where he was to serve two years imprisonment for some offence against the German forces. He managed to escape from his guards and has not been seen since. On Tuesday six people, four relatives and two friends were summoned to the German police office and told that they would be put in prison of they did not produce Buckingham by three o'clock next day. They came to us to see whether we could do anything for them. We took them to the Bailiff and they gave him an assurance that they had neither seen nor heard from Buckingham since he escaped. At 12.30 yesterday the Bailiff, Mr Martel and I went to see the General at La Corbinerie on the matter. The Bailiff said how surprised he was to hear that it was intended imprisoning innocent people on such a pretext and the General agreed that it would serve no useful purpose. He asked us to inform the people concerned that they need not report at the police office that afternoon but he asked the Bailiff to issue a notice in the newspapers informing the public that they would get into severe trouble if they harboured or assisted Buckingham and that they should assist in his apprehension. This we regarded as a bargain and the Bailiff agreed to publish the notice. The Germans asked that it should be submitted to them by five o'clock the same afternoon. We drafted it after lunch naturally stating that all instructions came from the Germans and I duly took it to the offices at La Corbinerie for approval at five o'clock. After making one or two unnecessary alterations they said that they would have to show it to the General and that they would let me know later whether it met with his approval. They telephoned later to say that we were not to publish the notice for they would put one in themselves.

Ted Dorey has a movie camera which he gave in in 1942 on the German order. A week or so ago Mr Krafft told me that a Major on the General's staff wanted to buy it. Ted was unwilling to sell as the camera was a present from his wife and I put that point to Grange Lodge. They passed on the information and the next we knew was that we received a requisition from the Germans claiming the camera for Military Purposes. We have no proof that this is a breach of the Hague Rules but it is certain that the military necessity for such a requisition will end with the end of hostilities. Perhaps I shall have a chance to get the camera back.

The war news is splendid. The Russians appear to have cut off the Germans in the Baltic states, Finland looks like asking for peace terms,

Turkey had broken off diplomatic and trade relations with Germany and in Normandy there is a general advance. The Americans on this side have advanced at least as far as Pontorson and the Germans say as far as Dol. I should imagine that Vaudin, Barnett and Guillemet have all made contact with our troops by now. I hope they are all safe.

José is two today.

FRIDAY, 4TH AUGUST TO MONDAY, 7TH AUGUST

José had a marvellous birthday party and all her friends ate until they could eat no more, quite a triumph in Occupation catering. John Warry, Anne Audoire, Nigel Roussel, Janet Mahy, Christopher and Marilyn Cambridge, Molly from the Misses Henry and Rosemary and Patrick Massy-Dawson came with parents etc. Everybody played with toys and José had so many presents she did not know which to play with first. She is a great lover of telephones and the Massy-Dawsons brought her a toy one. She was sitting on the floor with her party frock billowing round her when we opened this parcel and when she saw what was inside her expression was of incredulity and bliss in about equal proportions.

She has seen so little of the beach that today when we had a bathe, against all German orders, she cried with fright! And she has lived two years with the sea outside the front door!

The war news is superlative. The Americans have spread out right through Brittany and the only fighting seems to be in the neighbourhood of the bigger ports. Apparently Brest and St. Nazaire on the west and St. Malo on the north are still holding out but from the terrific explosions which are shaking the house this afternoon I doubt whether the latter port will last long. There is no doubt that a very large proportion of the Germans have lost heart and stories are widespread of Germans expressing their satisfaction at being here and at the fact that the end of the war is so close. Both Queenie and I have been told this by German soldiers. The Americans seem to have spread eastward as well as west from Avranches and are said to be very near Le Mans on the way to Paris. At Caen, or rather south of that town, we are advancing slowly against the full weight of the German main defence line and it is difficult to see any good reason why the war should continue much longer on this side. In Poland the battle for Warsaw seems to be going entirely in favour of the Russians and they have entered East Prussia. In Italy the fighting is fierce in the Florence district.

We have received a letter from George Vaudin dated July 27th, when he was still in Granville.[23] Four days later the town was in American hands and

---

23 See Item 57: Vaudin to Leale, 27 Jul 1944, p.392.

we hope he is now in England. Barnett and Guillemet went into hiding and most probably are safe.

The past fortnight has given us a close-up view of the end of the war and it only remains for us to wonder how we shall be situated when it comes. I do not foresee any difficulty with the Germans here. They become more human every day, especially as they realize that their number is up.

TUESDAY, 8TH AUGUST TO TUESDAY, 15TH AUGUST

We hear that we have landed today in southern France and that the opposition is not strong. This is bound to have tremendous repercussions in Italy and the Balkans.

In France an encirclement of the Germans is almost complete the only gap being a small one somewhere between Argentan and Falaise. The Brittany ports are still holding out.

Last Saturday afternoon we watched columns of black smoke rising from Alderney. It appears that H.M.S. *Rodney* bombarded the island with her 16 inch guns.

On Sunday night there was a running fight between a German convoy on the way here from Jersey and some Allied warships. We watched the tracer shells flying between the ships over a sea as smooth as oil and tried unsuccessfully to pick out the ships in the light of the flares sent up by each side. There were damage and casualties on the German ships. Of course we have no idea what happened to our own.

Mr Leale was invited to meet Count von Helldorff last Friday afternoon and yesterday morning the Count was introduced to several local officials and discussed with them problems of supply. I am attaching my minute of the meeting.[24]

Mr Leale asked him whether he knew what had happened to our letters to the Red Cross and the Protecting Power. He said that they had been sent on but that he did not know what had become of them. He thought there was nothing further we could do in the matter for the time being.

WEDNESDAY, 16TH AUGUST TO MONDAY, 21ST AUGUST

Germans continue to take grass from farmers. The other morning when I was at the Foulon, a horse wagon belonging to the horses stabled there drove into the yard and emptied a load of grass straight into a shed. A quarter of an hour later a farmer, White by name, came in on his bicycle having traced the wagon. The grass had been taken without permission from one of his fields.

---

24 See Item 58: Meeting with P.K.: Island supplies, 14 Aug 1944, p.395.

Now that food stocks are getting short, not only does Timmer buy vegetables and fruit all over the Island for the military, but soldiers buy large quantities in the markets and from private growers and farmers. In many cases the growers do not want to sell but it has been noticed that often when a refusal of this kind has been given, produce disappears during the next night when the grower cannot get out because of the curfew. Another factor is that the growers have had a disastrous year this year and the troops usually offer higher prices than the controlled price. I am afraid that some are tempted to make good some of their losses in this way. In February last a notice appeared stating that the Germans were to take precedence in shops and this is used coupled with a threat of punishment when refusals are met with. We are trying to get the Germans to issue an order to their men that they are not to buy fruit and vegetables since they already get their allowance through Timmer, but although Grange Lodge have put our case for us, the military will not issue such an order. The fact is that they are trying to get all the food they can for themselves. Doubtless we will take the matter further.

The gap in Normandy is closed and it looks as though that battle is an unqualified victory for us. Some of our spearheads have crossed the Seine and are reported in the outskirts of Paris. The landing in southern France is quite successful and the French themselves seem to be rising everywhere. The fighting spirit in France seems as strong as ever it was. Fighting in Russia is fierce but the advance continues if slower. It is said that Mr Churchill watched the landing in the south from a destroyer about a mile or so from the shore.

Many people here saw two of our war vessels patrolling off the southern coast all Friday afternoon. On Saturday afternoon six or seven boats left here, presumably for Jersey. About an hour later we heard heavy gunfire from the direction of Jersey and the coastal guns here opened up as well. We have not heard yet what happened to the convoy. On Sunday evening we watched two vessels steaming up the Russel, presumably for Alderney, and pitied the men who had been ordered to sea in broad daylight and for a port within fifteen miles of one of our naval harbours.

Sixteen years ago last Sunday I joined the Civil Service and today I gave in my application for the new post of Assistant Supervisor.

In Brittany Brest, St. Nazaire and Lorient are still holding out. Apart from that the war is moving steadily farther away from us.

TUESDAY, 22ND AUGUST TO SUNDAY, 27TH AUGUST

About half past one on Friday morning, Mr Jehan of Les Crabbes, St. Saviour's and his son were guarding their potato crop against theft. They found someone digging potatoes and chased them. Mr Jehan was shot at three times by the soldier concerned and the third bullet killed him. The Bailiff has written to the General (copy herewith[25]) and the Bailiff and Mr Leale are going to the funeral tomorrow. There will be a wreath from the Bailiff and people of Guernsey.

The Germans have issued a notice to the effect that members of the German forces are not allowed to buy fruit or vegetables direct from farmers or growers and only small quantities from recognised retailers. The troops have also been warned that stealing from civilians will be punished with long terms of imprisonment. There is little doubt that the troops are on comparatively short rations and many of them are complaining of hunger. They also feel bitterly the lack of news from their homes. We point out to them that we have had four years of waiting for news.

Practically every day British ships are to be seen off the south coast of the Island and sometimes they come fairly close in as though inviting the coastal batteries to open fire. None have been hit.

Apparently the convoy which left here for Jersey last Saturday week only received superficial damage en route.

Queenie went to visit a friend at hospital this afternoon and Dick, José and I went with her and went on to Albecq while waiting for her. The demolitions are rather an improvement than otherwise and with a light westerly breeze and brilliant sunshine the bay looked just as it must in the imaginations of our exiles in England and Germany. How we long for them to be back with us!

We started digging our potatoes this week and although we did not have a heavy crop there is no disease. The rest of the crop is not ripe yet, but it promises to be really good. Meanwhile we are working till dark most nights, preparing the terraces for next year.

Paris is now in our hands and was taken almost entirely by the French themselves. Toulon has fallen in the south, Brest is being heavily bombarded from the air and by our navy. Rumania is fighting with us, Bulgaria is asking for peace terms and the Germans are again cornered in a pocket in Normandy, this time on the west bank at the mouth of the Seine. They are getting across the river as best they can under heavy fire but are leaving all their equipment behind.

To save electricity the power station now closes down every night from midnight to six o'clock. The saving is about ten tons of diesel oil per month.

All applications for the post of Assistant Supervisor had to be in by last Friday. The Appointments Board are meeting next Wednesday.

---

25 See Item 59: Bailiff to General: Murder of Bertie Jehan, 26 Aug 1944, p.399.

MONDAY, 28TH AUGUST AND TUESDAY, 29TH AUGUST

Colonel von Helldorff called on the Bailiff at Le Vallon on Sunday to express, on behalf of the General, their deep concern over the death of Mr Jehan and to assure him that everything was being done to find the culprit.

Mr W.J. Corbet told me yesterday morning that Mr Cross (of the North Cinema) had told him that I was the man who had sent him to Germany – he was deported in 1942 by the Germans. I am asking for the holding of a proper enquiry into the matter and have sent a letter to Mr Leale on the subject.[26]

Cross further says that the new position of Assistant Supervisor was created for me. Both these statements he seems to be making everywhere at St. Sampson's. As far as the second one is concerned, of course it is ridiculous. The subject was opened in a letter from the Supervisor to the Board of Administration in which he says that the amount of work to be done after the war, plus the fact that he will be retiring as soon as possible, makes it necessary to appoint an Assistant. The Board approved the appointment but, of course, had no power to create such a post. They therefore placed the matter before the Bailiff who ruled that such a post-war necessity could not be discussed by the States under present conditions. As the matter is urgent, because the work will have to begin as soon as possible after the end of the Occupation, the matter was passed on to the Controlling Committee. They sanctioned the creation of the position and asked the Appointments Board to invite applications and make the appointment. The appointment is to be for one year only, so that other applicants may put in for the post when they are able. There are twenty one applicants for the job and the Appointments Board are meeting tomorrow to discuss them. For the post to be made for me, it would mean that the Supervisor, the Board of Administration, the Bailiff, the Controlling Committee and the Appointments Board had all agreed together on my behalf.

WEDNESDAY, 30TH AUGUST TO MONDAY, 4TH SEPTEMBER

At last the little rock fortress of Cézembre, off St. Malo, has given in after several weeks of fighting. One wonders whether the commander should be applauded for heroism or condemned for wasting life. I incline to the former view. Meanwhile Brest, Lorient and St. Nazaire are still holding out, although we are probably the nearest territory with organized German resistance and yesterday morning we watched two hundred and fifty American heavy bombers passing over to attack Brest. One flight came too

---

26 See Item 60: Guillemette to Leale: Cross enquiry, 29 Aug 1944, p.400.

close over the Island and the flak hit one plane. Flames streamed out from one wing and the burning part, said by some people to be an engine was promptly detached and fell into the sea off Cobo. The plane flew on.

For three consecutive nights newspapers in German were dropped by British planes. There must have been thousands of copies each time.

Our advances both on the eastern and western fronts have been spectacular during the past week and our troops are well inside Belgium and going on at such a rate that it is difficult to follow them. In Rumania the Russians are making for the Yugoslav frontier and have taken the oil-fields. In Italy we have broken through the Gothic line and in southern France we are past Lyon. The end is surely in sight this time.

Two small motor ships came in from Jersey a few days ago with mail. Apart from that we have had no communication with the outside world. Still everybody is quite calm and the improvement in the news has come so gradually that there is no great excitement.

I have appealed verbally for the return of the radios or, if that is not possible, for permission to use crystal sets which use no electricity. The P.K. promised to take up the matter for us but today I was told that there is no chance of obtaining such permission. All my eloquence about the psychological effect of isolation on our people was of no avail.

We are notified that we are to receive the quota of military petrol promised us at our recent meeting with Colonel von Helldorff. The Germans have published an order stating that troops are forbidden to buy fruit and vegetables, with the exception of melons and tomatoes, from any civilian source. Both these measures are some indication of recent changes in the German attitude here.

Last Wednesday the Appointments Board chose me for the post of Assistant Supervisor, for one year. The appointment was published in the newspapers and I have received a good share of kind wishes plus many indications that I do not meet with universal approval. I hope I may succeed in proving my worth and that I am neither a rogue nor an interloper.

TUESDAY, 5TH SEPTEMBER TO MONDAY, 11TH SEPTEMBER

We were not satisfied with the refusal from the P.K. regarding the use of radios so we found enough reasons for a visit to the General and the Bailiff and I went to put the point to him direct. That we met with no success is shown by the memorandum attached hereto.[27]

Last Saturday afternoon in broad daylight and brilliant sunshine a convoy of small craft came up from Jersey. It is said that a British warship

---

27 See Item 61: Meeting with P.K. and General, 6 Sep 1944, p.401.

was on patrol, as usual, off our south coast, but be that as it may, the ships came in unmolested. They brought, amongst other things, a hundred and sixty four tons of Jersey wheat for us and two hundred tons of potatoes for the Germans. Our bread ration will now continue into December.

Owing to shortage of gas the Germans have ordered that *The Star* be no longer published and that the *Evening Press* appear only four times per week.

The Allies continue to drop German newspapers by air most nights. Everybody sees them. They have also dropped cigarettes and half-mark notes with vulgar rhymes on the back.

I have started with the Supervisor on the study of post-war problems and schemes which we shall have to operate. They include immigration and emigration, rehousing, repairs to properties, restaffing and claims for damage.

Meanwhile, at home, we have lifted a very good crop of potatoes, at least 17 cwt from 8 perches and are continuing with the terracing. It is so pleasant doing strenuous gardening and I feel so fit that I believe I shall look back on these days with some pleasure.

The war news includes the declaration of war on Bulgaria by the Russians and an appeal from the former country for an armistice within twenty four hours; the building up of forces on Germany's western frontiers, the taking of Dieppe, Ostend and Le Tréport, the terrific bombardment of Le Havre from the air and the fact that Brest has not yet fallen, although there is now fighting in the streets of that town.

It appears that, in Jersey, the Bailiff on behalf of the Superior Council, has submitted to the Germans a memorandum setting out the position of the civilian population as regards supplies and a hint that it would not help Germany if Jersey had to report that the German decision to continue the siege was not in conformity with the occupying power's responsibility towards the well-being of the population. The matter seems to have been brought to a head by a German statement that the siege could continue till the end of next January. Already the island is without gas, which finished on the 1st of September.

TUESDAY, 12TH SEPTEMBER TO MONDAY, 18TH SEPTEMBER

By far the most exciting news this week is that concerning the war. Following on the fact that we have pierced the German West Wall in several places comes the news that a huge air-borne army has landed in Holland – on Sunday afternoon.[28] Apparently there were more troops than the contingent

---

28 Operation Market Garden, the ill-starred attempt to secure a bridgehead across the Rhine at Arnhem.

dropped in Normandy at the beginning of the Invasion. Meanwhile it is said that the Russians are preparing for the greatest attack in history.

Last Tuesday night, although an Allied plane flew low over the Island during the night, no newspapers were delivered. The plane dropped flares, however, an unusual occurrence and in the light shed by them many people saw parachutes falling.

I neither thought nor heard any more of the parachutes till Friday when I was told at Grange Lodge that an envelope, with a waterproof one inside, had been found in their letter-box. The inner envelope was addressed to General von Schmettow in person and was marked Secret. It had originally been sealed but the seals had been broken. I was asked whether I had heard anything of such an envelope being dropped by planes because it was wondered whether the whole matter was a hoax engineered by some civilian here. What the envelope contained my questioner did not know. I knew nothing and said so and I came away thinking that if the envelope contained an ultimatum or any other message from the Allies it would be a pity for it to be ignored because of broken seals.

I thought no more about it until next morning when Mr Leale mentioned casually that he had been informed that a civilian here had found a parachute with cylinder attached containing a message to the Germans and that he had grown frightened and was keeping it. I pricked up my ears and later in the day began to trace the story back. I reached a man who was actually two removed from the finder. Without telling him what I knew I asked him to tell me his story. According to him the civilian who found the parachute had a friend who had worked for the Germans for some years and could speak the language to some extent. Together they unscrewed the nose of the cylinder, which was marked "Not explosive", and found inside an envelope. There were at least three layers of envelopes, the innermost being of oiled silk and addressed personally to General von Schmettow. They opened this envelope and found inside a letter in German containing a questionaire of sorts, one question concerning the condition of civilian food supplies and instructions to get into telephonic communication with France at a certain date and time. The telephone line to be used was indicated. This proved conclusively that such a letter had been dropped and when my informant added that he knew that the letter had eventually found its way to a German office I felt certain that the one at Grange Lodge and the one about which I was hearing were one and the same letter.

We wondered whether we should assure the Germans that the letter was genuine but I had promised all concerned that I would divulge no names. We decided to think the matter over during the week end.

This morning I was talking to a shopman in town when he said casually that he had been told that the General had received two copies of a letter

236

from the Allies. I asked him how he knew and he said that he had been told by a German dentist of his acquaintance. He further added that the General had received the letters on the fourteenth. One had been picked up by a German and delivered immediately. The other had been found by a civilian and had been delivered eventually to a German office which had forwarded it to the General. Nobody knew the contents of the letters. And there the matter stands.

A man named Help was sentenced to five years penal servitude and twelve strokes of the birch last Saturday. This morning he created mild excitement in Town by escaping from prison. Apparently the thought of the 'cat' had driven him to try to escape. He is still at large. His crime was rape and robbery.

Le Havre is in our hands, Brest and the other west Brittany ports of Lorient and St. Nazaire are still holding out.

Mr Leale wrote to Cross, after the matter had come before the Controlling Committee, asking him to appoint someone on his behalf as a member of a Committee of Enquiry regarding my actions in the matter of his deportation. Mr Leale added that it was suggested that the results of the enquiry be made public and if Cross did not wish to hold an enquiry the Controlling Committee would feel at liberty to publish that fact too. Cross wrote back a most unsatisfactory reply, saying nothing about holding a public enquiry but as my next step would be proceedings before the Court I have decided that such an action would savour too much of a steam hammer being used to crack a nut and have given up the matter. I did suggest taking him up on the public enquiry but Mr Leale feels that he might make damaging statements which might be left unanswered for days through adjournment of the sittings and that for this reason a public enquiry would be unfair to me.

TUESDAY, 19TH SEPTEMBER AND WEDNESDAY, 20TH SEPTEMBER

Yesterday morning I received a telephone message from the Germans asking me to make arrangements for Colonel von Helldorff to meet the Bailiff. The meeting was fixed for four thirty yesterday afternoon at Le Vallon and the Bailiff asked me to take tea with him and remain for the meeting.

A visit to Le Vallon is always a treat. There is a mellowness about that little bit of Guernsey which could never be achieved in a new property – and the Bailiff's great-grandfather made it all out of a furze brake – woods and lawns and warm old walled-in fruit and flower garden and a feeling of spaciousness which I have never found elsewhere in Guernsey. And Victor Carey at home is a charming old gentleman and such a perfect host that one realizes that there is something to be said for the older and less headlong method of living.

The Colonel arrived and we had our meeting. It was an exciting one as the memorandum will show.[29] He was so eager to give us his news that he started speaking almost before he was seated and I received the impression that he wanted us to know that they are doing their utmost to do all we ask for the well-being of the population. Apparently they get very little more news than we do, except that for one hour a day some personal news comes through over their radio but this is only very important messages to individual members of the forces. It appears that they do not often fire at the newspaper plane, which is still fairly regular, because they are expecting a German plane.

Meanwhile a fast German boat has turned up, presumably from Jersey, and there are rumours that it has brought someone to inform the Germans here of the terrible conditions in that Island. I think this false, but no doubt, with no gas, they are beginning to feel the siege more than we do.

We went to the funeral of Tom Ozanne today, at a little chapel near here which he was instrumental in building and of which he has been the mainstay for over forty years. He was our only confessed Labour member in the States and was respected by everybody and loved by many. He had no money so he was loved and respected for his character alone – a fine record it seems to me.

THURSDAY, 21ST SEPTEMBER

I was at Grange Lodge this morning and Schneberger asked me whether the Bailiff had seen Colonel von Helldorff this week. I said that he had and that I had been present at the meeting.

"Then there is no need for me to tell you the news," he said.

I replied that I might as well check up to make certain that I had not misunderstood the Colonel. I thereupon went carefully over all the details regarding messages to both the Red Cross and German Government, including the fact that permission is being sought for the Germans here to contact the Allies. He agreed that the facts as I related them were correct. I said that what we were wondering was when we were likely to get a reply but he thinks that although the messages will get there quickly, the questions involved will not be decided upon in five minutes.

I gather that the Bailiff of Jersey has received a reply to his letter to the Germans and that he is told in it that more good will result from discussion than from threats.

It looks as though the idea of getting into touch with the Allies may have resulted from my suggestion at our meeting with the General on the 6th

---

29 See Item 62: Meeting with Colonel, Le Vallon, 19 Sep 1944, p.403.

of this month (see memorandum).[30] Our Bailiff told me the other day that rumour has it that when he and I saw the General at La Corbinerie we stayed to dinner and were seen coming away afterwards. This is to be reported to the British Government! Of course we did not stay to a meal but had our talk carried on over a meal-time we would certainly have been justified, in my opinion, in staying on to achieve our object.

FRIDAY, 22ND SEPTEMBER

Last night Allied planes dropped flares over the south of the Island and in their light many people saw small parachutes descending. This is exactly what happened last week when the message for the General was dropped and naturally I set to work at once this morning to discover if any such message had been picked up by civilians. I saw and telephoned many people living in the south of the Island but nobody had seen any actually land. I asked at Grange Lodge whether the General had received another message and drew blank. They told me this afternoon that all the parachutes had fallen in the sea and from civilian reports which I received I believe they were right.

Anyway this event faded into insignificance this afternoon when I was told there was an Allied ship off the south coast flying an undiscernable ensign and a huge white flag amidships and that a German boat had left St. Peter Port Harbour and had contacted the Allied vessel. News came through from the south coast at about half past four that the two ships had parted company and that the German one was making for the harbour again. They had been together for nearly two hours. The Spur was crowded with German officials when she came in and ten minutes later the General passed up the Grange with two or three other officers in his car and following behind was a smaller car with his interpreter, a very polite young German who graduated from Cambridge and whom I have met several times.

I went to Grange Lodge and Raymond Falla came with me to see Schneberger. I reminded him that he had promised us some months ago that if the Germans received any ultimatum they would let us know immediately; and asked whether this afternoon's contacts were likely to result in such an ultimatum. They had heard nothing of the affair and were wild with excitement, as I was. However, we know nothing further of the outcome of the meeting and although my telephone is nearly red-hot with use tonight, I have done little more than scotch fantastic rumours. I wonder what tomorrow will bring forth?

I hear today that the E boat in the harbour is one of several which made a dash for it from Brest just over a week ago. She brought kind regards from

---

30 See Item 61: Meeting with P.K. and General, 6 Sep 1944, p.401.

a German naval man called Herman who was working at the harbour and was very kind to our fishermen. He apparently was a port official at Brest and we hope he is still alive.

The newspaper plane has just passed over and I heard the light explosion of the newspaper container bursting in mid-air.

SATURDAY, 23RD SEPTEMBER AND SUNDAY, 24TH SEPTEMBER

I am attaching to this sheet a translation of correspondence published in the local German newspaper on the 11th of this month.[31]

Yesterday morning I went to the office ready for anything. I went straight to Grange Lodge where Schneberger told me that he had not yet been able to contact the General and so had no news. He was hoping to see him during the morning and promised to telephone me if he had any information. As he had not phoned by 12.30 I went up again. He said that as far as he knew the Americans had made some suggestion which was contrary to the German tradition, that the General had not gone out to the American boat (I heard afterwards that the Adjutant went instead) and that nothing was likely to come of the visit. He promised to let me have more information later and during the evening Mr Krafft telephoned on his behalf to say that there was nothing to worry about, so far as the civilian population was concerned.

Meanwhile, during the morning Mr Leale, Mr Martel and I met the Bailiff and decided that we should try to make an appointment with Colonel von Helldorff to find out what we could about the whole matter and to suggest that, if a further contact was to be made with the Americans, we be given an opportunity, either through the Germans or direct, to put before the Americans the food, fuel and medical position of the population. We thought this might have the effect of hurrying on the representations already made to the International Red Cross by the Germans.

After some difficulty I finally managed to make an appointment for five fifteen and Mr Leale, Mr Martel and I walked up to Summerland to meet him. We were kept waiting for nearly half an hour and were then shown into his office. What transpired is contained in the memorandum of the meeting which was quite friendly.[32]

Later in the evening I heard indirectly that the Americans had actually asked the Germans whether they were aware of what was happening in France and whether they wished to be given an opportunity to contact the American General in charge of this section in France. I should think this is

---

31 See Item 63: Newspaper article: Letter from Goebbels, 19 Sep 1944, p.405.
32 See Item 64: Meeting with P.K.: Meeting with Allies, 23 Sep 1944, p.406.

correct and it would explain why the Germans did not wish to have anything to do with the matter.

The Bailiff telephoned to me this morning to say that a bullet had been fired through one of his windows during the night and he thought the Germans should be informed. He said that he had reported the matter already to our Police and I suggested he should wait until he had received their report before taking the matter any further, especially as he had not heard any shot fired. The German Feldgendarmerie were called by our Police and it was discovered that what broke the window was not as bullet but a ball-bearing, probably fired from a catapult.

Help was caught some days ago. The Bailiff has appointed a committee to enquire into the matter of his escape and on conditions in general in the prison.

Yesterday afternoon a convoy came in, again in broad daylight, from Jersey. The ships brought 200 tons of Jersey wheat for the civilian population. It must be admitted that, in this, at any rate, the Germans are doing their duty by us, because German lives were definitely risked to bring us this food.

MONDAY, 25TH SEPTEMBER TO THURSDAY, 5TH OCTOBER

On Tuesday September 26th I received a telephone message from Schneberger to say that he had heard an announcement over the German radio regarding the visit of an Allied warship to this Island. The details were, in essence, those I have related already. Yesterday in the House of Commons, a question was asked concerning conditions in the Channel Islands and the answer was that the Germans had been given an opportunity to surrender and had refused. There was no evidence that the population of the Islands was not being properly treated. Meanwhile we have heard no more regarding the talks which are supposed to be going on between the British and German governments regarding the provision of essentials for our civilian population (see memorandum of meeting held on 23rd September).[33] As conditions are at present we can get no fuel released for the Dairy and the Hospitals and their stocks are almost exhausted. I have pressed for a decision on this matter but Grange Lodge say we shall have to wait a few more days. We understand that the General and Colonel von Helldorff are in Jersey and that there is nobody here with the power to make the decision.

The German troops here receive personal messages every day now over one of the German broadcasts. The messages are in stereotyped form.

33 See Item 64: Meeting with P.K.: Meeting with Allies, 23 Sep 1944, p.406 and Item 65: Leale to von Helldorff: Preparing for siege, 23 Sep 1944, p.408.

Numbers of mark notes coming into the bank each month are much bigger these last months, mainly, I think, because the public do not want to hold more than necessary, but also because the troops received an increase of R.M. 30 per month from the date of the invasion, thereby having more to spend in the Island. According to the order we received early in the year we are supposed to hand over all the notes we purchase from the banks to the German paymaster, but when, a month or so ago, we found we had to buy more than a million we decided not to hand them all over. This last month has been a record one and we have had to buy well over a million and a half notes. It had been decided to hand over a million and a quarter but when I had a request for even a small number over a million we were just in time to stop the order to the bank and instead of R.M. 1,250,000 we handed over 1,050,000 and I was thanked profusely for the favour!

Of course the more notes we give the Germans, the more they will have to spend on purchases of local produce, thereby pushing up prices, in spite of all our attempts at control, until our people cannot compete for necessities.

We are spending an increasing amount of time nowadays on post-war problems – control of imports with the least possible amount of red tape, control of immigration and emigration with the same proviso, control of the foreigners who are here should the Germans capitulate before the Allies arrive, restaffing throughout the administration to meet the needs of departments like the Duty on Goods which have not been functioning during the Occupation and many other problems. Everything we do is tentative since we know nothing of conditions outside the Island nor of the policy we shall be asked to adopt.

In the middle of all this work, I managed to get a permit to use the boat for three days, last Sunday to Tuesday, and Dick, Skipper, George, Nigel, Harry Bichard and I went to Herm and Jethou ormering. We had a variety of weather but plenty of sunshine and wind and delightful sails across the Russel in the mornings soon after high water with big swells and a little broken water and a liveliness everywhere which made us forget the war altogether. We did not get many ormers – I had three dozen altogether – but I can still feel the glow from those three days in the open air.

The war news is much less sensational than it was a month ago. Generally speaking we have come up against the German line of resistance on the borders of their country and although this is probably only a crust it is very thick and very tough.

Leaflets have not been dropped here for more than a month now.

FRIDAY, 6TH OCTOBER AND SATURDAY, 7TH OCTOBER

I am informed today by Grange Lodge that the talks between the British and German governments are continuing.

The Germans have cleared the airport of obstacles and we learned yesterday that each soldier has been allowed to write one letter for transmission to Germany. I went to Grange Lodge on hearing this news and asked that the Bailiff be allowed to send a letter to each of the camp seniors in Germany so that our internees may have news of us and also, although I did not say so, some such news might get through to England. Schneberger telephoned headquarters to see whether this was possible and received the answer that all available space had already been allocated but that they would keep our request in mind for next time. I said I thought two extra letters would make no difference at all but I was refused. I stressed the misery of most of the population with loved ones in England who might thereby get some news through, especially mothers of children who left the Island in 1940, but met with no success. Today, however, when I arrived at Grange Lodge, I was told that the Bailiff might write these letters, provided they were handed in this morning. I saw the Bailiff immediately and we drafted short letters (see copy attached).[34] We hope they will reach their destination. Being entirely dependent upon the Germans for their delivery made it impossible to say all that we should have liked to say, but no doubt Mr Sherwill will be able to read between the lines.

SUNDAY, 8TH OCTOBER TO TUESDAY, 10TH OCTOBER

The mail plane arrived on Saturday night at midnight and left again at two o'clock on Sunday morning. Krafft received news that his home had been destroyed completely but that his people were all safe. The letter was dated 2nd October and Nuremburg has had at least one raid since. His wife was still in the city when she wrote!

The General and Colonel von Helldorff arrived back from Jersey yesterday afternoon and today I was handed a letter addressed to the Bailiff enclosing a note for insertion in tomorrow's newspaper. (Copy herewith).[35] The general impression seems to be that the information will be welcomed by the population. Actually from information I have received from the Germans it seems that talks are already taking place between the British and German governments.

34 See Item 66: Letters to Camp Seniors at Biberach & Laufen, 7 Oct 1944, p.415.
35 See Item 67: Newspaper article: Supplies for Channel Islanders [nd], p.416.

Apparently I shall have to be more careful of whatever opinions I offer in future. The Bailiff of Jersey's letter to the German authorities on the food and general supply position has been circulated freely in Guernsey and public opinion on it is divided. Its terms appeal to many people but some think it is purely window dressing. I ventured the opinion, amongst friends, a week or two ago, that it might be a little premature in view of present conditions and this has been elaborated to such an extent that I understand that the members of the United Club, or some of them, think I am hopelessly swollen-headed because I say that the letter is childishly written, etc. It seems that my promotion, if it is an indication of what those who know most about the Civil Service and its work think of me, is also an opportunity for making me a cockshy for all and sundry without their bothering to discover what my work really is. I am getting quite accustomed to such efforts to smirch my name but I am thankful to say that without exception those with whom I have come into direct contact in my work have been unstinting in their congratulations.

Yesterday at Grange Lodge Schneberger told me that the new financial arrangement regarding the Regal Cinema would mean that the States would not have to pay the proprietors for seats taken by members of the civilian population but that, on the contrary, we should benefit to the extent of fifteen marks in entertainments tax for every performance. I said that every little helps but if they really want to help us it would be more to the point to keep down the demands of the military for R.M. I said that with less and less goods to purchase, the increasing demands for purchasing power on behalf of the military meant inevitably a rise in commodity prices despite any control of prices or otherwise we might try to enforce. I instanced the statement which is being made to us almost daily that German units are offering £50 per ton for sugar beet although the controlled price is £28. The result is that the poorer members of the population get less and less of local products. The last straw is the fact that we have to buy back the R.M. so spent by the military. I ended by saying that the present currency position in the Island must be the maddest ever seen.

WEDNESDAY, 11TH OCTOBER TO SATURDAY, 21ST OCTOBER,

The first mail plane on leaving here, was followed by radio to Strasbourg where she touched down for petrol. She then continued into Germany where she was shot down. Some of the mail was saved but we do not know whether the Bailiff's letters to the camps were destroyed. Anyway, we have sent on new letters to Grange Lodge to go on the next plane. The pilot of the first plane was an officer who has been flying to besieged garrisons for years. He did at least one trip to Stalingrad.

It is said that prices of over £100 per ton have been offered by Germans for sugar beet. Dried beans, of which we expected to collect a big crop through subsidising, are not coming through at all. They are being sold at prices which make the subsidy ridiculously small and a large proportion is going to the Germans.

In the middle of last week I mentioned to Mr Leale that I thought it time for the Controlling Committee to show their teeth. Two days later Mr Martel expressed the same view to me. We all agreed and I amused myself one evening in roughing out a letter to the General. I submitted it to Mr Leale on Monday and on Tuesday at a meeting of the Committee I read the draft. Since then we have received a letter from Colonel von Helldorff disclaiming responsibility for feeding the population and one from Grange Lodge requisitioning 60 tons of dried beans. All this has strengthened our case and yesterday afternoon, after hours of work, we agreed the final draft. It is now signed, by the Bailiff and Mr Leale jointly, and should be delivered to the General's office on Monday. (Copies of this correspondence herewith).[36] What the result will be remains to be seen but nobody has any doubt that in refusing point-blank to hand over food to the Germans at this stage the Controlling Committee is doing the only thing possible. Naturally, my first draft has been added to and changed almost beyond recognition.

I have drafted for Mr Wilfred Corbet a requête for submission to the States on reform of membership of the States of Deliberation. If big reforms are to come the period immediately after the war seems to me the most appropriate one.[37]

SUNDAY, 22ND OCTOBER TO TUESDAY, 31ST OCTOBER

I went to see Mr Cross last Monday week. Jack Hart arranged the meeting, thinking that we might benefit mutually from a talk over States affairs and I agreed to go on the understanding that we talked first about his accusation that I sent him to Germany. The conversation started safely and he told me his version. Apparently his present wife went first to Grange Lodge with his letter asking for his exemption from deportation and was told to go to Hirzel House to get a counter signature. This was quite new to me and I said so. Naturally, if such a signature was needed we would not have refused one – Mr Leale had signed many such letters – and after some discussion Mr Cross and I agreed that there had been an misunderstanding. I think we are both happier now. At any rate the remainder of the evening was

36 See Item 68: P.K. to Leale: Responsibilities of Occupying Power, 18 Oct 1944, p.417.
37 See Item 69: Requête: Review of Constitution, Oct 1944, p.422.

quite pleasant and when once I had acquired the knack of getting over his inarticulate delivery, I found him very interesting.

Mr Krefft told me that Crete had been evacuated by agreement between the British and German governments and that the Germans had been given a safe passage to the Balkan mainland.

We received no reply to the letter to the General until last Friday afternoon, when the letter arrived through Grange Lodge.[38] It was dated the Monday previous. The translation speaks for itself and is a total unmasking of the Germans' policy for the remainder of the siege. We never dreamed that they intended to be quite so ruthless. It was signed by the General with Colonel von Helldorff's initials as draftsman. The latter had, until then always striven to give the impression that our welfare was very near his heart! Nobody, in our opinion, could have regarded the letter sent by the Bailiff and Mr Leale as other than a sincere effort to place before the Germans the difficulties confronting the administration and I cannot help feeling that the hysterical reply betokens guilty consciences. Mr Hollard settled down to translating it roughly and excitement was intense as each page came off his typewriter and I took it down to Mr Leale's room to read it to those members of the Controlling Committee who happened to be there. We gasped at the statements made in the letter and felt more than ever before the grimness of our present situation.

I sent a copy to the Bailiff at Le Vallon and next morning Mr Leale and I went to see him at the Court House. He asked me to draft a reply and this I did during the day, giving him a copy to study over the week end. On Monday the Bailiff met the Controlling Committee to study the draft and it was accepted with surprisingly few amendments. Today it has been sent off to the General, with a copy to Grange Lodge for their information.[39]

As the public – and to a greater extent the States – are clamouring for news of the steps we are taking to counter the ever-increasing German demands on our supplies, the Bailiff had thought of sending a copy of his first letter to the General to each States member but now that the reply has arrived and a further letter sent to the General it seems wrong to make public only part of the correspondence. On the other hand he cannot obviously hand copies of German letters to States' members without German approval, so he has decided not to take any active measures for the time being. However, members of the Controlling Committee, being directly affected, are entitled to copies of the correspondence and are not forbidden to shew these copies, in strict confidence, to such members of the States as are interested. As the Controlling Committee are responsible

---

38 See Item 70: General to Bailiff: Resp. of Occupying Power, 23 Oct 1944, p.423.
39 See Item 71: Bailiff to General: Resp. of Occupying Power, 30 Oct 1944, p.426.

to the States for their actions I do not see why the information should remain secret.

Meanwhile, yesterday afternoon Raymond Falla received a verbal order from Grange Lodge for 20 tons of potatoes. After consultation with the Controlling Committee he indicated the depot from which the Germans could collect the potatoes. What else was there to do? If we refused to tell them where to get the potatoes, they would obviously take indiscriminately – and probably our best potatoes. The spectre of complete German control and the troops running wild over the Island is ever before us and we think it best to give up the luxury of telling them to boil their faces since this would doubtless mean sacrificing the population to worse treatment than they would otherwise get.

As far as one can see, one of four things must happen.

1. The British Government will send us supplies until the war ends.
2. The British Government will arrange for the total evacuation of the Island's civilian population.
3. The Island will be attacked and the Germans thrown out.
4. We shall be left to fight a losing battle against ever-increasing German demands until the end of the war.

The only alternative we can base our plans on at present is the last one, and if, in doing so, we appear to help the Germans to some extent it is only because we cannot afford to give them an excuse to throw out civilian control completely.

My personal opinion is that even if the British Government does not wish to help us, the members of our families who are in England will be making such a clamour by now that something will have to be done.

Mr Leale wrote on quite new lines to P.K. this morning on the subject of the requisition of the potatoes. His letter is entirely in keeping with the best in his character and is written in all sincerity. I shall be interested to see how it can be answered adequately.[40]

The monthly call from us for R.M. came through Mr Krefft to me a day or two ago. The paymaster asked whether, for once, he could have his money on the first of the month instead of the fifth. That means that although he had R.M. 50,000 more than ever before, last month, it did not last him a complete month. And yet the General says that the troops do not get more money than before! A quarter of a million R.M. will be handed over tomorrow.

The past week has shewn the veneer of straight dealing torn off and greed and a total disregard for responsibilities to the civilian population

---

40 See Item 72: Leale to P.K.: Potato Requisition, 31 Oct 1944, p.430.

underneath. There is not even the excuse of bad behaviour by the civilian population to be made for such ruthlessness and diplomatic manners and conversation will always be transparent to me – and to all of us – in the future.

WEDNESDAY, 1ST NOVEMBER TO SUNDAY, 5TH NOVEMBER

Some wheat arrived for us from Jersey during the week and the Germans resorted to extraordinary methods to get some of it. I shall attach reports on the subject later.[41]

At the States meeting last Wednesday questions were asked regarding present stocks and the dates on which they will run out. Sir Abraham Lainé and Doctor Symons gave very full answers (copy herewith).[42] Questions were also asked as to the reasons for the creation of the new post of Assistant Supervisor and these also were answered in full by Mr Leale.

On Wednesday and Friday we went ormering. On Wednesday we went to Godin. Rain was threatening and there was a strong breeze from the north east. We made good time and anchored in the bay at Godin just before it came on to pour. We crept under the mainsail and ate our lunch whilst waiting for the rain to stop. The wind howled in our scanty rigging and I hoped very much that our ripe anchor rope would not part. We went ashore and found a few ormers and then we came back across the Russel through fine big seas and with a strong wind behind us.

On Friday the only other fishermen at St. Sampson's when we arrived to go aboard the boat were Captain Fred Noyon and Enticott.[43] They told us they were going to look for ormers but were going to put down their net first. We remarked on the fine large baskets they had – apparently full of oilskins and nets – and ragged them about the catches they would need to fill them. We went to the back of Herm under sail and did not get two dozen ormers between the four of us. I had none at all. Saturday morning we heard that Fred and Enticott had not been seen since the previous afternoon!

This morning Dick, José and I strolled along to Nick Hubert and had just settled down in his greenhouse for a chat when Henry Bisson came hurrying in to say that Mr Leale wanted to speak to me on their phone, ours being out of order. Mr Leale told me that the Bailiff had received a message from Krafft to the effect that the General had given permission for a message to be sent by us to the International Red Cross over their radio transmitter. We were to go immediately to Le Vallon to compose the

41　See Item 73: Harbourmaster to Leale: Unloading ships, 4 Nov 1944, p.431.
42　See Item 74: Present stocks of essential commodities, 1 Nov 1944, p.433 and Item 75: Present stocks of medical supplies, 1 Nov 1944, p.439.
43　For details of this escape, see Kreckeler (1978).

message. I changed and rode along to Vernon Le Maître where I picked up a motor cycle and went on to catch Mr Leale who had left ahead of me. I came up with him at Le Val des Terres and he left his cycle at the top of the hill and rode on the pillion to the Vallon. Here we met Sir Abraham with the Bailiff and wrote out as much as we could of the message. Then I left the others and went on to Dr Symons for details of medical supplies, to the Grange Club to see Jurat de Putron regarding bread, to Hirzel House to type the message, to Miss Riderer to get translated into German, to Grange Lodge where Krafft checked the translation and to Queen's Road where I handed the completed article to Herr Schneberger.[44] He made me try his piano and gave me a drink and I asked him questions for which I had been wanting answers. I arrived back for lunch at 3.30, well satisfied with my morning.

The question which is occupying all our minds is, why has the General changed his mind about giving us facilities for getting into touch with the outside world? According to Herr Schneberger the reason is that he told Colonel von Helldorff that we must be granted such permission and that the idea was put into his mind by Percy Dorey and Raymond Falla at a recent meeting at Grange Lodge. If he really believes this his memory of our requests during the past four or five months must be very short. So many possibilities spring to mind that I have not the patience to set them out here. They must be obvious to everybody.

MONDAY, 6TH NOVEMBER TO TUESDAY, 14TH NOVEMBER

Up to the present there has been no news at all of the fate of the Bailiff's radiogram, except that we were told last week that it was sent off on the Monday morning.[45] They suggested at Grange Lodge that the Bailiff should notify the public, through the newspaper, that he had sent the message but I said that it would be better to wait until there was something definite to announce, since our people are getting to the stage when their reaction to this sort of news is, 'We've heard that one before!' However, a day later the Bailiff was told to put the notice in the paper and he published a non-committal one.

There is still no reply to the Bailiff's letter to the General nor to Mr Leale's to the P.K., regarding the requisition of potatoes. The matter of potatoes, however, has become very much more serious. On the 7th the P.K. wrote to the Controlling Committee ordering the immediate delivery of 500 tons of potatoes and the collection of a further 500 tons without delay.[46]

---

44 See Item 76: Bailiff to Red Cross, 5 Nov 1944, p.440. These are the original texts as signed by the Bailiff, and the edited version actually transmitted to Geneva.
45 A radiogram was the term for a telegram sent by radio.
46 See Item 77: P.K. to C.C.: Potato Requisition, 7 Nov 1944, p.442.

The memorandum of the meeting held at Grange Lodge next day sets out the position and the decision to continue the ration for the time being.[47] Early on Friday we received written instructions to cut the ration to 5 lbs per head and, from the stocks held by the Potato Board, 120 tons were taken by the troops. On Monday morning P.K. telephoned to the Potato Board instructions to stop the issue of a potato ration from stores this week. They added that if we wished to issue any ration we must get the necessary potatoes from the producers. We knew quite well that P.K. could not help us in the matter and it was decided that the Bailiff, Raymond Falla and I should make an appointment to see the General. I telephoned this morning to ask for the meeting but up to now have received no reply.

Meanwhile this afternoon the Controlling Committee met to discuss this and other matters and had almost decided in their misery that they were becoming nothing but agents for the collection of food supplies for the Germans, when Krafft telephoned to say that the potato ration might be issued this week.

I went to Grange Lodge about five o'clock this afternoon to see whether I could find out any more about future rations of potatoes but the people I wanted to see were out. However, I had a chat with Krefft who told me that there is a rumour that the Bailiff sent Fred Noyon to England. I said that of course we expected the Germans to think this but that there was no truth whatsoever in it. I added that all our appeals for help so far had been made through the Germans and it was quite likely that our people in England regarded them as inspired by the Germans. I suggested it would be much better to let some Guernsey official make a trip to England – and to return to the Island. If ever there were secrets to hide the British must know them all by now, with the number of people who had escaped from the Islands recently. He said it might be worth while putting forward the suggestion but he did not think we ought to press for it yet.

Mr Johns, Dr Symons and Raymond Falla have been visiting the Douzaines and reading the correspondence between the Bailiff and the General. In three out of four cases the douzaines concerned have passed unanimous votes of confidence in the Controlling Committee. Arrangements are being made for visits to the remaining douzaines.

There have been scarcely any roots to buy in the shops lately and stories are coming in of people suffering acutely from hunger. It seems that always, in spite of all efforts, the poor and the friendless are the people to suffer.

Rumours are still as prevalent as ever. British troops (or French troops) are massing at Cherbourg, Carteret, Granville and St. Malo for the relief of the Channel Islands; the British and the German governments are discussing

---

47 See Item 78: Meeting with P.K.: Potato Requisition, 8 Nov 1944, p.443.

an exchange of troops from the Channel Islands for the same number of prisoners of war from Germany; de Gaulle has broadcast a statement to the effect that the French ports and the Channel Islands are to be freed by French forces.[48]

Up to now there have been no repercussions because of Noyon's escape.

A ship which loaded foodstuffs for Alderney over the weekend was discharged again in St. Peter Port Harbour yesterday. Why?

On Sunday we built a copper for the manufacture of sugar-beet syrup.[49] I started work before daylight and finished at dusk. The actual work was done by Skipper.

WEDNESDAY, 15TH NOVEMBER AND THURSDAY, 16TH NOVEMBER

Potatoes are still the main worry. Yesterday, having finished collecting their 120 tons, the Germans continued taking from the Potato Board depots and up to this morning a total of over 160 tons had gone. We received no intimation whatever from the Germans that they were carting away the potatoes and this morning Mr Leale, Raymond Falla and I went to Grange Lodge about the matter. We were assured that they would not take all the potatoes from the depots and that the earlies would be left. The ration would continue at 5 lbs. We breathed a sigh of relief – until they said that they wanted immediately a full list of producers with their addresses, the area planted and the amount they would be allowed to keep calculated at 90 lbs per head of each household for eating, plus seed for next season! They read a document which would be carried by the Germans who would collect the surplus from individual producers – if it was decided to make such a collection – and added that the producer would be paid cash – in marks! Then to console us they explained that such potatoes would only be taken into safe custody. The hopes of civilians of ever eating any of those potatoes are too slim to talk about and we said so.

While we were there we put forward a new idea of the Controlling Committee, namely the slaughter of unproductive cattle on the grounds that we have not enough roots to feed such animals and human beings as well. They are submitting the matter to the Division.

We have not received a reply to the Bailiff's request for a meeting with the General.

Conditions have deteriorated so gradually here that now that we can see the horrid pit of starvation opening before us it is hard to realize that six

---

48 This refers to the French ports which were also still held by German garrisons, namely at Dunkirk, Lorient, La Rochelle and Royan.

49 The copper was in the shed at the back of La Platte for many years. It was heated up from underneath to boil sugar beet into syrup.

years ago competition was really keen for the sale of every kind of food and indeed of all luxuries too. Strong men wake in the night and cannot sleep again for hunger. They have to get up and go to work with one piece of bread to drive them, they eat a few potatoes for dinner and come home to a fireless grate in the evening with soaked clothing and no way of drying it. Families of children have to be deprived of the food they need, people wait in long rows in the markets for a few roots – and when their turn comes at the stall they often find that stocks have gone. And the winter is upon us. Our only hope is that food and fuel will be sent to us by our countrymen in England but we know that our government may have good reasons for sacrificing us and we do not hope too much. And we hear that in England they have to resort to propaganda to entice the public to eat bacon! Those of us who have been lucky enough to grow some food for ourselves, or who have farmer friends who have sold us roots and maize, are not yet desperate, but we know that we will never be able to eat our fill with the knowledge that others are hungry and we shall all go down together in the end. Morale, generally, is good, though, and, as usual in adversity, pettiness is beginning to disappear and is giving place to kindness and generosity and a growing will to resist the common enemy.

FRIDAY, 17TH NOVEMBER

Still the Bailiff has not been allowed to see the General. Krefft told Mallett confidentially yesterday that we should be receiving supplies of food from outside within a fortnight. We have not yet been informed of any reply to the radiogram to the Red Cross. The boom has been removed from the mouth of St. Peter Port Harbour. So we wonder whether the Germans are working hard to get supplies of food from us before they notify us of the decision of the Red Cross and whether the General has not yet given the Bailiff a date for an interview because he does not want to be embarrassed by having to answer a direct question as to whether an answer has been received.

The Germans are talking now of unglazing all greenhouses other than those served by windmills. They are so ignorant of glasshouse culture that they do not realize that such an act would kill all the tender crops in the houses. However, we have not been notified officially of this yet.

José can put on her own panties.

SATURDAY, 18TH NOVEMBER TO TUESDAY, 21ST NOVEMBER

The first information I received on arriving at the office on Saturday morning was that the General would see the Bailiff at noon and that there was an important letter at Grange Lodge from the General which the Bailiff should see before his visit. This letter proved to be, amongst other things, a warning of further reductions in rations (see copy).[50] We also received a letter from the P.K. regarding requisitions of potatoes.[51]

At twelve o'clock the Bailiff, Mr Leale, Mr Johns and I went to the Corbinerie where we met the General and Colonel von Helldorff. We left there at one o'clock and I came back to the office where I cooked and ate my lunch and then typed out the memorandum of the meeting.[52] By half past two it was finished and we went off to discuss it at Sefton. This meeting with the General was the first to take place since the exchange of correspondence and it was rather frigid at first. By the time we left we all felt better.

One of the Irish colony wrote a letter recently to the Irish ambassador in Berlin asking for help in getting supplies to the Islands but I do not know whether it has been sent off yet.

This morning at Grange Lodge I asked whether any reply had been received from the Red Cross and was assured that none had arrived. I said that I thought sometimes they knew more than they told us about this matter but they repeated that they knew nothing at all. I had hardly left the room when Krafft came running after me to say that they had just received an answer and when I returned they said that soap and medical supplies were coming. I arranged to call again this afternoon to hear more details and was then informed that in addition to soap and medicaments they thought that food parcels would be coming and perhaps a representative too. Meanwhile I heard that a Grange Lodge officer had given this news previously to a girl-friend of his, a Frenchwoman and I gather that when I asked this morning they must have known although they denied such knowledge. We have so lost confidence that we will not believe until we see the goods but there is no denying the fact that the relief is tremendous.

I expect we shall receive news if the Red Cross open communication for us and I fear this will be a mixed blessing since we have so many of our frinds and relatives fighting on the continent.

We had a preliminary talk at Grange Lodge this afternoon about the unglazing of greenhouses because of the lack of water when electricity and petrol give out. They say that the unglazing will only be resorted to when all other means of watering fail and we sincerely hope so when such a measure would mean a loss of hundreds of thousands of pounds to the Island, especially if it meant that the greenhouses could not be used next year if our English markets are again open to us.

We shall be starting the slaughter of unproductive cattle within the next few days.

---

50 See Item 79: General to Bailiff: Reduction in food rations, 16 Nov 1944, p.445.
51 See Item 80: P.K. to C.C.: Collection of potatoes, 17 Nov 1944, p.446.
52 See Item 81: Meeting with P.K. and General, 18 Nov 1944., p.447.

WEDNESDAY, 22ND NOVEMBER AND THURSDAY, 23RD NOVEMBER

We are now told that the 200 cattle which are to be slaughtered immediately will be killed by the Germans in their own slaughter house and that
they will keep all the offal![53] The Germans are hoping to organize alternative
methods of watering greenhouses which at present use waterworks water
or are served by electric, petrol or gas pumps. They talked of watering by
buckets when we met them yesterday!

I have discussed with the P.K. several times lately the wording of the
Bailiff's notice informing the public of the General's promise to take not more
than 500 tons of potatoes. Today they wanted us to word the notice so that
we would admit that the requsition was in accordance with Article 52 of the
Hague Rules. I refused flatly to suggest any such alteration to the Bailiff and
we are not going to do it. Eventually we agreed a form of words which will be
published in tomorrow's newspaper. In the same paper will be published a
Controlling Committee order for the delivery by potato producers of all but
90 lbs per head – of household – of their stocks. These potatoes are to be used
as a ration for those of our population who have no stocks of their own.

FRIDAY, 24TH NOVEMBER AND SATURDAY, 25TH NOVEMBER

No Red Cross ship yet but the beginnings of interference from the Germans,
who seem to consider, rightly or wrongly, that they must have a hand in
the distribution of whatever comes. I told them yesterday that the Essential
Commodities Department could easily distribute parcels through the
grocers who have all the necessary machinery already set up. Today when I
walked in they said that they had decided to entrust the distribution to our
Red Cross Bureau. I said that obviously they did not realize that the Bureau
is not known to the Red Cross proper and that the personnel is composed
mainly of temporary States staff whose work is to see that messages are
sent off and distributed properly. They repeated that some Red Cross
representative should take charge and I mentioned that Dr Collings was
a Red Cross representative acknowledged by the British Red Cross. I have
seen him since and I think he may act as liaison between the Red Cross and
the Essentials Committee.

This morning M.V.R. Schneberger said that my minute on last Saturday's
meeting was wrong concerning the acceptance of potatoes already taken
(see page 2, last sentence on potatoes)[54]. I asked whether this meant that
they were going to take more and he answered that they would not accept

---

53 See Items 82 and 83 for the continuation of this argument.
54 See Item 81: Meeting with P.K. and General, 18 Nov 1944., p.447.

about 100 tons which were not edible. They would therefore be taking a further 100 tons to replace them. This was such a barefaced piece of cheek that I lost my temper and told them what I thought of their promises. I added that they probably did not realize that, as in the past when they have taken our potatoes, our people would soon be paying high prices for potato peelings to eat and what the Germans found uneatable would be eaten by many civilians very thankfully. If they were going to break their promise, I claimed that we must see the potatoes they were rejecting before they took any more. I asked what further proof we could have that the paymaster would not throw into the pile many of his other rotten stocks. They agreed to arrange a meeting between our officials and theirs.

During the lunch hour I received a telephone message from Krafft saying that I should not pass on the statement they had made about potatoes since, after consultation with Colonel von Helldorff, it had been decided not to take any more potatoes. I cannot see the catch yet but I have altogether given up believing anything they say and mean to press on for a full settlement of the matter.

SUNDAY, 26TH NOVEMBER AND MONDAY, 27TH NOVEMBER

I took Ronald Mallett of the Potato Board with me to Grange Lodge this morning to compare our figures with theirs regarding recent requisitions of potatoes. There are such big differences that we brought back a copy of their figures and are to submit to them a report on individual figures. While there I asked if we could regard the matter of further requisitions as closed. Herr Schneberger said that he had submitted my minutes to Colonel von Helldorff and that they claimed the right to demand extra for uneatable potatoes. It is difficult to keep cool when such statements are made, but I managed it today. Anyway, I said I would like to know on what date they thought of basing such a claim. We told them that the removal of the potatoes from one store to another would be bound to result in a deterioration of the lasting qualities of the potatoes and naturally there would be more uneatable ones each day. Herr Schneberger said he thought it was too late to make any claim now and added that when, on Saturday, he told the Colonel what I had said, he decided not to make any claim. He said that, however, he did not know what the Paymaster would say on the matter. I said that we wanted a clear decision, since if they intended to take any more we were going to put in the strongest possible protest. In addition we had no doubt that if any more potatoes were requisitioned we would never again enjoy the confidence of our people and neither would the Germans.

From other German sources we hear continually that the Controlling Committee are getting the blame for the necessity of requisitioning. They say we gave false figures earlier in the season but the fact is that we never promised to contribute potatoes towards their food supplies. How could we when, even with quite large importations of foodstuffs from France we have never succeeded in producing sufficient potatoes for ourselves!

This afternoon I introduced Dr Collings at P.K. They said they wanted him to take charge of the distribution of Red Cross supplies and that a scheme should be prepared at once so as to be ready when the goods arrive. He agreed provided that the detailed work be undertaken by the Essentials Committee.

It is strange how little they realize the efficiency of the rationing scheme and the detailed knowledge available after four and a half years of strict rationing. If they were friends instead of enemies, their lack of confidence in the people who have worked so hard and so long for the Island would be heartbreaking. They asked questions showing plainly how little they knew about the complexities of distribution. However, they treated Dr Collings with the respect due to the Red Cross and I have no doubt that this new broom will be of great help to us. Having accepted him, they cannot, for instance, fail to let him know when the ship is due to arrive. They took his telephone number and invited him to get in touch with them if he wanted to ask any questions. They did not ask him to approach them through me. The doctor told me later that he had received a visit from Miss Trouteaud, our manageress of the Red Cross Bureau, last Saturday evening, and it appears that the P.K. had approached her direct regarding the taking over of distribution – without consulting us at all.

TUESDAY, 28TH NOVEMBER

This morning Mallett and I went to Grange Lodge again. He had checked his weights with the weighbridge figures and with receipts held by the depots, and although there were discrepancies in the case of nearly every depot, the principal differences resulted from false figures for two depots. When we came to this subject in the morning's talk, I said that although there were many differences in the figures we were willing to give them the benefit of all but two depots. They were delighted until they asked what these differences amounted to and I told them that the amount under dispute was about forty-nine tons. We were able to press home the point since the potatoes from the two depots in question were all weighed over the States' weighbridges. Thus we could prove, by their own figures in all but two cases and weighbridge weights for the remaining ones, that they had taken between 509 and 510 tons. I said that we therefore wanted nine tons returned to us. They laughed but I said it was no laughing matter, seeing that nine tons was a considerable part of a week's rations and that we meant to press for them. Whether my tactics of going over to the attack instead of keeping on the defensive will clinch the matter in our favour remains to be seen.

WEDNESDAY, 29TH NOVEMBER TO THURSDAY, 7TH DECEMBER

The potato argument is not finished yet but as I have written a full memorandum on it, I shall not repeat myself here.[55]

By far the most exciting news of the past week was telephoned to the Bailiff by the P.K. last Tuesday afternoon. A ship carrying Red Cross supplies leaves Portugal today (Thursday) for the Channel Islands. The Bailiff was summoned to see the General yesterday morning and I went with him. We were given details, again included in a memorandum.[56]

Meanwhile, the local Red Cross, St. John Ambulance and Essential Commodities Department are going ahead with the arrangments for the storage, guarding and distribution of the parcels – if there are parcels.

FRIDAY, 8TH DECEMBER TO TUESDAY, 12TH DECEMBER

No sign of the ship yet but plenty of rumours. The Germans tell that she is the *Vega* and in the shipping list she is given as an old Swedish ship carrying about 1500 tons. The weather has been foul and even if the ship left Lisbon last Thursday it is unlikely that she can be here yet. Meanwhile it is freely said that Question was asked in the House today concerning shipments to the Channel Islands and the Home Secretary replied that foodstuffs and medical supplies would be sent in ships which have been guaranteed a safe passage by the Germans. I think there was probably more in the answer but it is difficult to separate rumour from fact.

Nearly every night last week German aircraft landed here bringing mail and taking off – so it is said – officers to fight in Germany.

Electricity is cut to a minimum now in an effort to make the diesel oil stocks last over Christmas. We can only use current from 6 to 10 p.m. The standard ration is 1½ units per household per week. Gas is only on from 8 to 9 in the mornings, 11 to 1 and 6 to 7.30 in the evenings. The gas has been cut off at Plémy because they exceeded their ration and as we are 800 cubic feet over during the past seven weeks we fully expect to be cut off too when next our meter is read.

Bread is down to three pounds a head per week and besides the whole of the wheat being put into the flour, a third of the whole bulk is made up with oats. The result is a loaf which is almost uneatable.

---

55 See Item 84: Leale to P.K.: Potato Ration, 29 Nov 1944, p.452.
56 See Item 85: Meeting with General, Arrival of Red Cross ship, 6 Dec 1944, p.454.

Milk is down to a basic ration of a quarter of a pint a day and if we get more, we count ourselves extremely lucky. Happily José still gets a ration of 1½ pints of whole milk a day and this extra keeps the children in reasonable health.

WEDNESDAY, 13TH DECEMBER

Early this morning I received a telephone message from P.K. that Baron von Aufsess, who is here from Jersey, was making an appointment to see the Bailiff at noon and that he had some good news to impart. The Bailiff telephoned for me as soon as he arrived at the office and told me the same thing. He asked me to attend the meeting and to ask Mr Leale to be there too.

The first thing we were told at the meeting was that the General had received news that the ship had been delayed by the tempest! Then the Baron continued that we might already know that the subject of supplies for the Channel Islands had been mentioned by the B.B.C. yesterday. He paused for some answer from us but we all looked completely blank or thought we did. He then read out the announcement as they had it, in German, having been translated by the German interpreter who heard the news and telephoned from Jersey.

The Baron then conveyed to the Bailiff the good wishes of the Bailiff of Jersey.

As far as I was concerned the most welcome piece of information was that it had been decided not to ask for potatoes to replace the 25 tons which were taken on the 31st October.

They also told the Bailiff that he would be the first to welcome the representatives of the Red Cross, since the shipment is for us and not for the Germans.

THURSDAY, 14TH DECEMBER TO THURSDAY, 21ST DECEMBER

It is said that the B.B.C. announced this morning that the ship *Vega* left Lisbon last night for the Channel Islands with 1,000 tons of food, clothing, soap and medical supplies and that she is flying the flag of the International Red Cross. After many false alarms, it really looks as if the boat is on her way to us this time.

The gas supply came to an end this morning at nine o'clock and we wonder when it will start again. Cooking by any other means is inconvenient, to say the least, and especially in this house which has no alternative cooking arrangements.

Dr Symons has been dismissed by the Germans. I have written a memorandum on a meeting we had with P.K. on the subject.[57] We have all spent hours this week to see the right way out of this serious situation and as a result of our meeting with P.K. I have had to make an appointment for the doctor to see Colonel von Helldorff – at the Colonel's request. It looks as if the matter will be settled.

The Germans are very keen on the planting of all potato seed in glasshouses, so as to have the earliest possible crop. Twice complete arrangements have been made and have been upset and today was the fourth meeting we have had on the subject with P.K. Tempers are apt to be a little frayed with the strain.

FRIDAY, 22ND DECEMBER TO WEDNESDAY, 27TH DECEMBER

The most exciting news – of purely local interest – since the beginning of the Occupation is that the International Red Cross ship, *Vega* arrived here today; berthing at six o'clock this evening.

Throughout the holidays we have waited for her coming. I have hardly left the house, waiting patiently for news from the Germans that she was in sight, but it was not until I arrived at Grange Lodge this morning that I was told what I so longed to hear. Although she was sighted at 10.45 she was not seen off the east coast until after lunch.

During the lunch hour Mr Krafft telephoned me to find out where he could contact the Bailiff, since he had to give him a message from Herr Schneberger. He told me that the ship would berth some time after three o'clock and that the Bailiff was the only civilian who would be allowed to be on the harbour to welcome the Red Cross representatives. I put him in touch with the Bailiff and then called up Mr Leale, Sir Abraham Lainé and Dr Collings. We all met in the Bailiff's rooms at about two o'clock, when a message came through from the P.K. that Schneberger and Krafft were coming down to see the Bailiff immediately. They came and said that the General had decided not to meet the ship but to send Colonel von Helldorff in his place. They suggested that the Bailiff should send a representative and meet the Red Cross people formally later. The Bailiff asked me to represent him. Colonel von Helldorff did not wait for the ship to come in but was taken out to her early in the afternoon and spent some hours aboard before she berthed.

We were also told that the Bailiff of Jersey was on his way over and would arrive at about four o'clock with Baron von Aufsess. He would be put up by Schneberger. The Bailiff was not asked whether he would like to entertain him.

---

57 See Item 86: Meeting with P.K.: Dismissal of Dr Symons, 18 Dec 1944, p.456.

At four o'clock I went to the harbour with Schneberger and about half an hour later the boat arrived from Jersey. The Bailiff and I were driven up by the Germans to the Royal Court where our Bailiff, Mr Leale, Sir Abraham and Mr Martel were waiting. Then I drove on with them to Camblez in the Queen's Road where the P.K. officers live and Schneberger and I drove back to the harbour. The *Vega* was just about to berth as we arrived and sure enough, there were the Red Cross representatives, surrounded by beaming German officers. I was introduced to them – by the Germans – and the senior one said how glad they were to be able to come to our aid. I replied as suitably as I could and so the historic contact was made.

There were quite large crowds of people on the shore side of the Careening Hard and some of the children cheered as the ship came in. A German photographer took photographs of the Red Cross representatives, surrounded by smiling Germans – but nobody thought of including the Guernsey representative in the groups.

1945

On Thursday morning the two Bailiffs, the Controlling Committee, Dr Collings, the Supervisor, Loveridge and I met at the Bailiff's Chambers just before 11 o'clock to welcome the Red Cross representatives. I went down to the entrance to meet them and they arrived with a group of German officers. I was asked immediately, before even we had entered the building, to give the names of three civilians to check the cargo on the quay and to receive it on behalf of the Bailiff. Colonel Iselin explained that his instructions were that the goods were to be handed over to the Bailiff from the ship and that he was to obtain from the Bailiff a receipt for them. I said that if they would come to the Bailiff's rooms I would consult him and other officials and would give them the names without delay. The Germans had told us that no civilians at all would be allowed at the harbour and I gather there had been some argument on the matter before the Germans agreed to the Colonel's demands. However, I obtained the names and went to the harbour myself to see the work started. At 1 o'clock work began and soon was going quite smoothly. We received strict instructions that our men were to have nothing at all to do with the crew of the ship.

On Thursday afternoon we had our first meeting at Rozel, Mount Durand. This finished after six o'clock and I came back to the office, telephoned for a shorthand typist and dictated my minutes. These were fair-copied and ready for distribution at eleven o'clock on Friday morning. I tried to get into touch with the Red Cross representatives to hand them the figures of goods discharged during the day, going down to the harbour at about half past eight, but I was not allowed to see them. Instead I had to write out the figures and hand them to a member of the security police stationed on the boat. I arrived home at 9.30 having eaten nothing but a little bread and butter since 9 o'clock that morning.

On Thursday morning Colonel Iselin invited the two Bailiffs to lunch on board the boat next day. On Friday morning he came to the Court House and asked to see the two Bailiffs privately. He thereupon explained to them that he had overlooked the fact that no British subject was allowed on board the boat. The Germans had also been invited and they went. A meeting had been arranged at Rozel for three o'clock that afternoon but we had to wait till four o'clock before they arrived.

Again we had a very good meeting, with the Germans interfering very little in our discussions with the Red Cross representatives. We finished soon after six o'clock and I drove Dr Symons home. He gave me some tea and I telephoned from his house for two typists. We met at Hirzel House at a quarter to seven and I dictated to them in relays. The fair copies were ready by 8.30 and I delivered them to the P.K. that evening. Meanwhile, I received a telephone message that some of the cargo had had to be left at the harbour for the night and they did not know what to do about a guard. I went down and discovered a few St. John Ambulance men still at the berth. Two of them agreed to stay the night and I asked the security police to arrange for them to have some food from the ship. I learned next morning they were nearly sick with all the rich food they were given. I just managed to get home by ten o'clock and was at work again at the harbour just after half past seven next morning. Distribution to the shops started at 7.30 and finished, to all intents and purposes by the end of the morning. The public collected their parcels on Sunday and food is the only topic of conversation since that time.

We were very fortunate to have the Bailiff of Jersey with us for the meetings and I thought he and Mr Leale were as perfect a combination as I have met. They both know their subject, avoid bickering and put their points with a simplicity and clarity which amounts almost to genius. If it does not, at any rate, I have not during my short but intensive experience of conferences, come across anyone else, English, French or German nearly as good.

Throughout their visit we were never allowed to meet the Red Cross representatives without the Germans being present. They were invited to visit the hospitals, but refused, whether because of German pressure I do not know.

It had been arranged that the Bailiff of Jersey should return to that Island on the Red Cross ship but at the last minute the Admiral would not allow him to do so.

We were favourably impressed by Colonel Iselin who appears to be very efficient and it was a treat to hear somebody with sufficient power to get his own way!

We all ask ourselves what will happen now. Will German requisitions increase, will life be more bearable or will we lose as much as we have gained? Certainly if we receive flour from England the Germans will be able to last out much longer, perhaps even until the next harvest.

There seemed something almost sinister about the orders and counter-orders, the jealous guarding of the Red Cross people, the bland faces of the Germans giving all these orders and the smaller people who had to deliver them to us. I must admit that to my mind there is not full harmony in the higher official German positions here and the strictest and strongest orders come always from the Admiral – over the Red Cross at any rate.

Photographs were taken at every meeting as well as on the quays. I must try to get some of them.

WEDNESDAY, 3RD JANUARY TO TUESDAY, 16TH JANUARY

We received a letter on the 5th stating that the fat ration was to be reduced to a minimum guaranteed to the British Government during negotiations between the British and the Germans. We managed to save the old ration for one week but have had to reduce since. The letter and memorandum of a meeting with Colonel von Helldorff are enclosed.[1]

During the meeting the Colonel said that he did not think we had been very clever in suggesting, in the minutes of the meetings with the Red Cross representatives and in the general report which we handed to the representatives, that the British Government might not be willing to send to the Islands fuel which could be used by the occupiers as well as the occupied. He added that the Germans had given us large quantities of fuel in the past and that we did not want them to have any gas.

There has been very little excitement here lately, thank goodness! Today we went to Herm in the boat and came back with enough ormers to make one or two good meals. As usual, it was a great treat to be on the water and we actually landed. We had tried to get permits to visit the Island and had failed, but the Customs at St. Sampson's insisted that we must take a guard in the boat and we were lucky enough to find a Major who wanted to go to Herm. So, we went with him, though I gather that, strictly speaking we were still acting against regulations. However, although there were one or two naval officers on the Island they said nothing and we have not been hauled over the coals yet.

The war news has been of German counter-attacks on the western front during the past month, but they have been unsuccessful and we are progressing very well again. The Russians have their winter offensives in full swing from north to south and are making good headway. We wonder whether the war may end this summer after all.

WEDNESDAY, 17TH JANUARY TO MONDAY, 5TH FEBRUARY

It has been so cold since last I wrote up this diary that I have not had the courage to leave the fire for the typewriter. As with every winter I can remember the weather has been the worst for the past fifty years.

---

1   See Item 87: P.K. to Bailiff: Fat Supplies, 5 Jan 1945, p.458.

We went to Herm again on the 17th, to take Raymond Falla who had a permit to land. We all landed and had a magnificent lunch with the Le Pages. We brought back between four and five hundredweight of pinewood and by the time we had landed it, carried it up the beach to the handcart and wheeled it home it was pitch dark.

The past three weeks have seen some strange correspondence between us and the Germans, all of which is attached hereto. We find it very difficult to guess what is behind such a letter, for instance, as the one dated January 14th and sent by Colonel von Helldorff to the Bailiff. Taken at its face value, it is the letter of a man hurt to the quick by our total lack of gratitude for all the Germans have done for us. All the figures are wrong, however, and we have never been told that coal and diesel had been supplied to us on loan.[2] It was a difficult letter to answer and the Bailiff, Mr Leale, Mr Martel and I talked the matter over for hours on end, without agreeing on the motive which prompted the Colonel to send it. Eventually, it was decided that I should try to get him to talk about the letter and the kind of reply he was expecting. I did see him on other matters but he froze so completely when I mentioned the letter that I could not continue the conversation.

Then there were letters mentioning a guarantee given by the German Government to the British, but as the details are given to us in the P.K. letter of January 25th, it would appear that the Germans have guaranteed NOT to give us more than 500 grammes of vegetables per day. This, of course, is nonsense.[3]

The condition of flour stocks is very serious just now. We will finish completely by or within a few days of the end of this week. At the end of last year the Germans took over our stock at the Charroterie Mills, on the undertaking that they would give us theirs at Braggs Mills which they were leaving and would make up the difference to us. We lost a large quantity in this way and have never been given any of theirs, with the exception of eighty tons during the past month. They have obviously been waiting anxiously to discover whether we shall receive flour from England and so have only given us a week's flour at a time. They radioed three times themselves for news of the boat and when they received no reply they asked the two Bailiffs to send a message themselves. Today we have received news that the boat should arrive during the next few days and that she has no flour aboard. The latter part of last week P.K. told me that they definitely could not let us have any more flour. Today we have received news from Jersey (dated January 10th and censored) that the P.K. there asked the Bailiff to lend us fifty tons and that he had agreed to do so.[4] The arrangement was that the flour should be

---

2   See Item 88: von Helldorff to Bailiff: Civilian supplies, 14 Jan 1945, p.462.
3   See Item 89: Schneberger to Bailiff: Fat Ration, 25 Jan 1945, p.463.
4   See Item 90: Bailiff of Jersey to Bailiff: Flour supplies, 10 Jan 1945, p.464.

handed to us from German stocks here and that the States of Jersey would hand over a like amount for shipment in due course. All this took place last month and the first fifty tons of the eighty mentioned above were, in reality, lent us by Jersey. Why did the Germans not tell us this and why has the Jersey mail been held up until today? Is it a coincidence? Last Saturday the Bailiff wrote the Colonel asking whether they were going to refund the flour they promised us when they took over the Charroterie Mills. To this we have received no answer but this afternoon Schneberger suggested to me that he should ask the Division to lend us some wheat to tide us over until ours arrives from the Red Cross. I said that something would have to be done because our people could not be left to starve but was careful not to agree to any discussion of a loan.

Negotiations of this kind are very complicated and German information and statements are so contradictory that we have learned not to place any reliance on them. What we cannot decide is whether the Colonel and his associates are playing a very deep game or whether they are naturally inaccurate in every word they utter.

The second Red Cross parcel was given out last Sunday week but as there were not enough to go round, children up to four, all inhabitants of Sark and families of four and over had to be sacrificed, in the last-mentioned case, the family losing one parcel.

About a week ago two Guernsey fisherman named Le Page and a Frenchman made off in a boat.[5]

Last Wednesday a radio message arrived from Mr Sherwill and the two Bailiffs sent a joint reply. P.K. suggested last week that they should supply our police with revolvers and ammunition for use when guarding food stores at night. It has not yet been decided whether to accept the offer.

I now have the negatives of the photographs taken on the first visit of the SS *Vega*. There are some quite good pictures.

Meanwhile, the war news is making history with stories of huge Russian advances everywhere and the Allies taking the offensive again on the western front. Planes fly quite frequently at night between the Germans in the Atlantic coast pockets and Germany. They come here too from these pockets as well as Germany.

TUESDAY, 6TH FEBRUARY TO MONDAY, 12TH FEBRUARY

The *Vega* arrived on Tuesday, with parcels and other necessaries but no flour. During the afternoon Schneberger came to Hirzel House with Krafft and suggested that the ration of flour be cut to make it last another week.

---

5   For details of this escape, see Kreckeler (1978) and Bell (2002), p.337.

At six o'clock that evening the Bailiff and Mr Leale were called to Grange Lodge to meet Mr Callias and Colonel von Helldorff and were told that no flour would arrive until March. On WEDNESDAY AFTERNOON we all met at Rozel for a conference (see memorandum attached).[6] During that lunch hour I received a telephone message from Grange Lodge saying that they had a letter from Colonel von Helldorff for the Bailiff and that he should have it before the meeting. It was an answer to the Bailiff's letter asking for a decision about the flour at the Charroterie Mills. Today the Bailiff has written further on the matter, the draft being approved by a majority of the Controlling Committee.

There is no doubt that our present lack of flour is due to a difference of opinion between the British and German Governments regarding the interpretation of Article 52 of the Hague Rules in this connection. The British Government say that the Germans have sufficient stocks from production in the Islands to feed us until the beginning of March and the Germans that they cannot feed us after the end of January. The net result is that we are to be three weeks without bread. We are distributing a Red Cross parcel to every member of the population during the first week, extra rations during the second, and a parcel during the third. Von Helldorff says that we may give a pound of meat per head during the second week.

Meanwhile, because we cannot supply two tons of butter to the troops this week, we shall have to go without ourselves and issue a double ration next week. Their consumption is only one ton a week but they insist on two tons per fortnight and will not take one ton this week.

Thieving is increasing every day – Skipper was visited on Saturday night and his food cupboard was cleared, leaving him nothing for breakfast on Sunday morning.

A new trial is house-to-house searching by the German police. They came to us last Friday and while they were quite polite, the impotent rage brought on by enemies poking amongst one's private cupboards can only be realized when one has actually undergone it.

One of our Red Cross men at the harbour during the unloading of the *Vega* was watching the ship from the quay when he saw some packets of cigarettes thrown up through the hatchway and kicked under a tarpaulin by the German officer on deck. He remained watching until another German officer came along the deck. The first officer, who had seen him watching, spoke to the second one who thereupon shouted to our Red Cross man that his duty was to watch the quay and not the ship and that he was to get away from the quayside. He did so and half an hour later was called to sign for a damaged case. He refused as he had not seen the case renailed – he was

---

6   See Item 91: Meeting with P.K. and Red Cross representatives, 7 Feb 1945, p.465.

called on board, by the way – but eventually he did sign, without prejudice. He reported the matter to Mr Callias who said it was a very small matter. The cigarettes were not seen again.

When I arrived at the office this morning the Supervisor told me that he had received news that his son, Bill, had been killed. I was shocked. Later in the morning he heard, through Mary Bird, that he had turned up as a prisoner at the camp where her fiancé has been since 1941.[7]

I have been very anxious about Vic for some months and during the morning I telephoned to the Bouet to find out whether they had had any news. I could get no reply. During the lunch hour I telephoned again and after a long wait Dad came to the phone. I asked for news and he burst into tears and said that Vic was killed on the 8th of August. I went to see them as soon as I could and found them so shaken and old that I wept, but so brave that I was prouder of them than ever before. I walked out to Madeleine and we tooks turns of swearing to relieve our feelings and then we went back to the Bouet together. Queenie, José and Zu came up too and we all had a cup of tea together. We are still blessedly numb.

On the way home I met Mrs McLean who won such distinction in our eyes as children by her unique flow of foul language. She had heard the news and she cried over Vic and laughed over jokes she had had with him.

The war has at last reached our doorstep and Vic, our lovable brother, is nothing but a pleasant memory. I never knew until now how much I wanted to see him again nor how much the loss of even one unit of our marvellous family would hurt.

I tried to think who could be blamed for this grief but I think it must be more the idiocy of Mankind than any one man. I looked at the Germans I passed, but they seemed no more savage than before, with their drawn, sad faces and the hopelessness in their eyes. Certainly the one I saw grubbing in a field for whatever he could find left over from last year's root crop was only worthy of sincere pity. Whether we can do anything to make sense of Vic's sacrifice needs thinking about.

And our family is one of millions throughout the world who are mourning some member who seemed perfect to them.

TUESDAY, 13TH FEBRUARY TO FRIDAY, 16TH FEBRUARY

Strangely enough, life seems to go on just as usual. We find something to laugh at, Mum and Dad refuse to believe that Vic is dead, we are deeply touched by messages of sympathy from our friends but feel, at least I do, that

7   Mary Bird was going out with Lieut James Symes, the commando who landed at Petit Port with Lieut Hubert Nicolle in 1940. See Bell (1998).

kindness to me will not bring back my brother who took such joy in living. I deserve no kindness.

In a few years time it will be difficult to recapture the feeling of utter isolation which prevails here. The news which came on the *Vega* was the first we had received since some Red Cross messages dated last February and since then have come the bloodiest months of the war, whilst we have lived ever more quietly. England has become almost legendary after five years, new faces – apart from German ones – would, I am sure, frighten us out of our wits. We shall be years getting accustomed to the new world when we are free again.

Meanwhile, disputes with the Germans continue fast and furious. The latest is over the meat ration for next week. As I mentioned last week, Colonel von Helldorff agreed that we should issue a ration of one pound per head in view of the fact that next week we shall have neither parcel nor bread. We have to apply to Grange Lodge each time we wish to kill animals and so, although we had permission for the extra ration, we had to tell them that we wanted to kill a number of animals. Actually, we started on Thursday morning at the slaughter house without permission and during the morning I had to let Grange Lodge know, since they have a German inspector at the slaughter house and would therefore know in any case. Schneberger said at first that we could not have such a big ration and mumbled something about a four ounce ration. I said there was no question of a small ration since a promise had been made to Mr Leale in the presence of witnesses. He said that the Colonel might have said that we could have the ration but that he had never heard of any promise. I was astounded! I said that, of course, the Colonel's word was a promise in our eyes, and that if, on top of refusing us bread from Island wheat, they broke their word over meat it would be the last straw with the population. I said that everybody knew that a pound ration had been promised us. Schneberger promised to telephone Jersey and let us know today the result of his conversation. (The Colonel is in Jersey at present.)

Today we received a letter to say that there was sufficient meat in the cold store and that we might keep the meat we had slaughtered yesterday but must hand over the animals we were going to kill today to the troops. Soon afterwards he asked to see Mr Leale and Mr Johns and I went to Grange Lodge with them.

We were told that the Colonel had left the settlement of the matter in Schneberger's hands and had said that if a promise had been made, of course, it must be honoured. Schneberger added that he had never heard such a promise made, although Mr Leale and Mr Johns both reminded him of the conversation at the Bailiff's Chambers and the part he had taken in it. Having told us that the matter was left in his hands, he proceeded to try his utmost to wriggle out of the promise although he has assured us time after time that his work is to look after the interests of the civilian population. We explained to him at length that we needed about twenty five more animals to make up the required number and after blaming Spann for giving him false information he told us that he would let us know his decision later. We confirmed some of our figures later in the day and Raymond Falla went to Grange Lodge with them this afternoon. It now appears that Schneberger has suggested that he will consent to the pound ration if we agree to forgo three future rations to bring the matter into line with the minimum guaranteed to the British Government. Mr Leale, quite rightly, refuses to have anything to do with such a suggestion and we wait to see what tomorrow will bring.

On Tuesday morning I received a telephone message that my boat had been sunk at St. Sampson's. I was so busy I did not have time to stop and attend to it, but as I passed along the Bridge there was just one bit of her visible above the surface, the tide being high. They told me that a German barge had run her down early that morning and I went on to Town with my heart truly in my boots and a rage against everything German which made me feel faint. I managed to find time during the afternoon to go down to the harbour and to my astonishment and delight I discovered that no damage whatever had been done to the hull. Dick and I brought the engine ashore and dismantled it. We dried it out and it seems none the worse for its soaking. On Wednesday morning I saw the Customs chief and asked permission to take the boat home. He said that I would have to get a written permit from the harbour authorities in Town, but agreed that I might get that later in view of the fact that I had to do the whole job during the morning and would not have time to go to Town first. The horse and trolley was ordered and the boat was just hoisted out of the water when he came down to say that I would have to get the permit before towing the boat away. With him was the Major who had asked to be taken to Herm on our last trip and he wanted to take over the boat for himself. He was fairly insistent and I began to look round for something heavy to finish the boat off rather than let him take her. However, he went off and I had to go to Town after all. Eventually we brought her home, having made complicated arrangements for the temporary removal of barbed wire from our front gates to allow us to get her in.

Mrs Vaudin had heard that George, our buyer in Granville, is safely in England. This is about the happiest piece of news I have heard this week.

The war news is terrific with the Russians pressing on into eastern Germany and the British and the Americans bombing from this side the cities just ahead of the Russians. Apparently most of these cities are glutted with troops, transport and refugees and the chaos baffles the imagination.

SATURDAY, 17TH FEBRUARY

We hear today that Maurice Guillemet, one of the Granville staff, is safe in England. We have not heard anything of Barnett yet.

This morning, Raymond Falla and I went to Grange Lodge to get a decision about slaughtering cattle for next week. Herr Schneberger told us that he hoped to speak to Colonel von Helldorff by telephone during the morning and would give us the gist of the conversation later so that Mr Leale could decide what he was going to do. I telephoned at the end of the morning and was informed that through a technical hitch it had been impossible to speak to the Colonel. I said I would telephone again at three thirty. This time Schneberger said that the Colonel had arrived back in the Island and that they were meeting at six o'clock. I said that I would get in touch with them later. An hour later Krafft telephoned to say that we could issue a half pound ration of meat next week, that it must include bone and that they were extremely angry to discover that in the past the ration had been issued as net weight of meat instead of including bone. I replied that if this was final, I was instructed to ask him to arrange an interview between the Bailiff and either the General or Colonel von Helldorff as soon as possible. Tonight I hear that the meeting has not yet been arranged.

Will they delay until it is too late? It appears to us that Colonel von Helldorff, although he may have no objection to the extra ration, is afraid of the repercussions of his promise either on the troops or on his government or both. Neither he nor Schneberger seem to want the responsibility of authorizing the ration now.

SUNDAY, 18TH FEBRUARY TO TUESDAY, 20TH FEBRUARY

It was not until twelve o'clock on Sunday that Krafft telephoned to say that Schneberger wanted to see Mr Leale before lunch. Luckily I had brought a Civil Transport taxi with me on Saturday night, so I picked up Mr Johns and Mr Leale and went to Town. The memorandum of the meeting is attached.[8]

It is interesting to see that the offer made at the beginning of the meeting was modified in our favour before we left. We feel certain that Schneberger was given authority to bargain with us and no doubt the protest made by Mr Leale led him to increase the offer.

---

8   See Item 92: Meeting with P.K.: Meat Ration, 18 Feb 1945, p.471.

On Saturday last the letter from Colonel Iselin to the Bailiff appeared in *The Star* with an unintelligible preliminary paragraph.[9] I discovered that it had been published on German orders and I actually saw the letter from the Division to the P.K. giving the instructions. The Bailiff decided to lodge a protest againt the unauthorized use of his private correspondence but before the letter was drafted I was informed, on Sunday, that it was to be published on Monday and on Wednesday. The Bailiff asked me to stop the publication and I telephoned to Schneberger who said, almost before I had opened the subject, that it had nothing to do with him. He eventually agreed to telephone Colonel von Helldorff and inform him of the Bailiff's wishes. Later in the afternoon he telephoned to say that the Colonel had decided to publish. I asked him whether he realized that publication would be against the Bailiff's wishes and he said he did.

The letter did not appear either on Monday or Wednesday.

On Tuesday P.K. asked, on behalf of Colonel von Helldorff, for the Bailiff's reasons for not wanting the letter published, especially as it had been published in Jersey by the Bailiff of that Island. The reply was that the letter was now out of date and therefore misleading, that the Bailiff had already published the relevant parts of the letter in his notice of the 10th of February, and that he was publishing next day a notice which contained mention of the fact that flour would be coming on the *Vega*'s next voyage. We received instructions to cut out from this notice all mention of flour.

The Bailiff has received an answer from the General regarding the requisition of flour stocks.

The Germans are getting more and more hungry and robbery is becoming quite prevalent. A few days ago an old farmer was attacked in his home – in the afternoon – bound and gagged and threatened with a revolver.

At home, to be in the fashion, we have a burglar alarm. It consists of a very large metal tray which we balance on the handle of the kitchen door. A few nights ago it fell three times and I galloped down to battle to find that wind was the cause of the fall. It was a bit irritating the third time.

We are discovering exactly how many indispensable parts of modern life we can do without. We are now without electricity as well as gas and for the past fortnight have been without bread. Yet we live somehow, with candles, sticks and sweetcorn.

Although it was decided some weeks ago that the foreigners living here should be given Red Cross parcels, the Germans have raised so many

---

9   See Item 93: Letter from Colonel Iselin, *The Star*, 24 Feb 1945, p.473.

difficulties that they have not yet been issued.[10]

This morning at Grange Lodge I was informed that General von Schmettow and Colonel von Helldorff have been relieved of their positions in the Channel Islands and that Admiral Hüffmeier will be Commandant with Korvettenkapitän Reich as quartermaster. We wonder what this may mean to us. Herr Schneberger says that the new quartermaster is easy to work with. I hope so.

FRIDAY, 2ND MARCH TO THURSDAY, 8TH MARCH

The *Vega* arrived on Tuesday with flour as well as parcels. The first bread is being issued today. We have not had any meetings with the Red Cross representative because he is not our usual man and has not German permission even to leave the boat. Apparently Callias was taken ill just before the boat left Lisbon and this man took his place at four hours' notice. However, we have managed to put some questions to him through the Germans and have received answers.

Mr Leale and I met the new quartermaster yesterday for the first time and we are both favourably impressed. He is obviously intelligent, he does not shout and he is direct. We have, of course, been favourably impressed by Germans before.

There is talk by the Germans of taking all separated milk up to 3½ litres per milch cow in the Island. This would mean the whole ration at present. The present consumers of whole milk would continue to get their ration. The matter is to be discussed soon, so we are given to understand.

The war news is excellent and Mr Churchill is supposed to have told the troops the other day that it only needed one good heave to finish the war. Cologne has fallen and we hold most of the west bank of the Rhine. The Russians are thrusting northwards and have reached the Baltic between Stettin and Danzig.

FRIDAY, 9TH MARCH TO THURSDAY, 22ND MARCH

I seem to have so much to do at home, and it is so difficult to work by candlelight, that I have to write my diary at the office now. We go to dancing class on Thursday afternoons and I stay at the office for lunch and write afterwards.

We did not get the petrol and diesel oil which came on the *Vega*. The diesel oil, apparently, was sent to replace that used by the cranes in discharging this and past cargoes and the petrol is said to have been a mistake. Both

---

10 See Tough (1995), pp.32-49.

items were taken over by the Germans by agreement with the Red Cross representative, and the Bailiff made a footnote to this effect on the receipt which he sent back to Lisbon for the cargo.

There is no further news of the second boat, except that her name is *Sirius*, but the Bailiff of Jersey received a letter from Mr Howard of the Home Office in which he talks of payment for the gas coal. Doubtless we shall hear something very soon.

Sure enough, as will be seen from the memorandum of our meeting with the Germans on Sunday, 11th March,[11] they have requisitioned the first six pints of milk (separated) per cow per day and the result is that we very seldom see any fresh milk at all, except the consumers of whole milk.

We have met the new quartermaster several times during the past fortnight and although the work we have had to do with him has been far from pleasant, we have all been impressed by the frankness with which discussions have been carried on. As someone remarked the other day, it would be strange if we found the Nazis who are now in charge, better than those with whom we have had to deal in the past. Up to the present and remembering always that we are dealing with the enemy we find that the meetings are carried on in a more understanding way than ever before.

The cutting down of the water supply has caused some excitement recently. The Germans sent out eight pairs of soldiers to put out of action lavatory flushes and other water apparatus which must not be used on waterworks. Some of their methods were primitive, such as cutting off lead pipes with heavy hammers. They caused floods in some houses. We have now come to terms and our own plumbers can put our apparatus out of action, after which the Water Board officials inspect and issue a certificate which will be accepted by the Germans. Meanwhile water for greenhouses is allowed once more and the diesel oil used for this will far outweigh the saving over domestic curtailments.

Thieving is now wholesale. Cattle are being stolen almost nightly, potatoes in glasshouses are pulled up almost as soon as they come through the ground and even, in some cases, the seed is dug up the night after planting; there has been one armed robbery of Red Cross flour from a bakery and another in which the thieves got in through the roof. It seems impossible to stop it and there can be little doubt that, as everybody and especially the Germans become more hungry, nothing will be safe.

In view of the water shortage we have radioed for supplies of medicines to counteract various fevers.

According to the German reports the Granville raid was a great success, the main object being the sacking of the town. We are waiting to see what

---

11 See Item 94: Meeting with P.K., 11 March 1945, p.474.

the repercussions will be, although I personally do not think that nuisance raids will make the taking of the Islands by force worth while.

Last Thursday we went to a musical afternoon. There were only about four of us in the entire party who were not performers and naturally the audience was near a perfect one as possible. Until we do something like this, we have become so obsessed with the necessity for finding food and so forgetful of the joys we are missing that we do not realize how primitive we have become during these past five years. But what a treat it is to come back, quite unsophisticated, to intellectual pleasures.

I am enjoying myself almost as much, but in quite another way, preparing my boat for the coming season. Dick and I spent the whole of Sunday from half past nine until dark, making new seats. It was a brilliantly sunny day and working in the fresh spring air made me realize how good it is to be alive, even during an occupation.

Talking of occupations, I was discussing our troubles with Inspector Zachau the other day. I said that our suffering although not physical, was very real. I instanced the strain of not being our own masters and of the splitting up of families for nearly five years and the fact that nearly a year has passed since we had a full batch of news from England. He said he understood but that German suffering was even worse. His last letter from his wife told of the bombing of his home town. His wife's mother and father, aged eighty three and eighty four were in the cellar of their house when it caught fire and burned down over their heads. They crawled out of the wreckage and walked for twenty minutes with no proper clothes and nothing on their feet to Zachau's wife, through thick snow. The fact that the same must have occurred in thousands of cases in England does not allow me to regret less that war should bring such suffering.

FRIDAY, 23RD MARCH TO TUESDAY, 10TH APRIL

The *Vega* has come and gone again. Once more the Red Cross officials – two doctors this time – were not allowed to see us because their credentials were not in order, but they were permitted to talk to Dr Collings, since he is a British Red Cross official. They came to make preliminary arrangements for the evacuation of invalids and we learn that a ship, called, I think, the *Britannia* has been chartered by the British Government and will take the sick direct from here to England if German permission is forthcoming. In any case the evacuation will not start for six to eight weeks.

The cargo does not run to one parcel per head but with reserves in hand we will have enough for one full issue and about eight thousand parcels over. Flour will be enough for five pounds of bread a week and there were clothes, footwear, seeds and other miscellaneous items. Now that potatoes have finished for the greater part of the population, however, food is so scarce that there is practically nothing to cook.

WEDNESDAY, 11TH APRIL TO TUESDAY, 24TH APRIL

The past fortnight has seen the most spectacular news of the war. Germany has been practically overrun, a full-scale offensive is driving the Germans back in northern Italy and one of the western French pockets – at the mouth of the Gironde – has been taken. The war in Europe is nearly over – that is agreed on both sides – but here we are still very much under the Germans. Today we met them to complain about their methods of obtaining more than their share of vegetables. It is all in the minutes of the meeting.[12] We asked permission to issue as a ration a small quantity of potatoes which we had saved from those dug early on account of thieving and tonight I am told that instead of granting permission they have requisitioned them for the troops.

Our patience is so nearly exhausted that I, for one, have scarcely the energy to continue the fight. I know now how wars start and I have no doubt that were we on an even footing here the time for discussion would be past. Instead we take it on the chin and lower our opinion to meet new circumstances.

At all events we have been having glorious weather and I have planted sweetcorn and pieces of potato which we save when we boil them. It is said that the crop is nearly as good as from proper seed. It has been pleasant in the open air in the garden and painting the boat. This evening I put a tarpaulin over her so that she will not be so conspicuous in her new paint. The Germans are taking every boat they can find for fishing and I fear that when they have finished with them they will be the worse for wear. They seem to take no pride in anything belonging to them or perhaps I have a somewhat distorted outlook tonight.

Somebody said the other day that this diary is not so interesting now as it used to be. I used to find little pleasures to put into it but they do not seem to come my way now. The world seems so threadbare and life so earnest. However, when I stop to consider, my family and my home are very delightful and especially now that José is becoming a friend as well as a daughter.

---

12 See Item 95: Meeting with P.K.: Distribution of Vegetables, 24 April 1945, p.478.

WEDNESDAY, 25TH APRIL TO MONDAY, 30TH APRIL

We have had sundry meetings with the Germans about vegetables and greenhouses. Baron von Aufsess is now in charge at Grange Lodge, the boat is ready to launch – and on the six o'clock A.E.F.[13] programme they said that unconfirmed reports from Sweden state that Himmler has had another meeting with Count Bernadotte in Denmark. The Count is the chief of the Swedish Red Cross and Vice-president of the International Red Cross and IT IS SUGGESTED THAT HE HAS WITH HIM AN OFFER OF UNCONDITIONAL SURRENDER TO BRITAIN, THE USA AND RUSSIA. In case I ever forget these hours, let me jot down that I am sitting at the dining table with the sun shining brightly between snow clouds, with the sea very blue and vigorous with white horses in the Russel and the water filling the bay in front of the house. I am drinking the last of the port and waiting for the nine o'clock news. While waiting I may say that Mussolini met his end yesterday at the hands of the Italians themselves, in Milan. He and eighteen of his followers including his mistress were tried before a people's court and shot. Their bodies were then hung up for all to see in a square in Milan. What a life – and what an end!

It is said also that Hitler is either suffering from a haemorrhage of the brain or is already dead. Berlin is being razed by the Russians and most of the rest of Germany is in our hands. Italy is within our grip. Everybody here, Germans and English alike, know that the war is virtually over. But we are still waiting for deliverance.

Nothing further at nine o'clock!

TUESDAY, 1ST MAY AND WEDNESDAY, 2ND MAY

The Germans have given out officially that Hitler is dead. Admiral Doenitz has taken his place and up to date there is no sign of surrender. The Germans in northern Italy and western Austria have surrendered, however, the document having been signed on Sunday. It came into force at noon today. In these Islands it is apparently the intention not to surrender. We shall see whether the troops will continue to hold out. Meanwhile, in England the blackout has ended and evacuees have started returning to London.

Today we had a meeting with the Germans at Summerland.[14] The room is not very imposing. It faces south but looks bedraggled, with holes in the wall, badly patched where stove-pipes have been and three rickety tables to sit at in a row. Korvettenkapitän Reich and the other officers come forward

---

13   Allied Expeditionary Force Radio.
14   See Item 96: Meeting with P.K.: Distribution of Vegetables, 2 May 1945, p.482.

to greet us as we enter and everybody German shakes hands with everybody English. We sit down and the meeting begins. We listen usually while the Korvettenkapitän talks in German to Mr Krafft, the interpreter. His voice is naturally gentle and very clear but today he obviously intends to be fierce. He has to keep himself up to the mark. He becomes gentle as soon as he forgets himself. If you look at the minutes of the meeting you will see what he says. The other officers look as serious as owls and as the veiled threats and accusations come pouring out I find myself thinking how very much more it would take to frighten us. I wonder what they are leading up to and remembering how Herr Hauschild, some weeks ago, advised us always to use the psychological approach, I form the opinion that they mean to get something out of us. My theory seems more and more correct as the meeting advances. They make one statement too many and Mr Leale interrupts to ask a leading question on it. They look at each other, talk in German and change the subject. They get into their stride and talk themselves to a standstill. Mr Leale rams home his points and keeps his temper and by sheer sincerity shows me – and surely them too – that their lack of it is self-evident. Then we get the sop – a good one – butter for the children. Right through I have the impression that Captain Reich who has always seemed to us to be an honest man, has let himself down badly by being swayed by the too-clever Hauschild.

After two hours we rise, everybody smiles and shakes hands again and one almost expects to hear, 'So kind of you to come …' as we go out.

[The Diary ends here]

TUESDAY, 8TH MAY

THE WAR IS OVER FOR GUERNSEY

German Officers Inform Bailiff of Surrender

HISTORIC STATES MEETING AT MID-DAY TO-DAY

AT 10-30 THIS MORNING "THE STAR" WAS OFFICIALLY INFORMED BY MR: LOUIS GUILLEMETTE, SECRETARY TO JURAT JOHN LEALE, [PRESIDENT TO THE CONTROLLING COMMITTEE OF THE STATES OF GUERNSEY] THAT THE WAR HAS, SO FAR AS GUERNSEY WAS CONCERNED, HAD ENDED.

PEOPLE OF GUERNSEY CAN TO-DAY AT 3 O'CLOCK, IF THEY ARE ABLE TO DO SO, LISTEN TO THE SPEECH MADE OVER THE BRITISH RADIO BY PRIME MINISTER WINSTON CHURCHILL. IMEDIATELY AFTER THAT HOUR FLAGS CAN BE FLOWN IN GUERNSEY AS A SIGN OF REJOICING.

At 10 a.m. to-day Korvetten Kapitan Reich and Baron von Aufsess called on the Bailiff of Guernsey at his Chambers at the Royal Court House. Jurat John Leale, Prsident of the Controlling Committee and his Secretary, Mr: Louis Guillemette, were also present. Kapitan Reich said that the war was over in the Channel Islands as well as elsewhere. He said that Mr. Churchill, the British Prime Minister, was making a speech at 3 o'clock this afternoon and that the German authorities had no objection to the hoisting of flags after the speech:

On the receipt of this news the Bailiff convened an extra-special States Meeting to be held at mid-day to-day where the full details of this momentous news was conveyed to members of the States.

OTHER IMPORTANT NEWS WILL BE PUBLISHED IN SUCCEEDING EDITIONS.

Appendix

Memoranda, Correspondence and other documents referred to in the Diary

List of Documents

Item 1: A Brief History of our Trip to Jersey, 6 May 1942

Halkett Hotel, Jersey
6th May, 1942.

We left Guernsey harbour finally just after eleven o'clock in the *Favourite*, and a few minutes before we had an 'alert', but nothing happened.

On the way down we managed to sleep for a short while under the tarpaulin on top of the forward hatch. Towards three o'clock, Frank was sleeping and the other two were walking the deck when came a grinding and scraping noise as we grazed over rocks. We then saw a height of rock in front of us and the boat went on over the reef until she finished up well and truly fixed and wrecked on the rocks. There was heavy fog at the time and the night was quite dark. A searchlight was used from the captain's bridge and soon we were all issued with lifebelts, we three being the last to receive same.

When it was realized that we could go no further in either direction a rope ladder was let down over the side of the boat and one of the members of the crew went down and scrambled on to the rocks with a line to make fast as an anchor. A plank was placed from the foot of the rope ladder to the rocks and, true to tradition, it was women and children first. There were two German nurses on board, the rest of the company being German, with the exception of we three, a Dutch crew and a French pilot.

All the passengers were transferred to the rocks whilst the crew stayed on board to do what they could. This happened about about three o'clock and until daylight came we had to remain there, not being at all sure where we were; some being under the impression we were on an island, some thinking it was the Jersey coast.

Before daylight Frank did a spot of mountain climbing and found a way over the cliffs for us and at daylight we set out. We three went one way whilst all the others were hauled up the side of the cliffs with ropes, leaving their luggage behind. We took ours with us. At the top we found a minefield and Charles, Frank and Len set out with a German officer to find help. Charles and Len were left at a non-finished blockhouse, while Frank went on with the officer.

Before they got back Charles and Len with their luggage and lifebelts in a 'borrowed' German wheelbarrow set out to follow them but missed them entirely and after walking for about a mile and half found an isolated anti-aircraft crew in a hut. There they gave us a cup of coffee and leaving the wheelbarrow and lifebelts with an airman we set off in search of a lift to town.

We visited an O.T. camp to learn that nothing could be done in our effort to get a lift to town – some twelve and a half miles – and so we started hiking again. Eventually we found the Centenier of St Ouen's who had the only phone for miles around. From there we telephoned to Mr A.C. Sarre who came to fetch us with his car. Meanwhile the Centenier had informed the German authorities that two Englishmen had arrived and he was asked to hold them till their identity had been established. Meanwhile the Centenier's family fed us with coffee and bread and butter and had given Charles iodine to dress his wounds.

Mr Sarre turned up and arranged with the German authorities by phone that he should be responsible for us and took us into town where we reported to them. Then he took us to his house where we had a hot bath and breakfast – the first spot of food since 8:15 the previous evening.

We then learned that Frank had turned up in town safely and had reached the Marrett's in Bond Street. He had gone off with the German officer and came back with help whom they assisted in bringing the luggage away from the ship. As he was starving a French parson gave him his last slice of bread with a ration of cheese. Then they came by bus with the only casualty, a German sailor who they dropped in hospital and Frank came on to Bond Street hoping to meet the others there.

After a good night's rest we were all feeling very much better but on the Tuesday we visited the M.O.H. Jersey who granted us a permit to purchase a bottle of brandy to 'bring us round' from our exhausted condition.

Later in the day the authorities took further compassion on us and granted us a ration of tobacco and the police fixed us for a decent meal.

We learned that various things had been taken by the German authorities from the boat which was badly holed and that later she turned right over and disappeared. The crew have been put in clink.

[Unsigned, but Louis implies the writer was Len Collins. Diary 9 May 1942]

Item 2: Meeting with FK: Fishing, 7 May 1942

<u>Memorandum of Meeting Held at Grange Lodge
on Thursday, May 7th, 1942</u>

<u>Subject: Fishing</u>

Present:

      Capt J.P. Franklin

      Messrs A.C. Richings, B. Bartlett, L.A. Guillemette

      Dr Pelz, Insp. Oser

Inspector Oser said that the German Authorities were not satisfied with the marketing and control of fish caught in Guernsey waters and he wished to discuss improvements with the Guernsey representatives.

De Pelz then outlined the revised Jersey Fish Marketing Plan, which is roughly as follows:–

Permits to fish are issued by the Hafenkommandantur on the recommendation of the Essential Commodities Committee. Each fisherman, before receiving his permit, is required to sign an undertaking to sell 90% of all fish caught. Of this saleable fish, 20% is handed to a special shop for purchase by the Germans. Fish is only sold at St Helier and St Aubin. There is one wholesaler (understood by the Guernsey representatives to be the States of Jersey) to whom all fish is delivered by the fishermen and who takes out the 20% for the German Authorities. The remainder of the fish is delivered to the retailers.

Dr Pelz was of opinion that a similar plan should be adopted in Guernsey and suggested that a central control should be set up at a point midway between the two fishing harbours of St Peter Port and St Sampson. Fishermen would then be required to deliver all fish to this control point, when they would be paid for it by the States. It would then be delivered to retailers in St Peter Port and St Sampson in equal individual shares, irrespective of the number of customers dealing with the retailer.

The Guernsey representatives pointed out the obvious disadvantages of such a scheme, the reasons being given:–

(a)   Lack of flexibility.

(b)   Additional transport in taking the fish backwards and forwards to the control point.

(c)   The injustice of giving equal amounts of fish to all retailers, irrespective of the size or intensity of population of the district.

They then went on to explain that the present system in operation in Guernsey, of which the German representatives did not appear to have full knowledge. It was decided that the Guernsey representatives should re-examine the present system in order to make certain that:–

1. The greater part of the fish caught is made available for those sections of the population which are most scantily provided with food, eg. the urban district of St Peter Port.
2. The German troops and civilians did not get more than the 20% to which they are entitled.

Messrs Bartlett and Richings pointed out during the meeting that the main leakage occurs in St Peter Port, between the Quay at which the fish is landed and the central point at which it is submitted for weighing, and it was agreed by the whole meeting that the sale of fish between these two points should be rigorously suppressed.

Dr Pelz promised to send over a copy of the present Jersey system for consideration by the Guernsey representatives.

With regard to fish caught by Sark fishermen, Mr Bartlett said that 20% was taken officially for consumption by German troops in occupation in Sark, and in accordance with the present order in operation another 20% is required to be taken when Sark fish is landed in Guernsey. Dr Pelz gave a ruling that the second 20% should not be taken when Sark fish is landed in Guernsey.

Item 3: Leale to Mueller: Fishing, 19 May 1942

The Controlling Committee of the States of Guernsey
Hirzel House, Guernsey
19th May, 1942

General Mueller
Officer Commanding
German Occupying Forces
Guernsey

Dear Sir,

We have received the following letter from the Nebenstelle Guernsey of Feldkommandantur 515:–

<u>Re: Fishing</u>

"Fishing is dangerous at all times in the areas shown on the accompanying sketch, due to the firing of hand weapons.

I request you to call the attention of fishermen and other persons concerned in an appropriate manner. The sketch is to be returned to me.

(signed) Dr BROSCH, K.V.R."

We presume that these instructions originated from your staff and with your approval.

We regard the matter as one of major importance to the welfare of the population and I should like to take this opportunity of bringing to your notice some of the hardships which the population has suffered and is suffering today.

Many people, some of whom have spent many years in the same homes, have been forced to leave. In some cases, only the scantiest of notice was given, in other cases, sometimes in the same, they were not allowed to take their goods with them. Equally they have been refused permission to remain in a small part of their homes with soldiers occupying the remainder.

We have had to give up vegetables which were badly needed for ourselves. A calamitous shortage occurred in the early months of this year.

We were, as a States, cutting down trees and rationing among those who needed the fuel 200-250 tons of wood weekly. The public wood cutting was stopped by your orders during the winter.

Hospitals and schools have been taken over together with approximately 8 percent of the agricultural land of the Island.

Cycles have been requisitioned and thus taking away one of the only means of transport.

It has been our constant endeavour to make the Occupation, to use the words of our first President of the Controlling Committee, a "model one". The generally excellent behaviour of the local population is, we think, proof that we have not been altogether unsuccessful in achieving our aim.

We hope we have not been unmindful of the difficulties of the Occupying Forces and fully realise that some hardship is inevitable in a situation such as we find ourselves today. Whenever we have claimed the protection to the Feldkommandantur of the Hague Convention we have been given the explanation that Military Necessity is the overriding consideration and sometimes we have even received the answer that the Island is regarded as a front line position and that in such circumstances the Hague Rules cannot be applied. We do not know on what basis such an explanation is founded.

In the case under consideration, the declaration that the areas indicated on the sketch which accompanies the Feldkommandantur's letter are dangerous <u>at all times</u> to fishermen appears to us to allow of some modification. The areas on the north and south coasts are at present of particular value as fishing grounds and the arrangements now in force whereby fishermen are warned by the Harbour guards when shooting practice is taking place have, in all but a few instances, operated quite successfully. With regard to the area on the west coast, its denial to us at this time comes as a great disappointment since we are at present in negotiation with the Feldkommandantur and the Customs and Harbour Authorities for the reopening of a fishing port at Perelle Bay, and the area concerned is one of the principal fishing grounds concerned.

I ought in conclusion to point out to you that there has been a most noticeable increase in the Death Rate and in the number of days lost in sickness during recent months. We are hoping to build up somewhat the health of the population this summer in anticipation of a winter which may prove the severest test of endurance so far imposed on our people and a drastic reduction in the quantity of fish available in place of the increase for which we are hoping, cannot but seriously affect our aim.

You will realise that these are difficult days for us in this Island and my approach to you is dictated by my responsibility. I feel that it is my duty to make a most earnest appeal to you for a reconsideration of your decision, and that before decisions are arrived at you will always give the fullest consideration to the hardships which, directly or indirectly, may thereby be inflicted on the civilian population.

Yours faithfully,
JOHN LEALE,
President.

Item 4: Leale to F.K.: Cold Storage, 23 May 1942

The Controlling Committee of the States of Guernsey
Hirzel House
22nd May 1942

Feldkommandantur 515,
Nebenstelle, Guernsey

Sir,

With reference to your letter of the 20th instant and to recent conversations regarding the cession of cold storage space to the Occupying Forces, I am writing to lodge the strongest possible protest on behalf of myself and the Controlling Committee at the seizure of vital storage space at the beginning of the most critical season of the year in regard to perishable commodities.

As you are aware, the food situation during the past winter has been so bad, partly owing to the forced delivery to the Occupying Forces of potatoes and other vegetables urgently needed for the civilian population, that statistics show an alarming increase both in the death rate and in the incidence of illness. We are, therefore, depending on the more plentiful supplies of food which should be available during the summer to restore as far as possible the general health of the population and to build up reserves of strength for what will obviously be another critical winter. Amongst the foods which will be so vitally necessary to achieve our aim are many which are especially perishable during hot weather and the wastage of even a small proportion of such foods through lack of adequate cold storage would be nothing short of calamitous.

As you know we buy supplies from the continent, and, for some of these goods, we must have cold storage.

It is obvious to us, of course, that the same problem faces the Military department responsible for the supply of food to the Occupying Forces but certain facts are unquestionable and are ever before us in our efforts to meet our responsibilities towards the civilian population. They are briefly as follows:-

1. The cold storage plant in this Island was erected to meet the requirements of the civilian population and is the property of the States of Guernsey.
2. Up to date, and including the space taken over as a result of the letter and conversations referred to above, the German Forces have taken over 22,008 cubic feet of cold storage space, leaving the States in the possession of 11,166 cubic feet. Although we do not know the total number of troops and civilians constituting the Occupying Force, it is obvious that it does not amount to 24,000 which is roughly the number of local civilians. Yet the space used by the former is practically double that available to the latter.
   In this connection, I should like to claim the protection of the Hague Convention, Article 52, the relevant words of which read as follows:-
   "Requisitions shall be in the proportion to the resources of the country."

3. It is absolutely impossible for the States of Guernsey to purchase and erect the additional plant which they require to meet present needs, although the German Forces have the advantage of drawing on the immense resources of their country in meeting their needs in this direction.

4. The collection and storage of security stocks of essential perishable foods is at least as vital to us as it is to the Occupying Forces.

In your last paragraph you say that foodstuffs must not be allowed to spoil. We shall do our utmost to prevent this, but unless we have adequate facilities we obviously may fail.

We cannot but view with the deepest concern our efforts on behalf of the civilian population being so entirely unsuccessful.

I should be obliged if you would inform the appropriate Military Authorities of the contents of this letter.

Yours faithfully
JOHN LEALE
President

Item 5: Meeting with F.K.: Cold Storage, 23 May 1942

Memorandum of Meeting
held at Grange Lodge, Saturday 23rd May 1942

Present:

Dr Brosch

Mr Wynne Sayer   Member of the Controlling Committee
in charge of the Cold Storage

Mr H.E. Marquand   States Supervisor

Mr W.M. Wilson   States Maintenance Engineer

Mr J.H. Loveridge   Secretary to the Committee for the
Control of Essential Commodities

Mr L.A. Guillemette   Secretary to the President of the
Controlling Committee

Subject: Cold Storage

Mr Guillemette opened the meeting by reminding Dr Brosch that during the conversation which they had had on the previous day he had undertaken to give a full report on the condition of the States Cold Stores. On enquiry he had discovered that certain matters connected therewith required urgent attention and were already the subject of a draft report by the States Maintenance Engineer. The local representatives had therefore approached Dr Brosch in order to give a preliminary verbal report. A full written report will be given as soon as possible.

Consumable Stores

The local representatives said that certain consumable stores were at present in short supply. Both the German Authorities and the States were making provision for a three months' security stock of perishable foods, but it was obviously useless to make such provision unless at least three months' supply of consumable stores, necessary for the working of the cold stores, was also in stock. Such consumable stores had already been ordered from France but it had been found almost impossible to obtain adequate supplies. It was therefore necessary to ask for the Feldkommandantur's help in obtaining them. It was decided that a full list of the stores necessary should be handed to the Feldkommandantur as soon as possible.

Working Conditions

It was explained to Dr Brosch that in the case of the Castle Cold Store vital machinery was contained in Cold Room No 1. At present this cold room was controlled entirely by the German Revictualling Authorities and the resident mechanic had been refused admission to this room. The lack of attention resulting from this refusal was already affecting the efficiency of the plant, and it was essential for authority to be given to the States Maintenance Engineer to enter this room as and when necessary.

The local representatives also complained that troops, in the course of their duty, had refused to take normal precautions to ensure the maintenance of the necessary low temperature. This refusal had resulted in additional strain on the already somewhat over loaded cooling machinery. Dr Brosch thereupon telephoned to the German Authorities concerned and made the following arrangements:–

1. The States Maintenance Engineer will be given the telephone number of a soldier who will be ready at any time during the day or night to attend with him at the Castle Cold Store in order to give him access to Room No 1.
2. Troops working at the cold store will be instructed to take all precautions deemed necessary by the resident mechanic in order to retain low temperature throughout the cold store.
3. Visits to the cold store by German Troops will be made as infrequently as possible.

It was further pointed out to Dr Brosch that the Castle Cold Store was designed for long term storage and that day to day removals and admissions of food-stuffs placed a strain upon the plant which it was never designed to bear. With regard to the Market Cold Store it was not necessary for the mechanic to enter cold rooms in German Occupation, except for checking temperatures.

Replacement of Worn and Damaged Parts

1. Castle Cold Store
The States holds stocks of customary spare parts for normal working conditions, but under present conditions where it was impossible to communicate direct to the makers for large replacements it was essential stocks of these should be laid in. Dr Brosch thereupon asked for a full report in detail on the working of both the Castle and Market Cold Stores, on the same line as reports submitted to him by Major Barritt Hills on the plant of the Electricity Works. The States Maintenance Engineer undertook to submit such reports as soon as possible.

2. Market Cold Stores
The States Maintenance Engineer said that we were short of spare parts for this plant, especially belts and packing. Belts which had been ordered from France had arrived too long and had to be sent back for shortening, and had not yet been returned from France. The danger of a breakdown was therefore acute. He stated, however, that most other spare parts could be made locally.

Controller of the States Cold Stores

Mr Guillemette reported that Mr Hill Cottingham had, until recently, been the Controller of Cold Stores but that as he was not in good health he had been replaced, by the Controlling Committee by Mr Wynne Sayer.

Key to the Markets

Mr Sayer stated that the German Authorities had demanded the key to the markets. In view of the present condition where civil meat was hung in the market and access to the civil cold storage rooms was not debarred, it was quite impossible to give the German Authorities the keys to the markets. Arrangements, however, would be made for a watchman to be placed on the markets during those hours when the Market Superintendent was not on duty, and that access to the markets at all times of the day and night would now be available.

Item 6: Meeting with F.K.: Fort George Cemetery, 26 May 1942

<u>Memorandum of a Meeting held at Grange Lodge</u>
<u>on Tuesday May 26th, 1942</u>

<u>Subject: Cemetery at Fort George</u>

Present:

      Inspector Zachau
      Mr L.A. Guillemette

Inspector Zachau said that the German Authorities wished to make the north side of the Soldiers' Cemetery at Fort George into a burial ground for German soldiers. At present there were some graves of British Soldiers on this side most of which appeared to be between 40 and 50 years old. It was suggested that the local authorities should either remove the bodies to another site, or remove the headstones only. They asked how the Controlling Committee would react to these suggestions.

    Mr Guillemette said that his own opinion was that the Controlling Committee would have nothing to do with such an action and that they would probably regard it as an insult to our dead. Inspector Zachau said that the suggestion was not put forward as an insult and should not be regarded as such. Mr Guillemette refused to give any further opinion on the matter and repeated that he would consult the Controlling Committee and give the Feldkommandantur an answer in due course.

(signed) L.A. Guillemette

Note: I duly consulted the Bailiff, Messrs John Leale, R.H. Johns and Dr A.N. Symons; they all confirmed my statement and I therefore replied to Grange Lodge that the Bailiff and the Controlling Committee were not agreeable to the removal of either the bodies or headstones.

Item 7: Müller to Leale: Fishing, 26 May 1942

Der Wehrmachtbefehlshaber
26th May 1942

To the President of the Controlling Committee
of the States of Guernsey

Your letter of the 19th May has been transmitted to me by the Nebenstelle Guernsey der Feldkommandantur.

I am aware of the difficulties in connection with the opening of fishing along the West Coast, which form the direct subject matter of your letter. I hope that these difficulties can be overcome. I will assist in the matter.

During my tours of inspection I daily have the opportunity of observing the conditions under which the Island population has to live nowadays. I do not underestimate the difficulties, but difficulties are there to be surmounted. If the necessities of war necessitate the taking away of agricultural land, the remaining portion must be worked all the more intensively. A slack utilisation of land and greenhouses cannot be tolerated. Work is necessary, now more than ever before. The last bit of ground must be cultivated to the utmost.

As you are aware, it is extremely hard to obtain coal. If justified from a tactical point of view, permission to fell trees will be granted to private persons. A financial burden for the States is not justifiable, all the less because everyone willing to work has the opportunity of earning his living.

The evacuation of private houses and use of other buildings, no more than the requisition of means of transport (bicycles and other vehicles), are not in contradiction with the Hague land warfare provisions.

Other supplies and services are only requisitioned in case of urgent military necessity. The resources of the country are taken into consideration. Since January 1st, 1942, the German Army pays out of its own means 75% of the expenses.

The occupying Forces take interest in a smooth development. You are well aware that I insist on strong discipline and punish every offence.

From the Island Authorities, I may expect loyalty and positive work.

(signed) Müller
Generalmajor

Item 8: Report to C.C.: Visit to Jersey, 11 July 1942

<u>Memorandum on Visit to Jersey by Dr A.N. Symons and Messrs
Wynne Sayer and L.A. Guillemette – 5th to 11th July, 1942</u>

Dr A.N. Symons and Messrs Wynne Sayer and L.A. Guillemette visited Jersey at the request of the President of the Controlling Committee and discussed the following matters with Jersey and German officials in that Island.

Potatoes

The question of the supply of potatoes by Jersey to Guernsey was discussed at a meeting of the Superior Council attended by the Guernsey delegates. The Bailiff invited Mr Sayer to explain to the meeting what Guernsey needed, and Mr Sayer began by thanking the Bailiff for the opportunity of discussing Guernsey's difficulties with the Council and explaining the reasons for the delay in accepting Jersey's recent invitation to Guernsey to send representatives to make arrangements for the supply of potatoes to the latter island. The fact was that Guernsey had been given access to figures at Grange Lodge which showed that Jersey would be required to deliver large quantities of potatoes to the Occupying Forces in the Channel Islands and that they did not wish to discuss the matter with Jersey until they were certain that that Island was in possession of all the available information. They felt that otherwise they would be asking for Jersey's help under false pretences.

The Bailiff replied that Jersey now considered that they had helped Guernsey indirectly by supplying the Occupying Forces in Guernsey with potatoes which would otherwise have been taken from Guernsey. They were not certain now whether their crop would be sufficient to meet the German requisitions, in addition to the requirements of Jersey's own population, and they could therefore no longer make any offer to Guernsey.

The Guernsey delegates asked whether it would be possible for Jersey to supply Guernsey with 500 tons of seed potatoes since the introduction of new seed would make a great difference to Guernsey's crop next year.

Jurat T.J. Brée said that Jersey could make no promise on this matter, but suggested that as Jersey potatoes were to be supplied to the Germans in Guernsey, it might be possible to arrange with the German Paymaster concerned the exchange of 500 tons of imported potatoes for a like quantity of the Guernsey glasshouse crop. The Guernsey delegates agreed that this suggestion, which had already been taken up in Guernsey with the Germans, might be practicable.

Oats

Dr Symons asked the Superior Council whether it would be possible for Jersey to supply Guernsey with a quantity of oats to be issued as breakfast food. Jurat Brée said that none was available from last season's crop, but as the present crop was most promising it might be possible to supply Guernsey with some tons. He could not make any promise on the subject at present.

Insulin

At present the supply of Insulin in Jersey is very short. Dr Symons informed the Superior Council that he would endeavour to let Jersey have a quantity from the Guernsey stocks.

Red Cross Parcels

The Guernsey delegates handed the Bailiff a letter from the President of the Controlling Committee enclosing a letter to the Feldkommandantur on the subject of sending Red Cross parcels to the Islands from England. It was suggested by Mr Leale that Jersey should make a similar request to the Feldkommandantur and that the two letters should be presented together.

The matter was discussed by the Superior Council and the Guernsey delegates and it was decided by the Council that, although they were of opinion that the continued sending of such parcels might prove embarrassing to the British Government and would probably not receive the sanction of the German Authorities, they would be quite willing to join Guernsey in asking to be allowed to request permission for Red Cross parcels to be send to the Islands for next Christmas only. The Guernsey delegates undertook to acquaint the President of the Controlling Committee with this decision and withdrew Mr Leale's letter.

Imports from France

(a) Cereals. At the meeting of the Superior Council attended by the Guernsey delegates, it was stated that Jersey would be practically self-supporting in wheat if this year's crop came up to expectations. Jersey's constant fear, however, was that they would be required, as at the beginning of this year, to supply wheat or flour to Guernsey if the French Intendant treated the revictualling of the Channel Islands as a whole, regarded Guernsey's crop as being less than it should be. Jersey felt that it was essential that the Intendant should receive definite orders to supply Guernsey with her full quota of flour, the only allowance to be made being Guernsey's actual production of wheat. It was also most important that three months' security stock of flour be supplied by France to both Islands.

The Guernsey delegates fully concurred with these views and it was decided that the Feldkommandant should be asked by both Islands to see that the French Intendant received these orders. At the meeting with the Feldkommandant on Friday, the 10th July, the subject was raised and Col Knackfuss agreed on the necessity for full deliveries from France. He said, however, that at present the food difficulties in France were considerable although he would do his utmost on our behalf.

(b) Fuel supplies. Col Knackfuss asked the Jersey and Guernsey officials for their opinion on conditions generally in their respective Islands.

On behalf of Guernsey, Dr Symons said that food supplies were adequate at present, but that he was very concerned regarding the coming winter. He pointed out that the question of fuel would be very serious since the States of Guernsey were no longer allowed to cut timber. Col Knackfuss promised to do his utmost to obtain larger supplies of coal from France.

(c) Shortages. Both the Jersey and Guernsey officials pointed out to Col Knackfuss that the French Authorities seldom delivered to the Islands the quotas of rationed commodities to which they were entitled. They instanced the three months' security stock of flour which they were never able to set aside as reserve because, when a large consignment which could be regarded as security stock had been received, the monthly quotas ceased until the consignment was practically exhausted. The practice of repudiating the Islands' claim to monthly quotas which had not been delivered intensified rationing difficulties. Col Knackfuss agreed to do his utmost to ensure that the French Authorities fulfilled completely their obligations to the Islands.

Security Stock: Cattle

Jersey expects to receive over 400 head of French cattle as her security stock. Guernsey expects to receive about half this number. The difficulties encountered are:–

(a)   Lack of cold storage space, resulting in it being essential to keep the cattle on the hoof;

(b)   Lack of pasture, which means that every head of imported cattle fed in the Islands results in less food for the local herds;

(c)   Imported cattle fed on grass only are bound to lose weight and, therefore, as they are paid for in France on their weight at the time of purchase, the loss is both financial and in food value.

To surmount these difficulties, it was decided at the meeting of the Superior Council attended by the Guernsey delegates to approach the Feldkommandantur for their help in importing hay and straw from France for feeding the imported cattle.

The matter was discussed with the Feldkommandant, and Col Knackfuss agreed that the importation of hay and straw was necessary and asked for requests from both Islands in writing.

Subsequently, it was agreed with Jurats Le Masurier and Brée that the request should be made by Jersey for both Islands and that amounts asked for should be:–

1,000 tons of hay	630 tons for Jersey, and
	370 tons for Guernsey
500 tons of oats straw	250 tons for Jersey, and
	250 tons for Guernsey

Agricultural and especially pasture difficulties are intensified in Jersey as in Guernsey by requisitioning of land. It is estimated that Jersey has so far lost 3,000 vergées.

Finance

(a) French financial credit to the Islands. The Guernsey delegates handed to the Bailiff of Jersey copies of the letter received by the President of the Controlling Committee on this subject from the Feldkommandantur and his reply thereto, dated respectively 29th June and 2nd July 1942. They asked for a discussion on the subject with the Jersey finance officials and met Jurat Dorey (President of the Finance Committee) and Mr H.F. Ereaut (States Treasurer).

Jurat Dorey agreed with the substance of Mr Leale's letter and it was decided that, on Dr Casper's return to Jersey he should have a preliminary talk with him and should acquaint Mr Leale with the result of their conversation. He also agreed to make arrangements, if possible, for an inter-island talk with the Feldkommandantur in Jersey in the near future.

(b) Sale of foreign currency. During a conversation with Jurat Dorey, he claimed that, since the beginning of the occupation, Jersey had supplied Guernsey with the same amount of foreign currency as Guernsey had supplied to his Island.

(c) Reichsmarks. The Bailiff of Jersey informed the Guernsey delegates that legislation concerning the issue of Reichsmarks as legal tender was contained in VOBIF[1] No 6. Regarding payment in Reichsmarks for purchases in France, the Bailiff of Jersey takes the view that as Reichsmarks are legal tender in that country we are entitled to make payments in that currency.

Medical Supplies from the Red Cross

The Bailiff of Jersey said that the recent joint letter from the two Islands was not forwarded by the Feldkommandantur because Dr Casper would not agree to the mention in the Guernsey correspondence of our inability to obtain further supplies of drugs from Germany. Even if such were the case in fact, politically it could not be accepted.

The Guernsey letter to the Feldkommandantur was cancelled and was replaced by one letter from Jersey on behalf of both Islands.

Red Cross Messages: Answers in Handwriting

The Bailiff said that, in Jersey's view, the work of their Red Cross Department would be hampered considerably if answers in handwriting were allowed. He also feared that if unnecessary work were imposed on the Red Cross in either Paris or Geneva the result might be the loss of some of the privileges already granted to the Islands.

The Guernsey delegates explained that it had already been decided by the Feldkommandantur that the present practice of typing of replies must continue. They also assured the Bailiff that the difficulties resulting from allowing answers in handwriting were appreciated by the Controlling Committee.

The Bailiff added that, as the matter had been ventilated in the Guernsey newspapers and as such newspapers reached Jersey, he thought it would stop further discussion in his Island if the Feldkommandantur's decision were published in the Guernsey newspapers.

The Guernsey delegates undertook to raise the question on their return to Guernsey.

---

1   VOBIF stands for Verordnungsblätt des Militärbefehlshabers in Frankreich, the Official Gazette of the German Military Governor of the German Occupied Zone of France.

APPENDIX

Collection of Radios

The Bailiff and Crown Officers of Jersey are of opinion that no steps whatever should be taken by them concerning collections ordered by the Occupying Forces. For this reason, the Bailiff refused to sign the executive notice regarding radio collections prepared for his signature by Dr Reffler. He also thinks that the issue of receipts by the States for radios collected through them is most dangerous, since legally it may make the States liable to meet claims for compensation in case of loss or damage.

The Guernsey delegates pointed out that the procedure adopted in their Island in connection with the collection of radios was designed entirely to make the execution of the German Order as easy as possible for the population and to facilitate the work which the Order would doubtless entail at some future date. The Bailiff of Guernsey had asked for an official receipt from the German Authorities for the total number of radios delivered to them and that would show the States to be merely the medium of collection.

Mr Guillemette reminded Col Knackfuss of this letter from the Bailiff of Guernsey, and it was decided to discuss it further during the Colonel's visit to Guernsey in the near future.

The Jersey officials are of opinion that the first consideration is that whatever claims might be lodged should be entirely between owners of radios and the German Authorities.

General

The Bailiff of Jersey thinks that there is a distinct possibility of the Channel Islands being cut off from France during the next few months with the launching of a British offensive, especially if a bridge-head is established on the Cherbourg peninsula. It would be then vitally necessary for the Islands to help each other if any ships at all were available; at any rate, the three months' security stock of all imported goods is essential. He is also of opinion that as the war progresses it may become increasingly necessary to discuss measures to be taken in the event of demilitarisation with some thousands of foreigners left in the Islands. Both the Guernsey delegates and the Bailiff of Jersey are of opinion that more frequent visits between the Islands would make for a better understanding of difficulties and would lessen friction which has so often occurred in the past.

It is very apparent that the Jersey officials possess a distinct advantage in being able to approach and discuss all matters with the chief officials of the Feldkommandantur. Many matters which would otherwise become the subject of German orders are discussed at the Feldkommandantur with the Bailiff and members of the Superior Council and the explanation of difficulties involved in their operation are often accepted. Instances have occurred where the Feldkommandantur orders have been rescinded after discussion with the Bailiff.

The Guernsey delegates wish to place on record the fact that they received the most courteous reception from all Jersey officials, all of whom showed a much clearer understanding of the difficulties peculiar to Guernsey than they have done during past visits.

Item 9: F.K. to Bailiff: Deportations, 15 Sep 1942

Feldkommandantur 515
Guernsey
15 September, 1942

To the Bailiff of the Island of Guernsey

St Peter Port

By Higher Order the following British subjects have immediately to be evacuated to Germany:

(a)　　Persons who have not their permanent residence in the Channel Islands for instance persons who were surprised there at the outbreak of war.

(b)　　All male persons from 16–70 years of age who were not born in the Islands and are of English Nationality together with their families.

For the execution of these directions I request you to send me at once lists separated by parishes of the persons above mentioned according to the attached example.

Der Feldkommandant
(signed) KNACKFUSS
Oberst

Item 10: Leale to F.K.: Deportations protest, 23 Sep 1942

The Controlling Committee of the States of Guernsey
Hirzel House
Guernsey
23rd September, 1942

Feldkommandantur 515
Nebenstelle
Guernsey

Sir,

    May I make the strongest possible plea to retain the services of my colleague Mr Wynne Sayer. Ever since the Occupation the aim of the Controlling Committee has been to maintain correct relations between the population and the troops and to adjust the life of the Island to the ever changing economic conditions. In carrying these aims into practice Mr Sayer has played a most prominent part.

    As you are aware our three production chiefs are Messrs Falla, Dorey & Sayer. We have many good growers and many good farmers on the Island, but the number of such with administrative ability is limited in the extreme. If Mr Sayer should be taken and anything happen to either Mr Dorey or Mr Falla, I literally do not know where I should turn to for men of the same class. Mr Dorey is over sixty years of age, Mr Falla's health has often caused us anxiety.

    I would, therefore, both on public and on personal grounds make the strongest possible plea for Mr Sayer to remain in the Island.

Yours faithfully
JOHN LEALE
President

Item 11: Memo: Toilet paper rationing [nd]

<u>Translation</u>

COMITÉ D'ORGANISATION DE REPARTITION DU PAPIER
Section Paper H
14 Boulevard Poissonnière
Paris 11

By virtue of circular Q.245 of the 6th May, 1941, of Order P.238 in the J.O. (Journal Officiel?) of the 7th June, 1941, it has been decided to regulate the sale, purchase and use of sanitary paper known as H.

Consequently, if you wish to benefit by this distribution, will you please let us have not later than the 1st May, 1942, the following documents:

1. 8 copies of a demand for registration with the "Groupement de répartition du Papier H" signed by the head of the household or by the managing director, manager or authorised person in the case of a commercial, industrial or hotel establishment <u>certified by the Commissioner of Police</u> of your district.

2. a statement of the W.C.s in each dwelling, workshop, office, factory or hotel. In the case of premises with only one W.C. for several tenants, the demand and statements should be signed by the caretaker of the premises.

3. a statement of the persons using the W.C. in your house or establishment (children under 6 years of age and old persons of over 93 years of age should not be included in this statement) showing the surnames, Christian names, age and nationality of the users.

4. a statement of the number of sheets of paper H per person during the year 1938 or, if preferable, the yearly average of sheets used per person according to the totals of the years 1937-1938 and the first half-year of 1939 doubled. <u>In no case will it be possible to take into account</u> consumption during the second half of 1939, the events of this period and their effect on the population having caused an abnormal consumption of paper H.

THIS DECLARATION SHALL BE MADE ON OATH.

Note: This declaration should be made in the same manner as the previous ones, signed by a responsible person; it should be accompanied by certificates of character of the users.

In conformity with order P.246/243 in the J.O. of the 26th April, 1941, the distribution for the second half of 1942 will be based on the consumption for the years 1937/38 doubled and the first half of 1939 doubled, making a reduction of 80% plus the coefficient 8.9, less 1/12th of the average monthly consumption, taking into account the percentage of the loss caused by the paper falling from the distributor and thus unusable, and which the Committee has, after investigation, fixed at 0.017 of the total monthly consumption.

In respect of persons who live abroad and for all new establishments subsequent to 1938, a demand may be made according to the following calculation:–

P being the number of users per W.C.

F bring the number of sheets to be ordered from the distributor

$$22\ V \qquad \frac{P\ 4 \times 365 - 52}{P.4 + 354 - 52} \quad = F$$

Obtaining lifting of ban

A request for lifting may be made in special cases (diarrhoea, enteritis, etc). This request should be signed by the manager of the establishment or by the head of the household, or in a case requiring it, by the caretaker of the premises certified by the Commissioner of Police, accompanied by one or more doctors' certificates, and addressed to the responsible director for investigation.

In any case, this lifting will not be granted to more than 5.8% of the users of the same W.C. (cases of constipation can be expected in the same proportion).

Penalties

As from the 1st May, 1942, the use of more than 4 sheets of sanitary paper per person per week is strictly prohibited. Offenders render themselves liable to punishment of from 3 months to 2 years' imprisonment. Persons repeating the offence will be liable to hard labour.

The responsible director advises the managers of undertaking to instal the special distributor with sheet counting device and alarm bell in order to avoid excessive use.

Seen:

The Government Commissioner	(signed) Illegible.
The Distributor	(signed) Illegible.
The responsible Director	(signed) Illegible.

Item 12: End of Season Supper Menu, 13 Oct 1942

<u>MENU</u>

Queue-boeuf à la Johns

———————

Oreille de Mer à la Guillemette – Audoire
Haricot beurre
Crème de pomme de terre

———————

Groseille à Maquereau fou

———————

CAFÉ

———————

Raisins à la Dorey.

Item 13: Leale to F.K.: Currency Transfer Protocol, 4 Dec 1942

The Controlling Committee of the States of Guernsey
Hirzel House, Guernsey
4th December, 1942

Feldkommandantur 515
Nebenstelle Guernsey

Dear Sir

On June 29th of this year you wrote me regarding a new method of accounting in respect of Channel Islands imports and exports. I replied on July 2nd urging reasons why the suggested arrangement, which might be so adverse to our interests, should not come into force. To this letter I received no reply whatever. You may therefore believe that it was with very considerable surprise that we have now learned from our Granville Office that a protocol dealing with this matter was signed by representatives of the German and French Governments on October 13th.

I feel I would be entirely lacking in my duty to the Island if I did not point out frankly to you the position as I see it.

The crux of the matter, from our point of view, is the possible implication that henceforth we shall be prohibited from continuing to discharge our debts with the money we earn. For instance, our electric current is generated from Diesel Oil, which I believe comes ultimately from a German source. We do not understand why we should be precluded from settling these Diesel Oil Accounts in the currency with which the German Authorities and Nationals buy goods and services, including electricity, from us.

Similarly, we buy commodities from France and again we are puzzled to know why we should not pay for these with the money we are bound to accept – for it is legal tender – from French nationals when they buy our goods. We seem to have thousands of French labourers on the Island who buy goods locally produced, like fruit and vegetables, and those imported, such as wines.

We earn Reichskreditkassen Notes only because the Troops or Foreign labourers buy goods and services from us. I am, of course, unaware how many German Troops or labourers are here or in France, but the number here seems large relative to our population. If the numbers were less, the same or other commodities could be grown for export and earn us currency with which to buy in France. I realise that an arrangement whereby we import more than we export may seem one-sided, but on looking further into the matter it is obvious that we export less because we have so many troops and labourers to supply with goods and services.

The present arrangement therefore appeals to me as eminently just, but, under the new suggestion, when we sell to the German Authorities or German nationals or Frenchmen in Germany or France we shall be able to use the proceeds, but when we sell to the German Authorities or German nationals or Frenchmen in Guernsey the proceeds will be blocked. Why?

I therefore feel bound to protest against the suggested arrangement and ask that we be allowed, as hitherto, to pay for our purchases with the currency with which Germans and Frenchmen here pay us for their purchases from us.

Should the new arrangement come into being and our export of Reichskredit-kassen Notes be stopped, it is assumed that the Reichskreditkassen will remain legal tender. If this were not so, traders would be entitled to refuse to sell goods or services to troops and labourers.

The States will then be faced with the alternatives of (A) informing the banks that they are not prepared to buy any more Reichskreditkassen Notes or (B) continuing to buy up all such notes on offer.

Alternative (A)

Reichskreditkassen Notes have so far been freely accepted by the public because they have been freely exchangeable for sterling by the Banks. This has been possible because the States needed the Notes for our Granville Purchasing Commission and have bought up at ruling rates all such notes as have been presented at the Banks. If once the link between the Reichskreditkassen Notes and sterling is removed, apart altogether from the fact that the people of the Island are British, they would – at the best – be taking risks by accepting notes whose ultimate date and rate of redemption must remain a matter for conjecture. The Banks would presumably be forced to protect themselves by opening accounts in Reichskreditkassen currency. The danger is that rather than risk holding notes or Reichskreditkassen balances the public will hasten to get rid of these by turning them into something durable like furniture. Traders in durable goods, however, would naturally consider whether their interests would not best be served by selling as little as possible and ultimately in closing down. Since prices are controlled one may expect an extension of the Black Market in which increasingly large amounts of Reichskreditkassen Notes will be offered for goods.

The agriculturist and horticulturist are in a somewhat different position. They deal largely in perishables – milk, vegetables and so on. They may be forced to take the Reichskreditkassen Notes or have these commodities left on their hands to perish. It would be optimistic to expect them on such terms to produce as much as previously.

These things will presumably not happen immediately, but as first one, then another, then another, realises the changed position and takes advantage of it or protects himself against it, as the case may be, the consequences may well be disastrous.

Those who have means may be able to avoid the worst trouble. The burden will fall most heavily on the poor who will have nothing but the unwanted currency with which to buy necessities. They may be faced with starvation or be driven to theft.

It has to be remembered that the States will be buying goods in sterling and selling these in Reichskreditkassen currency and will themselves be accumulating Reichskreditkassen Notes in large quantities. You will appreciate that the Controlling Committee cannot be indifferent to the risk of loss in which the States will thus be involved.

In addition, this alternative would be very complicated to work, and only its operation would reveal all its implications and imperfections.

Alternative (B)

On the other hand the States can continue the system now in force of buying up the Reichskreditkassen Notes. This involved the Island in an ever increasing accumulation of Reichskreditkassen Notes which eventually might not be realisable at anything approaching the price at which they had been acquired. Under this alternative (B) there is, in addition, a considerable risk of these Notes being brought into the Island for the express purpose of being turned into sterling balances. Whatever action we took against this risk would probably not be wholly effective. This might involve the States in a loss so large as to be outside the ability of the Island to meet.

Alternative (C)

Owing therefore to the difficulties and dangers attendant on the prohibition of the export of Reichskreditkassen Notes, we therefore again request that the arrangements hitherto prevailing remain unaltered.

Should the export of Reichskreditkassen Notes be nevertheless prohibited, we would press that the troops and their ancilliaries pay in francs for what they buy from us and that we be allowed to utilise these francs on the continent.

If this is not possible, then we ask:–

1. To be allowed to settle accounts for goods emanating from a German source by payments in Reichskreditkassen Notes through the local Paymaster;
2. That money receivable for Motor Vehicles bought in the Island be paid through Barclays Bank, Jersey, into the Office des Changes;
3. And that Billeting and other Refunds be similarly dealt with.

It is because of the complexity of the subject and because the interests of both Islands are involved that we request permission for a delegation to visit Jersey to confer there with the local Administration in the first place and, doubtless, later with the Feldkommandantur 515, Jersey.

Yours faithfully,
JOHN LEALE
President

Item 14: Meeting with Bank Managers: Foreign Currency, 9 Dec 1942

<u>Memorandum of meeting held on Wednesday, 9th
December, 1942 at States' Office, St Peter Port</u>

Subject: Influx of Reichskreditkassen Notes

Present:

Jurat John Leale	President, The Controlling Committee of the States of Guernsey
Mr H.E. Marquand	States Supervisor
Mr H.G. Broughton	States Auditor
Mr C.W. Jones	Manager, Westminster Bank Ltd.
Mr H.M. de la Rue	Acting Manager, National Provincial Bank
Mr A.S. Iles	Manager, Lloyds Bank Ltd
Mr A.E. Le Mesurier	Manager, Midland Bank Ltd
Mr L.J. Corfield	Manager, Barclays Bank Ltd
Mr A. Bichard	Acting Actuary, Guernsey Savings Bank
Mr H.C. Chapell	Acting Head Postmaster
Mr L.A. Guillemette	Secretary to the President of the Controlling Committee of the States of Guernsey

Mr Leale said that the main purpose of the meeting was the discussion of the possible danger of foreign currencies, in particular Reichskreditkassen Notes, being imported in large quantities, not in payment for goods bought or services performed locally, but by foreigners wishing to hold sterling credits in local banks in preference to any foreign currency. At present all accounts in local Banks are kept in sterling and therefore any monies paid into any local banking account is automatically converted into sterling. Should such an influx of Reichskreditkassen Notes take place, the result would be extremely serious to the Island, since it would be impossible to dispose of the whole amount for goods on the Continent even if the export of R.K. Notes continued to be sanctioned. He reminded the meeting of the recently signed Protocol which, if and when put into operation, implied the cessation of export of R.K. Notes.

Already the States hold a cash amount of approximately £250,000 in France in Granville and surplus R.K. Notes are accumulating in the local banks at an astonishing rate (November £80,000).

Jurat Leale said it was this monthly accumulation which worried the Controlling Committee and caused them to wonder whether foreigners were already aware of the possibilities of dumping R.K. Notes here and acquiring sterling balances in their place.

The meeting discussed the various sources from which the monthly increases in R.K. Notes were derived.

The following is a list of the main sources mentioned:–

1. £20,000 received in wages by Guernsey people working for and paid directly by the Germans.

2. £10,000 (say) paid in by Timmer Ltd for vegetables sold to the Occupying Forces.
3. Payments for Guernsey firms working for Germans (Building contractors, Garages, &c).
4. Individual purchases by troops and foreign labourers with R.K. Notes paid them as wages monthly.
5. Difference between total R.K. receipts and payments of the States.

The Bank Managers all agreed that Bank Deposits in general are rising, and suggested that this was due to:–
1. The profits of business undertakings.
2. The savings of small business people and private individuals, the total rate of savings having recently increased considerably.
3. The sale of capital goods, including the stocks normally held by business undertakings, as well as goods normally in the possession of private households and individuals but for which there is an abnormal demand at present, especially on the part of foreign workmen.

All the Bank Managers were of the opinion that any unusual influx of R.K. Notes would shew itself clearly and that no dumping of foreign currencies was taking place at present. They were asked whether it would be possible to give the Controlling Committee a monthly return of the inward and outward payments in all accounts classified under standard headings, but explained that owing to:
(a)   difficulties of classification
(b)   outstanding debts owed by and to account holders at date of the return, the return would be valueless

They undertook, however, to keep close watch over all accounts and to inform Jurat Leale if and when they noticed any unaccountable increase in any account. They also decided to meet to examine the possibility of setting up some form of accountancy machinery which would preclude foreigners opening banking accounts from claiming sterling at a future date for any foreign currency which they might pay into such accounts.

With regard to the Soldatenkaufhaus which has an account with the National Provincial Bank Ltd. it was decided that Mr Leale would write to the Manager of the Bank informing him that the States would not buy any more R.K. Notes from that source.

Mr Leale said that at the present rate of the influx, even taking into account our considerable purchases of goods on the Continent, we were continuing to accumulate much more foreign currency than we required. If the export of R.K. Notes were prohibited, the matter would be even more serious. The value of this foreign currency after the War was highly problematical. He asked whether the Bank Managers had any suggestions to put forward.

The Manager of the Guernsey Savings Bank was of the opinion that the high price of agricultural products was partly the cause of the increase in deposits and suggested that this matter should be dealt with as soon as possible.

Regarding the possibility that the export of R.K. Notes may be prohibited, Mr Bichard made the following suggestion:

1. The States withdraw its offer to purchase all R.K. Notes available at the Banks.
2. This leads to the banks converting all accounts into R.K. Notes. On application by individuals the States offer to convert all surplus R.K. balances into States bonds repayable at some fixed future date.

The advantage claimed re:–

1. That it would stop any panic which might occur if the R.K. Notes were not guaranteed at all.
2. That it would decrease inflation since the tendency would be to keep as little R.K. Notes as possible in circulation and to tie up all other money in States Bonds.
3. That the States would not of necessity have to honour all R.K. Notes in circulation at the end of the war.

Against these advantages Mr Broughton suggested that the tendency would be for ordinary trading to be carried out to an ever increasing extent with States Bonds as currency, resulting in a States debt not appreciably smaller than it would be if the States continued to guarantee the Reichskreditkassen Notes.

Item 15: Meeting with F.K.: Currency Problems, 21 Dec 1942

Memorandum of meeting held at Grange Lodge on Monday 21st December, 1942

Present:

Victor G. Carey, Esq	Bailiff of Guernsey
Jurat John Leale	President, The Controlling Committee of the States of Guernsey
A.J. Sherwill, Esq	Procureur
Colonel Knackfuss	Feldkommandant
Major Kratsa [Kratzer]	
Dr Casper	O.K.V.R.
Dr Brosch	K.V.R.
Mr L.A. Guillemette	Secretary to the President of the Controlling Committee of the States of Guernsey

Subject: Present-day currency problems

Matters of a minor and more or less transitory importance were first discussed, but on being invited to bring forward any other questions the Guernsey representatives referred to the currency problems which are of such vital importance to the Island's financial future and the solution of which appears so urgently necessary.

The subject was introduced by Jurat Leale, which explained it was divisible into two separate problems. They were:–
1. That the Controlling Committee has not been informed whether they would be allowed to continue to buy goods in France when the recently signed protocol between the German and French Governments is put into operation, with the Reichskreditkassen Notes which accumulate in the Islands through purchases by and services to the Occupying Forces and their ancilliaries;
2. That even if such R.K. Notes continue to be spendable in France, the rate at which they accumulate in the Island far more than meets the Controlling Committee's requirements for purchases on the Continent, the result being an ever growing amount in this currency purchased and held by the States.

1st Problem

Dr Casper, who has attended meetings in France on the subject, said that as regards the first problem, it had been agreed that on payment of an amount of R.K. by the States to the Standort paymaster here, francs to the same value would be released in Granville for our French purchases.

This is the present system of transfer of currency to our Granville purchasing commission and it will continue to operate.

When the protocol is put into operation however it will be illegal:
(a)   to export francs used in the Islands;

(b)   for francs to be used as currency for internal trading in the Islands.

The Feldkommandantur will therefore publish a notice informing the public of these facts and stating also that any francs held by civilians may be exchanged for R.K. on application to the Standort paymaster.

At the time of the Notice similar instructions will be issued to the Troops.

It was agreed that Jurat Leale should request the banks forthwith not to accept francs in future.

The States will be allowed to pay Barclays Bank, Jersey, any francs they may hold when the protocol comes into effect.

2nd Problem

Jurat Leale gave details of the present situation in this connection, saying that up to date all R.K. surplus to the requirements of the banks had been purchased by the States and transferred to Granville. They were there paid out to the Purchasing Commission in francs and at present the Commission held about two and a half million R.K. worth of francs. In addition we were still owed large sums by the Germans for billeting and for motor vehicles purchased in the Island by them. The monthly purchases of R.K. from the local banks by the States averaged 800,000 R.K. and our monthly purchases on the Continent cost in the neighbourhood of 600,000 R.K. It followed, therefore, that each month the States' holding of R.K. increased by 200,000.

Dr Casper said that the States should be thankful that they held such a balance in Granville which could be used for purchases of other than rationed commodities. If the Germans had not contributed towards the costs of billeting during 1942 nor paid for the cars they took over, the balance would not be so large. He added that it was known to both the Feldkommandantur and to higher German authorities that we received more R.K. than we could spend but they see no danger in this state of affairs.

Jurat Leale pointed out that we do not know what the value of either francs or R.K. will be after the War and that we do not wish to hold large quantities of either currency.

Colonel Knackfuss said that this was a political question which would be solved by the nation which won the war. Jurat Leale remarked that Guernsey might well be the loser whichever side won. Dr Casper replied that if Germany won, R.K. would keep their value, if England then that country would attend to the matter. Jurat Leale asked whether that statement could be looked upon as a promise and Dr Casper said that he could promise for Germany but not for England.

Jurat Leale continued that with these large sums of R.K. already in hand and continuing to accumulate, we would not need the money which we were due to receive from the tomato crop which is to be exported next year. Dr Casper said that if we did not need it for current purchases it would be very useful after the war when more goods were available for purchase. Mr Sherwill added that we were of opinion that it would be better to produce, instead of tomatoes for export some crop which would provide food for our own population. Colonel Knackfuss said that before the War Guernsey exported much larger quantities of tomatoes and still managed to live very well. It was explained to him that we received in exchange for our crop large quantities of goods from England and in answer to his reply that we now received goods from France in return the Guernsey representatives said that the quantities of goods received from France could not be compared with those received formerly from England.

Jurat Leale stressed that the fact that we did not know what the value of the R.K. held by the States would be after the war was a constant source of worry to the Controlling Committee who felt themselves responsible to the Island in this matter.

Colonel Knackfuss said that as there was no doubt that Germany would honour her debts in R.K. after the war, it was useless discussing the matter further.

Jurat Leale said that a further danger which was envisaged by the Controlling Committee was that there might be persons on this Continent who would prefer to hold sterling balances rather than continental currency. Such persons might take steps to have such currency paid into an account in a local bank, when it would automatically be transferred into a sterling balance. He had discussed the matter with the local bank managers who were of opinion that no such transfers had been made to date. Nevertheless, it was difficult to account for much of the 80,000 R.K. which the banks have available for sale to the States every month.

Dr Casper said that, under the recently published Currency Order, such transfers were illegal and added that this Order would be applied rigorously.

Jurat Leale expressed the thanks of the Controlling Committee to those F.K. officers who had been instrumental in obtaining the ruling that the R.K. accumulating in the Islands could continue to be used for all purchases on the Continent and the Bailiff added his thanks to those expressed by Jurat Leale.

(signed)
Victor G. Carey
John Leale
A. Sherwill
L.A. Guillemette

Item 16: Letter from Major Stockwell: Conditions in Biberach [nd]

Major Alick Stockwell was deported to Germany in 1942. He wrote this letter on a standard POW letter form to Louis shortly after his arrival in Biberach – see Diary entry for 23 January 1943. Unfortunately the first few lines of his letter have been lost due to the way in which the letter was sealed.

... you will have heard of our last camp. Three deaths – Mr Walters, Mrs Manning & a child – Skipton. Men were vaccinated, inoculated against typhoid and in the case of my barrack, deloused. It was a 29 hour journey to this camp in the 2nd Cl carriages. Very cold on arrival and many suffered from coughs and 'tummy' trouble. Our Red X people under Drs McGlashan & Donaldson, worked like Trojans and we are deeply indebted to them. Health of the camp is now, I believe, very much better. I should have said that men without feminine responsibilities here proceeded to another camp to this. We number about a thousand here. The camp is well situated, hilly country, the site is dry and we think from 1500 to 2000 ft up. The buildings are newly constructed brick bungalows accommodating about 100 persons. Rooms vary in size – 18, 12, 8, 6, 4 and even 2 persons. (Mrs S and I are both in large 18 rooms – women in one set of buildings, the men in another). The rooms are stove heated & we get a tri-weekly issue of patent fuel. The lavatory & washing accommodation is clean and generally satisfactory. Once a week we have a hot shower baths, 60 or 80 men or women at a time in a really fine bath room, tiled walls, non-slip floors & plenty really hot water. 80 people cleaned in 15 or 20 minutes. We could well copy this bath room – and the method of community bathing. We have the same bread ration as in Guernsey, with sufficient margarine, cheese or jam to eat with it! We draw herbal tea at 7.30 and soup at noon & 5pm. In addition to our own rugs, we all have two blankets – women and men over 60 have received a third. The children go to school, short sessions. Education is under Mr Foote of Jersey. There are classes also, for adults, but things have not yet got into their full stride. C of E and the Free Churches hold one service each per Sunday & a RC padre has been up once from the neighbouring church, but we hear he is a busy man. The weather is glorious, cold out of the sun, with bright sunshine – as warm as G'sey can be on a Dec day. We had a good fall of snow a while ago & as much as 6° of frost, but rain cleared the snow. In spite of the change of diet, our surroundings & everything else, the atmosphere of the camp is cheery and already we are arranging for reunion dinners. Now that is all about ourselves. We naturally talk a lot about Guernsey and wonder how you are all progressing. I trust you and Mrs G keep well. The wife joins me in best wishes. Will you please let Verity[2] read this letter as we are sending her a pc only on this occasion (Our post is limited to 3 letters & 4 pc monthly). We have a barrack and room leaders & Garland camp captain. Yesterday we each received a wonderful Red X Xmas parcel & previously about 1½ ordinary parcels. We anticipate a regular issue at future intervals.

Regards & best wishes to friends. Write & tell us how you are.

Yours sincerely, A. Stockwell.

---

2   Received her letter.

Item 17: Meeting with F.K.: Intensification of Work, 7 Apr 1943

Memorandum of meeting
held at Feldkommandantur 515, Grange Lodge on Wednesday, 7th April, 1943

Subject: Labour Problems

Present:

Victor G. Carey, Esq.	Bailiff of Guernsey
Jurat John Leale	President, Controlling Committee of the States of Guernsey
R.H. Johns, Esq.	Labour Officer
J.E.L. Martel, Esq.	Acting Attorney-General
Colonel Knackfuss	
Major Kratzer	
Mr L.A. Guillemette	Secretary to the President of the Controlling Committee of the States of Guernsey

After the usual introductory formalities, Colonel Knackfuss said that he had asked the Guernsey representatives to meet him so that any matters of interest might be ventilated.

One or two matters of minor importance were discussed and then Mr Leale said that the Controlling Committee were very concerned over labour problems at the moment. The Colonel and Major Kratzer said immediately that this was the subject which they most wanted to discuss and the Colonel continued that the German Forces had to find labour and must depend upon the States to help them. He suggested that it might be possible to cut down shop staffs and numbers of shops and introduce longer shop hours. He then quoted remarks made by Jurat James Carey in the Royal Court on 3rd April which were reported as follows:

"When you see all these young fellows hanging about town, the theatres still going on, and nobody apparently worrying how we are to produce the food, I wonder what is to happen."

Mr Leale said that he had already written Jurat Carey asking for the names of the men concerned, and Mr Johns explained that some young men might be seen in the Town on Saturday afternoons, since this was the recognised half-holiday in most trades and industries, and on Wednesdays when men working in German kitchens were allowed time off.

The Colonel thought more effort could be put into most work and said that at present throughout the Continent and indeed probably throughout the world work is being intensified. He therefore considered it justifiable for the German Authorities to ask for a greater effort here, although they did not ask the impossible. He suggested that as Guernsey's principal industry before the war was catering for holiday-makers, the inhabitants had become unused to hard work. This suggestion was strongly denied by all the Guernsey representatives who explained that the tomato industry was the chief one, and that during the summer months employees worked practically from daylight to dark. The Colonel suggested that the work involved in the greenhouses at present was less than formerly and this was also denied.

Mr Leale asked how far the requisition of Guernsey labour was to go. Up to date about 2,000 civilians, or one eleventh of the total population, were working directly for the Germans and the demands of agriculture and horticulture for labour at this time of the year, coupled with the German requisitions, gave Mr Johns an impossible task to perform. The Colonel said that they are very content with what Mr Johns has done, but must still ask for more. Mr Leale asked that the German requisitions be stopped and the Colonel said he appreciated the difficulties involved. He asked that the Controlling Committee satisfy themselves that every able-bodied person is fully employed.

Mr Johns gave a summary of the steps he has already taken to satisfy himself on this matter. He said that for some weeks past the Island Police, acting on his instructions, had accosted all loiterers and taken their names and addresses and particulars of their work. Regarding shops, offices, etc, he had a record of all employees and had supplied the Feldkommandantur with lists of employees who were surplus to minimum requirements. He was constantly receiving complaints from employers because of their difficulties in running businesses with reduced staffs. He has warned the Manager of the principal bank that bank clerks would be requisitioned during the summer to help with clerical work in connection with the export of tomatoes and that he also intended using the more intelligent shopkeepers for such work.

He then went on to give figures of men in the younger age groups, showing that in the four age groups 19-22, out of a total of 643 men, 242 were already working directly for the Germans, 214 were employed in agriculture and horticulture. Of the total only 83 might possibly be spared for German employment although even of this number most were probably already doing vital civilian work. He also states that there are nearly 4000 compulsorily insured women. Of these only 1000 are domestics, leaving 3000 working in other capacities. Many work on the land, especially on small-holdings cultivated by men who depend to a large extent on the help of their wives.

Mr Johns further mentioned that he had recently received from the Feldkommandantur a list containing the names of eleven men whose services had been requisitioned by the Germans and who had been pronounced medically unfit by German doctors. It was possible that these men would be seen by German Officer who would not realise that they had already been discarded. There would then be further criticism because the work they were doing might be done by women. They had all been in employment before they were requisitioned.

Mr Leale then referred to the problem, closely allied to the labour shortage, of the dual wage rates which are in operation in the Island at present. He explained that German employers pay wage rates which are much higher than the civilian employers can afford. The result is that men want to leave agriculture and horticulture and although Mr Johns has the power to refuse applications for such transfers action of this sort causes great dissatisfaction amongst the men. The Controlling Committee in addition, must sympathise with married men who want to take advantage of higher wages.

The Colonel said that theoretically there were three solutions to the problem:

The first was the civilian wage rates be raised to the German level; but he realized that this would incur a general rise in commodity prices and was therefore undesirable.

The second was the lowering of German wage rates; but this he thought was impossible.

The third was the continuation of the present system with refusal to allow men to leave important civilian work.

Mr Leale then pointed out that dissatisfaction meant bad work, and on being reminded that in the German army men often found themselves in receipt of less money than they had been accustomed to, he said that army and civilian life were not comparable.

The Colonel said that everywhere the agricultural worker received less than the industrial worker but usually received some food in addition to pay.

Mr Leale reminded him that in Guernsey, with food rationed, it was impossible to give extra to agriculturalists and that men working for the Germans received extra money plus extra food from German stocks.

The Colonel said that the matter was receiving their attention and asked for suggestions from the Controlling Committee regarding the solving of the problems involved.

Item 18: Birthday Entertainment 1: Doctors Sutcliffe & Rose

This poem was written about Doctors Sutcliffe and Rose by the other friends who had their birthdays in April. Everyone slept the night at Louis and Queenie's home La Platte, Bordeaux. Abraham's Bosom is at St Sampson's Harbour. [José Day]

Of all the doctors in the land,
There's none like Brook or Rosie,
They treat you when you're not too grand,
And leave you feeling cosy.

On motorbikes they flash around,
Distinguished by Red Crosses,
In gents Spring Suitings, I'll be bound,
From Burtons, Hipps, or Moss's.
We all agree they're debonair,
We love our Brook and Alistair.

And when their patients coalesce,
And feel more hale and hearty,
They make them see its for their good,
To give an all-night party.
They give them permits booze to get,
  so everythings hunky-dory,
But what goes on when comes the dawn,
  is quite a different story.
Enough to say, they get quite friskey,
Drinking other peoples whiskey.
Two hours asleep, a shave, then up,
"By Gum" says Alistair, "The night's a pup".
Then back to work, these worthy sages,
A-mopping up some hem-or-ages.

The daily round, the common task,
  the fees are moderate that they ask;
On payment they've an open mind,
  with pound notes, reichmarks or in kind.
For eggs and butter, cheese or onions,
They'll remove protruding bunnions,
An eye for an eye, is no longer valid,
They do it for a tin of salid.
Their cigarettes and whiskey comes,
Through clearing pimples from babies bums,
While to take out a lung or two,
Is really more than they will do,

Unless you've something to offer them,
A little stronger than Or-Lem.
They're expert men these medicos,
At hacking off your little toes.
With frightful yells, and gleaming scalpel,
They'll split in to your Adam's Apple.
A fractured pelvis, or a punctured bladder,
Won't leave you feeling any badder,
They'll sew you up with the greatest gusto,
In such a way you'll never busto.
Now vaccination is their forte,
On beautiful maidens under forty;
But not on the arm, to them its inferior,
They'd much prefer a rounded posterior.

By Brook we are told to be patriotic,
They both think shootings idiotic,
So they fight for their country, in manner aesthetic,
By bumping off Germans with strong anasthetic,

Now their surgery hours are two to three,
Which they must both attend,
And this is where I fear me,
Their manners they must mend;
It's really quite unnecessary, to have to bare you solar
Plexus for the doctor, to remove an aching molar;
Or to be told you must undress, in accents stern and haughty,
When having massage to your knees, is little short of naughty.

No maids in trouble need apply,
To have their fears relieved,
To their pleas they get a Brunt reply,
And go out feeling peeved.
When day is done, and shadows fall,
They'll hang their boats up in your hall,
Produce their ukes, and with song and patter,
Persuade you that your cares don't matter.

And in days to come, if they should die,
We'll be very sad to lose 'em
And hope they'll find a place to lie,
On Abraham's hairy bosom.
So birthday greetings to your Brook, and life without a care,
And Fate, may you be kind also, to little Alistair.

Item 19: Birthday Entertainment 2: Controlling Committee au Cabinet

The Controlling Committee au Cabinet

The Sketch is played behind the stage curtains which are kept completely drawn. In the centre of the curtains is hung a card with the following legend:–

CONTROLLING COMMITTEE IN SESSION. NO ADMITTANCE.

The audience must therefore imagine themselves to be members of the public waiting in the hall at Hirzel House on an ordinary Occupation afternoon.

Mr Leale:	Gentlemen, let us start the proceedings as usual with our motto – and reverently please –
All together:	Favours for us few – the remainder for the rabble.
Mr Leale:	Our business need not delay us long today, especially as Jimmy Travers has only enough for one round for twenty people and he opens in a quarter of an hour. Well Sir Abraham, what is this rumour we hear about the cheese?
Sir Abraham:	Er, well, as a matter of fact ...
Mr Leale:	Is it on your boots, Raymond, or have you fallen in the pig-sty? And for goodness sake, take your boots off the table.
Raymond:	OK Jack.
Sir Abraham:	Well, as I was saying ...
Mr Leale:	Are those Coronas you're handing round Perce? Don't be tight and er, Aslett, fetch up the Black and White. By the way, did you say there were only twenty cases left?
Aslett:	Yes Sir.
Mr Leale:	Stop the doctors' ration immediately. What do you say Symons?
Dr Symons:	Hear, hear, the beggars are only handing it round to their patients now.
Mr Leale:	We're all waiting to hear you on cheese, Abe, and gentlemen in case you are not fully cognisant of the facts, they are as follows. A most awful damn stink has been spreading through the High Street lately and people with sufficient courage have traced it to the bottom of Lefebvre Street where the cheese is stored. The matter has been brought to a head by the Central Douzaine who are a week late with their meeting waiting for a favourable wind to let them get to the Constables Office. They demand the removal of the cheese and the main question we are asking Abe is, why have not the Controlling Committee received their rake off of a consignment of cheese which has been in stock a whole month? Mr Johns, do take the typist off your lap, and Leila, pull your frock down like a good girl, you're putting Raymond off his stroke.

Mr Johns:	All right Jack, but you see my wife doesn't understand me.
Sir Abraham:	There seems to be some misunderstanding, Mr President. As usual, on receipt of the invoice for this consignment, I entered into a contract with the Guernsey Railway Co for its destruction on arrival. The delay is caused by the press of work at the incinerator due to the burning of surplus stocks of macaroni, chocolate, cream, butter, fruit, etc. I hope that the cheese will be destroyed during the next week.
Mr Leale:	Thanks, Abe, for a most lucid and satisfactory explanation. If only such explanations could be made public there would certainly be no more uninformed criticism from the common horde.
Sir Abraham:	I might add, Mr President, that I did remonstrate with Mr Stead, the manager of the Guernsey Railway Co over the delay in regard to this cheese but found it wiser to desist when he informed me that too great a pressure on my part would interfere with the Committee's usual weekly supply of fish.
Mr Leale:	By the way, Symons, I noticed this morning that our coffee was made with skimmed instead of whole milk.
Dr Symons:	That's right, Jack, we're getting short of full cream milk these days.
Mr Leale:	Good heavens, man, cut off the babies' ration at 18 months instead of two years. What's that Raymond?
Raymond:	I fight like a tiger! This morning at half past five I had a phone message from Grange Lodge thaat the Colonel and Oser wanted me to show them how to run the Feldkommandantur. I got up, found my teeth under the pillow of one of my girls, and went off to give my advice. The General and H were with the Colonel and they all greeted me cordially. Of course I know them all very well – travelled hundreds of miles with them in France. My wife and H's wife were bosom pals at school. We had breakfast – I had five eggs and a big rasher of bacon I took with me in my cap – and then I took them down for a bathe. I dived off the 25 foot board and landed on my belly – with hardly a splash.
Mr Leale:	(very quietly) What was the result of your visit, Mr Falla?
Raymond:	Three marks fine for being on the roads before 6 am.
Mr Leale:	Are you weeping, Mr Dorey, or are you trying to smile? No, gentlemen, I believe he is trying to say something! Silence please. Johns, surely you can drink without making that drain-like noise and for goodness sake take your nose out of the glass – if you can.
Mr Dorey:	Say something! I've never heard such nonsense. They'll never finish the war without me. They want a man like me – a born organiser – to show them how to start the second front. As for the Germans, they say they are the premier race. Huh! I've never found one as good as me yet. If I were in Germany I'd be made Fuehrer at once.
Mr Leale:	By the way, Percy, what's all this criticism of prices in the vegetable market?
Mr Dorey:	Well the prices I fix are all right, but it's those women stall holders. They take no notice of me at all and since one of them hit me in the

	ear-hole with a ripe tomato I'm afraid to go near them.
Mr Leale:	Please wake up Mr Johns. I want to ask him a question. Ah, thank you. Now Mr Johns, I am told by Grange Lodge that they asked you a month ago for ten gardeners and that they have not yet seen anything of them.
Mr Johns:	I can't help that, Sir. The men have just finished planting my spuds at Lowlands and when they have re-laid my bowling green next week I have to send them to the Supervisor to clean up his front garden. By the end of the summer we may be able to spare them to the Germans for a few days.
Mr Leale:	Guillemette, you'd better make that clear to Grange Lodge. (There is a short silence). Where is Guillemette? Is he sitting behind you, Raymond?
Raymond:	No, but his wife told me that they have no more wood at home. He must be in Herm.
Mr Leale:	Our next and last job is the weekly share-out of booze and baccy. I've had it all stacked at the other end of the room this time to make sure that there is no pilfering by members. You will remember that last week Raymond was caught with his breeches full of loose whisky and it has come to my knowledge, by the way, that some of you are swapping baccy for children's chocolate rations. I don't mind that provided that you don't upset normal black market operations by offering too favourable rates. Remember always, gentlemen, that business is business. I need hardly quote that occupation classic:

> Remember what happened to Bertram Bartlett,
> He who was king of the Island's black market.

	Now to work. What's yours Raymond?
Raymond:	I'll have two thousand Club and three dozen whisky plus a couple of extra for my trouble last week in getting hold of those two pigs for you.
	(There is a sound of a heavy body moving in the room and the President calls sharply.)
Mr Leale:	Stay where you are Raymond until we are all ready!
Raymond:	OK but I'll have to be going soon. I've two fine heifers waiting for me in my office, with marvellous hind quarters. Dr Symons would love 'em.
	(Another hurried and heavy movement and then –)
Mr Leale	Stay where you are I tell you. Collar him, boys, he'll get away with all the swag.
	(There are signs of a most violent scuffle, with many grunts and groans, and then Raymond is projected – in ordinary attire – stern first to the audience.)

324

Item 20: Meeting with F.K.: Reduction of Food Rations, 30 Apr 1943

<u>Memorandum of meeting held at Grange Lodge
on 30th April, 1943</u>

Present:
   The Bailiff
   Sir Abraham Lainé
   Dr Kratzer
   K.V. Ass. Hertig
   L.A. Guillemette, Secretary to President

<u>Subject: Reduction of civilian food ration</u>

Dr Kratzer said that he had been ordered by higher authority to inform the Guernsey representatives that on the 27th April, 1943, the Royal Air Force had carried out attacks on German supply ships on the way to this Island. Amongst other goods a large quantity of potatoes had been lost. When former attacks by the Royal Air Force had been carried out, the Feldkommandantur had informed the Controlling Committee that if such attacks were repeated certain counter-measures might have to be taken. As such attacks might be against the interest of the civilian population, orders had arrived from higher German Authorities regarding the reduction of rationed foodstuffs.

A letter on the subject was then handed to the Bailiff and was translated by the German interpreter for the benefit of the Guernsey representatives. The translation is as follows:–

Feldkommandantur 515
Mi. Verw. Gr. (Az. Pol. 02.)   Jersey, 30.4.43

To: The Bailiff of Guernsey, St Peter Port

<u>Re: Reduction of food rations for the English civilian population of the Channel
   Islands on account of the disturbance of shipping by enemy attacks</u>

The Commander in Chief of the Army, as indicated in more detail in the announcement published in the press, has, after the attacks directed against supply ships, ordered a reduction of the food rations for the English civilian population.

By superior orders, the following reductions are immediately to be effected in the rations of the English population of the Channel Islands:
   1. The bread ration for all English subjects from 21 years of age and over is reduced to 175 grammes per day.
   2. The meat ration for all English subjects from 21 onwards is reduced to 60 grammes a week.
   3. The fat ration for all English subjects from 21 onwards is reduced to 150 Gr. a month.

4. The cheese ration for all English subjects from 21 onwards is reduced to 150 Gr. a month.

The extra rations (for instance for heavy workers) remain as before.

The following groups of persons are exempted from the reduction:
1. All non-English subjects incl. Irish.
2. All expectant mothers and nursing mothers.
3. All invalids in hospitals.
4. All sick persons, if and as soon as a medical certificate has been approved by the Feldkommandantur.
5. All employees and workmen employed direct by German Departments, as well as those employed for the Germans under Billeting Service on the part of the States, in both cases including the members of their families belonging to their household.

(signed) DR KNACKFUSS
Oberst und Feldkommandant
(signed) DR KRATZER
Major

Dr Kratzer continued that he was not yet informed how long such reductions would be in force. The measures included all the Islands of the Bailiwick and he requested the Bailiff to inform the Dame de Sark of the contents of the letter. He then asked whether the Guernsey representatives had any questions.

Sir Abraham Lainé said that the matter must be carefully considered. He did not see how such measures would remove the cause since we have no control over the British Government. Dr Kratzer said that the answer to that statement could only be given by higher authority. Sir Abraham added that the Island is urged to grow as much foodstuffs as possible. If the food potential of the population is reduced the growing of foodstuffs would become more and more difficult. Dr Kratzer said that this matter would have to be taken up again in putting measures into operation.

The Bailiff said that with regard to point 5 of the letter, our present difficulties, owing to the dual wage rates in operation in the island, would be accentuated. Dr Kratzer answered that this matter also would have to be taken up in discussing the carrying out of the instructions contained in the letter. In any case, the whole matter would have to be talked out at special meetings which he did not think would be necessary for the Bailiff to attend. He then went on to say that in connection with attacks by the Royal Air Force, it would be necessary to see that all civilian air raid shelters were in good condition and that everybody knew where to go in case of bombing attacks.

Sir Abraham then referred back to the main subject under discussion and asked whether these reprisals applied to Jersey as well as to this Bailiwick. Dr Kratzer said that they did, but that he did not like the use of the word reprisal. He preferred the word "retorsion", which he interpreted as meaning "answering an unfair measure by moderate counter-measures". Sir Abraham said that he assumed that the Germans accused the English Government of taking unfair measures. Dr

Kratzer answered that that was so. Sir Abraham continued that on that account he assumed the Germans were inflicting punishment on the civilian population who have no present connection with the British Government and were not responsible for the actions of that Government. The answer to this statement, as translated by the German interpreter, was "this is always within the contents of such measures and if fewer foodstuffs arrive then only fewer foodstuffs can be given out".

Dr Kratzer then said that if no further questions of principle were to be raised, the meeting could regarded as being closed. Sir Abraham said that since the Guernsey representatives had had no notice beforehand of the subject of the meeting, they assumed that they had the right to make further representations. Dr Kratzer replied that as mentioned before, questions regarding the carrying out of the measures would arise and would have to be taken up with K.V.Ass. Hertig. Sir Abraham then repeated his question asking whether the Island Government could make representations regarding the principles involved. Dr Kratzer said that the principle was decided by higher authorities, and could not be discussed further by the Feldkommandantur. Sir Abraham then asked whether representations could be forwarded through the Feldkommandantur to such higher authorities. Dr Kratzer said that the right of appeal, as in all other matters, was open to the Island Government.

Item 21: Meeting Bailiff & C.C.: Reduction of Food Rations, 30 Apr 1943

<u>Memorandum of a Meeting held at the Bailiff's Chambers,
Royal Court House, on Friday, 30th April 1943</u>

Present:

Victor G. Carey, Esq.	Bailiff
Rev. John Leale, Jurat	President of the Controlling Commmittee of the States of Guernsey
Sir Abraham Lainé, KCIE	Vice President
Dr A.N. Symons; Messrs. R.H. Johns; R.O. Falla; Percy Dorey;	Members;
J.E.L. Martel	Deputy Attorney General
H.M. Marquand	States Supervisor
L.A. Guillemette	Secretary to the President of the Controlling Committee;
J.H. Loveridge	Secretary to the Committee for the Control of Essential Commodities.

The Bailiff stated that the meeting had been called in order to discuss the Order of the German Authorities with regard to the reduction of food rations for the English civilian population of the Channel Islands on account of the disturbance of shipping by enemy attacks and he asked Mr Guillemette to read the memorandum of a meeting held at Grange Lodge that morning (copy attached to original hereof).

The Bailiff thought further representation should be made and he asked Advocate Martel how the position was affected by International Law. The latter said that it depended whether or not this action was a reprisal. If a reprisal, it would appear to be governed by Article 50 of the Hague Convention which states that no collective penalty, pecuniary or otherwise, may be inflicted on the population on account of the acts of individuals for which it cannot be regarded as collectively responsible.

Mr Leale pointed out that Dr Kratzer had stated at the meeting that he did not like the word "reprisal" preferring the word "retorsion" although this did not seem to alter the meaning at all. The German Authorities had stated that as less food would arrive from France the rations would have to be reduced. Mr Leale said that the proposed rations made it impossible for the persons concerned adequately to perform their work. He also doubted whether it would be possible to export any tomatoes to France as required by the German Authorities. If this order were enforced, he thought we should appeal to the Red Cross for supplementary supplies.

Sir Abraham Lainé said the question as to whether or not this was a reprisal should be raised. If not a reprisal, it would surely apply to all members of the population. Further, he wondered how we were expected to inform the British Government of this Order.

In reply to a question, Mr Johns said that probably approximately 12,000 persons would be affected. With regard to heavy workers, the basic bread ration would be reduced but not the extra ration. Sir Abraham Lainé said the proposed rations would be as follows:–

Bread	2 lbs 5 ozs per week
Meat	1.940 ozs per week
Fat	5.291 ozs per month
Cheese	5.291 ozs per month

Mr Dorey said it was impossible for the men working under his Department to work on these rations and he could not ask them to do so. He thought we should point out to the German Authorities that it would not be possible to carry out their cropping plan.

The Bailiff said this order would cause many men to leave their present employment to work for the German Authorities. He also thought the opinion of the Medical profession should be obtained.

Mr Johns thought the time had come when we should claim that a representative of another power should be sent to the Island, through whom representations could be made to the Red Cross and to the British Government.

Sir Abraham Lainé said that it should be pointed out to the German Authorities that the Controlling Committee might be obliged to resign if they were forced to carry out these orders.

After further discussion on the individual rations, Mr Leale was asked to prepare a letter to the German Authorities conveying the various points raised and it was resolved that an effort should be made for the Bailiff to speak to the Bailiff of Jersey in order to obtain the reaction of the Jersey Authorities. It was further resolved that a letter from the Medical profession should be sent to the German Authorities together with the above mentioned letter.

Item 22: Meeting Bailiff & C.C.: Reduction of Food Rations, 1 May 1943

<u>Memorandum of a Meeting held at the Bailiff's Chambers,
Royal Court House, on Saturday 1st May, 1943</u>

Present:

Victor G. Carey	Bailiff
Rev. John Leale, Jurat	President of the Controlling Committee of the States of Guernsey
Sir Abraham Lainé	Vice-President
Dr A.N. Symons; Messrs R.H. Johns; R.O. Falla; Percy Dorey	
	Members
J.E.L. Martel	Deputy Attorney General
H.E. Marquand	States Supervisor
L.A. Guillemette	Secretary to the President of the Controlling Committee

The Bailiff said that he, together with Mr Leale, had spoken to the Bailiff of Jersey that morning with regard to the order for the reduction of certain rations. The Jersey Authorities were adopting the same attitude as we were. In view of the fact that the rations of non-English inhabitants would not be reduced, this was in the nature of a reprisal and the Bailiff of Jersey also proposed to invoke the assistance of the neutral power which looked after the interests of prisoners and internees, ie. Switzerland. He proposed that each Island should send a letter to the Swiss Ambassador in Berlin forwarding all the relative correspondence and asking him to intervene on our behalf. The Bailiff thought we should do this and also ask for a representative of the Swiss Government to visit the Island.

Mr Leale pointed out that Jersey's position differed from ours in that they were self-supporting in wheat and therefore shipping difficulties should not affect their bread ration. The Bailiff of Jersey was also therefore putting the point that there was no economic reason for this reduction of bread in that Island. Mr Leale thought therefore that we should appeal to the Red Cross asking for a 6 months' supply of the deficit. This would amount to approximately 200 tons of flour and 55 tons of wheat.

Mr Falla said we were self-supporting in butter and that consequently only the cooking fat ration should be cut. Dr Symons said he was making a separate report to a German Doctor who had come from Jersey and would assume that the butter ration would not be cut.

Mr Leale then read the draft letter to the German Authorities on which the Bailiff of Jersey had passed no comments except on the first paragraph. The Bailiff of Jersey thought that Article 50 of the Hague Convention could not be invoked in this case as the attacks on shipping were not the acts of "individuals" but of a belligerent. He based his main argument on International Law which allowed reprisals only in extreme cases and he said that raids on shipping were legitimate acts of war and therefore not subject to reprisals. Mr Leale, however, although wishing to give the fullest support to the Bailiff of Jersey wondered whether it would be wise to state that raids on ships bringing food to Guernsey for the civilian population were legitimate acts of war – such a statement might rebound on us later.

Dr Symons suggested the word "customary" instead of "legitimate" and Sir Abraham Lainé said it might cover the point by stating that raids on "hostile shipping or shipping under hostile control" or "shipping which appears prima facie to be used for hostile purposes" were legitimate acts of war.

After further discussion the draft letter, with the exception of the first paragraph, was approved, the re-drafting of the first paragraph being left to the Bailiff, Mr Leale, Sir Abraham Lainé and Advocate Martel. The Bailiff said he would prepare a letter to the Swiss Ambassador and asked Mr Leale to prepare a letter to the Red Cross.

Item 23: F.K. to Bailiff: Food Ration Order, 3 May 1943

Feldkommandantur 515
Mil. Verw. Gr., Az. Wi. 15
Jersey, 3.5.43

To the Bailiff of Guernsey, St Peter Port

In amendment to my letter of 30.4.43, the bread rations, for the civilian population, are fixed as follows, until further notice:

1. Heavy workers, male, over 21.
    Previously: 2718 Gr. = 6 lbs.
    Now: 2175 Gr. = 4 lbs 12 ozs.
2. Heavy workers, female, over 21.
    Previously: 2377 Gr. = 5 lbs 4 ozs.
    Now: 1903 Gr. = 4 lbs 3 ozs.
3. Normal consumers above 21.
    Previously: 2036 Gr. = 4 lbs 8 ozs.
    Now: 1630 Gr. = 3 lbs. 10 ozs. (roughly)

The cheese ration is to be fixed at 150 Gr. monthly.
The other food rations remain as in the previous allotment.

The Feldkommandant
(signed) KNACKFUSS
Oberst

F.d.R. Dr. Kratzer, Major

Item 24: Meeting with F.K.: Reduction of Food Rations, 6 May 1943

The Feldkommandant
(signed) Knackfuss
Oberst

<u>Memorandum of a Meeting held at Grange Lodge
on Thursday, 6th May, 1943</u>

Present:

Victor G. Carey, Esq	Bailiff of Guernsey
Rev. John Leale, Jurat	President of the Controlling Committee of the States of Guernsey
Messrs. J.E.L. Martel	Deputy Attorney General
L.A. Guillemette	Secretary to the President of the Controlling Committee
Major Kratzer	
K.V. Ass. Hertig	

<u>Subject: Reduction of civilian rations</u>

Note: On Wednesday 5th May, letters from the Bailiff to the Feldkommandantur, the Swiss Minister in Berlin and the Secretary General of the International Red Cross Organisation, Geneva, together with a report from the Health Services Officer to the Bailiff were delivered to the Feldkommandantur by Mr L.A. Guillemette, who intimated that the Bailiff, Mr Leale and Mr Martel would be pleased to discuss the subject of the letters with Major Kratzer when he had had time to read them. It was arranged that a meeting should be held and this memorandum sets out the discussion which took place.

Major Kratzer opened the meeting by asking the Bailiff why the Guernsey representatives had asked for an interview, whereupon the Bailiff replied that, as arranged, they had come to discuss the letters which had been delivered to the Feldkommandantur. He went on to say that the present rations were the very minimum on which the Island community could work and expressed the opinion that any reduction would mean not only a reduction in local production but perhaps some violence as well.

Major Kratzer said that he had read the letters and thought that if read by a third person who was without the full knowledge of the conversations to date, that person would not realise that there had been two German orders and that the second modified the first considerably. He presumed that this was because the letters were already in draft when the second Order was received by the local Government. The Bailiff said that this was not so and that although it must be admitted that the original order had been modified, it would still be impossible for the community to carry on on the reduced rations. In amplification of this point, Mr Leale submitted figures of days lost in sickness by some 3,500 persons, mainly men, who were

333

members of the Friendly Societies which had come under States' control some two years ago by German order. The totals were as follows:–

      1941   47,107 days lost

      1942   53,979 days lost

The number of persons concerned was less this winter than during the previous one, but the number of days lost was greater. The States Insurance Authority had had the same experience and medical opinion was that this was due to the fact that when persons became ill now they had more difficulty in regaining health and were therefore ill for longer periods. He maintained that with smaller rations this evil would be accentuated.

Major Kratzer said that he was afraid the same thing was happening all over Europe, due to the cutting off of food supplies from other parts of the World and Mr Leale replied that this did not alter the fact that a reduction of rations would mean that Island work would suffer.

Major Kratzer then quoted from Dr Symons' letter in which he mentioned cases of Hunger Oedema. These cases had been examined by German doctors who had stated that they had been wrongly diagnosed. Mr Leale asked whether Dr Kratzer meant that the German and local doctors had disagreed and the discussion was immediately switched back to the letters from the Bailiff.

Major Kratzer said that the point of view of the Feldkommandantur regarding the question of appeals against the German order was different from that of the Guernsey representatives and he reminded them that, at their meeting last Friday, he had expressed the personal opinion that the order could not be regarded as a reprisal. The Jersey Feldkommandantur had now given an assurance to the Bailiff of Jersey on the subject. At the Major's request the text of the assurance was read. It was as follows:–

> "The delegation (of the Superior Council) received the assurance of the Feldkommandant that the 20% reduction of the present bread ration of the entire civil population over 21 years of age is dictated by the existing war situation and is in no sense a punishment against the civil population."

He continued that he would have appreciated it if the Bailiff's appeal to the Swiss Minister had presented a somewhat different aspect from that actually presented. As a further explanation of his point he said that if the enemies of the German Reich sank all existing ships it would be useless appealing to the German Government. In such a case it would be necessary to appeal to the British Government.

He continued that on the previous day the German Radio had given out the following statement in English:–

> "The food rations of the civil population on the Channel Islands had to be reduced as was announced yesterday. It will now no longer be possible to transport as many foodstuffs as heretofore as attacks endanger the steamers crossing between the Islands and which are visibly marked as Supply ships.

It will solely depend upon the future whether the allocations for the British civil population living on the Channel Islands have to be reduced still further."

The Bailiff, said the Major, would be interested to know that the Bailiff of Jersey had decided not to appeal either to the Feldkommandantur or to the Protecting Power. He had submitted to the Feldkommandantur an order for the reduction of rations which would be published on Friday 7th instant. It was as follows:–

Bread Rationing

"As from Monday, May 10th, 1943, the bread ration for the civil population is, until further notice, fixed as follows:

Manual worker, male, over 21 years of age, 4 lbs 12 ozs
Manual worker, female, over 21 years of age, 4 lbs 4 ozs
Other adults over 21 years of age, 3 lbs 12 ozs.

The bread ration of the rest of the Civil population remains unchanged."

(signed) Le Masurier
Department of Essential Commodities

F.K. Approval

In addition the following notice would appear in the Jersey newspaper on the same day:–

"During the past few days the Feldkommandant and a delegation of the Council have held conferences with reference to the sinking of ships by Allied Forces in the waters adjacent to the Channel Islands and to the possible effect of such sinkings on insular supplies.

The delegation received the assurance of the Feldkommandant that the 20% reduction of the present bread ration of the entire civil population over 21 years of age is dictated by the existing war situation and is in no sense a pubishment against the civil population.

Future events will show the time during which it may be necessary to continue the reduction."

On behalf of the Council
(signed) A.M. Coutanche
Bailiff
May 5th, 1943.

The Major suggested that the Bailiff should publish a similar notice, although he could not order him to do so.

In Jersey nothing had been made known regarding the cheese ration mentioned in the German order since lack of supplies made it impossible to issue such a ration.

The quantities of bread had had to be adjusted to a very small extent to ease matters for the bakers. He asked when we intended introducing the new bread ration and added that as the position was now clear it should be introduced on Monday next, the 10th instant.

Mr Leale said that he appreciated the fact that Jersey was starting on Monday but that he could not give a date without consulting the Essential Commodities Committee. He asked Mr Guillemette to telephone the Secretary of the Essential Commodities Committee to find out when they could start. As a result of the telephone conversation, Mr Guillemette explained that it would be impossible for the new ration to be in full operation on Monday, but he suggested that, if it was definitely ordered that the new rations must take effect from Monday, the Order could be inserted in the newspaper on Friday, to take effect on Monday officially, and the actual rations would be brought down to the new level as soon as practicable. This was accepted by the Feldkommandantur.

The Major then asked whether, in view of the changed situation, the Guernsey representatives still wished the appeals to go forward. The representatives asked for a day in which to consider the matter. The Major added that no Feldkommandantur approval would be needed to be attached to any notice which the Bailiff might wish to write to accompany the Rationing Order, but that any such notice must in fact be submitted to the Feldkommandantur before publication. He asked whether the Island representatives had any further questions to put to him.

Mr Leale asked what answer the Feldkommandantur gave to the question of the continuation of work on the season's tomato crop, since the shortage of shipping seemed to be so acute. The community needed the space given over to the crop for the production of crops for local consumption.

The Major replied that this must be the subject of a further meeting but that he thought the export could be carried through. However future events would throw further light on the subject.

The Guernsey representatives then asked whether, in view of the difficulties of working with fractions of pounds, it would be possible for the rations, in practice, to be issued to the nearest half pound above the ration as stated in the German Order. It was decided that the request should be passed on to Jersey and that Mr Guillemette should be informed of the answer.

The Bailiff further asked that arrangements be made for him to speak over the telephone with the Bailiff of Jersey. The Major said that he would ask the Colonel's permission and would inform Mr Guillemette.

Note: Information was received that it would not be possible for bread rations to be issued to the next highest half pound and also that the Colonel refused permission for the Bailiff to speak to the Bailiff of Jersey on the telephone.

Item 25: Bailiff to F.K.: Reduction of Food Rations, 7 May 1943

The Bailiff's Chambers
Royal Court House
Guernsey
7th May, 1943

The Feldkommandant
Feldkommandantur 515
Jersey

re: Reduction of Food Rations

I have received your letters of 30/4/43 and 3/5/43 with the utmost consternation and alarm.

1. It is my duty to the inhabitants of Guernsey and Sark to stress most emphatically that the result of your Order, even in its modified form, will be disastrous to the health of these communities. In support of this, I enclose a report from Doctor A.N. Symons, the Health Services Officer. Even with the present food rations the output of work is decreasing and workers continually complain that they have not sufficient food for their sustenance. Our Health Insurance statistics reveal this complaint is fully justified. Any reduction in rations must therefore result in a still further decrease of output, which means that we shall not be able to produce as much foodstuffs as we are doing now and our essential public utility (e.g. gas, electricity, water, &c) and administrative services will suffer to a very great extent.

2. If this Order is made because your Superiors are afraid that boats will not reach us, we must adjust our economic life accordingly. We must abandon all ideas of exporting tomatoes, for not only will the export boats be equally affected, but tomatoes being perishable will not stand delays. In any case, we now, in our dire position, need the valuable space in which to plant other crops to make us a little more self-supporting.

3. There are bound to be many other repercussions arising from the operation of your Order with which I do not propose to deal at this stage.

4. In view of the perilous position in regard to our food situation, the time has come when I feel it is my duty to apply immediately to the International Red Cross Organisation for help. I am appealing to that Organisation and I request that my letter be forwarded immediately. Further, as I regard it as absolutely essential that personal contact be made with the Red Cross Organisation at this stage, I am ready to send a delegation of responsible Island Officials to Geneva if it is found impracticable for the Red Cross to send representatives here. I should be obliged, therefore, if you would ascertain whether the necessary facilities would be granted.

5. Furthermore, I feel that the time has come when my duty to the inhabitants of Guernsey and Sark compels me to demand an investigation of our position by the Protecting Power, namely Switzerland. I am therefore enclosing an appeal to the Minister of that State accredited to your Government in Berlin,

together with a copy of the relevant correspondence, which I request you to forward to him with the least possible delay.

6. In view of the immediate and disastrous effects of this Order, I must ask that it be suspended, at all events until we have heard the result of our appeals to the Swiss Minister and to the Red Cross Organisation. Should this Organisation grant us the help asked for, then there would be no economic reason at all for the enforcement of your Order.

(signed) Victor G. Carey
Bailiff

Item 26: Health Services Officer report, 7 May 1943

Hirzel House
Guernsey
7th May, 1943

The Bailiff of Guernsey
Royal Court House
Guernsey

Sir,

From the purely medical point of view, I would like to draw your attention to the effects we may expect from the reduction in rations ordered by the German Command. The <u>daily</u> ration for the ordinary individual will be:–

	Per day	Calories
Bread	8.2 ozs	808.7
Meat	0.57 ozs	38.5
Potatoes	11.42 ozs	260.0
Butter	0.57 ozs	125.0
Cooking Fat	0.28 ozs	62.5
Sugar (*)	0.57 ozs	66.4
Jam	0.28 ozs	23.1
Breakfast Food	0.85 ozs	83.7
Separated Milk	10.00 ozs	88.4
Salt	0.28 ozs	-
Coffee	0.14 ozs	-
Cheese (amount received negligible)		
		1556.3 say 1600

(*) marked high as some sugar replaced by Saccharine.

It is said that a 12 stone man doing light work required 3500 calories a day, therefore another 1900 calories are required.

A small number of people keep rabbits and/or poultry. A few fortunate ones may have been able to retain some tinned provisions.

The large majority have none of these things and must depend on vegetables. I am informed by the Horticultural Department that until July, peas, carrots and cabbage only will be available. One pound of peas will give 114 calories, carrots 108, cabbage 192, average 138. Therefore to secure the correct number of calories a man would require to east over 14 lbs a day of these vegetables to remain at full strength, which is absurd. This is not taking into account that without sufficient fat and first class protein good health is impossible.

Of first class protein of which each man should have 37 grammes a day, we have 9.2 grammes a day from the half pint of separated milk and average 3.4 a day from the 4oz of meat a week, making only 17.6 grammes – in all under half of the proper amount.

The reduction of the bread will mean a great loss in good quality second class protein.

We must therefore be on the look out for cases of Hunger Oedema.

In theory we are supposed to receive cheese but it so seldom comes that we must ignore it in our calculations.

Returning to calories – it is understood that a man resting in bed requires 1600 calories to exist. For a man doing light work I suggest the danger level to be about 2000. The rations give 1600. Therefore he must eat at least 3 lbs of vegetables as well as his potato ration a day to continue, without doing any hard work.

Should it be stated that as the people have survived so far on the rations, the loss of 14 lbs of bread to the ordinary man and 20 ozs to the heavy worker will not make an appreciable difference, I would reply that there has been a slow but progressive deterioration in the vitality of the population. This has shown variation with the availability of extra vegetables to supplement the ration. It was most noticeable when there was a shortage of potatoes in the first months of 1942. This proves that the rations themselves are quite insufficient to maintain normal life, and points out the hardship in making a reduction of the bread rations, the shortage of which has been a constant cause of complaint. The increase in Tuberculosis and the cases admitted to Hospital for actual starvation in the early part of last year are evidence of the accuracy of these statements. Our statistics of working days lost owing to sickness add further proof.

For those who have no private stores remaining, keep no rabbits or chickens and are unable to obtain other food I can see nothing else but a steady degeneration not only in health but in character.

From the medical aspect I ask you to bring your influence to ameliorate such deplorable conditions.

> I have the honour to be, Sir,
> Your obedient Servant,
> A.N. Symons
> Health Services Officer.

Item 27: Bailiff to Swiss Minister: Reduction of Food Rations [nd]

The Bailiff's Chambers
Royal Court House
Guernsey

His Excellency
The Swiss Minister
BERLIN

Your Excellency

I write to you on behalf of the Inhabitants of the Islands of Guernsey and Sark which form part of the Bailiwick of Guernsey of which I am the Bailiff as I understand that your Country is the Protecting Power in so far as British subjects are concerned vis-à-vis Germany.

As you are doubtless aware the Islands of this Bailiwick were occupied by the German Military Forces in June 1940 and are still so occupied.

Previous to the Occupation a considerable proportion of the inhabitants evacuated to England but the present civilian population exceeds 25,000 persons.

These Islands, even previous to the Occupation, were not self supporting in the essentials of life and the position has not improved since. With the permission of the Occupying Forces we have been able to obtain certain food-stuffs from France to supplement locally produced food and thereby we have been able to exist. Our medical men, however, report that tuberculosis is on the increase and manual workers in particular complain with good reason of lack of sustaining food.

On April 30th 1943, I received an Order from the German Feldkommandantur 515 that we had to reduce considerably the present food rations of the English civilian population (except those including their families, who are employed by or for the German departments). The reason given for this Order was attacks directed against supply ships. I enclose a copy of this Order (Annexe 1). On the same day (30/4/43) there appeared a Notice in the local newspaper from the Oberfehlshaber der Armee which apparently is the notice referred to in the German Order to me. I enclose a copy (Annexe 2).

I have subsequently received an amending Order (dated 3/4/43) of which I enclose a copy (Annexe 3).

I have written to the Feldkommandantur 515 stating that I regard the Order as a reprisal which is not justified under International Law and I also enclose a copy of my letter (Annexe 4). I request that your Excellency will kindly with the least possible delay make representations to the German Government so that the Order may be withdrawn as being unjustifiable.

If, however, the German Government refuses to admit that the Order is illegal then I beg your Excellency to plead with the German Government that the Order may be withdrawn on humanitarian grounds. It will be quite evident to your Excellency that if the reduced scale of rations is to be enforced then the health of the community will suffer very seriously – in fact the results will be calamitous not only immediately but in the future. In this connection I also enclose a copy of the Report which I have received from our Health Officer (Annexe 5).

As you will see by the German Order the ration of cheese is to be reduced but in point of fact we rarely have an issue of that commodity.

I feel that the time has arrived when on account of our perilous food position I must appeal to the International Red Cross Organisation for help and I enclose a copy of my letter to that Organisation (Annexe 6).

May I request your Excellency to use your good offices in support of this Appeal?

I would greatly welcome a visit from a representative of your Government in order that the whole position may be fully and impartially investigated.

I shall be grateful if you will let me know as soon as possible if you are able to undertake this mission on our behalf and if so the result of your intervention.

Thanking you in anticipation,

I have the honour to be,

Your Excellency's obedient Servant
VICTOR G. CAREY
Bailiff

Annexes:

1. Copy of German Order dated 30.4.43.
2. Copy of newspaper Notice of 30.4.43.
3. Copy of German Order dated 3.5.43.
4. Copy of letter dated this day to the Feldkommandantur.
5. Copy of Report from Health Officer.
6. Copy of Appeal to Red Cross Society.

Item 28: Bailiff to Red Cross, Reduction of Food Rations, 7 May 1943

The Bailiff's Chambers
Royal Court House
Guernsey
7th May, 1943

The Secretary-General
Committee of the International Red Cross Organisation
Geneva
SWITZERLAND

Dear Sir,

Owing to the War our food position in this Island has become so perilous that I feel the time has come when it is my duty as Civil Head of the Bailiwick of Guernsey to appeal to your Organisation for help.

As you are doubtless aware, these Islands were occupied by the German Forces in 1940. Since then we have existed on what we have been able to produce locally, supplemented by various imports from France. But even on these rations the health of the people in deteriorating and local medical opinion greatly fears for the future.

Notwithstanding the inadequacy of these rations, our bread ration has now been reduced by German order to:–

Heavy Working Males, over 21 years of age	4 lbs 12 ozs	2154.6 grams
Heavy Working Males, under 21 years of age	6 lbs 0 ozs	2721.6 grams
Heavy Working Females, over 21 years of age	4 lbs 4 ozs	1927.8 grams
Heavy Working Females, under 21 years of age	5 lbs 4 ozs	2381.4 grams
Children, over 10 and under 21 years of age	4 lbs 8 ozs	2041.2 grams
Children, under 10 years of age	3 lbs 0 ozs	1360.8 grams
Children under 18 months	1 lb 8 ozs	680.4 grams
All other consumers over 21 years of age	3 lbs 12 ozs	1701.0 grams

We estimate that to make good the reduced rations for the next six months we should require 200 tons of flour and 1 ton of cheese. There are many other commodities which we should greatly appreciate, but I have only asked for what would be required to replace the rations by which we shall be reduced under the new German Order.

We have greatly appreciated the medical supplies which you have sent us in the past and your action in sending parcels to those of our inhabitants who have been evacuated to Germany. I sincerely trust that you will be able to help us in our present distress.

Apart altogether from the questions raised by the above-mentioned German Order, we regard the establishment of personal contact with your Organisation as so essential that we would urge you to arrange for one of your representatives to visit Guernsey to investigate our position. While such a visit would have obvious advantages over any other course of action, should this prove impracticable we are prepared – should the German permission be forthcoming – to send a delegation to Geneva to lay all the relevant facts before you.

In order that you may appreciate the gravity of our position, I might add that our present civilian population exceeds 23,000 persons.

Thanking you in anticipation,

I remain,

Yours faithfully
(signed) VICTOR G. CAREY
Bailiff of the Island of Guernsey
and its Dependencies

Item 29: Rumball to Leale: Currency Transfer, 7 May 1943

Etats de Guernesey
G.M. Vaudin
2, Rue Lecampion
Granville

Jurat Leale
President
Controlling Committee of the States of Guernsey
Hirzel House
Guernsey

Dear Jurat Leale

I have just returned from a visit to the Office des Changes where I discussed the question of the mark transfers from the Islands.

I enclose a copy of a letter they have written me in this connection, from which you will see they have received permission from the Ministère de l'Economie Nationale et des Finances to allow these transfers to continue by credit through the clearing.

The practical effect of this manner of procedure will be that all sums I receive arising from mark transfers will have to be paid to the Société Générale, Granville, who will transfer them to the Office des Changes. The Office des Changes in their turn will credit the Islands with the sterling equivalent via Barclays Bank Ltd, less of course their commission.

You will appreciate that this transfer to the Island of all francs I receive will leave me without funds, and I spoke about this point to the Office des Changes who informed me that transfers must now be made by you to me via the Clearing.

I should be glad if you would therefore pay Barclays Bank the equivalent of 20,000,000 Francs (twenty million francs) for the credit of the States of Guernsey at the Société Générale, Granville. As soon as I receive advice that this money is to hand, I will credit you with the surplus francs I have in hand.

I have just received a transfer of Fr. 15,000.000.– via the Feldkasse, and I will hope to be able to send the whole of this back as soon as I receive your transfer. If the transfer is delayed, however, I may be forced to use part of the funds to carry on, in which case, of course, I would return the balance only.

I still have about Frs. 2.000.000.– in the bank account on which I can draw, but as you will see from the letter of the Office des Changes, Société Générale has instructions to transfer any sums received from now direct to the Office for transfer back to the Islands. The result of this is that I am obliged to retain the transfers now received in cash in the till and I shall have to revert to settling accounts in cash money when my free bank balance is exhausted. I should be glad therefore if you make the transfer as soon as possible.

This concludes my negotiations with the Office des Changes on the major questions concerning the Clearing, and as they have imposed no limit on the quantity of marks which can be transferred back to you, you will be able to receive sterling credit for all you can send.

Kindly advise me when the deposit with Barclays has been made so that I can hurry up the credit from the Office des Changes.

I suggest we make future transfers via Mr Ereaut as you have already suggested, and if you are still in agreement, will you kindly write Mr Ereaut, informing him of the arrangement. I will then make further demands for transfer of funds from him sending you of course a copy of the letter.

With kind regards,
Yours sincerely, W.N. Rumball

Office des Changes
Service de la Compensation
8, rue de la Tour des Dames, Paris, 9eme
Paris, le 1er Mai, 1943

Monsieur Rumball
Representant des Etats de Jersey et de Guernesey
2, rue Le Campion, Granville (Manche)

Objet: Iles Anglo-Normandes. Application du protocole du 13 Octobre, 1942

Ref: Vos lettres des 15.25 et 30 Mars 1943; Ma lettre du 2 Avril 1943

Monsieur
Comme suite à nos lettres respectives citées en référence, et relatives à la question des versements qui vous sont faits par les soins des autorités d'occupation à Granville au titre des échanges de billets-reichsmarks contre francs, j'ai l'honneur de vous faire connaître que le Ministère de l'Economie Nationale et des Finances, Direction du Trésor, a decidé d'autoriser le transfert des avoirs en cause, de France vers les Iles, par la voie du clearing.

En conséquence, j'avise par même courrier l'agence de Granville de la Société Générale de la levée des mesures de blocage concernant le compte special sur lequel elle a dû inscrire les remises de l'espèce.

Ainsi que je le lui précise, elle pourra désormais porter les versements de cet ordre que vous lui ferez au crédit du compte général ouvert sur ses livres au nom des Etats de Jersey et de Guernesey et débiter ensuite ce dernier de ces mêmes montants par le crédit du compte ouvert à la Banque de Francs, Paris, au nom de l'Office des Changes, en vue du transfert envisagé.

Je vous serais obligé, en conséquence, de donner à la Société Générale les instructions nécessaires pour qu'elle effectue à l'Office le versement des sommes de Frs. 6.000.000 et Frs. 10.000.000 visées dans vos lettres des 15 et 25 Mars citées en référence, que mes services transfèrent à la Barclays Bank, par le clearing, sous déduction de la taxe habituelle de 3%.

Veuillez agréer, Monsieur, l'Expression de ma considération distinguées.
Le Chef du Service de la Compensation.

Item 30: Leale to F.K.: G.U.B. Concerns, 22 May 1943

The Controlling Committee of the States of Guernsey,
Hirzel House, Guernsey
22nd May 1943

Feldkommandantur 515
Nebenstelle Guernsey

Sir,

I am enclosing a letter from the President of the Glasshouse Utilisation Board which raises very serious concerns.

As you will remember an attempt was made some time age to make the glasshouse industry remunerative. The foundation of the scheme was the export of tomatoes at prices which would enable private growers to operate.

The new prices offered by Mr Chatam are so low that they will throw the industry into a state of chaos. Unless we take some immediate steps private growers will be unable to continue and the States will once more have to shoulder the burden for a very large area under glass.

Having studied the question carefully we have come to the conclusion that the only way to save the situation is to offer an immediate subsidy on beans and potatoes as outlined in Mr Dorey's letter. Some of the growers should then have a reasonable chance of meeting their expenses. If we delay, however, the time for planting beans will have passed.

Recent events, moreover, have given a clear indication of the precarious nature of sea transport to and from this island and so have emphasised the urgency of our growing more food for ourselves.

We feel therefore that we have no option but to ask you to inform Mr Chatam that the number of chips he will receive under this new price list will, especially later in the season, be greatly reduced.

Mr Dorey's letter also reveals the difficulties in getting the private growers supplies on the market. The difficulty is largely economic. The grower, faced with big risks and difficulties of transport, takes every opportunity that offers of increasing his receipts quickly. When the properties were returned to private ownership last autumn we visualised that the G.U.B. would function with about 500-600 vergées. Growers, however, shouldered their responsibilities well and this did not materialise. Because we have far better control over our own produce we consider it essential that the G.U.B. should return to 500-600 vergées and propose shortly to invite those private growers who desire to do so to hand back their properties to us.

You will appreciate that the Glasshouse industry has proved a most difficult problem during the whole occupation. In peace time it grew up as an export trade. When this fails there is no escape from States intervention and help. That was true at the time of the Occupation. Mr Chatam's prices make it true today.

In view of the extreme urgency of the matter we would press for a decision in the very near future and are ready if necessary, to discuss any points we have raised.

Yours faithfully,
John Leale, President.

The Controlling Committee of the States of Guernsey
Hirzel House, Guernsey
May 13th, 1943

The President
The Controlling Committe of the States of Guernsey

Dear Sir,

The glasshouses in the Island, with the exception of 300 vergées, have been under Private control for a period of six months, and I submit herewith the following report which I trust will be of interest:–

One of the main reasons why it was thought necessary for greenhouses to revert to private control was the avoidance of the loss made by the G.U.B. but I find that in a large number of cases this loss, or a considerable portion of it, will have to be borne by the private growers.

I am being told continually by private growers that they are unable to make their glasshouse properties pay, and I am anticipating that the G.U.B. will be asked to again take control in the near future, of quite a considerable number of glasshouse properties.

The growing of vegetables under glass is very precarious, crops in many instances do not come up to expectations and, again, often it is impossible to obtain maximum prices. Further, very severe losses are being sustained by thieving. One very regrettable feature is that during periods of scarcity, the population of the town is not supplied with vegetables as well as it should be as, owing to lack of transport facilities, growers dispose of their produce as far as possible to:–

1. Country shops
2. Private persons and employees
3. O.T. and Military
4. Timmer Ltd.

It is with the utmost difficulty that growers are maintaining their properties in a satisfactory state of cultivation and this again is partly due to finance, as they are relcutant to engage extra hands even when obtainable, they actually cannot afford to pay for what can be termed a sufficiency of labour.

I feel that I must inform you that I have had to bring considerable pressure to bear on growers to plant the prescribed area in tomatoes.

With regard to the tomato crop, the growers, generally speaking, have been reluctant to plant such a large area, their main objections being the amount of labour necessary for the production of this crop, which is at least one-third more than for other vegetable crops; also fear of this crop being unremunerative and, further, the extra labour and time which will be necessary for the conveyance, by truck or wheelbarrow, of the tomatoes from their glasshouse properties to the various receiving depôts.

This situation has been aggravated by the recent cut in the bread ration, as growers inform me that their workmen will not be able to stand up to heavy work and especially overtime, as overtime is certainly going to be necessary if the tomato crop is to be looked after and harvested.

During 1942, under the administration of Dr Brosch, the question as to whether the glasshouse industry could be placed on a sound financial basis was frequently discussed and I informed Dr Brosch that this might be possible if tomatoes were grown in sufficient quantity and exported at remunerative prices, and the price I asked for was 6d. per 1 lb or 1/1.2d per kilo.

During 1943, several interviews have taken place between Inspector Oser, Mr H.R. Bichard and myself relative to tomato prices and on March 13th, the following prices were tenantively agreed upon:–

	First quality			Second quality		
	per kilo P.F.G.S.	per chip of 12 lbs (s.d.)	per chip of 12 lbs nett (s.d.)	per kilo P.F.G.S.	per chip of 12 lbs (s.d.)	per chip of 12 lbs nett (s.d.)
To July 15th	50	5/9¼	4/5¼	40	4/7½	3/3½
July 16th – 31st	44	3/1¼	3/9½	55	4/0¾	2/5¾
Aug 1st – 20th	39	4/6	3/2	30	3/5½	2/1½
Aug 21st to end season	32	3/8½	2/4½	24	2/9¼	1/5¼

On April 13th, a meeting took place at the Feldkommandantur, at which Mr Chatam was present and arrangements were gone into in respect of shipping, empties, etc. No alteration in price was made at that meeting other than Mr Chatam informed me that he would not be able to accept tomatoes after September 3rd, but he was taking the suggested price-list to Paris for confirmation by the German Authorities.

At an interview on the 14th May at the Feldkommandantur, between Inspector Oser, Mr H.R. Bichard and myself, I was informed that the prices Mr Chatam would pay for tomatoes would be as follows:–

	First quality			Second quality		
	per kilo P.F.G.S.	per chip of 12 lbs (s.d.)	per chip of 12 lbs nett (s.d.)	per kilo P.F.G.S.	per chip of 12 lbs (s.d.)	per chip of 12 lbs nett. (s.d.)
To July 15th	50	5/9¼	4/5¼	40	4/7½	3/3½
July 16th – 31st	35	4/0¾	2/8¾	27	2/6¾	1/4¾
Aug 1st – 10th	25	2/10¾	1/6¾	20	2/3¾	11¾
Aug 11th to end season	20	2/3¾	11¾	12	1/4½	½

These new prices are a very considerable reduction from those given me previously and are quite unremunerative.

I calculate that there are approximately 850 vergées under glass planted in tomatoes and, should this area produce 4945 tons, this leaves a net sum to the growers of £100,000, whereas the previously arranged prices left a net amount to the growers of £154,000, this resulting in a reduction of £45,000 or £53 per vergée.

I have no hestiation whatever in stating that growers cannot possibly meet their expenditure with these prices.

The whole question of the glasshouse industry has been very carefully considered by myself and my colleagues who comprise the glasshouse Board and we are by no means satisfied that we are yet on the right lines, and our unanimous conclusion is that the best solution would be a States subsidy on two main crops which could be disposed of in Guernsey, i.e. Potatoes and Beans, and the details of the proposal are roughly as follows:–

> To plant 600 vergées of Early Potatoes, under glass, which should produce 900 tons. If this could not all be absorbed in Guernsey, no doubt a portion could be disposed of in Jersey or in other directions, as these potatoes mature at an earlier date than the outdoor.
>
> To plant 500 vergées of Early Beans and 600 vergées of Late Beans, to follow the potatoes.
>
> These 1100 vergées of Beans should produce about 275 tons, and these beans to be dried and would constitute a valuable winter food for the community.

A subsidy of 1d per 1 lb on Potatoes and 1/6d per 1 lb on Beans would cost the States say £50,000, but this would be, in my opinion, preferable to aiding the growers financially, when there is no prospect of recovery.

This proposed subsidy to commence to operate during the latter half of 1943, and to be paid on dried beans harvested during the latter half of this year, and also on any potatoes planted in glasshouses from next June onward, the crop from which would be harvested next October, November, December.

There are about 1800 vergées of glass in the Island cropped either by Private growers or the G.U.B. If 1100 vergées are utilised for Beans and Potatoes, this leaves 700 vergées for vegetable and fruit crops. The produce from the 700 vergées will be augmented by the proportion which can be double-cropped.

I consider that the effect of the G.U.B. taking over properties of private growers who are unable to continue working same through lack of finance or other valid reasons, would result in our having under G.U.B. control something like 500 to 600 vergées.

In this connection, may I point out that one advantage of States control of greenhouses is that the public do get what is grown, whereas, under private control, it is most difficult to trace what becomes of the produce; it certainly in many instances does not find its way into the shops.

Yours faithfully,
PERCY DOREY
President

Item 31: Meeting with F.K.: Requisition of Food Store, 26 May 1943

Memorandum of a Meeting held at Grange Lodge
on Wednesday, 26th May, 1943

Present:

Rev John Leale	President, Controlling Committee of the States of Guernsey
Mr J.H. Loveridge	Secretary to the Essential Commodities Committee
Major Kratzer	
Inspector Zachau	
Mr L.A. Guillemette	Secretary to the President of the Controlling Committee

Subject: Requisition of Store at St George's Esplanade used by the Essential
Commodities Committee and belonging to Messrs P.B. Young & Co Ltd

Mr Leale explained that the Guernsey representatives had called at Grange Lodge to ask for the help of the Feldkommandantur in stopping the requisition of Young's Store. He said that it was the main store for food under the Essential Commodities Committee's control, and that, in view of the fact that the German Authorities had already taken practically every available store in the Island, the matter was extremely serious for us.

Major Kratzer said that the store had been promised to the German Authorities in his absence but that St George's Hall was offered to us in return.

Mr Leale said that St George's Hall was certainly bigger than Young's Store, but that it was not a store but a skating rink with many entrances, making it particularly liable to pilferage. In addition it was not vermin proof, and being built of wood and bordered on two sides by a timber yard, there was constant danger of fire. The recent German Order in the newspapers made it clear that, from the German point of view, the risk of fire had increased considerably recently.

Major Kratzer said he was very sorry but the ruling had been made, and Young's store would have to be vacated.

Mr Leale said that in that case he was forced to appeal on grounds of International Law. He quoted the Article from the Hague Convention which states "requisitions ... shall be in proportion to the resources of the Country," and he claimed that in view of the fact that the German Authorities intended taking the last store suitable to our needs, their requisition was definitely out of proportion to the Island's resources.

Major Kratzer said that the reason for vacating St George's Hall was that if Young's store was taken instead there would be a saving in the number of guards necessary for the protection of the food supplies.

Mr Leale stated that in that case it appeared to be a military convenience rather than a military necessity which was the cause of the proposed transfer, and he doubted whether in that case they had any right to requisition at all.

Major Kratzer replied that it was necessary to save men everywhere and that the Occupying Forces could requisition what they wanted and had the right to decide themselves what consistuted military necessity.

Mr Leale reiterated that they only had a right to requisition in proportion to the Country.

Major Kratzer said that obviously the Occupying Forces would take the better building for themselves, and he suggested that if the Island were occupied by British Forces, they would do likewise.

Mr Leale claimed that that was not an answer to his contention, and Major Kratzer replied that the decision had been taken and that the transfer would be made.

Mr Leale said that he assumed that he was expected to give away the rights of the Guernsey population under International Law, and the reply was that he need not give his consent since the transfer was ordered by the Occupying Authorities and not by him.

Mr Leale said he must consider what else he could do and that he would certainly put his protest in writing.

Major Kratzer said that he was ready to place Mr Leale's appeal before the Feldkommandant if Mr Leale so desired.

Mr Leale said that he was giving notice of appeal, and asked that the Order be suspended until the result of such an appeal had been made known to him.

Major Kratzer said that International Law did not apply but that he would agree to suspend the Order for the time being if the work of emptying St George's Hall had not proceeded too far. He undertook to get in touch with the German Authorities concerned immediately, and, whether the work could be stopped or not, to forward the Controlling Committee's protest to the Feldkommandant at the earliest possible date.

Item 32: Leale to F.K.: Requisition of Food Store, 26 May 1943

The Controlling Committee of the States of Guernsey
Hirzel House, Guernsey
26th May, 1943

Feldkommandantur 515
Nebenstelle, Guernsey

Sir

Following our interview this morning regarding the proposed requisition of Young's Store, Esplanade.

We hold in this store a variety of goods, chiefly flour, sugar, pulses and farinaceous foods (including security stocks) held by the Essential Commodities Committee. The average stock is about two hundred and fifty tons.

A food store must be adequately protected against thefts, particularly in view of what is happening in this Island just now, it must as far as possible be fire-proof particularly in view of our being warned to take every precaution in regard to air-raids, and it must be vermin proof.

You suggest we move our goods to St George's Hall. This property, built originally as a roller skating rink, has many entrances which render it liable to pilferage; it is a building which might easily catch fire and adjoins a timber yard, and it is not vermin proof, and therefore entirely unsuitable for the purpose of holding our stocks.

I appeal against this requisition on the grounds that we have no store which could replace Young's: Article 52 of the Hague Convention reads "Requisitions ... shall be in proportion to the resources of the Country". Mr Guillemette reported to me that on Wednesday afternoon you agreed not to requisition Young's Store if we could find a suitable store for you for flour only. Nothing which was or could be made available met your requirements. This fact fully justifies our argument that in this further requisition you are making a demand which is beyond our resources. It will leave us without adequate means of holding securely stocks of foodstuffs for the civilian population. It is therefore a contravention of International Law.

Yours faithfully
John Leale
President

Item 33: Knackfuss to Bailiff: Requisition of Food Store, 1 Jun 1943

<u>Translation</u>

Feldkommandantur 515
Mil Verw. Gr.
Jersey 1.6.43

To: The Bailiff of Guernsey, St Peter Port
Through Nebenstelle Guernsey Ger F.K. 515

<u>Re: Handing over of the civilian "Young's Stores" to the Troops.
       (Your letter of 29.5.43)</u>

The States' food stores "Young's Stores" are to be immediately handed over to the troops and cleared. The skating rink hitherto used by the troops is placed at your disposal as a substitute.

Young's Stores are situated in the immediate neighbourhood of the other stores of the Verpflegungsausgabestelle and directly connected to the latter. The flour can be properly handled and stored there. The new stores effect a saving in store-keeping and watching personnel, and also in petrol due to shorter carting distance. Young's Stores are therefore better suited than any other for the storage and distribution of food to the troops. The other stores visited do not in any way fulfill these requirements.

On the other hand, the State's objections cannot be taken into consideration. As the skating rink in St George's Hall has up to now been found adequate for the troops, it should also meet the requirements of the States. The defects mentioned can be remedied, or else put up with, as hitherto done by the troops.

The appeal to Art. 52 and the alleged infringement of international law do not apply under the circumstances and are rejected. The resources of the country are in no way exhasuted by this exchange. On putting forward the above final motives, preference must be given to the requirements of the occupying force.

The Feldkommandant
Knackfuss
Oberst.

Item 34: Memo: Soldiers' Cemetery, Fort George, 6 Jul 1943

<u>Transfer of British Graves – Soldiers' Cemetery, Fort George, Guernsey</u>

On May 26th, 1942, the question of the transfer of certain British graves at the Soldiers' Cemetery at Fort George was raised by the Feldkommandantur and was turned down by the Bailiff and the Controlling Committee of the States of Guernsey.

The subject was re-opened with me by the Feldkommandantur towards the end of May, 1943, the reason given being lack of space now that so many Germans had been buried in this cemetery. They explained that they wished to have their soldiers buried together and that it would be better for all British graves to be grouped likewise.

I explained that the cemetery did not belong to the States of Guernsey but to the British Government War Office Department and that it was doubtful whether even the Bailiff (as Lieutenant Governor) had power to make any changes therein.

They said that of course they could make transfers themselves, but that they thought it would be better for us to supervise and perform the work.

I said that I would place the matter before the Bailiff, and as a result of my report it was decided that the Bailiff and the Dean of Guernsey, with Feldkommandantur officials, should pay a visit to the cemetery before taking any final decision.

On Tuesday, 1st June, I accompanied the Bailiff, the Dean and Feldkommandantur officials to the cemetery, and we were shown the graves which they wished to transfer.

At least three quarters of the cemetery is now occupied by German graves, and the result of the moving of the graves concerned would be that one more terrace would be made available to the Germans.

It appeared to us to be doubtful whether room could be found in terraces containing only British graves for the eight graves which were required to be transferred, and the German Authorities were therefore informed that the work would be done provided that it did not mean the crowding of the British graves to suit German convenience.

The view taken by the Island representatives is that it will probably be more satisfactory to the British Government for the transfer to be made reverently by English people rather than by the Germans themselves and that the division of the cemetery into two distinct sections – one British and one German – would meet the wishes of the War Office.

The supervision of the work of transference was given to the firm of Lovell & Co, and on the 3rd June, 1943, I went to the cemetery, accompanied by Mr W.D.M. Lovell, Mr E. Bourgaize (Registrar of the Ecclesiastical Court), Mr Renouf (of the Foulon Cemetery) and a representative of the firm L. Fevrier (Stonemasons). After careful measurement it was decided that it would be possible to make the necessary transfers without crowding.

The work was put in hand and was finished by Tuesday, 6th July, when the Very Rev, the Dean of Guernsey conducted a religious ceremony at the transferred graves. The service was attended by the Bailiff, Mr W.D.M. Lovell and Mr E. Bourgaize.

A Faculty was obtained from the Ecclesiastical Court granting permission for the transfer to be made, and it was decided that the cost of transfer and formalities should be charged to H.M. Receiver General on behalf of the Crown.

(signed) L.A. Guillemette
Secretary to the President of the Controlling
Committee of the States of Guernsey

Hirzel House
Guernsey, 6th July 1943.

Item 35: Meeting with F.K.: Escape, 18 Aug 1943

<u>Memorandum of Meeting held at Grange Lodge on the 18th August, 1943</u>

Present:

Rev John Leale	President, Controlling Committee of the States of Guernsey
Mr J.E.L. Martel	Deputy Attorney General
Major Kratzer	
Mr L.A. Guillemette	Secretary to the President of the Controlling Committee

<u>Subject: Measures to be taken as a result of the flight from the Island of certain Guernsey people</u>

Mr Leale stated that in September, 1940, a similar incident took place. Mr Sherwill, who was then President of the Controlling Committee, issued a notice in the local newspapers, the third and fourth paragraphs of which read as follows:–

> Any further such departures or attempts thereat can only result in further restrictions. In other words, any persons who manage to get away do so at the expense of those left behind. In these circumstances, to get away, or attempt to get away is a crime against the local population, quite apart from the fact that the German authorities will deal very severely with persons who are caught making the attempt.
> In the event of a repetition of any such incident there is a grave possibility that, by way of reprisal, the male population of this island will be evacuated to France.

Major Kratzer said he remembered the incident. Mr Leale continued that Mr Sherwill's words were perfectly clear. Since then much had happened in the Island, but the behaviour of the population had been good under very trying conditions.

Major Kratzer said he appreciated this fact, and added that the Occupying Forces had also done their best to make the occupation as easy as possible. The measures which had caused hardship to the population had had to be introduced for military reasons.

Mr Leale then said he would like an assurance that, in deciding on the measures to be taken in the case under review, the good behaviour of the population would be fully taken into account.

Major Kratzer said that the measures to be taken were designed to avoid similar occurrences. They would be:

1. Cessation of fishing for the time being.
2. Prohibition of beaches to all civilians except those civilians holding permits for the collection of seaweed.

The reason why this latter had been decided upon was that some of the party who left the island last week end had mixed with bathers on the beaches, and were thus helped in leaving unobserved by German guards. Major Kratzer continued that notices would be issued in the local newspapers making these measures known to the public. He hoped that fishing from boats would be allowed later under stricter control and after the issue of new permits. Probably new permits would be issued only to reliable professional fishermen without relatives in England. Relatives in this case are to be regarded as children, parents and wives. He was of opinion that these measures could be regarded as mild ones, and he hoped there would be no further cases of attempted escape.

Mr Leale said that what Mr Sherwill had said in 1940 was still the official view and that it was also the view of all responsible people in the Island.

Major Kratzer asked whether the local representatives thought it advisable to reprint Mr Sherwill's notice with a short introductory sentence to precede it. He stressed that the decision to republish this notice was a matter for the local Government.

The notices regarding the measures which are to be taken read as follows:–

> Guernsey, 18th August, 1943
> Taking effect from the day of publication all civilians are forbidden to set foot on the beaches of the Island of Guernsey. This revokes all permits given either generally or personally for bathing and for fishing from the shore.
> Permits for the gathering of seaweed remain valid.
>
> der Feldkommandant
gez Knackfuss
Oberst

> Guernsey, 19th August, 1943
> All authorisations issued for fishing in the areas of Guernsey and Sark are hereby withdrawn. Any permits granted on such authorisations as well as personal permits are now declared invalid and must be returned to the Hafenueberwachungstelle, St Peter Port (House "Chez Nous") by the 21st August, 1943.
> Applications for new permits should be addressed to the Hafenueberwachungstelle, St Peter Port.
>
> der Feldkommandant
gez Knackfuss
Oberst

(signed) L.A. Guillemette
Secretary to the President of the
Controlling Committee

Item 36: Meeting with F.K.: Storage of Photo Apparatus, 22 Oct 1943

<u>Memorandum of Meeting held at Grange Lodge on Friday October 22nd, 1943</u>

Present:

The Bailiff	
J.E.L. Martel, Esq.	Acting Attorney General
Postmaster	
Major Kratzer	
Kriegsverwaltungsrat Melzer	
Mr L.A. Guillemette	Secretary to President of the Controlling Committee

<u>Subject: Storage of Photographic Apparatus confiscated June 1942</u>

Major Kratzer explained the present situation regarding the photographic apparatus in question. He said that the present store at Victoria Road Chapel had been found unsuitable owing to dampness etc, and that he had received orders from Colonel Knackfuss that the apparatus had to be handed over to the States who would be held responsible for it, as had been done in Jersey. He asked whether the Bailiff had any objection to this being done, and referred to the Bailiff's letter to him of the 19th instant on the subject. He said that of course the present condition of the apparatus would be taken into consideration when it was handed over to the States, and that the States would not be held responsible for any damage done before such handing over. Experience had shown them that the cameras must be examined from time to time. Legally, the apparatus was still the property of the owners.

Mr Martel said that if the States had to store the apparatus, they could not assume responsibility for any thieving taking place. Major Kratzer said that the States would only handle the matter on behalf of the Feldkommandantur and would be held responsible only if negligence on their part was proved. Mr Martel asked whether, in the opinion of the Feldkommandantur, it would not be better for them to retain custody of the apparatus themselves, and appoint a civilian to keep the apparatus in good condition. He thought it seemed unfair to ask the States to undertake responsibility for war material requisitioned by the Occupying Forces. Major Kratzer said that the apparatus was not to be regarded as war material, it was only collected to prevent espionage. He thought, personally, that Mr Martel's suggestion was a good one and he would place it before the Colonel for his approval.

Kriegsverwaltungerat Melzer asked what were the States reasons for not wishing to undertake responsibility for the apparatus.

Mr Martel said that they were:–

1. That the States did not wish to take responsibility for the safety of the apparatus.
2. That in some cases where deterioration had already set in, it would probably be impossible, whatever was done, to stop it at this stage.

The Bailiff expressed the opinion that the requisitioning came under Article 53 of the Hague Convention. The Major said that even if that was so, although he did not agree with the Bailiff's contention, it would still be within the power of the Feldkommandantur to require the States to take responsibility for the apparatus. The Guernsey representatives claimed that the Feldkommandantur could only give this order if they admitted their responsibility for the payment of indemnity at the end of the war. The Major agreed that the occupying power must pay all deterioration, and the reason for asking the States to take over the apparatus was a practical one, namely, to stop further deterioration and was in no way an attempt to be unfair to the local administration.

It was decided that when the change of store was completed (the transfer being commenced today), the keys of the new store would be held by the Feldkommandantur, pending the decision of the Colonel on the whole matter.

Copy forwarded to:–
The Bailiff
Mr J.E.L. Martel
Mr. John Leale
Mr L.A. Guillemette

Item 37: Meeting with F.K.: New Postage Stamps, 22 Oct 1943

<u>Memorandum of Meeting held at Grange Lodge on Friday October 22nd, 1943</u>

Present:

The Bailiff	
J.E.L. Martel, Esq.	Acting Attorney General
Postmaster	
Major Kratzer	
Kriegsverwaltungsrat Melzer	
Mr L.A. Guillemette	Secretary to President of the Controlling Committee

<u>Subject: Issue of new Postage Stamps to help Island Social Welfare</u>

1. Major Kratzer said that the suggestion had been made to the Feldkommandantur that a new Postage Stamp be issued – probably a 2½d stamp – and that it be sold at 5d; the additional 2½d to be handed to some central organisation for us in social welfare. He stressed that it was not his own idea, but added that he thought it well worth examination. Buyers of stamps would be probably mainly Germans, and the result of the measure would therefore be a contribution from the German Reich to Island Social Welfare.

2. The Guernsey representatives acknowledged that social welfare was an excellent cause for which money should be collected. Their reasons against the suggestions under discussion, however, were:–

   a. It is against the recognised policy of the British Post Office, and therefore neither the Guernsey Postmaster nor the Bailiff (as Crown Official) has authority to sanction its operation.

   b. The financial position of island charities in general seems to indicate that such a measure is unnecessary at present.

   c. The fact that buyers of stamps would be largely Germans means that the balance to the credit of the States in Barclays Bank, Jersey, would rise. It remained to be seen what value this credit would be after the war.

3. Major Kratzer, during the conversation, said that as the Bailiff had already sanctioned the issue of 1d and ½d stamps he could also sanction the suggestion under discussion. It was explained that if these stamps had not been issued the postal service would have been severely hampered, if not stopped altogether. There was no such necessity evident with the present suggestion.

4. Major Kratzer asked whether the Bailiff objected to giving the necessary instructions to the Post Office. The Bailiff explained again that he did not possess the power, and the Major said that the Feldkommandantur did not wish to give the instructions themselves.

5. Major Kratzer thought that the Postmaster should welcome a 2½d stamp, especially as this was the normal charge for postage. The Postmaster said that when the Bailiff applied for the issue of 1d and ½d stamps, the

Feldkommandantur had stipulated that stamps should only be issued when absolutely necessary, as it was possible to buy smaller denomination stamps to the value of 2½d he had regarded the issue of a 2½d stamp as unlikely to be favoured by the Feldkommandantur. He added that in practice the number of letters requiring a 2½d stamp was a relatively small proportion of the total posted.

6. Major Kratzer said that Mr Blaikie-Webster had informed him that the "Star" Help-the-Children Fund was in urgent need of money. The Guernsey representatives gathered that the suggestion for a new stamp issue came from Mr Webster. Mr Webster also wished to start new communal kitchens, at which no charge would be made for meals. Mr Webster also felt that his efforts were entirely disregarded by the local administration.

The Guernsey representatives pointed out that communal kitchens were already operating in the island, and that although the charges for meals were extremely low, the kitchens were not generally patronised very well. The Bailiff said that he personally kept in close touch with the communal kitchens and was not aware of the necessity for new ones. Regarding Mr Webster's general attitude, the Bailiff said that he was disinclined to disregard the efforts of all other charitable organisations, and therefore there was some overlapping.

7. The Bailiff agreed to see Mr Webster and to discuss his difficulties with him.

8. The matter of the issue of the new stamp was not discussed further.

Item 38: Meeting with F.K.: Reduction in Food Rations, 26 Oct 1943

<u>Elaboration of discussion at meeting held at Grange
Lodge on Tuesday, 26th October, 1943</u>

<u>Subject:– Reduction in Rations – Civilian Population</u>

Mr Leale said that the Controlling Committee viewed most seriously the Feldkom-mandantur's letter of the 19th October, 1943 and he wished to place before Major Kratzer the position as viewed by the Committee.

The Major said that he had received very definite instructions from Jersey on the matter.

Mr Leale continued that, with winter coming, the Controlling Committee were worried over the position regarding rationed foods. The meat ration is only half the present French ration and half what we were receiving last winter. In addition we had received no cheese for several months and the short deliveries on our quota of farinaceous foods had been cancelled by the French Authorities.

The Major replied that shortages on quotas occurred in France as here and were due to bad French organisation and to the British blockade.

Mr Leale continued that the Feldkommandantur claimed that we receive too much fat. In making such a statement they should also say that we get too little meat, cheese, etc. Here the September rations were quoted and the Major agreed that the position was serious, but claimed that a three months' reserve must be kept. It was explained to him that, as the Island produces its own butter fat, there is no need to keep a three months' security stock, since possible stoppage of shipping is the reason for making such a reserve of imported goods.

The Major said that the reserve stock of butter had to be kept for military reasons. In the event of a blockade, animals would have to be slaughtered and therefore milk and butter production would fall.

Mr Leale claimed that we could continue to produce sufficient butter even with a smaller number of cows and said that if we were expected to keep a 3 months reserve of butter we should keep 12 months' reserve of flour.

The Major said that he was willing to submit the Controlling Committee's suggestions to Jersey and stressed that the instructions had been given for the good of the civilian population.

Mr Leale claimed that the civilian population would not benefit if too great a reserve were kept at the expense of current consumption. He suggested that the ration be kept at its present figure until the end of the year, meanwhile the Controlling Committee would keep the matter under careful review.

Item 39: Kratzer to Bailiff: De Saumarez Monument, 24 Nov 1943

Nebenstelle Guernsey der
Feldkommandantur 515 Az.10/4
24.11.43

To: The Bailiff of Guernsey

Re: Monument in Delancey Park

Following military orders, the Monument in memory of Admiral Lord de Saumarez in Delancey Park must be removed.

The 4 bronze panels on the base of the column may be removed by the States. This however, must be done immediately. The column and base will then be removed by the troops, unless the States wish to do it themselves. In the latter case, please let me know by return.

Dr Kratzer, Major

The Bailiff's Chambers, Guernsey
November 25th, 1943

Feldkommandantur 515
Guernsey

I have read your letter of the 24th instant notifying me of the intended removal of the monument at Delancey Park erected a century ago by the people of Guernsey to the memory of Admiral Lord de Saumarez, GCB, KS, DCL.

On behalf of the people of this Island, I protest as strongly as possible against the removal of this historic monument. According to Article 56 of the Hague Rules the destruction of or damage to historic monument is strictly forbidden. Great damage would inevitable be caused to the monument by its removal.

This monument is the Island memorial to one of the greatest Guernseymen in history. During the past century it has reminded people of many nations of the career of a man who enjoyed International fame and respect during his illustrious life.

I understand that the decision to demolish this monument was taken by General von Schmettow, and it is with regret I learn that my request for an interview with him on this subject cannot be granted at present. I understand also that his representative is of opinion that no plea which I might advance to the General could cause him to alter his decision. Nevertheless I should be obliged if you would forward this my protest to the appropriate military authorities.

(signed) Victor G. Carey, Bailiff

Nebenstelle Guernsey der
Feldkommandantur 515 Az.10/4
26th November 1943

To the Bailiff of Guernsey, St Peter Port

Re: Memorial in Delancey Park (Letter of 25.11.43)

The communication handed by your secretary Mr Guillemette, stating that the States were not in a position to have the memorial in Delancey Park removed, has been duly noted. The troops will therefore blow up the column.

I have submitted your letter of the 25th inst. to the Miliary Command.

To the legal question raised by you, we have the following remarks to make: Article 56, paragraph 2, of the Hague Convention only refers to artistic or historical monuments which are irreplaceable or at least difficult to replace. This cannot be said of the Column in memory of Admiral Lord de Saumarez, at any rate after the bronze panels have been removed. Furthermore, the article refers to "intentional" destruction or damage; this is not the fact if, as in this case, there exists an urgent necessity on military grounds.

(signed) Dr Kratzer, Major.

Item 40: C.C. Meeting: Reduction of Fat Ration, 28 Dec 1943

<u>Controlling Committee: Meeting held 28th December, 1943</u>

Present:
>   Sir Abraham J. Lainé, K.C.I.E, Jurat, Vice-President in Charge
>   Dr A.N. Symons
>   Messrs R.O. Falla, Percy Dorey, J.E.L. Martel, Acting Attorney General

Also present:
>   Messrs R.E. Chilcott, Manager, States Dairy
>   R.T. Short, Secretary

<u>Butter and Cooking Fat: Reduction of ration</u>

Sir Abraham Lainé read the following letter from the Feldkommandantur 515:–

>   Re: Food Rationing, 26.12.43
>   The monthly fat ration for normal consumers is, with effect from
>   January 1st, to be brought in line with the French ration of 310
>   grammes. This ration is to be maintained until the prescribed 3
>   months' fat reserve (36 tons) had been completed.
>   The heavy workers approved by the Feldkommandantur Nebenstelle
>   are to receive, in addition to 450 grammes of meat, an extra 300
>   grammes of fat per month.
>   It is pointed out that the above fixation of fat rations are to be adopted
>   in the interest of the population.
>   Dr Kratzer, Major R.

He pointed out that, even if this letter had not been received, it would have been necessary to cut the rations of butter and cooking fat. He thought it right that a reserve should be kept to cover unforseen circumstances. He did not expect any further imports of cooking oil or margarine.

Mr Falla agreed but did not think the ration should be reduced to the level ordered by the Feldkommandantur.

Mr Chilcott said that, if a weekly ration of 4 ozs of butter and a fortnightly ration of 2 ozs of cooking fat were issued, there would be no reserve at the end of the winter. If the proportion of whole milk added to separated milk were reduced, it would be possible to increase the production of butter.

Mr Short stated that stocks of butter on the 25th December amounted to 16 tons. Production to the end of March was estimated at 28 tons. If a total ration of 4 ozs was issued weekly, the stock on the 31st March would amount to 9 tons, which might be increased by approximately 2 tons to be produced from the whole milk previously issued on medical certificates. Production during April and May would, it was expected, be sufficient to provide a 4 ozs ration, after which it should be sufficient to provide a 6 ozs ration.

Mr Dorey thought the Committee should insist on maintaining the combined ration at 4 ozs and should refuse to reduce it further.

Dr Symons agreed, but pointed out that, if the German Authorities held the President personally responsible for the refusal, the decision should be left to the President. It was agreed, however, that any letter to the Feldkommandantur should point out that the person signing it did so on behalf of the Members of the Committee.

Sir Abraham Lainé pointed out that the letter stated that the reserve should be 36 tons, but the maximum capacity of the butter cold store was from 22 to 23 tons. Storage of the balance would present a difficulty.

It was then resolved that the meeting be adjourned till 2.30 p.m.

Controlling Committee: Meeting held 28th December, 1943

Present:

Sir Abraham J. Lainé, K.C.I.E, Jurat, Vice-President in Charge
Dr A.N. Symons
Messrs R.O. Falla, Percy Dorey
J.E.L. Martel, Acting Attorney General,
R.H. Johns

The minutes of the meetings held on the 3rd, 10th and 17th December, 1943, respectively were approved.

Before proceeding to the business of the meeting, Mr L.A. Guillemette was asked to express to the President the sorrow of the members of the Committee at his indisposition and their best wishes for a speedy recovery.

Arising out of the minutes of the 17 December, Mr Martel said he thought the question of application to the International Red Cross for assistance should be pursued, and after consideration it was resolved that it be suggested to the Bailiff that he might enquire from the Feldkommandantur 515 whether anything had transpired from his appeal in May, 1943.

Butter and Cooking Fat: Reduction of Rations

Referring to the meeting held that morning, Sir Abraham Lainé read a letter, dated the 20th October, 1943, from the Agricultural Officer to the Feldkommandantur 515 and a letter, dated the 23rd October, 1943, from the Health Services Officer to the President. It was clear that, in view of the continued and rapid decline of production, the ration could not be maintained at 6 ozs weekly, but the States Dairy was confident that they could maintain the combined rations at 4 ozs weekly throughout the winter. Potato stocks would be exhausted within three weeks, and there was not a large supply of roots available. He thought the security stock of fats should be based not on consumption alone but on the difference between local production and consumption.

Mr Dorey wondered what the Feldkommandantur meant when they stated that the reduction ordered was "for the benefit of the civilian population". He did not think the Controlling Committee should take the responsibility of reducing the ration to 310 grammes monthly. It would be possible to issue a ration of 5 ozs weekly if leakages could be eliminated.

Mr Falla said that, if the ration was cut to too low a level, farmers would be tempted to make more butter. Farmers in France were more generously treated than Guernsey farmers.

Mr Johns thought that in cases of illegal sale, the buyer should also be prosecuted and fined heavily when convicted. He thought the time had come when we would be justified in obtaining secret information. In such cases the informer should be given a substantial reward to be paid by the convicted person. He thought the German Authorities should be told that we cannot accept the comparison with France as we issue separated milk in order to produce more butter. We should therefore propose reducing the ration to 4 ozs weekly for a limited period.

Mr Guillemette suggested that it should be pointed out to the Feldkommandantur that it was not in the interests of the population to reduce the ration to 310 grammes per month but that the Committee agreed to reduce the ration to 4 ozs weekly. This reduction would enable the Dairy to maintain a reserve of 10 tons during the worst period of the year.

Sir Abraham Lainé pointed out that instructions should be given to the Dairy by the 30th instant. He therefore suggested that an order reducing the ration to 4 ozs weekly be submitted for approval, together with a letter giving reasons why it was not possible to reduce it further.

After further consideration it was resolved to authorise the Essential Commodities Committee, in conjunction with the States Dairy, to make the necessary arrangements for a reduction of the consolidated fat ration from 6 ozs to 4 ozs as from the week commencing the 2nd January, 1944. It was also resolved that a draft Order giving effect to this resolution be submitted for the approval of the Feldkommandantur 515, together with an explanatory letter, to be drafted by Messrs Martel and Guillemette. It was further resolved to meet on the 29th instant at 2 pm for the purpose of approving the letter.

Item 41: C.C. Meeting: Reduction of Fat Ration, 29 Dec 1943

<u>Controlling Committee: Meeting held 29th December, 1943</u>

Present:

Sir Abraham J. Lainé, K.C.I.E, Jurat, Vice-President in Charge
Dr A.N. Symons
Messrs R.H. Johns, R.O. Falla, Percy Dorey
J.E.L. Martel, Acting Attorney General.

<u>Butter and Cooking Fat: Reduction of ration</u>

The Committee took into consideration the draft letter to the Feldkommandantur 515 regarding the reduction in butter and cooking fat rations.

After considerable discussion the draft was approved subject to the following amendments:–

Paragraph 1.	The addition after the word "thereof" of the words "and in our President's unfortunate absence owing to illness".
Paragraph 2.	Deletion of the words "are causing us deep concern at present" and the substitution therefor of the words "have been causing us the deepest concern for some time past".
Paragraph 3.	The insertion, after the word "weeks" of the words "unless additional supplies are in the meantime forthcoming".
Paragraph 4.	Deletion of the word "verbally". Deletion of the words "contend with", "although even if a quarter of the cattle population were slaughtered, we could still maintain a four ounce fat ration after the end of April" and the substitution therefor of the word "face".
Paragraph 5.	The addition of the word "temporarily" after the word "reducing". The substitution of the word "paramount" for the word "primary".
Paragraph 6.	The substition of the words "help to maintain" for the word "safeguard".
Paragraph 7.	The substitution of the word "through" for the words "indicated cases of", the insertion of the word "were" after the word "necessity" and the substitution fo the word "unreasonable" for the word "frivolous".
Paragraphs 8 & 9.	To be deleted and replaced by the words "In view of the above, we submit that the accompanying Order is a reasonable one and we hope it will meet with your approval."

Item 42: Lainé to F.K.: Reduction of Fat Ration, 29 Dec 1943

The Controlling Committee of the States of Guernsey
Hirzel House
Guernsey.
29th December 1943

Feldkommandantur 515
Nebenstelle, Guernsey

Sir

Food Rationing

Your letter of the 26th instant (Az.16/1) has been received and immediately on receipt therefor and in our President's unfortunate absence owing to illness a meeting of the Controlling Committee was convened when the matter of our food supply was fully discussed.

You are aware, from conversations on this matter and from Mr Leale's letter and enclosures of the 25th October last as well as from Mr R.O. Falla's letter of the 20th October, that certain aspects of the food supply problem have been causing us deepest concern for some time past. On our part we know from the experience of the past three years that the Feldkommandantur are also interested in the welfare of the population.

You will realise therefore that your instruction to reduce the fat ration has caused us grave anxiety especially as the next few months are the most critical from the point of view of the health of the Island and in view of the fact that the present extreme shortage of meat makes any cut in another vital food doubly serious. In addition, the ration of potatoes will, unless additional supplies are in the meantime forthcoming, end during the next two weeks and supplies of root vegetables as a substitute are far from adequate.

In your letter you state that the cut in the fat ration is in the interest of the population and we gather than the reason is because has to be made for a three month reserve to be drawn upon in case of siege. We have indicated to you that our reserves of fat are always available in our herds of live dairy cattle. In answer we have been told that it might be necessary in case of stoppage of shipping to requisition cattle for slaughter for feeding the troops. We agree therefore, that it would be injudicious to attempt to continue the present fat ration of six ounces per week while we have this possibility to face.

We have therefore considered most seriously the possibility of reducing temporarily the ration as far as possible to provide a margin of safety and to meet your wishes, remembering always that the maintenance of the health of the population in this, the most critical period of the year, must be our paramount objective.

The conclusion we have reached is that a normal fat ration of four ounces per week should to some extent help to maintain the health of the population and would also go a considerable way towards meeting your wishes.

The fact that during the past three and a half years we have done our utmost to carry out orders of the Feldkommandantur even when such orders through military necessity were opposed to the interests of the civilian population, will make it obvious to you that in our efforts to further the welfare of our population and to ease their burden we have refrained from any unreasonable opposition to the orders of the Occupying Forces.

In view of the above, we submit that the accompanying Order is a reasonable one and that it will meet with your approval.

Yours faithfully,
A.J. LAINÉ
Vice-President in Charge.

Item 43: C.C. Meeting: Reduction of Fat Ration, 30 Dec 1943

Controlling Committee: Meeting held 30th December, 1943

Present:

Sir Abraham Lainé, K.C.I.E, Jurat, Vice-President in Charge,
Dr A.N. Symons,
Messrs R.H. Johns, R.O. Falla, Percy Dorey,
J.E.L. Martel, Acting Attorney General.

The Committee again considered the draft letter to the Feldkommandantur as amended on the previous day.

After consideration, it was resolved to delete the last paragraph of the amended letter and to substitute therefor the following two paragraphs:–

> We ask you to believe that, in informing you that we do not feel justified in putting into full effect the order contained in your letter, we are continuing our policy of carrying out your orders as fully as possible, always bearing in mind the fact that the welfare of the local population is the raison d'être for this Committee.
>
> Attached thereto is a draft Order reducing the standard fat ration to four ounces per capita per week and we should be obliged if you would inform us whether it meets with your approval so that it may be published as soon as possible.

Item 44: C.C. Meeting: Reduction of Fat Ration, 31 Dec 1943

<u>Controlling Committee: Meeting held 31st December, 1943</u>

Present:

      Revd John Leale, President,

      Sir Abraham Lainé, K.C.I.E, Jurat,

      Dr A.N. Symons, Messrs R.H. Johns, R.O. Falla, Percy Dorey,

      J.E.L. Martel, Acting Attorney General.

      Also Present:

      Mr L.A. Guillemette, Secretary to President.

<u>Butter and Cooking Fat: Reduction of rations</u>

On being asked to report on an interview which he had had with Major Kratzer, of the Feldkommandantur 515, on the previous evening, Mr Guillemette said that the following translation of a letter signed by Dr Kratzer had been read to him, viz:–

<u>Re: Food Rationing, Your letter of 29.12.43</u>

The Order of 26.12.43 holds good.
With reference to the last paragraph of the above Order, I request you
to immediately draw up and submit the amended Order.

Major Kratzer had then quoted the following points:
1. The instructions of the 26th instant constituted an Order and were not the wish of the Feldkommandantur. The matter has been long debated by all the German Authorities concerned.
2. Urgent military reasons were paramount in making the Order.
3. If the Controlling Committee had reduced the ration after the Feldkommandantur's letter of the 19th October last, there would be no necessity for such a drastic reduction at present.
4. If the Controlling Committee found it impossible, for practical reasons, to reduce the ration to 310 grammes monthly, they would be permitted to increase this to an amount not exceeding 3 ounces weekly.
5. In the event of a siege, this Order would definitely work in the interests of the civilian population.
6. The sooner the Order was put into effect, the sooner would normal rations be resumed.

Major Kratzer had further added that the Order giving effect to these instructions must be published on the 31st instant. Mr Guillemette had told Major Kratzer that the Controlling Committee took a serious view of this matter and would require a certain time to discuss it. Mr Guillemette explained that he had endeavoured unsuccessfully to get into touch with Sir Abraham Lainé. He had, however, spoken to Advocate Martel, and this meeting had been arranged.

Advocate Martel thought that, if there was likely to be a question of resignation, the President should be present at the meeting. Sir Abraham Lainé said that, if it were decided to resign, the members would hand their resignation to the President, who would then have to decide whether he should hand his resignation to the Bailiff.

The President said this matter should be considered very seriously. If he handed in his resignation to the Bailiff, the latter would have to find some other person who would sign the Order. He wondered whether such a procedure would be in the interests of the Island. It was difficult to visualise what the Island would be like without this Controlling Committee. Members should remember that the Committee was acting for the States and any decision taken should be communicated to the Bailiff. He thought it might be better to issue the Order and then ask the Bailiff to ascertain privately whether the Committee still had the confidence of the States. If it was found that they had forfeited that confidence, they would have no option but to resign.

Advocate Martel pointed out that the question at issue concerned only 1 ounce of fat, and he wondered whether it would be possible to increase the amount of whole milk added to the separated milk and to increase the number of invalids who were granted a whole milk ration. He also suggested that the Feldkommandantur be asked to issue the Order which would then be carried out by the Essential Commodities Committee. If the Committee decided to issue the Order, it should be stated that it was issued on German orders.

Sir Abraham Lainé agreed with the latter suggestion. He thought that, in the event of the Committee resigning, the German Authorities would take over the butter Cold Store and control the Dairy in order to ensure an issue of only 3 ozs of fat weekly. This would cause considerable confusion.

Mr Dorey said that resignation would not be in the Island's interests, and he supported the President's suggestion. He also agreed that it would be preferable for the matter to be discussed by the States in private.

In reply to Mr Johns, Mr Guillemette said that Point No. 2 meant that, in the event of a siege, the German Authorities would slaughter a number of cattle, which would cause a reduction in milk and butter production.

After further discussion, it was resolved as follows:–

1. That the Order reducing the ration to 3 ounces weekly should be issued by the Committee under "The Additional Powers (The Bailiff and the Controlling Committee) Law, 1943".
2. That the President should write to the Feldkommandantur 515 stating that the Controlling Committee had felt that they should comply with the Order but that, if the Committee lost the confidence of the public through this action, they would be obliged to resign. They also reserved to themselves the right to take up the question with Colonel Knackfuss on his next visit to the Island.
3. That the President should send a copy of the correspondence to the Bailiff, asking him to take such steps as he thought necessary in order to ascertain whether the Committee still had the confidence of the States.

Item 45: Leale to Bailiff: Reduction of Fat Ration, 4 Jan 1944

Controlling Committee of the States of Guernsey
4th January, 1944

The Bailiff
Royal Court House
Guernsey.

Sir,

During the latter part of October, I received a letter from the German Authorities that as from November 1st the Fat Ration had to be reduced to roughly 2½ ozs a week so as to build up an Emergency stock of 36 tons. We immediately made strong representations both verbally and in the form of letters and the matter remained in abeyance until early last week when a second letter, couched in much the same terms as the first, arrived. I was unfortunately ill at the time but Sir Abraham Lainé immediately convened a meeting of the Controlling Committee who while willing to agree to a reduction to 4 ozs a week in view of the milk situation, could not agree to anything lower. A letter to this effect was sent to Grange Lodge. On Thursday evening news was received that this letter had been rejected and saying that an Order must appear in the newspaper the next day giving effect to the Feldkommandantur's demands.

The Committee was thus placed in a most unenviable position. It had either to refuse to carry out the German demands or to issue an order which in its judgement was an ounce too low. The sole concession granted was the 2½ ozs was raised to 3 ozs. Had the Committee refused to carry out the Order it must have ceased to function either by its resignation or by its dismissal (it being too optimistic to think the Occupying Forces would overlook a flat refusal). Others would have had to be found (either by the States or the Germans) to take our place and the newcomers' first duty would have to be to do what we had refused to do. Rightly or wrongly the Committee came to the conclusion that either resignation or refusal while they might savour the heroic would lead nowhere and would be detrimental to the Island's interests.

As you may well imagine this episode has caused us the greatest misgiving and we would like to feel that the States agree we took the only rational course open to us, and that neither by our failure to obtain more than the smallest concession nor by our signature have we forfeited their confidence.

Believe me Mr Bailiff we do appreciate the sympathetic understanding the States have shown us since our inception. We do not forget that we are acting for and on their behalf.

What steps you care to take to assure me that we have acted as the States would have wished us to act is, of course, for you to decide.

Yours faithfully,
JOHN LEALE
President.

Item 46: Leale to F.K.: Reduction of Fat Ration, 4 Jan 1944

Controlling Committee of the States of Guernsey
4th January, 1944

Nebenstelle Guernsey der
Feldkommandantur 515

Sir,

It is with the deepest concern that I have received your letter dated 26th December last dealing with Food Rationing. Although our views on this matter are irreconcilable there are a few points I would like to bring to your notice.

Your order that we must keep a reserve stock of 36 tons. I hesitate to comment as I have not been informed of the basis on which this figure is fixed. It seems however to assume that under siege conditions we should be able to distribute just over 4 ozs butter ration weekly but would produce none at all. I would be glad of information on this point.

Ever since the occupation we have not spared ourselves to ensure that we have received from the producers for distribution the utmost possible amount. The severe cut is going to make our task much harder. The demand for illicit supplies will inevitably increase and producers will be tempted to indulge in irregular practices. We are already making arrangements to employ more inspectors.

A further serious point is this. Our failure in this important question will make many people question our ability to discharge our duty. (It makes me question my own ability). Should it become apparent that we have lost the confidence of the States I would, of course, have only one honourable course open to me and that would be to hand my resignation to the Bailiff.

During 1943 the Bailiff wrote once to the Swiss Minister in Berlin as the Protecting Power and twice to the Red Cross at Geneva. No replies have been received. Might we have your assurance that these letters safely reached their destination.

I would ask that a copy of this letter be forwarded to Colonel Knackfuss.

Yours faithfully,
JOHN LEALE

Item 47: Kratzer to Leale: Reduction of Fat Ration, 6 Jan 1944

Nebenstelle Guernsey der
Feldkommandantur 515
6.1.1944

To the President of the Controlling Committee of the States of Guernsey

Re: Food rationing (Your letter of 4.1.44, 5/3/3)

The temporary reduction of the fat ration to 3 ozs a week proved to be unavoidable in view of the general sitation.

Your remark regarding the confidence shown to you by the States is not quite understandable to me. I readily place myself at your disposal for a personal conversation in the matter.

The risk of a falling back of milk supplies as a result of the reduction of the fat ration is not unrecognised. I request you, however, to counteract this tendence by explaining the necessity and the temporary nature of this measure, as well as by a sharper watch on the delivery of milk supplies. The better this duty is fulfilled, the sooner the necessary reserve will be built up.

The communications of the States to the Swiss Embassy in Berlin and the Red Cross in Geneva, sent on 7.5.43, have been forwarded by me. Whether they have reached their destination, I cannot ascertain from here.

I have submitted to the Feldkommandant a copy of your letter of the 4th inst.

Dr Kratzer
Major

Item 48: Meeting with F.K.: Reduction of Fat Ration, 31 Jan 1944

<u>Memorandum of Meeting Held at Grange Lodge,</u>
<u>31st January, 1944</u>

Present:

Revd. John Leale, Jurat	President of the Controlling Committee of the States of Guernsey
Major Dr Kratzer	
Mr L.A. Guillemette	Secretary to the President of the Controlling Committee.

<u>Reduction in fat ration</u>

Major Krazter said that he did not understand Mr Leale's suggestion (Mr Leale's letter of 4th January, 1944) that he might no longer enjoy the confidence of the States.

Mr Leale explained that the States, seeing that the fat ration was reduced, and assuming that a protest had been made by him to the Feldkommandantur, might think that some other person might be more successful in fighting their battles and might therefore want to change.

The Major answered that no other person would have been more successful, since it was necessary for the Feldkommandantur to order the reduction.

Mr Leale said that even if that were so, the fact that he had suffered several failures, as for instance with Children's Allowances, might cause the public to wish to put somebody else in his place.

The Major continued that regarding the reduction in the fat ration, he had no personal wish to make such a reduction unless circumances made such action necessary. The Controlling Committee should realise that if there were a siege, the population would be hungry if no food could come in and they could blame the Feldkommandantur and the Controlling Committee if a wrong decision were taken now.

Mr Leale said that the Controlling Committee did not understand this argument, since the Island is self-supporting in fat, and the Major answered that if the Island were isolated for some time, production of fat would fall off due to the slaughter of cattle to feed the troops.

Mr Leale asked why the required reserve had been fixed at 36 tons and the reply was that it was calculated on the basis of the ration and on statements made by the Essential Commodities Committee. Mr Leale asked what ration the Major referred to and he replied that he was not certain but thought something between 5 and 6 ounces per week. Mr Leale continued that he assumed therefore that during a siege the Feldkommandantur would like the population to receive 6 ounces of fat weekly. The Major said that he could not answer that question at present, but if a siege did occur, there would be a meeting at the Feldkommandantur to decide such matters.

Mr Leale reminded him that from the 36 tons reserve a ration of 4 ounces could be issued for 3 months without taking current production into consideration.

The Major thought we should be happy to have plenty of fat during a siege. The orders from higher quarters were for the production of a 3 months reserve but the siege might last as long as a year.

Mr Leale asked again what ration for the siege would be and the Major said that it could not be fixed beforehand. It depended on the success or failure of the Forces landing in France.

Mr Leale asked how many cattle per month the Major thought would be claimed for the troops. The Major did not know but thought that they would be killed to supplement the tinned meat supplies already in the Island. It was possible that the troops would supply the civilian population with some tinned meat in return for the cattle slaughters.

Mr Leale thought that the number of animals slaughtered could not make such a vital difference to the fat production since we have over 2,400 cattle in the Island and the Major answered that during fighting many animals might be killed by bullets or gas.

The question of a temporary increase in the fat ration during very cold weather was then raised by Mr Leale. The Major gave no answer at all to the question except to say that he hoped that the reserve would soon be built up and that we would then return to our normal rations.

The Bailiff's letters of May, 1943 to the Red Cross and the Protecting Power

In reply to a question from Mr Leale, the Major said that the Feldkommandantur were making enquiries to discover what had happened to these letters, for which the Bailiff had never received acknowledgement.

Mr J.E.L. Martel

Mr Leale said that at a meeting with the Major recently, he had mentioned that the introduction of new and complicated legislation would be hampered by the fact that the only Law Officer in the Island is Mr J.E.L. Martel. He was under the impression that the Major did not realise fully the seriousness of this position. Mr Martel was, in his opinion, the hardest worked man in Guernsey and if anything happened to him we should have to ask for Mr Sherwill's return. The Major said that we should not count on being granted such a request. Mr Leale compared the Guernsey and Jersey position saying that in Jersey there were two experienced Law Officers and a draftsman in addition to the Bailiff.

Item 49: Melzer to Bailiff: Occupation Costs, 8 Feb 1944

Nebenstelle Guernsey der
Feldkommandantur 515 Az. 03/10. Mlz/Kl.
8.2.44

URGENT

To the Bailiff of Guernsey

Re: Occupation Costs – Provision of troops with money

In accordance with an Order of the Chief Intendant to the Befehlshaber in Frankreich, dated 24.12.43, the provision of money for the troops is, from the 1.1.44, to be effected in the Channel Islands in such a way, that the States shall every month place the stocks of Reichskreditkassen notes in their possession – as the case may be, by withdrawing them from the Banks – at the disposal of the Feldkasse, up to the required amount. For this purpose, an account shall be opened for the Island of Guernsey with the Westminster Bank, Guernsey (Konto der Feldkasse A) into which the stocks of RKK notes shall be paid. The amounts paid will be credited as contribution to occupation costs.

By the 10.2.44, 12 o'clock noon, the Nebenstelle Guernsey is to be notified what is the total amount of RKK notes available. This amount is immediately to be paid into the "Konto der Feldkasse A", Westminster Bank, Guernsey. In future, the States shall notify by the 5th of each month the total amount paid into the said account during the preceding month.

(signed) Melzer.

Item 50: Meeting with F.K.: Occupation Costs, 11 Feb 1944

<u>Memorandum of meeting held at Grange Lodge</u>
<u>Friday, 11th February, 1944</u>

Present:
    Jurat John Leale, President, Controlling Committee of the States of Guernsey
    Mr L.A. Guillemette, Secretary to President.
    M.V.R. Melzer
    Sonderfuehrer (z) Krefft.

<u>Subject: Feldkommandantur's letter of 8th February, re Reichskreditkassen</u>
    <u>Notes purchased by the States from the local Banks</u>

The meeting was asked for by Jurat Leale in order to talk over the effect of the order contained in the Feldkommandantur's letter of the 8th February, and to discuss whether anything could be done to lessen its burden on the States.

Mr Leale pointed out that the occupation costs would be raised from the present Budget figure of £250,000 to about £1,000,000 in 1944 and in reply to M.V.R. Melzer's remark that no levy had yet been made on the island, he said that the new amount of occupation charges would bankrupt the Island.

The Feldkommandantur put forward the argument that as we have always said that Reichskreditkassen Notes cannot be looked upon as of any value, no harm would be done by taking them for use by the Occupying Forces. Mr Leale replied that we had never said that. We had stressed that they were of problematic value afterwards. The Feldkommandantur appeared to think that no credit had been allowed in the Budget for stocks of Reichskreditkassen Notes in the Banks. They were thereupon corrected and the actual figures in the Budget were indicated to them.

Mr Krefft read an extract from a letter from headquarters in Berlin to Paris written at the time when the discontinuance of repayment of 75% of occupation costs by the Germans was under discussion. Apparently Berlin had pointed out that in England state expenditure was at the rate of £117 per head and that similar expenditure in the Channel Islands would amount to a total of between £6,000,000 and £7,000,000. As taxation was much below this figure they saw no reason for thinking that the Islanders needed help in the payment of occupation costs.

Jurat Leale replied that no comparison could be made between the resources of a small island like ours and England, more especially as since the Occupation incomes had fallen drastically here.

After further discussion during which the Feldkommandantur's representatives hinted their belief that we would be helped financially after the war by England, Jurat Leale asked the following question:–

> "Is your belief that we can bear these costs based on the assumption
> that after the war England will come to our rescue?"

The reply was that this could be looked upon as a private and not the official German opinion and later Mr Krefft said that they held no opinion, official or private, on the matter.

Jurat Leale explained that we are financially independent of England.

The Feldkommandantur's representatives asked what in Jurat Leale's opinion, was the limit of the financial burden which the island could stand. Jurat Leale replied that that limit had already been passed, even without the new and additional burden.

Jurat Leale said that on 19th July, 1943 he had protested in writing against having to pay for a consignment of electric light bulbs imported for the Germans and had received a reply from the Feldkommandantur dated 22nd July, 1943, stating that this was not in contradiction of the Hague Rules and that the Island finances were not yet in such a state that we were unable to meet the account. Jurat Leale said that whatever our financial position was at that time we certainly could not afford to pay for German imports now and he asked therefore that other German imports eg. coal, diesel oil, should be paid for by themselves in France. He did not think the Feldkommandantur's letter of 22nd July, 1943 could possibly be written today.

It was finally decided that a letter should be sent to the Feldkommandantur for transmission to higher authorities, making the following points:–

1. That Guernsey is financially independent of England.
2. That the limit of bearable financial burden has already been passed.
3. That stocks of Reichskreditkassen money show as a credit in the 1944 Budget.
4. That we ask that imports for which we pay, and which are used by Occupying Forces, eg. coal, diesel oil, be paid by the Germans in France.

Copies to:
President, Controlling Committee of the States of Guernsey
Mr L.A. Guillemette

Item 51: Bailiff to F.K.: Occupation Costs, 18 Feb 1944

The Bailiff's Chambers, Guernsey
18th February 1944

Feldkommandantur 515, Jersey

In connection with your letter of 8.2.44 Az.03/10 Mlz/Kl re Occupation Costs, the President of the Controlling Committee has reported to me that he has had an interview with you on the subject, and I wish to make the following observations.

In a letter of July 22nd, 1943, Az.03/7a to the President of the Controlling Committee dealing with Payment of Invoices under Billeting Services in reply to his protest against Guernsey having to pay for imports used by the German Forces, you stated:

> "The demands made are not in contradiction with the provisions of the Hague Convention under which services or objects demanded by the Occupying Forces should be in proportion to the resources of the country. In this case, the standard is the financial capacity of the States which still exists at present."

I estimate that the money you demand will increase our occupation costs this year from £250,000 to £1,000,000 and throw our Budget out accordingly. Surely £1,000,000 a year is altogether disproportionate to the financial capacity of the States. This Island is an always has been financially independent of England.

In my opinion our present financial situation is already extremely serious, and the multiplication of our occupation costs by four will be disastrous for us. I am therefore compelled to protest strongly against your decision and ask for its reversal.

I wish now again to raise the question raised in July, as in view of your latest demands the position has been fundamentally changed. I ask that you should pay the suppliers on the continent for imports such as diesel oil and coal and that we should repay you in Guernsey in RK notes for the proportion used for civil requirements and similarly with regard to imports for the island of Alderney.

(signed) Victor G. Carey, Bailiff.

Nebenstelle Guernsey der
Feldkommandantur 515
Az.05/5 Mlz/Li.
6.3.44

To the President of the Controlling Committee, Guernsey

Re: Money transfers to France. Your letter of 3.3.44. Ref. 5/1/24

I have noted your protest. If the States hold the view that the method of payment ordered in my letter of the 25.2.44 required from the States payments which do not belong to occupation costs, it may be answered that the occupation costs from the past years are considerably higher and that the payments only represent part-payments, and not exact monthly instalments from now on.

(signed) Melzer, M.V.R.

Nebenstelle Guernsey der
Feldkommandantur 515
Az.05/7 Mlz/Li.
6.3.44

To the Bailiff of Guernsey, St Peter Port

Re: Occupation costs. Your letter of 18.2.44. Ref. 5/1/24

In reply to your letter, the Feldkommandantur Jersey writes as follows:

> To the States' anxiety that the present regulation of payments might lead to bankruptcy for the States, it may be objected that the resulting indebtedness, owing to the fact that the RKK notes can no longer be used for purchases in France, will only lead to an indebtedness towards France. As, however, an unlimited credit is granted for this debt, no States bankruptcy is to be expected. If the burder of debt exceeds capacity of payment of the States, attention should be drawn to the point of view of the Reichsfinanzminister, ie. that the debt in question is an Empire debt, and not one of the hitherto financially independent Island States. As the matters stand, the former financial independence of the States cannot be taken into consideration.

(signed) Melzer, M.V.R.

Item 52: Meeting with F.K.: Firemen's contracts, 20 Mar 1944

<u>Memorandum of Meeting held at "Summerland" on 20th March 1944</u>

Present:

Jurat John Leale	President of the Controlling Committee of the States of Guernsey
Lt Col Count von Helder	[von Helldorff]
Mr L.A. Guillemette	

The Colonel said that he wished to discuss Mr Leale's letter of the 14th March, regarding contracts which civilian firemen were being asked by the German Authorities to sign.

He did not think that such an undertaking was in conflict with International Law. In Jersey the Fire Brigade consisted solely of civilians and no difficulty had been experienced in obtaining their signatures to a similar document. He visualised buildings, chiefly in the Town, catching fire during aerial attacks and he wished for an assurance from the civilian Members of the Brigade that they would be willing to perform their fire-fighting duties even during attacks. He thought it made no difference whether such buildings were in civilian or German occupation the danger of fires spreading being the same in either case. German fortifications were of steel and concrete and therefore could not catch fire.

Mr Leale said that he did not think it fair that in the event of a British landing on the Island British civilians might be called upon to extinguish fires in building purposely set afire by their own countrymen. He suggested that if the Germans wished the firemen to sign any undertaking, such document should contain a clause to the effect that they would not be expected to do work against their own country.

The Colonel gave an assurance that of course men would not be obliged to work against their own country and agreed to the insertion of these words. He suggested that Mr Leale submit to him a suitable document to which there would be no objection to the firemen appending their signatures.

Item 53: P.K. to C.C.: Delivery of Butter, 22 Jun 1944

Platzkommandantur I St Helier
Nebenstelle Guernsey, Az.16/5
22.6.44

To the President of the Controlling Committee
of the States of Guernsey

Re: Delivery of butter from civilian stocks to the Troops

On superior orders the troops are to be supplied weekly with 1½ tons of butter from the reserve stock or current production. The first delivery shall take place on Monday the 26th June, 1944.

This supply does not imply a shortening of the present fat ration for the civilian population. It may also be reckoned upon that in case of need pork fat will be placed by the troops at the disposal of the civilian population.

After each delivery, an invoice is to be sent here.

(signed) Schneberger, M.V.R.

The Bailiff's Chambers, Guernsey
June 24th, 1944

Platzkommandantur I St Helier,
Nebenstelle Guernsey

The President of the Controlling Committee has shown me a copy of yours of 24.6.44. Re: Delivery of butter from civilian stocks to the Troops. Az.16/5. I have asked him to allow me to reply to it.

We were most reluctant to make the reduction necessary to build up this reserve. See the Controlling Committee's letters of 26th December, 1943 and 4th January 1944.

Dr Kratzer in a letter dated 26th December, 1943, wrote that this reduction has "to be adopted in the interest of the population".

It is therefore with surprise that I learned of your letter requisitioning weekly 1½ tons of butter from the reserve which the population sacrificed in mid-winter to build up.

The matter assumed an added importance in view of the fact that our meat ration may not be more than a monthly issue in future.

I understand your letter to mean that should our fat ration fall below its present level you will place pork fat at our disposal to make up the difference.

(signed) Victor G. Carey, Bailiff

Item 54: Bailiff to P.K.: Taking of Hay, 15 Jul 1944

The Bailiff's Chambers, Guernsey
July 15, 1944

Platzkommandantur I St Helier
Nebenstelle Guernsey

With further reference to my interview with you on Tuesday last the 11th instant regarding the recent taking of hay by the German Authorities from various privately owned fields in this Island. I would like to draw your attention to Article 52 of the Hague Convention which is to be found as an annexe to the Convention contained in appendix 6 and signed at the Hague on the 18th October 1907. The Article is as follows viz:–

> "Des réquisitions en nature et des services ne pourront être réclamés des communes ou des habitants que pour les besoins de l'armée d'occupation. Ils seront en rapport avec les ressources du pays et de telle nature qu'ils n'impliquent pas pour les populations l'obligation de prendre part aux operations de la guerre contre leur patrie.
>
> Ces réquisitions et ces services ne seront réclamées qu'avec l'autorisation du commandant dans la localité occupée.
>
> Les prestations en nature seront, autant que possible, payées au comptant; sinon, elles seront constatées par des reçus et le paiement des sommes dues sera effectué le plus tôt possible."

I would point out that no requisition has been made unless the notice in the newspapers made by the German Authorities can be considered a requisition, and neither has it been suggested that the hay should be paid for in ready money or alternatively that receipts should be given for the hay taken.

I would therefore ask if you would let me have your observations on this matter, as it would appear that a breach of Article 52 of the Convention has been committed.

I should also like you to confirm the assurance which you gave me verbally that there was no intention of interfering with the harvest of corn and oats, but on the contrary that you were willing to assist us to collect the harvest by placing at our disposal a number of horses for that purpose.

Victor G. Carey, Bailiff.

Platzkommandantur I St Helier
Nebenstelle Guernsey
20.7.44

To the Bailiff of Guernsey

Re: Festungkommandant's Notice of July 1st, 1944 regarding the
        mowing of standing hay. (Your letter of 15h July, 1944)

The object of the Notice in question was not the taking away of hay, but to have the standing grass from getting entirely spoilt. The grass was for the greater part parched ("woody") and fit to be used for litter rather than as fodder. This condition had repeatedly been pointed out to Mr Falla. The troops have therefore helped to put an end to a state of emergency, so that one cannot speak of a break of, or non-compliance with Art. 53 of the Hague Convention. It may also be remarked that the troops have placed horses at the disposal of landowners for the hay harvest.

It is entirely unnecessary to give an assurance that it is not intended to interfere with the cereal harvest. I may refer you to the enclosed copy of a letter from the Platzkommandantur to the President of the Controlling Committee dated 17th inst. according to which troop horses are already being placed at the disposal of the civilian sector.

I hope that the matter is thus settled.

(signed) Schneberger, M.V.R.

Platzkommandantur I St Helier
Nebenstelle Guernsey, Az.15/9
17.7.44

To the Controlling Committee of the States of Guernsey

Re: Army Horses

After conferring with the Military Commandant, army horses may further be placed at the disposal of the civilian sector for carrying out work. The conditions are as follows:–

1.   The horses must be entirely fed by the farmer, free of charge.
2.   Where a driver is provided by the troops, he will be fed by the troops.
3.   If the horses are kept in the farmer's stables, the horses shall remain under the supervision of the Inselveterinaer.
4.   It is intended to leave the horses for a fairly long time at disposal even if lent in answer to an immediate call.

Please let us know as soon as possible how many horses are required and where they are to be used. For the moment, we are thinking of 40 to 50 horses.

It is to be ascertained whether the wood obtained by felling trees could also be transported by means of these horses. The vehicles could also be lent by the troops.

Schneberger, M.V.R.

Item 55: Bailiff to P.K.: Letter to Red Cross, 26 Jul 1944

The Bailiff's Chambers
St Peter Port, Guernsey
July 26th, 1944

Platzkommandantur I St Helier
Nebenstelle Guernsey

On the 11th July, 1944, I wrote to you enclosing a letter addressed to the International Red Cross. The object of the letter was the continuance of Red Cross correspondence in the event of total isolation from France.

I understand that my letter has been dispatched to France and as it is so vital to the interests of the population I should be obliged if you would keep me informed of any delay which may occur on its way to Geneva.

As the arrival of essential supplies for the civilian population has now been at a standstill for many weeks and as stocks will begin to run out in the near future, I am of opinion that the time has arrived to make whatever provision we can for feeding the population during the coming winter should the isolation of the Islands be complete.

I should be obliged therefore if you would arrange for us to discuss with General von Schmettow and yourself the question of approaching the International Red Cross for the dispatch to the Island of essential supplies for the civilian population.

Victor G. Carey, Bailiff.

Item 56: Bailiff to Red Cross, 29 Jul 1944

The Bailiff's Chambers
St Peter Port, Guernsey
July 29th, 1944

The Secretary-General
Committee of the International Red Cross Organisation
Geneva, Switzerland

Sir,

As you may be aware the Islands of the Bailiwick of Guernsey, of which I am the Civil Head, have been occupied by the German Forces since July, 1940.

The Islanders have never been self-supporting in foodstuffs, and during the past four years we have received essential imports from France through Granville.

You will doubtless realise that the present fighting in Normandy makes transport precarious between the Islands and the French mainland, and, indeed, since the beginning of the invasion we have received virtually no imports of foodstuffs.

Fortunately, we held at the beginning of the invasion some reserve stocks of vital imports, but eight weeks have passed and our stocks will not last more than a few weeks longer.

Formerly our revictualling organisation was built up in the Department of La Manche, but now that the war has spread to that area supplies from that source are no longer obtainable. Headquarters are therefore to be transferred from Granville to Saint Malo, with Brittany as our potential source of supply. Even if such an organisation could be adequately re-established, we have no guarantee of how long it would be able to operate.

I am therefore writing both to you and to His Excellency the Swiss Minister at Berlin, as representative of our Protecting Power, asking that arrangements be made for the delivery here of essential supplies with the least possible delay.

A visit from a representative of either your Organisation or the Protecting Power would be of the greatest benefit to us. In case this is impracticable, however, I enclose herewith lists of essential supplies representing our <u>minimum</u> monthly requirements.

In order that you may appreciate the gravity of our position, I may add that our present civilian population exceeds 23,000 persons.

I have the honour to be
Your obedient servant
Victor G. Carey
Bailiff of Guernsey.

Essential Imported Foodstuffs: Minimum Monthly Consumption

Flour	184	metric tons
Farinaceous foods	17	metric tons
Sugar	13	metric tons
Baby patent foods	2	metric tons

Essential Drugs: Minimum Monthly Consumption

Morphine	100	grammes
Cocaine	10	grammes
Chloral Hydrate	10	kg.
Glucose	8	kg.
Myped. Tabs Hyoscine	1000	tablets
Tab. Luminal 0.06 gm.	1000	tablets
Tab. Luminal 0.03 gm.	1000	tablets
Tab. Medinal 0.5 gm.	1000	tablets
Suprafin 10% 50	6 x 60	cc.
Suprafin Ampoules	55	ampoules
Coramine	30	ampoules
Compelon Ampoules 2cc.	100	ampoules
Cotton Wool	120	kg.

Hirzel House, Guernsey
July 1944.

Item 57: Vaudin to Leale, 27 Jul 1944

GRANVILLE, July 27th, 1944

Jurat Leale, President, States Controlling Committee
Hirzel House
GUERNSEY

Dear Mr Leale

I am told there may be a boat from Malo in a day or so, therefore on the chance of a letter reaching you, I shall try and give you a resumé of the happenings during the past six weeks. I have made no notes so shall have to trust to memory, for I have been rather ill during the past five weeks with diptheria, and under the conditions of living and the attention it is possible to have just now, this type of illness does not make it any the easier. Still, I am on the road to recovery, and with the exception of a partial paralysis of the palate, also whatever I drink partly comes back through the nose at once, plus a general weakness, I feel O.K. Doctors are so hard worked that they only see one once a week. I have had serum injections and am now having strichnine injected twice daily.

I had been in bed two days at the hotel with a temperature when we had to leave there in a hurry early in the morning of the 20th June, so I walked up to the Hotel de l'Arrivée a mile up the road, got to bed and have been there since. Three weeks ago last Friday, a German officer came to my room, told me to dress, as he was taking me to St Pair as a witness. We got there in his car, but after having got through the witness job, Kirschner "from Jersey" and I were told we must walk back, the car being required by the Major. I, like a fool feeling fairly well at the time, made no comment, so we started off and walked 5 kilometres to Granville. I got to bed, and nearly packed up, as this put me back quite a lot. However, matters are now improving. Enough of my aches and pains, and to business.

After the 6th June we kept the office open until the 13th. We three chaps had been on parole from Office to Hotel during this time, the embargo being somewhat relaxed after this date. Circumstances were such that most of our staff had left Granville, and transport being absolutely stopped, we could get no goods from anywhere to Granville. Our lorries were requisitioned, so we closed the Office, one or two members coming down every other day for a short time in case there was something to do. We still had a few local accounts to pay, which had to be collected as there is no post. We have also had no light for two months, or water except at odd times.

On the 20th June, even though the shutters at the Office were up, all the windows were shattered. We cleared out of our Hotel opposite on the same day. The owner had left for the country some days earlier, we being the only ones left there to sleep, and had our meals outside. Now there is but one Restaurant open in Granville, and this is at our Hotel, l'Arrivée. All the shops here are closed.

I very much regret that it was impossible to load our goods in the last boat which came to Guernsey with those 250 tons of coal. At this time, I had 91 tons of flour in the warehouse at the Port, 150 tons flour and wheat at Beguin's mills at Granville, awaiting shipment, four railway trucks of charcoal on the Quay, and the store full of goods awaiting shipment, including 3 sacks of Mangold seed which you badly required, and which you should have had at the end of May. I enclose a list of the good actually in store at that date and which could have come on the coal boat. It was heartbreaking to see all this stuff left behind, especially the wheat and flour after the hard work we had put in regarding flour and wheat during March, April and May, always with the thought in my mind that the next might be the last boat. The Dept responsible for giving us loading space has not helped us all they could, also as long as there were wagons loaded on the quay, they would not allow us to load from the store, wagons having to be cleared on arrival, put in store if no boat, then left there if wagons arrived at time of loading. I spoke to Mr Kihm about the fact that all our goods and flour could have been cleared if the boat had not taken the coal, and he told me it was an order from Ins. Pokorni from Jersey that the coal must be loaded, which coal will give you about an extra 5 days gas, whereas the flour and wheat would have given you a ration for two months at a reduced rate, which I take it you are now having. The bread ration here is 100 grammes per day, some day none at all.

When all this happened, there was supposed to be flour in Granville for the population for one month, but this turned out to be three days, so much for the capabilities of the Maire here. I gave them 19 tons from the 91 tons in the warehouse on the quay, the Military authorities taking the remainder. I again gave them 43 tons from Beguin to carry them on until June, the Authorities again taking the remainder. I have sent accounts to the Maire for the 19 and 43 tons, also to the German authorities for the balance taken by them.

The goods in store were left there for a time, then when the store was broken into, I had the whole lot removed elsewhere. This was further necessary, as we were not allowed on the Port after a certain date.

A fortnight ago, Mr Kihm (who certainly has been of great help to us and has worked hard on our behalf as regards getting the flour, wheat, etc down by rail), told me that he had orders to transfer the office from here to St Malo, and from there, send over to the Islands flour, meat and butter if we could get the latter. He asked me if I would go to Malo, and I replied, Yes, if its to work, but when I am fit to go which is not yet. I told him that we did not need much staff at Malo, and that I did not wish to confuse the two Offices. As the Malo office was to deal with a few items only, it would be best to leave the Granville office as it was, with Quatenens looking after Jersey interests, and Mme Plessix, my secretary, to look after Guernsey interests. Quatenens and I had already arranged that as from end July, the staff would be released, only he, myself and my secretary and Madame de Querillis as cashier staying on, the latter looking after the financial interests of both Islands, and she had been the one who had done all the work for Hall with the Office des Changes, and was therefore au courant with this work.

I told Kihm we start a fresh lot of books at Malo, not many being required, and that all we needed there was Kirschner (who had come over from Jersey), myself and Mme de Querillis, the latter to do the clerical work, also our two men for loading:- Barnett and Guillemet. To this he agreed. Kirschner went down to Malo.

Kihm went to St Germain for permission to obtain flour and meat for the Islands, and came back with news that they allowed us 1,000 tons flour, 200 tons to come immediately for Guernsey, also 60 head of cattle per month for both Islands. We have made arrangements with the O.T. at Malo to secure the cattle, and the first 60 will go 40 Guernsey, 20 Jersey, the latter having had 60 head a month ago from here when they loaded some for the German authorities in Jersey. These sixty were due to Jersey, they being this number behind as against we being up-to-date then. I hope some flour and cattle will be loaded for Guernsey early next week, as I am told that one boat is coming direct. As soon as I am fit I shall go to Malo, also Mme de Querillis who has been looking after me during my illness, and without her, I don't know what I should have done. She has been a brick to me, and being a widow and entirely on her own, can more easily come to Malo than any of the others who have their homes at Granville, plus she being the most capable for the work.

I have been alone here for the past fortnight, Barnett and Guillemet met having cleared out in hiding somewhere. They had already gone two or three times before, but always turned up a few days later, but this time I don't know where they have gone, and although I have made enquiries everywhere, I can get no information whatever as to where they might be. I specially wanted them now to go to Malo but Kirschner and myself shall have to attend to the lot there, as I don't think we shall see the chaps again around here. I personally found the position awkward, but decided to stay here whatever happened, there being the goods to see to and the Office in general, even though we could get no further supplies down. Had we been able to ship all our stuff on that coal boat, there would have been nothing to actually keep me here.

Since having cleared our goods from the store on the Quay, we have loaded all Jersey goods and taken to Malo, and I have also loaded three lorries of Guernsey goods plus another one today for Malo, and I trust these shall come by boat which leaves for Guernsey. I still have a few loads here which I shall send down to Malo trusting they shall arrive safely at Guernsey.

Jersey owes us about 24 million francs, but I have transferred 12 million to Guernsey today which had come for Jersey from the Office des Changes, thus leaving about another 12 million due. All purchases of flour, meat, etc at Malo shall be paid by Guernsey to be reimbursed later, Jersey having no credit at the Bank. All meat and flour bought for Malo has to be paid cash, and we shall keep a strict account of what is for each Island. It is possible that some goods for Guernsey may get only as far as Jersey, for instance, Kihm told me that the goods we are sending down to Malo from here would go to Jersey then await there a boat for Guernsey. Since then, it appears a boat is loading direct for Guernsey, and we may have those goods already sent to Malo come direct. In future, however, further goods may go to Jersey for us.

I have done best from memory to give you a resumé of happenings here. It may be a bit jumbled up, but I trust you may sort it out. Have typed this out in my bedroom, and am now going to lie down and rest. Kind regards,

Yours sincerely
G.M. VAUDIN.

Item 58: Meeting with P.K.: Island supplies, 14 Aug 1944

<u>Meeting held at Royal Court House</u>
on 14th August, 1944

Present:

Colonel Count von Helldorff
M.V.R. Schneberger
Sfr. Krefft
Jurat John Leale, President of the Controlling Committee
Mr L.A. Guillemette, Secretary to the President.

The meeting was held to acquaint Colonel Count von Helldorff with present conditions regarding Island supplies, and the various local officials were invited to attend to set out the position of their respective departments.

1. Flour. (Jurat Pierre de Putron)

The wheat crop is now being harvested. It would not normally be fit for milling for several weeks, but enough of last year's wheat is being retained to give a mixture of 50 per cent of last year's and 50 per cent of this year's crop. This mixture should be ready for milling from the middle of September.

The two mills being used at present – Charroterie Steam Mills and Bragg's Mill, Glategny Esplanade, together produce 80 tons of flour working 12 hours per day and 6 days per week.

Our supplies, including this year's harvest, will last until the beginning of November on the basis of the revised bread ration.

We produce 100 pounds of bread from 75 pounds of flour and 98 per cent of the wheat goes into the flour.

Rusks made from white flour are produced for invalids, and the bran extracted from such flour is returned to the stocks of standard flour.

We need 500 tons of wheat in addition to present stocks to enable the issue of the original bread ration to the civilian population to the end of January next.

As a large quantity of wheat is to be imported from Jersey to be milled here for both military and civilians, it will probably become necessary to work both mills 24 hours a day in the near future.

Six ounces of flour per head is issued to the civilian population once every other week.

Colonel Count von Helldorff is to ascertain whether it is possible for the Town Mills Bakery, formerly requisitioned for the Organisation Todt, to be used for baking civilian bread, thereby saving both petrol for transport and coke for fuel.

2. Wood Fuel. (Jurat Pierre de Putron)

We have, during the past few weeks, been producing about 300 tons of wood fuel weekly for civilian consumption.

<u>Petrol for Haulage</u>: An order has been received that no further petrol will be allowed for the haulage of timber to the cutting centres.

Enquiries are being made regarding the use of tractors for this work, and a report thereon will be submitted to the Platzkommandantur.

A ration of 56 pounds of wood per household means 200 tons of wood per week, and the consumption of pterol for the haulage of this quantity is 100 gallons.

The delivery of the wood from the cutting centres to consumer can be done without the use of petrol.

Electric Saws: Statistics of the amount of current being used at present for electric saws are to be submitted to Platzkommandantur. Meanwhile, the use of such saws is to continue until further notice.

Details are to be submitted to Platzkommandantur, for Colonel Count von Helldorff's information, of the type of electric motors used for saws. The Colonel is to make enquiries as to whether portable dynamos are available for driving such saws in place of electric power from the Electricity Department's mains.

Hand Saws: Colonel Count von Helldorff offered to lend hand saws if required and advised that such saws be used as much as possible, so that workmen may become accustomed to them. Jurat Pierre de Putron is to let him know if any are required.

3. Hospital Laundry. (Dr Symons)

Dr Symons stated that German Orders had been received to stop the use of an electric motor at the laundry at Les Cotils Convent. He explained that this laundry worked for the States' Convalescent Hospital at Blanchelande and that great difficulties would be experienced by its stoppage.

It was agreed that the motor might continue to be used one day per week on work for the Blanchlande Hospital.

4. Petrol Rationing. (Mr A.C. Richings)

Mr Richings reported on details of the cuts he had made to comply with present German Orders. He had cut as many as possible by 50 per cent, but advised that in some cases such a cut would have a very serious effect on efficiency.

The result of the cuts was a reduction to 20,500 litres per month as compared with 29,000 litres consumed in July. The former figure makes no provision for the haulage of wood fuel which would require 2,000 litres per month extra.

On Mr Leale's suggestion it was decided that Mr Richings should submit to the Platzkommandantur a scheme whereby the consumption of petrol over the next 6½ months, including the second half of August, should not exceed a monthly average of 20,000 litres. Colonel Count von Helldorff agreed to a total consumption within these limits.

5. Water. (Mr G. Heggs)

The public water of the island comprises two systems.

(a)   Domestic filtered water.

(b)   Irrigation supply – unfiltered.

With the stoppage of electric power from the Electricity Department's mains, the irrigation supply would cease since it is pumped entirely by electric motors.

This supply, together with private supplies pumped by electricity, furnishes water for nearly one quarter of the glasshouses of the island, and these properties would therefore either go completely out of production or become very much less efficient. It would be impossible to pump adequate quantities of water by hand.

At present the Domestic system is supplying 40,000,000 litres per week and the Irrigation system 11,000,000.

The Domestic system is not entirely dependent on the Electricity Department, as sufficient pumps are driven by diesel engines to maintain a reduced output. An adequate reserve of diesel oil is to be set aside to keep the system in operation for some months. Colonel Count von Helldorff is to inform the Controlling Committee as to the amount of this reserve.

One-and-a-half gallons of petrol per week for actuating the starting compressors of diesel engines is absolutely essential.

Chemicals: Stocks of chlorine will last until the end of December, and the purity of the water will be maintained thereafter with chloride of lime.

Lubricating oil: Present stocks will only last until the beginning of December. Consumption is about 450 litres per month. Colonel Count von Helldorff will try to provide lubricating oil for the Water Board.

6. Gas. (Mr R.G. Luxon)

With the 750 tons of coal handed over to the Gas Company by the German Authorities it should be possible to produce gas at the present rate until the first week in December.

As this coal is of poor quality, it will have to be mixed with the Company's present stocks to get the most efficient results.

At present the Company is using abouot 150 tons of coal per week.

Last quarter Military consumption was 16,000,000 cubic feet.

Last quarter Civilian consumption was 25,000,000 cubic feet.

All civilian water heaters are now disconnected.

Lubricating oil: The Company's stocks of lubricating oil will be exhausted by the middle of October. Consumption is 40 gallons per month.

Colonel Count von Helldorff is to try to obtain supplies of lubricating oil for the Company and also a motor-driven conveyor belt for loading the coal handed over by the German Authorities at St Sampson's.

7. Electricity. (Major F. Barritt Hills)

At the present rate of consumption electricity will continue for 16 weeks if no reserve of diesel oil is made for the Water Board.

Ways and means of saving electricity were discussed.

(a)   A cut in the domestic ration. In the last December quarter – which is always a heavy one for domestic lighting – the civilian domestic consumption amounted to only 11 per cent of total consumption. During the three summer months any cut in the domestic ration would make a very small reduction in total consumption.

(b)   Stoppage of plant at night. This would effect a considerable saving since quite a large amount of current is needed to keep the mains energised even if none is used by consumers.

Col. Count von Helldorff said that there were many difficulties involved with the stoppage of the plant, but undertook to examine the question again.

Major Barritt Hills said that on receipt of instructions the plant could always be re-started at five minutes' notice.

There was further discussion on the provisions of emergency electricity supply for essential services in case of the failure of the main plant. This is contained in a report from Major Barritt Hills attached hereto.

8. Glasshouse Utilisation Board.

The Platzkommandantur have recently put forward the suggestion that provision be made to supply 30 tons of glasshouse vegetables per week to the Military during the months of December to March inclusive. Mr Dorey thought that glasshouses would not be available for the production of such quantities.

He also mentioned the fact that private purchases of vegetables by the Military, and purchases by Timmer Ltd. from private growers made it difficult to maintain civilian supplies during periods of shortage. Such a period would be starting by the middle of September.

Count von Helldorff said that he would issue instructions that such private purchases were to stop.

9. Equipment for labour engaged on clearance work.

Col. Count von Helldorff undertook to try to obtain shovels, wheelbarrows and light railways for use in clearance work by civilian labour.

Item 59: Bailiff to General: Murder of Bertie Jehan, 26 Aug 1944

The Bailiff's Chambers, Guernsey
August 26th, 1944

Major-General Count von Schmettow
Guernsey

I have been very shocked to learn that Mr Bertie Jehan of Les Crabbes, St Saviour's, died yesterday as a result of being shot presumably by one of your soldiers whilst he was guarding his potatoes early that morning.

I shall be glad of your assurance that you are taking all possible measures to trace the culprit and to prevent the recurrence of such a crime.

(signed) Victor G. Carey, Bailiff.

Item 60: Guillemette to Leale: Cross enquiry, 29 Aug 1944

29th August, 1944

The President
Controlling Committee of the States of Guernsey

Dear Sir,

I am informed by Mr W.J. Corbet that, in conversation with Mr C.H. Cross this morning, the latter gentleman stated that I was the man who sent him to Germany.

Mr Cross, I take it, referred to his deportation to Germany in 1942 and as at that time I was engaged in making representations to the German Authorities on behalf of the Controlling Committee for the exemption from deportation of many of our population, such a statement at the least casts a serious slur on my work as a civil servant. At the worst – and this is its most literal meaning – it may be interpreted as an accusation that I made representations to the Germans to ensure that he be deported.

During the German Occupation of this Island, in my almost daily contacts with the Occupying Authorities on behalf of the Bailiff and the Controlling Committee and individual members of the public, I have always taken a pride in doing my utmost to further our interests and I am convinced that the statement made by Mr Cross is the result of some misunderstanding which can be explained, should an opportunity arise to do so.

As however, Mr Cross made no secret of his opinion, I can only suppose that he had voiced it, since his return to the Island, to others of his large circle of acquaintances, and both for his sake and my own I would therefore welcome an enquiry into the matter by persons nominated by Mr Cross and the Controlling Committee respectively.

Should the Controlling Committee and Mr Cross agree to the holding of such an enquiry, I would suggest that the result be made public.

Yours faithfully
L.A. Guillemette
Secretary to the President

Item 61: Meeting with P.K. and General, 6 Sep 1944

Memorandum of Meeting held at "La Corbinerie",
Wednesday, 6th September 1944

Present:

>Victor G. Carey, Esq. Bailiff of Guernsey
>Lt. General von Schmettow
>Colonel von Helldorff
>L.A. Guillemette

1. Threatening of Civilians with Revolvers

The Bailiff handed the General a translation of a letter which he had received from the Acting Police Inspector reporting on two cases of civilians being threatened with revolvers by members of the German Forces. He asked that a general order be given to the troops that such actions be forbidden. The General said that such an order was already in force and that the strictest possible measures would be taken to punish any offenders who were caught. The General added that investigations were still proceeding in the hope of discovering the murderer or murderers of Mr Jehan who was killed by a revolver shot some two weeks ago. Already some 5,000 army boots had been examined since footprints on the scene of the crime showed nails missing from the soles of the boots. Also, as the revolver bullet, which had been recovered, was of a special type over 100 revolvers had been examined but unfortunately the culprit had not yet been found. The investigation would continue.

2. Letters to the International Red Cross and Protecting Power

The Bailiff reminded the General that in July last he had written first to the International Red Cross to ask for the continuance of some kind of mail service to the Island, and, secondly to both the International Red Cross and the Swiss Minister in Berlin asking for arrangements to be made for the supply of essential foodstuffs in case of the total isolation of the Island and serious food shortages. The Bailiff asked the German Officers if they had any knowledge as to whether the letters had reached their destination. Colonel von Helldorff said that they had no such knowledge, but suspected that, at any rate, the second letters had travelled no further than St Malo which was cut off soon after the letters left the Island. Mr Guillemette asked whether it would be possible to make enquiries as to whether the letters had reached their destination. The German Officers said that this was quite impossible.

Later in the meeting, Mr Guillemette asked whether it would be possible for some civilians to be allowed to make contact with the Allied Forces in France so that arrangements could be made for food supplies. Colonel von Helldorff said that at present this was impossible but that if there was any serious shortage of any essentials, for instance, medicines, it would be possible to send a wire.

3. Radios

The Bailiff asked whether, now that the Island was completely isolated, permission could be granted for the use of radio receiving sets by the civilian population. He stressed the fact that islanders had no contact whatsoever with the outside world and that the psychological effect on their morale caused him anxiety. He added that crystal receiving sets used no electric power whatsoever and that their use would, therefore, have no affect on the Diesel oil stocks of the Island. The General explained that the Order for the confiscation of radio sets had been given, not by the Officer Commanding the Islands but by Headquarters in Germany. He did not possess the power to rescind such an Order. Colonel von Helldorff added that the Order had never been popular with the Commanding Officers of the Islands. The Bailiff asked whether it would be possible to obtain permission from German Headquarters since the Officers here could not grant such permission. The reply was that German Headquarters had other troubles at present.

4. Alteration of Punishment of Mrs L.M. Le Gallez

The Bailiff reminded the General that he had written to him on the 23rd ultimo setting forth the request of Mrs L.M. Le Gallez, of Le Grand Belle, St Andrew's, that the sentence of seven weeks' imprisonment, recently passed on her by a German Court, should be altered so that she might pay a fine instead. The General said that he had been into the matter and discovered that Mrs Le Gallez had not placed the full facts before the Bailiff. A letter was being addressed to the Bailiff by an official of the German Court which had tried her. The facts were that Mrs Le Gallez' son was suspected of stealing from the German Forces. The Feldgendarmerie had called at the house to search and had been abused by Mrs Le Gallez. When they threatened her with punishment she had tried to bribe them with gifts of farm produce. The General feared that he could not accede to the Bailiff's request.

Item 62: Meeting with Colonel, Le Vallon, 19 Sep 1944

<u>Memorandum of meeting held at Le Vallon, September 19th, 1944</u>

Present:
      Victor G. Carey, Esq., Bailiff
      Colonel von Helldorff
      L.A. Guillemette

<u>Note:</u> The meeting was held at Colonel von Helldorff's request.

<u>Letters to International Red Cross</u>

Colonel von Helldorff said that as no replies had been received to the Bailiff's letters of 29th July addressed to the International Red Cross and the Protecting Power respectively, long telegrams (presumably by radio) had been sent to the International Red Cross and the German Government regarding supplies of essentials for the civilian population. As examples as to what he meant by essentials he gave medicaments and sugar. The German Authorities here had also asked permission to get into touch with England (presumably on the same subject). No reply had been received as yet and the Colonel wondered whether the necessary permission would be given.

<u>Investigation into the murder of Mr B. Jehan</u>

The Colonel said that although investigations were still continuing he regretted very much that the murderer of Mr Jehan was not yet found. The soldier, however, who had threatened a civilian with a revolver (see Memorandum of meeting held on 6th September) had been caught and was being severely punished. In addition, all pistols had been taken from Russian Units and orders had been given that no German soldier was allowed to enter any civilian houses; with the exception of the Feldgendarmerie and the Officer of the Quartieramt when such visits were necessary.

<u>Coal for Gas Works</u>

The Colonel said that he hoped to be able to give more coal to the Gas Works. He made no promises, however, as yet. He had had to sent 500 tons of coal to Jersey for their Electricity Works.

<u>Protest by Bailiff of Jersey</u>

The Colonel mentioned that he had received a long letter from the Bailiff of Jersey who was very angry. He said that they were doing all they could to help the civilian populations in both Islands.

Message from Allies to Lt General von Schmettow

Mr Guillemette said that there was a strong rumour in the Island that a message had been dropped by parachute. He asked whether there was any truth in this and the Colonel replied that it was true but that the message only contained instructions to get in touch with the Allies by telephone. The cables were destroyed and such communication was therefore impossible.

Guernsey Star Company and States Printing

The Bailiff told the Colonel that he had received notification from the Guernsey Star Company, who are the States' Printers, that they had been ordered by the Pressestelle to close down completely. At present the States accounts, Billet D'Etat was in course of preparation and as it is one of the most important Billets of the year the position was very serious. The work on this Billet involved special printing and members of the Star staff were the only men with the necessary knowledge in the Island. He asked that arrangements be made for work on this Billet D'Etat to continue. The Colonel said he would see that such arrangements were made forthwith.

Copies to:
> The Bailiff
> Controlling Committee files (2 copies)
> L.A. Guillemette (2 copies)

Item 63: Newspaper article: Letter from Goebbels, 19 Sep 1944

Exchange of Messages between Dr Goebbels and Graf von Schmettow

Your wireless message of 11.9 in which you informed me that the German Soldiers of the fortresses of Guernsey, Jersey and Alderney had collected RM. 1 003 450.– for the German Red Cross, has duly reached us. This Fund has caused me much pleasure as an expression of confidence in victory and solidarity with the Fatherland. This splendid collection result was broadcasted on the 15.9 by the New Service of the German Radio.

I send you and all your comrades hearty greetings and wish you all Soldier's luck.

Heil Hitler!
Yours, Dr Goebbels
Reichspropagandaministerium

The Commandant of the Channel Islands sent the following answer:

For your personal message of the 19.9, which came through to me via my Naval Commandant's station regarding the Red Cross Collection made in the fortresses of Guernsey, Jersey and Alderney which sent under my command. I send you my best thanks on behalf of the troops of occupation. This collection was made among the Guernsey Division.

In our complete isolation on British soil for many months past, we particularly appreciate the broadcast as well as your personal greeting.

The three island fortresses, conscious of their strength and following the example of other fortresses, will faithfully hold out to the last.

With this in mind, we salute our Fuehrer and the Fatherland.

The Commandant of the British Channel Islands
(signed) Graf von Schmettow, Generalleutnant.

Item 64: Meeting with P.K.: Meeting with Allies, 23 Sep 1944

<u>Memorandum of Meeting held at Summerland,
Mount Durand, on Saturday 23rd September, 1944</u>

Present:

Jurat J Leale	President of the Controlling Committee
J.E.L. Martel, Esq.	Acting Attorney General
Colonel von Helldorff	
L.A. Guillemette, Esq.	Secretary to the President

<u>Meeting off South Coast of Guernsey between American
and German War Vessels</u>

Mr Leale said that everybody knew of the meeting which had taken place on Friday afternoon off the South coast of the Island between an American war vessel and a German boat from St Peter Port harbour. He reminded the Colonel that he had invited the local administration to approach him whenever they needed help. The Guernsey representatives had therefore arranged this interview with the object of discovering whether the Colonel could tell him anything of interest to the local community regarding the said meeting. The Colonel said that nothing happened at the meeting except that the Americans had asked some silly questions which had nothing at all to do with the civilian population. In reply to a question he said that quite definitely fighting would not ensue in the Island because of the German replies to the American questions. The Germans did not intend to discuss their position with the Americans. Discussion with the British would be a different matter.

The Colonel continued that, as Mr Guillemette knew, the Bailiff had been informed last Tuesday, at a meeting held at The Vallon, that the German Authorities in the Island had sent telegrams to the International Red Cross and to the German Government regarding supplies of essentials for the civilian population. The Colonel had now been informed that the two Governments were in communication through a neutral power on the subject. The Germans offered to allow the importation of food, medical supplies and fuel. The telegrams gave the finishing dates for all essentials at a few days before the actual date at which supplies would peter out in Jersey; that Island in almost every case being in a worse position than Guernsey. As an instance he said that the telegrams had given the 15th October 1944 as the date on which medical supplies would finish. Actually the real date for Jersey is somewhere in the neighbourhood of the end of October.

The Guernsey representatives put forward the suggestion that the plea for the importation of essentials might be strengthened if some Guernsey official would join the Germans in their representations, especially if further direct contact was to be made with the Americans. The Colonel pointed out that the matter was already under discussion between the British and German Governments and that in his opinion it was possible that the next news we should receive would be the arrival of a ship from England or some neutral country laden with supplies. It would then be possible to send further orders for supplies with the returning ship.

Present position regarding food, fuel and medical supplies

Mr Leale handed to the Colonel documents giving the present position regarding the above essentials, signed by himself, Mr Pierre de Putron and Dr A.N. Symons respectively. He said that the position regarding food had been altered that afternoon by the arrival from Jersey of 200 tons of wheat. He asked the Colonel to peruse the documents and to suggest a date and time for discussion thereon with Mr Pierre de Putron, Dr A.N. Symons and himself sometime during the coming week.

Sales of Fruit and Vegetables

Mr Leale said that Mr Percy Dorey, President of the Glasshouse Utilisation Board, had informed him that he had heard from the Platzkommandantur that changes were likely to be made in the recent German Order regarding sales of fruit and vegetables to members of the Forces. The Colonel denied that any change was to be made in the order.

Public announcement regarding recent contacts between Germans and Americans

Mr Leale asked whether the German Authorities could make some announcement through the newspapers informing the general public of the results of the meeting. The Colonel said he would ask the General's permission to do so.

Item 65: Leale to von Helldorff: Preparing for siege, 23 Sep 1944

Hirzel House, Guernsey
23rd September, 1944

Oberstleutnant von Helldorff,
"Summerland", Mount Durand
St Peter Port

Sir

I am in receipt of your letter of 12th September, 1944. Several weeks ago you informed me that we ought to prepare for a six months siege, and that if we had any particular difficulties I should report them to you and you would endeavour to help us.

Later I sent you a report on certain problems which would be presented to us on the cessation of electricity.

I feel the time has come for me to acquaint you with the position as we see it in case of a failure of the gas supply and/or of its derivative, coke. I accordingly asked Jurat Pierre de Putron, Fuel Controller, to report to me on the matter. This report I forwarded to Dr Symons, Medical Services Officer, for his comments.

These reports are enclosed herewith. I also enclose a report on food, the situation will become very serious during November.

You have freely acknowledged that your duties towards the civilian population under International Law are very real and we appreciate the grave responsibility that is borne by the Occupying Authority in deciding how long the siege shall last. We on our side feel it incumbent on us to inform you with the utmost frankness of the situation as we visualise it.

It is our considered opinion that should gas fail the standard of life of the community will sink below that to which even under present circumstances it has a right. It is superfluous to comment on the very serious conditions which will exist should medical supplies fail. Similarly with food.

I should be glad of an opportunity of meeting you with Jurat de Putron and Dr Symons.

Yours faithfully,
John Leale, President

COAL AND COKE

1. With the exception of 150 tons handed over by the Military for Communal Cooking Civilian Coal stocks are exhausted.
2. This shortage seriously affects the maintenance of Essential Services, i.e. Hospitals and States Dairy. In the course of a conference at Grange Lodge on 8th June instructions were given that a three months' supply of coal should be sent to them from the coal stocks remaining and that they should continue to be supplied with coke.

The coal supplied to them will be exhausted at the end of September and as shown under further supplies of coke are not available.

Their requirements are 14 tons of coal and 26 tons of coke per month.

3. If, as seems probable, coke will not be available a corresponding amount of coal in its place would enable them to continue. The total amount of coal required would be 40 tons.

    This would be distributed as follows:–

	Coal	Coke		Coal
Emergency Hospital	4	10	or	14
Town Hospital	3	4	or	7
Blanchelande Hospital	1	2	or	3
King Edward Sanatorium	1	3	or	4
Emergency Hospital (mental)	1	2	or	2
Prison	1	1	or	2
States' Dairy	4	4	or	8
	14	26	or	40

The fuel does not provide for internal heating. Although a small allowance of wood can be provided it will be impossible to maintain a reasonable temperature by the use of wood alone and a certain amount of coal would seem essential for the hospitals.

From this it is apparent that unless 40 tons of coal can be made available monthly these services cannot continue after the end of September.

COKE

4. The position is stated fully in a letter to the Platzkommandantur dated September 18th, of which, to save repetition, a copy is attached for reference.
5. The general position can be summarised as follows:–

    Owing to the decrease in Gas produced, the amount of coke available for disposal has fallen from 135 tons in August to 75 tons in September. The figure for October will probably be lower still.

    The requirements of the German Forces are:–

    | H.U.V. | 35 tons |
    | A.E.G. Electrical Station | 60 tons |

    A total of 95 tons as compared with an output of 75.
6. If the whole of the coke required for the Bakers 55 tons is drawn from the reserve, the balance remaining on 30/9/44 will be 44 tons 5 cwt., which will only be sufficient to provide for the first three weeks of October. Owing to losses due to weather and pilfering it is improbable that the full amount will be found in this reserve. Nearly all the bread is baked in Patent ovens which cannot be fired with wood and other ovens are not available to replace them.
7. It is clear therefore that unless a supply of suitable fuel is made available from sources outside civilian control the baking of bread will come to an end automatically after the middle of October. Further developments in this

respect are dependent on the decision of the Platzkommandantur in relation to the letter of the 18th instant which is under consideration.

8. There are approximately 2,000 households or 25% of the population which have neither gas nor electricity for cooking.

   The last ration of coal issued in April amounted to ½ cwt of coal with a similar quantity of Pan Ash residue, a fuel of little heating value.

   In May and June the ration consisted of ½ cwt of Anthracite dust and ½ cwt of Pan Ash residue. No further quantities of these are available and therefore household fuel is dependent on the supply of wood fuel.

WOOD FUEL

9. On 3rd June we were informed by the Platzkommandantur I St Helier (Az Wi 11-22 of 31.5.44) that further supplies of coal could not be expected from France and that efforts should be made to purchase wood fuel in France. Orders, however, had already been placed by our agents for over 1,500 tons of wood but before any of this could be delivered the Invasion of Normandy put an end to the possibility of any supplies arriving.

   During the first year of the Occupation a number of trees were felled by the Forestry Department and distributed for fuel, but these activities were discontinued on the instructions of the Feldkommandantur when imports of coal commenced to arrive. From that time permits were restricted to individual owners and the States organisation disbanded.

10. At a conference with the Platzkommandantur at Grange Lodge on 8th June, the request was made for the lifting of the ban on tree felling by the States and approval was given for further felling of trees organised by the States, subject to the condition that any arrangements were put into force whereby trees for felling were selected by Mr Lloyd de Putron accompanied by a German officer and were blazed as approved. The felling was carried out by contract, depôts were organised for sawing the timber into logs by power saws, and transport was provided by the Civil Transport Department.

    The work was just beginning to progress when it was brought to an abrupt stop by the placing of a ban on the use of the lorries and of the power plants.

11. After a conference with Col. Count Helldorff on the 14/8/44 the ban on the use of power for the saws was removed immediately and an allowance of 100 gallons a week sanctioned for the lorries. The work was re-started but a certain amount of disorganisation was inevitable which reduced the output temporarily. The selection and marking of trees is handicapped considerably by reason of the fact that the trees are scattered and there are no densely wooded areas which can be drawn on. Equally the number of trees available for cutting is limited and it seems unlikely that felling can continue for long.

12. During the period 26/6/44 to 9/9/44, 1,350 tons were felled or an average of 123 tons per week.

    Taking into consideration the interruption in the work it is not possible to reckon on more than 150 tons per week which, allowing 17½% for shrinkage and waste in cutting, would provide 125 tons of wood fuel. Shorter days and winter conditions will reduce this figure to 100 tons, if not less. The work is dependent to a great extent on petrol for transport and electric power for saws. If petrol cannot be supplied the output will fall considerably and this will be the case equally in the case of power for the saws.

Taking all these factors into consideration it is doubtful if tree felling can be continued after 30th November owing to shortage of trees, and the weekly output must fall steadily from 150 tons per week to less than 100 tons in November.

COMMUNAL COOKING AND BAKING

13. A request was received from the Platzkommandantur to make arrangements for the provision of cooked food for persons dependent on gas for cooking in the event of a suspension of the supply of gas. On June 8th an allocation of 150 tons of coal was made for this purpose and was subsequently handed over to the Island Administration. The households dependent on either gas or electricity for cooking may be estimated at 75% of the population of which the majority are in the built up areas of the Town, St Sampson's and the Vale parishes. To meet this eventuality arrangements have been made as follows:-

    (a)   to extend as far as possible communal cooking and feeding centres at which persons obtain one cooked meal per diem.

    (b)   to re-open a number of brick ovens which have fallen into disuse and in some cases to build new ovens which persons can take meals which they have prepared for baking once a day, and also by a system of registration to ensure that the fullest use is made both of the supplementary ovens and also the ovens in regular use for baking bread.

    (c)   to provide centres for which persons who are unable owing to distance or for some other reason, to prepare their own meals and take them to the bakehouse, can draw a daily ration of hot stew in exchange for part of their ration of potatoes and meat.

14. A census of the population has been taken and all have been allocated to centres organised under the above three heads. Cards for this purpose have been prepared for issue to individual households pending the time when the scheme will have to be put into operation.

    The disused ovens have been put in order and the necessary staff engaged provisionally. Suitable fuel, faggots of furze and brushwood have been accumulated either at the bakehouses or in a central depôt at the Western Counties Association Yard.

    Since tree felling commenced all brushwood and small branches have been collected and stored for this purpose. Men have also been employed cutting furze for storage. Similarly any timber from demolished greenhouses which is suitable for firewood has been reserved by order of the Controlling Committee and stored pending its requirement.

    A reserve of 80 tons of logs has been set aside for the use of communal cooking centres, and the stock of faggots and furze accumulated (100 tons) represents approximately 8 weeks consumption.

Allocations have also been made to all ovens in which bread is regularly baked and to which dishes can be taken after the completion of baking.

15. These arrangements have been worked out carefully, and appear to be the best which can be made in such circumstances. The fact however cannot be ignored that however satisfactory these arrangements work, considerable hardships are inseparable from such a scheme.

It is inevitable that there will be many cases in which the distance from the house to the bakehouse or centre will be appreciable, no unimportant factor in winter conditions involved exposure to the elements of young and old alike to say nothing of the fact that in most cases the dish will need to be re-heated at home if it is to be eaten hot.

In any case unless household fuel is available as well no provision is possible either for reheating food or for the heating of milk or water for the purposes of preparing a hot drink from the various substitutes which now take the place of tea and coffee.

From this it follows that the provision of one baked dish per day will be inadequate to feed the population unless a certain amount of wood fuel is available to heat food in their homes. The minimum amount required for the cooking necessary for a household getting one meal a day baked in the public ovens can be reckoned at 1 cwt. per week.

16. To provide for 8,000 households at this rate would require 400 tons per week, apart from quantities required for Institutions, sick persons, young children and old people, which would require a further 100 tons per week, making a minimum requirement of 500 tons per week. To meet these requirements the most that can be anticipated is 150 tons per week which will steadily drop to 100 tons owing to weather conditions and cease at the end of November owing to the shortage of trees which can be felled. It may be added that the above requirements only provide for cooking, and the only form of heating available will be that obtainable from the wood fire for cooking.

From the above it is clear that while it is possible to issue a limited ration of wood fuel to those households which have neither gas nor electricity, until the supply of gas fails, it will be impossible to meet more than a fifth of the requirements of the population as regards wood fuel once that has occurred.

19th September ,1944.

BREAD AND FLOUR

The stock allowing for the maintenance of the present reduced bread ration and an issue in alternate weeks of 6 ozs per person as breakfast food, will last until the 11th November, 1944.

Macaroni

The stock allowing for the issue of the present ration (in alternative weeks) of 6 ozs per person as breakfast food will last until the 11th November, 1944. When flour stocks are exhausted and weekly issues will have to be made stocks will last until 16th December, 1944.

Butter and Cooking Fats

The present ration of 4 ozs butter and 2 ozs cooking fats per person per week, in addition to the 1.5 metric tons requisitioned weekly by the German Forces, can be maintained until the 18th November, 1944, after which the ration will depend on production.

Sugar

The ration of sugar previous to the 28th August, 1944, was 8 ozs per week for children under four years of age and 3 ozs per week for all other consumers. In addition to all the population received an extra ounce of sugar per week in the form of a monthly jam ration. On this basis, but with no jam ration, and allowing for bakers and chemists requirements, the stock would have lasted until the 9th December, 1944. From the 28th August, by order of the Occupying Authorities which we strongly contested, the ration of sugar for all consumers aged eighteen years and over was reduced to two ounces per week, and allowing for bakers and chemists requirements and with no jam ration or sugar in lieu thereof, the stock of sugar will last until 13th January, 1945.

Salt

The ration from the 3rd January to 8th July, 1944 was 1 oz per person per week. From 9th July, 1944, no ration could be issued. There is only sufficient salt for bread making and the production of butter to 4th November, 1944. A scheme for the distribution of brine has been in force since 9th July, 1944, the average issue being 2,354 gallons per week, equivalent to 5 cwt. 2 qtrs. 0 lbs, or assuming all the population take advantage of this scheme which through lack of transport and other difficulties is only available to a fraction thereof, a ration of 4 ozs per week per head of population.

Potatoes

The stock of potatoes is sufficient to last on the basis of the present ration to the 31st January, 1945.

Cheese

On the basis of monthly rations of 6 ozs per person the stock will last until the 30th November, 1944.

Chocolate

The stock is sufficient for an issue to all consumers of 3 ozs per person or for four issues of 4 ozs per head to children under fourteen years of age.

Tinned Meat (Sardines and Meat Paste)

Not sufficient for a general issue. Consideration is being given to an issue to adolescents and elderly persons.

Dried Beans

According to the Glasshouse Utilisation Board sufficient beans will be available at the end of September, 1944 to provide for an issue of a ration per head of 1 lb.

Item 66: Letters to Camp Seniors at Biberach & Laufen, 7 Oct 1944

The Bailiff's Chambers, Guernsey
7th October, 1944

My dear Sherwill,

The German Authorities have given me this opportunity of writing to you and I gladly avail myself of it so that those of our people who are in your company may know how we are getting on here.

First and foremost, although we were on the fringe of the bombing zone at the beginning of hostilities on the Continent, I am thankful to say that there have been no casualties here and comparatively little damage to property. The war, of course, is now far from us.

Up to the present we have not run out of either food or medical supplies, but the position is becoming much more serious every day. Our main difficulty, as in Jersey, is fuel, and if we do not receive help soon the bakers will have to stop making bread. We look like being reduced to wood fuel and we have already drawn considerably on stocks. There is, of course, very little fuel for domestic consumption and rations of gas and electricity have had to be cut very drastically.

We understand that negotiations are proceeding between the British and German Governments regarding the supply of essentials to the civilian population of the Islands.

Meanwhile lack of news, especially personal news from England is causing considerable mental suffering amongst our people. If you have any news please send it on to me at the first opportunity – above all news of people who are ill or wounded in England. One young man of whom news is anxiously awaited is the son of Mr G. Le Marchant of the National Provincial Bank.

If you can, put in a word anywhere about re-starting the Red Cross news service, we should all be most grateful, especially as we have received no message dated later than February last.

Please give my kindest regards to all internees; we are hoping to see you all again soon.

With kindest regards, Yours sincerely,
Victor G. Carey, Bailiff of Guernsey

P.S. Mrs Sherwill and the boys are in good health & spirits.

Note: A similar letter, except the postscript, was sent to Mr G.G. Garland at Biberach.

Item 67: Newspaper article: Supplies for Channel Islanders [nd]

Re: Supplies for the Channel Islanders

In order to keep the population informed about the question of supplies and to stop injurious rumours, the Commander of the Channel Isles has authorised the "Evening Press" to publish the following information:

> The Channel Isles had virtually been cut off from all supplies already a month before the invasion. From that moment the population lived on the produce of the island and from stocks which had been formed according to instructions from the Occupying Power. In view of the possibility of a state of siege, agriculture and industry had been adapted as far as feasible to make the fortresses self-supporting.
>
> As the population, however, cannot be supplied indefinitely from the stocks of the fortresses or from the produce harvested or manufactured within them, the Commander of the Channel Isles some time ago took the precaution of getting into touch with superior authorities and has informed the German Government of the situation.
>
> This action was appreciably facilitated by reports about the most essential commodities, supplies of which were running out in the near future, submitted by the States of Guernsey in the interest of the population of Guernsey.
>
> The German Government has intimated its intention of taking the necessary steps in this matter with the Protecting Power. For this purpose the Commander of the Channel Isles has submitted a report about the Islands' monthly requirements of essential commodities.
>
> Any action the Protecting Power may decide to take on this information is now, of course, beyond the control of the Occupying Authorities.

Item 68: P.K. to Leale: Responsibilities of Occupying Power, 18 Oct 1944

Befehlshaber der Kanalinseln
St. Qu., 18th October, 1944

Confidential

To the President of the Controlling Committee of the States of Guernsey
St Peter Port

Due to a trip to Jersey, your letter of the 23rd September can only be answered today. First of all, a fundamental error on your part must be cleared up, which is due to the fact that you believe the Occupying Power to be the responsible beseiger. As already announced to the Bailiff in September, the competent Protecting Power for the Islands was acquainted in detail, by the Occupying Power, many weeks ago, with the serious position of the civilian population, and it only depends on the good will of England whether and when supplies requested from here for the civilian population will be forthcoming.

As far as is in the power of the Occupier, everything will continue to be done to avoid serious hardship. The responsibility, however, no longer rests with the said occupier.

(signed) von Helldorff

Platzkommandantur I St Helier
Nebenstelle Guernsey
Az.16
19th October, 1944

Controlling Committee of the States of Guernsey

Re: Dry beans crop

The whole of the dry beans crop is to be collected by the G.U.B. A thorough collection must be guaranteed. Any deficits are to be reported immediately.

From the amount to be expected, 60 tons are to be delivered to the Verpflegungsausgabestelle.

(signed) Schneberger, Militaerverweltungsrat

The Bailiff's Chambers
Royal Court House
Guernsey
21st October, 1944

To: Generalleutnant Graf von Schmettow
Guernsey

On the 13th instant you authorised a statement to appear in the newspaper. Part reads as follows:–

> "Any action the Protecting Power may decide to take on this information is now, of course, beyond the control of the Occupying Authorities."

In a letter, dated the 18th October, 1944, Colonel von Helldorff is more explicit and concludes:–

> "As far as is in the power of the Occupier everything will continue to be done to avoid serious hardship. The responsibility, however, no longer rests with the said Occupier."

This is a matter of vital importance to us because as it stands this statement appears to mean that should England – or for that matter of that the Protecting Power or the Red Cross – not send us supplies, you will disclaim responsibility for the consequences.

This is not our conception of the matter. To us the Hague Convention is one and indivisible. We hold that so long as you continue to exercise, under it, the rights of an Occupying Force, you cannot escape from your responsibilities thereof. The only way you can divest yourselves of your responsibilities is by giving up your rights, that is, by ceasing to be an Occupying Force.

May we take an example? You claim under International Law the right to requisition food and money with which you buy food. How, therefore, can you assert that shortages in the island are not your responsibility?

We hope we have misunderstood Colonel von Helldorff's letter. If so, we shall be glad to be corrected. The remainder of this letter is on the assumption we have misunderstood it.

You will doubtless agree that, since the isolation of the Island from the French mainland in July last, the task of maintaining the civilian population has become increasingly difficult.

You will recollect that the first step we took was to write to the International Red Cross asking for the resumption of some form of message service and that you forwarded the letter for us. We have never been informed whether that letter reached its destination.

As it become increasingly certain that communication with France would be cut off and would not soon be resumed, we wrote to the International Red Cross and to our Protecting Power setting out the position of the civilian population regarding essential supplies and asking that preliminary arrangements be made for the shipment here of essentials should we become isolated. You have informed us that in your opinion those letters never left Saint Malo for their destination.

Since the beginning of August last we have kept you constantly informed regarding stocks of essentials and have made all possible economies in consumption. We have further asked several times for the transmission of some communication to the Protecting Power on our behalf.

We have learned recently, through conversations with Colonel von Helldorff and from the notice appearing in the "Guernsey Evening Press" on the 13th instant that you have sent messages, both to your own Government and to the Protecting Power, setting out the conditions under which the civilian population of the Channel Islands are living and asking for supplies to be sent to us.

We understand that the messages contained, inter alia, a statement to the effect that medical supplies would end by the 15th October and, since this information was in the hands of the Protecting Power some weeks ago, we are of opinion that that body would almost certainly have given some indication by now of their intention of sending in supplies, had they meant to do so. As we have received no such indication, we must assume that outside help will not be forthcoming and that we should proceed with our planning without taking such help into account.

This being so, we wish to emphasise certain factors which we regard as seriously affecting the interests of our people. They are:–

1. Purchasing Power in the hands of the Occupying Forces.
    The quantity of money obtained by your Paymaster from the States has greatly increased recently. We ask for your assurance that the Troops (both units and individuals) are not now put in possession of more money than they were before last June. The relative purchasing power of soldiers and civilians is a factor which cannot be disregarded in any realistic attempt to see that the population is fed in times of scarcity.

2. The requisition, during the past four-and-a-half months, of butter reserved at great sacrifice for civilian consumption.
    We claim that the present ration of butter, taking into account the negligible issues of commodities, such as meat, cheese and fish, which might serve to augment fat, is quite inadequate. We have asked several times recently that you fulfil your promise to issue to us pork fat in return for the butter you have requisitioned and have even gone so far as to ask that a panel of local and German doctors study the question and that you act on their advice. We have received no reply whatsoever to this request. Meanwhile, if the siege is to continue, there can be no doubt that any butter you may requisition at this stage is altogether beyond the resources of the Island and therefore contrary to Article 52 of the Hague Convention. We ask that such requisitions should now cease.

3. The Vegetable Position.
    We have recently been carefully into the vegetable position. Past experience has shown that during the Occupation there has been a shortage of vegetables – particularly roots – during the early months of each year. This winter, as

other foods become scarcer, there will be a greater demand for vegetables than ever before.

We believe that our resources in roots would only suffice to satisfy the civilian needs until the end of March. Any requisitions by the military by whatsoever method will have to be met by a corresponding reduction in the length of the siege. We were told in early August that we should be prepared for a six months' siege. It is, however, our considered opinion that unless military acquisitions of vegetables are reduced from what we believe is their present level, our resources cannot stand the strain of a siege as long as to the end of January. You have stated to us that you are bound under International Law to ensure the wellbeing of the population, and indeed Article 52 of the Hague Convention is quite explicit that requisition must be in proportion to the resources of the country. Should the public supply fail owing to your acquisitions, you will obviously lay yourselves open to a charge of taking beyond our resources.

As an illustration of the position in which the Island and its Authorities are being placed, we have just received the following order from the Platzkommandantur:–

19th October, 1944
Controlling Committee of the States of Guernsey
Re: Dry beans crop

The whole of the dry beans crop is to be collected by the G.U.B. A thorough collection must be guaranteed. Any deficits are to be reported immediately.
From the amount to be expected, 60 tons are to be delivered to the Verpflegungsausgabestelle.
(signed) Schneberger, Militärverweltungsrat

This collection is impossible. The Glasshouse Utilization Board do not expect to receive more than 20 tons of dried beans, and this will not be nearly sufficient for the civilian population. The Hague Convention expressly forbids an Occupying Power to requisition under such circumstances, and we therefore cannot carry out this order.

At the request of the Platzkommandantur we are considering a scheme for some form of control of vegetables, but in view of the preremptory order for beans, we are not proceeding further with the matter until we have discussed the whole position with you.

We feel, therefore, that, in view of our vegetable, as well as our general situation – particularly as regards fuel and medicines (see letter from the President of the Controlling Committee to Colonel von Helldorff, reference 5/3/4, dated 23rd September, 1944, with enclosures) – it is incumbent on the German Authorities most seriously to consider an earlier closing date of the siege than the end of next January in the light of their responsibilities accepted by them under International Law.

We take this opportunity of making formal application to be put into direct communication with our Protecting Power, so that arrangements may be made for us to be supplied with food, medical supplies and other essentials before the position becomes impossible. We ask that you should allow us to do this by your wireless to avoid delay and the risk of correspondence going astray.

In view of the gravity of the outlook which confronts us, we ask that you will meet us with the members of the Controlling Committee to discuss the situation.

(signed) Victor G. Carey
Bailiff of Guernsey

(signed) John Leale
President
The Controlling Committee of the States of Guernsey

Item 69: Requête: Review of Constitution, Oct 1944

Guernsey, October 1944

To The Bailiff
Royal Court House, Guernsey

The humble Petition of the undersigned members of the States of Deliberation sheweth:

1. That on the First day of January, 1900, membership of the States of Deliberation was increased by the inclusion therein of nine Deputies of the People;
2. That after a due period of successful trial, the number of Deputies was increased to eighteen on the First day of January, 1921.
3. That experience in all countries during the last twenty-five years has vindicated the democratic system of government; and
4. That the time has therefore arrived, both from an Island standpoint and in view of world experience, to study once more the question of direct representation in the States of Deliberation, as well as other means whereby the government of the Island may be brought more into line with present day requirements.

These Premises considered, your Petitioners humbly pray that this Petition be laid before the States of Deliberation with the request:

(a)   That a Committee be appointed to study carefully and to report to the States of Deliberation regarding the desirability of increasing the number of Deputies of the People from 18 to such number as will give to this section of the States of Deliberation a majority of the total voting power;

(b)   Any other alternatives in either the constitution of the States or in the rules and customer regulating procedure therein whereby this House may be brought more into conformity with the requirements of present day government.

And your Petitioners will ever pray.

Item 70: General to Bailiff: Resp. of Occupying Power, 23 Oct 1944

<u>STRICTLY CONFIDENTIAL</u>

GUERNSEY

Befehlshaber der Kanalinseln

23.10.44

To The Bailiff of Guernsey, Victor G. Carey

I hereby acknowledge receipt of your letter of the 21.10.44. Its form and contents are not, to my regret, of such a nature as to preserve the good collaboration which has hitherto existed and the confidence which I have always placed in the co-operation of the States.

I cannot get rid of the impression that, in drawing up the letter, you, Mr Bailiff, availed yourself of the services of an advisor who, instead of acknowledging the great efforts made by the Occupying Power and by myself in the interests of the population, now expresses views and makes assertions which in no way correspond to the actual facts.

Already before the invasion, the supplies for the population were constantly obtained by the importation of the necessary commodities and ensured the feeding of the population in accordance with the rations in force in France. Only the attacks made by the English Air Force, long before the invasion, on supply ships and on the harbours, led to important disturbances and delays in sea transport. They not only cost losses of personnel among the naval forces who performed transport work in the interest of the civilian population, but also losses in shipping space and, consequently, in valuable commodities.

The Occupying Power, in the interest of the supplies for the island population, put up with these losses and, conscious of its responsibilities, carried on the supply shipping service.

Since the beginning of the invasion, the attacks have increased, and in consequence I had to request my superiors to call the attention of the British Government to the consequences of these attacks as regards the population of the islands, with the remark that, should such attacks continue, the Occupying Power could no longer, due to the impossibility of further transport, guarantee supplies to the population.

This menace on transport continued to increase, so that about one month before the invasion no supplies arrived to speak of. The islands were then left to depend on their own provisioning, or on what they produced. At that time there only remained an adjustment to be made between the islands regarding certain commodities such as cereals and potatoes.

It is to the credit of the German Military Administration that, looking to the future, it succeeded in obtaining, partly against the wishes of the States, an increase in the cultivation of cereals and potatoes at least in Jersey.

These measures made the islands independent of supplies from the Continent, at least for many things.

To all appearances, the States of the Islands could not liberate themselves from the thought of profitable exports – of tomatoes in particular.

With better judgement and greater social insight it would have been possible, even in Guernsey, to adjust the agricultural production, in good time, in the interests of the population.

In the Islands, you do not know the war, you do not know what war means. You cannot realize its effects as felt daily by German towns, the whole of France, London and South England, nor the sacrifices and sufferings which the affected countries have to live through. Compared to these, the islands have not felt even breath of it. You only feel the burden of occupation – an occupation, however, the Command of which, conscious of its responsibilities, has made every effort to prevent every hardship that could be avoided. The necessities of war can, however, not be disregarded.

The Occupying Power has reported in detail to the German Government the position of and the cares in connection with the civilian population, and has been informed that the Reich Government has applied for the sending of representatives of the International Red Cross.

If, a long time ago, the States were asked to co-operate in making a 6-months' plan for the civilian population, this was only a precautionary measure since effective assistance from outside could not be expected within a shorter time. This had however nothing to do with the duration of the occupation of the islands. I can only describe it as entirely irrelevant to make the Occupying Power responsible for the prolongation of the time of occupation and the consequences thereof for the civilian population. The besiegers are the Allied Forces, and we the besieged. The inhabitants of the island fortresses are British subjects.

Now the islands are cut off, I can no longer provide for the population.

With the further continuation of the siege by the Allied Forces, it will become necessary, under certain circumstances, in order to maintain the power of resistance of the island fortresses, to draw on the products of the country and on its stocks, without any other consideration and contrary to the moderation hitherto shown. All consideration for the besieged also disappears in the case of fighting activities. In such cases, the besieger alone bears the responsibility for his compatriots.

It is understandable that the States should hope for an early termination of the war, but not that they should base, on this hope, opinions or measures which do not correspond to the actual situation.

The German Army does not build fortifications of such strength without holding them with the greatest bitterness and until the exhaustion of its power of resistance. Even if, in the long run, a calamitous situation should arise for the population – for which the besieger alone would be responsible – this would not in any way alter the case.

In brief reply to the different points of your letter – which could have been cleared up previously with the Platzkommandantur – I would inform you that the troops not only receive no greater amount of money, but that, as your representatives know quite well, the purchase of fruit and vegetables for the troops has been forbidden for some time past. This is a measure which is probably unprecedented in the history of occupations.

As regards the requisition of butter stocks, this cannot be looked upon as a requisition. The troops receive at present 1 ton only per week, which is much below the amount they could claim on the basis of the country's production.

Vegetables are no longer levied as in the past years. In spite of this, the cultivation of vegetables has been increased by about 1000 vergées in order to improve the troops' supplies. Therefore, should the supplies for the civilian population fail, the States alone are responsible because they have not carried out the orders given and not properly supervised the growing of vegetables.

As regards the dried beans, your representatives reported the sowing of beans to an extent which, according to their own statement, should have produced an amount of 150 to 200 tons. As has been ascertained in the meantime, the report made to you of only 20 tons is based on a deliberate untruth.

I would therefore expressly warn you that if the plans and orders of the Platzkommandantur, made on the basis of careful calculations, are boycotted from any quarter, only your responsible officials and the population will have to suffer.

If you repeatedly refer to International Law, it is of little use to interpret it one-sidedly from your own point of view, while disregarding all necessities arising from the war.

A single example in this connection: The fortress of Le Havre was besieged by the Allied troops. Three times the Commander requested the Allied Commander to let the French population out of the fortress. Three times the request was rejected and the town so powerfully bombed that thousands of inhabitants lost their lives.

The request to establish direct communication with the Protecting Power – which by the way acts for both sides – is physically impossible and in any case could not be permitted by us. I must also abstain from personal conversations as long as the views and the unheard-of accusations put forward in your letter against the Occupying Power continue to be maintained.

(signed) VON SCHMETTOW

Item 71: Bailiff to General: Resp. of Occupying Power, 30 Oct 1944

STRICTLY CONFIDENTIAL

The Bailiff's Chambers
Royal Court House
Guernsey
30th October 1944

To
Generalleutnant Graf von Schmettow
Festungskommandant
Guernsey

I have to acknowledge receipt of your letter of the 23rd instant and to say that your regret at the contents of our letter of the 21st is equalled by my regret that you should find so much to displease you therein.

I have re-read our letter most carefully and can find neither false argument nor any part which is written other than in all sincerity and in the hope that your previous willingness to help with the well-being of the population would lead you to assist us in our present difficulties.

You must know that Jurat Leale, President of The Controlling Committee, shares with me responsibility for the administration of the Island and that, as the signatures would suggest, our letter of the 21st was written by Jurat Leale and myself in collaboration. His sense of justice is so well known to all who come into contact with him – civilian and German alike – that I cannot bring myself to believe that your mention of an advisor who disregards past German efforts on our behalf refers to him.

I am quite willing to admit that, in these Islands, we have seen and suffered little from the war so far. It is, however, my duty to see that the people under my charge are guarded as much as possible from future suffering, and the fact that civilians in other parts of Europe – including England – have suffered grievously does not absolve me from my responsibility.

You say quite frankly that if the siege continues you may have to disregard the well-being of the population in order to maintain the power of resistance of the Island fortresses. That is your duty as you see it. You further deny categorically that you can provide for the population now that the Islands are cut off. We have always understood from you previously that you regarded the feeding of the German and civilian populations as of equal importance under all circumstances, and this new statement from you makes my responsibility heavier than ever.

I must therefore, ask you to regard the problems that we have placed before you not as an effort to make your work more difficult, but as one to do our own duty to the very best of our ability.

I am still of opinion that some of these problems can be eased very considerably by talks between the officials concerned on either side, and now that I have explained our attitude, I hope that your objection to meeting us will disappear.

Three points in your letter, however, I must answer at once.

As it became increasingly certain that communication with France would be cut off and would not soon be resumed, we wrote to the International Red Cross and to our Protecting Power setting out the position of the civilian population regarding essential supplies and asking that preliminary arrangements be made for the shipment here of essentials should we become isolated. You have informed us that in your opinion those letters never left Saint Malo for their destination.

Since the beginning of August last we have kept you constantly informed regarding stocks of essentials and have made all possible economies in consumption. We have further asked several times for the transmission of some communication to the Protecting Power on our behalf.

We have learned recently, through conversations with Colonel von Helldorff and from the notice appearing in the "Guernsey Evening Press" on the 13th instant that you have sent messages, both to your own Government and to the Protecting Power, setting out the conditions under which the civilian population of the Channel Islands are living and asking for supplies to be sent to us.

We understand that the messages contained, inter alia, a statement to the effect that medical supplies would end by the 15th October and, since this information was in the hands of the Protecting Power some weeks ago, we are of opinion that that body would almost certainly have given some indication by now of their intention of sending in supplies, had they meant to do so. As we have received no such indication, we must assume that outside help will not be forthcoming and that we should proceed with our planning without taking such help into account.

This being so, we wish to emphasize certain factors which we regard as seriously affecting the interests of our people. They are:–

1. Purchasing Power in the hands of the Occupying Forces.
   The quantity of money obtained by your Paymaster from the States has greatly increased recently. We ask for your assurance that the Troops (both units and individuals) are not now put in possession of more money than they were before last June. The relative purchasing power of soldiers and civilians is a factor which cannot be disregarded in any realistic attempt to see that the population is fed in times of scarcity.
2. The requisition, during the past four-and-a-half months, of butter reserved at great sacrifice for civilian consumption
   We claim that the present ration of butter, taking into account the negligible issues of commodities, such as meat, cheese and fish, which might serve to augment fat, is quite inadequate. We have asked several times recently that you fulfil your promise to issue to us pork fat in return for the butter you have requisitioned and have even gone so far as to ask that a panel of local and German doctors study the question and that you act on their advice. We have received no reply whatsoever to this request. Meanwhile, if the siege is to continue, there can be no doubt that any butter you may requisition at this stage is altogether beyond the resources of the Island and therefore contrary to Article 52 of the Hague Convention. We ask that such requisitions should now cease.

3. The Vegetable Position.

    We have recently been carefully into the vegetable position. Past experience has shown that during the Occupation there has been a shortage of vegetables – particularly roots – during the early months of each year. This winter, as other foods become scarcer, there will be a greater demand for vegetables than ever before.

    We believe that our resources in roots would only suffice to satisfy the civilian needs until the end of March. Any requisitions by the military by whatsoever method will have to be met by a corresponding reduction in the length of the siege. We were told in early August that we should be prepared for a six months' siege. It is, however, our considered opinion that unless military acquisitions of vegetables are reduced from what we believe is their present level, our resources cannot stand the strain of a siege as long as to the end of January. You have stated to us that you are bound under International Law to ensure the wellbeing of the population, and indeed Article 52 of the Hague Convention is quite explicit that requisition must be in proportion to the resources of the country. Should the public supply fail owing to your acquisitions, you will obviously lay yourselves open to a charge of taking beyond our resources.

As an illustration of the position in which the Island and its Authorities are being placed, we have just received the following order from the Platzkommandantur:–

19th October, 1944
Controlling Committee of the States of Guernsey
Re: Dry beans crop

The whole of the dry beans crop is to be collected by the G.U.B. A thorough collection must be guaranteed. Any deficits are to be reported immediately.
From the amount to be expected, 60 tons are to be delivered to the Verpflegungsausgabestelle.
(signed) Schneberger, Militärverwaltungsrat

This collection is impossible. The Glasshouse Utilization Board do not expect to receive more than 20 tons of dried beans, and this will not be nearly sufficient for the civilian population. The Hague Convention expressly forbids an Occupying Power to requisition under such circumstances, and we therefore cannot carry out this order.

At the request of the Platzkommandantur we are considering a scheme for some form of control of vegetables, but in view of the preremptory order for beans, we are not proceeding further with the matter until we have discussed the whole position with you.

We feel, therefore, that, in view of our vegetable, as well as our general situation – particularly as regards fuel and medicines (see letter from the President of the Controlling Committee to Colonel von Helldorff, reference 5/3/4, dated 23rd

September, 1944, with enclosures) – it is incumbent on the German Authorities most seriously to consider an earlier closing date of the siege than the end of next January in the light of their responsibilities accepted by them under International Law.

We take this opportunity of making formal application to be put into direct communication with our Protecting Power, so that arrangements may be made for us to be supplied with food, medical supplies and other essentials before the position becomes impossible. We ask that you should allow us to do this by your wireless to avoid delay and the risk of correspondence going astray.

In view of the gravity of the outlook which confronts us, we ask that you will meet us with the members of the Controlling Committee to discuss the situation.

(signed) Victor G. Carey
Bailiff of Guernsey

(signed) John Leale
President
The Controlling Committee of the States of Guernsey

Item 72: Leale to P.K.: Potato Requisition, 31 Oct 1944

The Controlling Committee of the States of Guernsey
Hirzel House, Guernsey
31st October, 1944

Platzkommandantur I St Helier
Nebenstelle Guernsey

Sir

I have learned with the utmost dismay that you are taking from us 20 tons of potatoes.

I can protest, but I cannot prevent you from taking them. I can claim that your action is contrary to International Law, but I know you will deny this. I have decided to sink all pride and appeal to you as man to man and in the name of humanity to replace the potatoes you take by other foodstuffs of equivalent food value. If your contention is that your troops must have potatoes, you cannot fail to understand the full implication of what I mean when I say our people must have food.

You are German, I am British, it may be a difference of outlook but I cannot reconcile you taking potatoes we so badly need with risking German lives to bring us supplies. Some day this dreadful war will have ended and the Occupation have become a matter of history. I think you know my outlook on life sufficiently well to believe that I speak in all sincerity when I say I would sooner pass into Post-War days encouraged by the thought of the latter action than soured by the memory of the former.

Yours faithfully,
JOHN LEALE
President

Item 73: Harbourmaster to Leale: Unloading ships, 4 Nov 1944

Harbour Master's Office, Guernsey
4th November, 1944

John Leale, Esq., Jurat
President
The Controlling Committee of the States of Guernsey

Dear Sir,

It may be of some interest to you, with the object of using this information when the Occupation is at an end, to relate what happened yesterday with respect to the wheat cargo brought from Jersey.

Two barges, the "Tourane" and "Saigon" arrived here about 11 a.m. yesterday from Jersey. They were both loaded with foodstuffs – flour, wheat and potatoes, the States of Guernsey having an interest in the "Saigon" only. A manifest declaring 150 tons wheat in 2322 sacks, consigned to the States arrived with the barge "Saigon" and was duly handed to me at the Jetty.

The General commanding this Division was on the quayside and gave instructions, which were passed on to me, that our share of the cargo must be requisitioned on behalf of the military.

I was not prepared to accept this decision and said so in no unmeasured terms to all and sundry on the quay. Further, I immediately got in touch with the Essential Commodities Department, informing Mr Loveridge of what had occurred, and asking him to take the matter up with the Platzkommandant at once. This he did, informing me by 'phone at 13:00 that we were to have as much wheat as Bragg's could take. I immediately got in touch with the necessary labour, transport, etc. but you will readily appreciate that during a meal hour is not the best time to obtain service. The Germans commenced discharge of both ships at 13:00, unloading flour, potatoes and wheat simultaneously. I was ready to receive cargo at about 15:00, some lorries by that time turned up, but was not allowed to do so until a quarter of an hour later. Work was continued from then until one hold had been emptied, 41 tons having by then been over the weighbridge to our account. Another hold was broached the following morning and emptied by 12:30. Coincident with this I had been loading lorries with potatoes, of which 30 tons were allocated to civilian use. At about 12:45 a quantity of potatoes remaining in the bottom of a hold, already being discharged by German labour for their use, was handed over to me with the remark that I could have what was left. On enquiry as to working hours, I was officially informed that they would work during the meal hour and in the afternoon. What actually happened was that at 13:00, the electric current was cut off, and the crane I was using was left swung out immobilized. Several tons of potatoes were still in the hold, which I was unable to cover up, not having use of the crane. Such potatoes as were on the quay were eventually loaded, no suitable lorries being available at the time, theft being kept down as far as possible by enlisting the goodwill of such German ratings as seemed disposed to help me.

A watch was kept over what was left in the hold until the electric current came on again at 18:00, when the hold was covered up and sealed by the German Harbour

Police. This seal was broken during the night, however, as I found when discharge was resumed this morning. Whether any potatoes were taken it is of course impossible to say. The total tonnage of wheat actually landed for the States was:–

Wheat	103 tons	17 cwt.
Potatoes	20 tons	14 cwt.

Total tonnage passing over the weighbridge for the German Forces:–

Wheat	185 tons	18 cwt.
Potatoes	160 tons	4 cwt.

Yours faithfully,
(signed) J.P. FRANKLIN

Item 74: Present stocks of essential commodities, 1 Nov 1944

<u>Replies to Questions asked by Deputy C.H. Cross at Meeting of the States of Deliberation held on the 1st November, 1944 with reference to the position in regard to food and other essential commodities, clothing, footwear, essential services and medical supplies as on 21st October, 1944</u>

Wheat and Flour

The present rations of bread, which were reduced by order of the German Occupying Authorities following the invasion of France are as follows:–

	lbs per week
Children under 18 months	1½
Children aged 18 months and under 10	3
Male Heavy Workers under 21 only	6
Female Heavy Workers under 21 only	5¼
Male Heavy Workers over 21	4¼
Female Heavy Workers over 21	4¼
All other consumers	4¼

The present ration of flour is 6 ozs per person per fortnight.

The stock of flour as on the 21st October, 1944 was 71 tons 11 cwts.

The stock of wheat as on the 21st October, 1944 was 392 tons 12 cwts which represents a stock of flour of 353 tons 6 cwts.

The total stock of flour, and of flour as represented by wheat, is therefore 424 tons 17 cwts.

This stock, together with the stock of flour held by the bakers, which represents one week's requirements, will provide bread and flour on the present very inadequate rations until the 13th January, 1945.

Macaroni

The stock on the 21st October, 1944, was 26 tons 7 cwts, which on the present ration of 6 ozs per person per fortnight, will last until the 6th January, 1945.

Meat

There is no stock of meat in the Cold Stores. We had hoped to be in a position to guarantee the very meagre fortnightly ration of approximately 4 ozs per person, but this may not prove practicable oftener than once in three or four weeks, provided, of course, that our livestock herds are not requisitioned.

Coffee Substitute

The last ration of 2 ozs of coffee substitute per fortnight for all consumers over 4 years of age was issued during the week commencing the 16th October, 1944. The stock on the 21st October, 1944 was 8 cwts. No further ration of coffee substitute can be issued, the small stock being reserved for hospitals.

Cocoa

No stock. We have been able to issue on extremely isolated occasions a ration of cocoa of 1 oz or 2 ozs per head of the population, the last ration being issued during the week commencing 25th September, 1944.

Sugar

The present weekly rations of sugar, which also were reduced by order of the German Occupying Authorities following the invasion of France are as follows:-

Children under 4	8 ozs
Children aged 4 and under 18	3 ozs
All other consumers	2 ozs

The stock of sugar on the 21st October, 1944, was 17 tons 12 cwts, which on the present inadequate rationing basis will last until the 6th January, 1945.

Tea

No stock. No ration has been issued since February, 1941.

Salt

The stock on the 21st October, 1944, was 18 cwts. No ration of salt has been issued to the population since the 10th July, 1944, as stocks were reserved for issue to Bakers for bread making and to the States Dairy for butter. The small stock of 18 cwts. which remained on the 21st October has since been exhausted. From now onwards the Bakers will have to use salt water for bread making and no salt will be used in the production of butter. Salt Water is being distributed weekly or fortnightly to the civilian population in certain areas by the States Chemical Department, the total quantity of salt obtained from the salt water averaging not more than 0.4 ozs per head of the pooulation per week. This is of course being supplemented to some extent by private enterprise.

Fats

The present ration of butter, also reduced by order of the German Occupying Authorities from 4 ozs of butter and 2 ozs of fat per person per week as from the 2nd October, 1944, is as follows:-

(a)	Butter – all consumers	3 ozs per week
(b)	Cooking Fat (Butter) – all consumers	1½ ozs per week

i.e. a total of 4½ ozs per person per week. The German Authorities are at present requisitioning one metric ton (19 cwts 72 lbs) per week but they have intimated that as from 1st November, 1944, their requisition may be reduce to ½ metric ton (9 cwt 92 lbs), per week. The stock of butter on the 21st October, 1944, was 18 tons 12 cwts. Provided that there is no reduction in the number of milch cows we expect to be able to continue the present meagre rations till the end of the year.

Jam

No stock. The last monthly ration of ½ lb jam per head of population was issued during July, 1944.

Cheese

The present ration of cheese is on an average 6 ozs per person per month. The stock on the 21st October, 1944, was 9 tons 2 cwts, which, on the present rationing basis, will last until 23rd December, 1944.

Milk

Provided that there is no reduction in the number of milch cows we hope to maintain the present ration at ½ pint of separated milk per person per day, but during the low productive periods it may have to be reduced to ⅓ pint per person per day.

Saccharin

The stock on the 21st October, 1944 was 2 cwts 101 lbs. Issues of saccharin have been made from time to time. The present stock, allowing for issues to diabetics and for pharmaceutical requirements, will enable one issue to be made of 50 pastilles per head of the population over four years.

Chocolate

The stock on the 21st October, 1944, was 1 ton 9 cwts. Issues have been made from time to time generally to children under 14 years of age. The present stock would provide 4 issues of 4 ozs or two issues of 8 ozs each to all children under 14 years of age.

Matches

Matches are issued at the rate of one box of fifty matches per head of the population per month. The stock on the 21st October, 1944, was 476 gross boxes of fifty matches. On the present controlled basis the stock will be sufficient to make two issues of one box of fifty matches per head of the population. The stock will therefore last until December, 1944.

Soap

(a) <u>Household</u>. No stock. No ration of household soap has been issued since August, 1944.

(b) <u>Toilet Soap Substitute</u>. The stock on the 21st October, 1944, was 33 lbs, which is being reserved for babies under six months of age. No ration of toilet soap substitute has been issued since July, 1944.

(c) <u>Soap Powder</u>. The stock on the 21st October, 1944, was 1 ton 3 cwts which is being reserved for the washing of the clothes of babies up to the age of 18 months.

(d) <u>Soda</u>. The stock on the 21st October, 1944 was 16 cwts. which is being reserved for farmers and milk depôts for the cleaning of utensils and for persons engaged on what is usually known as "dirty" work.

(e) <u>Shaving Soap</u>. The stock on the 21st October, 1944 was 15 lbs. No ration can be issued or has been issued since July, 1944.

Coke

No stock. The coke produced by the Guernsey Gas Light Co Ltd is being consumed by bakers. This supply will cease when the supply of gas ceases about the end of December, 1944. No ration of coke has been issued since February, 1944.

House Coal

No stock. In July of this year the German Authorities handed over 150 tons of coal to be reserved exclusively for communal cooking. No ration of coal has been issued since May 1944.

Wood Fuel

Apart from a reserve of 80 tons of logs and 100 tons wood faggots for communal cooking, which will last about eight weeks, there are no stocks of wood fuel as it is issued to the public as soon as it has been cut up.

During October two hundredweight was issued for cooking to households without gas and a similar quantity would be required to provide a ration of 1 cwt each for sick and infirm.

To meet all these requirements we cannot produce more than 100 tons a week. This will only provide a reduced ration for cooking and for the sick and infirm, and consequently it will be impossible to provide a general heating ration or any heating for schools, offices or business premises.

Petrol

The stocks of civilian petrol are exhausted and we now rely upon receiving a monthly allocation from the German Authorities.

Paraffin Oil

The stock on the 31st October was 950 gallons. Under orders of the German Authorities supplies are only released for very essential services the average monthly consumption including supplies to hospitals for lighting purposes during the electricity curfew amount to 150 gallons, plus an additional average of 132 gallons requisitioned by the German Authorities. On the present basis of rigid control and requisition of the German Authorities the stocks will last until the end of January, 1945.

Electricity

On the present basis of rationing, which provides for eleven hours supply per day, and providing the civilian population and military authorities keep within their present allowances, electricity will last until about Christmas time.

Gas

On the present basis of rationing, which provides for 4½ hours supply per day, and providing the civilian population and military authorities keep within their present allowances, gas will last till approximately the end of December, 1944. The present very meagre civilian rations are as follows:–

For one person in household a ration of 135 cubic ft. per week

For two person in household a ration of 230 cubic ft per week

after which an increase of about 30 cubic ft per additional person in the household is allowed.

Footwear

Ladies' Wood Soled Street shoes, in sizes 4, 5 and 5½ only, 698 pairs. Will probably be exhausted by 30.11.44

Ladies' Rubber or leather soled street shoes. No stock.

Men's wood soled street shoes, 702 pairs. Will probably be exhausted by 30.11.44

Men's rubber soled street shoes (size 9 being the smallest size available) 375 pairs – will probably be exhaused by 30.11.44

Workmen's Rubber Boots. No stock.

Workmen's Leather Boots. Only sufficient material on hand to manufacture 100 pairs to meet the requirements of over 900 approved applicants on the labour Officer's list.

Schoolchildren's shoes and boots with leather uppers and wood soles, 2,702 pairs. Will probably be exhausted by 28.2.45.

Schoolchildren's shoes with leather uppers and leather or rubber soles (only in certain sizes), 408 pairs. Will probably be exhausted by 30.11.44

Infants Bootees and shoes with rexine uppers and rubber soles, in sizes up to and including size 8. 143 pairs. Will probably be exhausted by 30.11.44.

Infants shoes with leather uppers and soles in sizes 3 to 7 only, 207 pairs. Will probably be exhausted by 30.11.44.

Repairs to Footwear

Sole leather. No stock. Sheet Rubber – 1,898 lbs. Will probably be exhausted by 31st December, 1944.
Pump leather – No stock.
Leather for repairs to Belting – only a very small stock sufficient only for emergency repairs.
Leather for harness repairs – No stock.

Clothing

Adult Female (16 years and over) – no stock of outer or under clothing.
Male (5-16 years). Woollen vests – 198. Will probably be exhausted by 31st December. All other stock of outer or under clothing exhausted.
Female (5-16 years). Woollen vests – 48. Will probably be exhausted by 30th November. Woollen knickers – 372. Will probably be exhausted by 31st December. All other stock of outer and under clothing exhausted.
Adult Male (16 years and over):

- 2 Piece Suits – 231. Will probably be exhausted by 30th Nov.
- Workmen's Trousers – 459 prs. ditto.
- Shirts – 268. ditto.
- Stock of all other items of clothing exhausted.

Male and Female (2-5 years of age). No clothing available for either sex.
Infants (newly born).

- Nightdresses – 87. Will probably be exhausted by 31st Dec
- Wrap vests – 71. ditto
- Napkins – 63 doz. ditto
- All other necessary stocks of clothing for infants are exhausted.

Knitting Wool

White wool (reserved for expectant mothers (mothers) – 100 lbs (est). Will probably be exhausted by 31st December.
White Wool for underclothing etc. 930 lbs. ditto.
Dark Grey Wool – 1696 lbs. ditto.

Medical and Surgical Supplies and Requisites

As regards medical and surgical supplies and requisites, I have asked Dr A.N. Symons, Health Services Officer, to reply, with your permission, to Deputy Cross' queries.

A.J. Lainé, President
Ladies' College, 1st November, 1944.

Item 75: Present stocks of medical supplies, 1 Nov 1944

1st November, 1944

<u>Reply to question asked by Deputy C.H. Cross at meeting of the States
of Deliberation held on 1st November, 1944 with reference to the
position in regard to Medical supplies as on the 21st October, 1944</u>

The position of the more important Medical supplies is very bad. For operations – rubber gloves are in a very bad condition, scalpel blades are badly worn, Catgut which is essential in important operations is estimated to last another month. Cotton wool gave out a long time ago. Rectified Spirit of Wine, which is used extensively in surgery will not last more than about two months. Its use in making up medicine is practically finished.

Owing to the shortage of catgut it has become necessary to make a rule that operations shall be restricted to those of emergency, including accidents and operations to save life. All operations of expediency such as rupture or haemorrhoids must be postponed until the supplies shall have been renewed.

The following important drugs have been returned as finished:– Heart Stimulants, Campolon, Cod Liver Oil. The manufacture of Fish liver Oil, which was an excellent substitute has ceased because little or no fish liver has come in since March.

The medicines for treatment of influenza are finished including Aspirin. No Chloral, Nyosein tablets, Extract of Ergot, Tincture of Nux Vomica or liquor Strychnine, Glycerine, Olive Oil, Vitamin B tablets, Bromides, (though the Hospital has some), Aperient Pills remain, and there are others.

We are fortunate in our stock of Anaesthetics and Insulin for Diabetes.

Difficult as the position is of the Medical Supplies it is the fuel position that is causing the greatest anxiety to the House Committee of the Emergency Hospital. We are continuing from hand to mouth should the supply actually stop the work of the Hospital must also cease.

A.N. Symons
Medical Services Officer.

Item 76: Bailiff to Red Cross, 5 Nov 1944

<u>Message To Be Sent Over German Wireless [as drafted] on 5th November, 1944</u>

Guernsey, 5th November, 1944

The Secretary General
International Red Cross
Geneva

Conditions rapidly deteriorating here. Will soon become impossible. We appreciate difficulties but civilian population need urgent supplies of essentials. We urge immediate visit of Red Cross representative. All rations drastically reduced.

- Bread finishes 15th December
- Sugar finishes 6th January
- Fat production much below consumption. Reserves finish end of January.
- Ration of separated milk will be reduced to one third pint per head by end of year
- Soap and other cleansers – Stocks completely exhausted.
- Vegetables generally inadequate to supply civilian population through winter. German consumption heavy.
- Salt stocks exhausted.
- Clothing and footwear stocks almost exhausted.
- Fuel – Gas and electricity finish at end of year. Coal stocks exhausted. Wood fuel quite inadequate.
- Many essential medical supplies already finished.

Victor G. Carey
Bailiff of Guernsey

APPENDIX

Message to Red Cross, 5 Nov 1944

Platzkommandantur I, St Helier
Nebenstelle, Guernsey
16 November, 1944

To the Bailiff of Guernsey, St Peter Port

I enclose the desired copy of the radio message sent to the General Secretary of the International Red Cross.

(signed) Schneberger, Militaerverwaltungsrat

---

5 November, 1944

To the General Secretary, International Red Cross, Geneva

Conditions rapidly deteriorating here. Will soon become impossible. We appreciate difficulties but civilian population needs urgent supplies of essentials. We urge immediate visit of Red Cross representative. All rations drastically reduced.

- Bread will last till 15th December.
- Fat production much below consumption.
- Soap and other cleansers – stocks completely exhausted.
- Vegetables generally inadequate.
- Salt stocks exhausted.
- Clothing and footwear – stocks almost exhausted.
- Coal stocks exhausted, wood fuel quite inadequate.
- Many essential medical supplies already finished.

Victor G. Carey, Bailiff of Guernsey

Approved by the General (signed) Obstlt.v.Helldorff.

Item 77: P.K. to C.C.: Potato Requisition, 7 Nov 1944

Platzkommandantur I St Helier
Nebenstelle Guernsey
Az. 16/5
7th November, 1944

The Controlling Committee of the States of Guernsey

Re: Potato crop 1944

In the cultivation plan 1943/44, a harvest of 6150 tons was forecasted.

On the basis of the actual cultivation carried out and of the condition of the plantations, a new estimation was made, according to which the harvest could only be estimated at 4700 tons.

In the estimation of consumption, 1500 tons were provided for seed for next year. After the figures had been submitted to the Commander of the Channel Islands, only 200 tons, in round figures, were provided for next year's seed. Out of the balance of 1300 tons, 1000 tons are to be immediately secured by the troops.

For this purpose, 500 tons out of the amount now stored are to be immediately handed over to the Division.

The further 500 tons, which are partly stored by farmers and partly still in the ground, are to be collected as quickly as possible.

Please keep us informed of the quantities collected.

(signed) Schneberger, M.V.R.

Item 78: Meeting with P.K.: Potato Requisition, 8 Nov 1944

Memorandum of meeting held at Grange Lodge, Wednesday, 8th November, 1944

Present:

Rev. John Leale, Jurat	President of the Controlling Committee of the States of Guernsey
Messrs. R.O. Falla	Agricultural Officer
T. Le M. Allez	Potato Controller
L.A. Guillemette	Secretary to the President
M.V.R Schneberger	Platzkommandantur
Oberinspektor Spann	Platzkommandantur

Subject: German Requisition of 1,000 tons of Potatoes

Mr Leale said that he had received that day a letter from the Platzkommandantur, dated the 7th November, 1944, requisitioning 1,000 tons of potatoes. He did not know whether the Platzkommandantur realised that by such a requisition the potato ration, on which 14,000 people depend, would cease immediately. Bread would finish in the middle of December, and without these two essentials work in the island would be bound to stop. M.V.R. Schneberger said that there were potatoes in the Island in the hands of producers. Mr Leale replied that apart from potatoes to which producers were legally entitled there might still be 100 tons, but not more, still to come in. It appeared to the Guernsey representatives that the German calculation – the result of which was shown in the letter received from them – was based on a 5 lb ration for every member of the population; in point of fact, the average ration being issued at present was 8 lbs, and Mr Leale's opinion was that this figure would be a fair one to use for the average consumption of potatoes throughout the Island, including producers. It would be seen, if this figure was taken that the total consumption would be in the neighbourhood of 4,200 tons yearly. The German estimate of total crop, namely, 4,700 tons, was, in the opinion of the Guernsey representatives, an accurate one; therefore, the difference between production and consumption was 500 tons. This amount would have to serve for seed, and from it would have to be deducted wastage and thieving.

It would be seen, therefore, that there were no potatoes available at all for German consumption, and this proof was borne out by actual fact. The amount in store at present was 570 tons, and with the 100 tons still expected from producers the ration should continue, at its present rate of 41 tons per week, for about fifteen or sixteen weeks. This would leave the later part of the winter without any ration for the civilian population.

Actually, the amount of seed declared, in response to the recent Order, was 328 tons to date, and it was not expected that many more returns would be coming in.

M.V.R. Schneberger suggested that all potatoes throughout the Island be collected into depôts and redistributed through the ration.

Mr Leale said that, firstly, this would be a breach of faith since the population had been asked to grow potatoes and had been promised the produce of 4 perches per head. It would be unfair to those who had spent their leisure in producing food if they were deprived of such food to help others, who, in many cases, had been too lazy to do similar work. Secondly, removal of potatoes at this stage always resulted in a large wastage.

M.V.R Schneberger said he was considering doubling his Inspectors and carrying out a search into producers' stocks.

Mr Leale suggested, as an alternative, that a declaration of stocks should be called for, and that the matter be reviewed when such statistics were available.

M.V.R. Schneberger agreed to place this suggestion before the Division, and instructed the Guernsey representatives not to deliver the first 500 tons for the time being, but to continue with the present ration until they heard further from him.

During the meeting M.V.R. Schneberger stated that the taking over of 1,000 tons of potatoes was not to be regarded as a requisition. The German Authorities were simply taking them into safe keeping. The Guernsey representatives pointed out that movement of potatoes at this stage meant a heavy percentage of wastage.

M.V.R. Schneberger also states that Guernsey could be compared with a ship and that both Germans and civilians were on it. We must be prepared to share alike.

(signed)
John Leale, President
R.O. Falla, Agricultural Officer
T. Le M. Allez, Potato Controller
L.A. Guillemette, Secretary to President

Item 79: General to Bailiff: Reduction in food rations, 16 Nov 1944

Befehlshaber der Kanalinseln
Qu.Abt. Az. 13v.
16 November, 1944

To Platzkommandantur I, St Helier
Nebenstelle, Guernsey

<u>re: Food suppliers for the civilian population</u>

For communication to the States of Guernsey

Now that the message regarding the position of food supplies for the civilian population of the Channel Islands has been in the hands of the English Government for some time, but that the said Government has given no sign of giving assistance, it has become necessary to save the supplies still further, even if considerable hardship should result therefrom. Measures of economy have also been taken on the side of the troops, in order to limit the claims on the products of the country.

For this purpose, 100 tons are to be taken from the Oats crop for human consumption, i.e. to be incorporated in the bread.

The bread ration must be reduced to 200 grammes per head per day.

A certain reduction of the fat ration to the figure of last winter cannot eventually be avoided.

It is to be hoped that the help requested from the Red Cross will be coming sooner or later. Meanwhile, however, it may be expected that the States will ensure with the utmost strictness the most essential feeding of the population. In this connection, the States should now see that the potato crop be collected by all possible means. Every possible assistance will be rendered by the troops.

It is not intended to claim potatoes for the troops beyond the measure originally agreed upon. It would however be regrettable that further reductions in the potato rations should have to be made as a result of insufficient deliveries.

It may be added that the Bailiff of Jersey, clearly aware of the situation, had promised his full cooperation for the taking of all these measures, and already started to do so.

(signed) von Schmettow

Platzkommandantur I, St Helier
Nebenstelle, Guernsey

Communicated in original to the Bailiff of Guernsey, St Peter Port

(signed) Schneberger, M.V.R.

Item 80: P.K. to C.C.: Collection of potatoes, 17 Nov 1944

Plaztkommandantur I St Helier
Nebenstelle Guernsey Az.16/7
17.11.44

Controlling Committee of the States of Guernsey

Re: Collection and storage of potatoes

Ref: Order of 7.11.44

Out of the 15000 tons of potatoes provided for next year's <u>seed</u> – <u>not as table potatoes</u> – or out of the estimated total crop of 4,700 tons, 200 tons of earlies must be laid aside for seed. Out of the balance of 1300 tons, 1000 tons of late are to be immediately put aside for the troops. The potatoes already delivered are included in this amount.

As a precaution, it is pointed out that, in order to also ensure the serving of persons entitled to rations, the growers are to be left 90 lbs per person in the household, and the excess quantities are to be placed in the States' stores. The privilege hitherto granted to the growers, of keeping the crop from 4 perches or at least 4 cwt. of potatoes per head of their household, cannot be maintained, this in view of the acute position regarding food supplies and <u>in the interest of all</u>.

Regarding the 200 tons of earlies reserved for seed, a list is to be made up, showing what quantities have been left to the different growers.

Please let us know immediately where and in what quantities the potatoes may be fetched by the troops.

It is important that one should act quickly and that no time should be wasted.

(signed) Schneberger, M.V.R.

Item 81: Meeting with P.K. and General, 18 Nov 1944.

<u>Memorandum of Meeting held at La Corbinerie, Saturday, 18th November, 1944</u>

Present:

Generalleutnant Graf von Schmettow	
Oberstleutnant von Helldorff	
Militaerverwaltungsrat Schneberger	
Victor G. Carey	Bailiff of Guernsey
Rev. John Leale, Jurat.	President of the Controlling Committee of the States of Guernsey
Mr R.H. Johns	Labour Officer
Mr L.A. Guillemette	Secretary to the President of the Controlling Committee

<u>Message to International Red Cross</u>

The Bailiff asked whether any answer had been received to his recent radio message to the International Red Cross. The General said that they had received no direct reply but that he was certain that the British Government were informed in detail of the position in the Islands, since both the Protecting Power and the International Red Cross had been notified. The Bailiff asked whether he might send a further message to the Red Cross in order to emphasise the seriousness of the situation and the General replied that it was his opinion that we must have confidence that the Protecting Power is negotiating on our behalf. It was known to the Germans, through experience in Greece, that such negotiations take time. The Bailiff of Jersey was also of opinion that now that the British Government is in possession of the facts we must wait.

Mr Leale said that he hoped the General would not misinterpret what he was going to say, but the position was becoming desperate and we wondered whether, all our appeals for help having come through German channels, the British Government viewed such appeals with suspicion. He asked, therefore, whether we might send delegates to England to discuss the position direct. The General replied that that would never be allowed, since such work is always entrusted to the Protecting Power or the Red Cross and the British Government was at liberty to send a representative of one of these bodies to the Islands to get first hand information. The Bailiff of Jersey had asked to get into direct touch with the Protecting Power and had been refused.

<u>Potatoes</u>

Mr Leale said that he had that morning received from the Platzkommandantur a letter stating that the Occupying Authority must be supplied with a total of 1,000 tons of potatoes, of which 500 tons were already in the Potato Board stores.

Colonel von Helldorff said that a mistake had been made by the Jersey branch of the Platzkommandantur, which had been ordered to take over all stocks of civilian foodstuffs with the exception of that required by the population up to the end of January next. They had never put this order into effect in Guernsey, but had assured the Division that 1,000 tons of potatoes would be available from this Island. He understood that the matter had been left too late now, many of the potatoes having already been eaten, and that it would be impossible to find this quantity. They would therefore take over 500 tons instead. The Colonel added that, last August, when the Platzkommandantur offered us potatoes, we refused them on the grounds that we already had all the early potatoes we needed for consumption to the end of the year. Mr Leale said that he had never heard of such an offer and M.V.R. Schneberger said that the offer had been a verbal one by Herr Spann to Mr Falla. The Colonel had visited the Potato Board Depôts during the last week and had there seen many tons of early potatoes. The way in which they were stored was very bad indeed, many tons being wasted through lack of proper attention. Mr Leale explained that the Germans had taken over all suitable stores and that those left in our hands were so inadequate that the potatoes had to be stored in much too small a space.

Mr Leale continued that we believed there were 1,000 to 1,100 tons of potatoes in the hands of producers at present. If the collection of these potatoes was perfect, there would be none left for the ration when the producers had been allotted their 90 lbs per head of household and the Germans had taken 500 tons.

The Colonel asked two questions:–

1. Why are there so many early potatoes in the Depôts now?
2. Why did we state that the late crop would amount to 2,400 tons and where are they?

Mr Leale said that he could not answer these questions at once but that he would give the Colonel a written reply if he wished.

The Germans here repeated that they no longer wanted 1,000 tons of potatoes, but would take 500 tons of lates. Mr Leale said that if we had to collect from the producers, the goodwill of this section of the community was essential. He therefore asked whether the Bailiff might publish in the newspaper that he had the assurance of the General that the Germans would take no more than 500 tons of late potatoes, including all those already taken since the 1st November and that all other potatoes collected would be for the civilian population. This permission and assurance was given by both the General and Colonel von Helldorff who added, in reply to a question to Mr Guillemette, that all potatoes already taken from the depôts would be accepted as part of the quota and that none would be returned to us as unsuitable.

Cut in the Bread Ration

Mr Leale referred to a letter to the General sent through the Platzkommandantur to the Bailiff that morning, in which it was stated that the bread ration would have to be cut to 200 grammes per day. He said that we realised that these were difficult days of siege but that the Bailiff had asked Mr Johns, the Labour Officer, to attend the meeting to emphasise the fact that, with such reduced rations, the men would not be able to work nearly as hard as before.

Mr Johns said that 200 grammes per day was about 25% of the normal peace time consumption of a heavy manual worker and he repeated that the effect of such a reduction on the work of the Island must be extremely serious.

Colonel von Helldorff explained that the former ration was an average one of 260 grammes per day and that the new one must also be regarded as an average. It was the duty of the local administration to issue it in whatever way they thought most suitable.

The General said that the suggestion of the cut in the bread ration came from the Bailiff of Jersey who was of opinion that it was the duty of every civilian to hold out as long as possible now that the British Government knew the position of the Islands. He had issued a proclamation to the people of Jersey to this effect.

A letter would be received from the Platzkommandantur regarding the reduction in the bread ration.

Roots and Cattle

Mr Leale said that, on Thursday last, he had submitted to the Platzkommandantur a matter which is of vital importance to the population. This was the Controlling Committee's decision that all cattle which were not milk producers, and would not become milk producers by April 30th next, as well as old and inefficient cows, should be slaughtered as soon as possible. The reason for this measure was the fact that there are so few roots available on the Island that they are not sufficient to feed all the cattle and all the human population.

Colonel von Helldorff said that they might place some of the animals on the airport but Mr Leale stressed that this would not meet the case since about 600 animals were involved. Since every head of live cattle continued to eat roots it would be better for the Island if such animals were killed immediately, even if the meat were thrown away, but he saw no reason why the population should not be given a weekly ration for the next few weeks if the Germans feared that the cold stores would not be workable after the middle of December. The Colonel answered that, when the unproductive cattle had been eaten, they would begin to slaughter the milch cows and that the former category should therefore be made to last as long as possible. He promised that the matter would be considered without delay and that we would receive an answer next Monday.

Victor G. Carey, Bailiff of Guernsey
John Leale, President, Controlling Committee of the States of Guernsey.
R.H. Johns, Labour Officer
L.A. Guillemette.

Item 82: Bailiff to General: Slaughter of cattle, 29 Nov 1944

The Bailiff's Chambers, Guernsey
November 29th, 1944.

To: Generalleutnant Graf von Schmettow,
Festungskommandant, Guernsey

At our interview at your headquarters on the 18th instant we put forward the suggestion that, in general, cattle which are not producing milk should be slaughtered. You will recollect that the primary reason for this suggestion is the shortage of roots. We know that, with the increasing shortage of foodstuffs, stocks of roots cannot possibly meet the demands of the German and civilian populations as well as those of the present cattle population, for more than a small part of this winter.

The President of the Controlling Committee reports to me that he has received a letter from the Platzkommandantur, dated 24th instant, setting out detailed instructions for the delivery to your butchers of the first batches of animals. The letter further states that the cattle are to be paid for by the Forces, I can only infer from this that all the animals are to be kept for German consumption.

Should my assumption be correct, I would ask for your immediate reconsideration of this decision since, of a total of 600 animals which we wish to slaughter, 500 is obviously far beyond any share claimable by the troops under Article 52 of the Hague Convention.

If it is not intended to take this number of cattle, I should be obliged if you would inform me as soon as possible how many you claim for German consumption. Further, I would stress our wish to slaughter our share of the animals in our own slaughter-house, so as to obtain the valuable offal for civilian consumption.

During conversations with the Platzkommandantur we have been assured that the requisition of the animals in question will not mean an increase in the German meat ration and that it is therefore useless to ask for an increase in the civilian ration. The civilian administration, on the other hand, taking into account the serious effects upon both the health and the work of the population which must result from the recent drastic cuts in other rations, urge that advantage be taken of the opportunity to issue a more generous allowance of the one article of food of which there is no serious shortage at present.

(signed) Victor G. Carey, Bailiff of Guernsey

Item 83: General to Bailiff: Slaughter of cattle, 30 Nov 1944

Befehlshaber der Kanalinseln
Qu. Abt. Az. 13v.
30 November, 1944.

To the Bailiff of Guernsey, Victor G. Carey

In reply to your letter of 29th November, I beg to inform you that the reason for slaughtering a large quantity of cattle is perfectly clear to me, but that I did not think it possible that the President of the Controlling Committee could have also contemplated an extraordinarily high distribution of meat to the civilian population.

The Occupying Power has hitherto refrained from any slaughtering of civilian cattle, in order not to reduce the Island stocks; that in future a supply to the troops from island stocks should become necessary, needs no explanation. It should however be clear to the Controlling Committee that it would be reckless extravagance, if the rations were to be increased just now.

If now a considerable proportion of the animals proposed for slaughter is taken over for feeding by the troops or placed in cold storage, this means that the troops [are] provided for [for] a long time. The Controlling Committee has been given the liberty of slaughtering animals for themselves and to place same in cold storage. Provided always that the meat rations should not be increased, so that the milk producing cattle should not have to be slaughtered in the near future. It is to be borne in mind that the bull calves must continue to be slaughtered in order not to reduce milk production. The electric supply for the cold stores should also be taken into consideration.

I request you once more, as regards such matters, when a settlement cannot be obtained with the Platzkommandandtur, to apply to Oberstleutnant v. Helldorff, in order to avoid long-drawn correspondence.

(signed) von Schmewttow

Item 84: Leale to P.K.: Potato Ration, 29 Nov 1944

Controlling Committee of the States of Guernsey
5th December, 1944
5/3/3

Platzkommandantur I, St Helier
Nebenstelle, Guernsey

Sir,

With reference to the recent conversations between you and Messrs Guillemette and Mallett, I have seen the letter from Oberzahlmeister Lange dated 30th November, 1944, regarding certain discrepancies between our own and German figures of totals of potatoes taken by you recently.

I would not have troubled you with a letter on the subject except that your Paymaster is claiming an extra 25 tons of potatoes because this amount was taken from the Leale Ltd depôt on the 31st October. Mr Guillemette informs me that Oberzahlmeister Lange's claim is that the Festungskommandant only undertook to include potatoes taken on or after the 1st November in the 500 tons requisitioned.

You will recollect that at a meeting with the Festungskommandant on Saturday, 18th November, we were informed that the Occupying Authorities would take a total not exceeding 500 tons of potatoes from the Potato Board's Depôts. It was our suggestion that, for purposes of publication that the potatoes already taken from the depôts would be included in the total of 500 tons.

Neither your representatives nor ours at that meeting were aware that 25 tons of potatoes were taken one day previous to the 1st November, and I cannot think that General von Schmettow, Colonel von Helldorff or yourself would wish to take advantage of such a circumstance.

With reference to the discrepancy regarding the total weight of potatoes taken from the "Wembley" depôt, and Oberzahlmeister Lange's suggestion that confusion may have occurred between figures for this depôt and those for "Le Bourg", Forest, we hold weighbridge certificates plus German receipts – the latter for the potatoes weighed at the depôts and not sent to this weighbridge – which together represent the total weight of 67 tons taken from "Wembley" and "Le Bourg". This disproves Oberzahlmeister Lange's contention.

Both these depôts were emptied by the troops with the exception of 2 tons left at "Wembley", and the Potato Board records of stocks at 11th November show that, before German drawings, there were 72 tons in the two depôts. This provides further check on the accuracy of our figures of potatoes drawn.

I should be pleased to hear that the matter may now be regarded as settled.

Yours faithfully,
JOHN LEALE
President.

Depôt	Weight (kgs)
La Moye, Vale	30,504
Stoneworkers' Hall, St Sampson's	30,623
Military Road, St Sampson's	25,766
Pleinheaume, Vale	54,371
Belle Vue, Castel	38,900
Doulieu, St Saviour's	67,897
Le Douit, St Peter's	47,189
Wembley, Torteval	35,375
Le Bourg, Forest	32,551
Legion Hall, St Martin's	31,557
Mauxmarquis, St Andrew's	29,700
Leale	73,774
Unknown Depôt	3,930
	502,137
Delivered in Sark	28,348
	530,485
Refund of Jersey Seed	21,063
Total delivered	509,422
Over supplied	9,422
	500,000

Item 85: Meeting with General, Arrival of Red Cross ship, 6 Dec 1944

<u>Memorandum of meeting held at La Corbinerie</u>
<u>Wednesday, 6th December, 1944</u>

Present:

Lt. Gen Graf von Schmettow, Festungskommandant

Lt. Col. Hübner, MVR Schneberger

Victor G. Carey, Bailiff of Guernsey

Mr L.A. Guillemette, Secretary to the President of the
Controlling Committee.

<u>Subject: Arrival of Ship with Red Cross Supplies</u>

The Festungskommandant said that he was pleased to be able to notify the Bailiff that a ship would leave Lisbon for the Channel Islands with Red Cross supplies on Thursday, the 7th December, 1944.

The ship would contain four tons of soap and 750 tons of food supplies. He was not informed of details concerning the types of food. He imagined that the ship would arrive on the 10th and it would enter the harbour in daylight. The ship was calling at Guernsey before proceeding to Jersey.

The Bailiff said he was glad of an opportunity of thanking the General for the effort he had made on behalf of the civilian population to procure Red Cross supplies for the Island.

The General continued that the discharge of the cargo and its transport to St George's Hall would be undertaken by the German Authorities and that thenceforward the local Red Cross would be in charge of its distribution. He thought that guards supplied by the local Red Cross should be stationed in St George's Hall and that local police should be on guard outside. In addition, German guards would be posted outside the Hall.

The General asked whether the Bailiff knew how the distribution was to be effected. The Bailiff said he understood that it would be done through the grocers and under the direction of the Essential Commodities Department. In answer to a further question, the Bailiff said that even if the supplies were not in the form of individual parcels but in bulk, the grocers could still be used for distribution, under the norman rationing arrangements.

The General said that presumably International Red Cross representatives would arrive with the ship and that the local Administration would have opportunities of discussing the Island food situation with them. In his opinion it would be better for supplies to take the form of bulk consignments of flour and potatoes rather than individual parcels.

It was arranged that as soon as the General receives further information he will inform the Bailiff and make arrangements for him to receive the representatives on arrival at the harbour. He further promised that a copy of any photograph taken of the arrival of the ship by members of the German Army would be handed to the Bailiff.

The representatives are to be entertained by the German Authorities and will be put up at "Rozel", Mount Durand.

The Bailiff mentioned that he had asked the local newspaper to put in a paragraph giving notice of the expected arrival of Red Cross supplies and that the German censor had refused permission for its insertion. The General said that on the contrary he would be delighted if the Bailiff would put in such a notice since he understood that rumours were current to the effect that the German Authorities had taken no steps whatever to obtain Red Cross supplies.

(signed) Victor G. Carey, Bailiff
(signed) L.A. Guillemette, Secretary to the
President of the Controlling Committee

Copies to: –

> The Bailiff
> L.A. Guillemette
> Dr B.S. Collings
> Essential Commodities Committee
> Files (2)

Item 86: Meeting with P.K.: Dismissal of Dr Symons, 18 Dec 1944

<u>Meeting held at Grange Lodge
on the 18th December, 1944</u>

Present:–

John Leale, Esq	President of the Controlling Committee
MVR Scheberger	
L.A. Guillemette	Secretary to President

<u>Subject: Dismissal of Dr A.N. Symons by the German Authorities</u>

Mr Leale said that he was very much concerned over the receipt by the Bailiff of a letter from the Platzkommandantur dismissing Dr Symons from his post of Medical Services Officer. He asked the reasons for this dismissal.

M.V.R. Schneberger said that Dr Symons' letter of 13th December, 1944 had been objected to by the Division, not because of the substance of the letter but because of the manner in which it was written.

Mr Leale said that the Platzkommandantur may not have realised that Dr Symons' manner was exactly the same with Englishmen and Germans and that it was not intended to be insolent because the Germans were enemies of our nation.

M.V.R. Schneberger said that there were probably better doctors available to fill his post.

Mr Leale insisted that Dr Symons was irreplaceable since there were no other retired medical practitioners available to do public work. Continuing, Mr Leale asked what the words "new ground" meant in the Platzkommandantur's letter to the Bailiff. Did they mean that there had been previous objections to Dr Symons? M.V.R. Schneberger said that he could remember two or three occasions, but they had not been mentioned to the States. In one instance, about a month ago, the Division had asked for his dismissal, but M.V.R. Schneberger had caused them to withdraw their demand.

Mr Leale said that Dr Symons had served the Island excellently for the four-and-half years of occupation and, indeed, had done much public work during the years before the war. He was 70 years of age, and would have been quite justified in claiming that he had already done sufficient without shouldering the burden during the occupation. With the many new food problems brought on by the lack of essentials, Dr Symons' knowledge and medical outlook had been invaluable to the Controlling Committee in arriving at important decisions.

M.V.R. Schneberger said that if the letter had passed through Mr Leale's hands he felt certain that it would not have arrived at the Platzkommandantur in its actual form and that, in his opinion, all letters should come via the President of the Controlling Committee in future. Mr Leale said that he wanted it clearly understood that he had seen the letter but that he did not wish to answer questions on the subject at the moment. He asked whether the Bailiff might write to the Division asking for a reconsideration of their decision. M.V.R. Schneberger said that he held out no hope at all but did not object to the Bailiff making such an appeal.

Before finishing the meeting, Mr Leale mentioned that he understood that the word "humane", used by Dr Symons in his letter, might be translated into a German word with a very ugly meaning. He asked whether the translation of Dr Symons' letter did contain such a mistake. M.V.R. Schneberger examined the letter and said that the translation, although not quite accurate, did not make this mistake.

Returning to the question of replacing Dr Symons, Mr Leale again insisted that his place on the Controlling Committee could not be taken by anybody else. It might be possible for Dr Revell, the States Medical Officer of Health, to deal with medical problems and to do the routine work previously performed by Dr Symons.

(signed) John Leale, President of the Controlling Committee
(signed) L.A. Guillemette, Secretary to President

Copy to:
      The President, Controlling Committee
      Bailiff of Guernsey
      Dr A.N. Symons
      Mr L.A. Guillemette
      Two Files.

Item 87: P.K. to Bailiff: Fat Supplies, 5 Jan 1945

Platzkommandantur I St Helier
Nebenstelle Guernsey Az 16/1
5.1.1945

To: The Bailiff of Guernsey

Re: Supplies of Fat

The Food parcels from the International Red Cross contain, in the form of butter, milk powder and cheese, a sufficient quantity of fat, which distributed over 4 weeks and added to the 8.6 grammes a day guaranteed by the Occupying Power in the course of the negotiations with England, represents suitable supplies of fats for the civilian population. The butter ration is, therefore, to be reduced to the guaranteed amount, beginning with the next issue. The excess derived therefrom will be taken over in the military cold storage rooms.

This will at the same time provide a reserve, permitting to make up any shortage resulting from non-arrival of ships, and preventing the civilian population from suffering therefrom.

(signed) Schneberger MVR

<u>Memorandum of Meeting held at Grange Lodge on 11th January, 1945</u>

Present:–

Victor G. Carey	Bailiff of Guernsey
Rev. John Leale, Jurat	President of the Controlling Committee
Col. von Helldorff	
M.V.R. Schneberger	
Mr L.A. Guillemette	Secretary to the President

<u>Reduction of Fat Ration: German Guarantees to British Government</u>

The Bailiff said that in the letter, dated 5th January, 1945, from Herr Schneberger regarding the reduction in fat ration, mention was made of a guarantee given to the British Government that a minimum fat ration, from local supplies, of 8.6 grammes per day would be maintained to the civilian population in this Island. He said that he had not realized that any such guarantee had been given, and he asked whether similar guarantees had been given for other commodities.

Col. von Helldorff said that, in addition to butter, guarantees had been given for meat and vegetables, these three commodities being produced in the Island and being always available. He did not know what guarantee had been given for meat, but he thought 50 grammes a week. At any rate, the minimum given in this case was that of the current ration in either Jersey or Guernsey (he did not remember which Island), whichever at that time was the greater. He undertook to inform the Bailiff as soon as possible regarding the exact figure guaranteed for both meat and vegetables.

Mr Leale said that we were specially interested in these two minimum figures since there was a possibility that we were now receiving less than the minimum in regard to meat if, as the Colonel had suggested, that minimum was 50 grammes per week.

Regarding vegetables, Mr Leale pointed out that in March and April vegetables would be in very short supply since crops in glasshouses did not mature in those months and stocks of roots from last season would be finished. Colonel von Helldorff was surprised to hear this statement, saying that they had been given to understand that some of the crops now growing in the glasshouses would be available for consumption in March and April and that January and February were the months in which vegetable shortage were most acute. Mr Leale further stated that thieving at present would have very serious effects on future production since immature crops – he instanced cauliflower as one – were being stolen.

Referring to the above letter of the 5th January, 1945, Mr Leale asked why it was intended to transfer butter stocks from civilian cold storage to military cold rooms if they were to be regarded as a reserve for civilian consumption. The Colonel said that if they were in German cold rooms, they could be guarded by the Military.

Mr Leale further stated that in informing the Red Cross of civilian requirements in the Island during the recent conferences, no account had been taken of the possibility of reduction in ordinary rations, and it was the opinion of the civilian administration that such reductions would reduce total food supplies below the minimum requirements of the civilian population.

Colonel von Helldorff agreed that rations would not be as much as was desirable, but he stressed that some reserve should be kept in case of delays in arrivals of Red Cross ships.

Taking over of Glasshouses by Military

Mr Leale said that the present position was not satisfactory and Col. von Helldorff replied that he had received information on the subject from Herr Schneberger, and would see to it that in future no German Unit would take over any glasshouses without written permission from the Platzkommandantur. This Department in turn would consult the Civilian Authorities before giving such permits.

Mr Leale said that he would like the same arrangement made for the requisition of outside land, and to this the Colonel agreed.

Regarding the proposed growing of glasshouse potato crops, for the German Authorities, Mr Leale pointed out that many growers, for patriotic reasons, were averse to signing contracts with the German Forces. In his opinion, inasmuch as if the grower refused to sign the agreement, he would be ordered to do so by the Platzkommandantur, it would be preferable if an order were issued in the first instance.

Evacuation of Invalids

Mr Leale said that in regard to the proposed scheme for the evacuation of invalids from the Island by the Red Cross, he had been asked whether it would be possible for the sick to be accompanied by next-of-kin. He instanced babies and husbands needing treatment who should be accompanied by mothers and wives respectively. Colonel von Helldorff explained that the only category which in no case could be allowed to leave the island was men of military age in good health, since such men would become soldiers to fight against the German Reich. On being asked what constituted military age, he said this category would include men between the ages of 18 and 50 years.

In reply to a question, Colonel von Helldorff said that the Red Cross hospital ship would probably come on more than one occasion.

It was decided that local doctors should be informed of the fact that it would be possible, subject to the approval of the Red Cross, for next-of-kin to accompany invalids.

Correspondence with Internees and Prisoners-of-War in Germany

Colonel von Helldorff said that civilians in this Island might re-start to write to internees and prisoners-of-war in Germany. He agreed that a notice to that effect should be published in the local newspaper and that such mail should be delivered to Grange Lodge.

Fishing

Mr Leale referred to his letter to the Platzkommandantur, dated 5th January, 1945, giving details of an Order whereby all professional fishermen were required in future to work for the German Authorities. Colonel von Helldorff said he had seen the letter and that the German Authority issuing the Order was not entitled to do so, and that the matter would be investigated.

Tar

Mr Leale said that he had been informed by Mr R.G. Luxon, the Manager of the Guernsey Gas Light Company, that the issue of tar to the civilian population had been stopped by order of the Platzkommandantur. He stressed the fact that, with the present shortage of fuel and the cold weather, it was most important that the ration of tar should continue. Herr Schneberger said that the Naval Authorities wanted tar for painting naval vessels and it was suggested that they should have some thousands of gallons of tar for this purpose. After discussion it was decided that no such quantity was needed for this work.

It was agreed that the usual monthly ration of tar (one gallon per household) should be issued for the month of January and that the Gas Company might continue to deliver tar to essential services within the limits of their monthly allocations.

(signed)
Victor G. Carey, Bailiff of Guernsey
John Leale, President, Controlling Committee
L.A. Guillemette, Secretary to President.

Copy to:–

    Bailiff of Guernsey
    Rev. John Leale
    Dr A.N. Symons
    Mr L.A. Guillemette
    Files: 3

Item 88: von Helldorff to Bailiff: Civilian supplies, 14 Jan 1945

Guernsey 14.1.45

To the Bailiff of Guernsey
Victor G. Carey

In order to dissipate the false rumours and assertions relating to measures taken by the Occupying Power, I should like to let you know what has been done so far, amongst other things, for providing the civilian population with supplies.

1. After provisioning from France had ceased to be possible, and when the civilian stocks were exhausted, the following goods from military stocks were supplied on loan, without payment, to the Island States:

    (a)   Coal   4,200 tons
    (b)   Diesel oil, to date   305 tons
    (c)   Petrol   30,000 gallons

2. As regards potatoes, out of the total crop in Guernsey – about 5,500 tons, only 500 tons were claimed, ie. only a fraction of what the troops could have claimed if they had used the land for their own purposes.

3. Wheat, that is to say bread-making cereals, was so to speak not grown at all on the island. The population obtained its cereals from France. The Occupying Power obtained therefore from the Continent the necessary seed, the produce of which was exclusively intended for the troops. In Guernsey, not one kilo of locally-harvested cereals has been taken from the population, but 500 tons of wheat from military stocks from Jersey were placed at that population's disposal.

4. The provision of supplies to the civilian population by International Red Cross ships, including foodstuffs, coal, oil, clothing and drugs has now been promoted by the Occupying Power since the beginning of August. In September, England was informed of the situation of the population and supplies suggested.

After long delays and repeated enquiries as to England's approval, the first I.R.C. ship arrived and the Representatives of the International Red Cross could, as desired by the Occupying Power, satisfy themselves as to the position of the islands. They were afforded every opportunity of freely conversing with the Island States.

It is therefore to be hoped that the population's position as regards supplies will soon improve.

I should be thankful to you for kindly acquainting your collaborators with the contents of this letter.

(signed) von Helldorff

Item 89: Schneberger to Bailiff: Fat Ration, 25 Jan 1945

Platzkommandantur I St Helier
Nebenstelle Guernsey
25.1.45

To the Bailiff of Guernsey

According to the information supplied by Oberstleutnant von Helldorff, the fat ration for the civilian population which has been guaranteed by the German Government to the English Government, is, as already mentioned, 8.6 grammes per head per day, the meat ration 50 gr per head per week, and the vegetable ration up to 500 gr per head per day, according to production.

The guarantee was made under the obvious provision that the production is maintained on the same level as during the past years.

(signed) Schneberger, M.V.R.

Item 90: Bailiff of Jersey to Bailiff: Flour supplies, 10 Jan 1945

The Bailiff's Chambers
Jersey
10th January, 1945

My dear Bailiff,

Baron von Aufsess has asked me if we can help you out with some flour until your Red Cross Supplies of flour arrive.

The Superior Council of the States has authorised me to offer you fifty tons of Jersey flour on loan, and I hope you will be able to accept this offer in the glad spirit in which we make it.

As I understand that your need is somewhat urgent, it is proposed by Baron von Aufsess that the flour should be sent to you at once through the Platzkommandantur. I hope you will see no objection to this course.

Yours very sincerely
(signed) A.M. Coutanche.
The Bailiff of Jersey

Item 91: Meeting with P.K. and Red Cross representatives, 7 Feb 1945

<u>Memorandum of Meeting held at Rozel, Mount Durand
on Wednesday, 7th February 1945</u>

Present:

Lt Colonel von Helldorff	
Monsieur Callias	Representative of the International Red Cross
Victor G. Carey, Esq.	Bailiff of Guernsey
Rev. John Leale, Jurat	President of the Controlling Committee of the States of Guernsey
Dr A.N. Symons	Medical Services Officer
Dr B.S. Collings	Representative of the British Red Cross
M.V.R. Schneberger	
Hauptmann Tettenborn	
Mr J.H. Loveridge	Secretary, Essential Commodities Committee
Mr L.A. Guillemette	Secretary to the President of the Controlling Committee, States of Guernsey

<u>Subject: Red Cross Supplies for Guernsey</u>

<u>Potatoes and other Vegetables</u>. Jurat Leale asked whether the Red Cross Representatives had been able to secure potatoes for shipment to the Islands. Mr Callias replied that it had not been possible to do so. He asked how long potatoes would last in the Island and was informed that rations would finish by the 10th March and that no potatoes would be available until the end of May when the glasshouse crop matured.

Regarding other vegetables, roots would last until the beginning of March, but from that time onwards there would be a great scarcity – if any at all were available. Jurat Leale mentioned that the greatest difficulty at present was the thieving of crops, both mature and immature. The thieving of immature crops was already affecting supplies and green vegetables on sale were largely the green leaves of broccoli plants of which the heart had been cut.

The agricultural and horticultural experts say that they cannot make any promise about vegetables even from the glasshouse crops which should be ready for consumption in June since it is uncertain that such crops will be allowed to mature. Potatoes being planted in glasshouses at present are in some cases being dug and stolen the day after planting.

Colonel von Helldorff suggested that it might be possible to get more flour in view of the potato and vegetable shortage, and Mr Callias agreed that this might be possible and undertook to put forward a suggestion for doubling the requests made for flour during his first visit to the Island, ie. flour to produce a ration of 600 grammes per day instead of 300 grammes.

<u>Shipping difficulties</u>. Mr Callias here explained that the main difficulty with regard to sending supplies to the Islands was the lack of shipping space and that all future

importations would be governed by this factor. He said that an extra ship had been asked for for the shipment of fuel but that discussions regarding this matter and the possibility of fuel shipments direct from England were still being continued between the British and German governments.

Requirements for Supply of Water. It was mentioned that 30 tons of Diesel oil per month were needed for the supply of water for domestic purposes only. It was therefore impossible to spare any for the watering of glasshouses although without such a water supply the cropping of a large proportion of the glasshouses on the Island was impossible. Mr Callias said that the question of the supply of Diesel oil for the pumping of water was still under discussion, but that he had received no news thereon as yet.

Diesel oil for Electricity Supply. Colonel von Helldorff further mentioned that 15 tons of Diesel oil per week were needed for the production of electricity in the Island.

Flour. The Bailiff read to the meeting a letter which Mr Callias had handed to him from Colonel Iselin, the contents of which are as follows:–

> "You will certainly have learned that 'Vega', in spite of a rather rough crossing of the Channel, got safely back to Lisbon after her first voyage to your lovely islands. As expected, the repairs of the ship took a good fortnight and thus her departure had to be postponed. If the notified schedule can be maintained, 'Vega' should reach St Peter Port on February 6th and St Helier a few days later.
>
> To my regret, the cargo does not entirely correspond to what had been agreed with you. The Portuguese Government did not authorise the export of 8 tons of soap, which had been applied for by the BRCS representative in Lisbon. Furthermore – and this is worse – 'Vega' will not bring you any flour, although there is flour available in Lisbon. I wish to add that I have continually stressed the point how important it was that this flour should reach you now, but the BRCS in London – for reasons unknown to me – have decided that the flour shall be loaded on the third voyage only. Instead you will receive a proportionally higher number of standard parcels. It must be hoped that the consequences this change may have, will not be too serious.
>
> As a souvenir of my first voyage to the Channel Islands, I am sending you herewith a few photos, which kindly accept with my sincere wishes that all future voyages will take place under the same good auspices."

Mr Callias said that he expected that the "Vega" would arrive here on her third voyage on the 5th March next and that she would have on board flour for the islands.

<u>Sugar.</u> The standard parcels contain insufficient sugar to meet the needs of the population. Mr Callias said that requests had been made for 300 grammes per month as a minimum ration for the civilian population. Present stocks in the Island will produce a ration for small children until the 10th March next, no provision being made whatsoever for older children or adults (see second report of the States' Committee for the Control of Essential Commodities).

<u>Seeds</u>. Mr Callias said that the list of seeds handed to him on his first visit has been passed on to the British Red Cross in London, but that no news had as yet been received thereon.

<u>Yeast</u>. Yeast will be available and will be sent on with the flour when this is shipped.

<u>Clothing and Footwear</u>. The request for clothing and footwear has been passed on to the British Red Cross but no reply has as yet been received by the International Red Cross.

<u>Petrol and Lubricating Oils</u>. No reply to our request has yet been received by the International Red Cross.

<u>Charcoal</u>. Jurat Leale asked whether, if petrol were not available, charcoal could be sent to the Island instead. Guernsey's requirements would be 25 tons per month.

<u>Advance News from the International Red Cross regarding Shipments to the Islands</u>. Colonel von Helldorff asked whether the International Red Cross in Lisbon could send radio messages through the German Authorities when they had news of future shipments and of movements of ships between Lisbon and the Channel Islands. He said that no news had been received in the Island until a day or so before the "Vega" arrived. Mr Callias daid that they had had to wait two weeks for news regarding the shipment of flour to the islands.

<u>Funds collected in the Island for the Red Cross</u>. The Bailiff handed to Mr Callias a letter for Colonel Iselin regarding funds collected in the Island. It was explained to Mr Callias that previous to the first visit of the "Vega" and dating from 1941, an Organisation had been set up in connection with the transmission of Red Cross Messages. The result of collections made in connection with this service was a credit balance of £2,290 at the Guernsey Branch of Lloyd's Bank, which had been earmarked for the International Red Cross. In addition, collections were now being made for Red Cross Funds and donations were being received, payable to the Red Cross Organisations of various countries. It was intended to pay this money over to the British Red Cross for distribution to the Red Cross Organisations concerned. Mr Callias said that at present it was impossible to transmit money between the Islands and Great Britain but that it might be possible to present a letter of credit from the States of Guernsey to a British Bank which might be willing to honour it on the understanding that payment would be made by the States at the end of the war. Such letter of credit should be made out in favour of the International Red

Cross Organisation, Geneva. It was decided to discuss the matter with the Manager of the Branch of Lloyd's Bank in Guernsey.

Gas Consumers. In answer to a question from Mr Callias, Jurat Leale said that out of 8,000 households in Guernsey, 6,000 were gas consumers.

Fuel for Bakers and other Essential Services. Jurat Leake asked whether, if it were impossible or inadvisable owing to our food situation, to obtain shipping space for the importation of gas coal, a consignment of, say, 120 tons monthly of coke could be sent from Lisbon.

Importation of Gas Coal. It was pointed out to Mr Callias that if the importation of gas coal were arranged, it would be important for consignments to continue to arrive regularly, since much damage would be done to the Gas Works should supply have to cease.

Soap. Mr Callias said that the British Red Cross had bought 8 tons of soap in Portugal for delivery to the Islands, but that the Portuguese Government had declined to allow it to leave the country.

Distribution of Parcels to Young Children. Jurat Leale asked whether it was usual for standard parcels to be issued to very young children, such as babies under one year old. Mr Callias said obviously such parcels were not suitable for babies but suggested that it might be possible to give them suitable items from the Diet Parcels. It was left to the local authorities to use their own judgement in this matter.

Flints and Candles. No answer has yet been received by the International Red Cross in reply to the Islands' requests for these articles.

Evacuation of Invalids. Mr Callias said that the question of the evacuation of invalids was under discussion betwewen the German and British Governments, but, here again, the difficulty was in finding a suitable ship. Only Swedish ships were acceptable and very few were available.

Dr Symons drew attention to the fact that in Jersey a notice had been issued by the Medical Officer of Health stating that no next-of-kin would be allowed to accompany invalids should the evacuation take place and that the number allowed to go would be restricted. Colonel von Helldorff said that there was no reason at all for making either of these statements since, as far as he was informed, the German Government had no objection to next-of-kin accompanying patients and no mention had been made of restricting the numbers.

Dr Symons said that in Guernsey 300 applications for evacuation, including next-of-kin, had been received so far and that a few were still expected. He stressed that if next-of-kin were not allowed to go, this number would be greatly reduced. Also if, as the Jersey Medical Officer of Health stated, only persons who are likely to be cured by treatment were allowed to travel, the number would be further diminished. The number mentioned by him included some incurables who wished to leave the island.

Dr Symons further asked who would be required to pay the expenses of such evacuees and Mr Callias answered that the question of payment would not arise since contributions to the Red Cross were purely voluntary. It was further ascertained that all evacuees would be sent to England whether they travelled through a neutral country of not.

General Health. Dr Symons handed in a report on the health of the population during the past month.

Requirements of Drugs. Dr Symons handed in a list of drugs urgently required. Mr Callias asked whether this list had been checked against the consignment of medical supplies arriving in the Island by the "Vega" on its present voyage, and Dr Symons replied that he would make this comparison but that he thought from a first glance at the list of drugs on the "Vega" the quantities of individual items were so small that the list might stand in its present form. He stressed, however that the present consignment was extremely valuable.

Red Cross Mail. Mr Callias said he had brought with him mail from civilian internees and prisoners-of-war in Germany and also about 1,500 civilian messages from England. He said that he would hand them to the German Authorities for distribution.

Jurat Leale asked whether any advance had been made with the suggestion of the Field Message Card Service. Mr Callias said that he knew of no developments in this matter, and Colonel von Helldorff added that the matter had been submitted to the German Government. Both Jurat Leale and the Bailiff stressed the great mental hardship which the civilian population was undergoing by reason of the fact that they had received no news of their relatives and friends from England and elsewhere for nearly a year, and asked that every effort be made to put some mail service into operation. Colonel von Helldorff undertook to take up the matter again with the German Government.

Payment for Bulk Cargoes. Mr Callias said that instructions would be received by the Local Authorities regarding payment for bulk cargoes when such cargoes arrive and if such payments were required.

Education – Oxford Local Examination. Jurat Leale asked whether the International Red Cross could get into touch with the University of Oxford and ask for examination papers to be sent to the Island so that children here could sit for the Oxford Local Examinations. He submitted a letter on the subject from the President of the States' Intermediate School. Mr Callias said that he would certainly forward the request if the German Authorities had no objection. Colonel von Helldorff said that no objection would be raised.

Parcels for Prisoners-of-War. Mr Callias said that he had brought parcels for French prisoners-of-war in the Island.

Parcels for Neutral and Allied Foreigners. In Jersey it has been decided by the Bailiff to issue standard Red Cross parcels to allied and neutral foreigners working for the German Forces. Jurat Leale said that on the "Vega's" first trip the shortage of parcels had been such that none could be spared for these civilians but that the matter would be considered on this occasion since the number of parcels received was more than enough for two parcels each for the civilian population. He asked Colonel von Helldorff whether he was correct in assuming that such foreigners in Jersey were still receiving ordinary rations from the German Authorities. The Colonel said that this was so.

Cost of Red Cross Parcels. During the meeting Mr Callias said that the Red Cross parcels sent to the Channel Islands were being paid for half by the British Red Cross and half by the British Government.

[Bailiff's Red Cross Supplies Committee files, 1943-45, BF39-13, Island Archives]

Item 92: Meeting with P.K.: Meat Ration, 18 Feb 1945

<u>Memorandum of Meeting held at Grange Lodge,
Sunday, 18th February, 1945</u>

Present:

Jurat John Leale	President, Controlling Committee of the States of Guernsey
R.H. Johns, Esq	Member, Controlling Committe of the States of Guernsey
M.V.R. Schneberger	
Mr L.A. Guillemette	Secretary to the President, Controlling Committee of the States of Guernsey

<u>Subject: Meat Ration for week ending 24th February, 1945</u>

Herr Schneberger said that as a ration of 1 lb of meat per head had been promised by Colonel von Helldorff, in principle it might be issued but that one half would be taken from future rations since otherwise too many milk producing animals would have to be slaughtered and this would result in the necessity of importing animals from Jersey. He continued that the ration would have to be issued on the basis adopted in Jersey, ie. that between 8–10% allowance for cutting up but no allowance made for bone. The stock of veal at present held in the Cold Stores is to be included in the week's ration. Herr Scheeberger added that children up to a certain age in Jersey did not get a meat ration, and the same must apply here in future. He said that he would find out the age concerned and let us know later.

Herr Schneberger read a letter addressed by the Platzkommandantur, Jersey, to the Bailiff of Jersey, in which it was stated that at a meeting between the correspondents it was agreed that a 4 oz ration would be issued in Jersey during the first breadless week. Regarding future rations, other meetings would have to be held.

Mr Leale said that he was most disappointed in that he had never understood that Colonel von Helldorff would introduce any qualification into his promise. Mr Leale had asked for an extra ration to help the population over the breadless period. He asked whether the new suggestion meant that the Controlling Committee were left to decide whether to issue a ½ lb ration of meat this week, without future sacrifices of rations, or issue 1 lb now and sacrifice 8 ozs, in addition to the 3½ ozs to which the civilian population are entitled this week, without sacrificing future rations.

Extra Potato Ration

Herr Schneberger said that the Bailiff of Jersey had been told that he could not expect any more potatoes to be handed over by the troops for civilian consumption, and that if he increased the potato ration this week the responsibility for future ration shortages would be entirely his. Herr Schneberger said that the same would apply here. With this Mr Leale agreed.

Return of Flour for civilian use

Herr Schneberger said that the General had received a letter from the Bailiff, dated 13th February, regarding the return of flour from the Charroterie Mills. The General objected to the tone of the letter, Mr Leale said that it was the duty of the local administration to safeguard the interests of the civilian population. There were bound to be clashes between military and civilian interests. This had been so during the whole of the four years of Occupation and there would continue to be these difficulties until the end. Regarding the question of the return of flour, Colonel von Helldorff was of the opinion that it would not help matters to have a conference at the moment.

Confidential conversation between Colonel von Helldorff, The Bailiff of Guernsey, Herr Schneberger and Jurat J. Leale

Herr Schneberger said that some days previously he had been informed by a civilian of the subject of the confidential conversation held on February 7th at Rozel. He began to go into details but Mr Leale interrupted him and pointed out that he had observed the confidence placed in him so strictly that neither Mr Johns nor Mr Guillemette knew what Herr Schneberger was talking about. As far as he was concerned he had mentioned it to one person and one person only and this was Mr J.E.L. Martel, and that it should be mentioned to Mr Martel had been agreed by Colonel von Helldorff. Herr Schneberger was asked the name of the civilian concerned in order that investigations might be made into this leakage of information. He said that he would conduct an enquiry himself. He did not divulge the name.

Copies:
> The Bailiff
> Jurat J. Leale
> R.H. Johns, Esq.
> Mr L.A. Guillemette
> Files (3)

Item 93: Letter from Colonel Iselin, *The Star*, 24 Feb 1945

Flour Supplies for the civil population of the Channel Islands

The Bailiffs of Guernsey and Jersey have received the following letter from the head of the International Red Cross in Lisbon, Col. Iselin, which has been agreed with you. The sey newspaper—

"To my regret, the cargo does not entirely correspond to what had been agreed with you. The Portuguese Government did not authorise the export of eight tons of soap, which had been applied for by the B.R.C.S. representative in Lisbon. *Furthermore—and this is worse—'Vega' will not bring you any flour, although there is flour available in Lisbon. I wish to add that I have continually stressed the point how important it was that this flour should reach you now, but the B.R.C.S. in London—for reasons unknown to me—have decided that the flour shall be loaded on the third voyage only.* Instead you will receive a proportionately higher number of standard parcels. It must be hoped that the consequences this change may have, will not be too serious."

ISELIN.

Image courtesy of the Priaulx Library newspaper collection.

Item 94: Meeting with P.K., 11 March 1945

<u>Memorandum of Meeting held at the Platzkommandantur
on Sunday, 11th March, 1945</u>

Present:

Rev J. Leale, Jurat	President of the Controlling Committee of the States of Guernsey
Dr A.N. Symons	Medical Services Officer
Mr R.O. Falla	Agricultural Officer
Kapitaenleutnant Reich	Quarter-Master
Militaerverwaltungsrat Schneberger	
Militaerverwaltungsrat Hauschild	
Major Haubs	
Leutnant Wilmers	
Mr L.A. Guillemette	Secretary to the President of the Controlling Committee of the States of Guernsey

<u>General</u>

Kapitaenleutnant Reich said that the Festungskommandant wished to thank the Local Administration for the way in which their work had been carried out in the past and hoped it would continue to be done in a like manner. Jurat Leale said the Island Administration had no intention of changing their methods. Kapitaenleutnant Reich said that, although they knew the Allied Forces at present on German soil were taking up an attitude very different from that adopted here by the German Forces, they also had no intention of altering their policy here. He added that especially on the Eastern Front it is known that the German population is not being treated as one would expect between cultivated peoples. Even on the Western Front Administration Offices and Courts Martial have been set up and the death penalty has been pronounced against children. The German Forces in the Island intended to continue to behave like decent soldiers.

Kapitaenleutnant Reich continued that Jurat Leale had some time previously called attention to a few cases of bad behaviour on the part of the troops. Jurat Leale here interrupted to say that he again had a case to report, and Kapitaenleutnant Reich said that he knew of this case and that the two soldiers, who a few weeks previously had fired upon a civilian on whose property they were stealing, had been very severely punished, their sentences being three years and two months and over one year respectively. He assured the local representatives that all cases would be severely dealt with if the culprits were caught. The German Authorities on their part expect the Civil Administration to deal in like manner if civilian cases occurred.

<u>Water Supply</u>

Kapitaenleutnant Reich said that in the few days since he took over his present position he had spent much time in studying current problems. Being familiar with the sea, the Local representatives would appreciate that the Island is like an anchored ship and that Germans and Islanders are all in the ship together. The most important problem at present was water supply. Since no more Diesel oil could be expected it was necessary to take very decisive measures to safeguard the drinking supply as long as possible. The essential services would receive the supply as before.

Later in the meeting, Jurat Leale said that the local Doctors were most disturbed about the new Water Supply Order, and asked that Local Representatives might meet Kapitaenleutnant Reich and other German Officers to place representations before them. It was decided that a meeting should be held on Tuesday 13th March at 10 a.m.

Supplies of Milk for the Civilian Population

Kapitaenleutnant Reich was pleased that the "Vega" had brought fresh supplies for the civilian population, and the Festungskommandant had asked him to stress that the guarantees arranged between the German and British Governments were being adhered to strictly. Additional supplies of food had also been supplied to the civilian population.

Since it was now the season of spring, the milk supply will rise steadily. He asked M.V.R. Hauschild to continue with the subject of the milk supply for the civilian population.

The M.V.R said that the guaranteed amount of 8.6 grams of fat per person per day could continue to be supplied if the farmers obeyed orders under which they worked. It was also intended to allow full milk to nursing and expectant mothers, children and invalids. To increase the milk supply in future there will be German helpers in the milk collection depôts, and, in addition, in accordance with the season, minimum quantities for delivery by the farmers would be fixed.

From a quantity of 3½ litres [see (*) Note] per cow per day, the special civilian cases mentioned above would be supplied and the remainder would be processed, the German Forces receiving the resultant separated milk. If farmers delivered milk in excess of this amount it would be processed and the separated milk placed wholly at the disposal of the civilian population. These measures would be put into force on Tuesday, 13th March, 1945, and any necessary announcements on the subject would have to be published in the newspapers on Monday, 12th March, 1945.

It was agreed that this German requisition of milk would be the subject of a letter from the Platzkommandantur to the Civil Administration.

Dr Symons asked whether those invalids who at present receive a proportion of their allowance in separated milk, as well as some whole milk, would continue to be supplied with separated milk. M.V.R. Hasuchild answered that it would depend on the amount required and that he would make a decision on the matter when Dr Symons could inform him of that amount.

Jurat Leale said that Kapitaenleutnant Reich had suggested that it was desirable that relations should be maintained in the future as in the past between the German Occupiers and the Civil Administration. Everyone agreed on that point, and from the Controlling Committee's point of view the reason that relations had been so good in the past was because there had never been any objection to the utmost frankness in putting the civilian point of view before the Occupiers. He continued that he was certain the Germans could not expect us to welcome this latest requisition of milk and that we hoped that they did not assume that the civilian population did not need the milk. He described how, having just finished a letter to the Red Cross stressing the difficulty of feeding the civilian population with supplies of roots, vegetables and potatoes failing, he had been informed by Mr R. Chilcott, the Manager of the States' Dairy, of the cessation of civilian separated milk supplies. M.V.R. Hauschild said this was not quite correct since the supply of milk will rise with the season and if the farmers act loyally. The proportion of milk taken by the troops in the past had been so small that their health had suffered.

Jurat Leale and Mr R.O. Falla said that the rise in the supply of milk during the next month would be very small. They quoted statistics showing that in 1943 and 1944 the rise in the same period of the year had been 1,600 gallons only. The M.V.R. said that he had studied the figures carefully and since there were less cattle there would be more fodder per head and therefore more milk.

Jurat Leale said that it seemed useless to argue further on the matter at this stage. In his report to the International Red Cross he had stated that the separated milk ration was one-third of a pint per head. He wishes, therefore, to amend the report since it was now more urgent than ever to obtain larger supplies of food from the Red Cross.

Kapitaenleutnant Reich undertook to acquaint M. Mariotta with Jurat Leale's wish and said that, if permission was obtained from Germany for conferences to be held in Jersey with M. Mariotta, he would allow Jurat Leale facilities for telephoning his amendments himself to the Bailiff of Jersey.

Jurat Leale reminded the German Officers that last November when an appeal was made to growers of potatoes to hand in quantities for the supply of a ration to civilians without any potatoes whatsoever, a promise had been given by General von Schmettow that he would not requisition more than the 500 tons already taken from the civilian stocks. This assurance had been published by the Bailiff and had encouraged potato growers to deliver supplies. He suggested that in the same way the Bailiff should publish an assurance from the Festungskommandant that the German Forces would not take more than 3½ litres per cow per day and that all milk over this amount delivered to the Dairy would go to the civilian ration. He further suggested that a draft should be prepared and submitted to the German Authorities this afternoon. To this Kapitaenleutnant Reich agreed.

Requisition of Roots by the Verpflegungsausgabestelle[3]

The Local Representatives said that the Verpflegungsausgabestelle had handed the Glasshouse Utilisation Board their requirements of roots for the weeks beginning 14th and 27th March, 1945. The Glasshouse Utilisation Board held no supplies whatsoever of roots and, therefore, could not meet the demand.

---

3   Military Rations Distribution Office.

Red Cross Empty Sacks

Kapitaenleutnant Reich said that the Red Cross Representative now asked that empty sacks should be prepared for return on the next voyage of the "Vega".

(*) Note: On the afternoon of Sunday, 11th March, 1945, when the Bailiff's notice was submitted for approval, the amount of 3½ litres per cow per day was reduced to 6 pints per cow per day. As this would free a little more milk for civilian consumption, it was agreed that invalids at present drawing part of their allocation in separated milk should receive their separated milk as first claim on supplies available for civilian consumption. It was further agreed that farmers and their households should continue to receive whole milk as at present.

Item 95: Meeting with P.K.: Distribution of Vegetables, 24 April 1945

<u>Memorandum of Meeting held at Summerland,
Mount Durand on Tuesday, 24th April, 1945</u>

Present:

Jurat J. Leale	President, Controlling Committee of the States of Guernsey
Mr P. Dorey	President, Glasshouse Utilisation Board
Korvettenkapitaen Reich	Quarter-Master
M.V.R. von Aufsess	
Lieutenant Colonel Seiler	
M.V.R. Hauschild	
Paymaster	
Paymaster	
Oberinspektor Spann	
Lieutenant Schumacher	
Mr L.A. Guillemette	Secretary to the President of the Controlling Committee

<u>Distribution of Vegetables</u>

Korvettenkapitaen Reich extended his greetings to the Guernsey Representatives and said that he had asked them to this meeting to discuss the distribution of vegetables. The German Representatives had met previously and he would ask M.V.R. Hauschild to put forward their suggestions. Before doing so, however, he asked whether the Guernsey Representatives wished to make any comments. Jurat Leake said that he would like to hear M.V.R. Hauschild first. Herr Hauschild said that the provisioning of the troops was becoming increasingly difficult especially because of the lack of fuel for transport. Under the present system vegetables were being collected all over the Island, taken to one distributing centre at the Fruit Export Co. Ltd. and then redistributed to Units in both town and country. Their suggestion was that each Unit be allocated a growing property or properties from which they would draw their vegetables. The growers supplying the troops would continue as private growers and would be paid for the produce they supplied. Herr Hauschild then placed before the meeting certain figures which he had calculated as follows:–

1. There are approximately 300 hectares under glass in the Island, say 280 hectares.
2. In addition, about 180 hectares of outside land are producing vegetables.
3. Of the 280 hectares of glasshouses, 45 hectares are in potatoes and, as this is only a six months crop, this area should be calculated at 23 hectares.
4. There are also 10 hectares in beans, therefore, from the 280 hectares must be subtracted 23 plus 10 = 33 hectares, giving a total in vegetables of 247 hectares.

He calculated that the total vegetables produced from this area would be in the neighbourhood of 6,175 tons per annum.

5. The 180 hectares of outside land, calculated at 30 tons per hectare, should produce 5,400 tons per annum. Therefore, the total vegetables to be produced in the Island should be 11,575 tons.

6. The troops need from 4,700 to 5,000 tons of vegetables per annum, say 5,000 tons, therefore approximately 6,600 tons are left for civilian consumption and to provide for a small export to the other islands.

7. 23,000 civilians at 500 grammes per day equals 180 kilos per head per annum, or 4,140 tons per annum. Deduct 6,600 – 4,200 and 2,400 tons are left. This shows that there are enough vegetables in the Island for both civilians and troops over a whole year.

The allocation of vegetables as mentioned above not only would save transport but would segregate growers producing entirely for troops from those growing for civilians. To put this scheme into operation, the troops would need 35 hectares of glasshouses in addition to those which they had already taken over and those worked by Timmer Ltd.

In addition, 40 hectares of outside land would then be handed over to work for the German Forces.

Jurat Leale said that it was difficult to comment on this scheme without seeing it on paper. He gathered, however, that the troops would require 35 hectares of glasshouses and 40 hectares of outside land. The German Representatives agreed. Jurat Leale continued that the main worry of the Civilian Administration at present was the immediate future, and the difficulty to be overcome was the effect of the Order published in Monday's newspaper giving the troops permission to buy vegetables in unlimited quantities from the shops. Korvettenkapitaen Reich had always allowed complete frankness and Jurat Leale wished to tell the meeting the effect of the Order upon the Controlling Committee. Firstly, they were very disappointed to see it. He reminded Korvettenkapitaen Reich that when last they met to discuss vegetables about four or five weeks ago, he had understood Korvettenkapitaen Reich was waiting for a report from the German Inspectors on the subject of vegetable production in the Island, and it had been arranged that a further meeting would be held to discuss the needs of the troops and the guarantee made by the German Government to the British Government, when this report was to hand. Korvettenkapitaen Reich had, shortly afterwards, left the Island and the meeting, naturally had to be delayed. On Friday last the civil Police reported that they had been informed by the Platzkommandantur regarding purchases by the German soldiers in the shops. Jurat Leale had seen Herr Schneberger who had given him to understand that no such Order would be published until an opportunity had been given to the Civilian Administration to discuss it with the German Authorities. No such opportunity had been given.

On one of the first occasions on which Jurat Leale had met Korvettenkapitaen Reich, the latter had said how he valued the relations which had existed between the military and civilians during nearly five years of occupation. Jurat Leale valued them no less highly, but this new Order was bound to cause great bitterness. He gave the example of a mother wanting vegetables and finding that the last vegetables in the shop had been bought by German soldiers. She would know that while these vegetables constituted her only source of supply, for the German soldiers they would be simply an extra to the rations supplied. Jurat Leale could see no advantage in increasing the bitterness between Guernsey women and German soldiers. In addition, he could not understand how the German Authorities could guarantee an amount of vegetables to the civilian population if the soldiers were allowed to buy unlimited quantities. The German officials might <u>hope</u> that there would be enough left for the civilians but to guarantee it would be impossible. The Guernsey Representatives had been trying to see how the Order would work. Mr Dorey had that day received an indent for 18 tons of vegetables from the Glasshouse Utilisation Board to be supplied during the next week, ie. 7 tons more than last week's indent. There was no doubt, however, that the Glasshouse Utilisation Board would receive less instead of more vegetables since the soldiers would buy from growers and Glasshouse Utilisation Board Depôts as well as from shops.

Korvettenkapitaen Reich here interrupted to say that German soldiers were strictly forbidden to buy from producers or from depôts. They were only to buy from retailers. Mr Dorey said that nevertheless soldiers were asking the growers to sell and the fact that they only buy from retailers was not made clear in the Order. Korvettenkapitaen Reich said that an Order had since been given to the troops to buy only from retailers. M.V.R. von Aufsess undertook to publish an official notice in the civilian newspaper to the same effect. Jurat Leale continued that as people found that they could not buy vegetables in sufficient quantities from shops, black marketing and buying from growers would increase with a resultant breakdown of control.

Regarding indents from the Glasshouse Utilisation Board, Jurat Leale had, at the last meeting, complained that they were too high. The latest ones were even higher. This difficulty was accentuated by the fact that the weighty vegetables, such as cabbage and broccoli, were finished now in the glasshouses and the crops which would be picked in the near future, such as peas, were very light.

Korvettenkapitaen Reich suggested that Herr Hauschild's plan be examined by the experts, both German and civilian. However, he did not think that the position was as bad as it appeared. There were amounts available above general requirements of vegetables, and therefore soldiers should partake in buying from retailers. He suggested that it might be possible to have some rationing system for civilians. Jurat Leale said that if the Germans were allowed to buy unlimited quantities from the shops, there might not be enough vegetables to supply a ration for the civilian population. Here M.V.R. von Aufsess said that perhaps the shops could be barred to the German troops in the mornings, and with this the Guernsey Representatives agreed. Korvettenkapitaen Reich added his assurance that he would see that the guarantee of 500 grammes of vegetables per head per day was maintained. It was finally decided that the experts would meet the next morning to discuss Herr Hauschild's suggestions and to find a way of supplying the civilian population with the guaranteed 500 grammes.

In reply to a question from Mr Dorey, an assurance was given that if the produce of the 35 hectares of glasshouses and 40 hectares of outside land was handed over to the troops, there would be no further indents on the Glasshouse Utilisation Board with the exception of small amounts at irregular intervals.

Potato Ration

M.V.R. von Aufsess explained to Korvettenkapitaen Reich that a small quantity of potatoes, about 10 tons, had been collected by the Potato Board and that the Controlling Committee wished to issue a potato ration of 1 lb per head this week. The Guernsey Representatives were informed that a reply to their request would be given at seven o'clock that evening. Jurat Leale stressed the fact that stealing of potatoes was getting steadily worse and that the potatoes collected for the ration had been dug to save them and for no other reasons. They were immature and would not keep. He did not think that the total glasshouse crop potatoes would exceed from 50 to 100 tons this year.

Cutting of timber at Saumarez Park

Jurat Leale asked that no more timber be cut by the troops at Saumarez Park since too much had already been taken and there was the great danger that this, the only property of its kind left in the Island, would be completely spoilt. Korvettenkapitaen Reich agreed to pass on Jurat Leale's request to the Officer-in-Charge of tree felling.

JOHN LEALE
President,
Controlling Committee of the
States of Guernsey

PERCY DOREY
President,
Glasshouse Utilisation Board

L.A. GUILLEMETTE
Secretary to President,
Controlling Committee of the
States of Guernsey

Copies to:–
    The Bailiff
    Jurat J. Leale
    Mr P. Dorey (2 copies)
    Mr R.O. Falla
    Mr L.A. Guillemette
    Files (3 copies)

Item 96: Meeting with P.K.: Distribution of Vegetables, 2 May 1945

Memorandum of Meeting held at "Summerland", Mount Durand
on Wednesday, 2nd May, 1945

Present:

Jurat John Leale,	President, Controlling Committee of the States of Guernsey.
Mr R.O. Falla	Agricultural Officer
Korvettenkapitaen Reich	
Lieutenant-Colonel Seiler	
MVR von Aufsess	
MVR Hauschild	
Lieutenant Schumacher	
Mr L.A. Guillemette	Secretary to the President of the Controlling Committee of the States of Guernsey
Uffz Kraft	Interpreter

Distribution of Vegetables

Korvettenkapitaen Reich said that at the last meeting Jurat Leale had mentioned several points regarding the rescinding of the German Order which allowed the unlimited purchase of vegetables by the troops. In the meanwhile a new notice had been published giving effect to the decisions taken at the above-mentioned meeting. He wished to make five points:–

1. It had been discovered that the vegetable shops were now shutting in the afternoons and that civilians were allowed inside the shops during those hours and after ordinary business hours.
2. Regarding the reports received periodically by the Platzkommandantur from Mr Falla of thefts of vegetables and animals, the German Authorities had received proof that in many cases produce was not actually stolen but was sold by the owner outside the regular channels. With regard to vegetables, Korvettenkapitaen Reich said that broccoli and potatoes were especially sold in this way.
3. Again, in regard to potatoes sold on the black market, it was especially serious in view of the fact that the potatoes were dug before maturity.
4. A proportion of cattle reported stolen had been, in reality, slaughtered and sold on the black market.
5. English civilians working for the German Forces were showing an increasing disinclination to work. Many complaints had been received regarding irregularity of attendance. Mr Leale had mentioned before the good relations prevailing between the German and Civil Administration. It appeared as if there were a certain section of the public who did not appreciate the reasons why such relations should continue. The German Authorities could not but arrive at the conclusion that this unsatisfactory

attitude amongst people working for them was at least a form of passive resistance and might even mean active resistance. If this state of affairs continued the Festungskommandant would be forced to consider putting into effect meansures which would lead greatly to the disadvantage of the population. Upon the future behaviour of the population depended:–

(a)   whether good relations continued between the two administrative bodies;

(b)   whether the food granted to the population, in addition to the guaranteed amounts, would continue to be allowed;

(c)   whether the German Administration would be in a position to allow the guaranteed foods to continue to be put at the disposal of the population.

Korvettenkapitaen Reich continuing said that he presented these difficult points to Jurat Leale because he regarded him as the proper person to place the matter before the population and to take appropriate action. He wished to stress the fact that the forces were in favour of continuing to co-operate with the Civil Administration. In the past the Germans had proved their appreciation especially by the granting of additional allowances of food. In the hope that a certain class of people would stop their disloyalty, the German Authorities were prepared to give a further proof of their goodwill.

According to reports received by Korvettenkapitaen Reich, potatoes in addition to areas declared, had been planted. Here Mr Leale interrupted to ask what potatoes had been declared, and Lieutenant-Colonel Seiler replied that Korvettenkapitaen Reich was referring to potatoes planted in glasshouses and outside, Jurat Leale pointed out that no declarations whatsoever had yet been received regarding potatoes planted outside.

The Germans here changed the subject and MVR Hauschild was asked by the Chairman to put forward the new suggestion regarding potatoes. He said that, although potatoes did not come within the guaranteed categories of food, the forces would be willing to turn over for civilian consumption a proportion of the area planted in potatoes. Jurat Leale here said that potatoes were a vegetable and Korvettenkapitaen Reich declared that in the German language potatoes did not come under this category. Upon Jurat Leale insisting that they must be regarded as vegetables, Korvettenkapitaen Reich said that it must be an error on Jurat Leale's part and that the matter was not decisive since the troops were willing to hand over part of the crop. MVR Hauschild continued that there were approximately 30 hectares of glasshouses planted in potatoes, apart from those glasshouses taken over by the troops. The suggestion was that of this are half should be allocated to civilians half to the forces. Jurat Leale, in reply, said that, firstly, the civilian population was not getting the guaranteed 500 grammes of vegetables per day, and, secondly, that he did not know how much the Germans expected to produce from the 30 hectares of glasshouses and that if thieving continued at its present rate the quantity would be extremely small. He agreed that some potatoes were probably sold on the black market but the fact remained that thieving was getting steadily worse. He quoted the figures which he had received from the police, showing the increase of reported thefts during the past month and especially during the last few days. He added that, in addition to these cases, there were many other cases not reported since the public knew that in most cases the police could do nothing to help them and were losing interest in reporting at all. Korvettenkapitaen Reich said that the amounts set down as possibly stolen by the troops could not be accurate since the soldiers had no opportunity to cook food without being caught by their superiors. Jurat Leale said he was not accusing the troops of stealing at all. He continued that it was impossible for him to say who the culprits were, but he knew that if the thieving went on the whole of the Island, German and civilians, would starve.

At the last meeting Herr Hauschild had put forward a suggestion regarding the allocation to the German Authorities of glasshouses and outside land. The scheme would be a failure since by the time the areas were taken over by the troops there would be nothing left in the ground. Korvettenkapitaen Reich replied that a section of the growers were not "playing the game". Jurat Leale said that he was glad that Korvettenkapitaen Reich had been frank but he must insist that thieving was the root of the trouble. He instanced a grower who had planted a glasshouse of potatoes, had spent time and money on it and had had all but a few rows stolen. For a poor man it was a great temptation to make good some of his financial loss by selling the few remaining potatoes on the black market. He agreed with Korvettenkapitaen Reich that the Island population was out of control to some extent but nothing he could do would put matters right unless stealing stopped. Korvettenkapitaen Reich said he knew that potatoes were sold on the black market since the troops had been caught buying them. Jurat Leale agreed and said that it would be very difficult to catch anybody since to avoid detection altogether an owner need only treat his crop so that it looked as though it had been thieved. Korvettenkapitaen Reich continued that the Germans caught buying on the black market had been punished very severely. Jurat Leale said that civilians had also been punished and he hoped that Korvettenkapitaen Reich appreciated that he was asking him to do something very difficult. He did not see how he could do anything in addition to what the police were already doing. Korvettenkapitaen Reich said that it was a States' affair to decide what to do. Jurat Leale asked whether Korvettenkapitaen Reich was acquainted with the terms of the Potato Order, and added that already there were Police and Inspectors whose work was to look for irregularities. Korvettenkapitaen Reich said it was unnecessary to continue discussing stealing. If it continued the Germans could not carry out the guarantee; on their part they had even sentenced people to death as punishment.

Jurat Leale said that with regard to the suggestion that half the potatoes in glasshouses be taken by the troops and half left for the civilian population, Korvettenkapitaen Reich must not expect to dig potatoes which would not be there in a month's time. Lieutenant-Colonel Seiler said that the idea was that areas be selected for supply to troops and civilians respectively.

The five points made by Korvettenkapitaen Reich were then repeated. In regard to point (1), Jurat Leale said that the Glasshouse Utilisation Board Inspectors would see that the shops did not make sales in violation of the German Order.

Regarding point (5), Jurat Leale said that unwillingness to work was not confined to men working for the forces; in most cases it was due to hunger and it was difficult to prove otherwise. Korvettenkapitaen Reich said that he must leave the solution of the matter to Mr Leale, as he did not want the German Authorities to have to give stricter orders which might be to the detriment of the population. Jurat Leale undertook to talk to Mr Johns, the Labour Officer. He thanked Korvettenkapitaen Reich for his frankness and said that he had especially refrained from making any promises, although he would give his serious consideration to what the German Representatives had said.

Here MVR Hauschild gave more details regarding the suggestion of potatoes. He said that, firstly, arrangements would be made for the allocation of the 30 hectares of potatoes under glass and that later in the season discussion would take place regarding outside crops. The suggestion was the the allocation should be made as soon as possible in co-operation with Mr R.O. Falla. In answer to a question from Mr Falla, it was agreed that growers would be allowed to keep an agreed quantity of potatoes per head of household. Mr Falla said that when potatoes were planted in the glasshouses he had received a verbal assurance from the Platzkommandant that what had been planted was for civilian consumption. It was on this understanding that 50 tons of civilian seed potatoes had been handed over to the troops. He asked whether this arrangement was now being altered. The German Officers present declared that they had never heard of this assurance, and Korvettenkapitaen Reich added that the offer of 15 hectares of potatoes for civilian consumption was in addition to the guaranteed quantity of vegetables already allowed by the troops.

Butter for Children

Korvettenkapitaen Reich said before closing the meeting he wished to give further proof of the goodwill of the German Authorities. He then read a letter addressed to the States of Guernsey stating that children up to 14 years of age would be allowed their 8.6 grammes of butter per day, in addition to the whole milk already received daily.

Arrival of Red Cross Ship

It was revealed that the s.s. "Vega" would probably arrive in Guernsey the next day, Thursday, 3rd May, 1945.

Ammonia for Market Cold Store

Korvettenkapitaen Reich mentioned that the stocks of ammonia for the Market Cold Store were completely finished and suggested that the Red Cross Representatives be asked to send some of the "Vega's" next voyage. Jurat Leale agreed to make the request.

Essential Medical Supplies

Korvettenkapitaen Reich suggested that various medicinal plants might be collected in the Island for the manufacture of essential medicines. He asked whether there was in the Island a Doctor versed in this requisite knowledge. It was decided that Dr Symons should get into touch with Dr Rupp on the subject.

Saumarez Park Trees

Korvettenkapitaen Reich said that, as requested by Jurat Leale, he had given orders that no more trees should be cut down at Saumarez Park, with the exception of a few at the back of the park, neither would trees be cut down at Castle Carey.

JOHN LEALE
President of the Controlling Committee of the States of Guernsey

R.O. FALLA
Agricultural Officer

L.A. GUILLEMETTE
Secretary to the President of the Controlling Committee of the States of Guernsey.

LAG/PLD/MMF

Copies to:
The Bailiff
Mr Leale
Mr R.H. Johns
Mr P. Dorey
Police Inspector
Mr R.O. Falla
Mr L.A. Guillemette.
Files.

Item 97: Ormers and Ormering

The ormer (*Haliotis tuberculata*) is a gastropod mollusc found in the rocky shores around the Channel Islands, where they are considered a delicacy.

Ormering involves searching for ormers clinging to the underside of boulders by turning them over, feeling the underneath or looking into rock crevices. They are prised off with a special ormering hook or a sharp tool.

This can only be done in winter months between 1st January and 30th April these days at very low tides when it is either a full moon or a new moon and two days following. They are very nutritious and supplemented the meagre occupation diet.

When the precious catch arrives home they need to be removed from their shells, beaten with a rolling pin or mallet, fried in Guernsey butter, seasoned and coated in flour and then cooked slowly in a casserole for a few hours.

Nowadays they are revered and very expensive. They are a very special treat to some of us!

José Day

Illustration by José Day

Bibliography

Archival sources

Central Register of Identifications – the Occupation ID system (IAS).
> This consists of some 22,000 identity card application forms, each with a passport type photograph attached. The register was set up by order of the German authorities and included all civilians over the age of 14. It was run by H.M. Greffier and records, inter alia, date and place of birth, occupation and postal address. See Tough (1995).

Controlling Committee – Minutes 1940-45 (IAS).
> See Tough (1978).

Lewis, Kenneth George – Occupation Diaries (IAS).

Bailiff's Chambers Archive – Biberach File B/A/W80/2 (Jersey Archive).

Printed sources

Bell, William M., *I Beg to Report: Policing in Guernsey during the German Occupation* (Guernsey, 1995).

Bell, William M., *Guernsey Occupied But Never Conquered* (Guernsey, 2002).
> Two colourful and detailed accounts, the first on crime and policing and the second on government and civilian life under enemy occupation. Wherever possible Bell presents corroboration from two or more contemporary sources, including official island records recently released and personal diaries which he has brought to light.

Bell, William M., *The Commando Who Came Home to Spy* (Guernsey, 1998).
> Lieutenant Hubert Nicolle's two espionage missions to his native Guernsey and his subsequent treatment by the Germans.

Bell, William M., 'Escape from Alderney', *CIOR*, No 26 (2000), pp.5-15.

Bertrand, L.E., *A record of the work of the "Guernsey Active Secret Press" 1940–1945* (Guernsey, 1945) (Pamphlet).
> Short but well-written account by the editor of this underground newsletter. Includes the activity of Louis's sister Madeleine Sims and her husband.

Cortvriend, V.V., *Isolated Island* (Guernsey Star, 1947).
> Contemporary chronicle written with access to official files, and interspersed with personal reminiscence.

Coutanche, Lord 'The government of Jersey during the Occupation', *Société Jersiaise Annual Bulletin* 19:1 (1965).
> A brief but authoritative account, especially on the legislative framework of Occupation government. The writer was Bailiff of Jersey 1935-1961. Government in Guernsey developed along similar lines, differing in detail but not in principle.

Cruickshank, Charles, *The German Occupation of the Channel Islands* (Imperial War Museum, 1975).
> Sponsored jointly by Guernsey and Jersey as an 'official history', this urbane account relies heavily on the release of British wartime archives under the 'thirty year rule' introduced in 1972.

De Jersey, Graham, *Bordeaux Wesleyan Mission Hall 1908: Bordeaux Methodist Church 2008* (Guernsey, 2008).

Duncan, Jonathan, *The history of Guernsey; with occasional notices of Jersey, Alderney, and Sark, and biographical sketches* (Guernsey, 1841).

Durand, Ralph, *Guernsey Under German Rule* (Guernsey Society, 1946), 2nd ed. (Guernsey, 2018).

> A prolific writer on imperial subjects, Durand was in effect appointed as an 'official historian' with contemporary access to CC minutes and files from 1940 to 1945. The second edition contains a full index and a useful introduction by Stephen Foote.

Falla, Frank, *The Silent War* (Brewin, 1968), 4th ed. (Blue Ormer, 2018).

> Journalist imprisoned for spreading BBC news. See www.frankfallaarchive.org.

Gibson, Richard, 'The Doctor's Story', *Channel Islands Monthly Review* – Journal of Channel Islands Refugees in Great Britain (July, 1945).

> Speech to mass meeting of refugees in Manchester by one of the eight doctors who were asked by the C.C. to remain in Guernsey in 1940.

Ginns, Michael, 'The Kommandant', *CIOR* (1981) pp.6-10.

> A succinct account of the various German commanders in the Islands and their titles.

Harris, Roger E., *Islanders Deported*, Part 1 (*CISS*, 1990), Part 2 (*CISS*, 1983).

> Published in two parts, the first a general history of the internment in Germany of selected British subjects from the Islands, and the second an account of the mail services to and from the internment camps.

Hubert, Frank, 'Occupying my mind 1940-1945', *CIOR* 28 (2001), pp.53-91.

> Excellent Occupation memoir. Includes detailed account of the shipwreck of the *Favoriet* off Jersey on 5 May 1942.

Kreckeler, D., 'Escapees from Guernsey and Alderney during the Occupation', *CIOR* (1978), pp.6-17.

> 12 vessels got away, carrying a total of 80 Islanders.

Lainé, A.J. & Loveridge, J.H., 'Committee for the Control of Essential Commodities: Report on Essential Supplies and Services during the Occupation of Guernsey by German Forces and the work of the Committee', Appendix to *Billet d'Etat XIV* 1946, pp.3-124.

'The Laws and Usages of War on Land', being Chapter XIV, as amended 1936, in the *Manual of Military Law*, HMSO, 1929 edition.

Leale, Jurat John, 'Speech to the States of Deliberation', printed verbatim in the *Guernsey Evening Press*, 23 May 1945 and in the Déliberations on *Billet d'Etat I* of 1945.

> An account of the work of the C.C., delivered by the Committee's president just two weeks after the Liberation. Sets out the thinking of the C.C. in its attempt to preserve civilian government under enemy Occupation. Louis would have been heavily involved in the drafting of this speech and his diary, with letters and documents attached, would have served as an aide-mémoire.

Le Page, Martin J., *A Boy Messenger's War – Memories of Guernsey and Herm 1938-45* (Guernsey, 1995).

> Lively account of country life in Herm.

Le Tissier, Richard, *Island Destiny - A true story of love and war in the Channel Island of Sark* (Seaflower Books, 2006).

> A detailed account of the Occupation in Sark, from both the German and the Sarkee point of view.

Marr, L. James, *Guernsey People* (Phillimore, 1984).

> Idiosyncratic collection of biographical summaries – useful for obscure facts.

Mayr, Leopold, *Waists getting waspish: wartime communication in 25 word snippets* (CISS, 2017).

> A chance discovery in the Guernsey archives of a file of messages impounded by the German censor has led this philatelic researcher to produce a classic piece of social history on the Red Cross message system – a form of pre-digital SMS texting in (very) slow motion between the Islands and Great Britain.

Packe, Michael St. J. & Dreyfus, Maurice, *The Alderney Story - 1939-49* (Alderney Society, 1971).

> A fluent and well-documented account. Discusses but does not entirely resolve the mystery as to why, at the crucial moment before mass evacuation, Judge French was unable to communicate with Guernsey.

Rose, Alistair, 'Impressions of the Occupation of Guernsey', *CIOR* 28 (2001), pp.6-28, CIOR 30 (2002) pp.49-72 and CIOR 36 (2008) pp.60-71.

> Doctor's memoir which gains in immediacy from having been written during the latter part of the Occupation.

Sanders, Paul, *The British Channel Islands Under German Occupation 1940-1945* (Jersey Heritage Trust and Société Jersiaise, 2005).

Sanders, Paul, Gilly Carr and Louise Wilmot, *Protest, Defiance and Resistance in the Channel Islands – German Occupation, 1940-45* (Bloomsbury, 2014)

> These two recent academic studies are fully referenced and provide a useful guide to records of the Occupation, formal and informal, British and German.

Sauvary, J.C., *Diary of the German Occupation of Guernsey 1940-1945* (The Self-Publishing Association, 1990).

> An excellent edition of this diary by a builder, grower, churchwarden and douzenier in St. Sampson's.

Sherwill, Sir Ambrose, *A Fair and Honest Book* (Lulu, 2006).

> Memoirs of the first president of the C.C., deportee and postwar Bailiff of Guernsey. Although incomplete and not revised for publication by the author, this is an important account by a key player. Contains contemporary diaries and correspondence.

Stoney, Barbara, *Sybil: Dame of Sark* (Hodder & Stoughton, 1978).

Stroobant, Frank, *One Man's War* (Guernsey Press, 1967).

Tough, Kenneth, 'The States of Guernsey 1939-1945', *CIOR* (1978), pp.45-56.

> Describes the creation of the C.C. and its extraordinary powers.

Tough, Kenneth, 'The Identity Card System in Occupied Guernsey', *CIOR* 20 (1995), pp.30-49.

von Aufsess, Baron, *The von Aufsess Occupation Diary* (Phillimore, 1985).

> A version of a personal diary of the siege in 1944-1945, edited and translated by Kathleen J. Nolan.

von Aufsess, Hans Max, *Tagebuch aus der Okkupationzeit der britischen Kanalinseln, 1943-45* (Osburg Verlag, 2020).

> The complete original text – or rather texts, for more than one version has survived – edited by Tobias Arand. No index. This is the only detailed account we have from the German point of view and is from a senior military government official rather than a soldier. Useful for his views on the character and ability of senior German officers from von Schmettow downwards and of leading figures in Jersey and Guernsey. An English translation of the complete original text is planned.

Wallbridge, Capt John (with Peter J. Bryans, and David Hocquard), *Channel Islands Merchant Shipping 1940-45* (*CIOS* Jersey, c.1975).

> Details of 45 vessels which helped to supply the Islands.

Winterflood, Herbert, 'The secret diaries – one man's war': a 24-page illustrated supplement to *The Guernsey Press & Star*, 4 May 2005.

> Substantial extracts from Louis's diary were published for the first time, with a commentary by 'Herbert Winterflood, one of the besieged'.

Wood, Alan & Mary, *Islands in danger - the story of the German Occupation of the Channel Islands, 1940-1945* (Evans, 1955).

> Remains the best introduction, researched when most of the actors, British and German, were still available for interview. Written in plain English, with no particular axe to grind.

Abbreviations

CIOR	*Channel Islands Occupation Review*
CIOS	*Channel Islands Occupation Society*
CISS	*Channel Islands Specialist Society*
IAS	Island Archives Service
QRGS	*The (Quarterly) Review of the Guernsey Society*
TGS	*Transactions of La Société Guernesiaise*

INDEX

G

H

I

Y

Z